Inside Excel for Windows 95

Bruce Hallberg

Contributions by:

    Daniel Hodges

    Sally Neuman

New Riders

New Riders Publishing, Indianapolis, Indiana

Inside Excel for Windows 95

By Bruce Hallberg

Published by:
New Riders Publishing
201 West 103rd Street
Indianapolis, IN 46290 USA

Printed in the United States of America 1 2 3 4 5 6 7 8 9 0

```
Hallberg, Bruce A., 1964-
    Inside Excel for Windows 95 / Bruce Hallberg.
      p.  cm.
    Includes index.
    ISBN 1-56205-379-5
    1. Microsoft Excel for Windows.  2. Business--
    Computer programs.  3. Electronic spreadsheets.
I. Title.
HF5548.4.M523H35  1995
005.369--dc20                      95-38442
                            CIP
```

Warning and Disclaimer

This book is designed to provide information about the Excel computer program. Every effort has been made to make this book as complete and as accurate as possible, but no warranty or fitness is implied.

The information is provided on an "as is" basis. The author and New Riders Publishing shall have neither liability nor responsibility to any person or entity with respect to any loss or damages arising from the information contained in this book or from the use of the disks or programs that may accompany it.

Publisher	*Don Fowley*
Marketing Manager	*Ray Robinson*
Acquisitions Manager	*Jim LeValley*
Managing Editor	*Tad Ringo*

Product Development Specialist
Ray Robinson

Acquisitions Editor
Alan Harris

Software Specialist
Steve Weiss

Production Editor
Sarah Kearns

Assistant Marketing Manager
Tamara Apple

Acquisitions Coordinators
Stacey Beheler
Tracy Turgeson

Publisher's Assistant
Karen Opal

Manufacturing Coordinator
Paul Gilchrist

Cover Designer
Karen Ruggles

Photographer
Larry Ladig

Book Designers
Paula Carroll
Sandra Schroeder

Production Manager
Kelly Dobbs

Production Team Supervisor
Laurie Casey

Graphics Image Specialists
Jason Hand
Laura Robbins
Craig Small
Todd Wente

Production Analysts
Angela D. Bannan
Bobbi Satterfield

Production Team
Aren Howell, David Garratt,
Angela Calvert, Dan Caparo,
Kim Cofer, Jennifer Eberhardt,
Kevin Foltz, Joe Millay,
Erika Millen, Beth Rago,
Erich J. Richter, Christine Tyner,
Karen Walsh

Indexer
Brad Herriman

About the Author

Bruce Hallberg is the Director of Information Systems for Genelabs Technologies, Inc., a biotechnology company located in Redwood City, California. He has been heavily involved with PCs since 1980, and has specialized in accounting and business control systems for the past seven years. He has consulted with a large number of local and national companies in a variety of areas, and has expertise in networking, programming, and system implementations. He works with a wide variety of PC computing platforms, including DOS, Windows, OS/2, Unix, and Macintosh.

Trademark Acknowledgments

All terms mentioned in this book that are known to be trademarks or service marks have been appropriately capitalized. New Riders Publishing cannot attest to the accuracy of this information. Use of a term in this book should not be regarded as affecting the validity of any trademark or service mark.

Dedication

For my brothers, Brian and Brad.

Acknowledgments

Thanks to Ray Robinson for doing a bang-up job in developing *Inside Excel*. His guidance on the project greatly helped us to more closely target the book to our previous customers.

Alan Harris should be thanked for coddling us through the process. Alan's a very professional acquisitions editor, evidenced by the fact that he hasn't pulled out all of his hair from all that we put him through. We would also be remiss if we forgot to thank Alicia Buckley for starting the acquisitions process on the book, so we won't—thanks Alicia!

Sarah Kearns took the mangled English we submitted and smoothed it out considerably. She also had to deal with our tardiness in getting her final changes. Thanks, Sarah!

Thanks also to Stacey Beheler for coordinating the myriad details involved, including coordinating our submission dates and politely telling us to get with the program when we were late!

Contents at a Glance

Table of Contents

3   Worksheet Formatting   89

9   Mastering Excel Analytical Tools   333

Part II: Databases   365

10   Excel Database Basics   367

Part IV: Macros   521

15 Understanding Macros   523

Part V: Excel Tools 641

Part VI: Appendixes 669

Introduction

Welcome to *Inside Excel for Windows 95*!

This book is *the* most complete guide to using Excel for Windows 95 available, with extensive information about using Excel, linking Excel to other applications, and developing your own custom uses with Excel. When designing the first edition of this book, we surveyed the marketplace of available Excel books and designed *Inside Excel* to offer what no other publisher can: the single most comprehensive source of information about Microsoft Excel. In revising and updating this book for its second edition, we incorporated feedback and suggestions in order to better meet the needs of our customers. We believe we have met our goals, and that *Inside Excel for Windows 95* is truly the only book you will never outgrow.

Microsoft Excel for Windows 95

Excel for Windows 95 is an important upgrade. It adds impressive features to an already feature-packed product, and synchronizes Excel with the new Windows 95. The most notable enhancements to Excel for Windows 95 include the following:

◆ *New File Open and File Save dialog boxes,* in which you can perform many more advanced operations when performing these functions. You can now create directories when you are saving your workbooks, for example, or you can rename your files in the dialog boxes. Also included is a new file preview mode that lets you get a glimpse of the files on your disk before you open them in Excel.

◆ A new *data map* capability, in which you can easily create geographic maps that are tied to data in your worksheet.

◆ The *Answer Wizard,* which lets you pose natural language questions of the Excel help database. You can type in queries like **Show me how to outline a worksheet** or **How do I audit cells**, and Excel's Answer Wizard will show you the information you need.

◆ A *new formatting dialog* for number formatting that makes it easier to get the formats you need.

◆ A new *AutoComplete* feature. When you type information into a cell and it appears to be a duplicate of information in other cells, Excel automatically fills in the rest of the characters for you.

◆ You can now get quick totals and statistics for selected ranges of cells with *AutoCalculate.* Just select a range and Excel shows you the sum, or other statistics, in a status area at the bottom of the display.

◆ *AutoFilter* now lets you choose the Top Ten entries for your filters.

◆ *Enhanced drag-and-drop editing,* where you can now more easily drag cell ranges to other sheets in your workbook.

◆ *ScrollTips* displays information about the area you will see as you drag the scroll bar. *CellTips* lets you more easily view attached cell notes by simply pointing to the red dot that indicates an attached cell note.

◆ Excel now benefits from the *AutoCorrect* feature that was introduced in Word 6. When you type a common misspelling, Excel automatically corrects it for you as you work.

◆ You can now let multiple people maintain worksheet lists simultaneously with the *new Shared Lists feature.*

◆ Many new, powerful templates have been added to Excel that let you automate many functions.

Inside Excel for Windows 95 shows you all these new features in detail, while also providing extensive coverage of every other Excel feature, complete with examples and step-by-step instructions.

How This Book is Organized

To keep the book well organized, *Inside Excel for Windows 95* has been divided into eight main sections, each one detailing a particular area of Excel.

Part I: Worksheets

Chapter 1, "Introducing Excel," is for you if you are completely new to Excel. In this chapter, you walk through all of the steps necessary to create a simple worksheet, format the worksheet, create a chart from the worksheet data, and then save your work. Along the way, you learn about the key parts of the Excel screen, how to manipulate Excel, and so forth. If you have used Excel before, you can skip this chapter.

Chapter 2, "Working with Worksheet Data," is devoted to working with data on worksheets. This chapter shows you all the ways to enter and manage data on an Excel worksheet. You learn about data entry techniques, addressing cells in a variety of ways, moving data around the worksheet, working with named ranges on an Excel worksheet, and using Excel's AutoFill feature.

Chapter 3, "Worksheet Formatting," shows you ways to format your worksheets in an attractive fashion. You learn to format numbers, dates, times, and text. You also learn to apply fonts, underlining and shading, cell borders, format styles, and so forth.

Chapter 4, "Printing Documents," shows you all of the tricks to printing your worksheets and charts. You learn about previewing printouts, how different fonts work with Excel, how to get the most from your printer, and more.

Chapter 5, "Working with Multiple Windows," teaches you about all the different ways in which Excel can work with different views of your workbooks. You learn about 3D cell references that enable you to build workbooks, linking pictures between documents, and setting up workbook templates.

Chapter 6, "Advanced Worksheet Features," explains all the more advanced features in worksheets, such as embedding sound objects, outlining, auditing tools, and the new PivotWizard.

Chapter 7, "Mastering Functions," teaches you to use Excel functions, which enable you to begin to really master Excel. You learn about entering functions, using parameters, and dealing with function error messages.

Chapter 8, "Complete Guide to Excel Functions," is a reference guide to all the Excel functions. Look here for detailed information about all the Excel functions.

Chapter 9, "Mastering Excel Analytical Tools," shows you how to use the more advanced analysis features in Excel that are part of the Analysis add-in. The Analysis add-in includes more technical tools that are not part of the base Excel package. These tools include functions for engineering and statistical analysis of your data.

Part II: Databases

The second part of *Inside Excel for Windows* 95 takes a detailed look at the database features in Excel.

Chapter 10, "Excel Database Basics," explains the process of creating databases, setting up fields, entering data, and editing data.

Chapter 11, "Using Microsoft Query," teaches you how to find query data in your Excel databases, how to use Microsoft Query to access other databases, and how to set up database reports.

Part III: Charts

Part III helps you learn about creating charts and graphics. It includes a complete guide to Excel charts, an advanced charting chapter, and a chapter on using the Excel drawing tools on worksheets and charts.

Chapter 12, "Complete Guide to Charts," takes you through all of the details about creating and changing charts. You learn to use the ChartWizard and to format and rearrange your charts. This chapter also includes a guide to all of the Excel charts, along with notes about each type of chart and how it is used.

Chapter 13, "Drawing and Adding Graphics to Documents," educates you on using the drawing tools in Excel to annotate your worksheets and charts. The drawing tools in Excel are even good enough to use for general drawing purposes, and might just replace any dedicated drawing programs that you use. This chapter also shows you how to import drawings from other programs, and then use them in various ways in Excel.

Chapter 14, "Advanced Charts for Business and Science," covers more advanced charting needs. You learn about stock charts and technical charting features, such as regression trend lines and error bars. You also learn about dual y-axis charts and about adding new data to an existing chart, as well as how to deal with missing data.

Part IV: Macros

Part IV marks the beginning of the part of the book devoted to automating Excel. Whether your needs are as simple as recording basic macros or learning the underlying techniques required to build complex applications using Excel, you can find the information you want in this section.

Chapter 15, "Understanding Macros," begins by exploring simple recorded macros. It continues with macro arguments and also discusses using Excel 4 macros in Excel for Windows 95.

Chapter 16, "Using the Excel 4 Macro Language," shows you how to write your own macros from scratch. You learn to create new macro sheets, assign your macros to shortcut keys or to the menu, design macros, and test them.

Chapter 17, "The Complete Macro Language Function Reference," is a guide to all the Excel macro commands, their arguments, syntax, and examples.

Part V: Excel Tools

Chapter 18, "Using Excel Add-Ins," instructs you in the use of the Excel add-in programs—features not considered part of the main Excel program, but included with Excel. These tools include an autosave feature that regularly saves your work, a report manager for generating recurring reports, and an advanced Solver, which finds optimal solutions to challenging problems that would otherwise require programming to solve.

Chapter 19, "Excel in Workgroups," covers all the features that let you take advantage of Excel when you share files with many people. You learn about shared lists, how file sharing works, and how to send people copies of your workbooks.

Part VI: Appendixes

Appendix A, "Getting Excel Help," details your choices when seeking additional help with Excel. From the built-in tutorials to Microsoft's technical support phone numbers to a complete guide to the CompuServe support areas for Excel, turn to this appendix when you are stumped with a problem and need further help.

Appendix B, "Keyboard Shortcuts," shows you, in one convenient place, all the shortcut keys in Excel that can make you more productive.

Conventions Used in This Book

To make this book more readable, a number of type conventions have been established. Table I.1 explains these conventions.

TABLE I.1
Inside Excel Type Conventions

Example	Description
Bold	Boldface type represents something that you actually type. An example might be as follows: Type **=(A5*100)/2.34** and press Enter.
Italic	Italic type is used to draw your attention to new terms as they are defined. Occasionally, italic type is also used for *emphasis*.
File, **O**pen	Excel makes liberal use of shortcut keys. All the shortcut keys available in Excel have been marked with bold underline type so you can easily identify them.
Key1,Key2	When you are supposed to press two keys in succession, the keys are separated by a comma, as in this example: Press Alt,Tab and then press Enter.
Key1+Key2	When you are to press two keys at the same time, the keys are separated by the plus sign. When you see this, hold down the first key and then press the second key while the first key is still held down. Then release both keys. For example, you might see something like this: Press Ctrl+Enter to create a new line.

Note   Excel for Windows 95 is a very flexible program. Don't worry if your program does not look exactly the same on the screen as shown in the figures. The author might have used a customized setup or rearranged some of the elements on his or her machine.

Icons

Inside Excel for Windows 95 includes a number of different icon sections to cover material that isn't part of the normal text.

Note A *note* is an aside that contains information—sometimes background information—about the current subject. Notes are not critical to the discussion, but often contain helpful information.

Tip *Tips* contain shortcuts that can speed your use of Excel. Tips also contain practical advice to make Excel easier to use.

Stop If the book is covering material that might be dangerous to your data or your computer, a *warning* appears. Warnings tell you to be especially careful about something. Pay very close attention to them.

AUTHOR'S NOTE

Author's notes generally are personal comments about the subject at hand. These notes might be witty or provide some additional information from the author's background that might be helpful for you to know.

Excel makes extensive use of buttons on the various toolbars. Near the beginning of some chapters, you can find a table that shows you the buttons covered in that particular chapter.

If you are an experienced Excel user and are interested mostly in reading about what's new to Excel for Windows 95, look for the following icon. It usually points out places where new features are discussed.

New Riders Publishing

The staff of New Riders Publishing is committed to bringing you the very best in computer reference material. Each New Riders book is the result of months of work by authors and staff who research and refine the information contained within its covers.

As part of this commitment to you, the NRP reader, New Riders invites your input. Please let us know if you enjoy this book, if you have trouble with the information and examples presented, or if you have a suggestion for the next edition.

Please note, though: New Riders staff cannot serve as a technical resource for Excel for Windows 95 or for related questions about software- or hardware-related problems. Please refer to the documentation that accompanies Excel or to the applications' Help systems.

If you have a question or comment about any New Riders book, there are several ways to contact New Riders Publishing. We will respond to as many readers as we can. Your name, address, or phone number will never become part of a mailing list or be used for any purpose other than to help us continue to bring you the best books possible. You can write us at the following address:

New Riders Publishing
Attn: Publisher
201 W. 103rd Street
Indianapolis, IN 46290

If you prefer, you can fax New Riders Publishing at (317) 581-4670.

You can send electronic mail to New Riders at the following Internet address:

rrobinson@newriders.mcp.com

NRP is an imprint of Macmillan Computer Publishing. To obtain a catalog or information, or to purchase any Macmillan Computer Publishing book, call (800) 428-5331.

Author's Note

A lot of people—authors, developers, editors, technical editors, proofreaders, and production people—have worked very hard to bring *Inside Excel for Windows 95* to you. I am extremely excited about the book and the impact it will have on the Excel community. If, however, you have any problems or suggestions about the book, I

would love to hear from you directly, and would love to incorporate your comments into the next edition. Write to me in care of New Riders Publishing at the address given previously, or e-mail me directly on CompuServe at 76376,515.

Enjoy the book!

Bruce Hallberg

Part I

Worksheets

Chapter Snapshot

In this chapter, you learn the basics of working with Microsoft Windows 95 and Microsoft Excel for Windows 95. Using what you learn here, you will be able to set up simple worksheets that contain numbers and formulas, create charts, and print your results. The following topics are discussed:

- ◆ Starting Excel

- ◆ The parts of the Excel screen

- ◆ The parts of the worksheet

- ◆ Moving around the worksheet

- ◆ Creating a simple spreadsheet

- ◆ Creating a simple graph

- ◆ Printing the worksheet and graph

- ◆ Saving your work

- ◆ Quitting Excel

Although these operations are just the basics, you will get some idea of the program's ease of use, and you'll be introduced to a touch of its power.

Introducing Excel

With most software products, you use 10 percent of the features 90 percent of the time. Excel is no different in this regard. If you want to get going easily with Excel, learn to use the most fundamental features and functions, and achieve quick success with the product, then this chapter is for you. After learning these basics, you will be able to perform the most common tasks yourself and use the rest of this book as a guide to the more advanced features of Excel.

Excel for Windows 95 adds terrific new functionality to Excel. If you are an experienced Excel user, you can skim much of this chapter. Excel's key new features include the following:

◆ **Answer Wizard.** Excel for Windows 95's newest Wizard lets you ask questions in plain English to receive visual, interactive, or step-by-step answers from Excel's Help for the feature, function, or procedure you're using.

◆ **AutoCorrect.** New to Excel, AutoCorrect fixes errors as you type. AutoCorrect can even be used to create your own custom shorthand—tables of frequently used terms, phrases, formulas, and other features—for quick recall into your current sheet.

◆ **AutoComplete.** While you type, AutoComplete scans your text and adjoining columns to see if it can provide AutoFill features for you. It also provides a previous entries list, which will help increase your data entry accuracy across cells and sheets.

◆ **AutoFilter.** AutoFilter lets you apply a "Top 10" filter to a range of cells, taking a lot of the guesswork out of filtering data, and making it easier to find specific types of information in your workbooks.

◆ **Find Fast.** Finding data across folders and drives is greatly enhanced with Microsoft's new Find Fast technology. Local hard drives can be indexed to make finding data and files faster and easier.

◆ **Table of Contents for Workbooks.** You can now right-click on the radio buttons of an Excel screen and see a menu of sheets in your workbook from which you can select.

◆ **Expanded Microsoft Query Functions.** Powerful tools that can be used to query many databases, including SQL databases, and then import the results of your queries into Excel.

◆ **32-Bit Version of Visual Basic for Applications.** An entirely new programming model, introduced for the first time in Excel 5 for Windows. Visual Basic for Applications is the new common macro language for all Microsoft products. (Of course, Excel for Windows 95 still supports all the macros written in the Excel 4 and 5 macro languages.)

◆ **Universal Support for OLE 2.** Excel for Windows 95 now supports both Container and Object drag-and-drop functions, enabling you to seamlessly embed information between applications.

◆ **Data Mapping.** New to Excel, data mapping enables you to plot your data on a map to see relationships between the data. For example, you can query your database as to the members in your association who donated more than $100 last year, and who also live west of the Mississippi River or are from a particular zip code range.

◆ **Template Wizard.** This new Wizard helps you turn your most commonly used worksheet formats into a template, and it can even help you export cells to a "tracking database," helping you track and compile company-wide information.

◆ **Spreadsheet Solutions.** Ten new templates are provided with Excel for Windows 95, which include preformatted and predesigned invoices, purchase orders, expense reports, time cards, and more.

Starting Excel

When you installed Excel, a program group was created on the Windows 95 Taskbar for Excel, as shown in figure 1.1.

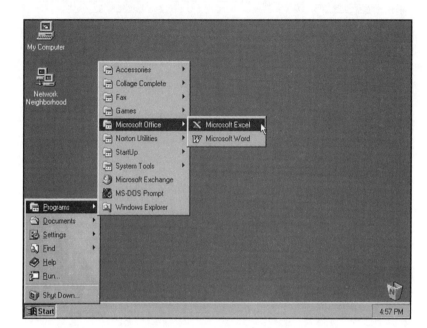

Figure 1.1

The Excel program group.

To start Excel, click on the Excel item on the taskbar. Excel opens and loads a blank worksheet, as shown in figure 1.2.

Understanding the Excel Screen

Excel makes extensive use of the graphical user interface with menus, buttons, icons, and many different mouse pointers. The main elements of the Excel screen control the program itself, as displayed in figure 1.3.

Figure 1.2

*The Excel
opening screen.*

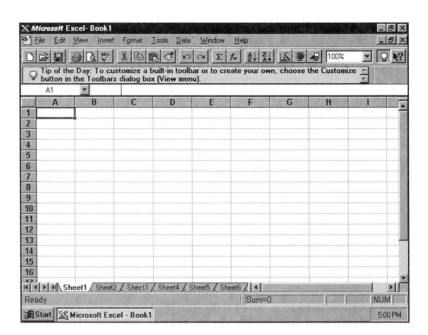

Figure 1.3

*Excel program
screen elements.*

Using Menus

Each menu item in the menu bar contains many choices, most grouped logically. The File menu, for instance, shows commands that deal with files, Edit shows editing commands, and so on.

You can access menus in Excel using your mouse by clicking on the menu item to activate it, sliding your mouse pointer through the menu to the command you want to activate, and then clicking to activate it. Where a menu item has more than one command available, a right-pointing arrow will be shown on the right side of the menu opposite the command name.

This method is nearly the same as that for Macintosh computers; however, the Macintosh requires that the mouse button be constantly depressed when sliding through menu options, whereas Windows 95 does not.

Menus can be accessed entirely using keyboard shortcuts, as well. To pull down a menu using only keystrokes, follow these steps:

1. Hold down the Alt key and press the letter on the keyboard that corresponds to the underlined letter in the menu. To activate the File menu, for example, hold down Alt and press the F key on your keyboard.

 Note   The underlined letter of a menu option is commonly called a "hot key."

2. After the menu appears, choose the option you want and press the letter on your keyboard that corresponds to the menu's hot key (you can just press the underlined letter to select a command within a menu).

Unlike the Macintosh, nearly every Windows or OS/2 menu option can be accessed exclusively from the keyboard using this method. Many people find this method faster than constantly having to reach between the mouse and the keyboard.

Introducing the Toolbar

One of the more recent innovations in Windows programs is the wide use of *toolbars*, those little rows of buttons that appear on your screen below the menu bar. These buttons typically show small icons; the icons represent the functions of choosing different command options and functions. To print, for example, you simply click on the small button that looks like a printer.

The buttons in the toolbar are designed to provide you with quick access to the functions you use most often. Mastering the use of the Excel toolbars can dramatically increase the speed at which you can work with Excel (and other Windows programs, for that matter).

When you open Excel for the first time, the Standard toolbar (the default) appears across the top of the window just below the menu bar, as shown in figure 1.4. The function of each button on the Standard toolbar is described in table 1.1.

Figure 1.4

The Standard toolbar.

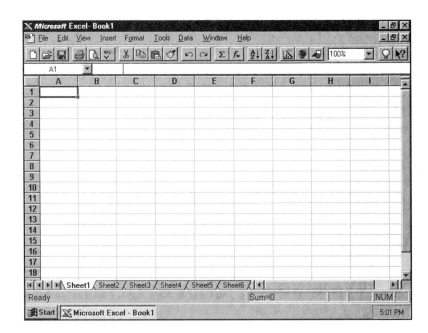

TABLE 1.1
Standard Toolbar Icons

Icon	Name	Description
	New Workbook	Opens a new workbook.
	File Open	Opens an existing workbook on your disk.
	File Save	Saves the workbook document to your disk.
	File Print	Prints the active document.

Icon	Name	Description
	Print Preview	Shows the document as it will look on the printed page.
	Cut	Cuts the currently selected area into the Windows Clipboard.
	Copy	Copies the contents into the active or marked cells into the Windows Clipboard.
	Paste	Pastes the contents into the Windows Clipboard, beginning at the current cell location.
	Format Painter	Enables you to quickly copy the formatting of one cell to other cells.
	Undo	Reverses the last action you took.
	Redo	Repeats the last action you took.
f_x	Function Wizard	Helps you use Excel functions and inserts the result into the current cell.
Σ	AutoSum	Automatically determines which cells to sum, depending on the location of the active cell. Proposes a summation range that you can modify before you press Enter. When you press Enter, Excel automatically enters the SUM formula for you into the active cell.
	Sort Ascending	Sorts the contents of the selected cells in ascending order (lowest to highest).
	Sort Descending	Sorts the contents of the selected cells in descending order (highest to lowest).

continues

TABLE 1.1, CONTINUED
Standard Toolbar Icons

Icon	Name	Description
	Chart Wizard	Automatically walks you through the process of creating a chart.
	Camera	Enables you to insert graphic images into your worksheets.
	Graphics	Brings up the Graphics toolbar, which contains the tools you use to draw in your current document.
100%	Zoom Control	Enables you to quickly zoom in and out of your document.
	Tip Wizard	When selected, displays a bar under the main toolbar. The Tip Wizard automatically shows you shortcuts in Excel as you work.
	Region Help	Provides instant online help for any item on the screen. Select this button, then click on the area with which you want help.

Using the Control Menu

The Control menu is the program's graphic icon in the upper left corner of the Excel window. It functions the same in Excel as in most other Windows programs, although each program's icon will be different. The Control menu is shown pulled down in figure 1.5.

Table 1.2 explains the functions of each Control menu option. On your system, some options might be grayed-out (not selectable), depending on whether they are appropriate options for the present context. Table 1.2 includes notes about grayed-out options.

TABLE 1.2
Excel Control Menu

Menu Name	Description
Restore	Restores the Excel window to the size it was before the Ma**x**imize command was issued. This option is grayed-out when Excel is not maximized.
Move	When Excel is *windowed*, or not maximized to take over the entire screen, you can select the **M**ove option, then use the arrow keys to reposition the Excel window on the screen.
Size	To resize the Excel screen using the keyboard, choose **S**ize from the Control menu, then press the arrow key for the edge that you want to change (up arrow to adjust the upper edge of the Excel window, right arrow to adjust the right edge, and so on). After you select the edge you want to change, use the arrow keys to shrink or enlarge the Excel window.
Mi**n**imize	Choose Mi**n**imize to shrink Excel to an icon on the desktop. Excel continues to run and process data while it is minimized.
Ma**x**imize	Ma**x**imize causes Excel to grow to take up the entire screen area.
Close	Choose **C**lose to exit Excel.

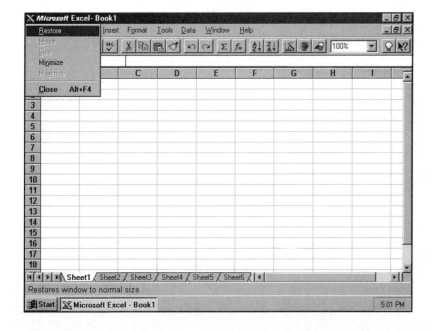

Figure 1.5

The Control menu.

Using Control Commands Shortcuts

Using the mouse or a keyboard shortcut is often a more convenient way to execute the Control menu commands. This section teaches you ways to accomplish similar tasks using a mouse or keyboard shortcut. Figure 1.6 displays a few instructions on using these shortcuts.

Figure 1.6

Control menu shortcuts.

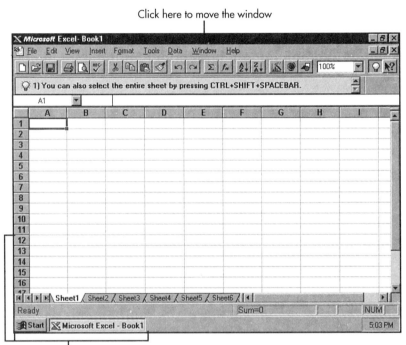

Click here to move the window

Click and drag any border or corner to resize window

Restore

To restore the Excel window to its windowed state so that it does not take up the entire screen, click once on the Restore button in the upper inside right corner of the Excel window. When Excel is in its windowed state, this button changes to a single window pane, which indicates that you can maximize Excel.

Move

To move the Excel window around on the desktop, click and hold on the Excel title bar, then drag your mouse to reposition the window.

Size

Resize the Excel window by carefully moving your mouse pointer to an edge of the Excel window. When the pointer is precisely over the edge, it changes shape and becomes a double-headed arrow. At this point, press the left mouse button and drag the mouse to resize that edge of the window.

 Tip Position the mouse pointer over the corner of the screen to control two dimensions at the same time. When your mouse is in the right place, the pointer changes to show two diagonal arrows.

Minimize

The Minimize button is located immediately to the left of the Maximize/Restore button. Click on it to immediately minimize Excel.

Maximize

The Maximize button is in the upper inside right corner of the Excel screen. When Excel is windowed, you can choose this button to cause Excel to take up the entire screen. When Excel is maximized, this button becomes the Restore button and the icon changes to reflect two cascaded screens.

Close

Although you can use the Excel command to exit the program (**F**ile, E**x**it), you also can exit by double-clicking on the Control Menu. Another alternative is to press Alt+F4 on the keyboard. Finally, you can click on the X icon in the top right corner of the Excel screen to close the current files and the application.

Understanding the Workbook

Excel for Windows 95 uses the metaphor of workbooks just as Excel 5 did. A *workbook* is a collection of different documents, all grouped together. Some documents contained in a workbook might be worksheets, charts, macro sheets, and so forth.

Excel has many different types of documents, as follows:

◆ **Worksheets.** Contain data and formulas. Worksheets also can contain other embedded objects, such as charts, pictures, and so forth.

◆ **Charts.** Contain graphs that you create using Excel. A chart can be in its own document or embedded in a worksheet.

◆ **Modules.** Visual Basic modules for Excel. These modules contain program code for the programs you write using Excel's built-in programming language, Visual Basic for Applications.

◆ **Dialog sheets.** Contain dialog boxes you can use in your Excel application. You can draw dialog boxes using dialog sheets and attach program code for each button and field.

◆ **Excel 4 Macro Sheets.** Contain macros from version 4 of Excel.

Each workbook shares certain controls for managing the workbook itself. These controls are used to scroll around the current sheet of the workbook, minimize and maximize the workbook within the Excel window, and so on. This section discusses these workbook controls. Figure 1.7 shows the controls and key parts of a worksheet.

Figure 1.7

Excel document controls.

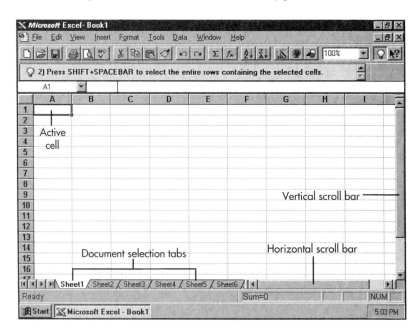

Understanding the Document Control Menu

The Document Control menu duplicates the functions of the Excel Control menu, but its commands affect only the current document itself, and not the overall Excel program. It contains the familiar commands **R**estore, **M**ove, **S**ize, Mi**n**imize, Ma**x**i-mize, and **C**lose. This menu, however, also contains a command not found in the Excel Control menu: Nex**t** Window. The Document Control menu can also contain a command called S**p**lit, which you learn about momentarily.

Each time you select Nex**t** Window, Excel brings to the front each successive work-book until it reaches the last document you have open. Then it returns to the first document. It "circulates" between open Excel workbooks.

Tip

Some other ways to move between sheets are as follows:

◆ You can quickly scroll through worksheet tabs by clicking the tiny upside-down "v" space to the right of the Sheet6 tab in figure 1.7.

◆ You can also right-click on the radio buttons to the left of the Sheet1 tab in figure 1.7 to show a menu of sheets from which to choose.

S**p**lit is available when you have a worksheet document open. This option enables you to split the worksheet into different sections so that you can work with and see different parts of the worksheet at the same time. This command is covered in detail in Chapter 5, "Working with Multiple Windows."

Exploring Other Document Controls

Excel offers several other document controls. You already learned to use these controls for the Excel program itself; this section shows you the way to use them in a workbook:

◆ Each workbook has its own Maximize/Restore, Minimize, and Close buttons, which are located at the upper right corner of the document screen. These buttons maximize or restore the workbook within the Excel window.

◆ Resize workbooks by positioning the mouse pointer over the edge of the workbook, then dragging the edge to resize the workbook. You can do this only when the workbook is not maximized.

◆ You can close the current workbook by double-clicking on the workbook's Control menu (as opposed to double-clicking on the Excel Control menu, which exits Excel) or by clicking on the X in the top right corner of the work-book window.

◆ Reposition—or move—the workbook by clicking and holding your mouse while your pointer is on the workbook's title bar.

Tip   Double-click on the title bar of the workbook (or Excel itself) to maximize or restore it.

Right-click on the title bar of the workbook (or Excel itself) to minimize, maximize or restore, or close it.

Identifying the Active Cell

The *active cell* is shown in figure 1.7. This cell is the one affected by whatever you type or whatever commands you execute (such as formatting commands).

Moving Around the Worksheet

During a typical Excel session, you move within one of the worksheets in your workbook, enter data in different places, view results in other places, and so on. Excel provides many ways to move around within the active workbook.

Tip   Some movements change the portion of the worksheet you are viewing without affecting the position of the active cell. This feature can be used to your advantage. If, for example, you want to view a different part of the spreadsheet before you enter some data, you can use the scroll bars to look at the information you want to see. Because using the scroll bars doesn't change the position of your active cell, you can just start entering data to immediately return to the active cell. You can also move the active cell simply by clicking on a cell after you have scrolled to the desired place on the worksheet.

Using Scroll Bars

Very few worksheets can be viewed entirely on a single screen; worksheets often take many, many screens of space to display. Given this fact, Excel enables you to scroll around the current document and view different parts of it at will.

You can use scroll bars in a number of ways, as follows:

◆ Click on the scroll bar button and drag it to a different position to change the area you are viewing. If you drag the vertical scroll bar to the bottom or the horizontal scroll bar to the far right, you see the bottommost or rightmost part of your current worksheet.

Tip In the upper left corner of the document, Excel shows you the row or column name that will appear after you release the scroll button. This "sneak preview" helps you avoid making guesses as to what will appear after you release the mouse button.

◆ Click on the arrows at either end of the scroll bar to move one cell in the direction of the arrow.

◆ Click on the blank area of the scroll bar (the area between the button and the arrow) to move an entire "screen full" at a time. You move in the direction away from the position of the scroll bar button. For example, if the vertical scroll bar button is in the middle of the vertical scroll bar, click once above the button to move your display up by one full screen.

Tip Excel's scroll bars are proportional to the area you are viewing on the screen. In other words, the button on the scroll bar itself will change size (larger or smaller) to more accurately reflect the size of the area you are viewing.

Moving Around the Document Using the Keyboard

The keys and key combinations listed in table 1.3 provide alternative ways to move around within the worksheet.

TABLE 1.3
Keyboard Movement Keys

Key	Action
Arrow keys	Moves the active cell in the direction of the arrow key, one cell at a time.
PgUp/PgDn	Moves the display one full screen up or down. The active cell moves with the display, but stays in the same relative position on the screen.
Ctrl+arrow	Hold down the Ctrl key while you press an arrow key to move the active cell in that direction until it encounters a cell that contains data. If no cells contain data in that direction, Excel moves the active cell all the way to the boundary of the worksheet.

continues

TABLE 1.3, CONTINUED
Keyboard Movement Keys

Key	Action
F5	Press F5 to open a dialog box in which you can enter the cell reference to which you want to jump. This dialog box also displays all your *named ranges* (areas of the worksheet to which you have assigned a name) so that you can just choose a named area. Otherwise, simply enter a cell reference (like AB255 or R3C4) and press Enter to immediately move the active cell there, and view that portion of the worksheet. This is also referred to as the "Goto" key.
Ctrl+PgUp Ctrl+PgDn	Changes the active sheet left or right.
Alt+PgUp Alt+PgDn	Shifts one screen at a time left or right.
Ctrl+Home	Moves you to cell A1 of the current worksheet.
Ctrl+End	Moves you to the last row and column of the current worksheet.

Creating a Worksheet

Now that you know the fundamentals of working with the Excel screen and of moving around the worksheet, it's time to set up a sample worksheet so that you can put these steps into practice.

In the following sections, you create a worksheet that shows sales projections for the ACME Corporation. As you create the worksheet, you learn additional information about working with Excel.

Before you begin this exercise, start with a new workbook. Pull down the **F**ile menu and choose **N**ew. If you have defined multiple template documents, a dialog box appears that asks you what type of document you want to create. Click on Workbook and then click on the OK button.

Entering Text

The first order of business in creating your sample worksheet is to create the title and headings for the worksheet. Follow these steps:

1. Move your pointer to cell A1. (If you started a new worksheet, A1 should already be your active cell.) To quickly move to cell A1, press Ctrl+Home.

2. Type **ACME Corporation Sales Projections** and press Enter.

As you type, you will see the text appear in the active cell on the worksheet, as well as in the formula bar above the worksheet cells, as shown in figure 1.8.

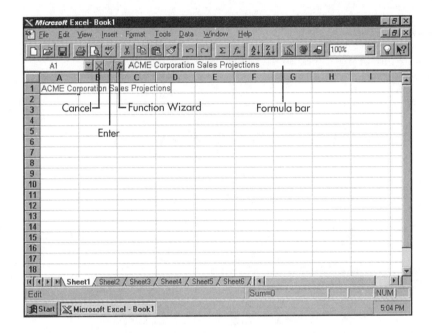

Figure 1.8

The formula bar.

Formula Bar

The formula bar shows you the reference of the active cell or cells, the data that you are typing, and the Cancel, Enter, and Function Wizard buttons (see fig. 1.8).

When you are entering data in the formula bar, you can use the normal editing keys (arrow keys, Backspace, Del, Ins, Ctrl+left arrow, Ctrl+right arrow, and so on) to change the data until you are satisfied with it. When you are finished typing or editing the data, click on the Enter button (the check mark), or simply press Enter. To cancel your changes, click on the Cancel button (the X) or press Esc.

Centering Text

You can center text across a selection of cells by using the Format, Cells command, as follows:

1. Click on cell A1, hold down the mouse button, and drag the cursor to the right until the cells from A1 to I1 are highlighted. Release the mouse button.

2. Pull down the Format menu and click on Cells. This action brings up the Format Cells notebook, shown in figure 1.9. This notebook enables you to control the way in which the cells you select are formatted. Each "tab" of the notebook corresponds to a different formatting topic or "page."

3. Because centering the title falls under the heading Alignment, click once on the tab marked Alignment.

4. On the Alignment page, click on the option button marked Center Across Selection.

5. To complete the change, click on the OK button.

Figure 1.9

The Format Cells dialog box.

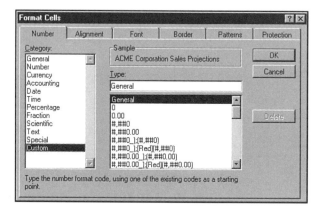

Continue entering the text labels for the exercise worksheet by entering the subtitle and two more labels, as follows:

1. Move to cell B1, type **By Region**, and press Enter.

2. Center the text using the Center Across Selection method described earlier.

3. Move to cell B4, type **Region**, and press Enter.

4. Move to cell C4, type **Q1**, and press Enter.

AutoFill

Excel contains a powerful feature to automatically enter sequential labels. In the example you are creating, you want the labels Q2 through Q4 to appear in cells D4 through F4. You could type each label into each cell, or better yet, you could use AutoFill.

In the lower right corner of your active cell, you see a small square. This square is the *fill handle* (see fig. 2.16 in Chapter 2 for a blowup of this handle). You can use this feature to fill the rest of the titles for you:

1. Move to cell C4. Click once on that cell or use the arrow keys to make it the active cell.

2. Position the mouse pointer immediately over the fill handle. When it is positioned correctly, the cursor will change to a small cross.

3. Press and hold down the left mouse button, and then drag the mouse to the right to highlight the cells up to F4. When cells C4 through F4 are highlighted, release the mouse button.

Voilà! Excel intelligently interprets what you're trying to fill and correctly places each successive label into the correct cell. The AutoFill feature also works with month names or other types of labels.

Tip If you drag the fill handle too far to the right, or not far enough, just grab it again and drag it to the correct position. Excel will refill the region correctly.

Continue with the following steps to complete the entry of the labels for the worksheet:

1. Enter **Total** into cell G4.

2. Move to cell B5, enter **North**, and then press Enter.

3. Repeat step 2 for the other three regions, as follows:

   ◆ Enter **East** into cell B6

   ◆ Enter **West** into cell B7

   ◆ Enter **South** into cell B8

4. In cell B9, enter **Total**.

At this point, you have entered all the labels for the worksheet. Your screen should look like figure 1.10.

Figure 1.10

*A sample
worksheet
with labels.*

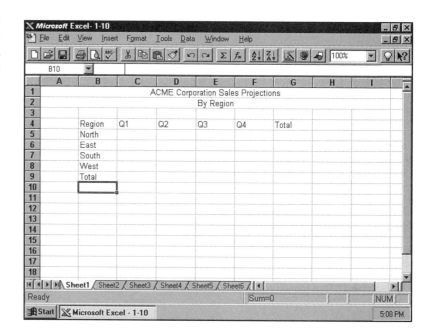

Entering Numbers

For this example, assume that you already know the actual results for the first quarter, and you want to calculate the projections for the following three quarters, as well as the yearly total. Enter these values into each of the first quarter cells:

◆ **25292** in cell C5

◆ **13510** in cell C6

◆ **8900** in cell C7

◆ **43250** in cell C8

When you enter numbers into Excel, notice that they automatically appear aligned to the right edge of the cell. This alignment is Excel's default, because it is the most common way to format numbers, with their right edges aligned. It also serves as a useful way of knowing whether Excel is interpreting what you type as a number or as text (sometimes it can fool you!).

Note   Normally, Excel correctly determines whether data is intended to be treated as a number or as text. Occasionally, however, you may want a number to be treated as text. Perhaps you are preparing a table in which each line is labeled 1, 2, 3, and so on. In this case, to force Excel to treat those numbers as text, you must enter them in with a leading apostrophe.

To force the number 145 to appear as text, for example, enter **'145** in the cell in question. The apostrophe does not appear in the cell once you've pressed Enter—only the number.

Entering Formulas

Continuing with your sample worksheet, assume that each region is experiencing a five percent quarterly growth rate. You want Excel to calculate the remaining quarterly sales based on the sales of the first quarter, plus a five percent increase. Follow these steps:

1. Move to cell D5. Enter the formula **=C5*1.05** and press the Enter key. Excel immediately calculates the result and displays the answer.

Note Excel, like most computer programs, uses the asterisk (*) to represent multiplication, and the forward slash (/) to represent division. Addition and subtraction are represented with plus (+) and a hyphen (-), respectively.

2. You now need to enter the formulas for the remaining calculated cells. You can enter the remaining formulas by hand, but why not let Excel's AutoFill feature do it for you? Grab the fill handle for cell D5, and drag it down so that the highlighted area extends from cell D5 to cell D8. Release the mouse button.

   Each cell now shows the correct amount: the cell to the left plus five percent of that amount. This calculation works correctly when you use AutoFill because Excel automatically adjusts any cell references so that they are *relative* to the cell that contains the formula. You can force Excel to look at a particular cell in a formula, as well. No matter where you copy such a formula, it still works. This feature is called an *absolute reference*. In Chapter 2, "Working with Worksheet Data," you learn to control this reference and to use any combination of relative and absolute references that you want.

3. Finally, copy the entire column of formulas (cells D5 to D8) two columns to the right so that all the quarterly sales are correct.

   Using the normal mouse pointer (the large plus symbol), select cells D5 to D8 (they should already be selected from the previous step). If not, move the pointer to cell D5, then click and drag the pointer down to cell D8. Release the mouse button after you have marked all the cells.

Tip   You can use the keyboard to quickly select multiple cells. Use the arrow keys to move to the starting cell, hold down the Shift key, then use the arrow keys to move to the ending cell. You also can click on the starting cell, hold down the Shift key, and then click on the ending cell to select the entire range of cells.

4. Grab the fill handle at the bottom of cell D8, and drag it two columns to the right. Excel now fills in all your formulas two columns to the right, and all the quarterly columns now show the correct sales figures. If everything has gone well for you, your screen should look like figure 1.11.

Figure 1.11

Completed sales figures.

X *Microsoft* Excel- 1-10								_ 8 X

| File Edit View Insert Format Tools Data Window Help | | | | | | | | _ 8 X |

A1 — ACME Corporation Sales Projections

	A	B	C	D	E	F	G	H	I
1			ACME Corporation Sales Projections						
2			By Region						
3									
4		Region	Q1	Q2	Q3	Q4	Total		
5		North	25292	26556.6	27884.43	29278.65			
6		East	13510	14185.5	14894.78	15639.51			
7		South	8900	9345	9812.25	10302.86			
8		West	43250	45412.5	27683.13	50067.28			
9		Total							
10									
11									
12									
13									
14									
15									
16									
17									
18									

Sheet1 / Sheet2 / Sheet3 / Sheet4 / Sheet5 / Sheet6

Ready   Sum=0   NUM

Start   X Microsoft Excel - 1-10   5:10 PM

Using AutoSum

To finish building the data for the worksheet, you need to calculate the totals for both the columns and the rows. To enter the total for cell G5, you have the following three choices:

◆ You can enter the formula to add up all the cells. Using this method, you enter **=C5+D5+E5+F5** into cell G5 and then press Enter.

◆ You can use one of the Excel math functions. You can type the formula **=SUM(C5:F5)** and press Enter. Notice the way the range of cells is given in the

formula. The first cell of the range to be summed is separated with a colon from the last cell. The colon tells Excel to work with all the cells in that range.

◆ You can use the Excel AutoSum tool, the fastest way to get totals of rows or columns of numbers. To use AutoSum, make G5 your active cell and click on the AutoSum button in the toolbar—the one that shows the Greek Sigma (Σ) icon. Excel automatically enters the SUM function, then determines which cells you most likely want to total, surrounding the suggested cells with a dotted line. If the range of cells Excel has guessed is correct, just press the Enter key. If the range isn't correct, use your mouse to select the correct cells and then press Enter.

After you have entered the formula in cell G5 to total row 5, use the fill handle to copy the formula down to cell G9. When you are finished, move to cell C9 and use the AutoSum button again to total up the sales for the first quarter. Then, use the fill handle to copy that formula across to cell F9. When you are finished, your worksheet should look like figure 1.12.

Tip Excel smartly handles AutoSum for you by entering the beginning of the formula (=SUM( ), leaving you to enter or edit the rest of the formula. If you enter the cells you want to have summed and forget to enter the closing parentheses, Excel will also smartly finish the sum for you.

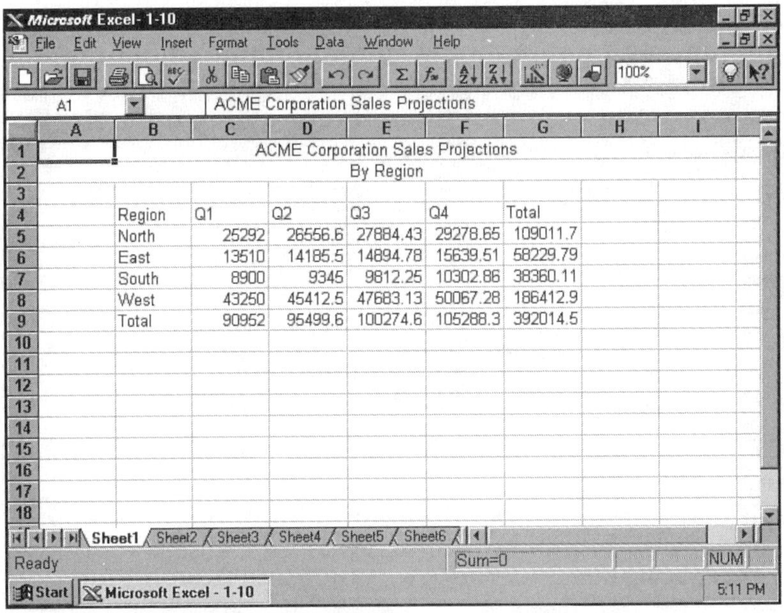

Figure 1.12

The completed worksheet.

	A	B	C	D	E	F	G	H	I
1				ACME Corporation Sales Projections					
2				By Region					
3									
4		Region	Q1	Q2	Q3	Q4	Total		
5		North	25292	26556.6	27884.43	29278.65	109011.7		
6		East	13510	14185.5	14894.78	15639.51	58229.79		
7		South	8900	9345	9812.25	10302.86	38360.11		
8		West	43250	45412.5	47683.13	50067.28	186412.9		
9		Total	90952	95499.6	100274.6	105288.3	392014.5		

Using AutoFormat

Although all the numbers in your spreadsheet are correct, the document is not yet very presentable. Excel contains many commands that enable you to control the way your worksheet is formatted. One of the most convenient of these methods is the AutoFormat tool, which automatically applies one of a number of predesigned formats to a table.

To use AutoFormat, make sure that the active cell is anywhere within the table (for example, cell C5). Then, pull down the Format menu and choose AutoFormat. The AutoFormat dialog box appears, as shown in figure 1.13.

Figure 1.13

The AutoFormat dialog box.

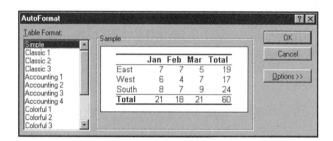

The Table Format list box contains many different predefined table formats for you to choose from. For this example, choose Financial 1 and click on the OK button. The result is shown in figure 1.14.

Figure 1.14

The formatted worksheet.

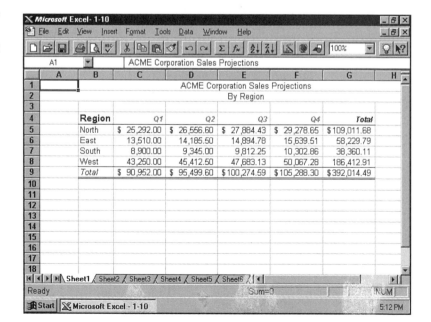

Creating a Graph

Excel contains one of the most powerful graphing functions contained in any software product. Part of this power comes from the simple, easy-to-use tool called the ChartWizard.

In this example, you want to graph the sales data for each region for each quarter. Later in the book, you learn to do this manually. For this introduction to Excel, however, use the easy ChartWizard. Follow these steps:

1. Select B4 to F8 as the range to chart. You do not want to graph the totals for this chart.

2. Click on the ChartWizard button in the toolbar. Excel prompts you to indicate where you want to place the chart, and changes the mouse pointer to a small cross with narrow lines. You can embed charts right alongside your data in Excel, or you can place them in a separate sheet in your workbook. For this example, you place the chart right below your data.

3. Using the small cross, drag a rectangle in the area immediately below the table, so that you create the outline (sometimes called a *marquee*) from cell B11 to cell G18.

Excel now walks you through the five necessary steps required to create a chart. At any point, you can cancel the process by clicking on the Cancel button or by pressing Esc. You can also go backward or forward in the process by clicking on the **B**ack or Next buttons.

1. The first step, shown in figure 1.15, verifies that you want to create the chart with the range that you selected. If the range was originally selected correctly, click on the Next button. If not, click on Cancel to go back and reselect it.

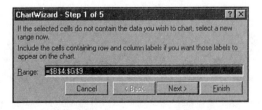

Figure 1.15

Step 1 of the ChartWizard.

2. The second step, shown in figure 1.16, provides samples of different chart types and asks you to choose one. For this example, click on **C**olumn, which should already be selected. Click on the Next button to go to the next step.

Figure 1.16

Step 2 of the ChartWizard.

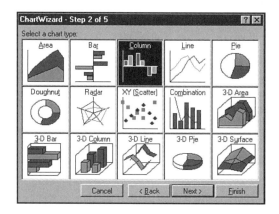

3. The third step shows you a different set of pictures (see fig. 1.17). These pictures represent all the different variations of the chart type you selected in the second step. Choose type 1 and click on the Next button.

Figure 1.17

Step 3 of the ChartWizard.

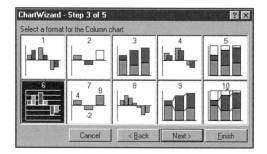

4. The fourth step, shown in figure 1.18, asks you to select the way in which the data should be charted. These options are covered in detail later in the book. For now, the default choices are fine; click on the Next button.

Figure 1.18

Step 4 of the ChartWizard.

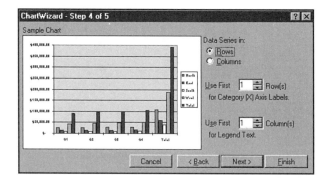

5. The fifth and final step asks for information concerning labels on the chart (see fig. 1.19). Everything is fine, except that you want to add a title to the chart. Click on the field under **C**hart Title, and type **ACME Sales Projections**. After you enter the title, wait a minute; the sample chart shows this text as it will appear. To complete the chart and place it into the worksheet, click on the **F**inish button.

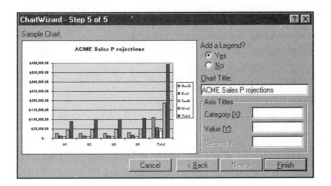

Figure 1.19

Step 5 of the ChartWizard.

The completed chart is shown in figure 1.20.

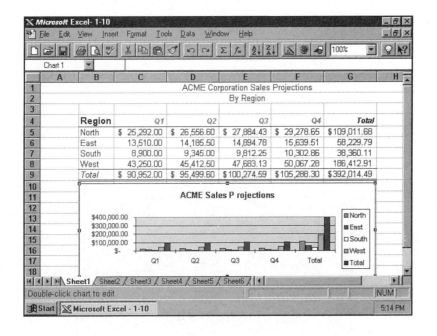

Figure 1.20

The completed chart, embedded in the worksheet.

Note The chart you see is *compressed*—you cannot see much detail because it is fairly small. To see the chart in more detail, click once on the chart to activate it, then drag up the upper handle (the small box in the middle of the top line). To return it to its original size, drag the handle back down.

When a chart is embedded into a worksheet, it is "floating" on top of the cells beneath it. If there was text in the cells behind the chart, that text is still there—it simply is covered by the chart.

Although charts are covered in detail elsewhere in this book, the following tips might help until you go through that information:

◆ If you need to delete a chart, click on the chart to select it. (You know it's selected when the small squares, called *handles*, appear at the corners and edges of the chart.) When the chart is selected, press Del to get rid of it.

◆ You can move the chart within the worksheet by selecting the chart and dragging it to a new location.

◆ You can resize the chart. To do this, select it, then drag one of the small handles at the perimeter of the chart.

Printing

To print the worksheet, select the area from cell A1 to cell H20, then pull down the **F**ile menu and choose **P**rint. This step brings up the Print dialog box, shown in figure 1.21.

Figure 1.21

The Print dialog box.

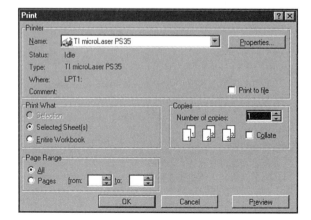

In the dialog box, click on the option button marked Selection. This option tells Excel to print only the selected area of the worksheet rather than the entire document. Finally, click on the button marked OK to print the document.

Saving Your Workbook

To save the completed workbook, pull down the File menu and choose Save As. This action opens the dialog box shown in figure 1.22.

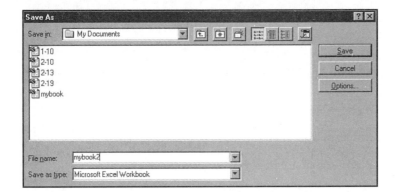

Figure 1.22

The Save As dialog box.

Enter the name of your workbook in the File Name field and click on the OK button to save the workbook. If you need to change the directory in which the workbook is saved, use the Drives and Directories list boxes to navigate to the location where you want your file stored.

After you have assigned a name to a workbook, you can save more quickly by choosing Save from the File menu.

Note Saving frequently is very important. Many people lose lots of time by forgetting to save their work. Then, when they lose power or their computer crashes, they lose all the work they have done since the last time they saved the file. Excel also includes an AutoSave feature. You learn about AutoSave in Chapter 18, "Using Excel Add-Ins."

Chapter Snapshot

Nearly all your time working with Excel will include manipulating the data in your worksheets. Entering data, moving it, cutting and pasting it, and even transforming it, are all functions you will spend significant amounts of time doing. This chapter teaches you the following tasks:

◆ Entering different types of data into an Excel worksheet

◆ Taking advantage of some large scale data-entry shortcuts

◆ Building simple formulas

◆ Referencing other cells—including combinations of cells—in your formulas

◆ Taking advantage of absolute versus relative cell addresses

◆ Understanding the difference between R1C1 cell addressing and A1 cell addressing

◆ Naming portions of your spreadsheet for better control and accountability

◆ Including detailed notes in individual cells

◆ Rearranging the data in your worksheet

By mastering the techniques presented in this chapter, you learn to work with your worksheet data and use Excel as efficiently as possible.

New Riders Publishing
INSIDE
SERIES

Working with
Worksheet Data

This chapter covers the basics of working with data—text, numbers, and formulas—on the Excel worksheet. You need to be able to enter and manipulate data in Excel in order to be productive with the program.

Entering Data

The first thing you have to do when you build a spreadsheet is enter data. You must also know how to enter labels for different parts of your worksheet, and you really need to know how to enter numbers and dates for calculations, as well as other information.

This section discusses entering text and numbers and how to make Excel accept a number and treat it as text when you need to do so. Through examples in the chapter, you learn how to enter and manipulate text so you can do an inventory spreadsheet in Excel. You enter different inventory items and the quantity and price of each. Then, you use Excel to calculate the inventory value.

Entering Text

To enter text, position the active cell where you want the text to appear, then begin typing. When you type the first letter, the text appears in the active cell *and* in the formula bar.

Tip   If editing in the cell is disenchanting for you, you can turn off the feature by accessing **O**ptions from the **T**ools menu, clicking on the Edit tab in the Options Notebook, and clicking on the line "Edit Directly in Cell" to remove the X.

The following steps tell you how to enter a title and headings for the different parts of the inventory spreadsheet:

1. Type **ACME Company Inventory** in cell C2. Then click once on the Checkmark button next to the formula bar or simply press Enter to store your entry. If you want to cancel what you have typed, click on the X button in the formula bar or press Esc.

2. In cell A4, type **Quantity** and press Tab.

3. In cell B4, type **Description** and press Tab.

    Description spans two cells, with the last part of the word covering part of cell C4. When no text or numbers are in an adjacent cell, Excel allows the text of one cell to continue and display to the right.

4. In cell C4, type **Model #** and press Enter.

When you enter the text, the final part of the word `Description` is obscured. Because of the label in C4, Excel cannot display the complete word, so it shows the contents of cell C4 rather than the final portion of the preceding cell.

5. In cell D4, type **Price** and press Enter.

Compare your spreadsheet to figure 2.1.

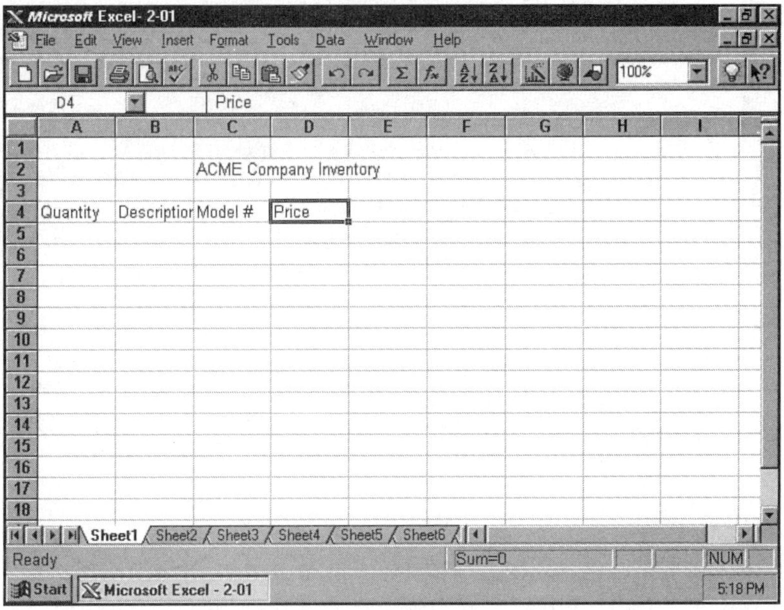

Figure 2.1

The spreadsheet with title and labels.

Before you continue, you should widen column B in the spreadsheet. Not only does text `Description` not fit, but the actual inventory descriptions you will enter are unlikely to fit, either. Use the following procedure to widen column B:

1. Position your pointer directly on top of the line that separates B and C at the top of the spreadsheet. When positioned correctly, the pointer changes to a vertical bar with two horizontal arrows.

2. When this vertical bar appears, click and hold the left mouse button and drag the mouse to the right until the column is close to twice the original size.

Tip

When the pointer has changed to a vertical bar with two horizontal arrows, you can simply double-click to have the column automatically size to the appropriate width.

3. Release the mouse button to finish the change (see fig. 2.2).

Entering Numbers

Move to cell A5, type **5**, and press Enter. The number immediately springs to the right of the cell after you press Enter instead of aligning to the left of the cell. Excel's default setting assumes that you want text to be left-aligned and numbers to be right-aligned.

Move to cell B5, and type the following description entry: **Paper Clips**.

Entering Numbers as Text

Type the model number **00587** for this item in cell C5 and press Enter. Excel displays 587, rather than 00587.

Normally, Excel correctly anticipates whether you want an entry to be treated as text or as a number. In this case, it interprets your entry as a number and eliminates the unnecessary leading zeros. You want this entry to be treated as text, however, for two reasons: you need to preserve the leading zeros for the model number to be accurate, and you want all the model numbers to be similarly aligned. Some are pure text. If you mix numbers and text, some entries are right-aligned, while others are left-aligned.

To make Excel treat a number as text, you need to enter the number differently. In cell C5, type **'00587** (note the leading single quote mark) and press Enter. Voilà! Excel knows you want the entry to be treated as text, and displays it accordingly. The single quote mark is all it takes.

To finish the first line of data, move to the Price column and enter **.75** to represent 75 cents.

Entering Times and Dates

Before you continue with the exercise, you should learn to enter times and dates into Excel.

Excel stores times and dates differently from the way it displays them. When you enter a time, Excel records two things: a number that represents a decimal fraction of a 24-hour day and a formatting command that tells Excel to display that number as a time rather than as a simple number. In Excel, you can enter times in the following formats:

◆ 21:45

◆ 21:45:50 (hours, minutes, seconds)

◆ 9:45 PM

◆ 9:45:50 PM

◆ 5/6/95 9:45 PM

In the last example, you also can combine dates and times in the same cell entry. Any valid date combinations can be used that follow with any of the valid time combinations.

You can enter dates in a variety of ways, as follows:

◆ 5/6/95

◆ 5-6

◆ 6-May-95

◆ 6/May/95

◆ May-95 (uses your computer's year)

◆ May 6 (uses your computer's day)

You can use /, -, or a space to separate the elements of a date. If Excel does not recognize your entry as a date, it treats it as a normal text entry and displays it accordingly.

Note   No matter how the date appears in the spreadsheet, it always appears with the format mm/dd/yyyy in the formula bar. For example, if you enter 5 May into a cell, you see 5/6/1995 in the formula bar. Seeing the way the date appears lets you know whether Excel correctly recognized your entry as a date or displayed it as normal text.

Excel stores a special number called a *serial number* when you enter a date. The serial number counts the number of days from the beginning of the century up to the date entered in the cell. For example, if you view the serial number for the date 1/1/2000, you see the number 36526. This number represents 365 days per year multiplied by 100 years (36500), plus the number of days added by leap years (25), plus one additional day (the first of January).

Tip   To see the serial number for a particular date, enter the date and press Ctrl+Shift+~, the shortcut key to force a cell to assume a numeric format (also called Normal formatting).

To return the cell to a date format, press Ctrl+Shift+#, which is the shortcut key for the standard date format.

Performing Data Entry

Entering large amounts of data is extremely boring, rife with the potential for error. By using some of Excel's data-entry shortcuts, however, you can reduce the chance of error and complete the task more easily and quickly.

Selecting the Data-Entry Range

Normally, you need many extra keystrokes to move from the end of one line to the beginning of the next when you enter several records. Fortunately, you can automate this process with Excel.

If you use the mouse to select the range of cells into which to enter data before you type the data, Excel moves between cells for you automatically. After you choose your data-entry area, use the keys listed in table 2.1 to move your active cell in an efficient manner for data entry.

TABLE 2.1
Data-Entry Key Actions

Key	Movement
Tab	Stores your entry and moves one cell to the right in the selected area. If you are at the right border of the area when you press Tab, the active cell moves to the beginning of the next row down.
Shift+Tab	Stores your entry and moves one cell to the left in the selected area. If you are at the left border, the active cell moves to the right end of the next row up.
Enter	Stores your entry and moves one cell down in the selected area. If you are at the bottom row, the active cell moves to the top row, one column to the right.
Shift+Enter	Stores your entry and moves one cell up in the selected area. If you are at the top row, the active cell moves to the bottom row, one column to the left.

Using the Numeric Keypad

If you are used to entering numbers with a 10-key calculator that automatically places the decimal point in the number, you will be pleased to know that Excel can emulate that capability. To activate this feature, follow these steps:

1. Pull down the **T**ools menu, then select **O**ptions.

2. The Options notebook appears, enabling you to change many global characteristics of Excel. In this notebook, first click on the Edit tab. The Edit notebook page appears. Click on the Fi**x**ed Decimal check box. The field below the check box should already have 2 in it, which indicates that two decimal points will be entered automatically.

3. Click on the OK button to close the notebook.

After you activate this option, all numbers have a decimal point automatically inserted two places from the right. So, if you enter 12345, Excel stores it as text 123.45. If you enter the number **5**, Excel stores it as .05, and so on. You can override this format in an individual cell by entering the decimal point by hand (for example, if you enter **5.**, you get 5). Excel uses the automatic decimal places until you uncheck the Fi**x**ed Decimal check box.

Special Data-Entry Keys

Often when you enter a large amount of data, certain parts of each line are repeated in the following line. For example, if you enter inventory locations in your inventory spreadsheet, many adjacent records share the same location. And then, sometimes you want to copy the formula in a cell, or automatically enter the date or the time into a cell.

The keys in table 2.2 perform such actions.

TABLE 2.2
Special Data-Entry Key Actions

Key	Effect
Ctrl+; (Semi-colon)	Enters the present date
Ctrl+: (Colon)	Enters the present time
Ctrl+' (Apostrophe)	Copies the formula from the cell above without adjusting the cell references
Ctrl+" (Quotation mark)	Copies the value (text or number) from the cell above

Completing Data Entry

Using the preceding tools, enter the remainder of the inventory information into your spreadsheet. Table 2.3 shows all the records, including the one you already entered. As you enter the data, remember the following points:

◆ Select cells A5 through D9 before you begin. Then, use the Tab key to move between cells.

◆ When you enter model numbers, remember to enter the number-only entries as **'nnn**, where *nnn* is the number you want to enter. The single quote mark forces the numbers to be treated as text.

◆ If you use the Fi**x**ed Decimal feature, remember to enter the numbers correctly. For example, to enter the number 31, you can enter **3100** or **31.** (with a decimal).

TABLE 2.3
Inventory Records

Qty	Description	Model #	Price
5	Paper clips	00587	.75
31	Faber #2 Pencils	2002	.05
12	Office Calendars	OCTZAB	12.95
93	Cs. Manilla Folders	12MAN	6.95
12	Rm. #20 Copy Paper	20#500	5.35

After you finish entering the data from table 2.3, your screen should look like figure 2.3.

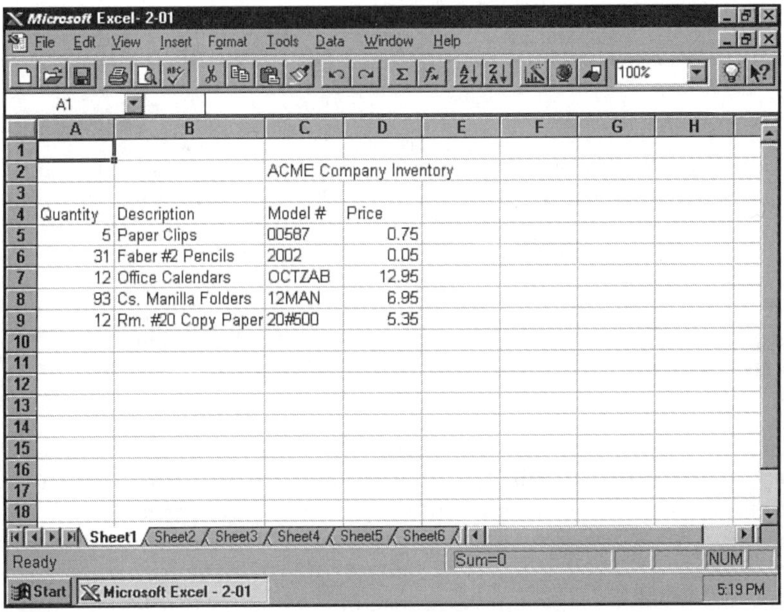

Figure 2.3

The completed inventory worksheet.

Working with Formulas

To add to your inventory spreadsheet, you might want to add a column that shows the value of the goods on hand, as well as a total amount for all of the inventory items. You can do this work by using a few simple formulas.

To begin, create a new column called Value in column E. Move to cell E4, type **Value**, and press Enter.

Using Cell References

Now, you must enter the formula. In this case, all you want to do is take the price in column D and multiply it by the quantity in column A—far from difficult, you shall soon discover.

Keyboard

You can enter this formula in two ways, using only the keyboard. Both methods are depicted in the following two examples. Use E5 as your active cell.

The first method is merely a matter of typing in the formula. In cell E5, type **=D5*A5** and press Enter. The result appears in your active cell. Notice, however, that the formula appears in the formula bar when a cell is selected. This display lets you see the basis for the result as you work in your spreadsheets.

The second method involves "pointing" with the arrow keys. Follow these steps:

1. Type an equal sign.

2. Press the left arrow once. The cell reference D5 appears in the formula bar, and a dashed line appears in cell D5 (showing the cell to which you point).

3. Type an asterisk (*) for multiplication. The dashed box (called a *marquee*) disappears, and =D5* appears in the formula bar.

4. Press the left arrow four times. The marquee moves one cell at a time to the left, until it rests on cell A5.

5. Press Enter.

Both methods produce the same result. The method you use is up to you. Sometimes the pointing method works better because your spreadsheet is too big for you to know which cell you want. In that case, you can arrow quickly to the cell you want as you build your formula without having to know the cell reference. In a small worksheet, however, like the one used in this example, you might find it faster to use the first method and directly type the formula.

Mouse

You also can enter the formula using the mouse by following these steps:

1. In cell E5, type an equal sign.

2. Move the mouse pointer to cell D5 and click once. The marquee appears, and D5 appears in the formula.

3. Enter an asterisk (*).

4. Move the mouse pointer to cell A5 and click once. A5 appears in the formula bar. You can press Enter to store the formula.

Another variation of this procedure is to use the scroll bars to locate the cell to which you want to point with the mouse. After you find the cell you want, click on it with the left mouse button. Then, enter an appropriate math symbol and your display automatically returns to the cell into which you are entering the formula. In a small worksheet, however, like the one used in this example, you might find it faster to use the first method and directly type the formula.

Working with Ranges of Cells

Finish the column of formulas. If you want to practice the methods you just learned, do so until each row has the inventory value in column E. If, however, you see that as drudgery and would prefer to circumvent it, copy the formula to the other cells automatically by using the following steps:

1. Select the range of cells from E5 to E9 by moving your mouse pointer to cell E5, clicking and holding the left mouse button, and dragging down to cell E9. After the cells are highlighted, release the mouse button.

2. Pull down the **E**dit menu, and select F**i**ll, then **D**own.

After you select the F**i**ll Do**w**n command, the formula you entered is copied automatically to all the cells below E5. Those cells should all display the correct result, as shown in figure 2.4.

 Tip   You also can press Ctrl+D instead of choosing **F**ill, **D**own from the **E**dit menu.

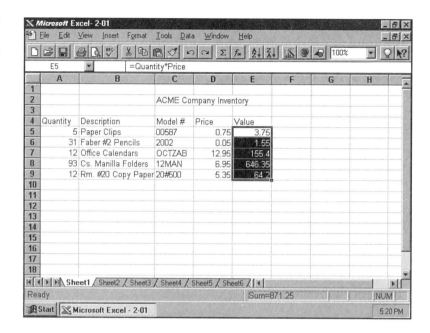

Referring to Multiple Ranges

Next, you want to total the Value column. You already know how to total it by entering a formula, =E5+E6+E7+E8+E9, in cell E10. If you have a spreadsheet that has a large
table (one that contains hundreds or thousands of rows), however, entering that
formula takes much too long. Furthermore, Excel cells are limited to 255 characters,
which is hardly enough if you enter formulas after such a manner.

Fortunately, Excel includes a function called SUM that can add a range of cells and
display the result. To use SUM, enter **=SUM(E5:E9)** in cell E10 and press Enter.

 Tip

You can enter the SUM function in several ways. You can type **=SUM(** and use the
keyboard arrow keys to indicate the range. (When you use the keyboard, you move
the marquee to the first cell, hold down Shift, and then arrow to the last cell.) After
you indicate the range, you can, if you wish, enter the closing parenthesis to
complete the formula, or you can press Enter and let Excel complete the formula
for you.

You can also use the mouse. Type **=SUM(** and select a range of cells, then type **)**
or just press Enter to complete the formula.

Lastly, you can use the Sum tool on the Standard toolbar, as discussed in Chapter 1,
"Introducing Excel."

The shorthand notation in the preceding SUM command is important. In Excel, you can refer to a range of cells by indicating only the beginning and ending cells, separated by a colon. If the range covers multiple rows and columns, you refer to the range by indicating the top left cell and the bottom right cell.

Also, for some formulas you might want to refer to many ranges of cells. For instance, you might want to total two columns with a column of text between them. In that case, you can separate each range of cells with a comma. For example, if you want to sum all of range C5 through C9 and E5 through E9, enter the formula =SUM(C5:C9,E5:E9).

Understanding Relative and Absolute References

By default, the cells you refer to in your formulas are treated as though they refer to cells that are relative to your current cell. For this reason, you can copy the formula in cell E5 to cells E6 through E9 and still get the correct answers for each different row. This type of referencing is called *relative cell referencing* and means that the cells you enter in your formulas are relative references. Most formulas use this relative method.

Excel also can use *absolute cell referencing*, meaning that your formulas always refer to a particular cell, no matter where you copy the formula.

Using Absolute References

To enter a formula in Excel using absolute cell referencing, add a dollar sign ($) before the row and the column. For example, in cell E5 enter **=$D$5*A5$**. If you copy this formula to a different cell, it still refers to cell D5 and A5.

Using Mixed References

Excel enables you to mix absolute and relative cell references. For example, you can enter the formula in cell E5 as **=$D5*$A5**; in essence, telling Excel that you want the column letters to be absolute, but that the row numbers can be relative. This formula still yields the correct answers in each cell because only the row number actually needs to change. If you copy the formula to the right, it still works because this formula always refers to the values found in columns A and D of the current row.

Tip After you enter a cell reference, you can use the F4 key to toggle between the different combinations of relative and absolute cell references. For an example of these combinations, select a blank cell and enter **=D8**. Then, before you continue, press F4 to cycle through D8, D8$, and D$8, which are the different combinations available. You also can use this method when editing a formula. Move to the formula you want to edit and press F2 to begin editing. Use the arrow keys to move the cursor so that it is in the cell reference you want to change, then press F4 to cycle through the changes.

Understanding A1 and R1C1 Cell Addressing

By default, Excel refers to cells using what is called the *A1 reference method*, which uses the alphabet to represent columns and numbers to represent rows. Columns are lettered from A through IV (A to Z, AA to AZ, BA to BZ, and so on, up to IV, which is the 256th column). Rows are numbered from 1 to 16384—a heck of a lot of rows!

Excel also can use a different reference method, called the *R1C1 reference method*, in which the rows *and* columns are numbered.

In the R1C1 method, cells are referenced by using a combination of their row and column number. The equivalent of cell A1 is R1C1 (meaning Row #1, Column #1). Cell E5, for example, would be R5C5, and so on.

Toggling Between A1 and R1C1 Addressing

To toggle Excel between the A1 and the R1C1 methods, pull down the **O**ptions, select **O**ptions, then click on the General tab in the Options notebook that appears. Select the check box marked R1C1, then click on the OK button. To toggle Excel back to the A1 method, choose the same menu item and check the A**1** option.

After you follow those steps, your formulas and cells are referenced using this different method. Table 2.4 shows two examples of the differences you observe.

TABLE 2.4
A1 versus R1C1 Formula Changes

A1 Cell	R1C1 Cell	A1 Formula	R1C1 Formula
E5	R5C5	=D5*A5	=RC[-1]*RC[-4]
E10	R10C5	=SUM(E5:E9)	=SUM(R[-5]C:R[-1]C)

 Note Using the A1 or the R1C1 method changes only the *appearance* of your worksheet. Nothing internal is any different about your spreadsheet. If you give a copy of your spreadsheet to someone using a different method, he or she sees the formulas in the method he or she is using, and the worksheet functions exactly the same as it did using the other method.

If you look at the first example, the R1C1 formula =RC[-1]*RC[-4], translated into English, reads:

"Take the value in the current row, one column to the left, and multiply it by the value in the current row, four columns to the left."

The second example, =SUM(R[-5]C:R[-1]C), translates to the following:

"Sum the values starting from the cell five rows up in the current column to the cell one row up in the current column."

These formulas refer to cell positions that are *relative* to the current cell. The formulas in cells R5C5, R6C5, R7C5, R8C5, and R9C5 are all *exactly* the same formula. When a number is not given after the "R" or the "C" in the R1C1 addressing method, Excel assumes you are referring to the current row or column. Because of this assumption, it is easy to understand how formulas copied to different locations in the spreadsheet refer to cells in the same positions, relative to the cell that contains the formula. So, for example, if you copy the formula =SUM(R[-S]C:R[-1]C) to cell R19C34, it sums the values found in cells R14C34, R15C34, R16C34, R17C34, and R18C34.

If you use the R1C1 method, you also can enter formulas that are not relative to the current cell but are absolute. If, for example, you enter the formula **=R5C1*R5C4**, the formula always refers to those two cells, no matter where in the worksheet you copy the formula.

Understanding the Importance of Names

One of the most useful, but least used, features of Excel is its capability to assign names to parts of the worksheet. In Excel, you can name ranges of cells, constant values, and formulas. Possibly, names are not used by many people because the normal cell references work just fine, and they don't want to take the time to learn something new. Or, perhaps, people think their worksheets won't grow large enough to benefit from using names, but then their worksheets do grow! In any case, consider the following advantages and features of using names in Excel:

◆ If you name cells or ranges of cells, you can then use those names in your formulas. It is far easier to remember to type =**Amount*****Quantity** than to know to type =**D5*A5**.

◆ Using names improves the ability to audit your worksheets. When you use names in your formulas, you can see easily that the formula =**Amount*****Quantity** is correct, but it is not as apparent that =**D5*A5** is correct.

◆ In Excel, you can assign a constant value to a name. For instance, if you work with many financial statements from many different companies, you can assign the name *Number_of_Periods* the value 12 or 13, depending on how many accounting periods the company uses. Then, use the *Number_of_Periods* name in your formulas in place of the number 12 or 13. When you need to use the same worksheet for a company with a different number of accounting periods, just change the value of the *Number_of_Periods* constant, and then all the formulas that use the name automatically are based on the new value.

◆ When you need to jump around a large worksheet, it is easier to use the name to which you want to jump with the Goto command (F5), as opposed to using, for example, cell BZ157. You can press F5 for the Goto command, then just enter **SALES** to jump to the cells named SALES.

◆ Using names can reduce the potential for errors. If you type in a formula with the column or the row even slightly wrong, Excel can give you the answer based on what is in the wrong cell, and you might think that the answer is correct. If you use a name incorrectly, however, Excel gives you a #NAME? error, instead of using an erroneous cell and possibly giving you an incorrect answer.

◆ The preceding advantage is even more important when you consolidate multiple worksheets. It is far easier to validate the formula =AUGSUM.XLS!Units than to validate =AUGSUM.XLS!AR214.

Note Technically, Excel has two types of names: book-level names and sheet-level names. Book-level names correspond to a named range that encompasses an entire workbook, while sheet-level names correspond to ranges within a single worksheet.

Creating Names

As you create and work with names, remember the following rules:

◆ **Names cannot contain spaces.** Instead, use the underscore (_) or the period (.) to separate words. For example, use West_Sales, West.Sales, or even WestSales rather than West Sales.

◆ **Use short names.** Excel allows names as long as 255 characters, but no cell can have an entry that exceeds 255 characters. Also, long names make it difficult to find the name you want when you search through a list of names in a list box.

You can name parts of your worksheet in two ways. The method you use depends on the way your data is structured and the way you want to use the names. Try both of the following exercises so you can understand the differences between the two methods.

Manually

To manually name a range, follow these steps:

1. Select the range of cells A4 through A9.

2. Pull down the **I**nsert menu, select **N**ame, then **D**efine. The Define Name dialog box appears, as shown in figure 2.5.

3. Click on the OK button.

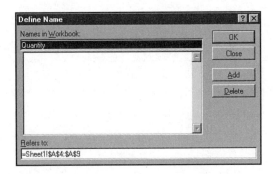

Figure 2.5

The Define Name dialog box.

Because you preselected the range you wanted to name, the dialog box already has filled in the range you want to name, as well as the name you want to use. (Excel uses the text found in the top row or far left column that you selected in order to "guess" the name.) If you don't select the range before you issue the Insert Name Define command, you have to type the name you want in the Names in Workbook field and the range of cells in the Refers to field. Excel has also used absolute cell references in the Refers To field, which is correct.

Automatically

In Excel, you also can create names for multiple ranges at the same time, which is most useful for tables, not unlike the inventory table you have created. To use this method, follow these steps:

1. Select ranges A4:A9, D4:D9, and E4:E9. Remember to hold down the Ctrl key when you select the second and third ranges. If you select all three ranges properly, your screen will look like figure 2.6.

Microsoft Excel- 2-01
File Edit View Insert Format Tools Data Window Help
100%
E4
Value
A B C D E F G H
ACME Company Inventory
Quantity Description Model # Price Value
5 Paper Clips 00587 0.75 3.75
31 Faber #2 Pencils 2002 0.05 1.55
12 Office Calendars OCTZAB 12.95 155.4
93 Cs. Manilla Folders 12MAN 6.95 646.35
12 Rm. #20 Copy Paper 20#500 5.35 64.2
871.25
Sheet1 Sheet2 Sheet3 Sheet4 Sheet5 Sheet6
Select destination and press ENTER or choose Paste
Sum=1050.3
NUM
Start
Microsoft Excel - 2-01
5:22 PM

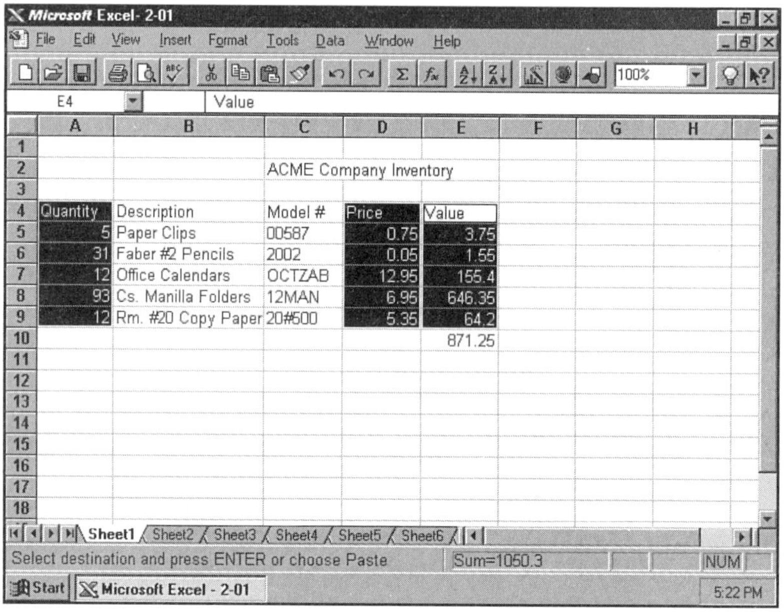

Figure 2.6
Multiple ranges selected.

2. Pull down the Insert menu, select Name, then Create Names. The Create Names dialog box appears (see fig. 2.7).

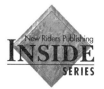

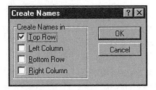

Figure 2.7

The Create Names dialog box.

In the Create Names dialog box, you can tell Excel where to look for the names you want to apply automatically to the ranges. Here, you want Excel to automatically use the titles in the top row for each range, so you need to make sure that the **T**op Row check box is selected.

If you are working in a table that has labels in both the top and left rows, you can select both of those check boxes (**T**op Row and **L**eft Column), which creates a name for each range. **Important:** You can have many names that all refer to the same cell. For instance, you might have vertical ranges named Q1_Sales and Q2_Sales, and horizontal ranges named West_Region and East_Region. In this example, each cell will be referenced by two different names, and you can use those two names appropriately in formulas. If you are creating a new row that adds West_Region and East_Region, you can enter those names. If you are creating a column that totals Q1_Sales and Q2_Sales to the right of your table, you also can use those names.

3. With the **T**op Row check box selected, click on the OK button.

After you click on the OK button, Excel opens a dialog box that asks if you want to replace any existing names (in this example, Quantity was defined earlier). Click on the OK or Cancel button in that dialog box. If your worksheet has no preexisting named ranges in the area in which you are working, nothing happens when the new names are created. You can, however, test these new named ranges. To test them, follow these steps:

1. Move to cell E5.

2. Enter the formula =**Quantity*Price** and press Enter.

If you created the named ranges correctly, you see the same result that previously existed in cell E5, but the formula bar shows your new formula. If the names did not exist, or if you mistyped them in the formula, you get a #NAME? error in that cell.

Applying Names

If you are working with an existing worksheet, it is hardly worth it to manually re-enter all your formulas the way you did for cell E5. Fortunately, in Excel you can take your new named ranges and automatically change all the applicable formulas to use those names. To do this with the inventory worksheet, follow these steps:

1. Select the ranges A4:A9, D4:D9, and E4:E10 (make sure to include the total at the bottom of the Value column). Press and hold down Ctrl while you use your mouse to select the second and third ranges.

2. Pull down the **I**nsert menu, select **N**ame, then select **A**pply. The Apply Names dialog box appears, as shown in figure 2.8.

3. Click on the OK button.

Figure 2.8

The Apply Names dialog box.

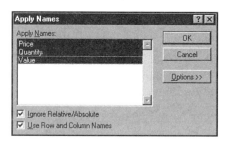

Before you use it, make sure that the names you want to apply are selected in the list box, which they are by default if you completed the range selection process in step 1. If the names are not selected, you need to select them using the mouse, holding down Ctrl if you want to apply more than one name.

The Apply Names dialog box has several options, as follows:

◆ **Ignore Relative/Absolute.** Controls the way Excel substitutes names for relative and absolute references. If this box is not checked, Excel applies only names that match the absolute or relative reference found in the original formula. You usually want to have this box checked.

◆ **Use Row and Column Names.** Controls how liberally Excel applies names. If this box is not checked, Excel applies only names that refer to the individual cells used in the formula rather than names that might refer to an entire column or row. If this box is checked (the default), Excel uses the name for the entire row or column. Normally, you want to leave this box checked.

Check around the worksheet. All the formulas have been replaced with the simpler, name-based formulas. Even the =SUM formula reads =SUM(Value), which is far easier to read and remember (and understand!) than =SUM(E4:E9).

Creating Named Constants

One often-overlooked feature in Excel is being able to create named constants. If you use Excel's name feature, constants don't even have to take up cell space.

Use a constant when parts of your worksheet depend on a single number. One example is a sales projection worksheet that uses a single value for sales growth assumptions, or, perhaps, a profit and loss statement that has an assumption about your gross margin. In either case, you can handle the numerical assumption in one of two ways:

◆ You can enter the assumption in a single cell on the worksheet, and then have your other formulas refer to that cell (using an absolute cell reference).

◆ You can define a named constant that contains the number.

Using the named constant keeps your worksheet a little neater and also makes it easier to see the ways your formulas work.

Tip　When you create named constants, use something consistent in the name to distinguish it as a constant rather than a named range of cells. For example, you could use only uppercase letters for the names of your constants. Or, you could begin the name of each constant with C_. For example, you might create a constant named C_GROWTH. Using this kind of visual clue helps you see quickly which names in your formulas are constants and which are named cells.

Using B_name for book-level range names and S_name for sheet-level names will also help you keep your naming conventions in check.

To create and work with named constants, use the following steps. You add a new column to the example worksheet that shows the retail value of the inventory in stock. As part of the exercise, you create a named constant called C_MARKUP that you use to calculate the retail value:

1. Move to cell F4 and select it, then type **Retail Value** and press Enter.

2. Reselect cell F4. Then, pull down the **I**nsert menu, select **N**ame, and then **D**efine.

3. In the Define Names dialog box that appears, move to the field called Names in **W**orkbook and type **C_MARKUP**.

4. Tab to the **R**efers to field and type **1.40**—a 40 percent markup after you use it in the formula to multiply against the Value.

5. Click on OK to return to the worksheet.

6. Move to cell F5 and type the formula **=Value*C_MARKUP** and press Enter. Cell F5 now shows you the retail value of the inventory in row 5.

7. Select the range F5:F9. While those cells are selected, pull down the **E**dit menu, select **F**ill, then **D**own.

8. While the range still is selected, pull down the **I**nsert menu, select **N**ame, then **D**efine.

9. The Define Name dialog box already has the name—Retail_Value—and the range of cells entered. So just click on the OK button.

10. Move to cell F10, enter the formula **=SUM(Retail_Value)**, and press Enter.

Your worksheet now has the new column, along with the total retail value in cell F10. To change the assumption contained in the constant value C_MARKUP (your retail markup assumption), follow these steps:

1. Pull down the **I**nsert menu, select **N**ame, then **D**efine.

2. In the Names in **S**heet list box, select C_MARKUP. Then, click in the **R**efers to field and change the value from 1.40 to 1.5.

3. Click on the OK button for your changes to take effect. The results are shown in figure 2.9.

Figure 2.9

The retail value columns after changing the constant C_MARKUP.

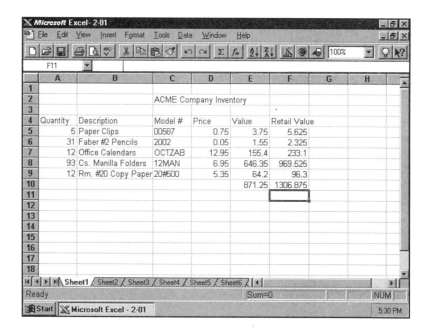

Immediately after you click on the OK button, the retail value of each item changes to reflect the new markup in the constant C_MARKUP. The total at the bottom of the column also changes to reflect the new value assumption.

Creating Named Formulas

Even as you can define a named constant, so too can you define a named formula. While named formulas have fewer uses, they can come in handy. One example in which named formulas are useful might be if your worksheet uses a single formula in many places. If you use a named formula, you can simply change the named formula, rather than finding and changing the formula in every cell in which it occurs.

To see how this works, create a named formula called Calc.Retail.Value. This named formula has the formula necessary to calculate the retail value. Follow these steps:

1. Select cell F5. Then, pull down the **I**nsert menu, select **N**ame, and then **D**efine.

2. In the Define Name dialog box, move to the **N**ame field and type **Calc.Retail.Value**.

Tip   For the same reason you want your named constants to have a distinct naming style from named ranges, you also want named formulas to have a distinct naming style. In this example, the named formula uses periods to separate the words and also has the word Calc at the beginning of the name, which helps you see that this name refers to a named formula.

3. Move to the **R**efers to field, type **=(E5*C_MARKUP)**, press Enter to create the name, and click on the OK button to close the Define Name dialog box.

4. Move back to cell F5, type **=Calc.Retail.Value**, and press Enter.

    Cell F5 now contains a reference to Calc.Retail.Value, which contains the formula that does the calculation. To complete this change, copy the new formula down to the other cells.

5. To copy the named formula to the rest of the column, select the cells F5:F9 and press Ctrl+D (the shortcut for **E**dit, Fi**l**l **D**own).

Deleting Names

Sometimes you have to delete names from a workbook. For example, if the name in question is no longer in use, you might want to remove it from the list to reduce clutter. To remove a name, use the following procedure:

1. Pull down the **I**nsert menu, select **N**ame, then **D**efine.

2. Click on the name you want to delete in the Names in **W**orkbook list box.

3. Click on the **D**elete button, then the OK button.

Stop   If you delete a name that is being used in other formulas, Excel doesn't warn you. What happens is, after you click on the OK button, a #NAME? error message appears in all the cells that have formulas using that name, as well as in any cells that refer to the cells using that deleted name. For example, if you delete the Price name from the example worksheet, all the cells in columns E and F show the #NAME? error because those cells depend on the Price name. To rectify such a mistake, you must re-create the name or edit the formulas in the affected cells.

Working with Notes in Cells

Naming parts of your workbook is only the beginning of documenting it. Often, you still have to explain *why* certain calculations were made or provide other information pertinent to the workbook. Here are a couple of reasons why notes make sense:

◆ If you need to look at the workbook again in several months, you might not remember why you made certain choices.

◆ If others work with your workbooks, they might not understand why you did certain things or the way in which you did them.

In Excel, you can attach notes to individual cells—notes that you can use to explain the worksheet. In essence, you can annotate your worksheet.

Adding Notes

In the worksheet in figure 2.10, the sales for Clyde Coyote are at zero for the month of April, but why the sales go to zero that month is totally inexplicable.

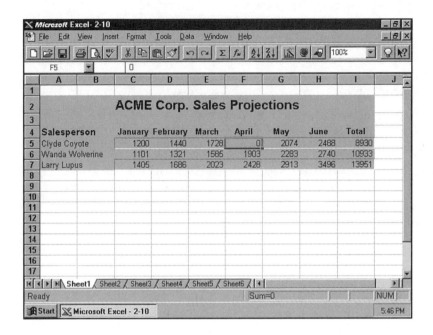

Figure 2.10

The ACME Sales Projections worksheet.

Any proper documentation must certainly explain that "zero" entry—a perfect occasion for Excel's note feature. To add a note that explains the lack of sales during April, follow these steps:

1. Move to cell F5.

2. Pull down the **I**nsert menu and select **N**ote. The Cell Note dialog box appears, as shown in figure 2.11.

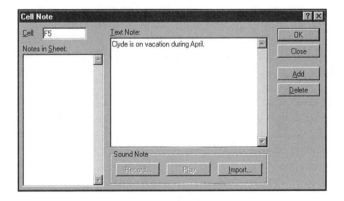

Figure 2.11

The Cell Note dialog box.

Note If the active cell moves down a row when you press Enter, you might want to turn off the feature that controls this action. Pull down the **T**ools menu and choose **O**ptions. Click on the Edit tab, then select or clear the option marked **M**ove Selection after Enter.

The Tab key moves you one cell to the right. When you are editing a cell and press the Tab key, the contents of the cell you just entered is saved before the active cell is moved. Similarly, press Shift+Tab to move one cell to the left.

If you pay attention to Excel's menu, you can see that most of Excel's shortcut keys are listed next to their respective menu options. In step 2, for example, Ctrl+D also performs the Fill Down operation.

Tip Press Shift+F2 to pull up the Cell Note dialog box.

The Cell Note dialog box has many fields and buttons, which are described in the following list:

◆ **Cell.** Indicates the cell to which this note is to be attached. You can attach notes only to single cells and not to ranges of cells.

◆ **Notes in Sheet.** Displays all notes that the worksheet contains. The notes are listed in order of cell location. Only the first 10 or so characters of the note appear in the list.

◆ **Text Note.** You type the complete note in this field. Also, if you browse in the Cell Note dialog box, you can see the complete note if you select it from the Notes in **S**heet list box.

◆ **Sound Note.** If your computer contains a sound board and a microphone, you can record a note and attach it to the cell. You also can import a sound clip and attach it to the cell. Double-click on the individual cells that contain the sound note to play the sound notes.

For this example, move to the **T**ext Note field and type **Clyde is on vacation this month**. To store the note, press Enter or click on the OK button.

A small red dot in the upper-right corner of a cell indicates the presence of a note (see fig. 2.12).

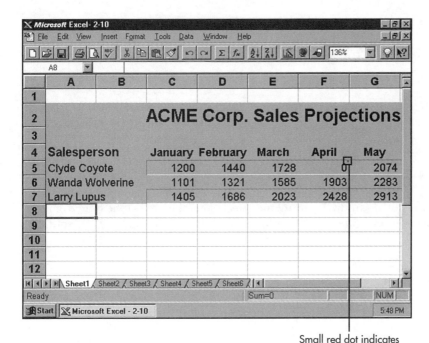

Figure 2.12

The Note indicator.

Small red dot indicates
note attached to cell

Showing Notes

If a note is indicated by the small red dot, press Shift+F2 after you select the cell to play the note or bring up the note dialog box.

You can turn off the appearance of the small red dot by following these steps:

1. Pull down the **T**ools menu, select **O**ptions, then click on the View tab.

2. On the View notebook page, find the check box marked **N**ote Indicator and click on it to deselect the check box.

3. Click on the OK button.

Finding Notes

To search the spreadsheet for a specific note, follow these steps:

1. Pull down the **E**dit menu and select **F**ind (or press Shift+F5). The Find dialog box appears.

2. In the Fi**n**d What field, type the word you want to find.

3. In the Look Indrop box, select Notes.

4. Click on the OK button.

Excel searches all the notes in the worksheet for the word you typed, and the cell that contains the note becomes the active cell. To bring up the note, press Shift+F2 when you are on that cell.

Editing Notes

To edit a note, pull down the **I**nsert menu, select **N**ote, then select the note from the Notes in **S**heet list box. After you select the note, you can edit it in the **T**ext Note field.

Also, after you select a note, you can click on the **D**elete button to remove the note from the worksheet.

Rearranging Data

One of the most powerful notions behind worksheets is that they enable you to work through an idea or analysis progressively. It is vital to know how to rearrange the data you enter into the worksheet as you decide to try new approaches, consider new information, and so on. Whether you want to analyze the data in a different way, rearrange the data to better graph it, or accomplish some other task, manipulating data and rearranging it are important skills. This section covers the following:

◆ Cutting data from one location and pasting it to another

◆ Copying data in your document

◆ Moving data in a single mouse movement

◆ Moving not only ranges, but also entire rows or columns

◆ Filling ranges of cells automatically with numbers or text

◆ Using AutoFill to complete various numeric and date progressions

Cut and Paste

The basic method for moving and duplicating data in a worksheet is to Cut and Paste or Copy and Paste—similar, but not duplicate, activities. You can cut or copy data into the "Clipboard," then paste it from the Clipboard to a new location.

For these examples, you use the inventory worksheet that you created at the beginning of this chapter:

1. Begin by selecting range B4:B9.

2. Pull down the **E**dit menu and select Cu**t**. A marquee surrounds the area you have cut, but it doesn't disappear right away (in many programs, your data disappears immediately after choosing Cu**t**, but not in Excel).

3. Move your active cell to location B12.

4. Pull down the **E**dit menu and select **P**aste.

 Note   When you cut and paste cells on which other cells are dependent, Excel automatically adjusts the references so that the formulas still work properly with the data in the new location.

Immediately, the data vanishes from its original location and reappears in the new location (see fig. 2.13). The pasted data starts in the active cell (B12) and fills the cells downward. The destination you select is always the upper left corner of the area you want to paste.

Figure 2.13

The pasted data in a new location.

	A	B	C	D	E	F	G	H
1								
2			ACME Company Inventory					
3								
4	Quantity		Model #	Price	Value	Retail Value		
5	5		00587	0.75	3.75	5.625		
6	31		2002	0.05	1.55	2.325		
7	12		OCTZAB	12.95	155.4	233.1		
8	93		12MAN	6.95	646.35	969.525		
9	12		20#500	5.35	64.2	96.3		
10					871.25	1306.875		
11								
12		Description						
13		Paper Clips						
14		Faber #2 Pencils						
15		Office Calendars						
16		Cs. Manilla Folders						
17		Rm. #20 Copy Paper						
18								

To reverse the process, select the data from cells B12:B17, then choose Cut from the Edit menu. Move your active cell to cell B4, then select Paste from the Edit menu.

Note   Of course, if you wanted to undo the cut and paste operation, you simply choose Undo from the Edit menu.

You cut, copy, and paste frequently in Excel, so you can save a great deal of time by learning to use the cut, copy, and paste shortcut keys. These keys are shown in table 2.5.

TABLE 2.5
Cut, Copy, and Paste Shortcut Keys

Function	Shortcut Key	Memory Cues
Cut	Ctrl+X	Think of "X" as similar to a pair of scissors, or think of crossing something out on a paper document with a big X.
Copy	Ctrl+C	"C" stands for copy.
Paste	Ctrl+V	Think of the "V" as an insertion point that you would make hand-editing a document.

AUTHOR'S NOTE

All these keys are on the keyboard in the order shown. Cut, copy, and paste are in the same order, from left to right, as X, C, and V on your keyboard. Excel is one of the few Windows programs that uses Ctrl+X, Ctrl+C, and Ctrl+V for these functions. Most Windows-based programs use Shift+Delete for Cut, Ctrl+Insert for Copy, and Shift+Insert for Paste.

These easier key combinations originated on the Macintosh, for which they have been standards ever since the Mac was developed more than 10 years ago.

Copying Data

Copying data works just like cutting and pasting. Instead of cutting from one location and pasting onto another, you copy the data from the selected range onto the Clipboard and then paste it onto the new location. The original data is unaffected.

For an example of how copying works, select the range B4:B9 and press Ctrl+C (for copy). Move your active cell to B12 and press Ctrl+V (for paste). You should see a copy of the data appear in the new location.

Also, because the data is still in memory, you can paste the copied data into an unlimited number of new locations, until you cut or copy something else, which overwrites the old data in the Clipboard. To see the way this works, move to cell C12 and press Ctrl+V again.

Deleting Data

To delete data from your worksheet, select a range such as C12:C17 in the example, pull down the Edit menu, and choose Clear, then All.

The cascading menu is shown in figure 2.14.

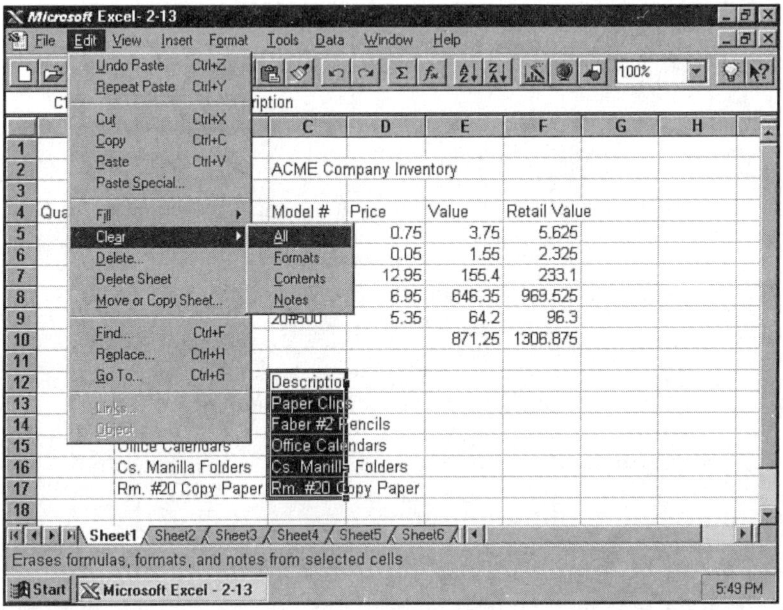

Figure 2.14

The Clear All cascading menu.

Tip   Pressing the Del key does the same thing as selecting Clear, All from the Edit menu.

The Clear cascading menu has four options, as follows:

◆ **All.** Removes the data in the selected range, as well as any formatting applied to the cell and any notes attached to the cell. When formatting is removed, the cell reverts to General—the default format.

◆ **Formats.** Causes the formatting for the cell to be removed. The cell reverts to the General format.

◆ **Contents.** Removes any cell contents, including formulas, numbers, and text labels, but does not affect the cell format or any notes attached to the cell. This is the default.

◆ **Notes.** Removes only the note attached to the selected cells. The cell contents and formatting remain.

In this example, you want to remove the entire range contents. Because the menu already is set to <u>A</u>ll, click on <u>A</u>ll.

Tip   To remove all cell contents quickly, select the range you want to clear and press Ctrl+Del. Pressing Del only removes cell contents, whereas Ctrl+Del clears everything from the selected cells.

Entire Rows and Columns

You can cut, copy, paste, or clear entire rows and columns. As an example, move column E to column G by using the following steps:

1. At the top of the worksheet, click once on the column marker labeled E. The entire column becomes highlighted.

2. Press Ctrl+X to cut the data from column E.

3. Click on the column marker for column G.

4. Press Ctrl+V to paste the data into the new location. Depending on your computer's available memory, you might see a dialog box that warns you that the section is too large to undo. If you are sure you want to proceed, click on the OK button.

You can perform the same operation on rows by selecting the numbered row label.

You also can perform the operation on multiple rows or columns. Hold down Ctrl as you select each row or column. If, by chance, you select an operation (such as <u>E</u>dit, <u>D</u>elete) that Excel cannot perform on multiple rows or columns, an error box appears.

Dragging

Cutting and pasting with Ctrl+X and Ctrl+V are quick methods, but Excel includes one other shortcut that lets you move data with a simple drag of the mouse. To see how shortcuts work, move the cells D4:D9 to G4:G9, as follows:

1. Select the range D4:D9.

2. Very carefully move your pointer to the outside border of the selected cells. When your pointer is in precisely the right place, it changes to a white arrow.

3. With your pointer in the arrow shape, click and hold down the left mouse button. With the button held down, move your mouse to the right. As you move it, a thick marquee moves.

4. Position the thick marquee so that it encloses cells G4:G9, and then release the mouse button.

This procedure works with both single cells and ranges. You even can use it with entire rows and columns!

Stop When you move sections of your worksheet that contain formulas or numbers used by formulas in other cells, be careful. Moving cells can mess up the formulas they contain or formulas in other cells that use the moved data. Often these problems appear as #REF! or #VALUE! errors in the affected cells.

Filling Ranges of Cells

Often, you need to copy the contents of one cell into many cells. You can copy the data into the Clipboard, then paste it into the new cells, but there are yet faster ways available to duplicate cell contents into many cells.

For these examples, begin a new worksheet. Pull down the **F**ile menu and select **N**ew. A dialog box prompts you for the type of document that you want to create. Select Workbook and click on the OK button.

Menu Commands

Follow these steps to see how to fill ranges of cells with menu commands:

1. Move to cell D6, type **Example**, and press Enter.

2. Select the range D6:D10.

3. Pull down the **E**dit menu and select **F**ill, then **D**own.

The word Example is copied into each of the selected cells. You also can do this to fill cells to the right by selecting a horizontal range and selecting **E**dit, **F**ill, **R**ight.

Tip You can fill down faster by pressing Ctrl+D. Filling right can be done using Ctrl+R.

Fill Handle

Using the fill handle is far easier than using the menu commands to fill ranges. The fill handle also has some neat tricks! For these examples, delete anything on the worksheet left over from the previous example. Select a range that includes all the worksheet contents and press Ctrl+Delete to clear the worksheet contents.

Use table 2.6 to set up several cells to use to explore the different ways in which the fill handle works. After you set up the worksheet, it should look like figure 2.15.

TABLE 2.6
Fill Handle Example Setup

Cell	Contents
B3	1
B4	1
C4	3
B5	January
B6	Jan
C6	Apr
B7	Quarter 1
B8	1/1/95
B9	1/1/95
C9	2/1/95

Tip You can use double-clicking to your advantage with the fill tool, as well. If you double-clicked the fill handle in the preceding exercise, it would automatically fill down the column only so far as the column on the left extended. If the column on the left is empty, it will fill down as far as the right column extends.

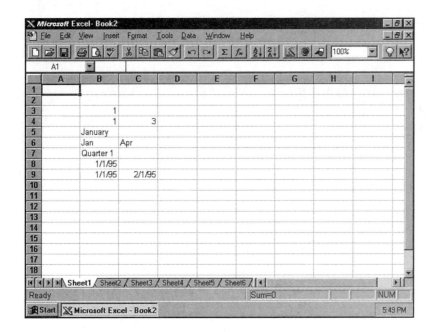

Figure 2.15

The worksheet for fill handle examples.

Follow these steps to start using the fill handle:

1. Make sure that cell B3 is your active cell.

2. Locate the fill handle. It is the small box at the lower right corner of the active cell (see fig. 2.16).

3. Carefully move your pointer until it is immediately on top of the fill handle. When positioned correctly, the pointer changes to a small cross.

4. Hold down the left mouse button and drag the mouse to the right until the thick marquee surrounds the cells from B3 to H3.

5. When the marquee is positioned correctly, release the mouse button.

The number 1 is automatically copied into each of the selected cells. You also can use the fill handle to fill on each of the other four directions.

Figure 2.16

The fill handle.

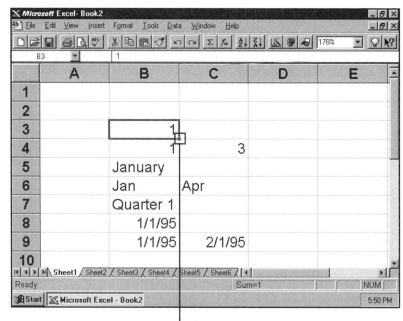

Fill handle

AutoFill

If you use the fill handle with a single number or a text label, Excel simply copies the data. Similarly, if you use the fill handle with a formula, Excel copies it, adjusting any relative cell references as it fills the formula.

Sometimes, however, the fill handle activates a feature called *AutoFill.* Follow these examples to see some of the ways in which AutoFill works.

Numeric Progression

1. Select the cells B4:C4

2. Drag the fill handle in the lower right corner of cell C4 until the thick marquee extends to H3 and release the mouse button. The results are shown in figure 2.17.

Excel determined that you had marked out two cells that contained a numeric progression. Excel assumed that you wanted to continue the numeric progression and filled the cells accordingly.

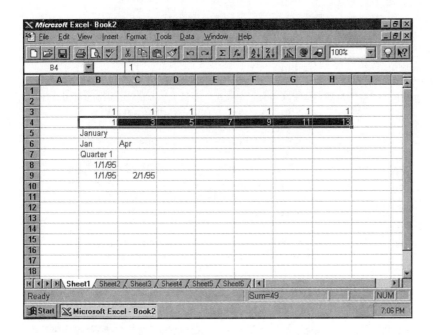

Figure 2.17

Numeric progression with the fill handle.

Date Progressions

AutoFill also is very intelligent about filling dates into cells. For each of the remaining lines in the example worksheet, use the fill handle to copy the contents to column H. In the two cases where two initial examples are provided (when column C has a value), remember to select both examples before dragging the Fill handle to the right. The results are shown in figure 2.18.

Table 2.7 contains some comments on each of these examples.

TABLE 2.7
Comments on AutoFill Examples

Row	Starting Data	Comments
5	January	Excel recognizes the word "January" as a valid month name. It automatically fills the remaining months into the filled cells.
6	Jan, Apr	Excel also recognizes Jan and Apr as valid month titles. Because you used two month names that are three months apart, Excel continues the series, even starting over again at Jan when it finishes the first year.

continues

TABLE **2.7**, CONTINUED
Comments on AutoFill Examples

Row	Starting Data	Comments
7	Quarter 1	Excel recognizes Quarter 1 as a common financial heading. It correctly fills the remaining three quarters, and then starts over again at Quarter 1. Excel also recognizes "Qtr1," and "Q1" as quarterly titles.
8	1/1/93	AutoFilling this range produces dates each one day apart. If you AutoFill many cells, you find that Excel knows the day on which each month ends and that it even takes into account leap years!
9	1/1/93,2/1/93	As you observed in previous progressions, Excel is fairly intelligent about assuming your desires. In this case, it automatically fills each cell with the first day of each month.

Figure 2.18

Completed examples of AutoFill.

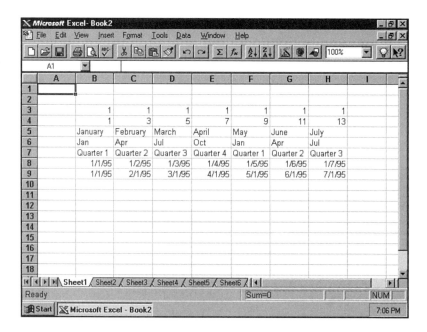

As you can see, Excel's AutoFill feature is very intelligent and saves you a tremendous amount of time.

Inserting and Deleting Data

Aside from cut, copy, paste, and clear operations, Excel also offers insertion and deletion areas on the worksheet. Using the **Edit**, **I**nsert and Edit, **D**elete commands, you can accomplish the following tasks:

◆ Insert new rows or columns, pushing the existing rows or columns down or to the right to make room.

◆ Insert blocks of data, pushing the existing data to the right or down.

◆ Delete entire rows or columns, moving the remaining data up or to the left.

◆ Delete ranges of data, moving the remaining data up or to the left.

Inserting Blank Space

To insert new blank space in your worksheet, select the area in which you want the new cells to appear, pull down the **I**nsert menu, then select **C**ells.

As an example, select the range C4:F7, pull down the **I**nsert menu, and then select **C**ells. The Insert dialog box appears, as displayed in figure 2.19.

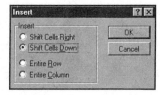

Figure 2.19

The Insert dialog box.

The Insert dialog box lets you choose from the following four options:

◆ **Shift Cells Right.** Makes new space by forcing the existing cells to the right of the new area.

◆ **Shift Cells Down.** Pushes the existing cells downward.

◆ **Entire Row.** Inserts entire rows in the selected range, pushing the existing rows down.

◆ **Entire Column.** Inserts entire columns, pushing the existing columns to the right.

For this example, select Shift Cells **D**own. The results are shown in figure 2.20.

Figure 2.20

*The inserted
blank range.*

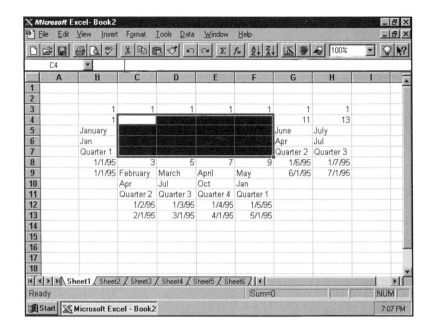

Inserting Data

You also can copy data from one location and insert it into a new location by selecting
the range you want to copy, pressing Ctrl+C to copy it to the Clipboard, positioning
the active cell where you want the data to be inserted, pulling down the **I**nsert menu,
and selecting **C**ell. The Insert dialog box appears, which enables you to shift the
existing cells to the right or down. After you make your decision in the dialog box,
Excel performs the insert operation, moving the existing cells in the direction you
specify.

Deleting Ranges

Deleting entire ranges is accomplished in a similar way. Select the range of cells to
delete, pull down the **E**dit menu, and select **D**elete. You will be shown a Delete dialog
box, which enables you to choose to shift the cells up, to the left, or to delete entire
rows and columns. Select the appropriate choice and click on the OK button.

Inserting and Deleting Entire Rows and Columns

Finally, you can insert and delete entire rows and columns by selecting the row or column. Click on the row or column label, then choose **I**nsert **R**ow, **I**nsert **C**olumn, or **E**dit **D**elete.

You also can select multiple rows and columns. Just hold down the mouse on the first row or column, then drag the mouse in the appropriate direction to select the desired rows or columns.

Special Paste Tricks Within Excel

Excel has a few other tricks up its sleeve concerning the rearrangement of data. Under the **E**dit menu is a command called Paste **S**pecial. Paste **S**pecial enables you to accomplish the following tricks:

◆ Selectively paste only cell values, formulas, formatting, or notes.

◆ Automatically take the originating range and perform a mathematical function with its cells on the destination cells.

◆ Transpose a series of cells, which has the effect of rotating the data 90 degrees.

To understand the way these features work, set up the worksheet as follows:

1. In cell B2, enter **1.**

2. In cell C2, enter **3.**

3. Use the Fill handle to AutoFill the numeric series to column G (select B2:C2 and drag the Fill handle to cell G2).

4. In cell B3, enter **2.**

5. In cell C3, enter **4.**

6. Use the Fill handle to AutoFill the numeric series to column G.

7. In cell B4, enter the formula **=B2*B3** and press Enter.

8. Use the Fill handle to copy the formula in cell B4 to all of the cells over to cell G4.

Your worksheet should look like figure 2.21.

Figure 2.21

A sample worksheet for Paste Special examples.

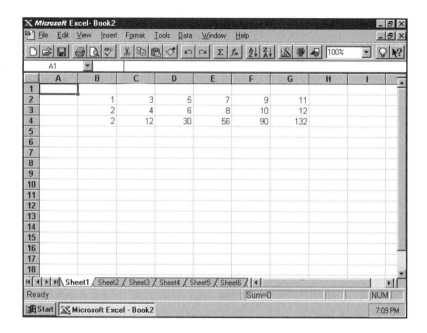

Pasting Values

Excel enables you to copy a series of formulas and paste only their results. You can, for example, select a series of formulas that result in numeric values and copy those formulas into the Clipboard. Then you can move to the destination cell, use Paste **S**pecial, and select **V**alues from the dialog box. Click on OK to complete the operation. The destination cells contain the results, not the formulas of the originating cells.

To perform this operation, do the following:

1. Select the cells B4:G4 and press Ctrl+C to copy them into the Clipboard.

2. Move to cell B6.

3. Pull down the **E**dit Menu and select Paste **S**pecial.

4. In the Paste Special dialog box, select **V**alues, and click the OK button.

If you look at the cell contents of the original cells (B4:G4), you can see that they contain formulas. The destination cells, however, contain only the resulting values. It is as if Excel took the values and simply typed the results for you in the new location (see fig. 2.22).

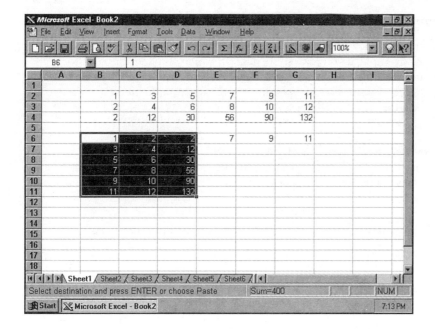

Figure 2.22

The first result of Transpose.

Performing Math Operations

Excel enables you to copy one series of numbers (either from a formula or simple, entered numbers), and then add, subtract, multiply, or divide those values against a different range.

To see how this operation works, follow these steps:

1. Select the series of cells B3:G3.

2. Press Ctrl+C to copy the cells into the Clipboard.

3. Move to cell B6, where the results of the previous example start.

4. Pull down the **E**dit menu and select Paste **S**pecial.

5. In the Paste Special dialog box, select D**i**vide, and click on the OK button.

Excel takes the numbers in the destination cells and divides them by the contents of the Clipboard. Using the same method, you also can add, subtract, or multiply two ranges of numbers against one another.

Transposing Data

You also can change the orientation of your data quickly using the Paste **S**pecial command. For example, if you have some data for which you want the rows to become columns and the columns to become rows, Paste **S**pecial enables you to "rotate" the data 90 degrees. This capability is separate from the new Pivot Table feature, which is discussed in a later chapter.

 Stop   When you transpose cells that contain formulas, you change any formulas in the transposed cells. To deal with this potential problem, select the Values option button when performing the Paste Special command. This option converts any formulas to pure numbers.

To see how the transpose feature in Paste Special works, follow these steps:

1. Select the range of cells B2:G4.

2. Press Ctrl+C to copy the cells to the Clipboard.

3. Move to cell B6.

4. Pull down the **E**dit menu and select Paste **S**pecial.

5. In the Paste Special dialog box, click on the Transpos**e** check box, then click on the OK button.

The results are shown in figure 2.23.

Excel rearranges the data 90 degrees from its original arrangement in the source cells. Also, notice that the far right column now shows primarily zeros. This rightmost column originally was the formula in row 4. Now that the data is rearranged, those formulas no longer refer to meaningful cells. To avoid this problem, select the **V**alues option when you select Transpos**e** if you have any formulas in the copied area that are dependent on other data or on data structure.

87

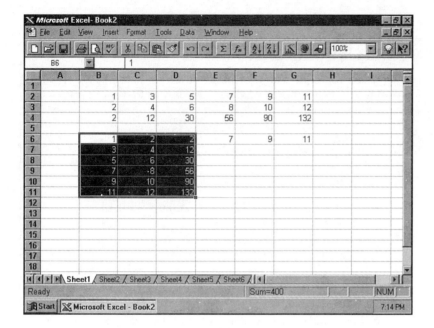

Figure 2.23

The second result of Transpose.

Chapter Snapshot

Now that you understand the basics of working with data in Excel, you need to know how to make the worksheet look more professional and appealing. In this chapter, you learn to use Excel's formatting tools to do the following:

◆ Format numbers for different display styles

◆ Change fonts in your worksheet

◆ Change the height of your rows and the width of your columns

◆ Dress up your worksheet with border lines and shading

◆ Control the alignment of the data in your worksheet, including how to center a title across the worksheet quickly

◆ Use Excel's styles to format your worksheets quickly

◆ Use Excel's AutoFormat feature to format a table quickly and easily

◆ Zoom in and out of your worksheet to see more area or more detail

A nicely formatted document helps you present your information much more effectively.

CHAPTER 3

Worksheet Formatting

Setting up a worksheet, entering the data, getting all the formulas to work, and structuring the worksheet in a useful way are usually only half the battle. Before you can use Excel to share information with others, you must be able to format the worksheet so you can communicate quickly and effectively.

Excel provides many tools to help you control the way your worksheet appears and prints. This chapter teaches you how to produce professional, eye-catching reports and worksheets.

Activating the Formatting Toolbar

This chapter shows you how to use the Style toolbar for faster and easier formatting. To open the Style toolbar, follow these steps:

1. Pull down the **V**iew menu and choose **T**oolbars. The Toolbars dialog box appears, as shown in figure 3.1.

Figure 3.1

The Toolbars dialog box.

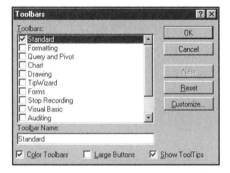

2. Click on the check box to the left of the word Formatting.

3. Click on the OK button or press Enter. The Formatting toolbar will appear directly beneath the standard toolbar.

Figure 3.2 shows all the buttons in the Formatting toolbar. The function of each button is described in table 3.1.

TABLE 3.1
Formatting Toolbar Buttons

Icon	Name	Description
Arial	Font Name	Chooses font name for selected range.
10	Font Size	Chooses font size for selected range.
B	Bold	Makes selected range bold.
I	Italic	Makes selected range italic.

Icon	Name	Description
U	Underline	Underlines selected range.
	Align Left	Makes selected range left-justified.
	Align Center	Makes selected range centered.
	Align Right	Makes selected range right-justified.
	Center Across Selection	Centers the text across selected range.
$	Currency Style	Applies the currency style to numbers in selected range.
%	Percent Style	Applies the percentage style to numbers in selected range.
,	Comma Style	Applies the comma style to numbers in selected range.
	Increase Decimal	Increases the number of digits after the decimal point for numbers in selected range.
	Decrease Decimal	Decreases the number of digits after the decimal point for numbers in selected range.
	Color	Chooses the color for selected cells.
	Borders	Chooses the border style for selected cells.
	Font Color	Chooses the color for text in selected cells.

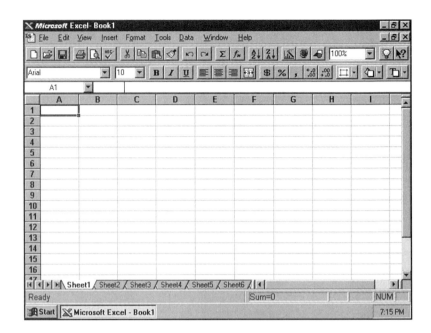

Formatting Numbers

The first step when you format a worksheet is to control the way numeric information appears in the individual cells. Many choices are available, as follows:

◆ Use commas for the thousands separator?

◆ Display negative numbers in red?

◆ Use brackets for negative numbers, and if so, what characters to use for the brackets?

◆ How many decimal positions to show?

◆ What format to use to display dates and times?

Because you can create your own numeric and date formats, the possibilities for using different numeric formats are virtually endless.

Using Built-In Formats

Excel uses format codes to control the way numbers are formatted in your worksheets. *Format codes* are collections of special formatting characters that Excel interprets in order to know how to format the numbers in the worksheet. Although

these format codes can be a bit cryptic, you learn in the following sections how to read and create them quickly.

Table 3.2 shows the different format codes used with Excel, along with examples of how each number appears when that code is used.

TABLE 3.2
Built-In Excel Formats

Format Section	Format Setting	Examples Positive	Negative
All	General	12345.67	–12345.67
Custom	(Shows formats that you create)		
Number	0	12346	–12346
	0.00	12345.67	–12345.67
	#,##0	12,346	–12,346
	#,##0.00	12,345.67	–12,345.67
	#,##0_);(#,##0)	12,346	(12,346)
	#,##0_);[Red](#,##0)	12,346	**(12,346)**
	#,##0.00_);(#,##0.00)	12,345.67	(12,345.67)
	#,##0.00_);[Red](#,##0.00)	12,345.67	**(12,345.67)**
Accounting	_(*#,##0_);_(#,##0);_(*"-"_);_(@_)	12,345	(12,345)
	_(*#,##0.00_);_(*(#,##0.00);_(*"-"??_);_(@_)	12,345.67	(12,345.67)
	_($*#,##0_);_($*(#,##0);_($*"-"_);_(@_)	$12,345	$(12,345)
	_($*#,##0.00_);_($*(#,##0.00);_($*"-"??_);_(@_)	$12,345.67	$(12,345.67)
Date	m/d/y	4/15/95	
	d–mmm–yy	15–Apr–95	
	d–mmm	15–Apr	
	mmm–d	Apr–95	
	m/d/y h:mm	4/15/95 6:31	

continues

TABLE 3.2, CONTINUED
Built-In Excel Formats

Format Section	Format Setting	Examples Positive	Negative
Time	h:mm AM/PM	6:31 AM	
	h:mm:ss AM/PM	6:31:00 AM	
	h:mm	6:31	
	h:mm:ss	6:31:00	
	m/d/yy h:mm	4/15/95 6:31	
	mm:ss	31:00	
	mm:ss.0	31:00.0	
	h:mm:ss	6:31:00	
Percentage	0%	12%	–12%
	0.00%	12.35%	–12.35%
Fraction	# ?/?	12345 2/3	–12345 2/3
	# ??/??	12345 65/97	–12345 65/97
Scientific	0.00E+00	1.23E+04	–1.23E+04
Text	@ (Text placeholder)		
Currency	$#,##0_);($#,##0)	$12,346	($12,346)
	$#,##0_);[Red]($#,##0)	$12,346	**($12,346)**
	$#,##0.00_);($#,##0.00)	$12,345.67	($12,345.67)
	$#,##0.00_);[Red]($#,##0.00)	$12,345.67	**($12,345.67)**

 Note Numbers that appear in bold in the preceding table appear in red on a color monitor.

Applying Built-In Formats

You can apply different numeric formats to your cells in two ways. The first way, using menu commands, is the most flexible. The second way is to use keyboard shortcut keys that are available for the most common formatting needs.

To apply a format using menu commands, use the following procedure:

1. Select the cell or range that you want to format.

2. Pull down the **F**ormat menu and select C**e**lls.

Tip   As a shortcut, after you select the cell or range to format, you can click on the selected range using the right mouse button to bring up the pop-up menu for the selection. From the pop-up menu, choose **N**umber to access the Number dialog box.

3. Step 2 causes the Format Cells notebook to appear. If it is not selected, click on the Number tab. You see the Number page, shown in figure 3.3.

4. Click on the appropriate category in the **C**ategory list box.

5. Click on the desired format in the **T**ype list box. Use the small sample at the bottom of the dialog box to help you determine which format you want.

6. Click on the OK button.

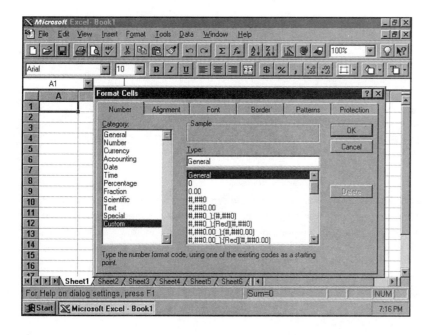

Figure 3.3

The Number format notebook page.

Excel also includes some key combinations that format the cells you select instantly with a number of commonly used formats. Table 3.3 shows a list of these shortcut keys.

TABLE 3.3
Excel Format Shortcut Keys

Key Combination	Format Code	Example
Ctrl+Shift+~	General	12345.67
Ctrl+Shift+!	0.00	12345.67
Ctrl+Shift+@	h.mm	6:31
Ctrl+Shift+#	d-mmm-yy	15-Apr-95
Ctrl+Shift+$	$#,##0.00);($#,##0.00)	$12,345.67
Ctrl+Shift+%	0%	12%
Ctrl+Shift+^	0.00E+00	1.23E+04

Creating New Formats

To create your own custom number formats, you need to understand how Excel interprets the format codes and learn the various available codes. Excel is extremely flexible for displaying numbers, times and dates, or text. This flexibility creates some complexity, but the following section clearly explains how these formatting codes work. You can begin writing your own formats in no time!

Note   When you create a new format using the symbols that follow, Excel automatically stores the new format in its list of formats. The formats you create, however, are stored only as part of the workbook in which you create them. Other workbooks have only the default Excel formats in the Format dialog box.

Format Code Structure

Each format code is divided into four parts, as follows:

```
Positive_Section;(Negative_Section);Zero_Section;Text_Section
```

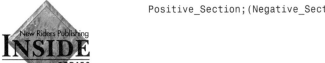

Codes that appear in the positive section format positive numbers; the negative section contains the format codes for negative numbers; the zero section formats zero values; and the text section formats any text entries. Each section is separated from the others with a semicolon. Only the first section, the positive section, is required. If the remaining sections are not specified, Excel provides default formatting for numbers that match those characteristics.

Consider the following format:

```
#,###;[Red](#,###);0;[RED]/"@/" "is not allowed. Entry must be a number!!"
```

The preceding format specifies that positive numbers appear with a thousands separator, that negative numbers are in red with parentheses, that a zero appears as "0", and that if text is entered into this cell, the message x is not allowed. Entry must be a number!!, where x is whatever you typed, appears in red instead of the text you enter. The preceding format uses several tricks. The section, "Format Codes," explains how the format works.

Format Code Conditions

You can define the conditions Excel will use for each section of the format. By default, the first section applies to numbers greater than 0, the second section to numbers less than 0, and the third section for all other numbers (generally 0).

If you use a conditional operator surrounded by square brackets at the beginning of the code section, you can specify the conditions for each of the three format code sections that Excel uses, rather than the default number ranges. Consider the following format code:

```
[>100][Blue]#,##0;[<-100][Yellow]#,##0;[Green]0
```

This code specifies that numbers greater than 100 are blue and that numbers less than 100 are yellow. Zeros and numbers less than zero are green. The reason that the third position applies to zeros and numbers less than zero is that the third section must format everything the first two formats don't control. Usually, only zero values are involved, because the first section typically formats all positive numbers, and the second section typically formats all negative numbers. When you change the numeric conditions of the first two sections, however, the third section has to take care of everything else.

Format Codes

You can use a variety of different codes in each format code. Table 3.4 lists each code symbol, along with an explanation of its function.

TABLE 3.4
Format Symbols

Symbol	Explanation
General	The word "General" is actually one of the format symbols. For example, you might have a specific format for positive numbers, but specify General format for negative numbers. An example follows: `$#,###;General`. The general format symbol displays numbers exactly as they were entered. The symbol 0 acts as a placeholder for a number. The 0 placeholder indicates that if the number being formatted does not have as many digits as the number of 0s in the format, a zero is to appear. For example, if the number 123 is formatted with the code 0.000; the result is 123.000. As another example, if the number 23.12 is formatted with 0000.000, the result is 0023.120; note that zeros appear in place of the missing digits.
#	The pound sign acts similarly to the 0 symbol, except that it does not force a digit to appear if the digit doesn't exist in the underlying number. For example, the number 123 formatted with `#,###.##` simply appears as 123.
?	The question mark functions like the pound sign (#), except that it inserts a space for the missing digits. This function is useful when you need to make decimal points align with numbers for which the number of digits that follow the decimal point varies. The question mark is also used for fraction displays, as in the format `# ???/???`, which displays the fractional portion of the number with up to three-digit accuracy.
.	The period enables you to define the number of digits that are to appear following the decimal point. If your format code specifies a decimal point, a decimal point always appears, even if no digits follow the decimal point. If the format code has one or more #s before the period, Excel displays numbers less than one as starting with a decimal point. To force Excel to always display at least one zero before the decimal point, use 0 before the period, as in the format `0.0#`.
%	If you use a percentage mark in your format code, Excel multiplies the number by 100 and then appends the % symbol to the number that appears.
,	The comma tells Excel to include commas as a thousands separator. Also, if you put the comma after a single placeholder, Excel divides the number by 1000 before displaying it. Following a placeholder with two commas divides the number by one million before displaying it. `#,` displays the number 145000 as 145, and `#,,` displays the number 12000000 as 12. This trick is very useful for financial statements displayed in thousands (000s) or millions.

Symbol	Explanation
e+,e–,E+,E–	The E symbol followed by a plus or minus causes the number to appear in scientific notation, along with the letter "E" in the appropriate place on the display. Table 3.2 displays an example of this format symbol.
–+/()$:(space)	Including any of these characters in your format code causes them to appear. If you need to display a character other than one of these, use the backslash followed by the character you want to display. For example, \" causes a double-quotation mark to appear—particularly useful when you want your format to display a character otherwise used as a formatting symbol. \# displays the pound sign, which is otherwise interpreted as a formatting symbol.
\	The backslash character is a special character that is not displayed in the format. Use it to tell Excel to display the character that follows it. For example, \? displays a question mark, which Excel normally interprets as a special format code symbol. If you need to display a backslash in your format, use two backslashes.
*	The asterisk is similar to the backslash, except that it causes the following character to repeat often enough to fill up the cell. The format code #,###;#,###;*! displays positive and negative numbers, but if a zero is entered, it fills the entire cell with exclamation points.
_	The underline is used to tell Excel to insert a space in its location. For example, in a format that surrounds negative numbers with parentheses, the decimal points of positive numbers do not align, because the negative number takes more space to the right of the decimal point to display the closing parenthesis. In this case, you use an underline at the end of the positive section of the format to tell Excel to save a space in that location for any possible parentheses.
"Text"	If you want Excel to display a text string, you should enclose it in quotation marks. The following example displays "DR" or "CR" (abbreviations for debit and credit) after positive and negative numbers, respectively: #,###"DR";[Red]#,###"CR";0
@	The at symbol represents any text that is entered into the cell. In the example given earlier, the @ is used to show what was entered, followed by a message that indicates the entry is not correct.
m	Displays the month number (1-12).

continues

TABLE 3.4, CONTINUED
Format Symbols

Symbol	Explanation
mm	Displays the month number, but with leading zeros for months 1–9.
mmm	Displays the month name using its three-letter abbreviation (Jan, Feb, Mar, and so on).
mmmm	Displays the full name of the month (January, February, March, and so on).
d	Displays the day of the month without leading zeros.
dd	Displays the day of the month with leading zeros.
ddd	Displays the three-letter abbreviation of the day of the week (Mon, Tue, Wed, and so on).
dddd	Displays the full name of the day of the week (Monday, Tuesday, Wednesday, and so on).
yy	Displays the last two digits of the year (00–99).
yyyy	Displays all the digits of the year (1900–2078).
h	Displays the hour without leading zeros. If the format contains an AM or PM, Excel uses the 12-hour clock; otherwise it uses the 24-hour clock.
hh	Displays the hour with leading zeros, if necessary. If the format contains an AM or PM, Excel bases the number on a 12-hour clock; otherwise it uses the 24-hour clock.
m	Displays the minutes without leading zeros, but must be preceded by an h or hh or Excel interprets them as a request for the month.
mm	Displays the minutes with leading zeros, if necessary. Note that the mm must be preceded by an h or hh or Excel treats it as a month code.
s	Displays the seconds without leading zeros.
ss	Displays the seconds with leading zeros, if necessary.
AM/PM	Forces Excel to use a 12-hour clock for the time display, and displays AM or PM in the location specified. You also can use am/pm (lower-case letters), A/P, or a/p to tell Excel to use those indicators.

Symbol	Explanation
[*color*]	If you place a color name in square brackets at the beginning of the appropriate section of the formatting code, Excel displays the matching number in that color. Valid colors are Black, Blue, Cyan, Green, Magenta, Red, White, or Yellow.
[*condition*]	As you saw in an earlier section, you can tell Excel which condition to use for each different section of the format code. Valid operators include <, <=, >, >=, =, and <> (not equal).

As an exercise, use the preceding format code explanations to examine what the standard Excel formatting codes do.

Changing Row Height

When you use different font sizes in your worksheets, the rows in which the text appears might need to be taller to accommodate the taller font. On the other hand, you might be designing a form in Excel and need taller rows to give your form the appearance you desire.

Note If you change the font in a given cell, Excel will automatically increase the column height to accommodate the taller letters.

You can alter the height of a row using the mouse or menu commands.

To use the mouse, follow these steps:

1. Move your mouse pointer over to the row labels. Carefully maneuver the pointer so that it is directly on top of the line at the bottom of the row you want to adjust. When you have positioned the pointer correctly, you see a horizontal line with two vertical arrows, one pointing up and one pointing down.

2. Press and hold the left mouse button and drag your mouse up or down to shorten or heighten the row as you see fit. Release the mouse button.

Tip While you are dragging the mouse up and down, the row height appears in the upper left corner of the Excel screen in the cell indicator box to the left of the formula bar.

As an alternative to this method, you can select multiple rows before you adjust the height of one. When you finish sizing one row, all the other selected rows use the new row height.

Tip   If a row doesn't display the full height of any text in the row, you can command Excel to set the row height automatically to display all text. To make that command, move your mouse so that it is on top of the line at the bottom of the row label you want to change and double-click your mouse. Excel uses a "best fit" method to determine the row size. This method also works if you select multiple rows before double-clicking on one of the rows' adjustment lines.

To change the height of a row using menu commands, follow these steps:

1. Pull down the **Fo**rmat menu and select **R**ow. You see the cascading menu shown in figure 3.4. The **R**ow menu offers the following choices:

   ◆ **H**eight. Brings up a dialog box in which you can enter the desired row height for the selected rows or the current row manually.

   ◆ **AutoFit.** Sets the row height to the tallest characters in the entire row.

   ◆ **H**ide. Hides the selected rows.

   ◆ **U**nhide. Reveals the hidden rows.

Figure 3.4

*The **R**ow menu selected from the **Fo**rmat menu.*

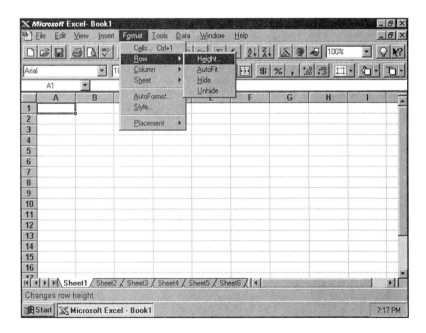

2. Select **H**eight from the **R**ow menu. The Row Height dialog box appears, as shown in figure 3.5.

New Riders Publishing
INSIDE
SERIES

Figure 3.5

The Row Height dialog box.

3. Enter the height you want for your row in the **R**ow Height field. Enter the value as a decimal figure in points.

4. Click on the OK button.

Tip In typographical terms, 72 points is approximately equal to one inch, so 36 points would be 1/2-inch tall, 18 points would be 1/4-inch tall, and so forth.

Hiding a Row

You hide a row the same way you change height. You can drag the height adjustment line for the row until the row height is zero, or you can use the **H**ide command. To use the **H**ide command, select the row or rows you want to hide, pull down the F**o**rmat menu, select **R**ow, then select **H**ide.

Tip When you have a row or rows selected, you can press Ctrl+9 to hide them.

Unhiding a Row

You unhide a row the same way you hide a row. Select the rows that include the hidden rows. If row 10 is hidden, for example, select rows 9 and 11. Then, pull down the F**o**rmat menu, select **R**ow, and then select **U**nhide.

Tip When you have selected the rows, including the hidden rows, press Ctrl+Shift+(to unhide the row.

Changing Column Width

Changing column widths is similar to adjusting row heights. The main difference is that you drag the line to the right of the column label to adjust a given column. You also can double-click on that column heading to have Excel examine all the entries in that column and adjust the column width so that all entries fit within the column's borders.

Tip When the pointer has changed to a vertical bar with two horizontal arrows, you can simply double-click to have the column automatically sized to the appropriate width.

Column Width Menu

To see the column width menu, pull down the Fo̲rmat menu and select C̲olumn (see fig. 3.6).

Figure 3.6

The Column Width menu.

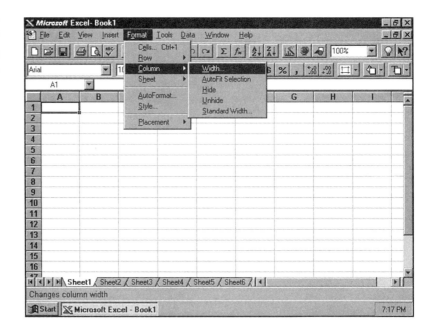

As you can see, the C̲olumn menu is much the same as the R̲ow menu, and it functions in the same way. The only difference is the addition of the S̲tandard Width option. Selecting S̲tandard Width opens a dialog box that enables you to change the default width for all columns in the worksheet (see fig. 3.7).

Figure 3.7

The Column Width dialog box.

Changing Worksheet Display Characteristics

You can change many of the characteristics of the Excel display to suit your tastes. Pull down the **T**ools menu and select **O**ptions. The Options notebook appears. Click on the View tab to see the view settings, shown in figure 3.8.

The notebook page has many settings, as shown in table 3.5.

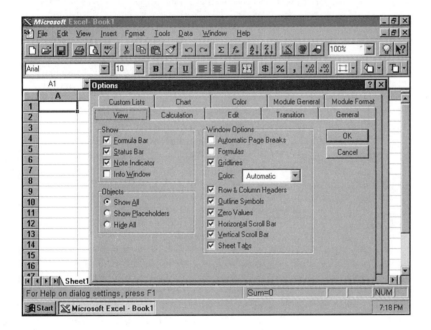

Figure 3.8

The View notebook page.

TABLE 3.5
View Settings

Section	Setting	Explanation
Show	**F**ormula Bar	Controls the presence of the formula bar. If this box is not selected, the formula bar is not shown.
	Status Bar	The status bar is the area at the bottom of the screen that shows you the status of various options in Excel. Deselect this check box to hide the status bar.

continues

TABLE 3.5, CONTINUED
View Settings

Section	Setting	Explanation
	Note Indicator	When you attach notes to cells, a small, red dot appears in that cell's upper right corner. If this option is not selected, the note indicator is not shown.
	Info Window	If this check box is selected, a new window is created that shows you all the details about the current cell. Use the **W**indow menu to move between the Info Window and the workbook. Deselect this check box to hide the Info Window.
Objects	Show **A**ll	If this option button is selected, all graphic objects in the workbook (buttons, graphics, etc.) are displayed.
	Show **P**laceholders	If this option button is selected, a gray rectangle appears on your screen in place of any graphic objects. This option can help you scroll through the worksheet more quickly.
	Hi**d**e All	This option button causes all graphic objects to be hidden. They are not printed.
Window Options	A**u**tomatic Page Breaks	This check box causes Excel's automatically determined page breaks to appear.
	Fo**r**mulas	Choose this check box to show the formulas in the cells instead of the results. At the same time, it doubles the width of the cells (so that they are likely to be capable of displaying the formula), and it left-justifies all the displayed formulas. This option is useful for checking the validity of the formulas in your worksheet or for documenting your work.
	Gridlines	Deselect this option to turn off the gridline display in the worksheet.
	Color	This option is a drop-down list that enables you to choose the color of the gridlines in the worksheet.
	Row and Column H**e**aders	Deselect this choice to turn off the labels for rows and columns. If you are developing worksheet-based forms, this option can be useful when you distribute the worksheet, because the people who are completing the form should have little need for the row and column markers.

Section	Setting	Explanation
Window Options	**O**utline Symbols	This check box controls whether Excel displays the symbols used when you are using the outline feature in Excel.
	Zero Values	If this option is unchecked, cells that have a zero value and are formatted using the General format are displayed as blank. Cells formatted with a specific format calling for zeros still display the zeros.
	Horizon**t**al Scroll Bar	This check box hides or unhides the horizontal scroll bar.
	Vertical Scroll Bar	This check box hides or unhides the vertical scroll bar.
	Sheet Ta**b**s	This check box controls the display of the workbook sheet tabs at the bottom of the screen.

Tip   Press Ctrl+', the left single quote, beneath the tilde (~) on most keyboards, to switch quickly between the normal worksheet and formulas. See Chapter 6, "Advanced Worksheet Features," to learn more about Excel's outlining features.

Changing Fonts

Excel has many tools that enable you to format the fonts—typefaces, sizes, and styles—that your worksheet uses.

Understanding Different Font Types

Depending on the font tools you have installed on your system, a wide variety of fonts are available with Excel. Each type of font appears differently on your screen and prints differently on your printer. The most popular types of fonts include the following:

◆ **Screen Fonts.** Windows has several screen fonts that approximate the fonts your printer uses. For these fonts to print correctly, your printer must have similar fonts built into it. Examples of screen fonts on a standard Windows system are Roman, Helvetica, Modern, Script, and Symbol. These fonts are available only in the sizes installed in your system: if you choose a size that your system doesn't have, Windows tries to approximate it on the screen, but the results are usually poor.

◆ **TrueType Fonts.** TrueType fonts were introduced in Windows 3.1. They include both *display fonts,* which you can see on your worksheet, and equivalent *printer fonts,* which Windows can generate for your printer when you print. Even if your printer does not contain that font, Windows (and therefore Excel) can make your printer use them. TrueType fonts can be scaled to different sizes, and the underlying Windows TrueType software generates the appropriate display and printer fonts automatically so that what you see on the screen is as close as possible to what you see when you print. Examples of TrueType fonts are Arial, Courier New, and Symbol. TrueType fonts have a 'TT' symbol before their names in the Excel font dialog box.

◆ **PostScript Fonts.** PostScript fonts are the most professional available, although the untrained eye often cannot distinguish between TrueType fonts and PostScript fonts. PostScript fonts can be printed in any size desired, from 1 point up to 999 points. If you have a PostScript printer, Excel can print these fonts, and has screen fonts that are roughly the same as what you see on paper. Examples of PostScript fonts are Courier, Times Roman, and Helvetica.

◆ **ATM (PostScript) Fonts.** Many Windows-based applications include a program called *Adobe Type Manager* (ATM), which gives the capabilities of TrueType fonts. You also can purchase ATM separately. If you have ATM installed, you can view and print PostScript fonts, even if your printer doesn't normally support PostScript fonts. ATM fonts include Courier, Times New Roman, and GillSans (similar to Helvetica).

Note   You should know that when you use ATM, PostScript, or TrueType fonts and your printer does not include TrueType or PostScript fonts, your printouts take longer because Windows has to draw the letters for your printer. In other words, rather than instruct the printer to print the letter 't' in a certain location and at a certain size, Windows must download the letter to the printer as a graphic image. This procedure slows printing.

Changing Fonts

Excel includes several tools to quickly change the current font. You can make the current font bold, italic, or underlined. You can change fonts, and you can change the size of the selected font.

Many of these functions can be accomplished using the toolbar. Figure 3.9 shows the toolbar buttons for these fonts styles.

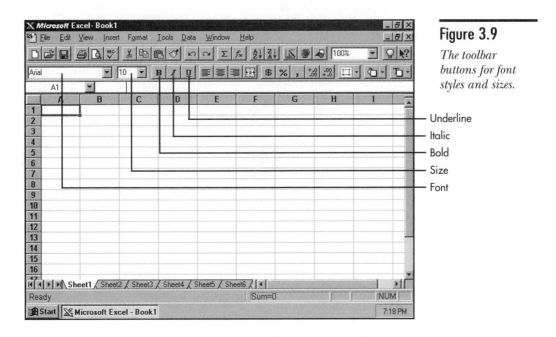

Figure 3.9

The toolbar buttons for font styles and sizes.

To use these buttons, select the cells you want to format and click on the appropriate button.

You also can change fonts and font styles by using the Font dialog box and following these steps:

1. Pull down the **F**ormat menu, select Cell, then click on the **F**ont tab in the Cell formatting notebook. You see the Font notebook page, shown in figure 3.10.

Tip

To access the Format Cells notebook quickly, select the cells you want to format and then click your right mouse button in the selected region. This procedure causes a pop-up menu to appear. From the pop-up menu, select Cells from the **F**ormat menu.

2. In the **F**ont box, select or enter the typeface you want to use. When you select the font, Excel shows an example of the font in the Preview window.

3. In the F**o**nt Style list box, select the display style of the font (Bold, Bold Italic, Italic, and so on).

4. You also can use the <u>U</u>nderline list box to select from a variety of underline styles.

5. Use the Stri<u>k</u>ethrough, Sup<u>e</u>rscript, and Su<u>b</u>script check boxes for those effects.

6. Finally, select the size you want from the <u>S</u>ize list box.

7. After you finish making the font choices you want, click on the OK button.

Figure 3.10

The Font notebook page.

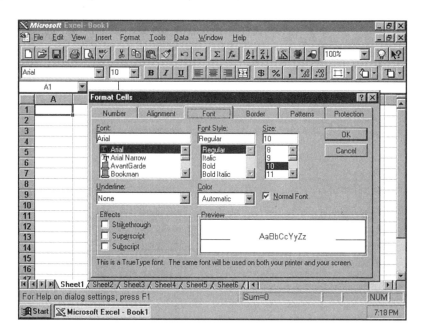

AUTHOR'S NOTE

Here is a bit of typography trivia: The term *font* is often used incorrectly. A set of letters in a particular style (like Courier, Times Roman, or Helvetica) is actually a *typeface.* When you take a typeface and define the size and attributes (bold, italic, and so on), you end up with a *font.* Many incorrectly call a typeface a font. The Excel dialog box makes this mistake, for example. Many programs do!

Excel also has some shortcut keys for many of the font attributes. Table 3.6 shows these shortcut keys.

TABLE 3.6
Font Style Shortcut Keys

Function	Shortcut Key
Bold	Ctrl+B
Italic	Ctrl+I
Underline	Ctrl+U
~~Strikethrough~~	Ctrl+5
Normal font	Ctrl+1 (Uses the font in the Normal style)

Using Borders

You can spice up your worksheets by using borders. By drawing lines around certain portions of your worksheets, you can make the worksheets more visually attractive, as well as separate them into distinct sections. Borders make your work more presentable and easier for others to understand.

Tip   You can make a border around a cell or group of cells quickly using the toolbar. An example of the Border button can be seen in figure 3.2 near the beginning of this chapter.

To use the Border button to quickly create a border, follow these steps:

1. Select the cell or group of cells that you want the border to surround.

2. Click on the down arrow next to the Border button, which causes a box of borders to appear, as you can see in figure 3.11.

3. Examine the border box to find the border style you want. After you find the border style you want, click on that particular box to select it for the selected cells.

After you choose a particular border, the Border button changes to show the most recently used border. You simply can click on that button to choose immediately the most recently used border.

Figure 3.11

The border box.

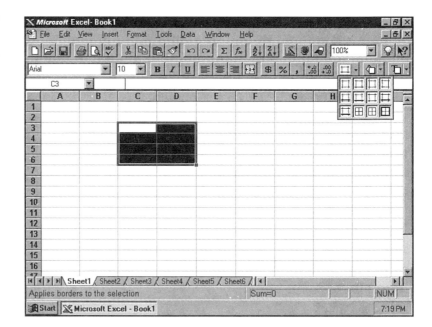

 Tip If you do a lot of work with borders, the border box accessed from the toolbar can be "torn off" and left right on top of your worksheet. To "tear off" the border list, pull down the list by clicking on the down arrow to the right of the border button. Then, click and hold the mouse button within the border box, and drag your mouse down out of the border list box. When your mouse leaves the region of the list, the border box is torn off and can be left on your worksheet to more quickly access it.

You can achieve even more control over the borders you create by using the Border page in the Format Cells notebook. To use this page, pull down the Format menu and select Cell. When you see the Format Cells notebook, click on the tab marked Border. The Border page is shown in figure 3.12.

Use the following fields to control the way the border lines are drawn:

◆ **Outline.** The outside edges of the selected cells. If you have selected many cells before pulling up the Border dialog box, only the outline of the selected cells is given a border.

◆ **Left.** All selected cells have a border line drawn on their left edges.

◆ **Right.** All selected cells have a border line drawn on their right edges.

◆ **Top.** The tops of the selected cells get a border.

◆ **Bottom.** The bottoms of the selected cells get a border.

◆ **Style.** This section presents a number of different border styles, from double lines to dashed lines.

◆ **Color.** This drop box lists the various color choices for the border lines.

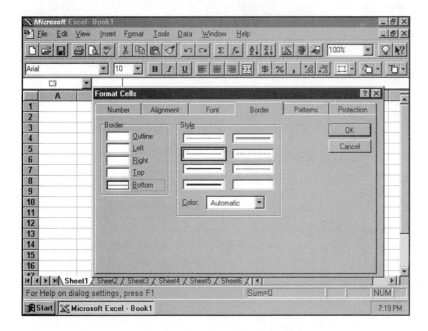

Figure 3.12

The Border page.

Shading and Coloring Cells

You also have many choices about changing the color and shading of cells in your worksheet, just as you did with the Border command. You can color cells and text with the Color and Font Color buttons on the Formatting toolbar. These buttons are shown near the beginning of the chapter in figure 3.2.

To change the color of specific cells, follow these steps:

1. Select the cells you want to color.

2. Click on the down arrow to the right of the Color button to show the colors available. This color box is shown in figure 3.13.

Figure 3.13

The color box.

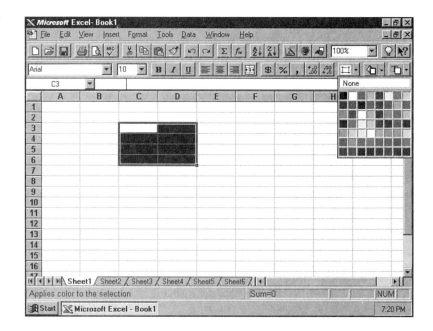

3. Click on the color you want for the selected cells.

The color and background pattern can be controlled in selected cells by using the Format Cells notebook. Follow these steps:

1. Select the cells you want to format.

2. Pull down the **F**ormat menu and select **C**ells. Then, click on the Patterns tab in the formatting notebook (see fig. 3.14).

3. Choose the color you want from the selection of colors available.

4. Open the drop-down box labeled **P**attern to see a variety of patterns that you can use. Click on the pattern you want.

After you choose a color and pattern, you can see an example of the way they look in the Sample box on the Pattern page.

The final coloring option comes from the Font Color button on the Formatting toolbar. You can change the color of the text in cells. Select the cells you want to affect, and then click on the down arrow to the right of the Font Color button. You see a list of colors that you can use. Choose one to change the text color for the cells you selected.

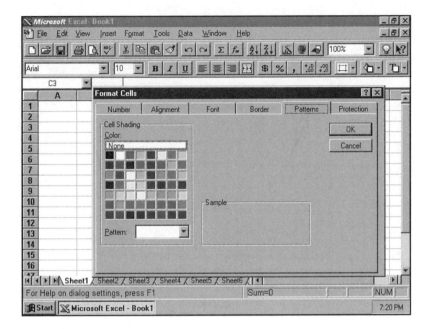

Figure 3.14

The Patterns page.

Aligning Text

By default, Excel aligns text to the left edges of cells and numbers to the right. You can override these default alignments.

The Formatting toolbar contains three buttons to control text alignment within cells. Figure 3.2, at the beginning of this chapter, shows these buttons.

To use the Toolbar alignment buttons, select the cells you want to realign and click on the desired alignment button.

Excel has some other text alignment tricks up its sleeve. You can align text vertically, and you can arrange text so that the words appear vertically. To access these options, do the following:

1. Select the cells you want to change.

2. Pull down the F**o**rmat menu and select **C**ells to cause the Format Cells notebook to appear.

3. Click on the Alignment tab. You see the page shown in figure 3.15.

Figure 3.15

The Alignment page.

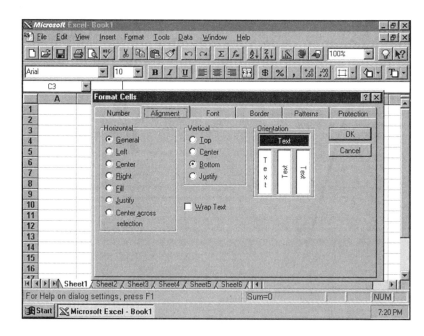

The page is grouped into three sections: Horizontal, Vertical, and Orientation. Table 3.7 describes some of these choices.

Table 3.7
Alignment Page Choices

Section	Button	Function
Horizontal	General	Aligns text using the default Excel alignments. Numbers are right-aligned and text is left-aligned.
	Left	Aligns cell contents to the left side of the cells.
	Center	Centers cell contents within the cells.
	Right	Aligns cell contents to the right side of the cells.
	Fill	Repeats the text as many times as necessary to completely fill the cell with whatever is entered.
	Justify	Attempts to spread the text so that it uses the entire width of the cell.
	Center across selection	When you select a range of cells that begins with a cell that contains text and choose this option, Excel takes the text contents of the first cell and centers it across all the cells you selected.

Section	Button	Function
Vertical	**T**op	Aligns cell contents against the top of the cells.
	C**e**nter	Aligns cell contents vertically between the top and bottom boundaries.
	Bottom	Aligns cell contents against the bottom boundary of the cells.
	Justify	Causes the text, when wrapped, to align against the top and bottom of the cell.

You can choose one of four different orientations to display the text, choosing among the displayed options for vertically arranging the text so that it reads from top to bottom or bottom to top. Finally, if you select the **W**rap Text check box, Excel causes text that is longer than an individual cell to wrap downward.

Centering Text Across a Range

Often, you want centered titles at the tops of your worksheets. Achieving a perfectly centered title can be difficult, however, given the number of columns in your worksheet, the width of each column, and the width of your title.

AUTHOR'S NOTE

In the early days of spreadsheets with VisiCalc, Lotus 1-2-3, Multiplan, and the like, the only way to center text across the page was to manually insert spaces in the title. With the advent of proportional typefaces, even that trick became impossible, because each letter takes up a different amount of space.

Excel can center text across a range automatically. To center text across a range, follow these steps:

1. Type the title in the far left column of the range in which you want the text to appear centered. For example, if you want the text centered between columns A and I, enter the text into column A.

2. Select the range of cells starting from the cell that contains your title, and extending to the right to the full width of your worksheet (or print range).

3. Click on the Center Across Selection button on the Formatting Toolbar. Alternately, pull down the F**o**rmat menu, choose **C**ell, click on the Alignment tab, and then choose the Center **a**cross selection option button. Then, click on OK.

Filling a Range with Text

Excel also can take a piece of text—a single letter, word, or sentence—and fill that text across a range. To do this, follow these steps:

1. Type the text to be repeated in the far left cell of the range you want to fill.

2. Select the range of cells starting with the cell that contains the text to be repeated and extending as far right as you want to repeat it.

3. Pull down the Format menu, select **C**ell, then click on the Alignment tab.

4. Choose the **F**ill option button and click on the OK button.

Figure 3.16 shows the effect of filling an asterisk across the visible worksheet in row 2.

Figure 3.16

The filled range.

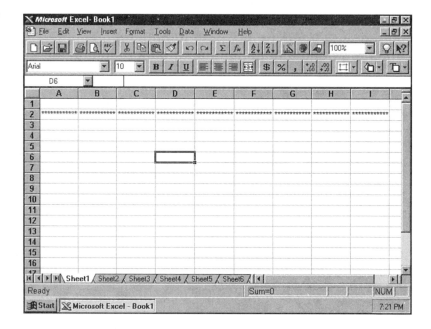

Protecting and Hiding Cells

When you develop worksheets for others to use, it is wise to restrict their choices. Certain cells should be unmodifiable, others should hide their formulas. This makes your worksheet easier for them to use and protects your work from being modified in such a way that it stops working properly.

By default, cells you create are marked as already being *locked*. After the entire document is protected, locked cells cannot be modified. You also can designate certain other cells as *hidden*, which doesn't mean that the cell itself is hidden, only that the underlying formulas are hidden.

To change the protection characteristics of a cell or group of cells, follow these steps:

1. Select the cell or group of cells you want to protect.

2. Pull down the **Fo**rmat menu and choose **C**ells. Click on the Protection tab to display the protection page. You see the page shown in figure 3.17.

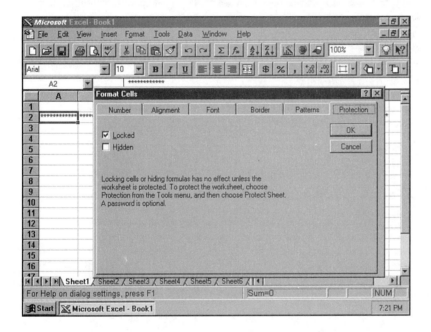

Figure 3.17

The cell protection page.

3. In the dialog box, click on the **L**ocked or Hi**d**den check boxes. Then, click on the OK button.

After you finish your worksheet, you need to protect the document so that these settings take effect. Follow these steps:

1. Pull down the **T**ools menu and select **P**rotection to display a cascading menu, from which you can select **P**rotect Sheet or Protect **W**orkbook. Selecting either option displays the dialog box shown in figure 3.18.

2. If necessary, enter a password in the **P**assword field (passwords are optional).

Figure 3.18

The Protect Sheet dialog box.

Stop   Passwords in Excel are case-sensitive. In other words, they depend on exact capitalization. Also, when you use a password in a document, be sure to use one that you can remember. If the document you work on is important to your company, make sure someone else knows your password. Your computer department may have stringent policies regarding the use of application-specific passwords. Follow them!

3. Choose from the remaining three check boxes:

   ◆ **Contents.** Causes the cells you mark as hidden to hide their formulas, or the cells you mark as locked to be unchangeable.

   ◆ **Objects.** Causes graphic objects in your worksheet to be made unmodifiable.

   ◆ **Scenarios.** Makes the scenarios in a workbook unmovable and unsizable.

4. With the appropriate options selected, click on the OK button to protect the document.

To unprotect the document, pull down the **T**ools menu, select **P**rotection and then select either Un**p**rotect Document or Unprotect **W**orkbook. If a password was used to protect the document, you need to enter it before the document becomes unprotected. If no password was used, the document or workbook is unprotected instantly.

Using Styles

Styles enable you to predefine collections of formatting settings and quickly apply those settings to selected cells. Rather than choose a range and then tediously select the typeface, font style, size, alignment, shading, and so on, you can define entire styles that you commonly use and then apply them to a cell or collection of cells quickly and easily.

Styles enable you to define the follow properties:

◆ Typeface (Font)

◆ Number format

◆ Cell alignment

◆ Borders

◆ Cell patterns

◆ Cell protection

Applying a Style

For styles that already exist, apply them by following these steps:

1. Select the cells you want to format.

2. Pull down the F**o**rmat menu and select **S**tyles. You see the dialog box shown in figure 3.19.

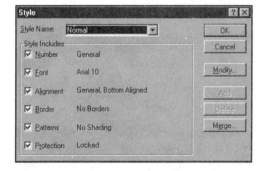

Figure 3.19

The Style dialog box.

3. Pull down the **S**tyle Name drop-down list and choose the style you want.

4. Click on the OK button to close the Style dialog box.

Creating a Style

To create a new style, use the Style dialog box that you saw in figure 3.19.

The first thing you probably notice on the dialog box is a series of check boxes: **N**umber, **F**ont, A**l**ignment, **B**order, **P**atterns, and P**r**otection. These check boxes define which formatting aspects the style contains. If you want a style that controls only the font, for example, deselect all of the check boxes except for **F**ont.

To begin creating your new style, click on the **S**tyle Name box and type in the name for your new style. Then, using the check boxes, choose the formatting elements that you want your new style to affect and click on the Modify button. This procedure brings up the Format Cells notebook. Any changes you make to it now, however, impact only the style you are creating. Use the notebook to change all the aspects of the style until they are satisfactory. After you are finished, click on the OK button to return to the Style dialog box.

You also see a button marked M**e**rge. Click on this button to import styles that you have created in other workbooks. The other workbooks must be open in a different Excel window before the styles in those workbooks can be available.

Note Styles that you create appear only in the workbook in which you create them. To move them to other workbooks, use the preceding merge procedure.

After you finish changing the style attributes, click on the **A**dd button to create the new style. The new style can then be applied just like any other style in the list. Similarly, if you want to delete an existing style, select it in the **S**tyle Name list box and click on the **D**el button.

To finish working with the Style dialog box, click on the OK button.

Using AutoFormats

Examine the worksheet in figure 3.20. You could spend a lot of time reformatting the table to give it a polished, professional appearance. Fortunately, instead of spending much time on reformatting, you can use the Excel AutoFormat feature to format a table quickly in one of many predefined, professionally designed formats.

Before you use AutoFormat, make sure that your active cell is within a table, and that the table elements are contiguous. If blank columns or rows are in the table, then select the entire range of cells that contains the table; otherwise Excel does not know where your table begins and ends. After you select the table, follow these steps:

1. Pull down the F**o**rmat menu and choose **A**utoFormat. The AutoFormat dialog box appears, as shown in figure 3.21.

2. Scroll through the list of formats. If you click on a format, you can preview the results of a particular AutoFormat in the Sample window.

3. After you find a format you like, click on the OK button to apply it.

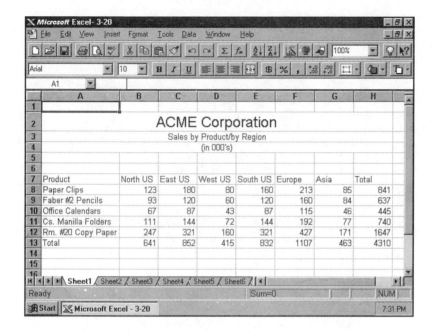

Figure 3.20

The sample sales table.

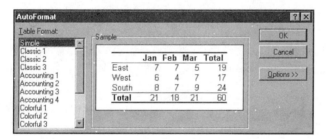

Figure 3.21

The AutoFormat dialog box.

When using the AutoFormat dialog box, you also can control which parts of the format to apply by clicking on the **O**ptions button, which expands the dialog box, as shown in figure 3.22.

The expanded AutoFormat dialog box enables you to select the aspects of the format you want to apply by using the various check boxes.

Figure 3.23 shows the example table with the List 1 table format applied.

Figure 3.22

The expanded AutoFormat dialog box.

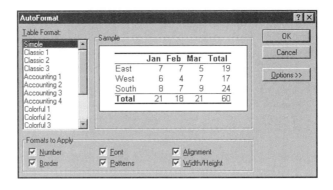

Figure 3.23

The formatted table.

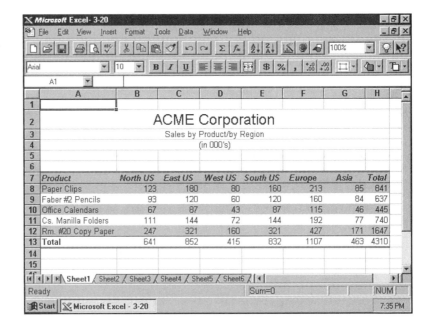

Chapter Snapshot

Putting your work on paper is one goal when using Excel. Whether you are printing to proofread your work, to get a better look at the overall picture your work represents, or to distribute your worksheets and charts to others, you need to master Excel's printing tools. In this chapter, you learn the following:

- ◆ Using different types of printers

- ◆ Using different types of fonts

- ◆ Printing with Excel

- ◆ Adjusting Excel's printing

- ◆ Creating and editing headers and footers

- ◆ Using Print Titles

- ◆ Using the Excel Report Manager

The tasks and tips you learn in this chapter help you produce high-quality, professional-looking worksheets every time.

Printing Documents

P rinting is usually easy: you select the area to print, click on a given print button, and that's it—you're done. In Excel, however, you can do a variety of printing tricks. This chapter covers these features.

Understanding Your Printer's Capabilities

Before you can understand your printer, you need to know what type of printer it is and which fonts are built into it. This section discusses different types of printers, built-in fonts, and print quality.

Dot-Matrix Printers

Dot-matrix printers fire little pins into an inked printer ribbon. The resulting pattern of the dots forms the letters and images that appear on the paper. Dot-matrix printers are relatively slow, and the output quality varies considerably depending on the model.

Some dot-matrix printers use 9 pins to form characters; these offer poor print quality. Some use 24 pins and perform better than their 9-pin counterparts, but still not as well as laser printers.

Dot-matrix printers typically have a limited number of fonts preinstalled, often at fixed sizes. If your printer supports graphics printing, as many do, Excel can use TrueType fonts to create different typefaces, sizes, and styles on the printer.

Impact Printers

Few impact printers are in use today. Impact printers form characters just like a typewriter: they hammer individually formed metal or plastic letters into an inked printer ribbon, which then hits the page. These printers are really slow and noisy in comparison to the other types of printers. Although text quality is very high, you are limited to the one font installed in the printer at a time, and generally have no graphics capabilities.

Inkjet Printers

Inkjet printers shoot small amounts of ink directly onto the paper. These printers are very quiet, form near-laser quality text and graphics, and are relatively inexpensive. The main drawbacks to inkjet printers are that they are fairly slow compared to laser printers, and they don't offer the same sharpness of printing as laser printers.

Most inkjet printers have a limited number of typefaces and sizes pre-installed. Due to the fairly high resolution (about 360 dots per inch) of these printers, however, you often can get good print quality by using TrueType fonts, which Windows prints on the inkjet printer as a graphic image. Printing this way is slower than using the printer's built-in fonts, but offers flexibility you don't otherwise have—an inkjet printer's built-in fonts rarely handle multiple sizes beyond the sizes of type built into the printer.

One advantage of inkjet printers over laser printers is that many good color inkjet printers are available. With a color inkjet printer, you can produce color charts and overhead transparencies. Equivalent color capabilities on laser-type printers still cost $7,000 or more, but color inkjet printers can be purchased for as little as $300.

Laser Printers

Laser printers set the standard for high-quality output in today's business world. They are fast, quiet, and have become fairly inexpensive in recent years, with some selling for less than $1,000.

Laser printers shoot a laser beam onto a drum. The drum picks up an electrical charge in the areas that the laser hits. The drum then is rolled through powdered ink, known as *toner*, which sticks to the charged places on the drum. The drum then rolls onto the paper, depositing the toner particles. Finally, the paper is rolled through a very hot roller called a *fuser*, which fuses the toner particles onto the paper.

Two major standards exist in the world of laser printers: PostScript and *Printer Control Language* (PCL). PostScript laser printers are the most expensive, but give you the greatest capabilities for accurate graphics and text. PCL printers have somewhat less capability, but more recent versions of PCL (version 5 and later) can scale the printer's built-in typefaces to different sizes. Hewlett-Packard sets the standard in the PCL world, although almost all laser printers are PCL-compatible and can emulate HP LaserJet printers. PostScript printers also are available from a number of different printer manufacturers.

Graphics

By default, Excel prints graphics at the highest resolution allowed by your printer. You can also change the resolution used if you use the Printer Setup dialog box to select a different resolution.

Fonts

Font support is one of the more complex areas of effective printing—so many fonts are available, and each one has its own limitations and abilities. Windows (and, therefore, Excel) offers four major font types, as noted and described in the following list. Knowing which types of fonts are best for different tasks and which fonts work best with your printer can make your job of turning out attractive output much easier:

◆ **Screen Fonts.** Windows has a number of screen fonts that approximate the fonts your printer uses. For a screen font to print correctly, similar fonts must be built into your printer. Examples of screen fonts on a standard Windows system are Roman, Helvetica, Modern, Script, and Symbol. These fonts are available only in the sizes installed in your system. If you choose a size your system doesn't have, Windows tries to approximate it on the screen, but with poor results.

◆ **TrueType Fonts.** TrueType fonts were new in Windows 3.1. They include display fonts that you can see on your Excel screen and equivalent printer fonts that Windows can generate for your printer. Even if your printer doesn't have a particular TrueType font or its equivalent, Windows can make your printer use them by printing each letter as a graphic image. TrueType fonts can be scaled to different sizes, and the underlying Windows software generates the appropriate display and printer fonts automatically so that what you see on the screen is as close as possible to what you print. Examples of TrueType fonts include Arial, Courier New, and Symbol. TrueType fonts have a "TT" symbol before their names in the Excel font list.

TrueType fonts work with any printer that can print graphics. The TrueType software in Windows prints these fonts at the highest resolution your printer allows. You also can adjust the resolution with which Windows prints TrueType fonts by accessing the Page Setup command in the **F**ile menu, then closing the **O**ptions button.

ote TrueType fonts are an economical alternative to PostScript fonts, at often only 1/100 the price. TrueType fonts are usually a better value because the quality compared to PostScript fonts is nearly comparable when printed on most laser printers.

As a general rule, use PostScript fonts if you are doing work that a professional printing company will print for you.

◆ **PostScript Fonts.** PostScript fonts are the most professional available, although the untrained eye cannot often distinguish between TrueType and PostScript fonts. You can print PostScript fonts in any size you want, from 1 point up to 999 points. If you have a PostScript printer, Excel is capable of printing these fonts, and displays screen fonts that approximate what prints on paper. Examples of PostScript fonts are Courier, Times Roman, and Helvetica.

To use PostScript fonts, you must have a PostScript-based printer or Adobe Type Manager, a special software that emulates a PostScript printer and prints the graphic images to a non-PostScript printer, rather than the actual fonts.

◆ **ATM (PostScript) Fonts.** Many Windows-based applications include a program called *Adobe Type Manager* (ATM), which provides capabilities equal to TrueType fonts. You also can purchase ATM separately. If you install ATM, you can view and print PostScript fonts, even if your printer does not normally support PostScript fonts. ATM fonts include Courier, Times New Roman, and GillSans (similar to Helvetica).

ATM functions like TrueType. If your printer can print graphic images, then ATM can print the PostScript fonts at the highest resolution your printer supports.

Printing Worksheets

Excel prints your entire worksheet automatically when you select the **P**rint command. To print your entire worksheet, pull down the **F**ile menu and select **P**rint. The Print dialog box appears, as shown in figure 4.1.

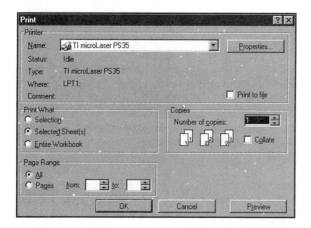

Figure 4.1

The Print dialog box.

Table 4.1 shows the options available in the Print dialog box.

TABLE 4.1
Print Dialog Box Options

Option	Description
Page Range	Here you choose whether to print **A**ll pages of the worksheet, or a range of pages by selecting Pa**g**es, then a starting page (**F**rom) and an ending page (**T**o).
Selectio**n**	If you select a range of cells prior to selecting the **P**rint menu, then click on the Selectio**n** option button, only the preselected range of cells is printed.
Selecte**d** Sheet(s)	Excel enables you to print multiple worksheets from your workbook simultaneously. You must click on the first sheet you want to print, then click on the remaining sheets while holding down the Ctrl key. When you print, use the Selecte**d** Sheet(s) option button to print only those sheets.
Entire Workbook	Choose this option button to print all sheets in your workbook.
Copies	The number you enter in this field is the number of copies of the worksheet Excel prints. In most office environments, it is easier, cheaper, and faster to use the photocopier than printing multiple copies of your documents on the laser printer.
Print Previe**w**	If you click on this button, Excel displays a rough representation of how the printed output should appear. You can use this option to resolve problems with different fonts, graphic positioning, and any other problems, without having to print each time. Because you usually need to print many times to resolve printing problems with your worksheet, using the Print Previe**w** option can greatly speed up this process.
Page **S**etup	Selecting this button brings up a new dialog box that enables you to control many aspects of your printouts, including headers, footers, and so on. This dialog box is explored completely in a later section of this chapter.
P**r**inter	Click on this button to choose which printer to use, if you have more than one printer.

After you select the options you want to use, click on the OK button to print your document.

Selecting Areas to Print

Often, you don't want to print the entire worksheet. Sometimes you do not need parts of the worksheet, or parts of the worksheet contain only support information used to generate the actual worksheet. For example, you might have detailed sales records in your worksheet, but you only use them to generate the totals you are using for a sales report.

In such cases, follow these steps:

1. Select the range of cells you want to print.

2. Pull down the **F**ile menu and select **P**rint.

3. When the Print dialog box appears, click on the Selecti**o**n option button to print only the selected area.

Excel shows you where the pages of your worksheet will break onto multiple pages with dashed lines. If these locations are not acceptable, you have several choices, as follows:

◆ You can reformat your worksheet to fit in the number of pages you want, usually by choosing smaller fonts and reducing the width of columns and the height of rows. You might also rearrange your data to print the way you want, inserting or deleting rows and columns in order to fit everything on the pages.

◆ You can insert page breaks to force Excel to break the pages earlier.

◆ You can use Excel's print-to-fit feature, which automatically shrinks the entire selected print area to fit on a single page. You also can choose varying levels of reduction or enlargement.

Working with Page Breaks

In Excel, you can print certain parts of your worksheet on certain pages by inserting page breaks into the document. To insert page breaks, do the following:

1. Decide where you want to begin a new page.

2. Move your active cell to immediately below and to the right of where you want the page break. The page break is created at the upper left corner of the active cell.

3. Pull down the **I**nsert menu and select Page **B**reak.

The page break indicator lines show the new page layout. Excel automatically adjusts the other page breaks accordingly. To remove an inserted page break, use the following procedure:

1. Move your active cell to immediately below and to the right of the page break.

2. Pull down the **I**nsert menu and select Remove Page **B**reak.

The Remove Page **B**reak menu option is in the same place on the menu as the Set Page **B**reak command, but appears in place of Set Page **B**reak when your active cell is next to an inserted page break. If you see the Set Page **B**reak command instead of the Remove Page **B**reak command, then your active cell is in the wrong location, or you are trying to remove a page break that Excel has inserted because no room is available on the page. You cannot remove Excel's automatic page breaks. You can, however, insert new page breaks before the Excel-inserted page breaks and let Excel reformat the rest of the document accordingly.

Using Print-To-Fit

You can instruct Excel to take a print area and reduce it automatically so that the entire area fits on one page. Of course, it might be reduced so much you can't read it, so this option doesn't prove useful if you ingeniously try to cram a twenty-page printout on a single page. The reduction in size is accomplished by Excel choosing exactly the right font shrinkage. To use the print-to-fit feature, do the following:

1. Select the range of cells you want to print.

2. Pull down the **F**ile menu and choose Page Se**t**up; the Page Setup notebook appears. Click on the Page tab. The Page notebook page appears, as shown in figure 4.2.

3. Click on the **F**it to option button (see fig. 4.2).

4. If you need to modify the number of pages into which Excel fits your selected area, change each field appropriately.

If you follow the preceding instructions, Excel automatically calculates the necessary percentage reduction, which you can see in the Re**d**uce/Enlarge field.

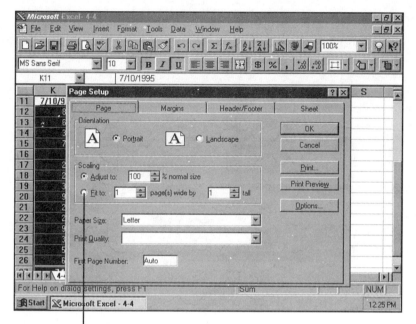

Figure 4.2

The Page Setup page.

Fit to option button

You also can manually adjust the percentage reduction or enlargement by selecting the Reduce/Enlarge button and entering a percentage amount.

Note If your printer doesn't support scalable typefaces, or you use fixed-size typefaces in your document, you might be unable to reduce or enlarge the page exactly as you want. To avoid this problem, try to use scalable typefaces (such as PostScript or TrueType fonts) as often as possible.

New to Excel for Windows 95 are two-up and four-up printing orientations (see fig. 4.3). This feature enables you to specify one-up, two-up, or four-up printing in either landscape or portrait orientation. This feature can give you a quick printout for filing, for thumbnail review, or simply to conserve paper, ink, and time.

Figure 4.3

The Printer Properties (layout) page.

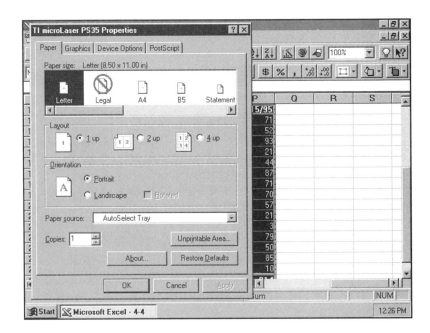

Using Headers and Footers

By default, Excel prints the name of your worksheet in a print header and the page number in a print footer. You can replace these with your own headers and footers. Some uses for headers and footers include confidentiality notices, specially formatted page numbers, dates and times, or author name.

Headers and footers are managed in the Page Setup dialog box shown in figure 4.2. Clicking on the Header/Footer brings up the Header/Footer notebook page, shown in figure 4.4.

Note Headers and footers are printed in a 1/2-inch border at the top and bottom of the page. If you use headers or footers that exceed this amount of space, your worksheet contents will probably print on top of the header or footer. To avoid this problem, change the top or bottom margins by using the Page Setup command in the **F**ile menu.

Note also that if you use a laser or inkjet printer, you may have as much as a 1/3-inch unprintable border on your pages.

One of the more thoughtful touches included in Excel is predefined headers and footers. To use these, pull down the He**a**der or **F**ooter drop-down list and select one of the many styles available from the list. Figure 4.5 shows the predefined headers list.

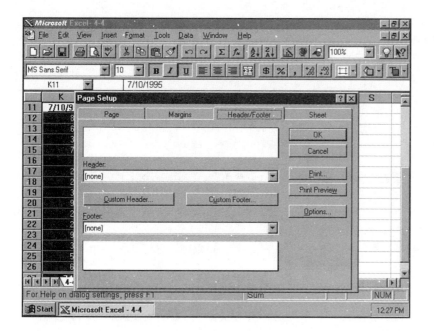

Figure 4.4

The Header/ Footer notebook page.

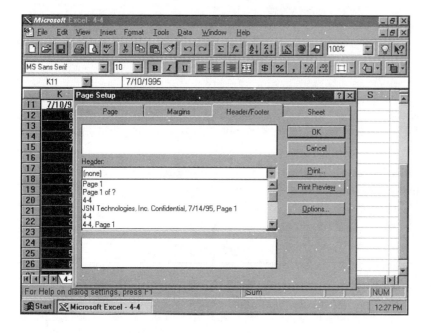

Figure 4.5

The predefined headers list.

In the Header/Footer page, you can see two windows. The top window shows you what the header will look like; the bottom window shows the footer. You cannot edit these two windows directly, because they are preview windows. To change the header or footer, you must choose from Excel's predefined headers and footers or create your own.

Creating headers and footers works the same way. The following example shows you the screens for creating a footer, but the steps shown work identically for headers. Click on the Custom Footer button. The Footer dialog box appears (see fig. 4.6).

Figure 4.6

The Footer dialog box.

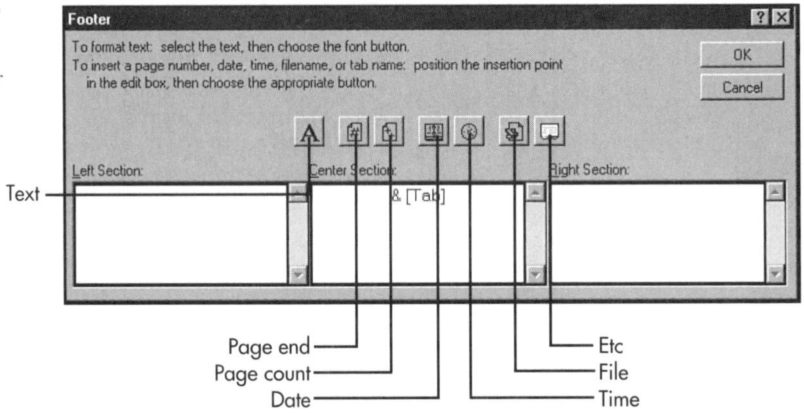

The Footer dialog box has three windows—the **L**eft Section, **C**enter Section, and **R**ight Section—which are used to enter information that should be left-aligned, centered, or right-aligned, respectively. In each window, you can enter text information or special codes. You use the special codes to insert things like the system date and time, the name of the worksheet, or formatting commands to select a particular font and type style.

To enter text in any window, simply click in that window and type the text you want. To insert a code, click on one of the buttons shown in table 4.2.

TABLE 4.2
Header and Footer Codes

Icon	Code	Result
 **A**	None	Use this icon to format the header or footer text. After you select the text to be formatted, click on this icon to bring up the Font dialog box. Code-based equivalents exist, but using this button and the Font dialog box is easier.

Icon	Code	Result
None	&"*fontname*"	The name used in *fontname* must be exactly as spelled in the Font dialog box, and the surrounding quote marks are required.
None	&*xx*	Replace *xx* with the point size of the font desired. Be sure to use two-digit point sizes, as in 06, 08, 12, and so on. Also, be sure to leave a space after the numbers for the font size.
None	&B	Makes the following text bold. The next &B turns bold printing off, then the next turns it back on, and so forth.
None	&I	Makes the following text italic. The second &I turns italic printing off, and so on.
None	&S	Causes the following text to be printed with strikethrough emphasis. The second &S turns strikethrough printing off.
None	&U	Underlines the following text. The second &U turns underline off, and so forth.
	&D	Prints the system date.
	&F	Prints the name of the worksheet.
	&T	Prints the system time.
	&P	Prints the current page number.
	&N	Prints the total number of pages. Useful for footers that read Page 1 of 12, which would be accomplished with this entry: Page &P of &N.

continues

TABLE 4.2, CONTINUED
Header and Footer Codes

Icon	Code	Result
None None	&P+*x* &P-*x*	These two header or footer code forms instruct Excel to print the page number plus or minus the number specified by *x* and are useful when your worksheet is part of a larger report. Use this code to have Excel print the correct page numbers for your report instead if its own page numbers. For example, if you have several sheets that need to be numbered from page 10 to page 15, you can use this code to start the page numbers at 10 instead of 1.
None	&&	Prints an ampersand. Because Excel normally interprets an ampersand as part of a header or footer code, the double-ampersand code is provided if you need to print an ampersand rather than have Excel try to interpret it as a code.

Figure 4.7 shows an example footer using some of these codes.

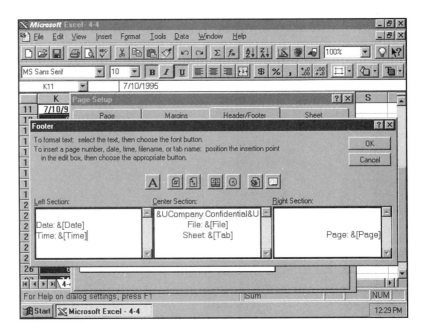

Figure 4.7

A sample custom footer.

Setting Up Repeating Titles

Tables that span many pages can make finding specific data difficult, because the labels that define the data are often on a different page. You can avoid this problem by using an Excel feature called Print Titles to automatically print the labels for the data on each page.

Consider the worksheet shown in figure 4.8.

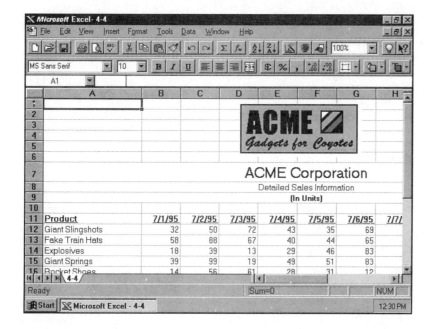

Figure 4.8

The large worksheet.

When you print your worksheet using a normal font, the results appear as shown in figures 4.9 and 4.10.

This example illustrates the problems that exist in a strictly horizontal format. In reality, you must work in both dimensions, sometimes crossing many pages. The cure is Print Titles, which causes part of your worksheet to repeat automatically on each page. You can select the rows or columns that contain the header information you want repeated so that it prints on each page.

Figure 4.9

The first page looks fine.

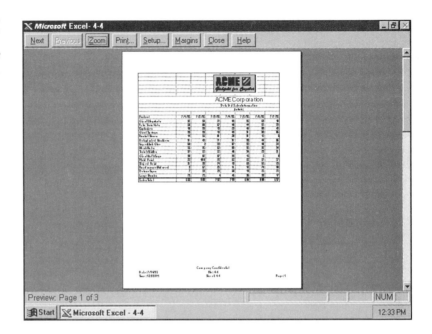

Figure 4.10

The second page is difficult to interpret.

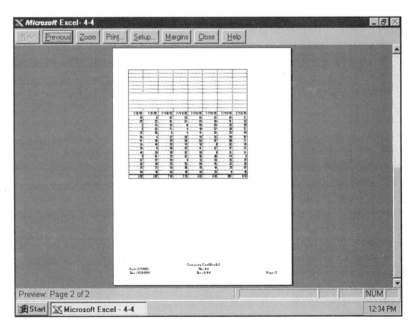

In this example, you want to make the row titles (the product names) into print titles. To make print titles, use the following procedure:

1. Pull down the **F**ile menu and select Print Se**t**up. The Page Setup notebook appears.

2. Click on the Sheet tab to display the Sheet page, as shown in figure 4.11.

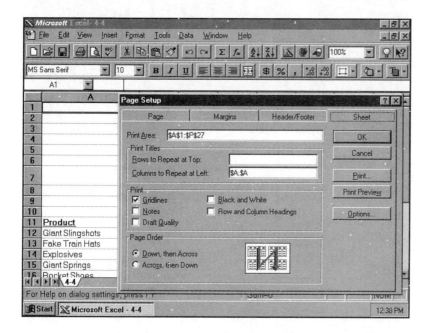

Figure 4.11

The Set Print titles page.

On the Sheet page, click once on **R**ows to Repeat at Top or **C**olumns to Repeat at Left field. Then, use your mouse to select the rows or columns you want to repeat. The rows or columns you select must be contiguous.

3. Click on the **C**olumns to Repeat at Left field.

4. Click on the A column label at the top of the worksheet. The column range is entered into the field automatically.

 Note You might need to move the dialog box in order to select the rows or columns you want to use. Also, either field will accept a named range of columns or rows rather than column letters or row numbers.

5. Click on OK to close the Page Setup notebook.

Figure 4.12 shows the new page 2 of the example printout, complete with titles.

Figure 4.12

Page 2 looks better with titles.

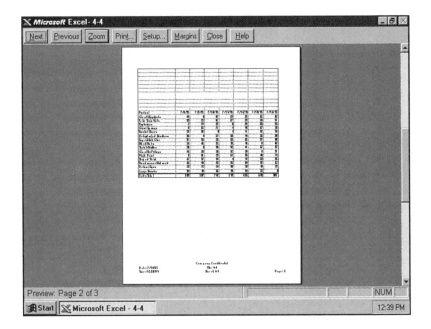

Previewing Your Printout

With Excel, you can preview your printouts before printing out hard copy. Excel shows you, as closely as possible, exactly what you will see when you print out to paper. You also can adjust certain print characteristics when you view the print preview, until you are happy with the results. When you are satisfied, you can print the final document quickly and easily.

To preview a document, pull down the File menu and select Print Preview. Alternately, click on the Print Preview button on the Standard toolbar. The preview appears, as shown in figure 4.13.

Along the top of the screen are a number of buttons, listed in table 4.3.

TABLE 4.3
Print Preview Buttons

Button Name	Function
Next	In a multipage document, click on this button to move to the next page. If no more pages remain, this button is grayed out.
Previous	In a multipage document, click on this button to move to the previous page. If you are on the first page, this button is grayed out.

Button Name	Function
Zoom	This button acts as a toggle switch. Click on it once to zoom in for a closer view of your document. Click on it again to view the entire page. You also can simply point to a particular region of the screen with the magnifying glass pointer. A zoomed view of that particular area then appears. Click again with the magnifying glass pointer to return to viewing the full page.
Print	Clicking on this button closes the preview window and returns you to the document, automatically bringing up the Print dialog box.
Setup	Click on this button to bring up the Page Setup dialog box. You can make any changes you want. When you click on the OK button, the preview window reflects your changes.
Margins	Clicking on this button brings up control handles that enable you visually to set the margins and column widths (see the next section).
Close	This button closes the preview window and returns you to your worksheet.

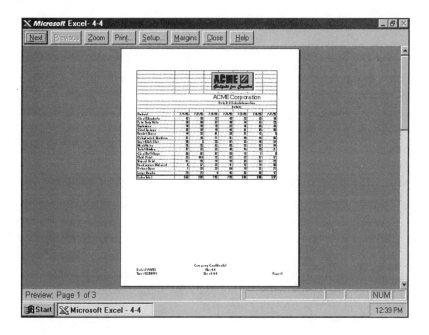

Figure 4.13

The Print Preview screen.

In this example, the document might benefit from a number of changes. Clicking on the **S**etup button enables you to make the following changes:

◆ Switch from Portrait to **L**andscape Orientation on the Page page.

◆ Remove the gridlines. Use the Sheet page and deselect the **G**ridlines check box.

◆ Remove the header and footer. Use the Header/Footer page. Pull down the **H**eader and **F**ooter list box and choose (none). The (none) entry can be found at the top of the list box.

◆ Automatically center the document vertically and horizontally. Use the Margin page and select the Hori**z**ontally and **V**ertically check boxes in the Center on Page section of the page.

After these changes are made in the Page Setup dialog box and the OK button is selected, the results appear (see fig. 4.14).

Figure 4.14

The Preview example after changes.

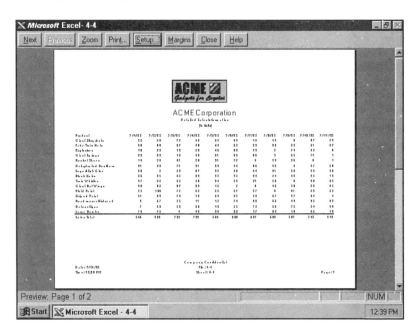

Adjusting Margins and Column Widths in Print Preview

When you are in the preview window, you can adjust the margin and column widths visually by clicking on the **M**argins button. Control handles appear, as shown in figure 4.15.

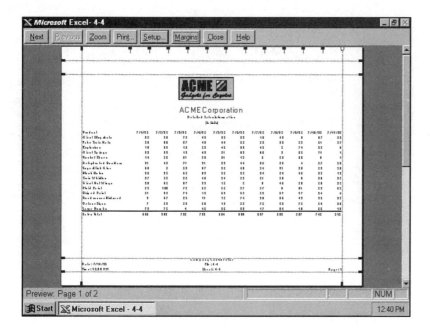

Figure 4.15

The margin and column control handles.

To adjust the margins or the column widths, position your pointer on top of the relevant control handle and drag it to the new position. The results appear instantly.

After you make adjustments to the preview, click on the **P**rint button to print the document.

Chapter Snapshot

One of the real strengths of Excel is its capability to help you manage complex data. You can view and work with large amounts of data fairly effortlessly, using the built-in tools designed for that purpose. You can view one or more documents in multiple windows or views and easily consolidate information from different worksheets—even when they are in different workbooks. You also can set up titles and different scrollable areas of a single worksheet to make them easier to work with. In this chapter, you learn about these tools, including the following:

◆ Viewing and working with multiple windows in the Excel work area

◆ Managing sheets within the workbook: inserting new sheets, deleting sheets, and renaming sheets

◆ Managing and switching between multiple workbooks

◆ Using three-dimensional references in your workbooks

◆ Linking data between multiple worksheets or workbooks

◆ Setting up and using Excel templates

By learning to manipulate multiple windows and views, you learn to work more efficiently. The features discussed in this chapter can help you put more of Excel's power to work for you.

Working with Multiple Windows

One of Excel's most valuable aspects is its capability to help you consolidate and analyze data that would otherwise be very cumbersome. Particularly with the workbooks in Excel for Windows 95, this task becomes even easier. The workbook-organizing metaphor makes it easier to keep similar types of data together, with different sheets for different parts of your data, for charts, or even for Excel programming instructions.

Splitting the Worksheet

In many cases, you might want to view different parts of a single sheet at the same time. You might, for example, want to keep the labels of a table visible, or to view multiple parts of the worksheet to better understand the way a complex formula works while you scroll across it.

Creating Multiple Viewing Areas

To split the worksheet into multiple *panes* (different scrollable portions of the same sheet) by using the mouse, drag the horizontal split bar down or the vertical split bar to the left. Figure 5.1 shows you the location of the two split bars. When you put your mouse pointer on top of the split bar, the pointer changes to two vertical or horizontal bars with arrows to indicate that you can move the bar. When your pointer is in the right place, click and drag the bar to the position you want.

Figure 5.1

Split bar locations.

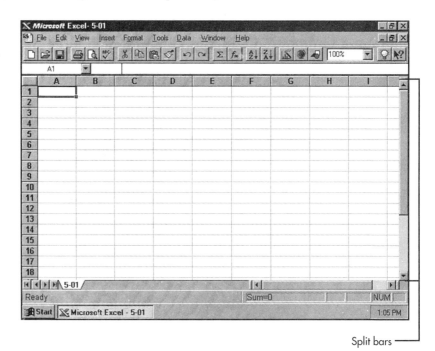

Split bars

Figure 5.2 shows the effect of dragging the vertical split bar to the middle of the worksheet.

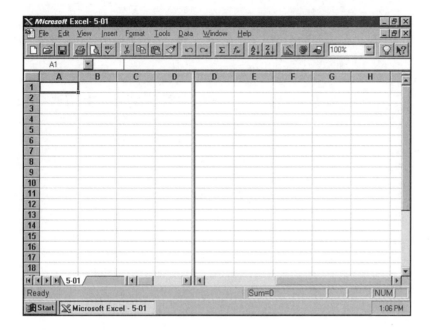

Figure 5.2

The vertical split bar.

You also can split the worksheet into four parts instantly with the menu command provided by using the following procedure:

1. Pull down the **W**indow menu.

2. Choose **S**plit from the menu.

You can move between panes simply by clicking your mouse in the pane with which you want to work. Each pane area can scroll independently of the other panes. As you see in figure 5.2, each pane gets its own scroll bars for this purpose.

Freezing Panes

You also can "freeze" the window panes in a single position. Freezing is useful when you are working with large tables. Look at the sales worksheet shown in figure 5.3, for example.

Figure 5.3

The table example.

	B	C	D	E	F	G	H	I	J	
10										
11	7/1/95	7/2/95	7/3/95	7/4/95	7/5/95	7/6/95	7/7/95	7/8/95	7/9/95	
12	32	50	72	43	35	69	10	49	8	
13	58	88	67	40	44	65	29	99	25	
14	18	39	13	29	46	83	43	2	74	
15	39	99	19	49	51	83	86	9	65	
16	14	56	61	28	31	12	6	53	36	
17	91	43	71	91	99	44	86	36	4	
18	60	2	53	87	92	48	54	31	50	
19	56	95	62	83	32	92	94	24	46	
20	97	22	22	48	94	23	21	50	0	
21	38	82	87	93	15	2	0	46	28	
22	25	100	72	62	22	27	57	8	81	
23	51	39	74	13	63	62	23	67	37	
24	3	67	25	11	12	74	98	66	43	
25	7	53	29	68	13	25	72	59	72	
26	79	75	4	46	36	99	17	84	18	
27	666	909	732	793	684	808	697	683	587	

When you look at the data to the right of the table, you really can't tell what each line represents, because the labels in column A are not visible (they are far to the left of the visible portion of the worksheet). This example shows the problem in only one dimension. If the table extended down farther, you would have similar problems with the dates at the top of the table—they would not be visible while looking at the lower parts of the table. To deal with this problem, Excel enables you to create independently scrollable portions of the worksheet. You then can continue to view one part of the worksheet (the labels, for example), while you scroll the other portion to see data located elsewhere in the worksheet. To see the way this command works, follow these steps:

1. Move to cell A1.

Tip Ctrl+Home quickly takes you to cell A1.

2. Pull down the <u>W</u>indow menu and choose <u>S</u>plit.

3. Position your mouse pointer directly over the intersection of the two panes. Drag the panes so that the two lines intersect at cell A11, as shown in figure 5.4.

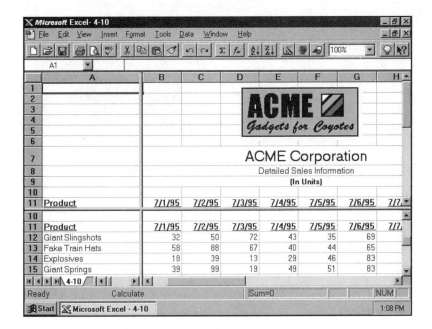

Figure 5.4

Correctly positioned split panes.

Tip   Excel normally creates the split above or to the left of the active cell. For the preceding example, you could position the active cell to B12 before using the **S**plit command to automatically create the split in the correct position.

4. Pull down the **W**indow menu again and choose **F**reeze Panes. The result is shown in figure 5.5.

Notice that several things have happened. First, the pane indicators are made up of fine lines rather than the thicker lines shown in figure 5.4. Second, the worksheet only has a single set of scroll bars, because you no longer can scroll the frozen portions independently as you could before you chose the **F**reeze Panes command. Now when you scroll the worksheet, you scroll everything *except* the frozen panes (in this case, rows 1 through 11 and column A). If, for example, the worksheet is scrolled down and to the right, the frozen pane areas still are visible, as in figure 5.6.

Removing Frozen Panes

To unfreeze the existing panes, pull down the **W**indow menu and choose Un**f**reeze Panes. You also can remove the panes without unfreezing them first by pulling down the **W**indow menu and choosing Remove **S**plit.

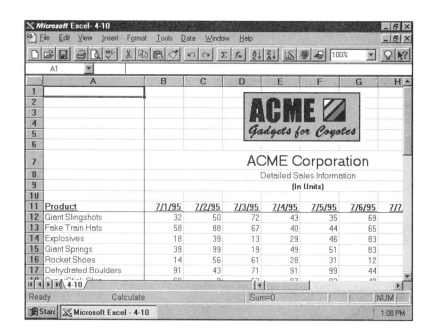

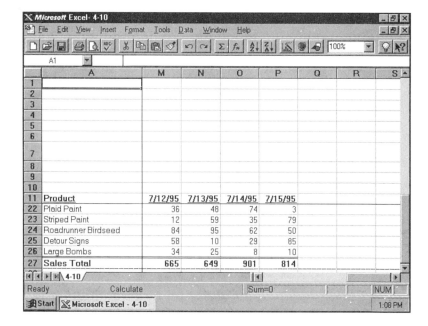

Using Multiple Views of a Single Workbook

Another useful trick is to work with multiple views of a single workbook, which enables you to have different pages of a single workbook on the screen at one time. Using a related feature, you also can show multiple workbooks on the screen at one time with this feature.

To open a second view of a single workbook, do the following:

1. Pull down the **W**indow menu.

2. Choose **N**ew Window.

This procedure creates a second *instance* of the workbook, so you can switch using the **W**indow menu, as shown in figure 5.7.

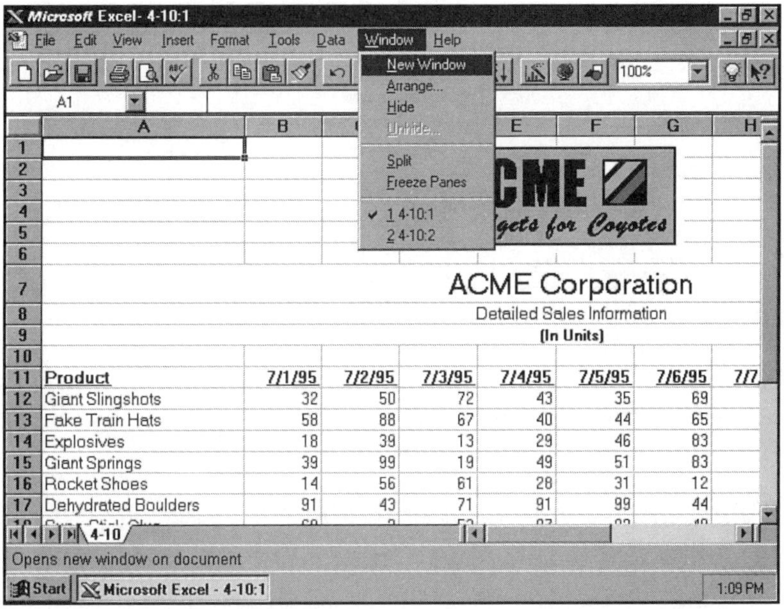

Figure 5.7

*The **W**indow menu.*

Choosing either window from the list takes you to that copy of the workbook. Notice that each workbook has a colon following its name, with a number after the colon, indicating these are different windows of the same workbook. Changes to one window are shown instantly in the other.

Arranging Windows

You also can arrange the windows on your screen so that you can view them all simultaneously. To make this arrangement using the mouse, first click on the Restore button. This button reduces the current view to a window that can be moved and resized on the Excel work area. Figure 5.8 shows what this view looks like after you click on the Document Restore button.

Figure 5.8

The windowed view.

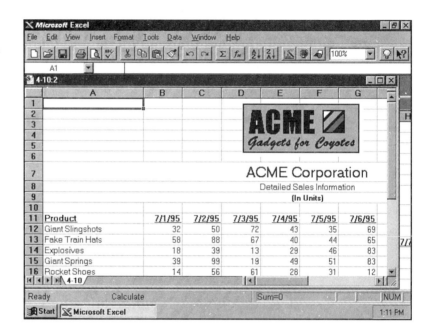

Arranging Automatically

Some Excel commands rearrange multiple windows automatically. You can follow these steps:

1. Pull down the **W**indow menu.

2. Choose **A**rrange. The Arrange Windows dialog box appears, as shown in figure 5.9.

Figure 5.9

The Arrange Windows dialog box.

The Arrange Windows dialog box offers several options, as follows:

◆ **Tiled.** Arranges windows so that they each use an equal portion of the screen, as in figure 5.10.

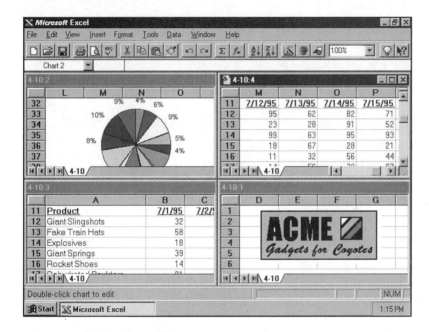

Figure 5.10

The Tiled option.

◆ **Horizontal.** Arranges windows so that they span the entire screen and are arrayed vertically, as in figure 5.11.

◆ **Vertical.** Arranges windows so that they stretch from the top of the screen to the bottom and are arranged next to each other, as in figure 5.12.

◆ **Cascade.** Arranges the windows vertically, as you can see in figure 5.13. The Cascade option gives each window the most space possible, while still enabling you to click on any of the windows at any time to bring it to the front.

The Arrange Windows dialog box also has a check box called Windows of Active Workbook. If this option is selected before you click on the OK button in the dialog box, Excel only includes different views of the workbook currently selected in the arrange operation.

You can close any of the views by double-clicking on that window's Control menu. The remaining views are renumbered accordingly.

Figure 5.11

The Horizontal option.

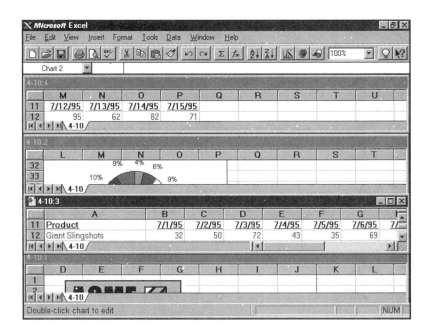

Tip

Normally, you switch between windows by using the **W**indow menu. You also can switch between all open windows by pressing Ctrl+Tab.

Figure 5.12

The Vertical option.

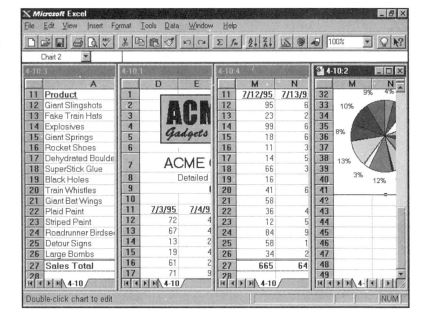

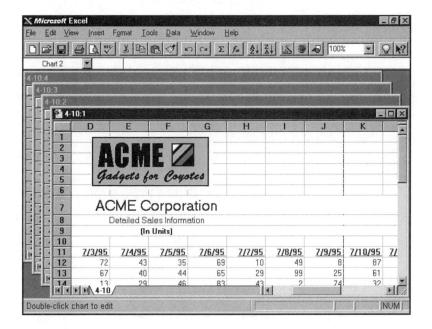

Figure 5.13

The Cascade option.

Hiding and Showing Windows

You can easily hide any of the open windows by using the **W**indow menu's **H**ide command. Make sure the window you want to hide is active, then select **H**ide. The window vanishes and does not appear in the **W**indow menu as it normally would. This option is valuable for worksheets that you distribute to others. You can hide the underlying details of the worksheet, if necessary.

To unhide a hidden window, pull down the **W**indow menu and choose **U**nhide. The Unhide dialog box, shown in figure 5.14, lists all currently hidden windows.

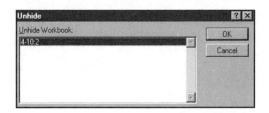

Figure 5.14

The Unhide dialog box.

Select the window you want to unhide from the list and click on OK.

Locking Down Windows

When you are developing workbooks for others to use, you might want to take away the user's ability to rearrange the windows. For example, perhaps your workbooks might be used by novice Excel users who might become confused and disoriented if they mistakenly closed a window in the workbook. Prevent this possibility by locking the windows of the workbook into your assigned positions.

To lock windows, follow these steps:

1. Arrange the windows in exactly the way you want them to remain.

2. Pull down the **T**ools menu, choose **P**rotection, and then choose Protect **W**orkbook. You see the Protect Workbook dialog box, shown in figure 5.15.

Figure 5.15

The Protect Workbook dialog box.

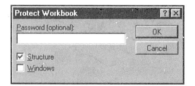

Before protecting the workbook, make sure that the **W**indows check box is selected. This step ensures that the border around each window that normally enables you to resize it is hidden. Also, attempts to use the **A**rrange option on the **W**indow menu are ignored.

To restore Excel's capability to arrange the windows, simply unprotect the workbook. Pull down the **T**ools menu, choose **P**rotection, and then choose Unprotect **W**orkbook.

Controlling Workbook Sheets

You can move easily between different worksheets in your workbook by clicking on the tabs found at the bottom of the workbook.

You also can switch between your active sheets using a keyboard combination. Ctrl+PgDn moves you to the next sheet in the workbook; Ctrl+PgUp moves you to the previous sheet.

Rearranging Sheets

To rearrange sheets in your workbook, click on the sheet tab you want to move, hold down the left mouse button, and drag to the right or left. A small arrow indicates where the sheet will be "dropped" when you release the mouse button.

You also can use the object menu to move or copy sheets in your workbook by using the following method:

1. Click the right mouse button on the sheet you want to copy or move.

2. From the menu, choose Move or Copy. You see the dialog box shown in figure 5.16.

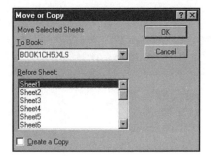

Figure 5.16

The Move or Copy dialog box.

This dialog box offers many options, as follows:

◆ **To Book.** Enables you to choose any other open workbook to which to move the sheet.

◆ **Before Sheet.** Enables you to choose where to position the moved sheet in the target workbook. Choose the sheet before which you want the moved or copied sheet to be inserted.

◆ **Create a Copy.** Tells Excel to make a copy of the sheet rather than moving it.

3. After you have selected the options you want, click on the OK button.

Tip

To see a list of sheets in the current workbook, right-click on the radio buttons to see a table of contents.

To see fewer or more tabs displayed on the tab line, grab the tab split box just to the left of the horizontal scroll bar left-pointing arrow and drag left or right for better visibility.

To see the next tab label quickly, click once on the tab split box to slide one tab to the right.

Creating Sheets

The easiest way to create new sheets in an existing workbook is to use the pop-up menu. Follow these steps:

1. Right-click on one of the sheet tabs.

2. Choose Insert from the pop-up menu. You see the dialog box shown in figure 5.17.

Figure 5.17

The Insert dialog box.

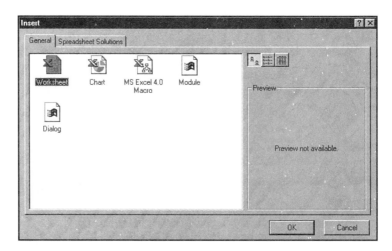

As you can see from the dialog box, Excel supports many types of sheets:

◆ **Worksheet.** A worksheet is an Excel spreadsheet. The sheet in the background of figure 5.17, for instance, is a worksheet.

◆ **Chart.** Excel supports charts embedded in worksheets or that exist as separate sheets in the workbook. If you want to create a chart on a separate sheet in the workbook, choose this option.

◆ **MS Excel 4.0 Macro.** The old macro language that was used in Excel 4 was replaced with Visual Basic Application tools. Excel for Windows 95 still contains support for the Excel 4 macros, however. To use a macro from Excel 4, include it in an MS Excel 4.0 macro sheet in your workbook.

◆ **Module.** Module sheets are Visual Basic Application modules. These sheets contain the programming code that defines your Excel application.

◆ **Dialog.** For use with modules, dialog sheets contain dialog boxes that accept input and choices from the user of the VBA application.

◆ **Slides.** A slide sheet coordinates a presentation based in Excel. These sheets contain commands designed to enable you to prepare a sequence of charts and worksheets for a presentation.

3. After you choose the type of sheet you want to insert, click on the OK button.

You also can insert new sheets by using the **I**nsert menu:

◆ To create a new worksheet, access the **I**nsert **W**orksheet command.

◆ To create a new chart, access the **I**nsert **C**hart command. Then, from the cascading menu, choose either **O**n This Sheet or **A**s New Sheet to tell Excel where to create the new chart.

◆ To create a module, pull down the **I**nsert menu and choose **M**acro. You then can choose, from the cascading menu, either **M**odule, **D**ialog, or MS **E**xcel 4.0 Macro.

Deleting Sheets

To delete a sheet or sheets in Excel, follow these steps:

1. Select the sheet you want to delete. If you want to delete more than one sheet, Ctrl+click to select additional sheets.

2. Pull down the **E**dit menu and choose De**l**ete Sheet. Alternately, you can access the pop-up menu from here by clicking your right mouse button on the sheet tab. From the pop-up menu, choose Delete.

Renaming Sheet Tabs

You probably will find it difficult to manage your sheets with the default names of Sheet1, Sheet2, Sheet3, and so on. Fortunately, Excel enables you to rename the tabs for each sheet so that each sheet has a more meaningful name. To rename tabs using the menus, follow these steps:

1. Select the sheet you want to rename.

2. Pull down the **F**ormat menu and choose S**h**eet. Choose **R**ename from the cascading menu.

3. Type the new sheet name in the dialog box that appears.

As with almost all Excel commands, you also can rename tabs using the pop-up menus. Right-click on the sheet tab and choose Rename from the pop-up menu.

Figure 5.18 shows the sample worksheet for this chapter with new tab names.

Figure 5.18

The renamed tabs.

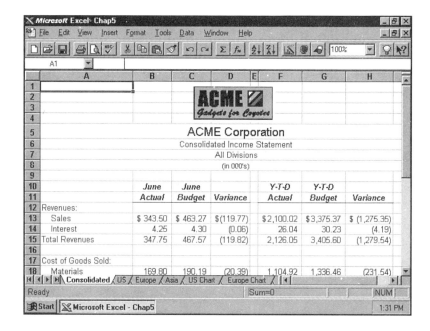

Adding an Existing Worksheet to a Notebook

To take an existing Excel 4 worksheet and add it to a workbook, follow these steps:

1. Open the workbook of which you want the existing worksheet to be a part.

2. Open the existing worksheet. It opens into a single-sheet workbook, with the file name where you normally see the tab name.

3. With the existing worksheet active, pull down the **E**dit menu and then choose **M**ove or Copy Sheet from the menu.

4. In the Move or Copy dialog box, select the name of the workbook in the **T**o Book drop box.

Tip   Sheets are inserted to the left of the active sheet by default.

5. In the list labeled **B**efore Sheet, select the sheet in the workbook before which you want the existing worksheet to appear.

6. Click on the OK button.

New Riders Publishing
INSIDE
SERIES

Linking Data Between Sheets

The workbook is one of Excel's most powerful features. It enables you to organize your worksheets more logically, with major sections of your project each contained in a single worksheet. Thus, you spend less time worrying about organizing your data and more time actually getting answers and analyzing your data. Also, workbooks make developing more complicated worksheets, such as multicompany spreadsheets, much easier.

Note The following sections discuss various ways to link data between different sheets, whether they are in the same workbook or different workbooks. Table 5.1 defines many terms you need to know in order to understand these sections.

TABLE 5.1
Linked Data Terms

Term	Definition
3D Reference	A reference to another sheet in the current workbook. These references are updated automatically when Excel recalculates the workbook.
Source Document	When linking different files, this document contains the source data.
Dependent Document	When linking different files, the dependent document is the one that relies on data in other documents.
External Reference	A cell reference that refers to cells in a different workbook.
Remote Reference	A remote reference refers to data in a file that was created by an application other than Excel. This data might be graphic data from a drawing program or word processing data from a word processor.

To access the full power of the workbook, however, you must learn to link data between the different sheets of the workbook. From these examples, you can learn to create a simple income statement, with individual sheets for each major division in the company and a sheet that combines all divisions into a consolidated total. The consolidated sheet is made of formulas that automatically total each of the other sheets in the workbook. After the consolidated sheet is completed, changes in any of the divisional sheets are reflected there automatically. Consider figure 5.19, which shows all four sheets in the same workbook.

Figure 5.19

The ACME consolidated 3D workbook.

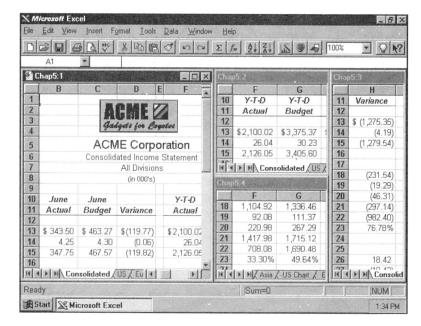

Creating 3D References

The easiest way to link cells from different sheets into a formula is to use the mouse. This section shows you how to perform mouse references and tells you what to type when you want to enter 3D references manually.

To see the way a 3D reference works, follow these steps:

1. Move to the cell in which you want the total placed from another sheet.

2. Type the equal sign to begin the formula.

3. Click on the tab of the sheet that contains the data you want.

4. Click on the cell you want to reference.

5. Press Enter to complete the formula.

After you press Enter, Excel returns to the sheet that contained the formula, and the data from the other sheet now appears in the cell. This data is said to be *dynamic*. In other words, if you change the source cell, the destination cell (which contains the formula) instantly changes to reflect the new number.

Also, as you can see, Excel entered the formula in the format:

```
=SheetName!CellName
```

Note Sheet names in a 3D reference always are absolute. Individual cells or ranges in the 3D reference can be absolute or relative.

This method is the general way in which references to other sheets are entered. The only exception is when you have spaces in the sheet name, in which case Excel surrounds the sheet name with single quote marks, as in the following example:

```
='Sheet with a Space'!CellName
```

Note When you enter references to other sheets using the mouse, Excel automatically uses the single quote marks, if needed.

The next step in entering multisheet references with the mouse is to perform some arithmetic. In figure 5.20, the formula bar shows one way to add cells from three sheets into a total in the consolidating sheet.

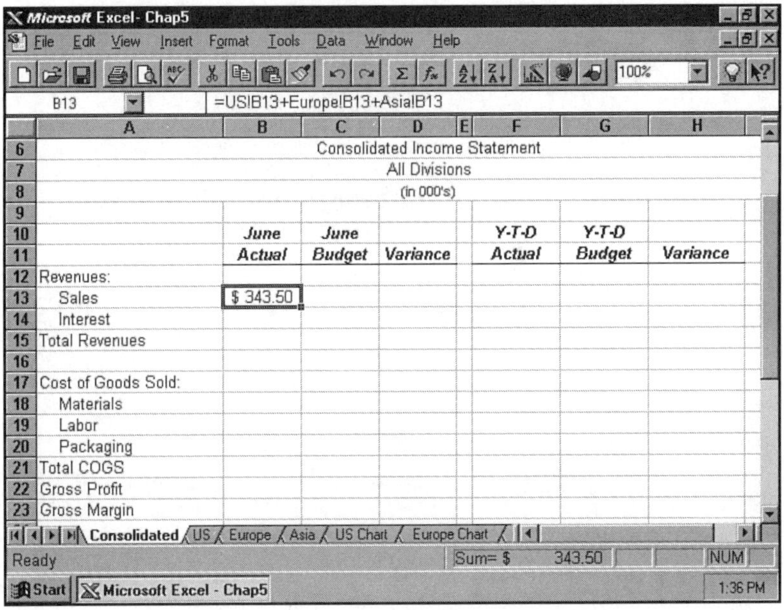

Figure 5.20

3D arithmetic.

Working with Sheet Ranges

Excel also enables you to use references that refer to many sheets all in one reference. The example in figure 5.20 is not very practical if you are consolidating tens or hundreds of worksheets (and Excel *can* handle hundreds of worksheets!). In these cases, you want to use the SUM function and enter the sheet names as a range. This operation can be done entirely with mouse commands, as follows:

1. Move to the cell that contains the formula.

2. Start the formula by entering =**SUM(**.

3. Switch to the first sheet in the range and then click on the cell you want to total, or select the range you want to use.

4. Shift+click on the last sheet in the range that you want included in the formula.

5. Press Enter to complete the formula.

Figure 5.21 shows the range of sheets with the completed formula.

Figure 5.21

The range of sheets highlighted in the formula bar.

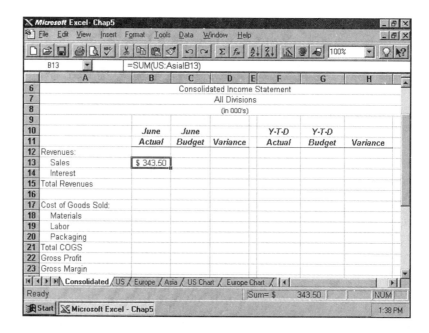

As you can see, multisheet references are given in the following form:

```
FirstSheet:LastSheet!Cell_Or_Range
```

Figure 5.22 shows this form using a range of cells in each sheet, with the resulting formula =SUM(Sheet2:Sheet3!A1:D6).

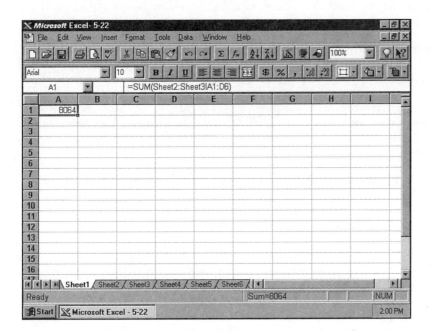

Figure 5.22

The 3D reference with range displayed.

 Stop If you rearrange the order of the sheets in your workbook, you might change the way sheet ranges are calculated. In the range Sheet4:Sheet8, for instance, if you move Sheet6 somewhere outside of the range in the formula, its cells are no longer part of the solution. Similarly, if you insert a new sheet in a range of sheets, the new sheet's data become part of the answer.

If you move the first or last sheet to an area outside of the original range, the formula adjusts to exclude that sheet. In the preceding example, if Sheet4 is moved to follow Sheet8, then the formula changes to Sheet5:Sheet8.

For this reason, be careful when you rearrange sheets in a workbook that contains 3D references.

Using References to Other Workbooks

Linking between different workbooks (and not just different sheets within a workbook) has many possible uses, including the following:

◆ **Look at different analyses of your data.** You can create new workbooks from your source workbooks to present key data in different ways without changing the structure of the original data. This procedure helps you look at your data differently.

◆ **Simplify complex workbooks.** Often, in very large workbooks, you can simplify the organization of your data by breaking it down into different workbooks.

◆ **Conserve memory.** You can conserve your computer's memory by breaking large workbooks into smaller pieces. In fact, if you are working with a workbook that includes many sheets, and you start getting Out of Memory error messages, break the large workbook into smaller workbooks.

◆ **Create a hierarchy of different workbooks for very large projects.** You can create multiple levels of linked workbooks, if necessary. In other words, workbook #1 can refer to workbook #2, which references workbooks #3 and #4 (or any other hierarchical organization that makes sense for your project).

◆ **Coordinate large projects.** You can use Excel to do your company's budgeting, for example, or prepare and distribute workbooks for budgeting managers. When the managers complete and return the workbooks, consolidate them into a single, company-wide budget workbook.

To link workbooks, you can use all the same tools about which you just learned. You can use the mouse, as you saw earlier, to create the links between the different workbooks. The only exception is that you should open the workbook you want to link, and use the <u>W</u>indow menu to switch between the workbooks instead of just clicking on the workbook tabs.

References to other workbooks that are open in Excel take the following form:

```
=[Workbook_Filename]Sheet_Name!Cell_Or_Range
```

When the workbook you want to reference is not open in Excel, the full path name of the workbook is added to the beginning of the reference, as in the following example:

```
='C:\EXCEL\DATA\[WORKBOOK.XLS]Sheet_Name'!Cell_Or_Range
```

 Note   Make sure that the entire sequence of path name, workbook file name, and sheet name is enclosed with single quote marks before the exclamation point.

Also, if the workbook you are linking is located in the same directory as the dependent workbook, you do not need to type the path name.

When opening a workbook that contains links to other Excel workbooks stored on your computer's disk, you see the message shown in figure 5.23.

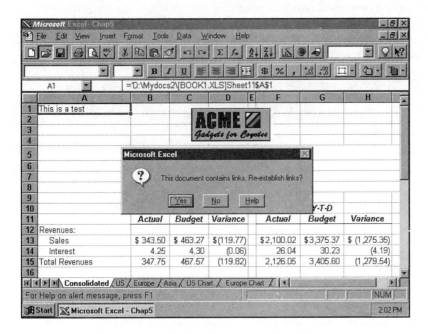

Figure 5.23

The Update Reference message box.

If you click on **Y**es, Excel automatically goes into the referenced workbooks to find the most recent data and updates all the formulas that access that data.

If you select **N**o, Excel simply shows you the most recent answer that was stored the last time you saved the dependent workbook. The links to the other workbook are still present, but are not necessarily accurate if the other workbooks are updated. You might want to choose the **N**o button when you are working with a very large workbook that contains many links to many different workbooks. If you do not need the most current data, you can save time by telling Excel to skip the update process.

Managing Workbook Links

You can manage the links between your workbooks to do the following tasks:

◆ Update the dependent workbook at any time

◆ Redirect a workbook link from one workbook to another

◆ Open the source workbooks

Note A *dependent document* is one that contains a formula that uses data from another document. The document that contains the original data is the *source document*.

To manage your document links, pull down the **E**dit menu and choose **L**inks. You see the dialog box shown in figure 5.24.

Figure 5.24

The Links dialog box.

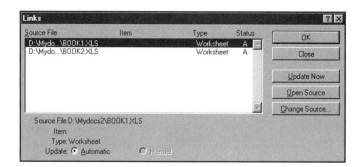

The Links dialog box shows you all active links in the current document. You can select the link with which you want to work by clicking on it. After you have selected a link, you can perform the following functions:

◆ Click on the **U**pdate Now button to update the links immediately with any new information in the source document.

◆ Click on the **O**pen Source button to open the source document.

◆ Click on the **C**hange Source button to tell Excel to link to a different workbook. You are shown the Change Links dialog box (much like the File Open dialog box). Use the Change Links dialog box to find and open the new document to which you want to link. The links automatically use the same ranges in the new source document that you select.

 Note The Links dialog box shows all the links available to control. Links are not limited to other Excel workbooks. Excel allows linked graphics, word processing files, and so on. The Links dialog box shows all these links for your current workbook.

Save the source workbook first when you are saving linked workbooks. This precaution ensures that the data is calculated properly before the dependent workbook is closed.

Be careful when renaming or moving workbooks. If you rename a source workbook, do the following two things to make sure that all the dependent references are properly updated:

1. Check to see that the source and dependent workbooks are open so Excel can automatically correct any dependent references to the renamed workbook.

2. Use the Excel Save **A**s command to rename the workbook, as shown in figure 5.25.

Figure 5.25

The Save As dialog box.

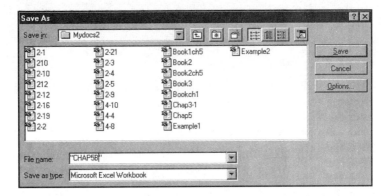

If a source workbook is renamed or moved using the File Manager, you must update the links in the dependent workbook manually, because Excel does not know what you did with the source workbook. When you open the dependent workbook, it automatically notes that the source workbook is no longer present and automatically brings up the Save As dialog box shown in figure 5.25. Use this dialog box to relocate the file that contains the source data, or to save your file with a new name.

Using Paste Special

Often, you want to share data in different sheets, but when you use the normal copy and paste between worksheets, you do not create a link between those sheets. Instead, you have to use Paste **S**pecial to copy data to a new sheet that still is linked back to the original sheet. To use Paste **S**pecial, follow these steps:

1. Select the source range of cells.

2. Pull down the **E**dit menu and choose **C**opy.

3. Move to the destination workbook, and click on the cell in which you want the data to be copied.

4. Pull down the **E**dit menu and choose Paste **S**pecial. You see the dialog box shown in figure 5.26.

5. Click on the Paste **L**ink button.

Figure 5.26

*The Paste Special
dialog box.*

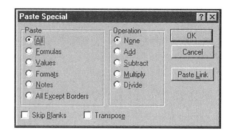

The data is placed in your destination cells, with an automatic link back to the source document.

Removing Links

To remove a link but retain the results, follow these steps:

1. Select the range you want to retain.

2. Pull down the **E**dit menu and choose **C**opy.

3. Pull down the **E**dit menu again and choose Paste **S**pecial. In the Paste Special dialog box, click on the button marked **V**alues and then click on the OK button.

When you follow the preceding steps, the links are removed, but the results that were present are converted to regular data, as if you simply retyped them.

Pasting Pictures from a Workbook

Excel enables you to take "pictures" of a series of cells and paste them into another worksheet or workbook so they appear as graphic images. These images can be resized, reshaped, and so on. Use the following procedure:

1. Select the range of cells of which you want to take a picture.

2. Pull down the **E**dit menu and choose **C**opy, or click on the Camera button on the toolbar.

3. Move to the destination worksheet.

4. If you copied the cells using the Camera button on the toolbar, simply click in the destination area to create the linked picture. If you used the **C**opy command, then hold down the Shift key while you pull down the **E**dit menu and choose Paste Picture **L**ink.

Although Paste Picture **L**ink creates a linked picture that changes if the source cells change, you also can create a simple picture that has no links and does not update if the source cells change. Simply hold down the Shift key while you pull down the **E**dit menu and choose **P**aste Picture, instead of Paste Picture **L**ink.

Linking to Other Applications

Many business and science documents are really *compound documents.* They are composed of information from a variety of sources: spreadsheets, charting programs, drawing programs, word processors, and so on. Instead of cutting or pasting information from all of these sources, you can use a Windows technology called *Object Linking and Embedding* (OLE, pronounced like a bullfighter saying "Olé!") to make the creation of compound documents much easier.

Excel versions prior to 5.0 used OLE 1.0, which enabled you to link data between different Windows-based applications. You could, for instance, take an Excel chart and link it to a Microsoft Word or WordPerfect for Windows document. The linked chart would be updated automatically if it was changed in Excel, so the word processor automatically showed the most current version of the chart. Also, if you were to double-click on the chart in the word processing program, Excel would be launched automatically with the chart loaded and ready for changes. Many Windows applications support OLE 1.0 and can perform these tricks.

Excel version 5 and Excel for Windows 95 support an updated version of OLE called *OLE 2.0.* Excel was one of the first applications to feature version 2 of OLE. Many other application developers also are working to include OLE 2.0 capabilities in their programs.

OLE 2.0 adds two key capabilities to OLE 1.0, as follows:

◆ **In-place editing of embedded (linked) objects.** If you double-click on an Excel chart embedded in a word processor that supports OLE 2.0, you are able to edit the chart without leaving your word processing document. The word processor's menus become Excel menus, and you have full access to Excel's power, almost as if Excel is built into the word processor!

◆ **Dragging and dropping of objects.** This capability enables you to grab data in one application and simply "drop" it into another application.

Using OLE

You can take information from one Windows application and link it to another application in two ways. You can take the source data and drag it to the destination, or you can use the **C**opy command in the **E**dit menu of the source program and then use some form of Paste **S**pecial in the destination program.

Note Although Microsoft programs generally use a command called Paste **S**pecial, other programs might call this command something else. For example, WordPerfect for Windows calls it Paste Link. When in doubt, consult the documentation for the program with which you are linking Excel.

Using Drag and Drop

Drag and drop might function differently, depending on the application you are using. Some applications, for instance, might interpret a drag-and-drop operation as a command to move data from the source application to the destination application. Other applications might assume you are attempting a link creation. The interpretation depends on the application you are using, and also on the specific data you are trying to drag and drop.

Note For drag and drop to work with Excel, you must enable a check box in the Options notebook. Pull down the **T**ools menu and choose **O**ptions. Then click on the Edit tab in the options notebook. Make sure that the check box labeled Allow Cell **D**rag and Drop is checked.

Figure 5.27 shows a chart that was dragged from Excel to Microsoft Word 7.0. Note that once the chart was dropped into Word, the original range from which the chart was created was restored to the Excel screen.

To perform the drag-and-drop function, follow these steps:

1. Arrange the applications on the screen so you can see them both at the same time.

2. Select the graphic object (such as a chart) or range of cells you want to drag and drop.

3. If you are selecting a graphic object, click on the object and hold down the left mouse button. Then drag the mouse to the destination application. If you are copying a range of cells, then select the border of the selected range before dragging.

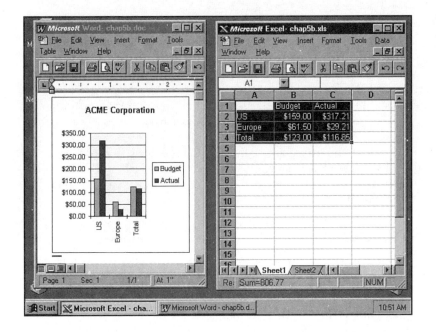

Figure 5.27

A demonstration of drag and drop.

4. Position the cursor in the destination application and release the left mouse button.

Tip

To force the drag and drop to insert the new data, hold down the Shift key while you perform the operation. To remove the data from Excel and place it in the destination application, hold down Ctrl during the drag-and-drop operation.

After the chart is dragged to the destination application, you can edit the data simply by double-clicking on it. This operation brings up Excel with the data ready for editing, or if Excel was not running when you double-clicked on the data, Word uses Excel's capabilities to help you edit the data. Excel is started in the background and "inserts" itself into Word so it still appears that you are working with Word, even though you have full access to all of the power of Excel (the menu commands appear in place of the Word menu commands, and so forth). This capability is called *in-place editing*.

AUTHOR'S NOTE

Microsoft is changing all its applications' menus so they are as standardized as possible. One reason for this change is to make the in-place editing process more "seamless."

Tip Use Shift plus drag and drop to cut from and then paste into another application.

Use Ctrl plus drag and drop to simply copy from one application to another.

Use Ctrl+Shift plus drag and drop to both cut and then copy and paste into another application. This latter option can handle pasting of simple formats or values from one worksheet to another, or from one workbook to another.

Some applications do not support in-place editing of Excel objects. In those cases, when you double-click on the Excel data in the destination application, Excel is launched with the data loaded in it. Edit the data in Excel and exit Excel to update the data in the destination application.

Controlling Link Requests

While Excel is running, it services any requests for link updates from other applications. You can control whether Excel responds to these requests by following these steps:

1. Pull down the **T**ools menu and choose **O**ptions.

2. Click on the Calculation tab in the notebook.

3. Select or deselect the check box labeled Update **R**emote References.

Using the Camera

You probably have wondered about the function of the Camera button on the Standard toolbar. It is used to prepare a "snapshot" of part of an Excel document that can be placed easily in another program (or another sheet in Excel, for that matter). If, for example, you use the **C**opy and **P**aste commands to move part of a worksheet into a Word document, you actually paste only the data; you do not place the data so that it appears with all of its formatting intact. Instead, use the Camera tool to prepare a snapshot of part of your worksheet (which includes all formatting), then place the resulting image into the other application. Follow these steps:

1. Select the part of your worksheet you want to present in a different application (in this example, Microsoft Word).

2. Click on the Camera button. A marquee appears around the selected cells, and your pointer changes to a small cross.

3. Click on another area of the worksheet to create the image. Figure 5.28 shows the resulting image on top of the worksheet.

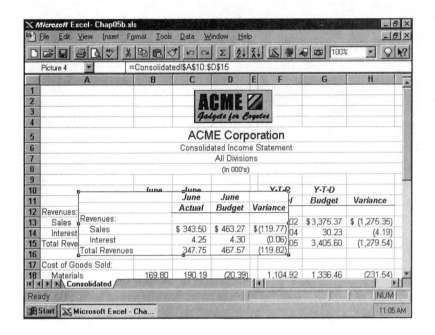

Figure 5.28

The worksheet image captured with the Camera tool.

The image created is dynamic. Even though you expect it to be a fixed image, you discover that if you change the data in the area you used for the image, the image changes.

After you have the image, you can drag it to another Windows application that supports OLE 2.0, or you can copy it to the Clipboard, then paste the object into the destination application so that the image is linked to Excel.

Setting Up Templates

One useful Excel application is setting up template workbooks that can be completed by people with whom you work. To set up template workbooks, follow these steps:

1. Prepare the workbook you want to make into a template.

2. Pull down the File menu and choose Save As.

3. In the Save As dialog box, click on the button to the right of the Save File as Type field to see a list of the different types of files you can save from Excel.

4. Choose Template from the list, enter a file name, then click on the OK button to save the document, which is given an XLT extension.

After you create the template and it is opened, a copy of the document is loaded and given a temporary name to preserve the original template file from changes.

To edit a template file, follow these steps:

1. Pull down the **F**ile menu and choose **O**pen.

2. Select the template file.

3. Hold down the Shift key while you click on the OK button.

This procedure opens the template file. Make any necessary changes and resave the template.

Chapter Snapshot

Excel has some advanced features that the typical user does not use on a day-to-day basis. When you do need these features, however, they can be real time-savers. In this chapter, you learn about the following advanced features:

◆ Embedding sound objects into your workbooks

◆ Using the Excel outlining feature

◆ Creating different scenarios using the Scenario Manager

◆ Using the PivotTable Wizard, which enables you to look at information in a table by rotating data categories to show new relationships

◆ Importing text files using the TextWizard

◆ Auditing workbooks

By taking advantage of Excel's powerful worksheet tools, you can go far beyond the basics and become an Excel "power user."

Advanced Worksheet Features

Excel includes many advanced features that are available to you when needed. This chapter discusses a number of these features—some of them new to Excel for Windows 95. The features included in this chapter are not needed by everyone who wants to benefit from using Excel; for those who do need them, however, they can be incredible time-savers.

Using Sound with Excel

In Excel, you can annotate your worksheets and charts with sound. These *sound objects* can be prerecorded sounds you use to emphasize a point or recorded voice annotations that explain certain features of the worksheet.

 Note You must have certain sound hardware to play or record sounds in Excel. You also have to set up Windows so that it can access the sound hardware.

Creating Sound Notes

Just as you can attach text notes to cells, you also can attach or record sound in addition to or in place of the written note. To record a sound note, follow these steps:

1. Click on the cell to which you want to attach the sound note.

2. Open the Cell Note dialog box by selecting No**t**e from the **I**nsert menu or pressing Shift+F2. The Cell Note dialog box appears, as shown in figure 6.1.

Figure 6.1

The Cell Note dialog box.

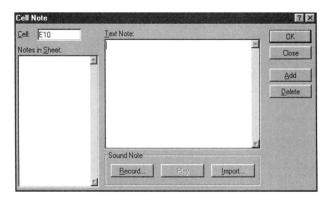

3. To record a sound using a microphone connected to your sound hardware, click on the **R**ecord button in the Cell Note dialog box. The Record dialog box appears, as shown in figure 6.2.

Figure 6.2

The Record dialog box.

4. Click on the **R**ecord button in the Record dialog box and begin speaking. After you finish your sound note, click on **S**top.

5. To check your sound note before you save it, click on the **P**lay button. If you don't like your sound note, click on the **R**ecord button again and re-record it.

6. After you are satisfied with your sound note, click on OK to save the sound note.

You also can use prerecorded sound notes that are stored on your disk as WAV files. To use prerecorded sound notes, follow these steps:

1. Select the cell to which you want to attach the sound note.

2. Open the Cell Note dialog box by selecting No**t**e from the **I**nsert menu or by pressing Shift+F2.

3. Click on the **I**mport button. You see the Import Sound dialog box, which functions like the standard **F**ile, **O**pen dialog box.

4. Find the WAV file on your disk by using the Import Sound dialog box. Select the file, then click on OK.

To play a sound note on the worksheet, select the cell that has the sound note and press Shift+F2 to call up the Cell Note dialog box; click on **P**lay to hear the sound note.

Importing Sounds into Excel

In Excel, you can import sound objects stored on your disk and embed them directly on the worksheet. After you embed the sound object, you can simply double-click on the icon shown in the worksheet to play the sound. To create an embedded sound object, follow these steps:

1. Select **O**bject from the **I**nsert menu. The Object dialog box appears (see fig. 6.3).

2. Select Wave Sound from the **O**bject Type list box and click on OK. This step creates the sound icon on your worksheet and starts the Windows Sound Recorder (see fig. 6.4).

3. To record a sound, click on the button in the Sound Recorder that looks like a microphone. After you finish speaking, click on Stop.

You also can use an existing sound file stored on your disk in WAV format. To use an existing sound file, select **I**nsert File from the Sound Recorder's **E**dit menu. The Insert File dialog box appears, which you can use to find the WAV file on your disk, and then click on the OK button.

Figure 6.3

The Object dialog box.

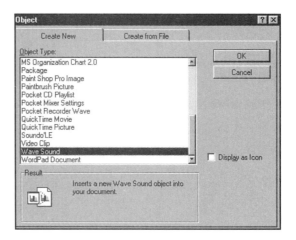

Figure 6.4

The Windows 95 Sound Recorder.

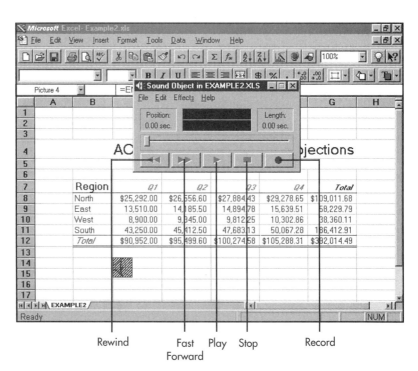

4. When you have finished recording or inserting the sound you want, select the **F**ile menu in the Sound Recorder and choose E**x**it and Return to *your_filename.xls*.

After you complete the preceding steps, you have an icon in your worksheet (see fig. 6.5).

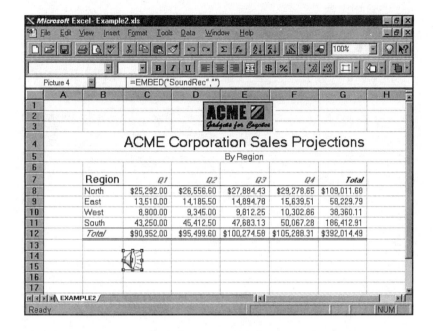

Figure 6.5

*An embedded
sound object.*

To play an embedded sound object, double-click on the icon in the worksheet. To edit a sound object, right-click on the sound object, select Wave Sound Object, and then select Edit. The Edit command brings up the Sound Recorder with the sound automatically loaded and ready to edit. To delete a sound object, select it and press the Del key.

Mastering Excel's Outlining Feature

Excel enables you to hide and show detail in your worksheets by using outlining. You can designate ranges of rows or columns and group them so that you can quickly hide or show their detail. You also can create *nested outline groups* (groups within groups) so that you can achieve exactly the level of detail you want.

Examine the worksheet shown in figure 6.6 and again in figure 6.7. This worksheet shows a detailed income statement (organized by quarter) that has been outlined.

Figure 6.6

An expanded income statement.

Click here to collapse monthly detail

Click here to collapse or show all cells at this outline level

Click here to collapse category detail

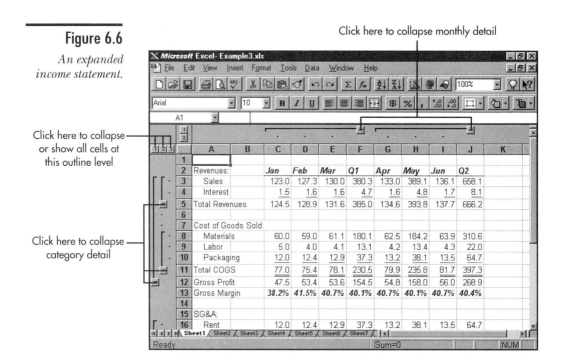

Figure 6.7

A collapsed income statement.

Click here to show monthly detail

Click here to expand to this outline level

Click here to show category detail

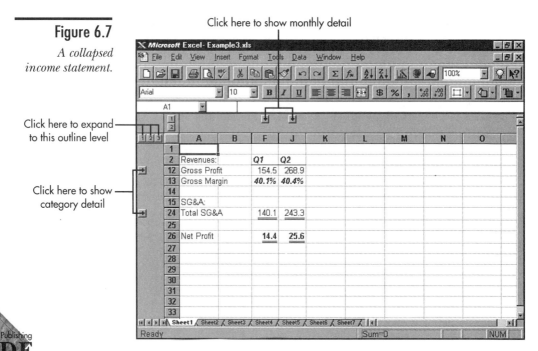

By using the outlining that has been added to the worksheet shown in figures 6.6 and 6.7, you can switch more quickly to any level of detail you want. In a large and complex worksheet, you can navigate faster with collapsed groups. When you get to the area in the worksheet in which you want to work with the detail, just click on the appropriate outline button to reveal the detailed information.

Creating an Outline Range Manually

To manually create an outline range, follow these steps:

1. Select a range of rows or columns. Be sure to select the rows or columns themselves, rather than cells within the worksheet.

2. Pull down the **D**ata menu, choose **G**roup and Outline, and then choose **G**roup from the cascading menu that appears.

 Tip
After you select a range of rows or columns, you can quickly group or ungroup them for the outline by pressing Alt+Shift+right arrow to group or Alt+Shift+left arrow to ungroup.

You don't always have to select whole rows or columns, as you did in the previous example. You also can select a range of cells on the worksheet before you select the **G**roup command. When you select a range of cells and then **G**roup them, the Group dialog box appears, asking whether you want to group the rows or columns for the selected range of cells (see fig. 6.8). Select **R**ows to group the rows that contain the selected cells, or **C**olumns to group the columns in the selected cell range.

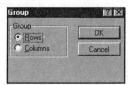

Figure 6.8

The Group dialog box.

Creating an Outline Automatically

With most worksheets, Excel can examine the structure of the worksheet and generate all the appropriate outlining levels automatically. Excel bases its decisions on factors such as location of formulas compared to actual data, location of SUM formulas, and so forth. Excel then creates an outline level for each consistent structure in the worksheet.

You can control how Excel looks for this consistency before you create the automatic outline by pulling down the **D**ata menu and selecting **G**roup and Outline. When you choose S**e**ttings from the cascading menu, the Outline dialog box appears (see fig. 6.9).

Figure 6.9

The Outline dialog box.

In the Outline dialog box, select the Summary rows **b**elow detail check box if your data summarize downward (in other words, if the totals are at the bottom of each range of data in the worksheet). If your summary formulas are above the detail they represent, deselect this check box. Also, if your column summaries are to the right of the detail they represent, select the Summary columns to **r**ight of detail check box.

If you select the **A**utomatic Styles check box, Excel formats your document with boldface in the summary cell locations, to help you distinguish summary information from detailed information.

If you want to create the outline from the Outline dialog box, click on the **C**reate button. Otherwise, pull down the **D**ata menu, select **G**roup and Outline, and then select **A**uto Outline. Excel then applies the rules you set in the Outline dialog box and automatically creates all the appropriate outline levels for your worksheet.

Tip

To restrict the area that Excel outlines with the **A**uto Outline feature, select the cells you want to outline before executing the command. Otherwise, Excel will outline the entire document.

If you restructure your data, you can select the **A**uto Outline command again to rebuild the outline levels based on the new data structure.

Deleting Outlines

Excel offers two ways to delete outlines. You can either delete individual outlines or you can delete all outlines in the worksheet with a single action.

To delete individual outlines, select the rows or columns in the outline level you want to remove. Then pull down the **D**ata menu, select **G**roup and Outline, then select **U**ngroup. You also can press Alt+Shift+left arrow instead of using the menu command.

To delete all outlines on your worksheet, begin with no rows or columns selected. Then pull down the **D**ata menu, select **G**roup and Outline, then select **C**lear Outline.

Using the Scenario Manager

Excel has a tool called the *Scenario Manager* that you can use to help track multiple scenarios of your data in a single workbook. The Scenario Manager enables you to define *changing cells* for a single worksheet. You then define different scenarios based on those changing cells. Using this feature, you can store multiple scenarios of your data in a single worksheet without having to maintain multiple copies of your data. This method is a fundamentally better way to accomplish multiple scenarios—if you change the formulas that make up your worksheet and are not using the Scenario Manager, you might forget to update all of the copies of your worksheet. When you use the Scenario Manager to model many scenarios, you need to make structural changes to your worksheet in only one place.

When you create different scenarios, you can use the Scenario Manager to switch quickly between the different sets of data, which lets you quickly examine and compare the different scenarios. As an example, you might have a budgeting worksheet for which you want to examine three budget "cases:" Projected (or expected), Best Case, and Worst Case. Or, you might define scenarios such as "Best case if the Johnson deal goes through" or "Projected profits if we freeze salaries."

 Note For even more complex and powerful analysis, use the Scenario Manager together with PivotTables. PivotTables are discussed in the next section of this chapter.

Examine the worksheet shown in figure 6.10. This worksheet shows a sales budget for four different regions in the company. Each region has a projected sales growth target, which is defined below in the Sales Growth cells.

 Note The easiest way to access the Scenario Manager is through the Workgroup toolbar, although you also can select the S**c**enarios command from the **T**ools menu. You activate the Workgroup toolbar by using the **T**oolbars command in the **V**iew menu.

One way to use the Scenario Manager might be to look at the total company sales if the regions experience different sales growth rates. This example defines simple Projected, Best Case, and Worst Case scenarios, but you could also define scenarios that examine different events in each of the individual regions (such as Projected: West Loses Sales Manager, or Best Case: New Product Introduction in East).

Figure 6.10

The Scenario Manager sample worksheet.

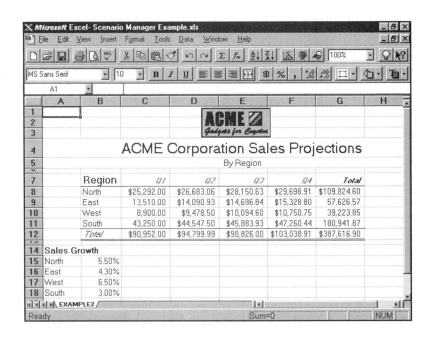

Creating a Scenario

To create a scenario, pull down the **T**ools menu and select **S**cenarios. The Scenario Manager dialog box appears, as shown in figure 6.11.

Figure 6.11

The Scenario Manager dialog box.

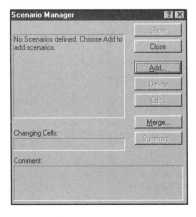

You begin to define the new scenario by clicking on the **A**dd button in the Scenario Manager dialog box, which brings up the Add Scenario dialog box, shown in figure 6.12.

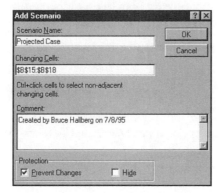

Figure 6.12

The Add Scenario dialog box.

Type the name of your scenario in the Scenario **N**ame field. Define the changing cells by clicking in the Changing **C**ells field, and then select the cells in the worksheet. Excel automatically generates your name and the date you created the scenario in the C**o**mment field, although you can easily edit it. The Add Scenario dialog box also has two check boxes: **P**revent Changes and Hi**d**e. Select the **P**revent Changes check box to prevent other users from being able to modify your scenario. Select the Hi**d**e check box to prevent the new scenario from appearing in the Scenario Manager dialog box.

After you select the changing cells (in this case, cells B15:B18), click on OK. The Scenario Values dialog box then appears (see fig. 6.13).

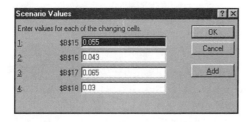

Figure 6.13

The Scenario Values dialog box.

Use the Scenario Values dialog box to define the values in the changing cells for the new scenario. You are limited to 32 changing cells per scenario. For each cell in the dialog box, there is a corresponding field in which you input the value for the cell. After you enter the values for the new scenario, click on OK.

Tip

If you need to define a scenario that uses more than 32 changing cells, create multiple scenarios—each of which changes a different range of cells. For example, you can define scenario #1 to change cells A1:A32, scenario #2 to change cells B1:B32, and so forth.

Creating a Scenario with the Toolbar

If you have the Workgroup toolbar visible, you can quickly create a scenario by following these steps:

1. Manually change the values in the changing cells in the worksheet for the new scenario.

2. Select the range of changing cells. If necessary, use Ctrl+click to select multiple noncontiguous ranges.

3. Click in the Scenarios field on the Workgroup toolbar, type the new name of the scenario, and press Enter.

Switching Between Scenarios

You can quickly switch between scenarios by using the Scenario Manager dialog box or the Scenarios drop-down list on the Workgroup toolbar.

To display different scenarios using the Scenario Manager dialog box, follow these steps:

1. Access the Scenario Manager dialog box by using the S<u>c</u>enarios command in the <u>T</u>ools menu.

2. Click on the desired scenario in the S<u>c</u>enarios field.

3. Click on the <u>S</u>how button.

After you click on the <u>S</u>how button, the scenario you selected appears. When you finish viewing scenarios, or have the scenario you want to work with, click on the Close button to return to the worksheet.

To display different scenarios using the Scenario drop-down list in the Workgroup toolbar, simply click on the drop-down arrow and choose the scenario name from the list. After you click on the name, the selected scenario appears.

Creating a Scenario Summary Report

You can create a summary report of your different scenarios that shows the different assumptions and the results you want to view based on each scenario. To create a scenario summary report, follow these steps:

1. Access the Scenario Manager dialog box by pulling down the <u>T</u>ools menu and selecting S<u>c</u>enarios.

2. Click on the S**u**mmary button in the Scenario Manager dialog box. The Scenario Summary dialog box appears, as shown in figure 6.14.

Figure 6.14

The Scenario Summary dialog box.

3. In the Report Type box, choose Scenario **S**ummary.

4. Click on the **R**esult Cells field, and then select the cells in your worksheet that have the results you want to see in your scenario summary report. In this example, select the range G8:G12. Remember, you can hold down the Ctrl key to select multiple ranges to view.

5. Click on the OK button to create the scenario summary report.

The preceding steps create the scenario summary report in a new sheet in your workbook (see fig. 6.15).

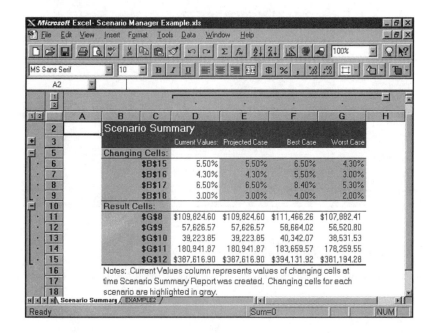

Figure 6.15

A scenario summary report.

Note the following features of the scenario summary report:

◆ Excel automatically creates the formatting you see in figure 6.15.

◆ Excel automatically outlines the report for you.

◆ You can view the comments (creation date and creator) for each scenario by clicking on the Outline button to the left of row 3 (the row that includes the scenario names).

◆ The scenario summary report is somewhat difficult to understand with only cell references for the categories in the report. You can correct this problem by using named ranges in your worksheet. Figure 6.16 shows a scenario summary report with named ranges.

Figure 6.16

A scenario summary report with named ranges.

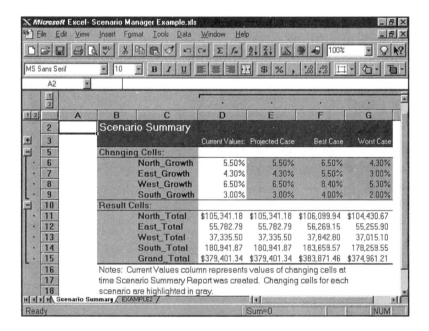

Creating a Scenario PivotTable

You can create a scenario PivotTable to view your scenarios by following these steps:

1. Access the Scenario Manager dialog box by pulling down the **T**ools menu and choosing S**c**enarios.

2. Click on the S**u**mmary button in the Scenario Manager dialog box. The Scenario Summary dialog box shown in figure 6.14 appears.

3. Select Scenario **P**ivotTable from the Report Type box.

4. Click in the **R**esult Cells field, then select the cells in your worksheet that contain the results you want to view in the summary report. In this example, you select the range G5:G9.

5. Click on the OK button to create the scenario PivotTable shown in figure 6.17.

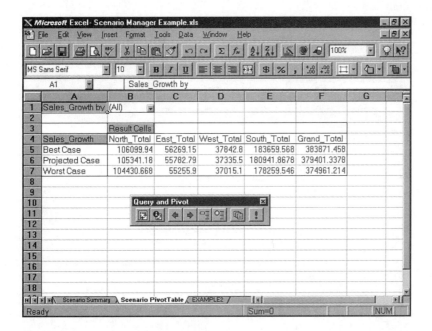

Figure 6.17

A scenario PivotTable.

Using PivotTables

One of the most powerful features in Excel for Windows 95 is the PivotTable feature. PivotTables enable you to summarize detailed information for easier analysis. You can use PivotTables to analyze the following:

◆ Detailed sales records

◆ Shipping cost statistics

◆ Purchase order details

◆ Engineering safety records

PivotTables have many other potential applications as well. You can summarize a detailed list or database records (such as those in the preceding list) into PivotTables, which show summary information only. You can then *rotate* the data with your mouse to analyze it in different ways.

This section teaches you about Excel's PivotTable feature by using sample call records from a call accounting system. Figure 6.18 shows the top of the worksheet that contains the detailed records.

Figure 6.18

Call records.

	A	B	C	D	E	F	G	H	I
1	Date	Month	Day	Length	Cost	Phone Number	Ext.	Destination	Type
2	09/28/93	Sept	Tuesday	0:00:24	1.81	0112341844716	2	NIGERIA	International
3	09/28/93	Sept	Tuesday	0:00:26	1.81	0112341844716	7	NIGERIA	International
4	09/28/93	Sept	Tuesday	0:00:26	1.81	0112341844716	4	NIGERIA	International
5	09/28/93	Sept	Tuesday	0:00:10	1.81	0112341844716	5	NIGERIA	International
6	09/28/93	Sept	Tuesday	0:00:24	1.81	0112341844716	3	NIGERIA	International
7	09/28/93	Sept	Tuesday	0:00:18	1.81	0112341844716	8	NIGERIA	International
8	09/28/93	Sept	Tuesday	0:00:24	1.81	0112341844716	2	NIGERIA	International
9	09/28/93	Sept	Tuesday	0:00:28	1.81	0112341844716	2	NIGERIA	International
10	09/28/93	Sept	Tuesday	0:00:58	1.81	0112341844716	4	NIGERIA	International
11	09/28/93	Sept	Tuesday	0:00:24	1.81	0112341844716	5	NIGERIA	International
12	09/28/93	Sept	Tuesday	0:00:24	1.81	0112341844716	6	NIGERIA	International
13	09/28/93	Sept	Tuesday	0:00:34	1.81	0112341844716	5	NIGERIA	International
14	09/28/93	Sept	Tuesday	0:00:08	1.81	0112341844716	6	NIGERIA	International
15	09/28/93	Sept	Tuesday	0:00:34	1.81	0112341844716	2	NIGERIA	International
16	09/28/93	Sept	Tuesday	0:00:24	1.81	0112341844716	1	NIGERIA	International
17	09/28/93	Sept	Tuesday	0:00:28	1.81	0112341844716	5	NIGERIA	International
18	09/28/93	Sept	Tuesday	0:41:18	44.45	0112341844716	7	NIGERIA	International

Note A *call accounting system* is software that runs on a computer connected to your telephone system. A call accounting system captures telephone statistics so you can manage your telephone costs. Most such systems can output their data into text files that Excel can read.

Approximately 500 call records have been imported into Excel for this example (although you can use thousands without any trouble). Table 6.1 shows the fields in the sample worksheet.

TABLE 6.1
Worksheet Fields

Field Name	Description
Date	The date the call was placed.
Month	The month in which the call was placed.
Day	The day of the week when the call was placed.
Length	The length of the call in minutes.
Cost	The estimated cost of the call (generated by the call accounting system).
Phone Number	The phone number dialed.
Extension	The extension number from which the call was placed.
Destination	The name of the geographic destination.
Type	The type of call: international, interstate, or intrastate.

If you were the telecommunication manager at your company, you might want to ask certain types of questions about the telephone data, such as the following:

◆ **What were the total dollars spent by each telephone extension?** Because you know who is assigned to each extension, you can figure out the amount each person spends from the data. You might even provide the data to accounting so that each person's department can be charged for its calls.

◆ **How much is spent on different call types?** In other words, how much is spent on international, interstate, and intrastate calls? This information might help you justify a different telephone carrier who has cheaper rates for the most common types of calls.

◆ **What are the most expensive destinations called?** If you can identify a couple of frequently called and expensive destinations, you can use that data to negotiate targeted discounts with your telephone carrier.

◆ **What are the traffic patterns by day of week or by time of day?** This data can help you look at different carriers' rates for different time periods. Also, if you make the assumption that outgoing call volume has a rough relationship to incoming calls, this information can help you schedule your telephone operators better.

◆ **What is the average time spent on each call for each extension?**
These statistics can indicate, for example, that you need to work with a couple of people to try to make their expensive international calls briefer.

The preceding questions are only a few of the valid questions you can ask with the data shown in the sample worksheet. You also can use Excel's capability to manipulate the records to ask even more questions. You might use the MID() function, for example, to strip out the area code called in the telephone number field and then get summaries by area code. Use Excel's extensive list of functions to massage your data into different categories, so you can ask different questions about the data. These questions, and many more, cannot be easily answered by looking through hundreds or thousands of data records. PivotTables work well with this type of application.

Figure 6.19 shows an example of a PivotTable created from the sample data. This PivotTable shows the total dollar amount of calls made by type of call (international, intrastate, or interstate) for each extension, and also has a Page field that enables you to look at all calls or just the totals for a given month.

Figure 6.19

A sample PivotTable.

	Ext.	International	Interstate	Intrastate	Grand Total
Month	(All)				
Sum of Cost	Type				
	1	26.77	0	3.08	29.85
	2	107.9	5.76	2.89	116.55
	3	15.67	7.36	3.04	26.07
	4	42.87	0.32	3.31	46.5
	5	110.87	4	2.74	117.61
	6	61.98	0.8	2.13	64.91
	7	70.87	1.6	3.09	75.56
	8	41.72	1.76	4.42	47.9
	9	15.82	1.16	5.04	22.02
	10	5.13	4.8	3.39	13.32
	Grand Total	499.6	27.56	33.13	560.29

Using the PivotTable Wizard

You use the PivotTable Wizard to generate the sample PivotTable shown in figure 6.19. To begin creating a PivotTable, pull down the **D**ata menu and select **P**ivotTable. The first page in the PivotTable Wizard appears (see fig. 6.20).

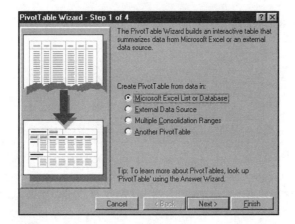

Figure 6.20

The PivotTable Wizard: step 1.

In step 1 of the PivotTable Wizard, you select from the four choices explained in table 6.2.

TABLE 6.2
PivotTable Wizard: Step 1 Options

Option	Description
Microsoft Excel List or Database	Choose this option to use data in a single worksheet in your workbook.
External Data Source	Choose this option to automatically start Microsoft Query, a tool that comes with Excel and is used to query other database files or sources.
Multiple **C**onsolidation Ranges	Choose this option to build the PivotTable from multiple worksheets in your workbook.
Another **P**ivotTable	If your workbook contains other PivotTables, choose this option to incorporate one of them in the new PivotTable.

For this example, select **M**icrosoft Excel List or Database, and then click on the Next button (or press Enter) to proceed to step 2 of the PivotTable Wizard (see fig. 6.21).

In step 2 of the PivotTable Wizard, you select the range of data on which you want to report. If the range Excel guesses for you is incorrect (Excel assumes you want to create the PivotTable using all cells contiguous with your active cell), use your mouse to select the range that contains the data. You also can click on the Bro**w**se button to select a file on the disk that has the data, if the data is in a different worksheet. After you select the range of data for the PivotTable, click on the Next button to go to step 3 of the PivotTable Wizard (see fig. 6.22).

Figure 6.21

The PivotTable Wizard: step 2.

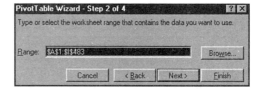

Figure 6.22

The PivotTable Wizard: step 3.

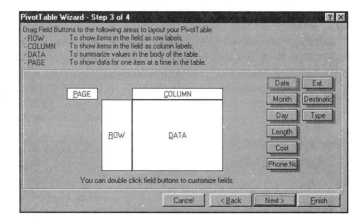

Step 3 of the PivotTable Wizard is the most important step. To the right a number of buttons are arrayed, one for each category of data. In the center of the page is the layout area, divided into four different sections (described in table 6.3).

TABLE 6.3
PivotTable Wizard Layout Sections

Section	Description
PAGE	Defines a section of the PivotTable in which you can select the records shown in the table. For example, you could drag the Type field to the **P**age section to enable you to show only international calls in the resulting PivotTable.
ROW	Enables you to choose which categories are shown in the PivotTable rows.
COLUMN	Controls which categories appear along the horizontal axis of the table.
DATA	Can be summarized in different ways. You can show totals, counts, or averages of the category in the **D**ata section.

New Riders Publishing
INSIDE
SERIES

After you drag the categories you want to report on into the layout area, click on the Next button to display the fourth and final step of the PivotTable Wizard (see fig. 6.23).

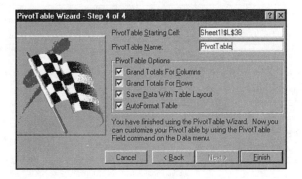

Figure 6.23

The PivotTable Wizard: step 4.

Table 6.4 shows the settings available in the fourth step of the PivotTable Wizard.

TABLE 6.4
PivotTable Wizard: Step 4 Settings

Setting	Description
PivotTable **S**tarting Cell	Use this field to tell the PivotTable Wizard which cell to use for the upper left corner of the PivotTable. After you select this field, you can click on your worksheet in the location you want.
PivotTable **N**ame	Some other functions in Excel (for example, the Scenario Manager) use the name of the PivotTable for certain features. Indicate the name here, or accept the default name.
Grand Totals for **C**olumns	If this check box is selected, the PivotTable Wizard automatically creates grand totals for all the columns in your PivotTable.
Grand Totals for **R**ows	If this check box is selected, the PivotTable automatically creates grand totals for all the rows in your PivotTable.
Save **D**ata With Table Layout	Normally, the PivotTable contains a copy of the source data in a hidden area. If you are having memory- constraint problems, you can clear this check box to avoid creating duplicate data.

continued

TABLE 6.4, CONTINUED
PivotTable Wizard: Step 4 Settings

Setting	Description
AutoFormat Table	Select this check box to automatically format the PivotTable with the default table AutoFormat.

Click on the **F**inish button to complete the creation of the PivotTable. Figure 6.24 shows the completed PivotTable.

Figure 6.24

The completed PivotTable.

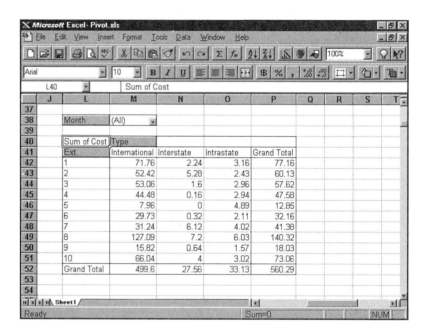

Changing the PivotTable

Not only can you use the PivotTable Wizard to create PivotTables, you also can use it to determine which categories to include in the PivotTable. To change categories, place your active cell anywhere in the PivotTable, then access the **P**ivotTable command in the **D**ata menu. The layout page of the PivotTable Wizard immediately appears; you can then drag categories and drop them in different locations. Just as you can drag new categories from the right into the layout area, you can delete categories by dragging them from one of the layout sections to a blank part of the screen.

Manipulating the PivotTable

Figure 6.25 shows a new PivotTable created from the sample data. This PivotTable shows the call totals by looking at the mix of calls placed on different days of the week. This PivotTable also has two Page fields: Month and Extension.

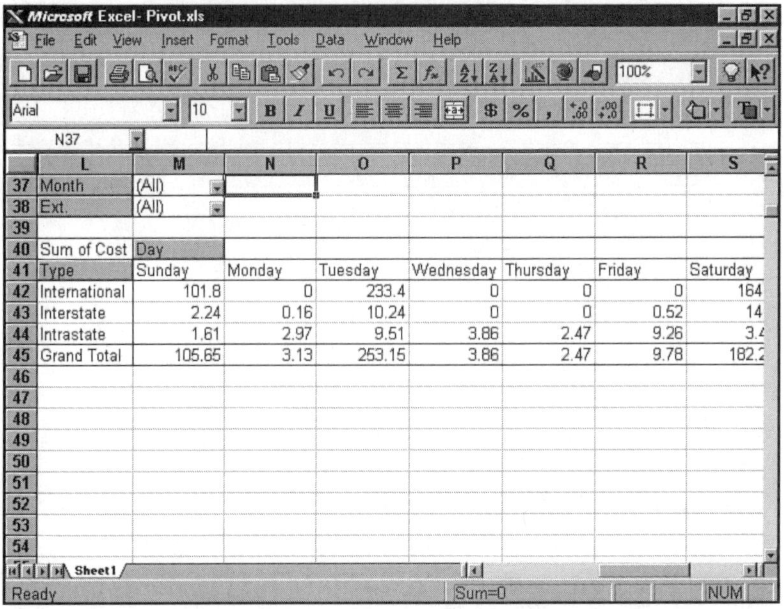

Figure 6.25

A sample PivotTable.

You use the Page fields to restrict the data being looked at. To use the Page fields, click on the drop-down arrow to display the valid choices. When you make a selection, your PivotTable shows only that category of data. On the sample PivotTable shown in figure 6.25, it is easy to show the information for only one extension by using the Extension Page field. You also can look at one extension in a given month or all extensions for a given month by using the appropriate combination of choices in the Page fields.

You can drag and drop the categories used in the PivotTable (this can be easier than reaccessing the PivotTable Wizard to change how the data is displayed). Figure 6.26 shows the result of dragging the Extension field to the vertical axis of the table. You then see that the breakdown is in call type by extension. You can see that whoever uses Ext. 1, for example, does most of his or her calls on Tuesday, and these calls are mostly international (at least in terms of dollars).

The new format is not useful if you want to compare the mix of calls made by each extension. For example, you now know that Ext. 1 makes many international calls, but does Ext. 1 make the most international calls? To change the PivotTable to show that information, drag the Ext. field to the right of the Type field so that the Ext. field becomes a subcategory of Type, as shown in figure 6.27.

Figure 6.26

Comparing the mix of type per extension.

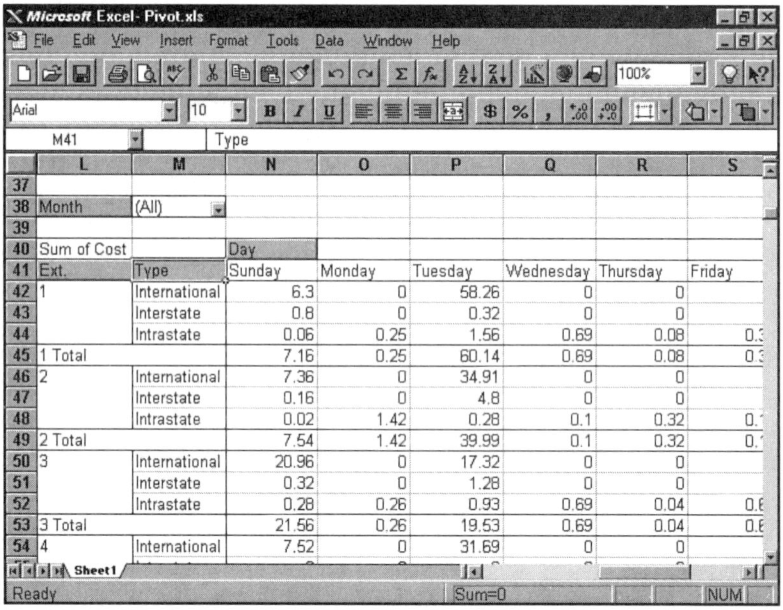

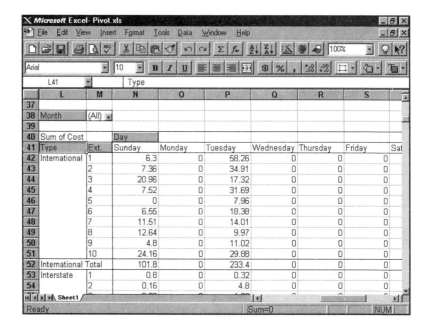

Figure 6.27

Comparing the type of call for extensions.

On the new PivotTable, you can easily see that Exts. 3 and 6 make more international calls than Ext. 1. When you scroll the PivotTable to the right to view the Grand Totals, you discover that Ext. 6 is the international call leader.

Figure 6.28 shows a new configuration of the fields in the PivotTable. The new arrangement shows only international calls and also shows that most international calls are made on Tuesday. This example was created by dragging the Type field to the page area (below the Month field), and then selecting International from its drop-down list.

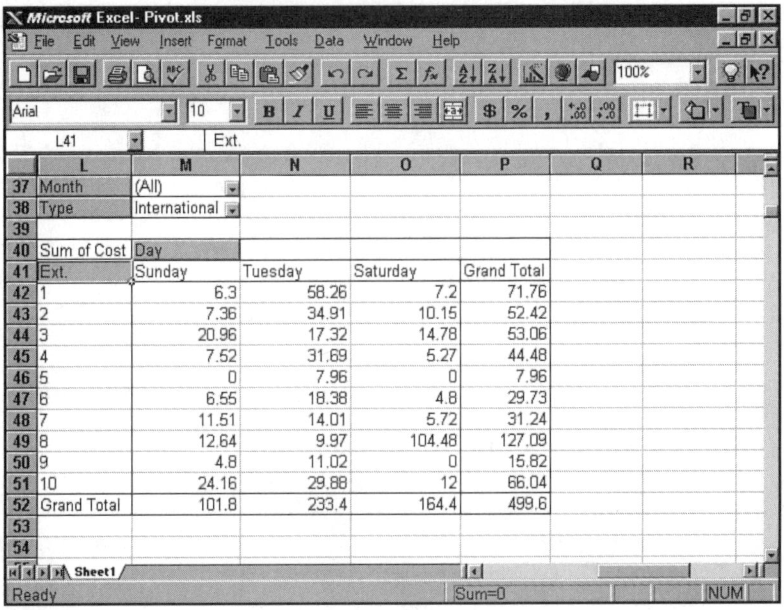

Figure 6.28

International call totals.

Ext.	Sunday	Tuesday	Saturday	Grand Total
Month	(All)			
Type	International			
Sum of Cost	Day			
Ext.	Sunday	Tuesday	Saturday	Grand Total
1	6.3	58.26	7.2	71.76
2	7.36	34.91	10.15	52.42
3	20.96	17.32	14.78	53.06
4	7.52	31.69	5.27	44.48
5	0	7.96	0	7.96
6	6.55	18.38	4.8	29.73
7	11.51	14.01	5.72	31.24
8	12.64	9.97	104.48	127.09
9	4.8	11.02	0	15.82
10	24.16	29.88	12	66.04
Grand Total	101.8	233.4	164.4	499.6

Note In figure 6.28, only three days are listed (Sunday, Tuesday, and Saturday). The PivotTable lists only these three days, because no international calls were made by any extension in the database on the other days of the week. PivotTables automatically filter out completely blank categories.

Controlling Fields

You can control the treatment of different categories by using the PivotTable Field command in the **D**ata menu. Before you select the PivotTable Field command, select the category you want to reformat. If you select an axis field, such as Extension, the PivotTable Field dialog box appears, as shown in figure 6.29.

Figure 6.29

The PivotTable Field dialog box.

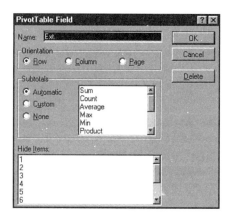

You can change the name of the category by typing a new name in the Name field. If you want to reposition the category without dragging and dropping, select the **R**ow, **C**olumn, or **P**age option button. If the category you format is divided into subcategories, select the different summarization options in the Subtotals box. Choose from the various methods listed, such as Sum, Average, Count, and so on. You can select as many subtotals as you want by clicking on each one individually. Finally, you can choose to hide parts of the data by selecting from the list in the Hide **I**tems list box.

You also can reformat the data portion of the PivotTable. For example, if you want to show the number of calls rather than total dollars spent, reformat the data area accordingly. Place the active cell in the data area of the PivotTable, then select the PivotTable F**i**eld command in the **D**ata menu. A somewhat different version of the PivotTable Field dialog box appears, as shown in figure 6.30.

Figure 6.30

The PivotTable Field dialog box with the data area selected.

Use the Na**m**e field to change the name of the subtotal. Select the type of subtotal from the **S**ummarize by list box in the PivotTable Field dialog box. Click on the **N**umber button to choose what number format to use to format the subtotals.

Refreshing Data

PivotTables do not automatically update data when the data in the worksheet changes. You have to use the **R**efresh Data command. Select the **R**efresh Data command from the **D**ata menu, or click on the Refresh Data button in the Query and Pivot toolbar (if the toolbar is displayed).

Removing Categories

You can remove categories by dragging them out of the PivotTable area. When you do this, your pointer changes to a category button that has a large X in it. If the X is displayed and you drop the category (by releasing the mouse button), you effectively remove the category from the table.

 Tip   Instead of removing categories from the PivotTable that you might want to use again later, you can drag the category to the Page area of the PivotTable and set it to display all records. You get the same result as far as the data shown in the table is concerned, and you can drag the category back into the PivotTable later without having to call up the PivotTable Wizard again.

Grouping Data in a PivotTable

Sometimes groups you might want to view in a PivotTable do not exist within the data you are using. In these cases, you can group together similar types of records. As an example, you could group interstate and intrastate call types together to compare international call and noninternational call costs.

To group data together, select the records you want to group in the PivotTable, then click on the Group button in the Query and Pivot toolbar or select the **D**ata menu, choose **G**roup and **O**utline, and then choose **G**roup. Figure 6.31 shows a PivotTable with the interstate and intrastate calls grouped.

After you create a group using the **G**roup command, you can then rename the group to make more sense for your data (here, noninternational would be a good name). You can then hide the subgroups by selecting the Type2 category, selecting the **D**ata menu, selecting **G**roup and Outline, then **H**ide detail. To show hidden detail, select the **D**ata menu, select **G**roup and Outline, and then choose **S**how detail.

Figure 6.31

Grouped records.

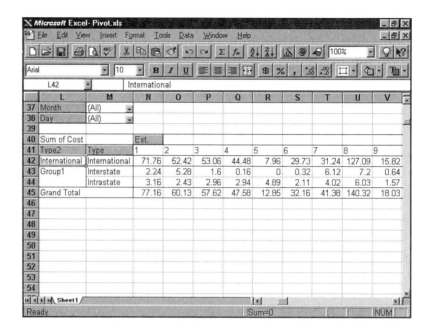

Charting PivotTables

You can create charts from your PivotTables using all the charting tools covered in Part 3 of this book. When you change your PivotTable, the chart is updated with the changes automatically.

Importing Text Files

Although Excel can read and write many different file formats, sometimes you have to import text files into Excel. Some examples of cases where you would want to import text files into Excel include the following:

◆ Downloading stock data from an online service such as CompuServe, and then importing the stock data into Excel.

◆ Taking the output of another program and importing it into Excel; for instance, you might want to import detailed measurements from a piece of test equipment. Most automated test devices have interface software that can export the test data into text files, which can then be used in Excel.

◆ Importing accounting data from your accounting system into Excel. Very few accounting systems can create Excel files for analysis, but almost all accounting systems can create a text file that can be used in Excel. After you load the detailed accounting data (General Ledger transactions, for example), you can use the PivotTable feature to analyze the data.

Any time you open a text file in Excel, the TextWizard starts automatically. The *TextWizard* is a tool that enables you to import almost any format of text data into Excel.

Using the TextWizard

To use the TextWizard, simply open a text file by accessing the **O**pen command in the **F**ile menu. If the file you open has an extension other than the normal Excel file extension (which it probably does), make sure that List Files of **T**ype is set to All Files (*.*). Select your file in the File Open dialog box, then click on the OK button.

Excel recognizes the file as a text file and starts the TextWizard, as shown in figure 6.32.

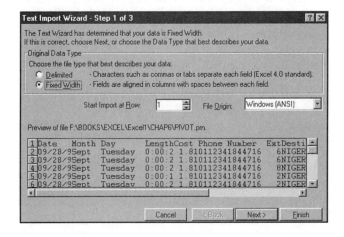

Figure 6.32

The TextWizard: step 1.

The TextWizard examines the data in the text file and guesses whether the fields are delimited in some way or the file is composed of fixed-width fields. *Delimited data* generally separates each field with a comma, but you can choose spaces, tabs, or other characters. Fixed-width records are set up in such a way that each field is at exactly the same horizontal position within each line. If Excel guesses incorrectly about your data, select the appropriate option button before proceeding.

The Step 1 page also has two other fields. The first field, Start Import at **R**ow, enables you to choose from which row in the data to begin reading. Often the first row or rows have header information for the file that you might not want or need. In those cases, set Start Import at **R**ow to the appropriate value. You can use the Preview window to help determine from which row the import should start. The second field is labeled File **O**rigin. You can choose from three file origins: DOS or OS/2 (PC-8), Windows (ANSI), and Macintosh. The File **O**rigin field determines the way certain control characters in the file should be interpreted. Usually, DOS or OS/2 (PC-8) is the most correct choice, although Windows (ANSI) works with almost all files as well. If the data you see in the Preview window is garbled, try another type of file origin. If the data appears garbled using any of the file origin choices, then the file is not a text file; you need to go back to the originating application and re-export the data into an ASCII or ANSI text-based format.

Importing a Delimited File

Assuming your file is delimited, select the **D**elimited option button before you click on the Next button to move to step 2, as shown in figure 6.33.

Figure 6.33

The TextWizard: Delimited step 2.

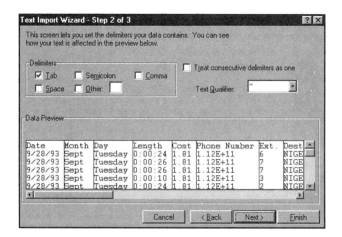

Note   If your file is fixed width, see the following section. Fixed-width files go through different steps in the TextWizard.

The second step for importing delimited files is to tell Excel what character was used to delimit the fields in each record. Examine the Preview window of this screen to see what the delimiter character is. In most cases, Excel correctly guesses what the delimiter character is, but you may need to change the check boxes shown if Excel guesses wrong.

In addition to the Delimiters section of this dialog box, you can set two other choices: Treat consecutive delimiters as one, and Text Qualifier. Selecting Treat consecutive delimiters as one has the effect of making the import records vary in length, so this option is not normally set. If, however, you want to discard blank records rather than just leave them blank in the Excel worksheet, select this check box.

You use the Text Qualifier field to indicate which character has been used in the text file to indicate textual data as opposed to numeric or date information. Most delimited text files surround purely textual data with quotation marks (" "). Because you want to import text data as text, and because you probably don't want the text qualifier character to be imported along with the text, this field is important to set.

To finish the TextWizard import of a delimited file, skip the following section.

Importing a Fixed-Width File

If you select Fixed Width in step 1 of the TextWizard, you see a different step 2 screen than if you choose Delimited (see fig. 6.34).

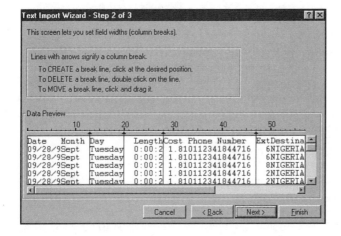

Figure 6.34

The TextWizard: Fixed Width step 2.

In step 2 of a fixed-width file import, you see a preview of the data with a ruler above it, as shown in figure 6.34. For fixed-width files, Excel does not have the capability to recognize where each field is separated from the adjacent fields; you need to indicate where each field starts and ends by clicking at the ruler position for each field. Each time you click in the Preview window, a new vertical line is created that shows where Excel will break the field. You can move these lines by clicking and dragging them to a new position, and you can delete these lines by double-clicking on them. After you place all the field markers, click on the Next button to proceed to step 3.

Using the TextWizard: Step 3

In the final step of using the TextWizard, you tell Excel what type of data each field should contain (see fig. 6.35).

Figure 6.35

The TextWizard: step 3.

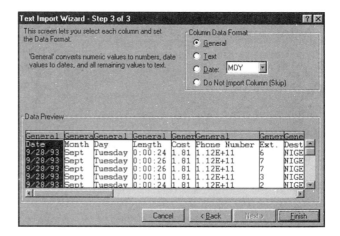

Each field has a button above it that has the type of data listed inside the button. By default, all fields are marked as General data type, which causes them to be created in Excel with the General cell format. To change the field format, click on the button for the field you want to change and then select the appropriate option button in the Column Data Format box. The Column Data Format box enables you to choose from the options listed in table 6.5.

TABLE 6.5
Field Format Options

Option	Description
General	This option uses the Excel General cell format when the data is imported.
Text	This option forces the field to be treated as text, even if it contains only numbers. It can be important to force some numeric fields to be treated as text, particularly if you want to retain any leading zeros.
Date	Select this option if the field contains dates. Furthermore, choose the format the dates are in by using the drop-down list to the right of the **D**ate option button.
Do Not **I**mport Column (Skip)	Select this option to avoid loading the selected field.

After you finish designating the fields in step 3, click on the **F**inish button to complete the operation and import the data into Excel.

Auditing Workbooks

Complex workbooks can quickly become difficult to validate or correct problems with. So many interdependencies develop that it gets particularly tough to make changes that don't cause many problems elsewhere in the workbook. You can help alleviate the situation by using named cells and cell notes, but even that doesn't always help sort out a complex workbook.

Excel for Windows 95 includes auditing tools that let you visually see how a worksheet or workbook is put together, and helps you to validate the results in the workbook. You access these features with the Auditing toolbar, shown in figure 6.36.

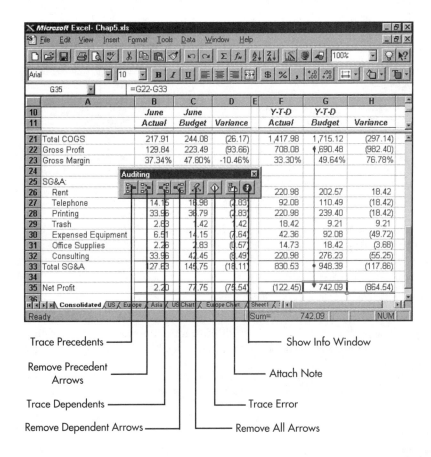

Figure 6.36

The Auditing toolbar.

Trace Precedents

Remove Precedent Arrows

Trace Dependents

Remove Dependent Arrows

Show Info Window

Attach Note

Trace Error

Remove All Arrows

To audit the sources for a particular cell in a workbook, first make that cell your active cell. Then, click on the Trace Precedents button, which reveals the immediate source of the data (see fig. 6.37).

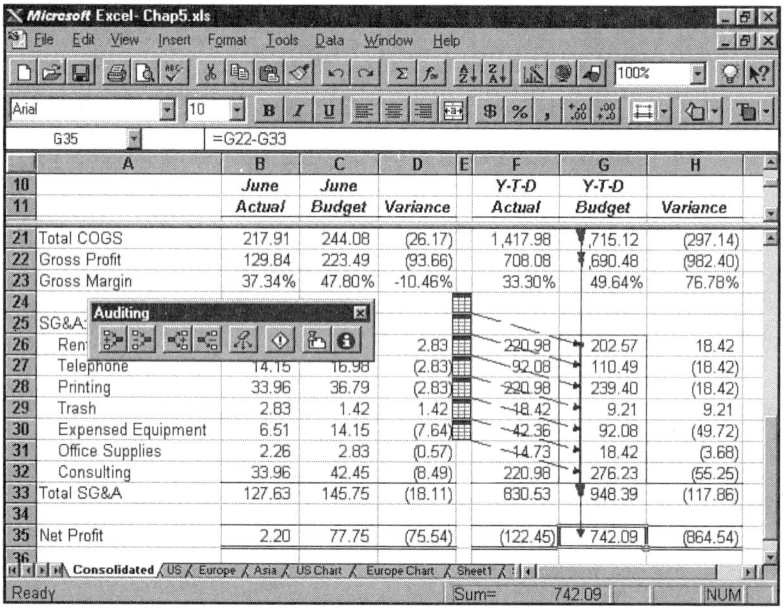

Figure 6.37

Clicking on Trace Precedents shows the source of your data.

To follow the formulas further back, continue clicking on Trace Precedents to see back to the original data on which the cell is based. For example, figure 6.38 shows the appearance of the screen after tracing precedents three more times.

If you are working in a multidimensional workbook, you may also see precedents that point to other sheets in the workbook. Figure 6.38 shows such references, indicated with small worksheet icons. You can jump to the source worksheet by double-clicking on the line that connects the icon to the cell it points to. This brings up the Go To dialog box, shown in figure 6.39.

The example in figure 6.39 shows three source sheets and cells, because the formula in this particular case sums the values across the U.S., Europe, and Asia worksheets. Select the sheet to view and then click on the OK button to jump to that sheet. Your active cell in the destination sheet will be the one referenced by the tracing action.

Tracing dependents works exactly the same as tracing precedents, except that you will see cells that are based on your active cell, rather than sources for your active cell.

When you're done tracing cells, click on the Erase All Arrows button to remove them from the workbook.

	A	B	C	D	E	F	G	H
10		June	June			Y-T-D	Y-T-D	
11		Actual	Budget	Variance		Actual	Budget	Variance
21	Total COGS	217.91	244.08	(26.17)		1,417.98	1,715.12	(297.14)
22	Gross Profit	129.84	223.49	(93.66)		708.08	1,690.48	(982.40)
23	Gross Margin	37.34%	47.80%	-10.46%		33.30%	49.64%	76.78%
24								
25	SG&A:							
26	Rent			2.83		220.98	202.57	18.42
27	Telephone	14.15	16.98	(2.83)		92.08	110.49	(18.42)
28	Printing	33.96	36.79	(2.83)		220.98	239.40	(18.42)
29	Trash	2.83	1.42	1.42		18.42	9.21	9.21
30	Expensed Equipment	6.51	14.15	(7.64)		42.36	92.08	(49.72)
31	Office Supplies	2.26	2.83	(0.57)		14.73	18.42	(3.68)
32	Consulting	33.96	42.45	(8.49)		220.98	276.23	(55.25)
33	Total SG&A	127.63	145.75	(18.11)		830.53	948.39	(117.86)
34								
35	Net Profit	2.20	77.75	(75.54)		(122.45)	742.09	(864.54)

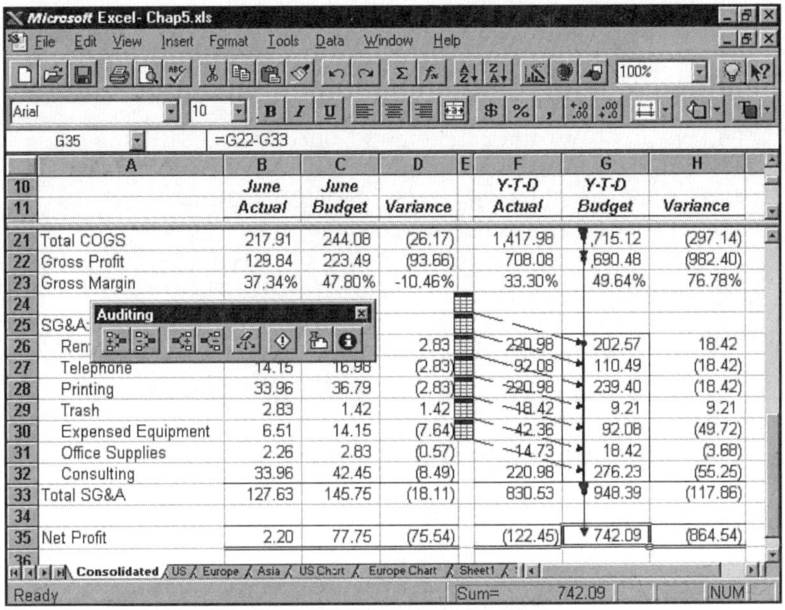

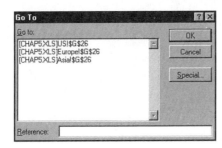

Figure 6.38

Continue tracing precedents to see more and more underlying detail.

Figure 6.39

The Go To dialog box.

Chapter Snapshot

This chapter covers the functions included in Excel. Knowing how to use these functions can help you create worksheets that solve what-if questions, assist with special analysis, and much more. Functions constitute the backbone of Excel's power. Chapter 7 shows you how to utilize Excel's power by including the following:

◆ Understanding what a function is

◆ Understanding the parts of a function

◆ Understanding how to create a function

◆ Using the Function Wizard

◆ Using functions to select prize winners

◆ Using functions to answer refinancing questions

◆ Troubleshooting functions

7

Mastering Functions

In this chapter, you will see how easy it is to use and master functions in Excel. Even if you feel that functions are sometimes intimidating, you can learn about tools like Function Wizard and Help, which make using functions simple. Using Excel to its full potential will make your life much easier.

Understanding Functions

How often do you have to repeat a certain task or calculation when you wish you could just snap your fingers and be done with it automatically? With the aid of functions in Excel for Windows 95, you can come quite close to just that. You can make your life significantly simpler—just automate procedures by using some of the methods covered in this chapter.

A *function* is a precoded formula that can automatically calculate results, perform worksheet actions, or assist with decision-making based on information you provide. You can use functions that Microsoft built into Excel for Windows 95, or you can write your own. This chapter discusses the functions provided with Excel, called *worksheet functions.*

Note   *User-defined functions,* those that you write, can be used in your worksheet just like normal worksheet functions. These functions, called *macros,* are discussed in Chapter 15, "Understanding Macros."

Functions are most commonly used to generate calculated results. You might, for example, want to find out your monthly payment if you refinance your house. Or, you might need to track revenues and expenses to calculate your profit margin. Maybe you are developing a marketing survey and want a statistical analysis. To answer these kinds of questions and more, Microsoft has included a wide variety of functions with Excel.

Function Groups

Excel has hundreds of built-in functions available to you. They have been categorized into the following groups:

◆ **Financial.** Calculate interest, depreciation, return on investment, and other types of financial information.

◆ **Date & Time.** Calculate the number of days between two dates based on a 360-day year, translate dates to serial numbers, and so on.

◆ **Math & Trigonometry.** Useful with basic engineering and math problems, such as calculating the cosine or tangent of a number.

◆ **Statistical.** Help with statistical problems, like calculating the binomial distribution probability.

- ◆ **Lookup & Reference.** Provides information about your worksheet, such as returning the column number of a reference or the number of areas in a reference.

- ◆ **Database.** Helps with database information, like selecting the minimum or maximum value from database entries.

- ◆ **Text.** Helps you manipulate text data.

- ◆ **Logical.** Produces results based on certain conditions in your worksheet.

- ◆ **Information.** Returns general information about your worksheet, such as formatting or the contents of a cell.

- ◆ **Engineering.** Useful for converting feet to meters, a binary number to hexadecimal, or complex numbers.

The organization of functions into these categories helps you find the right function quickly.

Components of a Function

No matter which type of function you use, you always express the function in the same way. You can see an example of a function in figure 7.1. This worksheet is a template for Kreative Kites' sales. As data is entered for different quarters, row 10 reflects Total Country totals and column G automatically reflects the YTD totals because formulas have been previously defined. The formula appears in the formula bar when you select a cell in the worksheet that contains a function. The formula bar shows an equal sign followed by the function name, then a set of parentheses enclosing the information that is used to calculate the result.

Each component provides meaning to the function so that Excel can determine how to process the information, as follows:

- ◆ **Equal sign.** This tells Excel to display the *results* of the function. Without the equal sign, there is no calculation made, and the cell shows the remaining function syntax as text.

- ◆ **Function name.** The referenced function can be any function provided by Excel or a user-defined function.

- ◆ **Parentheses.** Every function requires at least one argument, and all of its associated arguments must be enclosed in a set of parentheses.

◆ **Arguments.** Different functions have their own requirements for the type of information that can be used for each of their arguments. There are numerous ways you can provide the data for an argument, however. Arguments can be literal (constants), formulas or expressions, references to cells, or other functions. Each argument is separated with a comma. Cell references and ranges are most commonly used as arguments in functions. When using functions within functions, called *nesting*, you are limited to seven nested levels. You do not use the equal sign in front of a nested function.

Figure 7.1

The form of a function.

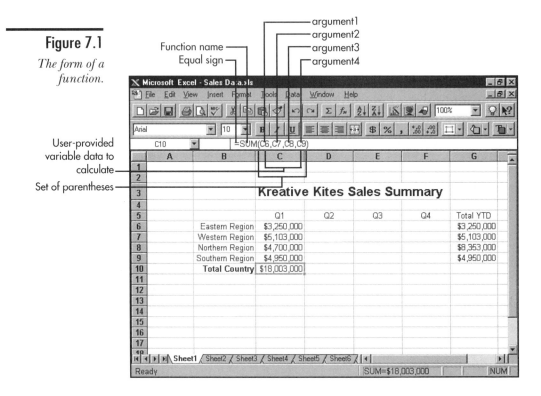

The components together provide a structure or format to the function. This format is defined by *syntax*, the rules or "model" you must follow to describe the information you want to use in the function. The syntax for each function is different. Thus, you must pay attention to the way Excel looks for information, or you might get some very strange results.

Using Arguments

The information you provide to a function is called an *argument*. A function can include more than one argument, because different kinds of information might be needed to calculate the desired answer. Each function includes a predetermined set of arguments, always separated by commas.

Tip Particular function syntax and arguments are documented in the Excel documentation. You also can use the Function Wizard or the online help, both discussed later in the chapter, to help you with your functions and argument lists.

In the example illustrated in figure 7.1, you need to calculate the total of first quarter sales for each territory in the United States. The function name, SUM, is followed by the information you want to sum enclosed in parentheses. Total first quarter sales for the first region, Eastern, is located at cell C6—this is *argument1*. Total first quarter sales for the Western, Northern, and Southern regions are located in cells C7, C8, and C9—these amounts represent *argument2*, *argument3*, and *argument4*. Simply put, arguments in a function tell the function what information to use when the function is calculated.

You can describe function arguments in several ways. The preceding example uses *cell references*. You told the Excel function SUM which cells to reference to find the information to calculate the sum. A better way to describe what you want to sum, however, is to use a *cell range*, or a group of cells. In the next example, you use a *cell range* to calculate the second quarter sales, because you anticipate a realignment of the Western region and think another territory might be added (see fig. 7.2).

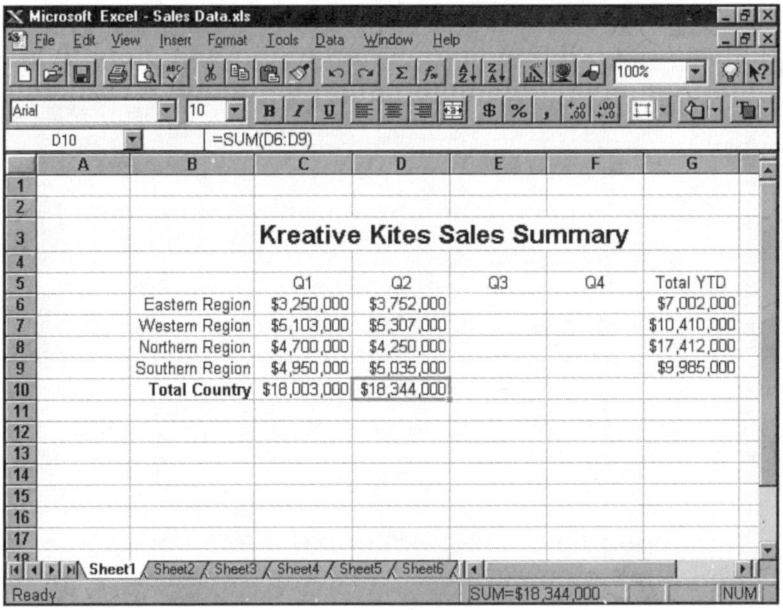

Microsoft Excel - Sales Data.xls
File Edit View Insert Format Tools Data Window Help
Arial 10 100%
D10 =SUM(D6:D9)
Kreative Kites Sales Summary
Q1 Q2 Q3 Q4 Total YTD
Eastern Region $3,250,000 $3,752,000 $7,002,000
Western Region $5,103,000 $5,307,000 $10,410,000
Northern Region $4,700,000 $4,250,000 $17,412,000
Southern Region $4,950,000 $5,035,000 $9,985,000
Total Country $18,003,000 $18,344,000
Sheet1 Sheet2 Sheet3 Sheet4 Sheet5 Sheet6
Ready SUM=$18,344,000 NUM

Figure 7.2

The SUM function using a cell range as an argument.

This example contains only one argument, the range D6:D9. This range includes cells D6 through D9 and all cells in between. One good reason to use a cell range and not individual cell references is because if you insert or delete rows or columns within a cell range, Excel automatically adjusts all references to reflect the new range. Excel does not adjust individual cell references to include a new row or column, because it doesn't know it is part of a range. You can also build this function by dragging across D6 through D9 after you insert the left parenthesis.

Look at Total first quarter sales, now located at C11 (see fig. 7.3). Notice that after you insert a row to add a new Central region, Excel changes the last two arguments in that SUM function to reflect the new location of the Northern and first quarter sales, C9 and C10. It does not change the first two arguments, C6 and C7, because the location of first quarter sales for the Eastern and Western regions did not change. If you were to add a number to show Central first quarter sales, C8, it would not be included in the total at C11.

Figure 7.3

The individual cell references not adjusted to include added row.

		Q1	Q2	Q3	Q4	Total YTD
	Kreative Kites Sales Summary					
Eastern Region		$3,250,000	$3,752,000			$7,002,000
Western Region		$5,103,000	$5,307,000			$10,410,000
Central Region						$0
Northern Region		$4,700,000	$4,250,000			$17,412,000
Southern Region		$4,950,000	$5,035,000			$9,985,000
Total Country		$18,003,000	$18,344,000			$44,809,000

C11 =SUM(C6,C7,C9,C10)

Microsoft Excel - Sales Data.xls

Now look at Total second quarter sales in D11, as shown in figure 7.4. The argument for the SUM function, cell range D6:D9, changed to D6:D10 after we added the Central region.

In this case, any second quarter sales for Central territory shown in D8 would be included in the sum at D11. Figure 7.5 illustrates these last two points.

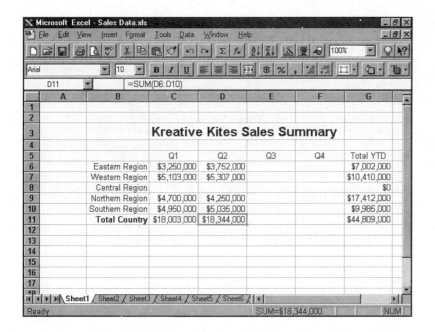

Figure 7.4

The cell range automatically adjusts to include the added row.

Figure 7.5

The C11 value is incorrect, but the D11 value is correct when Central region sales are added.

Keep in mind that although the formula for grand total YTD in G11 is correct, the value calculated is incorrect. G11 sums the range C11 through F11, but total first quarter, C11, is in error. This common problem emphasizes why you should use care when constructing formulas—a simple error in one cell can throw off the accuracy of the entire spreadsheet.

Tip

If all you want to do is get a quick look at the sum of group of numbers, take advantage of the AutoCalculate feature. Look at the status bar at the bottom of figure 7.5—the AutoCalculate box is there showing the sum of the G11 because that is the currently selected cell. Just make a selection of a range of cells and the answer is automatically displayed on the status bar. You no longer need to use a calculator or use a temporary formula in a worksheet when you want to quickly check a total. You can also average the numbers or count the entries by clicking on the Auto Calculate area in the status bar with the right mouse button.

Function Wizard

Mastering function construction is one of the most difficult steps to becoming a proficient Excel user. Fortunately, Microsoft has made it easier. To assist you in choosing functions and determining the information Excel needs to calculate them, Excel provides the *Function Wizard*, a step-by-step tool that helps you choose and build functions in your worksheet.

Activate the Function Wizard by choosing **I**nsert, **F**unction, or by clicking on the Function Wizard tool on the Standard toolbar (see fig. 7.6).

To understand the way the Function Wizard works, the next demonstration adds a logical function to the worksheet. In the following exercise, you need to know which territories met their sales quotas, because those salespeople win a trip to Bora Bora.

On the Disk

Open file EX07.XLS located on the disk provided with *Inside Excel for Windows 95*. Your Excel worksheet should look like figure 7.7.

Total year-to-date sales for each region are shown in cells G6 through G10. Annual quota by region is in cells J6 through J10. You use those numbers to determine which regions' sales associates win the trip. If sales were greater than or equal to quota, you want Excel to put an asterisk (*) in column H. To begin, select H6, then activate the Function Wizard. A dialog box appears, as shown in figure 7.8.

The first dialog box of the Function Wizard shows the function categories on the left and specific function names on the right. As you select different categories, the function list changes. Below the list boxes, Excel provides a description of the currently highlighted function and its syntax.

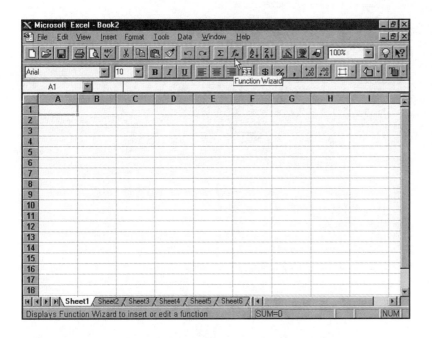

Figure 7.6

The Function Wizard tool.

Figure 7.7

The Sales Data.xls spreadsheet.

Figure 7.8

The Function Wizard: step 1.

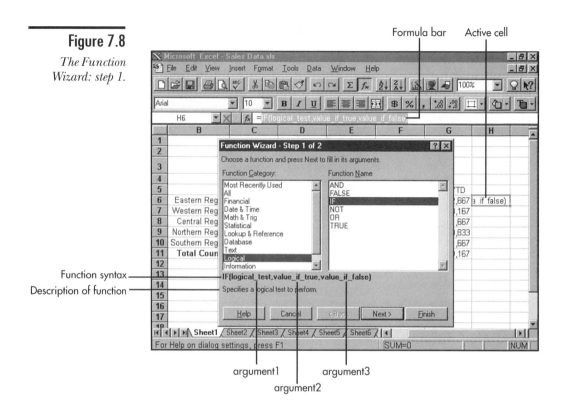

Function syntax

Description of function

argument1

argument2

argument3

For this example, click on the category Logical, then select the IF function by clicking on the function name or by pressing the Tab key and then the arrow keys. The Function Wizard tells you that *argument1* for this function is *logical_test*, *argument2* is *value_if_true*, and *argument3* is *value_if_false*. Also notice that the Function Wizard has automatically begun constructing the IF function in the formula bar and in the active cell, H6.

Tip   This information might be enough for you to complete your function. If you need more guidance, click on **H**elp or press F1 to activate Help. The Microsoft Help utility will further explain the current function you are working with, complete with examples. To exit Help, select E**x**it from the **F**ile menu or press the Close button (see fig. 7.9).

Now click on the Next button in the Function Wizard dialog box. You see the second step dialog box, as shown in figure 7.10.

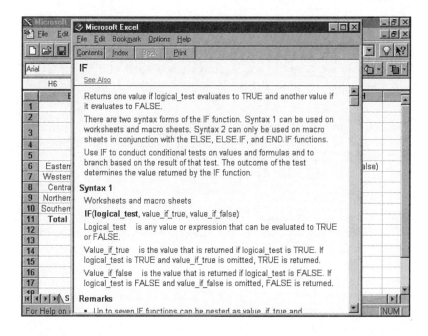

Figure 7.9

Help for the IF function.

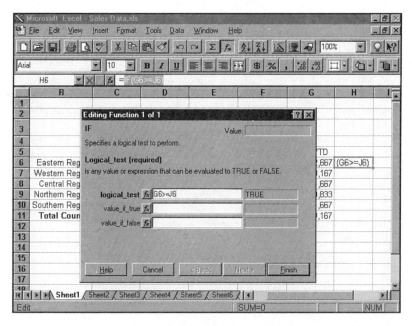

Figure 7.10

The Function Wizard: step 2.

The Function Wizard gives you three edit boxes in which you can provide the three arguments for the IF function. Notice that the first argument, *logical_test*, is bold, which means it is required. You must enter a value or expression that can be evaluated to TRUE or FALSE. In the example, you want to know if Total YTD Sales for the Eastern Region, cell G6, is greater than or equal to Eastern Region Annual Quota, cell J6.

Enter the expression **G6>=J6** into the *logical_test* box. Because this expression can be evaluated to TRUE or FALSE, it is a legitimate logical test. In this case, the expression evaluates to TRUE. Notice that the expression also appears in the formula bar, because the Function Wizard builds the function as you proceed.

 Tip   When an argument is in bold type, it is required. If it is in regular type, it is optional. If you omit the optional arguments, Excel applies an assumed value. This assumption is documented in the Help file and also in the Excel documentation.

To enter *argument2, value_if_true,* click on the second box or press Tab. You want H6 to show an asterisk if sales met the quota, so enter * in the second edit box (see fig. 7.11). Because *value_if_true* is optional, you could omit this argument, and Excel would assume the value TRUE, as you learned from reading the Help screen in figure 7.9.

Figure 7.11

Enter argument2.

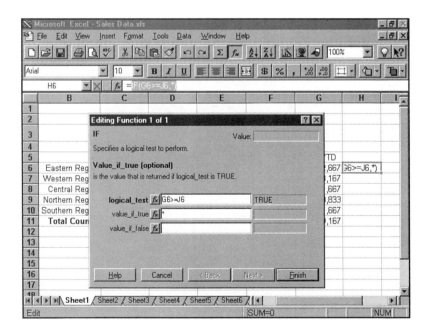

To enter the third argument, *value_if_false*, click on the third edit box or press Tab. If sales did not meet quota, you want H6 to be blank, so you press the spacebar (see fig. 7.12). (This argument also is optional, so you could omit this argument and Excel would assume the value FALSE.)

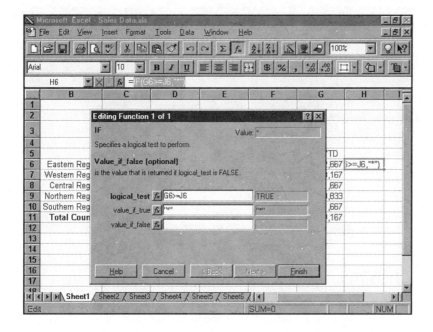

Figure 7.12

Enter argument3.

You now are finished building your function. Click on the **F**inish button or press F. Pressing F puts the function in the edit box. Figure 7.13 shows the completed IF function in the formula bar and the * at H6 to show that Eastern sales met quota. The Formula Wizard put quotation marks around the asterisk in *argument2* and the space in *argument3*. The Formula Wizard understands that you want these entries to be treated as text values (all text values must be enclosed in quotation marks).

Select H6 through H10 and choose **D**own under the Fill option from the **E**dit menu. Now cells H7 through H10 contain similar IF functions to show which other territories win the trip. Your analysis shows that Western and Central salespeople will also be going to Bora Bora.

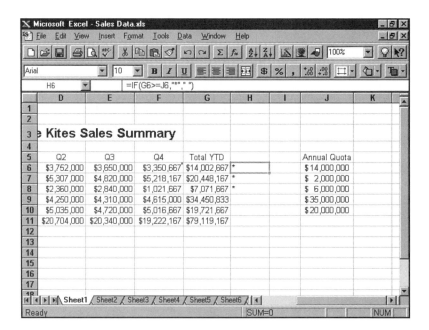

Figure 7.13

The completed IF function.

Nesting Functions

Excel enables you to include functions inside other functions. This process is called *nesting* functions. You can use functions and nested functions as arguments. Suppose, for example, the vice president of sales gets to accompany her sales team to Bora Bora if Total National YTD sales is greater than or equal to the sum of all quotas. One way to construct the IF function might be as follows:

```
=IF(SUM(G7:G11)>=SUM(J7:J11),"*****"," ")
```

The SUM function is nested within the IF function.

Entering Functions

On the Disk

Now take look at a worksheet that is designed to calculate mortgage payments based on mortgage amount, points, interest, and term. Open file Refinance.XLS from the disk provided with *Inside Excel for Windows 95*; it should look like figure 7.14.

For this analysis, you want to finance the fees and points along with the mortgage. To calculate the total amount financed, you again use the SUM function. Select cell C10 and enter **=SUM(C6:C8)** so your worksheet looks like the one illustrated in figure 7.15.

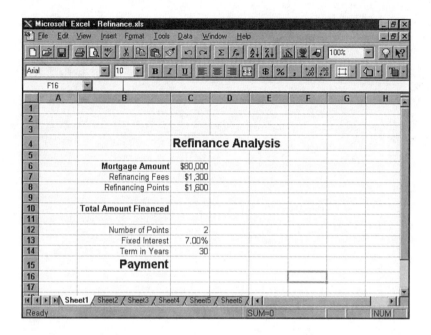

Figure 7.14

The Refinance Analysis worksheet.

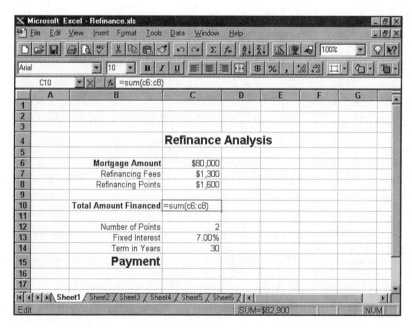

Figure 7.15

The SUM function keyed from the keyboard.

Figure 7.16

*The SUM
function
calculated.*

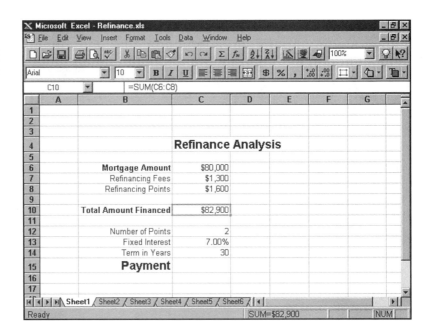

Notice that the function appears in C10, as well as in the formula bar. When you press Enter, Excel calculates the equation, and $82,900 then appears in cell C10. Also, notice that SUM is in capital letters in the formula bar, telling you that Excel recognizes the function and can calculate the formula based on the argument you specified, the range C6:C8, as shown in figure 7.16.

The next step is to construct the payment function. You can enter it from the keyboard as you did in C10, use the Function Wizard step by step as you did in your sales recap worksheet, or use a combination of methods. For this function, use the Function Wizard to get the syntax of the PMT function, paste information from the worksheet for part of the arguments, and then edit the formula bar to get the final result.

1. Select cell C15.

2. Activate the Formula Wizard.

3. Select the Financial Category and Function Name PMT. Your screen should look like figure 7.17.

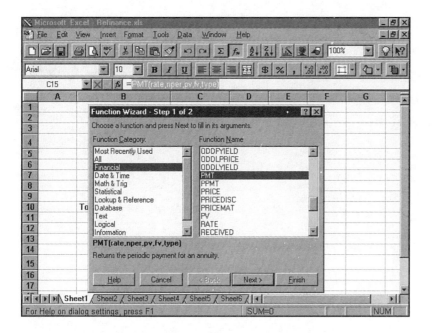

Figure 7.17

The PMT function activated by the Function Wizard.

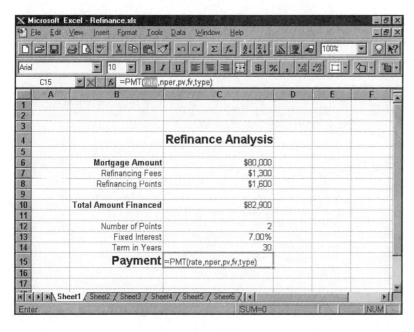

Figure 7.18

The PMT function syntax put into the formula bar by the Function Wizard.

Figure 7.19

The cell reference for rate pasted into the PMT function.

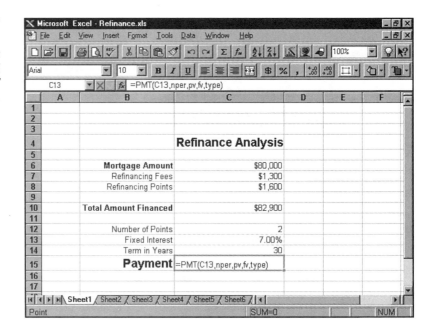

Click on Finish or press Alt+F. Bypass step 2 of the Function Wizard to get the syntax of the PMT function into the formula bar. If you were to continue with the Function Wizard, you would enter argument information into the dialog box. Instead, you want to get information from the worksheet, and then edit it (see fig. 7.18).

Figure 7.20

The PMT function Help screen.

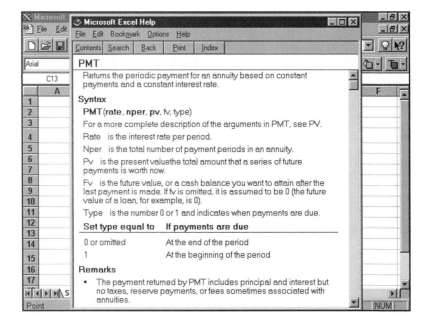

Notice that *rate*, the first argument of the PMT function, is highlighted in the formula bar. Click on cell C13 to paste that cell reference into *argument1* (see fig. 7.19).

The next step is to edit the rest of the arguments: *nper, pv, fv,* and *type.* If you want help with this part of the function construction, activate the Help screen. Press F1 or choose **H**elp, Answer **W**izard, then enter **PMT** and press Enter. The PMT function Help screen is shown in figure 7.20.

Notice that *rate, nper,* and *pv* are in bold because they are required arguments. The *fv* and *type* variables are optional arguments. As discussed in Help, *rate* is the interest rate per period; *nper* is the total number of payment periods in an annuity; *pv* represents the total payments' present value; *fv* is the future value, or cash balance after the last payment is made; and *type* indicates when payments are due.

Note   Note the second remark: you must be consistent about the units you use for specifying *rate* and *nper.* If you use monthly payments on a four-year loan at 12 percent annual interest, use 12%/12 for *rate* and 4*12 for *nper.*

To put this into more simple terms, you are making monthly payments, so your units must be in monthly terms. Our annual interest rate of 7 percent must be divided by 12 to get the monthly interest rate; the period for the loan (30 years) must be multiplied by 12 to determine the number of monthly payments throughout the life of the loan. *pv* is the total amount financed, because that is what the future payments are worth now. The value of *fv* is zero, because the mortgage balance will be zero after all payments are made. *type* tells when the payments are due, assumed to be the end of the period.

So, for the example, *rate* is C13/12, *nper* is C14*12, and *pv* is C10. You can omit *fv* and *type,* because they are assumed to be zero, as desired. To place these arguments into the PMT function, first complete *rate* to show C13/12.

Select E**x**it from the **F**ile menu or press the Close button to exit the Help screen.

1. The I-beam is to the right of C13 in the formula bar. Enter /**12**. The first argument now is complete.

2. Select *argument2,* nper, by dragging the mouse across it, or by double-clicking on it.

3. Click on C14 to paste it into the argument list.

4. The I-beam is to the right of C14 in the formula bar. Enter *****12** to complete *argument2.*

5. Select *argument3,* pv, by dragging the mouse across it, or by double-clicking on it.

Figure 7.21

The PMT function complete.

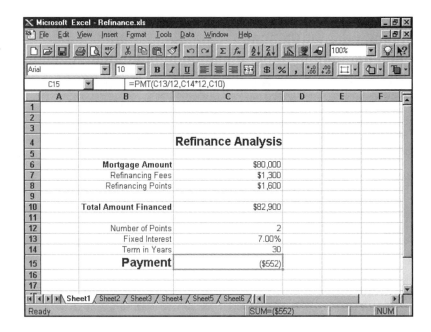

6. Click on C10 to paste it into the argument list. This step completes *argument3*.

7. Select ,fv,type in the formula bar by dragging the mouse across it. Press Del. This step removes the optional arguments.

8. Press Enter to calculate the monthly payment at C15. Your worksheet should look like the one in figure 7.21.

Note that the payment appears as ($552). The parentheses mean it is a negative number—money paid out.

Note You can use the Function Wizard in the following ways:

◆ When you enter a function from the keyboard, enter the equal sign and function name and press Ctrl+A to display Function Wizard step 2, then use it to assist you when you enter arguments.

◆ When you select a cell that contains a function and then activate the Function Wizard, Function Wizard Edit mode opens so that you can make changes to arguments.

◆ Use the same order of precedence for Excel functions as you do for other Excel formulas. Excel performs operations in the following order:

()	Parentheses
:	Range
Space	Intersection
,	Union
-	Negation (single operand)
%	Percent
^	Exponentiation
*	Multiplication
/	Division
+	Addition
-	Subtraction
&	Text joining
=	Equals
<	Less than
>	Greater than
<=	Less than or equal
>=	Greater than or equal
<>	Not equal

Troubleshooting Function and Syntax Messages

If a function name remains in lowercase after you complete the formula and press Enter, check for spelling errors in the function name.

Tip Get into the habit of using lowercase so that Excel can help you spot spelling errors.

When Excel displays an error message rather than a calculated result from the worksheet function, check the following:

◆ Check for typing errors.

◆ Make sure all your parentheses match.

◆ Make sure all the required arguments are defined and in the order that Excel expects to see them.

◆ Make sure all data types are valid for the argument.

◆ Make sure cell references contain valid data. Use the auditing tool to help trace any dependencies your referenced cells have on other cells.

◆ Make sure you leave out commas in numbers, or Excel will think you are separating arguments. (1,000 should be entered as **1000**, for example.)

◆ When you omit an optional argument and you want to define another argument later in the list, make sure you place a comma (,) as a placeholder for the omitted argument.

Excel also displays formula errors instead of function results when you make an error in a formula that serves as an argument. These errors include #DIV/0, #N/A, #NAME?, #NULL!, #NUM!, #REF!, and #VALUE!.

Chapter Snapshot

This chapter picks up where the last chapter left off, showing in more detail the functions available in Excel for Windows 95. This reference explores the following information about each function:

- ◆ The function's group or category, as defined by the Function Wizard

- ◆ The purpose of the function

- ◆ The correct syntax of the function

- ◆ The function's available arguments or variables

Keep this function reference in mind as you use functions in your daily Excel life.

Complete Guide to
Excel Functions

The last chapter discussed ways to use functions in your Excel spreadsheets. This chapter provides you with a complete guide to the functions available in Excel.

Note All of the functions discussed here are included with Excel; they are not, however, all automatically available from a typical installation. Run Excel's Setup program (or Office Setup and choose Microsoft Excel) and select Add/Remove components. Make sure the Add-Ins box is checked and click on the Configure button. Check the box for the Analysis ToolPak and choose OK twice (three times for Office Setup). Now you can add the remainder of the functions from the **T**ools menu. Select Add-**I**ns_ and click on the Analysis ToolPak check box. This adds almost another hundred functions to the Function Wizard's listings. See Chapter 9, "Mastering Excel Analytical Tools," for more information about installing the Analysis ToolPak.

The functions are divided into the groups you see in the Function Wizard for easy reference, as shown in the following list:

◆ Financial

◆ Date and Time

◆ Mathematical and Trigonometric

◆ Statistical

◆ Look-Up and Reference

◆ Database

◆ Text

◆ Logical

◆ Information

◆ Engineering

◆ DDE and External

Within each category, functions are listed alphabetically. An explanation of what each function does is provided, as well as its correct syntax and options.

Note The category DDE and External Functions is not included for use by the Function Wizard, but is included with Excel and documented in the Help Function Reference.

Tip To see examples of each function in use, consult the built-in help that accompanies Excel. From the Help Contents tab, click on Reference Information, and then click on Worksheet Functions. Select the function category to access examples of the functions alphabetically by function name.

In addition, you can open the worksheet SAMPLES.XLS, which you can find in the EXAMPLES folder within the EXCEL folder. This worksheet contains examples of almost all the Excel worksheet functions correctly formatted and operating. Several of the other example spreadsheets in this directory also help to illustrate using worksheet functions.

Financial Functions

The financial functions provided by Excel enable you to make financial calculations a part of your worksheets. You can calculate principal and interest for loans and make several related calculations. You also can calculate depreciation and yields for a variety of assets. Examples of using many of the financial functions are provided in the spreadsheet shown in figure 8.1.

	A	B	C	D	E	F
1	Double-declining balance depreciation	$1.32				
2	Future Value	$2,301.40				
3	Interest Payment	($66.64)				
4	Number of Periods	59.67386567				
5	Payment for an Annuity	($1,037.03)				
6	Present Value	($59,777.15)				
7	Monthly interest rate	1%				
8	VDB Depreciation Example	$1.32				

Figure 8.1

A sample spreadsheet showing the use of financial functions.

Many financial functions require the use of a code indicating the day count basis to be used. Table 8.1 gives the codes used by the financial functions for this purpose.

TABLE 8.1
Codes for Day Count Basis

Code	Basis
0 or omitted	US (NASD) 30/360
1	Actual/actual
2	Actual/360
3	Actual/365
4	European 30/360

Financial functions also use codes for different year bases. Table 8.2 shows the codes used for year basis.

TABLE 8.2
Year Basis Codes for Financial Functions

Code	Year Basis
0	360 days (NASD method)
1	Actual
3	365 days in a year
4	360 days in a year (European method)

In addition, certain financial functions need codes that represent the timing of payments. Table 8.3 shows the codes used for this purpose.

TABLE 8.3
Payment Timing Codes for Financial Functions

Code	Timing of Payments
0	Payment at the end of the period
1	Payment at the beginning of the period

Tip Many of the functions in Excel need their date values expressed as serial date numbers. For instance, if you wanted to represent a date value for January 1, 1996, the serial date number entered in the formula would be 35065. (The number is based internally on the number of days since 01/01/1900.) Instead of figuring the serial date number yourself, being mindful of leap years, use a nested DATE(*year, month, day*) function.

ACCRINT

Purpose: Calculates accrued interest for a security paying periodic interest.

Syntax: ACCRINT(*issue, first_interest, settlement, rate, par, frequency, basis*)

Arguments: *Issue* is the security's issue date. *First_interest* is the first date the security paid interest. *Settlement* is the settlement date for the security. *Rate* is the annual coupon rate. *Par* is the par value for the security. If you omit *par*, Excel assumes a par value of $1,000. *Frequency* is an integer representing the number of coupon payments in one year. *Basis* is day count basis code from table 8.1 in the introduction to the financial functions. Date arguments need to be expressed as serial date numbers.

ACCRINTM

Purpose: Calculates the accrued interest for a security that pays interest at maturity.

Syntax: ACCRUINTM(*issue, maturity, rate, par, basis*)

Arguments: *Issue* is the issue date of the security (entered as a serial date number). *Maturity* is the maturity date (entered as a serial date number). *Rate* is the coupon rate. *Par* is the par value. If you omit *par*, Excel assumes a value of $1,000. *Basis* is the day count basis from table 8.1.

AMORDEGRC

Purpose: Calculates the depreciation for each accounting period. (This function is provided for those using the French accounting system.)

Syntax: AMORDEGRC(*cost, date_purchased, first_period, salvage, period, rate, year_basis*)

Arguments: *Cost* is that amount of the asset cost. *Date_purchased* is the purchase date for the asset. *First_period* is that date that ends the first period. *Salvage* is that value of the asset at the end of its life. *Period* is the period. *Rate* is the depreciation rate. *Year_basis* is the year basis to be used from table 8.2.

AMORLINC

Purpose: Calculates the depreciation for each accounting period. (This function is provided for those using the French accounting system.)

Syntax: AMORLINC(*cost, date_purchased, first_period, salvage, period, rate, year_basis*)

Arguments: *Cost* is that amount of the asset cost. *Date_purchased* is the purchase date for the asset. *First_period* is the date that ends the first period. *Salvage* is that value of the asset at the end of its life. *Period* is the period. *Rate* is the depreciation rate. *Year_basis* is the year basis to be used from table 8.2.

COUPDAYBS

Purpose: Calculates the number of days from the beginning of the coupon period to the settlement date.

Syntax: COUPDAYBS(*settlement, maturity, frequency, basis*)

Arguments: *Settlement* is a serial date number for the settlement date. *Maturity* is a serial date number for the maturity date. *Frequency* is the number of coupon payments annually. *Basis* is the day count basis from table 8.1 in the introduction to the financial functions.

COUPDAYS

Purpose: Calculates the number of days in the coupon period containing the settlement date.

Syntax: COUPDAYS(*settlement, maturity, frequency, basis*)

Arguments: *Settlement* is a serial date number for the settlement date. *Maturity* is a serial date number for the maturity date. *Frequency* is the number of coupon payments annually. *Basis* is the day count basis from table 8.1 in the introduction to the financial functions.

COUPDAYSNC

Purpose: Calculates the number of days from the settlement date to the next coupon date.

Syntax: COUPDAYSNC(*settlement, maturity, frequency, basis*)

Arguments: *Settlement* is a serial date number for the settlement date. *Maturity* is a serial date number for the maturity date. *Frequency* is the number of coupon payments annually. *Basis* is the day count basis from table 8.1 in the introduction to the financial functions.

COUPNCD

Purpose: Calculates the next coupon date after the settlement date.

Syntax: COUPNCD(*settlement, maturity, frequency, basis*)

Arguments: *Settlement* is a serial date number for the settlement date. *Maturity* is a serial date number for the maturity date. *Frequency* is the number of coupon payments annually. *Basis* is the day count basis from table 8.1 in the introduction to the financial functions.

COUPNUM

Purpose: Calculates the number of coupons payable between settlement and maturity dates.

Syntax: COUPNUM(*settlement, maturity, frequency, basis*)

Arguments: *Settlement* is a serial date number for the settlement date. *Maturity* is a serial date number for the maturity date. *Frequency* is the number of coupon payments annually. *Basis* is the day count basis from table 8.1 in the introduction to the financial functions.

COUPPCD

Purpose: Calculates the previous coupon date before the settlement date.

Syntax: COUPPCD(*settlement, maturity, frequency, basis*)

Arguments: *Settlement* is a serial date number for the settlement date. *Maturity* is a serial date number for the maturity date. *Frequency* is the number of coupon payments annually. *Basis* is the day count basis from table 8.1 in the introduction to the financial functions.

CUMIPMT

Purpose: Calculates the cumulative interest paid between two periods of a loan.

Syntax: CUMIPMT(*rate, nper, pv, start_period, end_period, type*)

Arguments: *Rate* is the interest rate, *nper* the number of payment periods, and *pv* the present value. *Start_period* is the first period for the purposes of the calculation, and *end_period* the last period for the calculation. *Type* is the payment timing, as shown in table 8.3 in the introduction to the financial functions.

CUMPRINC

Purpose: Calculates the cumulative principal paid between the starting period and ending period of a loan.

Syntax: CUMPRINC(*rate, nper, pv, start_period, end_period, type*)

Arguments: *Rate* is the interest rate, *nper* the number of payment periods, and *pv* the present value. *Start_period* is the first period for the purposes of the calculation, and *end_period* the last period for the calculation. *Type* is the payment timing, as shown in table 8.3 in the introduction to the financial functions.

DB

Purpose: Calculates depreciation for an asset using the fixed-declining balance method for a specified period.

Syntax: DB(*cost, salvage, life, period, month*)

Arguments: *Cost* is what you paid for the asset, *salvage* its value after depreciation, *life* the number of periods in the useful life of the asset, *period* the period over which to calculate depreciation, and *month* the number of months in the first year. (If *month* is omitted, Excel assumes a value of 12.)

DDB

Purpose: Calculates depreciation for an asset using the double-declining balance method, or another method you specify.

Syntax: DDB(*cost, salvage, life, period, factor*)

Arguments: *Cost* is what you paid for the asset, *salvage* its value after depreciation, *life* the number of periods in the useful life of the asset, *period* the period over which to calculate depreciation, and *factor* the rate at which the balance declines. (If *month* is omitted, Excel assumes a value of 12.)

DISC

Purpose: Calculates a security's discount rate.

Syntax: DISC(*settlement, maturity, pr, redemption, basis*)

Arguments: *Settlement* is a serial date number representing the settlement date. *Maturity* is the serial date number representing the maturity date. *Pr* is the price per $100 of face value of the security. *Redemption* is the redemption value per $100 of face value. *Basis* is the day count basis, given in table 8.1 in the introduction to the financial functions.

DOLLARDE

Purpose: Converts a dollar price written as a fraction to a dollar price written as a decimal.

Syntax: DOLLARDE(*fractional_dollar, fraction*)

Arguments: *Fractional_dollar* is the number of dollars expressed as a fraction. *Fraction* is the integer used as the denominator of the fraction.

DOLLARFR

Purpose: Converts a dollar price written as a decimal number to a dollar price written as a fraction.

Syntax: DOLLARFR(*decimal_dollar, fraction*)

Arguments: *Decimal_dollar* is the dollar price as a decimal number. *Fraction* is the denominator for the fraction you wish to use in the conversion.

DURATION

Purpose: Calculates the annual duration with periodic interest payments for a security.

Syntax: DURATION(*settlement, maturity, coupon, yld, frequency, basis*)

Arguments: *Settlement* is the serial date number representing the security's settlement date. *Maturity* is a serial date number representing the security's maturity date. *Coupon* is the annual coupon rate, *yld* the annual yield, and *frequency* the number of payments in a given year. *Basis* is the day count basis given in table 8.1 of the introduction to the financial functions.

EFFECT

Purpose: Calculates the effective annual interest rate.

Syntax: EFFECT(*nominal_rate, npery*)

Arguments: *Nominal_rate* is the nominal interest rate involved. *Npery* is the number of periods for compounding the interest in a given year.

FV

Purpose: Calculates the future value of an investment that has constant periodic payments and a constant interest rate.

Syntax: FV(*rate, nper, pmt, pv, type*)

Arguments: *Rate* is the interest rate expressed as a per period value. *Nper* is the total number of payment periods. *Pmt* is the payment made each period. *Pv* is the present value. *Type* is the payment timing code shown in table 8.3 in the introduction to the financial functions.

FVSCHEDULE

Purpose: Calculates the future value of an investment with variable or adjustable interest rates.

Syntax: FVSCHEDULE(*principal, schedule*)

Arguments: *Principal* is the present value of the investment. *Schedule* is an array of interest rates that apply.

INTRATE

Purpose: Calculates the interest rate for a security that is fully invested.

Syntax: INTRATE(*settlement, maturity, investment, redemption, basis*)

Arguments: *Settlement* is a serial date number that represents the settlement date, and *maturity* is a serial date number that represents the maturity date. *Investment* is the amount invested, *redemption* the amount received at maturity, and *basis* the day count basis given in table 8.1 in the introduction to the financial functions.

IPMT

Purpose: Calculates the interest payment over a given period of time for an investment based on constant periodic payments and a fixed interest rate.

Syntax: IPMT(*rate, per, nper, pv, fv, type*)

Arguments: *Rate* is the constant interest rate, *per* the period over which you want to calculate the interest rate, and *nper* the total number of periods in the investment. *Pv* is the present value. *Fv* is the future value you want to attain. (If *fv* is omitted, Excel assumes the future value of a loan, or 0.) *Type* is the payment timing code shown in table 8.3 in the introduction to the financial functions.

IRR

Purpose: Calculates the internal rate of return based on a series of cash flows.

Syntax: IRR(*values, guess*)

Arguments: *Values* is an array or reference containing the numbers representing the cash flows. *Guess* is a number representing your estimate of the result of the calculation. The guess parameter is optional—the default for *guess* is 10 percent (0.1). Excel uses the guess as a starting point for calculating the result. After 20 attempts at resolving the calculation without success, Excel returns the #NUM! error value. If you get the #NUM! error message, try a different value for *guess*.

 Note For the purposes of this function, your initial investment should be entered as a negative number, such as –$70,000.

MDURATION

Purpose: Calculates the modified Macauley duration for a security. The function assumes a par value of $100.

Syntax: MDURATION(*settlement, maturity, coupon, yld, frequency, basis*)

Arguments: *Settlement* is a serial date number representing the settlement date. *Maturity* is a serial date number representing the maturity date. *Coupon* is the annual coupon rate. *Yld* is the annual yield. *Frequency* is the number of coupon payments annually. *Basis* is the day count basis from table 8.1 in the introduction to the financial functions.

MIRR

Purpose: Calculates the modified internal rate of return for a series of cash flows. The function includes the cost of investment and interest on reinvestment of cash.

Syntax: MIRR(*values, finance_rate, reinvest_rate*)

Arguments: *Values* is an array or reference of numbers that represent the cash flows. *Finance_rate* is the interest rate paid on the money used for the cash flows. *Reinvest_rate* is the interest the reinvested cash flows generate.

NOMINAL

Purpose: Calculates the nominal annual interest rate.

Syntax: NOMINAL(*effect_rate, npery*)

Arguments: *Effect_rate* is the effective interest rate, and *npery* the number of compounding periods in one year.

NPER

Purpose: Calculates the number of periods necessary for an investment.

Syntax: NPER(*rate, pmt, pv, fv, type*)

Arguments: *Rate* is one period's rate of interest, *pmt* the payment made during each period, *pv* the present value, *fv* the future value, and *type* is the payment timing code given in table 8.3 in the introduction to the financial functions.

NPV

Purpose: Calculates the net present value for an investment, assuming a discount rate and a series of periodic cash flows representing future payments and income.

Syntax: NPV(*rate, value1, value2, ...*)

Arguments: *Rate* is one period's discount rate. The *values* are up to 29 values that represent the future payments (negative values) and income (positive values).

ODDFPRICE

Purpose: Calculates the price per $100 face value for a security with an odd first period.

Syntax: ODDFPRICE(*settlement, maturity, issue, first_coupon, rate, yld, redemption, frequency, basis*)

Arguments: *Settlement* is a serial date number representing the settlement date. *Maturity* is a serial date number representing the maturity date. *Issue* is a serial date number representing the issue date. *First_coupon* is a serial date number representing the first coupon date. *Rate* is the interest rate, *yld* is the annual yield, *redemption* the redemption value per $100 of face value, *frequency* the number of coupon payments per year, and *basis* the day count basis given in table 8.1 in the introduction to the financial functions.

ODDFYIELD

Purpose: Calculates the yield of a security with an odd first period.

Syntax: ODDFYIELD(*settlement, maturity, issue, first_coupon, rate, pr, redemption, frequency, basis*)

Arguments: *Settlement* is a serial date number representing the settlement date. *Maturity* is a serial date number representing the maturity date. *Issue* is a serial date number representing the issue date. *First_coupon* is a serial date number representing the first coupon date. *Rate* is the interest rate, *pr* the security's price, *redemption* the redemption value per $100 of face value, *frequency* the number of coupon payments per year, and *basis* the day count basis given in table 8.1 in the introduction to the financial functions.

ODDLPRICE

Purpose: Calculates the price per $100 of face value for a security with an odd last period.

Syntax: ODDLPRICE(*settlement, maturity, last_interest, rate, yld, redemption, frequency, basis*)

Arguments: *Settlement* is a serial date number representing the settlement date. *Maturity* is a serial date number representing the maturity date. *Last_interest* is a serial date number representing the last coupon date. *Rate* is the interest rate, *yld* is the annual yield, *redemption* the redemption value per $100 of face value, *frequency* the number of coupon payments per year, and *basis* the day count basis given in table 8.1 in the introduction to the financial functions.

ODDLYIELD

Purpose: Calculates the yield for a security with an odd last period.

Syntax: ODDLYIELD(*settlement, maturity, last_interest, rate, pr, redemption, frequency, basis*)

Arguments: *Settlement* is a serial date number representing the settlement date. *Maturity* is a serial date number representing the maturity date. *Last_interest* is a serial date number representing the last coupon date. *Rate* is the interest rate, *pr* the security's price, *redemption* the redemption value per $100 of face value, *frequency* the number of coupon payments per year, and *basis* the day count basis given in table 8.1 in the introduction to the financial functions.

PMT

Purpose: Calculates the payment for an annuity built on fixed payments and a fixed interest rate.

Syntax: PMT(*rate, nper, pv, fv, type*)

Arguments: *Rate* is the interest rate per period, *nper* the number of periods in an annuity, *pv* the present value, *fv* the future value, and *type* the payment timing code given in table 8.3 in the introduction to the financial functions.

PPMT

Purpose: Calculates the payment on the principal in a given period for an investment built on fixed payments and fixed interest.

Syntax: PPMT(*rate, per, nper, pv, fv, type*)

Arguments: *Rate* is the interest rate per period, *per* identifies the period, *nper* is the number of payment periods, *pv* the present value, *fv* the future value, and *type* the payment timing code given in table 8.3 in the introduction to the financial functions.

PRICE

Purpose: Calculates the price per $100 of face value for a security paying periodic interest.

Syntax: PRICE(*settlement, maturity, rate, yld, redemption, frequency, basis*)

Arguments: *Settlement* is a serial date number representing the settlement date. *Maturity* is a serial date number representing the maturity date. *Rate* is the annual coupon rate, *yld* the annual yield, *redemption* the redemption value per $100 of face value, *frequency* the number of payments annually, and *basis* the day count basis given in table 8.1 in the introduction to the financial functions.

PRICEDISC

Purpose: Calculates the price per $100 of face value for a discounted security.

Syntax: PRICEDISC(*settlement, maturity, discount, redemption, basis*)

Arguments: *Settlement* is a serial date number representing the settlement date. *Maturity* is a serial date number representing that maturity date. *Discount* is the discount rate, *redemption* the redemption value per $100 of face value, and *basis* the day count basis given in table 8.1 in the introduction to the financial functions.

PRICEMAT

Purpose: Calculates the price per $100 of face value for a security that pays its interest at maturity.

Syntax: PRICEMAT(*settlement, maturity, issue, rate, yld, basis*)

Arguments: *Settlement* is a serial date number representing the settlement date. *Maturity* is a serial date number representing the maturity date. *Issue* is a serial date number representing the issue date. *Rate* is the interest rate at date of issue, *yld* the annual yield, and *basis* the day count basis given in table 8.1 in the introduction to the financial functions.

PV

Purpose: Calculates the present value for an investment.

Syntax: PV(*rate, nper, pmt, fv, type*)

Arguments: *Rate* is the interest rate per period, *nper* the number of payment periods in an annuity, *pmt* the payment for each period, *fv* the future value, and *type* the payment timing code given in table 8.3 in the introduction to the financial functions.

RATE

Purpose: Calculates the interest rate per period for an annuity.

Syntax: RATE(*nper, pmt, pv, fv, type, guess*)

Arguments: *Nper* is the number of payment periods in an annuity, *pmt* the payment for each period, *pv* the present value, fv the future value, *type* the payment timing code given in table 8.3 in the introduction to the financial functions, and *guess* your estimate of what the rate will be. If you do not give a guess, Excel assumes a guess of 10 percent. If Excel returns a value of $NUM! error, try a different *guess*.

RECEIVED

Purpose: Calculates the amount received at maturity for a security that is fully invested.

Syntax: RECEIVED(*settlement, maturity, investment, discount, basis*)

Arguments: *Settlement* is a serial date number representing the settlement date. *Maturity* is a serial date number representing the maturity date. *Investment* is the amount invested, *discount* the discount rate, and *basis* the day count basis given in table 8.1 in the introduction to the financial functions.

SLN

Purpose: Calculates straight-line depreciation for an asset over one period.

Syntax: SLN(*cost, salvage, life*)

Arguments: *Cost* is the initial cost of the asset, *salvage* the value of the asset after the depreciation period (salvage value), and *life* the number of periods over which you depreciate the asset (useful life of the asset).

SYD

Purpose: Calculates the sum-of-years' digits depreciation for an asset over one period.

Syntax: SYD(*cost, salvage, life, per*)

Arguments: *Cost* is the initial cost of the asset, *salvage* the value of the asset after the depreciation period (salvage value), and *life* the number of periods over which you depreciate the asset (useful life of the asset). *Per* is the period in question.

TBILLEQ

Purpose: Calculates a Treasury bill's bond-equivalent yield.

Syntax: TBILLEQ(*settlement, maturity, discount*)

Arguments: *Settlement* is a serial date number representing the settlement date. *Maturity* is a serial date number representing the maturity date, and *discount* is the discount rate.

TBILLPRICE

Purpose: Calculates a Treasury bill's price per $100 of face value.

Syntax: TBILLPRICE(*settlement, maturity, discount*)

Arguments: *Settlement* is a serial date number representing the settlement date. *Maturity* is a serial date number representing the maturity date, and *discount* is the discount rate.

TBILLYIELD

Purpose: Calculates a Treasury bill's yield.

Syntax: TBILLYIELD(*settlement, maturity, pr*)

Arguments: *Settlement* is a serial date number representing the settlement date. *Maturity* is a serial date number representing the maturity date, and *pr* is the price per $100 of face value.

VDB

Purpose: Calculates the depreciation of an asset over a specified period using the depreciation method you specify.

Syntax: VDB(*cost, salvage, life, start_period, end_period, factor, no_switch*)

Arguments: *Cost* is the initial cost of the asset, *salvage* the value of the asset after the depreciation period (salvage value), and *life* the number of periods over which you depreciate the asset (useful life of the asset). *Start_period* is the starting period for the depreciation calculation. *End_period* is the ending period for the calculation. *Factor* is the rate of decline for the balance (assumed as 2 if factor is omitted). *No_switch* is a logical value that causes the calculation to switch to straight-line depreciation if depreciation is greater using this method. (TRUE enables the switch, and FALSE disables it. Excel assumes FALSE if you omit this argument.)

XIRR

Purpose: Calculates the internal rate of return for a nonperiodic schedule of cash flows.

Syntax: XIRR(*values, dates, guess*)

Arguments: *Values* is an array of cash flows. *Dates* is an array of payment dates corresponding to the cash flows. *Guess* is your estimate of the result of the function.

XNPV

Purpose: Calculates net present value for a nonperiodic schedule of cash flows.

Syntax: XNPV(*rate, values, dates*)

Arguments: *Rate* is the discount rate. *Values* is an array of cash flows. *Dates* is an array of payment dates corresponding to the cash flows.

YIELD

Purpose: Calculates yield for a security that pays periodic interest.

Syntax: YIELD(*settlement, maturity, rate, pr, redemption, frequency, basis*)

Arguments: *Settlement* is a serial date number representing the settlement date. *Maturity* is a serial date number representing the maturity date. *Rate* is the annual coupon rate. *Pr* is the price per $100 of face value, *redemption* the redemption value per $100, *frequency* the number of coupon payments per year, and *basis* the day count basis given by table 8.1 in the introduction to the financial functions.

YIELDDISC

Purpose: Calculates the annual yield of a discounted security.

Syntax: YIELDDISC(*settlement, maturity, pr, redemption, basis*)

Arguments: *Settlement* is a serial date number representing the settlement date. *Maturity* is a serial date number representing the maturity date. *Pr* is the price per $100 of face value, *redemption* the redemption value per $100 of face value, and *basis* the day count basis given by table 8.1 in the introduction to the financial functions.

YIELDMAT

Purpose: Calculates the annual yield for a security paying interest at maturity.

Syntax: YIELDMAT(*settlement, maturity, issue, rate, pr, basis*)

Arguments: *Settlement* is a serial date number representing the settlement date. *Maturity* is a serial date number representing the maturity date. *Issue* is a serial date number representing the issue date. *Rate* is the interest rate at date of issue. *Pr* is the price per $100 of face value, and *basis* the day count basis given by table 8.1 in the introduction to the financial functions.

Date and Time Functions

Date and time functions enable you to look up dates and times and to perform mathematical calculations on dates and times with ease. Excel for Windows 95 uses a serial number system to work with dates. Although this system might seem strange at first, it provides efficient calculation of dates and times.

Each date between January 1, 1900, and December 31, 2078, is assigned a serial number between 0 and 63,918. Times also are assigned serial numbers as well, so you can represent a date and time string with a decimal number. The number to the left of the decimal is the date serial number, while the number to the right is the time serial number. The number 367.5, for instance, represents 12:00 noon on January 1, 1901.

Many of the date and time functions work with serial numbers. Their use is demonstrated by the spreadsheet shown in figure 8.2.

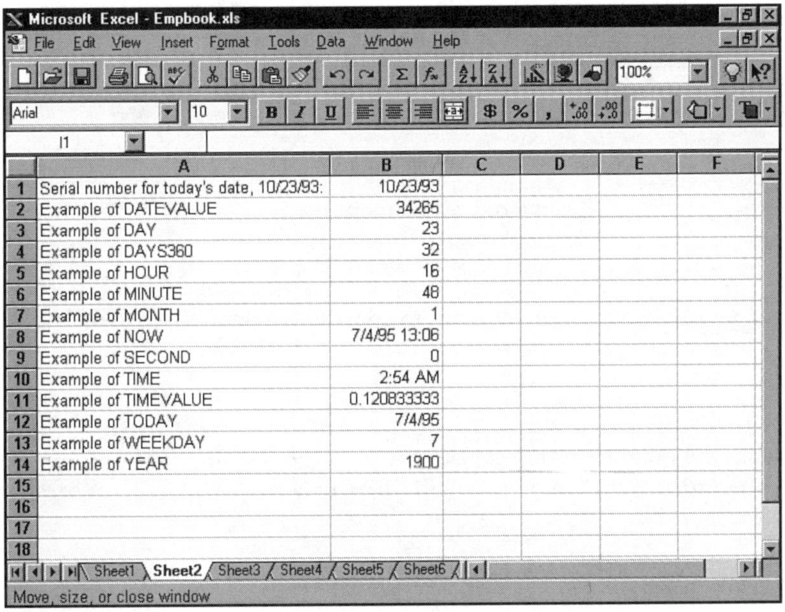

Figure 8.2

A spreadsheet showing the use of date and time functions.

DATE

Purpose: Returns a date's serial number.

Syntax: DATE(*year, month, day*)

Arguments: Each argument is a number representing the *year, month,* and *day* for which a serial number is desired. If the *day* value is larger than the number of days in the month indicated, the *month* value is incremented and the extra days are added to the *day* value for the incremented month. DATE(91,1,35) gives the same serial number as DATE(91,2,4), for example.

DATEVALUE

Purpose: Returns a serial number for a date written as text, as long as the date falls between January 1, 1900, and December 31, 2078.

Syntax: DATEVALUE(*date_text*)

Arguments: The only argument is a date written as text. If the year is not present, Excel assumes the date refers to the year set on the system clock. If the year is included, separate it with a comma. The format is better expressed as DATEVALUE(*month day, year*) where *month* is at least the first three characters of the month, *day* is simply the day of the month, and *year* is either a 2-digit or 4-digit number representing the year. Notice that with our alternate syntax, there is no comma between *month* and *day.*

DAY

Purpose: Converts a serial number to a day of the month.

Syntax: DAY(*serial_number*)

Arguments: *Serial_number* is a number you want to convert to a date.

DAYS360

Purpose: Calculates the number of days between two dates based on a 360-day year (twelve thirty-day months). This function is used when an accounting system is based on twelve thirty-day months.

Syntax: DAYS360(*start_date, end_date, method*)

Arguments: *Start_date* and *end_date* can be text strings (for example, "03/02/96" or "03-02-1996") or serial numbers. *Method* takes a value of 1 if you are using the U.S. (NASD) method. *Method* is 2 if you are using the European method of calculating a 360-day year. If you omit *method*, Excel assumes the U.S. convention.

EDATE

Purpose: Gives the serial number for a date the indicated number of months afterward or before.

Syntax: EDATE(*start_date, number_of_months*)

Arguments: *Start_date* is serial number for the date in question. *Number_of_months* is the number of months after *start_date*. You can use a negative number to calculate the number of months before a date.

EOMONTH

Purpose: Gives the serial number for a date at the end of the month, for the indicated number of months afterward or before.

Syntax: EOMONTH(*start_date, number_of_months*)

Arguments: *Start_date* is serial number for the date in question. *Number_of_months* is the number of months after *start_date*. You can use a negative number to calculate the number of months before a date.

HOUR

Purpose: Converts a serial number for a date into an hour, represented as an integer (0 through 23).

Syntax: HOUR(*serial_number*)

Arguments: *Serial_number* is a serial number that represents a date-time code. You also can include the time string as text.

MINUTE

Purpose: Converts a serial number for a date into a minute expressed as an integer (0 through 59).

Syntax: MINUTE(*serial_number*)

Arguments: *Serial_number* is a serial number that represents a date-time code. You also can include the time string as text.

MONTH

Purpose: Converts a serial number for a date into a month returned as an integer (1 through 12).

Syntax: MONTH(*serial_number*)

Arguments: *Serial_number* is a serial number that represents a date-time code. You also can include the time string as text.

NETWORKDAYS

Purpose: Calculates the number of working days, excluding weekends and identified holidays, between two dates.

Syntax: NETWORKDAYS(*start_date, end_date, holidays*)

Arguments: *Start_date* and *end_date* are serial numbers representing the dates in question. *Holidays* is an optional list of serial numbers to exclude from the count of working days.

NOW

Purpose: Gives the serial number for the current date and time.

Syntax: NOW()

Arguments: None. The current data and time is determined from the computer's internal clock.

SECOND

Purpose: Converts a serial number for a time into a second returned as an integer (0 through 60).

Syntax: SECOND(*serial_number*)

Arguments: *Serial_number* is a serial number that represents a date-time code. You also can include the time string as text.

TIME

Purpose: Gives the serial number for the time indicated. A time serial number is reported as a decimal fraction (for example, .99999, 11:59:59pm).

Syntax: TIME(*hour, minute, second*)

Arguments: *Hour* is a number (0–23) indicating the hour, *minute* a number (0–59) indicating the minute, and *second* a number (0–59) indicating the second.

TIMEVALUE

Purpose: Gives the serial number (0–0.99999) for a time represented as text.

Syntax: TIMEVALUE(*time_text*)

Arguments: *Time_text* is a text string that represents the time in question.

TODAY

Purpose: Gives the serial number for the current date.

Syntax: TODAY()

Arguments: None. The date is determined from the computer's internal clock.

WEEKDAY

Purpose: Converts a serial number to a day of the week.

Syntax: WEEKDAY(*serial_number, return_type*)

Arguments: *Serial_number* is the serial number to be converted or a text representing the date. *Return_type* takes values from table 8.4.

TABLE 8.4
Return Types for WEEKDAY

Return_type	Range for Number Returned
1 (or omitted)	1 (Sunday) – 7 (Saturday)
2	1 (Monday) – 7 (Sunday)
3	0 (Monday) – 6 (Sunday)

YEAR

Purpose: Gives the year (1900–2078) associated with a serial number.

Syntax: YEAR(*serial_number*)

Arguments: *Serial_number* is the serial number to be converted. You also can use a text string to represent this date.

YEARFRAC

Purpose: Gives the fraction of the year represented by the number of whole days between two dates.

Syntax: YEARFRAC(*start_date, end_date, basis*)

Arguments: *Start_date* and *end_date* are the serial numbers representing the two dates. *Basis* is a value from table 8.5.

TABLE 8.5
Values of Basis for YEARFRAC

Basis	Description
0 (or omitted)	30/360 (US/NASD)
1	Actual/Actual
2	Actual/360
3	Actual/365
4	30/360 (European)

Mathematical and Trigonometric Functions

Excel's math and trig functions, of course, perform a variety of calculations. They form the core of Excel's mathematical capabilities. Examples of their use appear in the spreadsheet shown in figure 8.3.

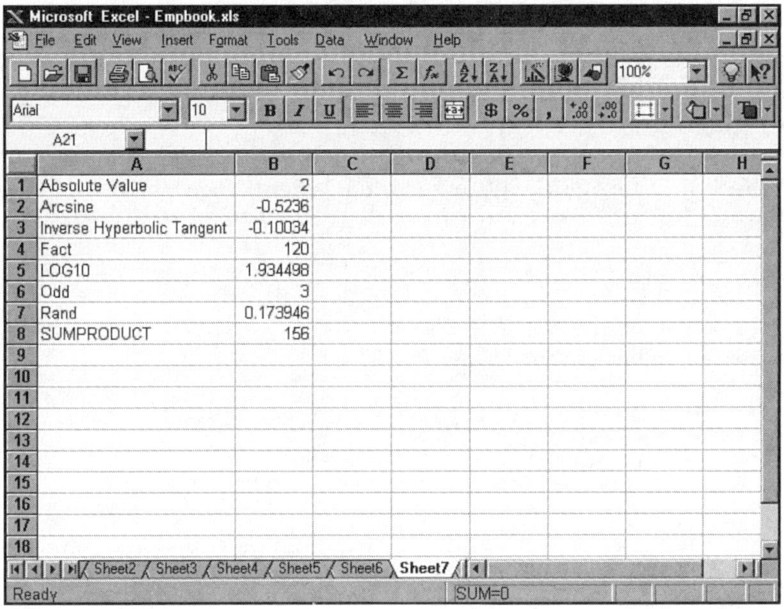

Figure 8.3

A spreadsheet showing the use of math and trig functions.

ABS

Purpose: Gets the absolute value of a number.

Syntax: ABS(*number*)

Arguments: *Number* is a real number for which you want the absolute value.

ACOS

Purpose: Calculates a number's arccosine.

Syntax: ACOS(*number*)

Arguments: *Number* is the cosine of the angle in question. It must range between 1 and –1.

ACOSH

Purpose: Calculates a number's inverse hyperbolic cosine.

Syntax: ACOSH(*number*)

Arguments: *Number* is a real number greater than or equal to 1.

ASIN

Purpose: Calculates a number's arcsine.

Syntax: ASIN(*number*)

Arguments: *Number* is the sine of the angle in question. It must range between 1 and –1.

ASINH

Purpose: Calculates a number's inverse hyperbolic sine.

Syntax: ASINH(*number*)

Arguments: *Number* is a real number.

ATAN

Purpose: Calculates a number's arctangent.

Syntax: ATAN(*number*)

Arguments: *Number* is the tangent of the angle in question.

ATAN2

Purpose: Calculates the arctangent from x/y coordinates.

Syntax: ATAN2(*x_num, y_num*)

Arguments: *X_num* is the x-coordinate and *y_num* is the y-coordinate of the point in question.

ATANH

Purpose: Calculates a number's inverse hyperbolic tangent.

Syntax: ATANH(*number*)

Arguments: *Number* is a real number ranging from 1 to –1.

CEILING

Purpose: Rounds numbers up to the nearest integer or multiple of significance.

Syntax: CEILING(*number, significance*)

Arguments: *Number* is the value to round, *significance* the multiple to which you want to round; CEILING(423, 5) equals 425, for example.

COMBIN

Purpose: Calculates the number of combinations for a number of objects.

Syntax: COMBIN(*number, number_chosen*)

Arguments: *Number* is the number of objects in the set from which to choose. *Number_chosen* is the number of objects selected in each combination.

COS

Purpose: Calculates a number's cosine.

Syntax: COS(*number*)

Arguments: *Number* is the angle in question, measured in radians.

COSH

Purpose: Calculates a number's hyperbolic cosine.

Syntax: COSH(*number*)

Arguments: *Number* is the number for which you want the hyperbolic cosine.

COUNTIF

Purpose: Counts the number of non-blank cells meeting the given criteria.

Syntax: COUNTIF(*range, criteria*)

Arguments: *Range* is the set of cells in which you want to count. *Criteria* is a number, expression, or text that defines whether a cell is counted. For text cells, enclose the text to be compared in quotes. For example, use "expense" to count all cells in the range that contain the word expense. For numeric cells, use >, <, =, and so forth as comparisons. >50 would include all cells with a value greater than 50 in the count.

DEGREES

Purpose: Converts from radians to degrees.

Syntax: DEGREES(*angle*)

Arguments: *Angle* is an angle measured in radians.

EVEN

Purpose: Rounds a number up to the nearest even integer.

Syntax: EVEN(*number*)

Arguments: *Number* is the number to round.

EXP

Purpose: Calculates *e* raised to a given power.

Syntax: EXP(*number*)

Arguments: *Number* is the value to be used as the exponent.

FACT

Purpose: Calculates the factorial of a number.

Syntax: FACT(*number*)

Arguments: *Number* is a positive number or 0 for which you want the factorial.

FACTDOUBLE

Purpose: Calculates the double factorial of a given number.

Syntax: FACTDOUBLE(*number*)

Arguments: *Number* is the number for which you want a double factorial.

FLOOR

Purpose: Rounds a number down to the nearest multiple of significance.

Syntax: FLOOR(*number, significance*)

Arguments: *Number* is the number to round, *significance* is the multiple to round to; FLOOR(728, 5) equals 725, for example.

GCD

Purpose: Calculates the greatest common divisor of two or more integers.

Syntax: GCD(*number1, number2, ...*)

Arguments: *Number* is up to 29 values to include in the calculation.

INT

Purpose: Rounds a number down to the nearest integer.

Syntax: INT(*number*)

Arguments: *Number* is a real number.

LCM

Purpose: Calculates the least common multiple for a set of integers.

Syntax: LCM(*number1, number2, ...*)

Arguments: *Number* is up to 29 values to include in the calculation.

LN

Purpose: Calculates the natural logarithm for a number.

Syntax: LN(*number*)

Arguments: *Number* is a positive real number.

LOG

Purpose: Calculates the logarithm of a number in a specified base.

Syntax: LOG(*number, base*)

Arguments: *Number* is a positive real number. *Base* is the value to be used as the base of the logarithm. If base is not present, Excel assumes the base is 10.

LOG10

Purpose: Calculates the logarithm of a number in base 10.

Syntax: LOG10(*number*)

Arguments: *Number* is a positive real number.

MDETERM

Purpose: Calculates the matrix determinant of an array.

Syntax: MDETERM(*array*)

Arguments: *Array* is an array of numbers with the same number of rows as columns.

MINVERSE

Purpose: Calculates the inverse matrix of a matrix stored in an array.

Syntax: MINVERSE(*array*)

Arguments: *Array* is an array of numbers with the same number of rows as columns.

MMULT

Purpose: Calculates the matrix product of two arrays.

Syntax: MMULT(*array, array2*)

Arguments: *Array1* and *array2* are the two arrays.

MOD

Purpose: Gets the remainder in a division problem.

Syntax: MOD(*number, divisor*)

Arguments: *Number* is the number for the numerator. *Divisor* is the number by which you want to divide.

MROUND

Purpose: Rounds a number to the specified multiple.

Syntax: MROUND(*number, multiple*)

Arguments: *Number* is the number to round. *Multiple* is the multiple to which you want to round.

MULTINOMIAL

Purpose: Calculates the ratio of the factorial of a sum of values to the product of the factorials.

Syntax: MULTINOMIAL(*number1, number2, ...*)

Arguments: *Number* is up to 29 values to include in the calculation.

ODD

Purpose: Rounds a number up to the nearest odd integer.

Syntax: ODD(*number*)

Arguments: *Number* is the number to round.

PI

Purpose: Returns the value of Pi calculated to 15 digits.

Syntax: PI()

Arguments: None.

POWER

Purpose: Raises the given number to the specified power.

Syntax: POWER(*number, power*)

Arguments: *Number* is the base. *Power* is the exponent.

PRODUCT

Purpose: Multiplies the specified numbers.

Syntax: PRODUCT(*number1, number2, ...*)

Arguments: *Number* is up to 30 values to multiply. You can use cell references.

QUOTIENT

Purpose: Calculates the integer portion of a division problem.

Syntax: QUOTIENT(*numerator, denominator*)

Arguments: *Numerator* is the number for the numerator, *denominator* the number for the denominator.

RADIANS

Purpose: Converts from degrees to radians.

Syntax: RADIANS(*angle*)

Arguments: *Angle* is an angle measured in degrees.

RAND

Purpose: Gets an evenly distributed random number between 0 and 1. This function gets a new number each time the worksheet is recalculated.

Syntax: RAND()

Arguments: None.

RANDBETWEEN

Purpose: Gets a random number between the specified numbers. This function gets a new random number each time the worksheet is recalculated.

Syntax: RANDBETWEEN(*bottom, top*)

Arguments: Bottom is the smallest integer to return, and top is the largest.

ROMAN

Purpose: Converts an Arabic numeral to text representing a Roman numeral.

Syntax: ROMAN(*number, form*)

Arguments: *Number* is an Arabic numeral. Form is 0 (or omitted) for a Classic Roman numeral. The values 1, 2, 3, and 4 specify increasingly concise (shorter) numerals. If form is TRUE, the number is classical; if FALSE, it is a simplified form.

ROUND

Purpose: Rounds a number to the number of digits indicated.

Syntax: ROUND(*number, num_digits*)

Arguments: *Number* is the real number to round. *Num_digits* gives the number of digits to which you want to round.

ROUNDDOWN

Purpose: Rounds a number down to the specified number of digits.

Syntax: ROUNDDOWN(*number, num_digits*)

Arguments: *Number* is the real number to round. *Num_digits* gives the number of digits to which you want to round.

ROUNDUP

Purpose: Rounds a number up to the specified number of digits.

Syntax: ROUNDUP(*number, num_digits*)

Arguments: *Number* is the real number to round. *Num_digits* gives the number of digits to which you want to round.

SERIESSUM

Purpose: Calculates the sum of a power series.

Syntax: SERIESSUM(*x, n, m, coefficients*)

Arguments: *X* is the input value. *N* is the initial power to raise, by which you want to raise *x*. *M* is the step by which to increase *n*. *Coefficients* is a set of coefficients for multiplying each successive power of *x*.

SIGN

Purpose: Gets the sign of a number, returning 1 if the number is positive, 0 if the number is 0, and −1 if the number is negative.

Syntax: SIGN(*number*)

Arguments: *Number* is a real number.

SIN

Purpose: Calculates an angle's sine.

Syntax: SIN(*number*)

Arguments: *Number* is an angle measured in radians.

SINH

Purpose: Calculates a number's hyperbolic sine.

Syntax: SINH(*number*)

Arguments: *Number* is a real number.

SQRT

Purpose: Calculates the positive square root of a number.

Syntax: SQRT(*number*)

Arguments: *Number* is any number greater than 0.

SQRTPI

Purpose: Calculates the square root of a number multiplied by Pi.

Syntax: SQRTPI(*number*)

Arguments: *Number* is any number greater than 0.

SUM

Purpose: Adds the numbers listed as its arguments.

Syntax: SUM(*number1, number2, ...*)

Arguments: *Number* is up to 30 numbers you want to add together.

SUMIF

Purpose: Adds the cells that match the criteria specified.

Syntax: SUMIF(*range, criteria, sum_range*)

Arguments: *Range* is a reference to a set of cells that contain the values tested by criteria. *Criteria* is a number, expression, or text string that determines which cells to sum. *Sum_range* is a reference to cells paired with range that are the cells containing the values to be summed.

SUMPRODUCT

Purpose: Multiplies the corresponding cells in two arrays and adds the products calculated.

Syntax: SUMPRODUCT(*array1, array2, array3, ...*)

Arguments: *Array* is from 2 to 30 arrays to include in the operation.

SUMSQ

Purpose: Squares its arguments, then adds the squares.

Syntax: SUMSQ(*number1, number2, ...*)

Arguments: *Number* is up to 30 numbers to include in the operation.

SUMX2MY2

Purpose: Squares the corresponding values in two arrays, determines the difference between the corresponding squared values, and adds the resulting differences.

Syntax: SUMX2MY2(*array_x, array_y*)

Arguments: *Array_x* and *array_y* are two arrays containing the x and y values for the calculation.

SUMX2PY2

Purpose: Squares the corresponding values in two arrays and then sums the squared values.

Syntax: SUMX2PY2(*array_x, array_y*)

Arguments: *Array_x* and *array_y* are two arrays containing the x and y values for the calculation.

SUMXMY2

Purpose: Determines the difference between corresponding values in two arrays, squares the differences, then sums the squared differences.

Syntax: SUMXMY2(*array_x, array_y*)

Arguments: *Array_x* and *array_y* are two arrays containing the x and y values for the calculation.

TAN

Purpose: Calculates the tangent of an angle.

Syntax: TAN(*number*)

Arguments: *Number* is the measure of an angle in radians.

TANH

Purpose: Calculates a number's hyperbolic tangent.

Syntax: TANH(*number*)

Arguments: *Number* is a real number.

TRUNC

Purpose: Truncates a number to an integer according to the precision you specify.

Syntax: TRUNC(*number, num_digits*)

Arguments: *Number* is the number to truncate. *Num_digits* is the precision of truncation. (If *num_digits* is omitted, Excel assumes a value of 0.)

Statistical Functions

Excel's statistical functions enable you to analyze the data you have stored in your spreadsheets. They form Excel's core analytical engine. You can use them to determine trends and make statistical decisions. Examples of their use appear in the example spreadsheet shown in figure 8.4.

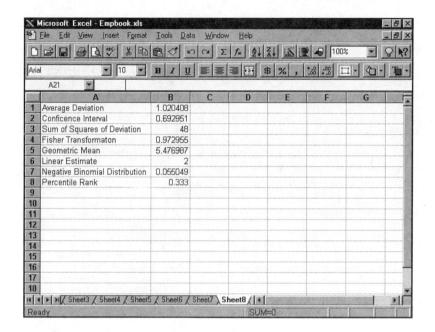

Figure 8.4

A spreadsheet showing the use of statistical functions.

AVEDEV

Purpose: Averages the absolute deviation of data points from the mean.

Syntax: AVEDEV(*number1, number2, ...*)

Arguments: *Number* is up to 30 numbers to include in the operation.

AVERAGE

Purpose: Calculates the arithmetic mean of its arguments.

Syntax: AVERAGE(*number1, number2, ...*)

Arguments: *Number* is up to 30 numbers to include in the operation.

BETADIST

Purpose: Calculates the cumulative beta probability density function. This function is used to study variation in a percentage across samples, as in the percentage of the day Americans spend driving automobiles.

Syntax: BETADIST(*x, alpha, beta, A, B*)

Arguments: *X* is the value at which to evaluate the function and is a value between *A* and *B*. *Alpha* and *beta* are parameters for the distribution. *A* and *B* are optional and represent the lower and upper bounds for the interval of *x*.

BETAINV

Purpose: Calculates the inverse of the cumulative beta probability density function. This distribution often is used to model the probable completion time of a project when you know the expected completion time and variability.

Syntax: BETAINV(*probability, alpha, beta, A, B*)

Arguments: *Probability* is the probability value for the beta distribution. *Alpha* and *beta* are the parameters for the distribution. *A* and *B* are the optional lower and upper bounds for the interval of x, the value that is the result of applying this function.

BINOMDIST

Purpose: Calculates the individual term binomial distribution probability. The binomial distribution is used to study problems consisting of a fixed number of trials with only two possible outcomes. A common example is predicting the outcome of a coin toss.

Syntax: BINOMDIST(*number_s, trials, probability_s, cumulative*)

Arguments: *Number_s* is the number of successes. *Trials* is the number of trials. *Probability_s* is the probability of success in a trial. *Cumulative* is TRUE for calculating the cumulative distribution function, the probability that there are at most *number_s* successes, and FALSE for calculating the probability mass function, the probability that there are *number_s* successes.

CHIDIST

Purpose: Calculates the one-tailed probability of the chi-squared distribution. This distribution is used when comparing observed and expected values in relation to contingency tables.

Syntax: CHIDIST(*x, degrees_freedom*)

Arguments: *X* is the value at which to evaluate the function. *Degrees_freedom* is the degrees of freedom associated with *x*.

CHIINV

Purpose: Calculates the inverse of the one-tailed probability of the chi-squared distribution. This function is used to compare observed results with expected results.

Syntax: CHIINV(*probability, degrees_freedom*)

Arguments: *Probability* is the probability associated with the distribution. *Degrees_freedom* is the degrees of freedom associated with the distribution.

CHITEST

Purpose: Calculates the chi-squared test for independence.

Syntax: CHITEST(*actual_range, expected_range*)

Arguments: *Actual_range* is a reference to the cells containing the observations to test against expected values. *Expected_range* is a reference to the cells containing the expected values.

CONFIDENCE

Purpose: Calculates a confidence interval for a population mean.

Syntax: CONFIDENCE(*alpha, standard_dev, size*)

Arguments: *Alpha* is the significance level. *Standard_dev* is the population standard deviation for the data. *Size* is the sample size.

CORREL

Purpose: Calculates the correlation coefficient for the values stored in two arrays. You use this value to study the relationship between two properties.

Syntax: CORREL(*array1, array2*)

Arguments: *Array1* and *array2* represent the two arrays to be correlated.

COUNT

Purpose: Determines how many numbers are in a list of arguments.

Syntax: COUNT(*value1, value2, ...*)

Arguments: *Value* is a reference to up to 30 spreadsheet regions that can contain any kind of data. Only numbers are counted, however.

COUNTA

Purpose: Determines how many nonblank values are in a list of arguments.

Syntax: COUNTA(*value1, value2, ...*)

Arguments: *Value* is up to 30 references to spreadsheet regions containing information of any type. Only nonblank cells, including cells containing "", are counted.

COVAR

Purpose: Calculates the covariance for data points stored in two arrays. Covariance can be used to study the relationship between two data sets.

Syntax: COVAR(*array1, array2*)

Arguments: *Array1* and *array2* are references to the arrays containing the two data sets.

CRITBINOM

Purpose: Determines the smallest value for which the cumulative binomial distribution is less than or equal to the criterion you set. This value is often used to determine the maximum number of defective products allowed off an assembly line before rejecting the entire lot.

Syntax: CRITBINOM(*trials, probability_s, alpha*)

Arguments: *Trials* is the number of Bernoulli trials. *Probability_s* is the probability of success of a trial. *Alpha* is the criterion.

DEVSQ

Purpose: Calculates the sum of squares of deviation of data points from the mean.

Syntax: DEVSQ(*number1, number2, ...*)

Arguments: *Number* is up to 30 values to include in the calculation.

EXPONDIST

Purpose: Calculates the exponential distribution, used to study problems in which the time between events is of interest.

Syntax: EXPONDIST(*x, lambda, cumulative*)

Arguments: *X* is the value at which to evaluate the function. *Lambda* is the parameter for the distribution. *Cumulative* is TRUE to calculate the cumulative distribution function, and FALSE to calculate the probability density function.

FDIST

Purpose: Calculates the F probability distribution used to study whether different data sets possess different degrees of diversity.

Syntax: FDIST(*x, degrees_freedom1, degrees_freedom2*)

Arguments: *X* is the value at which the function will evaluate. *Degrees_freedom1* is the degrees of freedom for the numerator. *Degrees_freedom2* is the degrees of freedom for the denominator.

FINV

Purpose: Calculates the inverse of the F probability distribution. You can use this function to compare the variation in two data sets.

Syntax: FINV(*probability, degrees_freedom1, degrees_freedom2*)

Arguments: *Probability* is the probability associated with the cumulative distribution. *Degrees_freedom1* is the degrees of freedom for the numerator. *Degrees_freedom2* is the degrees of freedom for the denominator.

FISHER

Purpose: Calculates the Fisher transformation at a given value. This function is used in hypothesis testing regarding the correlation coefficient.

Syntax: FISHER(*x*)

Arguments: *X* is the value for which to calculate the transformation.

FISHERINV

Purpose: Calculates the inverse of the Fisher transformation. This function can be used to analyze the correlations between data sets.

Syntax: FISHERINV(*y*)

Arguments: *Y* is the value for which to calculate the inverse transformation.

FORECAST

Purpose: Calculates predicted values for the x and y terms of a linear regression model. This function is used to predict unknown values, like future sales, in a correlation study.

Syntax: FORECAST(*x, known_y's, known_x's*)

Arguments: *X* is the value for which to predict a y value. *Known_x's* and *known_y's* are references to cells containing known x and y values.

FREQUENCY

Purpose: Calculates a frequency distribution as a vertical array of cells. This function sorts the data values into a set of intervals so you know how many values occur within each interval.

Syntax: FREQUENCY(*data_array, bins_array*)

Arguments: *Data_array* is an array or reference to an array of values within which you wish to count the frequencies. *Bins_array* is an array or reference to an array that contains values defining the intervals over which to count the frequencies. The numbers in *bins_array* represent the endpoints of the frequency intervals. The array {10,20,30} defines intervals of 0–10, 11–20, and 30 to the endpoint of the data.

FTEST

Purpose: Calculates the one-tailed F test, the one-tailed probability that the variances of two arrays of values are not significantly different. You can use this test, for instance, to compare the test scores of students entering public and private universities.

Syntax: FTEST(*array1, array2*)

Arguments: *Array1* and *array2* are references to the two sets of data to be compared.

GAMMADIST

Purpose: Calculates the gamma distribution, used to study variables whose distribution might be skewed, as in queuing analysis.

Syntax: GAMMADIST(*x, alpha, beta, cumulative*)

Arguments: *X* is the value at which to evaluate the distribution. *Alpha* and *beta* are the parameters of the distribution. *Cumulative* is TRUE to calculate the cumulative distribution function, and FALSE to calculate the probability mass function.

GAMMAINV

Purpose: Calculates the inverse of the gamma cumulative distribution, used in studying variables whose distribution might be skewed.

Syntax: GAMMAINV(*probability, alpha, beta*)

Arguments: *Probability* is the probability associated with the distribution. *Alpha* and *beta* are parameters for the distribution.

GAMMALN

Purpose: Calculates the gamma function's natural logarithm.

Syntax: GAMMALN(*x*)

Arguments: *X* is the value for which you want the natural log of the gamma function.

GEOMEAN

Purpose: Calculates the geometric mean of positive data points. This function often is used in calculating issues like growth rates that involve compound interest with variable rates.

Syntax: GEOMEAN(*number1, number2, ...*)

Arguments: *Number* is up to 30 numbers to include in the calculation. You can substitute a single array or reference to an array instead of listing the numbers as arguments.

GROWTH

Purpose: Calculates an exponential curve to fit known data points and calculates predicted y values for x values you supply.

Syntax: GROWTH(*known_y's, known_x's, new_x's, const*)

Arguments: *Known_y's* and *known_x's* are arrays of known values. (*Known_x's* are optional.) *New_x's* are x values for which you want corresponding y values. *Const* is TRUE (or omitted) to calculate the constant b normally, FALSE to force b to equal 1.

HARMEAN

Purpose: Calculates a data set's harmonic mean, the reciprocal of the arithmetic mean of reciprocals.

Syntax: HARMEAN(*number1, number2, ...*)

Arguments: *Number* is up to 30 values to include in the calculation. You can use a reference to an array.

HYPGEOMDIST

Purpose: Calculates the hypergeometric distribution, used to study problems within a finite population, in which observations are either successes or failures, and from which each subset is chosen with equal likelihood.

Syntax: HYPGEOMDIST(*sample_s, number_sample, population_s, number_population*)

Arguments: *Sample_s* is the number of successes appearing in the sample. *Number_sample* is the sample size. *Population_s* is the number of successes appearing in the population. *Number_population* is the size of the population.

INTERCEPT

Purpose: Calculates the y intercept for a regression line.

Syntax: INTERCEPT(*known_y's, known_x's*)

Arguments: *Known_y's* and *known_x's* are sets of data that represent the x and y values defining the regression line.

KURT

Purpose: Calculates the *kurtosis*, the relative peakedness or flatness of the curve describing the data distribution, for a data set.

Syntax: KURT(*number1, number2, ...*)

Arguments: *Number* is up to 30 values to include in the calculation. You can use a reference to an array.

LARGE

Purpose: Gets the *k*th largest value in the data set.

Syntax: LARGE(*array, k*)

Arguments: *Array* is the array of data from which to select the value. *K* is the position from the largest value to return.

LINEST

Purpose: Fits a straight line to describe a data set using the least squares method.

Syntax: LINEST(*known_y's, known_x's, const, stats*)

Arguments: *Known_y's* and *known_x's* are the set of known data points that will define the line. (*Known_x's* is optional.) *Const* is TRUE if the constant b is to be calculated normally, FALSE if b is to be forced to 0. *Stats* is TRUE to return regression statistics, FALSE (or omitted) to return only the m coefficients and the constant b.

LOGEST

Purpose: Fits an exponential curve that best describes a data set.

Syntax: LOGEST(*known_y's, known_x's, const, stats*)

Arguments: *Known_y's* and *known_x's* are the set of known data points that will define the curve. (*Known_x's* is optional.) *Const* is TRUE if the constant b is to be calculated normally, FALSE is b is to be forced to 1. *Stats* is TRUE to return regression statistics, FALSE (or omitted) to return only the m coefficients and the constant b.

LOGINV

Purpose: Calculates the inverse of the lognormal cumulative distribution, used for analyzing logarithmically transformed data.

Syntax: LOGINV(*probability, mean, standard_dev*)

Arguments: *Probability* is the probability associated with the distribution. *Mean* is the mean and *standard_dev* the standard deviation of ln(x).

LOGNORMDIST

Purpose: Calculates the cumulative lognormal distribution for a given value. This function is used to analyze logarithmically transformed data.

Syntax: LOGNORMDIST(*x, mean, standard_dev*)

Arguments: *X* is the value at which the function is to be evaluated. *Mean* is the mean and *standard_dev* is the standard deviation of ln(x).

MAX

Purpose: Gets the maximum value from its argument list.

Syntax: MAX(*number1, number2, ...*)

Arguments: *Number* is up to 30 numbers from which you want to select the maximum value.

MEDIAN

Purpose: Calculates the median for a set of numbers.

Syntax: MEDIAN(*number1, number2, ...*)

Arguments: *Number* is up to 30 numbers to include in the calculation.

MIN

Purpose: Gets the smallest number from the list of arguments.

Syntax: MIN(*number1, number2, ...*)

Arguments: *Number* is up to 30 numbers from which you want to select the minimum value.

MODE

Purpose: Gets the most frequent value in a data set.

Syntax: MODE(*number1, number2, ...*)

Arguments: *Number* is up to 30 numbers for which you want the mode.

NEGBINOMDIST

Purpose: Calculates the negative binomial distribution, the probability that there will be a given number of failures before a given success.

Syntax: NEGBINOMDIST(*number_f, number_s, probability_s*)

Arguments: *Number_f* is the number of failures, *number_s* the threshold number of successes, and *probability_s* the probability of a success.

NORMDIST

Purpose: Calculates the normal cumulative distribution with a given mean and standard deviation.

Syntax: NORMDIST(*x, mean, standard_dev, cumulative*)

Arguments: *X* is the number for which to evaluate the function, *mean* is the mean for the distribution, *standard_dev* is the standard deviation for the distribution. *Cumulative* is TRUE to calculate the cumulative distribution function, FALSE to calculate the probability mass function.

NORMINV

Purpose: Calculates the inverse of the normal cumulative distribution with a given mean and standard deviation.

Syntax: NORMINV(*probability, mean, standard_dev*)

Arguments: *Probability* is the probability associated with the distribution, *mean* the mean for the distribution, and *standard_dev* the standard deviation for the distribution.

NORMSDIST

Purpose: Calculates the standard normal cumulative distribution function, which has a mean of 0 and standard deviation of 1.

Syntax: NORMSDIST(*z*)

Arguments: *Z* is the value for which to calculate the distribution.

NORMSINV

Purpose: Calculates the inverse of the standard normal cumulative distribution.

Syntax: NORMSINV(*probability*)

Arguments: *Probability* is the probability associated with the distribution.

PEARSON

Purpose: Calculates the Pearson product moment correlation coefficient (r) for two data sets.

Syntax: PEARSON(*array1, array2*)

Arguments: *Array1* is the set of independent values, and *array2* the set of dependent values, for the calculation.

PERCENTILE

Purpose: Calculates the k-th percentile for a range of values. This function is often used to calculate thresholds, as when deciding to examine only job candidates who score above the 90th percentile on an evaluation criterion.

Syntax: PERCENTILE(*array, k*)

Arguments: *Array* is the range of data defining relative standing, and *k* is the percentile value desired.

PERCENTRANK

Purpose: Calculates the percentile rank for a given value in a set of data.

Syntax: PERCENTRANK(*array, x, significance*)

Arguments: *Array* is a reference to an array of numeric values defining relative standing. *X* is the value to be ranked. *Significance* is an optional value expressing the number of significant digits to include in the percentage value returned. (Three significant digits are included by default.)

PERMUT

Purpose: Calculates the number of permutations for a set of objects to be selected from a larger set of objects.

Syntax: PERMUT(*number, number_chosen*)

Arguments: *Number* is an integer expressing the number of objects, and *number_chosen* is an integer expressing the number of objects in each permutation.

POISSON

Purpose: Calculates the Poisson distribution, used for predicting the number of events in a fixed period of time.

Syntax: POISSON(*x, mean, cumulative*)

Arguments: *X* is the number of events, *mean* the expected numeric value. *Cumulative* is TRUE to calculate the cumulative probability function, and FALSE to calculate the probability mass function.

PROB

Purpose: Calculates the probability that a set of values are between two limits.

Syntax: PROB(*x_range, prob_range, lower_limit, upper_limit*)

Arguments: *X_range* is the range of values for x with associated probabilities. *Prob_range* is the probabilities associated with *x_range*. *Lower_limit* and *upper_limit* represent the lower and upper bounds of the value for which you calculate the probability.

QUARTILE

Purpose: Calculates the quartiles for a data set.

Syntax: QUARTILE(*array, quart*)

Arguments: *Array* is a reference to the values to be split into quartiles. *Quart* is which quartile to return.

RANK

Purpose: Determines the rank of a number in a given list of numbers.

Syntax: RANK(*number, ref, order*)

Arguments: *Number* is the number to be ranked, *ref* is an array or list of numbers, and *order* is 0 (or omitted) if reference is to be sorted in descending order of a non-zero value or if reference is to be sorted in ascending order.

RSQ

Purpose: Calculates the square of the Pearson product moment correlation coefficient, a value that gives the percentage of the variance in one factor y attributable to the variance in another factor x.

Syntax: RSQ(*known_y's, known_x's*)

Arguments: *Known_y's* and *known_x's* are the set of data points for which you want the squared correlation coefficient.

SKEW

Purpose: Calculates the *skewness*, the degree of asymmetry in a distribution's curve, for a set of data.

Syntax: SKEW(*number1, number2, ...*)

Arguments: *Number* is up to 30 numbers to include in the calculation. You can use a reference to cells.

SLOPE

Purpose: Calculates the slope of a linear regression line.

Syntax: SLOPE(*known_y's, known_x's*)

Arguments: *Known_y's* is an array of dependent data points, and *known_x's* an array of independent data points.

SMALL

Purpose: Gets the k-th smallest value in a set of data.

Syntax: SMALL(*array, k*)

Arguments: *Array* is an array of data from which to select the value. *K* is the position from the smallest value to make the selection.

STANDARDIZE

Purpose: Normalizes a value from a distribution with a given mean and standard deviation, transforming it to a value on a scale with a mean of 0 and a standard deviation of 1.

Syntax: STANDARDIZE(*x, mean, standard_dev*)

Arguments: *X* is the value to normalize, *mean* the mean of the distribution, and *standard_dev* is the distribution's standard deviation.

STDEV

Purpose: Estimates the standard deviation based on a sample.

Syntax: STDEV(*number1,number2,...*)

Arguments: *Number* is up to 30 values to be included in the calculation. You can use a reference to a range of cells.

STDEVP

Purpose: Calculates a standard deviation based on an entire population.

Syntax: STDEVP(*number1,number2,...*)

Arguments: *Number* is up to 30 values to include in the calculation. You can use a reference to cells.

STEYX

Purpose: Calculates the standard error of predicted y values for the x values in a regression problem.

Syntax: STEYX(*known_y's, known_x's*)

Arguments: *Known_y's* and *known_x's* are arrays of dependent and independent data points, respectively.

TDIST

Purpose: Calculates the T distribution, used for hypothesis testing in small data sets.

Syntax: TDIST(*x, degrees_freedom, tails*)

Arguments: *X* is the value for which to evaluate the function, *degrees_freedom* is the number of degrees of freedom, and *tails* is the number of tails (1 or 2).

TINV

Purpose: Calculates the inverse of the T distribution with given degrees of freedom.

Syntax: TINV(*probability, degrees_freedom*)

Arguments: *Probability* is the probability associated with a two-tailed text, and *degrees_freedom* is the number of degrees of freedom.

TREND

Purpose: Calculates values along a linear trend.

Syntax: TREND(*known_y's, known_x's, new_x's, const*)

Arguments: *Known_y's* and *known_x's* are arrays of known values. (*Known_x's* are optional). *New_x's* are x values for which you want corresponding y values. *Const* is TRUE (or omitted) to calculate the constant b normally, and FALSE to force b equal to 0.

TRIMMEAN

Purpose: Calculates the mean of an interior data set. You use this function to exclude spurious outliers from your data analysis.

Syntax: TRIMMEAN(*array, percent*)

Arguments: *Array* is the range of values to use, and *percent* is the fractional number of data points to trim from the data set.

TTEST

Purpose: Calculates the probability value associated with the t-test, which determines whether two samples come from the same or different underlying populations.

Syntax: TTEST(*array1, array2, tails, type*)

Arguments: *Array1* and *array2* are the two data sets. *Tails* is the number of tails in the test (1 or 2). *Type* is the kind of t-test to perform (1=paired, 2=two-sample equal variance, 3=two-sample unequal variance).

VAR

Purpose: Calculates the variance of a sample.

Syntax: VAR(*number1, number2, ...*)

Arguments: *Number* is up to 30 values to be included in the calculation. You can use a reference to cells.

VARP

Purpose: Calculates the variance for an entire population.

Syntax: VARP(*number1, number2, ...*)

Arguments: *Number* is up to 30 values to be included in the calculation. You can use a reference to cells.

WEIBULL

Purpose: Calculates the Weibull distribution, used in reliability analysis.

Syntax: WEIBULL(*x, alpha, beta, cumulative*)

Arguments: *X* is the value at which the function will evaluate, *alpha* and *beta* are parameters for the distribution, and *cumulative* determines the form of the function (TRUE for the cumulative distribution, FALSE for the probability mass function).

ZTEST

Purpose: Calculates the two-tailed probability value associated with the z-test, used to determine whether data was drawn from the same or different populations.

Syntax: ZTEST(*array, x, sigma*)

Arguments: *Array* is the data set to test. *X* is the value to test for the likelihood it was drawn from the population. *Sigma* is the population standard deviation. (If omitted, the sample standard deviation substitutes.)

Look-Up and Reference Functions

The look-up and reference functions provided in Excel enable you to access cells on your worksheet by address, row, and column. You can use these functions to convert row-column addresses to row numbers and column numbers. Using these functions, you easily can navigate your worksheet. Examples of their use appear in the sample worksheet shown in figure 8.5.

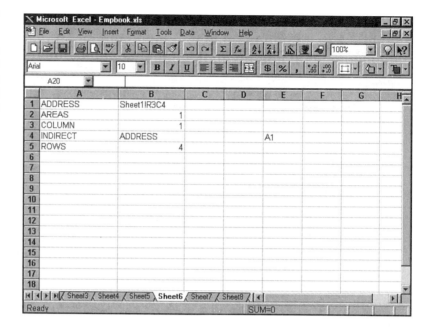

ADDRESS

Purpose: Converts a cell address to text, given specified row and column positions.

Syntax: ADDRESS(*row_num, column_num, abs_num, a1, sheet_text*)

Arguments: *Row_num* is the row number. *Column_num* is the column number. *Abs_num* is 1 (or omitted) for an absolute reference, 2 for an absolute row but relative column reference, 3 for a relative row but absolute column reference, or 4 for a relative reference. *A1* is TRUE (or omitted) for an A1 style reference, or FALSE for an R1C1 style reference. *Sheet_text* is a text string that names the worksheet or macro sheet to be used as external reference. (If omitted, no such name is used.)

AREAS

Purpose: Gets the number of areas, ranges of contiguous cells, or single cells in a given reference.

Syntax: AREAS(*reference*)

Arguments: *Reference* is a cell or a range of cells. You can refer to multiple areas.

CHOOSE

Purpose: Selects a value from the list provided using an index number.

Syntax: CHOOSE(*index_num, value1,value2,...*)

Arguments: *Index_num* is the index number indicating the position in the list to choose. The *values* represent the values in the list. You can include up to 29 values.

COLUMN

Purpose: Gets the column number for the specified reference.

Syntax: COLUMN(*reference*)

Arguments: *Reference* is a cell or a range of cells for which you need a column number.

COLUMNS

Purpose: Gets the number of columns in an array or a reference.

Syntax: COLUMNS(*array*)

Arguments: *Array* is an array, array formula, or range of cells for which you want to count the number of columns used.

HLOOKUP

Purpose: Searches the top row of an array for value and returns the value in the cell indicated.

Syntax: HLOOKUP(*lookup_value, table_array, row_index_num, range_lookup*)

Arguments: *Lookup_value* is the value you are searching for in the first row of the array. *Table_array* is the reference to the table of information. *Row_index_num* is the row number in the table from which you want the data returned. (It serves as the offset from the first row for selecting the cell from which to return information.) *Range_lookup* is TRUE (or omitted) if you want an approximate match or FALSE if you want an exact match.

INDEX

Purpose: Gets the reference to a cell or set of cells, or value of a cell in an array, or an array of values from an array.

Syntax: This function has two forms:

```
INDEX(reference, row_num, column_num, area_num)
INDEX(array, row_num, column_num)
```

The first form returns a reference to a cell or cells. The second form returns the value of a cell or array of cells in an array.

Arguments: *Reference* is a reference to cells in the worksheet. *Array* identifies an array. *Row_num* is the row number, *column_num* is the column number, and *area_num* identifies the area in a reference for use.

INDIRECT

Purpose: Gets the reference of a reference stored in a cell.

Syntax: INDIRECT(*ref_text, a1*)

Arguments: *Ref_text* is a reference to a cell containing a reference. The reference stored in the cell may be expressed in A1 style, R1C1 style, or as a name. *A1* is TRUE (or omitted) if the style of *ref_text* is A1, or FALSE if the style is R1C1.

LOOKUP

Purpose: Looks up and returns values in a vector or array.

Syntax: The function has two forms, the first for vectors, the second for arrays.

```
LOOKUP(lookup_value, lookup_vector, result_vector)
LOOKUP(lookup_value, array)
```

Arguments: *Lookup_value* is the value you search for. *Lookup_vector* is a reference to one row or column, and its values must be in ascending order. *Result_vector* is a reference to a single row or column and must be the same size as *lookup_vector. Array* is a range of cells containing values, which can be text, numbers, or logical values and must be in ascending order. If the function cannot match the specified value, it does an approximate match.

MATCH

Purpose: Gets the relative position of an array element that matches a specified value and in a specified way.

Syntax: MATCH(*lookup_value, lookup_array, match_type*)

Arguments: *Lookup_value* is the value to find. *Lookup_array* is a reference to the array to search. *Match_type* is 1 if you want to match the largest value less than or equal to *lookup_value*, 0 if you want an exactly equal match, or —1 if you want to match the smallest value greater than or equal to *lookup_value*. If *match_type* is 1, the array must be in ascending order. If *match_type* is —1, the array must be in descending order. If *match_type* is 0, the array can be in any order. If you omit *match_type*, Excel assumes a value of 1.

OFFSET

Purpose: Gets a reference of a specified row and column height offset from another reference of a given number of rows and columns.

Syntax: OFFSET(*reference, rows, cols, height, width*)

Arguments: *Reference* is a reference to the region serving as the basis for the offset. *Rows* is the number of rows up (negative) or down (positive) specifying the upper left cell of the new region. *Cols* is the number of columns right (positive) or left (negative) specifying the upper left cell of the new region. *Height* is the number of rows high the new region will be. *Width* is the number of columns wide the new region will be. If you omit either height or width, the height or width for reference is used.

ROW

Purpose: Gets the row number of a reference.

Syntax: ROW(*reference*)

Arguments: *Reference* is a reference to the cell or cells for which you want the row number.

ROWS

Purpose: Gets the number of rows in a reference or array.

Syntax: ROWS(*array*)

Arguments: *Array* is an array, an array formula, or a reference to cells that defines the array.

TRANSPOSE

Purpose: Shifts the vertical and horizontal orientation of an array, returning the array's transpose.

Syntax: TRANSPOSE(*array*)

Arguments: *Array* is a reference to the array that you want to transpose.

VLOOKUP

Purpose: Looks up a value in the far left column of an array, and returns the value of the cell indicated.

Syntax: VLOOKUP(*lookup_value, table_array, col_index_num, range_lookup*)

Arguments: *Lookup_value* is the value to find in the first column. *Table_array* is a reference to the table to be searched. *Col_index_number* is the column number from which the value should be returned. *Range_lookup* is TRUE (or omitted) if you want an approximate match, or FALSE if you want an exact match.

Database Functions

Database and list management functions in Excel enable you to extract information from a database or list and to perform operations on information you have extracted. With these functions, you can access databases you have defined within Excel and databases you maintain with database software external to Excel. If you are working with an external database, you should bring your data in with SQLREQUEST and then manipulate the data using functions that work on databases internal to Excel. All database function examples refer to figure 8.6, which shows a sample database defined by the range A1:E10.

Note When you enter a function into a spreadsheet cell, remember to include an equal sign (=) before the function name.

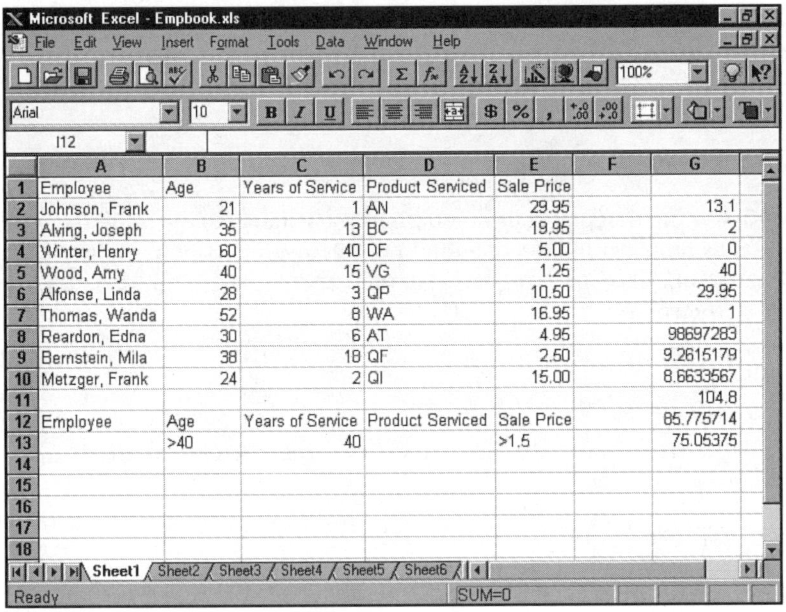
Microsoft Excel - Empbook.xls

	A	B	C	D	E	F	G
1	Employee	Age	Years of Service	Product Serviced	Sale Price		
2	Johnson, Frank	21	1	AN	29.95		13.1
3	Alving, Joseph	35	13	BC	19.95		2
4	Winter, Henry	60	40	DF	5.00		0
5	Wood, Amy	40	15	VG	1.25		40
6	Alfonse, Linda	28	3	QP	10.50		29.95
7	Thomas, Wanda	52	8	WA	16.95		1
8	Reardon, Edna	30	6	AT	4.95		98697283
9	Bernstein, Mila	38	18	QF	2.50		9.2615179
10	Metzger, Frank	24	2	QI	15.00		8.6633567
11							104.8
12	Employee	Age	Years of Service	Product Serviced	Sale Price		85.775714
13		>40	40		>1.5		75.05375
14							
15							
16							
17							
18							

Sheet1 Sheet2 Sheet3 Sheet4 Sheet5 Sheet6 — Ready — SUM=0

Figure 8.6

A sample Excel spreadsheet using database functions.

DAVERAGE

Purpose: Arithmetically averages the database entries you have selected.

Syntax: DAVERAGE(*database, field, criteria*)

Arguments: *Database* is the range of cells that defines the database. *Field* is the named field or range of cells representing the column to average. *Criteria* is the named field or range of cells containing any criteria that define which values of field to include in the average.

DCOUNT

Purpose: Counts the number of cells matching the criteria defined in the last argument that contain numbers.

Syntax: DCOUNT(*database, field, criteria*)

Arguments: *Database* is the range of cells that defines the database. *Field* is the named field or range of cells representing the column in which to count. (The field argument is optional. If it is absent, the count applies to the entire database.) *Criteria* is the named field or range of cells containing any criteria that define which fields containing numbers to include in the count.

DCOUNTA

Purpose: Counts the number of cells matching the criteria defined in the last argument that are not blank.

Syntax: DCOUNTA(*database, field, criteria*)

Arguments: *Database* is the range of cells that defines the database. *Field* is the named field or range of cells representing the column in which to count. *Criteria* is the named field or range of cells containing any criteria that define which nonblank fields to include in the count.

DGET

Purpose: Gets a single value from a database that matches the criteria identified in the third argument.

Syntax: DGET(*database, field, criteria*)

Arguments: *Database* is the range of cells that defines the database. *Field* is the named field or range of cells representing the column from which to extract the value. *Criteria* is the named field or range of cells containing any criteria that define which record to extract. This function returns the #VALUE! error value if no match is found. It returns the #NUM! error value if more than one match is found.

DMAX

Purpose: Gets the largest number in a column of data records.

Syntax: DMAX(*database, field, criteria*)

Arguments: *Database* is the range of cells that defines the database. *Field* is the named field or range of cells representing the column in which to find the maximum value. *Criteria* is the named field or range of cells containing any criteria that define any constraints on the search for a maximum value (such as within all the employees whose name begins with "J" represented in the "Years with Company" column).

DMIN

Purpose: Gets the smallest number in a column of data records.

Syntax: DMIN(*database, field, criteria*)

Arguments: *Database* is the range of cells that defines the database. *Field* is the named field or range of cells representing the column in which to find the minimum value. *Criteria* is the named field or range of cells containing any criteria that define any constraints on the search for a minimum value (such as within all the employees whose name begins with "J" represented in the "Years with Company" column).

DPRODUCT

Purpose: Multiplies (takes the product of) the numbers in the column identified by the field parameter that matches the stated criteria.

Syntax: DPRODUCT(*database, field, criteria*)

Arguments: *Database* is the range of cells that defines the database. *Field* is the named field or range of cells representing the column in which to multiply. *Criteria* is the named field or range of cells containing any criteria that define which fields to include in the product.

DSTDEV

Purpose: Calculates the standard deviation for a sample of cells in the column named in the field parameter. The criteria parameter defines the way in which the sample is selected.

Syntax: DSTDEV(*database, field, criteria*)

Arguments: *Database* is the range of cells that defines the database. *Field* is the named field or range of cells representing the column for which to calculate the standard deviation. *Criteria* is the named field or range of cells containing any criteria that define which fields to include in the calculation.

DSTDEVP

Purpose: Calculates the standard deviation for a sample of cells in the column named in the field parameter as if the cells defined were the entire population. The criteria parameter defines the way in which the sample is selected.

Syntax: DSTDEVP(*database, field, criteria*)

Arguments: *Database* is the range of cells that defines the database. *Field* is the named field or range of cells representing the column for which to calculate the standard deviation. *Criteria* is the named field or range of cells containing any criteria that define which fields to include in the calculation.

DSUM

Purpose: Sums the numbers in the column named by the field parameter that meet the criteria defined in the criteria parameter.

Syntax: DSUM(*database, field, criteria*)

Arguments: *Database* is the range of cells that defines the database. *Field* is the named field or range of cells representing the column of numbers to sum. *Criteria* is the named field or range of cells containing any criteria that define which fields to include in the calculation.

DVAR

Purpose: Estimates the variance for a sample of cells in the column named in the field parameter. The criteria parameter defines the way in which the sample is selected.

Syntax: DVAR(*database, field, criteria*)

Arguments: *Database* is the range of cells that defines the database. *Field* is the named field or range of cells representing the column for which to calculate the variance. *Criteria* is the named field or range of cells containing any criteria that define which fields to include in the calculation.

DVARP

Purpose: Calculates the variance for a sample of cells in the column named in the field parameter as if the cells defined were the entire population. The criteria parameter defines the way in which the sample is selected.

Syntax: DVARP(*database, field, criteria*)

Arguments: *Database* is the range of cells that defines the database. *Field* is the named field or range of cells representing the column for which to calculate the variance. *Criteria* is the named field or range of cells containing any criteria that define which fields to include in the calculation.

SQLREQUEST

Purpose: Uses the Excel add-in XLODBC.XLA to connect to an external database and collect information. The information enters Excel as an array.

Syntax: SQLREQUEST(*connection_string, output_ref, driver_prompt, query_text, column_names_logical*)

Arguments: *Connection_string* supplies information required by the external database in its own format. Sample formats for three databases appear in table 8.6.

TABLE 8.6
Sample Connection Strings for Three Databases

Database	Connection_string
dBASE	DSN=STind;PWD=woof
SQL Server	DSN=Server;UID=fhoulet; PWE=123;Database=Pubs
ORACLE	DNS=My Oracle Data Source;DBQ=MYSER VER; UID=ForrH;PWD=Quack

Output_ref is the cell in your Excel spreadsheet in which you want the completed connection string placed. *Driver_prompt* is a number that defines the way in which the dialog box for the external database driver is displayed. Its values are shown in table 8.7.

TABLE 8.7
Driver_prompt Values

Driver_prompt	Description
1	Dialog box is always displayed.
2	Dialog box is displayed only if there is not enough information in the function parameters to complete the connection to the external database and all options are available.
3	Dialog box is displayed only if there is not enough information in the function parameters to complete the connection to the external database and only necessary options are available.
4	Dialog box is not displayed. If no connection is made, the function returns an error.

Query_text is the text of the actual query statement you are sending to the external database. *Column_names_logical* takes a value of TRUE if you want column names returned as the first row of results and FALSE if you do not. This function returns an array of data if it is successful, and the #N/A error if it is not.

Text Functions

Excel's text functions enable you to manipulate text in your worksheets. You can format text, search for text, substitute text, and perform other such operations outlined for each function. Examples for functions described in this section appear in the example spreadsheet in figure 8.7.

Figure 8.7

An example spreadsheet showing the use of text functions.

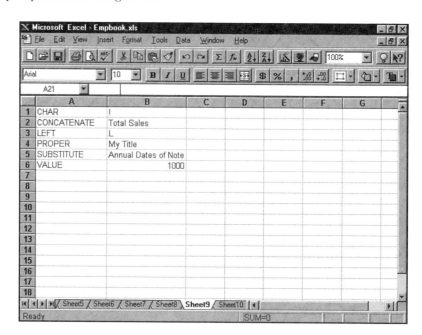

CHAR

Purpose: Gets the character associated with a code number.

Syntax: CHAR(*number*)

Arguments: *Number* is the number that represents the ASCII code for the character you want.

CLEAN

Purpose: Strips nonprintable characters from text.

Syntax: CLEAN(*text*)

Arguments: *Text* is the worksheet information you want to clean of nonprinting characters.

CODE

Purpose: Gets the numeric code associated with the first character in a text string.

Syntax: CODE(*text*)

Arguments: *Text* is the text string for which the function returns the code of the first character.

CONCATENATE

Purpose: Links several text strings into a single text string.

Syntax: CONCATENATE(*text1, text2, ...*)

Arguments: *Text* is up to 30 text strings that you want to concatenate into a single text string. You can use references to cells containing text as arguments.

DOLLAR

Purpose: Converts a number to text in an appropriate currency format.

Syntax: DOLLAR(*number, decimals*)

Arguments: *Number* is a numeric value, a formula that evaluates as a numeric value, or a reference to a cell holding a numeric value. *Decimals* is the number of decimal places to include. (If decimals is omitted, Excel assumes a value of 2.)

EXACT

Purpose: Returns TRUE if the text strings in the argument list are exactly the same.

Syntax: EXACT(*text1, text2*)

Arguments: *Text1* and *text2* are the two text strings to compare.

FIND

Purpose: Searches for a string of text within another string of text. The return value is the position of the first character in the found string. This function is case-sensitive and will not accept wild-card characters.

Syntax: FIND(*find_text, within_text, start_num*)

Arguments: *Find_text* is the text to find. *Within_text* is the text to search in. *Start_num* is the position in the string at which to start the search.

FIXED

Purpose: Rounds a number to the given number of decimal places and converts the number to text with the appropriate use of periods and commas.

Syntax: FIXED(*number, decimals, no_commas*)

Arguments: *Number* is the number to round and convert. *Decimals* is the number of decimal places. *No_commas* is a logical value. If TRUE, no commas appear in the text returned. If FALSE or omitted, the text returned includes commas.

LEFT

Purpose: Returns the far left number of characters specified from a text string.

Syntax: LEFT(*text, num_chars*)

Arguments: *Text* is the text string from which to get characters. *Num_chars* is the number of characters to get. (If omitted, Excel assumes a value of 1 for *num_chars*.)

LEN

Purpose: Gets the number of characters that make up a text string. This function counts spaces as characters.

Syntax: LEN(*text*)

Arguments: *Text* is the text whose length is determined.

LOWER

Purpose: Converts a text string to all lowercase.

Syntax: LOWER(*text*)

Arguments: *Text* is the text to convert.

MID

Purpose: Gets the specified number of characters from a text string, starting at the position you indicate.

Syntax: MID(*text, start_num, num_chars*)

Arguments: *Text* is the string from which to get characters. *Start_num* is the position at which to begin selection. *Num_chars* is the number of characters to get.

PROPER

Purpose: Capitalizes the first letter in a text string, as well as any letters that come after characters that are not letters, like spaces and punctuation marks. All other characters are converted to lowercase. This function can be used to capitalize all words in a title.

Syntax: PROPER(*text*)

Arguments: *Text* is the text to convert.

REPLACE

Purpose: Replaces a given number of characters starting at a given position with a new set of characters.

Syntax: REPLACE(*old_text, start_num, num_chars, new_text*)

Arguments: *Old_text* is the text in which characters are replaced. *Start_num* is the position of the character to be replaced. *Num_chars* is the number of characters to replace. *New_text* is the text that replaces characters in *old_text*.

REPT

Purpose: Repeats a text string a specified number of times. This function can fill a cell with a fixed number of instances of the same text string.

Syntax: REPT(*text, number_times*)

Arguments: *Text* is the text to repeat. *Number_times* is the number of times to repeat.

RIGHT

Purpose: Gets the far right number of characters specified in a text string.

Syntax: RIGHT(*text, num_chars*)

Arguments: *Text* is the text string or reference to a cell containing text from which to get characters. *Num_chars* is the number of characters to get. (If omitted, Excel assumes a value of 1 for *num_chars*.)

SEARCH

Purpose: Gets the number of the character at which the specified text is found, going from left to right, in a text string. This function accepts wild-card characters.

Syntax: SEARCH(*find_text, within_text, start_num*)

Arguments: *Find_text* is the text to find. *Within_text* is the text to search within. *Start_num* is the position within *within_text* at which to start the search.

SUBSTITUTE

Purpose: In a text string, substitutes the new text you specify for the old text you specify.

Syntax: SUBSTITUTE(*text, old_text, new_text, instance_num*)

Arguments: *Text* is the text string or reference to a cell holding text in which to substitute characters. *Old_text* is the text to replace. *New_text* is the text to substitute in place of the *old_text*. Use *instance_num* if you want to specify which occurrence of *old_text* you want to replace with *new_text*. Otherwise, every occurrence of *old_text* in *text* is changed to *new_text*.

T

Purpose: Gets the text referred to by a value. (Generally, you do not need to use this function because Excel automatically performs this action for you.)

Syntax: T(*value*)

Arguments: *Value* is the value to test. Value can be a reference to a cell, a text string, or any other value. If value refers to text, the text is returned. Otherwise "" is returned.

TEXT

Purpose: Converts a numeric value to text in the numeric format you specify.

Syntax: TEXT(*value, format_text*)

Arguments: *Value* is a number, a formula that evaluates a number, or a reference to a cell containing a number. *Format_text* is the number format in text form that you want to use.

TRIM

Purpose: Standardizes the spacing in a text string by removing all spaces but the single spaces between words.

Syntax: TRIM(*text*)

Arguments: *Text* is the text string or reference to a cell holding text from which you want the spaces removed.

UPPER

Purpose: Converts a text string to uppercase.

Syntax: UPPER(*text*)

Arguments: *Text* is the string or reference to a cell holding text that you want to convert.

VALUE

Purpose: Converts the text to number.

Syntax: VALUE(*text*)

Arguments: *Text* is the text string or reference to a cell holding text that you want to convert.

Logical Functions

Excel's logical functions enable you to make decisions about information in various cells on your worksheets. You can check to see whether certain conditions are true. If they are, you can take appropriate action with another function. The logical functions enable you to take complex actions using Excel's simple functions.

In many uses of logical functions, you will need to build logical expressions—several types of logical expressions can be evaluated. Comparisons are a common form and can be numeric, text, and date expressions using <, >, =, <=, >=. Nonzero numbers are evaluated to TRUE, zero returns FALSE. The text values of "true" or "false" are converted to their corresponding values of TRUE or FALSE—any other text value results in the #VALUE! error. Examples of their use appear in the sample worksheet shown in figure 8.8.

Figure 8.8

*A sample
spreadsheet
showing the use
of logical
functions.*

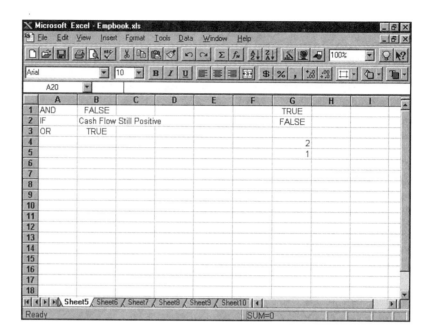

AND

Purpose: Evaluates to TRUE if all the arguments are TRUE, FALSE if one or more arguments are FALSE.

Syntax: AND(*logical1, logical2,...*)

Arguments: Each *logical* represents a condition that can evaluate to TRUE or FALSE. You can include up to 30 conditions.

FALSE

Purpose: Returns the value FALSE.

Syntax: FALSE()

Arguments: None. You may even omit the parentheses with this function, and Excel will interpret it as the FALSE condition.

IF

Purpose: Returns a value if the logical test evaluates as TRUE and some other value if the test evaluates as FALSE.

Syntax: IF (*logical_test, value_if_true, value_if_false*)

Arguments: *Logical_test* is an expression or value that can evaluate to TRUE or FALSE. *Value_if_true* is the value returned if *logical_test* evaluates to TRUE. *Value_if_false* is the value returned if *logical_test* evaluates to FALSE.

NOT

Purpose: Converts the value of the argument to its reverse.

Syntax: NOT (*logical*)

Arguments: Logical is any value or expression that can evaluate to TRUE or FALSE.

OR

Purpose: Returns a value of TRUE if any argument evaluates to TRUE, and a value of FALSE if all arguments evaluate to FALSE.

Syntax: OR (*logical1, logical2, ...*)

Arguments: Each *logical* is a condition that can evaluate to TRUE or FALSE. You can include up to 30 logicals.

TRUE

Purpose: Returns the value TRUE.

Syntax: TRUE ()

Arguments: None. Similar to the FALSE function; you may omit the parentheses and Excel will interpret it as the TRUE condition.

Information Functions

Excel's information functions enable you to collect information about the cells on your worksheets. You can determine the nature of information stored in any cell. You also can collect information about error types. Relevant examples of using these functions are shown in the sample spreadsheet in figure 8.9.

Figure 8.9

A sample spreadsheet showing the use of information functions.

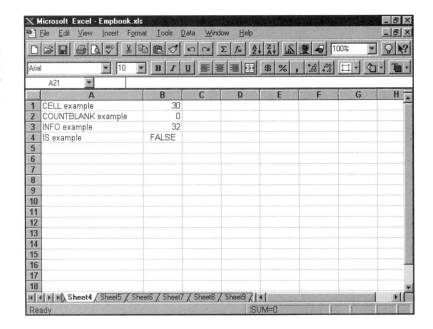

CELL

Purpose: Gets information regarding formatting, location, or contents for the upper left cell in a reference.

Syntax: CELL(*info_type, reference*)

Arguments: *Info_type* is a text string that identifies the type of information requested. Appropriate text strings are shown in table 8.8.

TABLE 8.8
Text Strings for Info_type

Info_type	Returns
"address"	First cell's reference.
"col"	First cell's column number.
"color"	1 if the cell is formatted in color; 0 if not.
"contents"	Upper left cell's contents.

Info_type	Returns
"filename"	File name containing the reference ("" if the worksheet has not been saved).
"format"	Text expressing the number format of the cell. "–" appended if cell is in color. "()" appended if parentheses for positive values or all values.
"parentheses"	1 if the cell uses parentheses for either positive or all values; 0 if not.
"prefix"	Text expressing the label prefix of the cell: "'" if text is left-aligned. """ if the text is right-aligned, "^" if text is centered, "\" if text is fill-aligned, "" if the cell contains anything else.
"protect"	0 if cell is unlocked, and 1 if cell is locked.
"row"	Row number for the first cell.
"type"	Text expressing the type of data in the cell: "b" if the cell is empty, "l" if the cell contains text, "v" if the cell contains anything else.
"width"	Cell's column width rounded to the nearest integer. Units of column width equal one character in the current font.

When info_type is "format," this function returns one of the codes shown in table 8.9.

TABLE 8.9
Return Codes for Info_type "Format"

Format	Code Returned
General	"G"
0	"F0"
#,##0	",0"
0.00	"F2"
#,##0.00	",2"
$#,##0_);($#,##0)	"C0'

continues

TABLE 8.9, CONTINUED
Return Codes for Info_type "Format"

Format	Code Returned
$#,##0_);[Red]($#,##0)	"C0–"
$#,##0.00_);($#,##0.00)	"C2"
$#,##0.00_);[Red]($#,##0.00)	"C2–"
0%	"P0"
0.00%	"P2"
0.00E+00	"S2"
# ?/? or # ??/??	"G"
m/d/yy or m/d/yy h:mm or mm/dd/yy.	"D4"
d—mmm—yy or dd—mmm—yy	"D1"
d—mmm or dd—mmm	"D2"
mmm—yy	"D3"
mm/dd	"D5"
h:mm AM/PM	"D7"
h:mm:ss AM/PM	"D6"
h:mm	"D9"
h:mm:ss	"D8"

Reference is the reference for any cell in the worksheet.

COUNTBLANK

Purpose: Gets the number of blank cells in a range.

Syntax: COUNTBLANK(*range*)

Arguments: *Range* is the range of cells in which you want to count the blank cells.

ERROR.TYPE

Purpose: Gets a number that corresponds to an Excel error value.

Syntax: ERROR.TYPE(*error_val*)

Arguments: *Error_val* is the error value whose number you want to have. Numbers associated with error values are shown in table 8.10.

TABLE 8.10
Error Values and Associated Error Numbers

Error Value	Error Number Returned
#NULL!	1
#DIV/0!	2
#VALUE!	3
#REF!	4
#NAME?	5
#NUM!	6
#N/A	7
Other values	#N/A

INFO

Purpose: Gets information about the current operating environment.

Syntax: INFO(*type_text*)

Arguments: *Type_text* is a text string that determines what information is collected. Valid values for *type_text* appear in table 8.11.

TABLE 8.11
Values for Type_text

Type_text	Value Returned
"directory"	Current directory or folder path.
"memavail"	Memory available, expressed in bytes.
"memused"	Memory used to store data.
"numfile"	Number of worksheets loaded.
"origin"	Absolute A1-style reference, as text, prepended with "$A:" for Lotus 1-2-3 release 3.x compatibility. Returns the cell reference of the top left cell visible in the window based on the current scrolling position.
"osversion"	Operating system version.
"recalc"	Recalculation mode that is current, either "Automatic" or "Manual".
"release"	Text expressing Excel version.
"system"	Operating environment, either "mac" for Macintosh or "pcdos" for Windows.
"totmem"	Memory available for use, including memory currently in use, expressed in bytes.

ISBLANK, ISERR, ISERROR, ISEVEN, ISLOGICAL, ISNA, ISNONTEXT, ISNUMBER, ISODD, ISREF, ISTEXT

Purpose: These nine functions test the type of a value or reference. They return TRUE if the value is of the type being tested for, and FALSE if not.

Syntax:

```
ISBLANK(value)
ISERR(value)
ISERROR(value)
ISLOGICAL(value)
ISNA(value)
ISNONTEXT(value)
ISNUMBER(value)
ISREF(value)
ISTEXT(value)
```

Arguments: *Value* is the value to be tested. These functions perform the tests indicated in table 8.12.

TABLE 8.12
Tests Performed by the Nine IS Functions

Function	TRUE If:
ISBLANK	The cell is empty.
ISERR	Refers to an error code except #N/A.
ISERROR	Refers to any error value, including #N/A.
ISLOGICAL	Is a logical value.
ISNA	Is the #N/A error code.
ISNONTEXT	Is any value, including a blank cell, that is not text.
ISNUMBER	Is a number.
ISREF	Is a reference.
ISTEXT	Is text.

N

Purpose: Converts a value to a number.

Syntax: N(*value*)

Arguments: *Value* is the value to convert. A number is, of course, converted to that number. Dates are converted to serial date numbers. TRUE is converted to 1. All other values are converted to 0.

NA

Purpose: Returns the "no value is available" (#N/A) error value.

Syntax: NA()

Arguments: None.

TYPE

Purpose: Gets the type of a value.

Syntax: TYPE(*value*)

Arguments: *Value* is the value whose type you want to know. TYPE returns the values shown in table 8.13.

TABLE 8.13
Return Types for the TYPE Function

Type	Return Code
Number	1
Text	2
Logical value	4
Formula	8
Error value	16
Array	64

Engineering Functions

Excel's engineering functions enable engineers to include specialized calculations and conversions in their worksheets. To use these functions, however, you must have installed the Analysis ToolPak Add-in.

BESSELI, BESSELJ, BESSELK, BESSELY

Purpose: These four functions return the values of different forms of the Bessel function. BESSELI returns the modified Bessel function In(x), BESSELJ the Bessel function Jn(x), BESSELK the modified Bessel function Kn(x), and BESSELY the Bessel function Yn(x).

Syntax: BESSELI(x,n), BESSELJ(x,n), BESSELK(x,n), or BESSELY(x,n)

Arguments: *X* represents the value at which the function evaluates. *N* is the function's order.

BIN2DEC, BIN2HEX, BIN2OCT

Purpose: These three functions convert binary numbers to other bases. BIN2DEC converts from binary to decimal, BIN2HEX from binary to hexadecimal, and BIN2OCT from binary to octal.

Syntax: BIN2DEC(*number*), BIN2HEX(*number, places*), or BIN2OCT(*number, places*)

Arguments: *Number* is the binary number for conversion. *Places* is the number of characters to use in the conversion. (If omitted, Excel uses the minimum number of characters necessary. If you specify extra characters, Excel pads with leading zeros.)

COMPLEX

Purpose: Combines real and imaginary coefficients and converts them to a complex number.

Syntax: COMPLEX(*real_num, i_num, suffix*)

Arguments: *Real_num* is the real coefficient, *i_num* is the imaginary coefficient, and *suffix* is the suffix to be used to identify the imaginary component of the converted complex number. (If *suffix* is omitted as an argument, the suffix "i" is used.)

CONVERT

Purpose: Converts numbers among several units of measurement.

Syntax: CONVERT(*number, from_unit, to_unit*)

Arguments: *Number* is the number to be converted from one unit to another. It is a value expressed in *from_units*. *From_unit* is a text string denoting the measurement system to convert from. *To_unit* is a text string denoting the measurement system to which you want to convert. Table 8.14 shows the text strings you can use in CONVERT.

TABLE 8.14
Text Strings for Use as From_unit or To_unit

Unit	Text String
Angstrom	"ang"
Atmosphere	"atm"
BTU	"BTU"
Cup	"cup"
Day	"day"
Degree Celsius	"C"
Degree Fahrenheit	"F"
Degree Kelvin	"K"
Dyne	"dyn"
Electron volt	"eV"
Erg	"e"
Fluid ounce	"oz"
Foot	"ft"
Foot-pound	"flb"
Gallon	"gal"
Gauss	"ga"
Gram	"g"
Horsepower	"HP"
Horsepower-hour	"HPh"
Hour	"hr"
Inch	"in"

Unit	Text String
IT calorie	"cal"
Joule	"J"
Liter	"l"
Meter	"m"
Minute	"mn"
mm of Mercury	"mmHg"
Nautical mile	"Nmi"
Newton	"N"
Ounce mass (avoirdupois)	"ozm"
Pascal	"Pa"
Pica (1/72 in.)	"Pica"
Pint	"pt"
Pound force	"lbf"
Pound mass (avoirdupois)	"lbm"
Quart	"qt"
Second	"sec"
Slug	"sg"
Statute mile	"mi"
Tablespoon	"tbs"
Teaspoon	"tsp"
Tesla	"T"
Thermodynamic calorie	"c"

continues

TABLE 8.14, CONTINUED
Text Strings for Use as From_unit or To_unit

Unit	Text String
U (atomic mass unit)	"u"
Watt	"W"
Watt-hour	"Wh"
Yard	"yd"
Year	"yr"

Table 8.15 shows the set of prefixes that can be added to the text strings for metric measurements.

TABLE 8.15
Prefixes for Use with Metric Measurements

Common Metric Prefix	Multiplier for Measurement Unit	Text String Prefix to Add in CONVERT
atto	1E-18	"a"
centi	1E-02	"c"
deci	1E-01	"d"
dekao	1E+01	"e"
exa	1E+18	"E"
femto	1E-15	"f"
giga	1E+09	"G"
hecto	1E+02	"h"
kilo	1E+03	"k"
mega	1E+06	"M"
micro	1E-06	"u"

Common Metric Prefix	Multiplier for Measurement Unit	Text String Prefix to Add in CONVERT
milli	1E-03	"m"
nano	1E-09	"n"
peta	1E+15	"P"
pico	1E-12	"p"
tera	1E+12	"T"

If a conversion is not possible for some reason, the function returns the #N/A error value.

DEC2BIN, DEC2HEX, DEC2OCT

Purpose: These three functions convert decimal numbers to other bases. DEC2BIN converts from decimal to binary, DEC2HEX from decimal to hexadecimal, and DEC2OCT from decimal to octal.

Syntax: DEC2BIN(*number, places*), DEC2HEX(*number, places*), or DEC2OCT(*number, places*)

Arguments: *Number* is the decimal number for conversion. *Places* is the number of characters to use in the conversion. (If omitted, Excel uses the minimum number of characters necessary. If you specify extra characters, Excel pads with leading zeros.)

DELTA

Purpose: Verifies that two numbers are equal, returning a value of 1 if so and 0 if not.

Syntax: DELTA(*number1, number2*)

Arguments: *Number1* and *number2* are the two numbers whose equality are verified.

ERF

Purpose: Integrates the error function between the specified lower and upper limits.

Syntax: ERF(*lower_limit, upper_limit*)

Arguments: The two arguments are the lower and upper limits for integration. If *upper_limit* is omitted, the function integrates between *lower_limit* and 0.

ERFC

Purpose: Evaluates the complementary ERF function between the value specified and 0.

Syntax: ERFC(*x*)

Arguments: *X* is the lower bound for the ERF function involved in the calculation.

GESTEP

Purpose: Determines whether a number is greater than the specified threshold value. This function returns the value 1 if number>=step, and 0 otherwise.

Syntax: GESTEP(*number, step*)

Arguments: *Number* is the number to be tested. *Step* is the threshold value. If *step* is omitted, the threshold of 0 is used.

HEX2BIN, HEX2DEC, HEX2OCT

Purpose: These three functions convert hexadecimal numbers to other bases. HEX2BIN converts from hexadecimal to binary, HEX2DEC from hexadecimal to decimal, and HEX2OCT from hexadecimal to octal.

Syntax: HEX2BIN(*number, places*), HEX2DEC(*number*), or HEX2OCT(*number, places*)

Arguments: *Number* is the hexadecimal number for conversion. *Places* is the number of characters to use in the conversion. (If omitted, Excel uses the minimum number of characters necessary. If you specify extra characters, Excel pads with leading zeros.)

IMABS

Purpose: Gives the absolute value in modulus form of a complex number.

Syntax: IMABS(*inumber*)

Arguments: *Inumber* is that complex number in x+yi or x+yj format for which you want the absolute value.

IMAGINARY

Purpose: Gives the imaginary coefficient of a complex number.

Syntax: IMAGINARY(*inumber*)

Arguments: *Inumber* is a complex number in x+yi or x+ji form for which you want the imaginary coefficient.

IMARGUMENT

Purpose: Calculates the argument of a complex number and returns it as an angle measured in radians.

Syntax: IMARGUMENT(*inumber*)

Arguments: *Inumber* is the complex number whose argument you want.

IMCONJUGATE

Purpose: Calculates and returns the complex conjugate of a complex number.

Syntax: IMCONJUGATE(*inumber*)

Arguments: *Inumber* is the complex number in x+yi or x+yj form for which you want the conjugate.

IMCOS

Purpose: Calculates and returns the cosine of a complex number.

Syntax: IMCOS(*inumber*)

Arguments: *Inumber* is the complex number in x+yi or x+yj form for which you want the cosine. *Inumber* is in text format.

IMDIV

Purpose: Divides two complex numbers in text format and returns the quotient.

Syntax: IMDIV(*number1, number2*)

Arguments: *Number1* and *number2* are complex numbers in x+yi or x+yj form. *Number1* is the numerator or dividend. *Number2* is the denominator or divisor.

IMEXP

Purpose: Calculates and returns the exponential for a complex number.

Syntax: IMEXP(*inumber*)

Arguments: *Inumber* is the complex number in x+yi or x+yj form for which you want the exponential.

IMLN

Purpose: Calculates and returns the natural logarithm for a complex number.

Syntax: IMLN(*inumber*)

Arguments: *Inumber* is the complex number in x+yi or x+yj form for which you want the natural logarithm.

IMLOG10

Purpose: Calculates and returns the common logarithm (base 10) for a complex number.

Syntax: IMLOG10(*inumber*)

Arguments: *Inumber* is the complex number in x+yi or x+yj form for which you want the common logarithm.

IMLOG2

Purpose: Calculates and returns the base-2 logarithm for a complex number.

Syntax: IMLOG2(*inumber*)

Arguments: *Inumber* is the complex number in x+yi or x+yj form for which you want the base-2 logarithm.

IMPOWER

Purpose: Calculates a complex number raised to an integer power.

Syntax: IMPOWER(*inumber*, power)

Arguments: *Inumber* is the complex number in x+yi or x+yj form that you want to raise to an integer power. Power is the integer.

IMPRODUCT

Purpose: Calculates the product of 2 to 29 complex numbers.

Syntax: IMPRODUCT(*inumber1, inumber2, ..., inumber29*)

Arguments: *Inumber1* and so on are the complex numbers in x+yi or x+yj form that you want to multiply together.

IMREAL

Purpose: Returns the real coefficient for the complex number specified.

Syntax: IMREAL(*inumber*)

Arguments: *Inumber* is the complex number in x+yi or x+yj form for which you want the real coefficient.

IMSIN

Purpose: Calculates the sine of a complex number.

Syntax: IMSIN(*inumber*)

Arguments: *Inumber* is the complex number in x+yi or x+yj form for which you want the sine.

IMSQRT

Purpose: Calculates the square root of a complex number.

Syntax: IMSQRT(*inumber*)

Arguments: *Inumber* is the complex number in x+yi or x+yj form for which you want the square root.

IMSUB

Purpose: Subtracts one complex number from another.

Syntax: IMSUB(*inumber1, inumber2*)

Arguments: *Inumber1* and *inumber2* are the complex numbers in x+yi or x+yj form that you want to subtract. *Inumber2* is subtracted from *inumber1*.

IMSUM

Purpose: Calculates the sum of from 2 to 29 complex numbers.

Syntax: IMSUM(*inumber1, inumber2, ..., inumber29*)

Arguments: *Inumber1* and so on are the complex numbers in x+yi or x+yj form that you want to add together.

OCT2BIN, OCT2DEC, OCT2HEX

Purpose: These three functions convert octal numbers to other bases. OCT2BIN converts from octal to binary, OCT2DEC from octal to decimal, and OCT2HEX from octal to hexa-decimal.

Syntax: OCT2BIN(*number, places*), OCT2DEC(*number*), or *OCT2HEX(number, places)*

Arguments: *Number* is the octal number for conversion. *Places* is the number of characters to use in the conversion. (If omitted, Excel uses the minimum number of characters necessary. If you specify extra characters, Excel pads with leading zeros.)

SQRTPI

Purpose: Calculates the square root of a the expression (number*pi).

Syntax: SQRTPI(*number*)

Arguments: *Number* is the number to be multiplied by pi before the square root is taken.

DDE and External Functions

Excel's external functions enable you to call routines in *dynamic link libraries* (DLLs), which are files of executable functions external to Excel. Using this feature, you can execute code that belongs to other applications or that you have programmed yourself and stored in a dynamic link library. External routines are the ultimate in customization. You can make Excel do anything you want it to, as long as you can program the function that will execute the activity. The catch is that you have to have a fairly sophisticated knowledge of Windows programming to create a DLL.

CALL

Purpose: Calls a function in a dynamic link library or other type of code resource.

Syntax: CALL(*register_id, argument1, ...*) or CALL(*module_text, procedure, type_text, argument1, ...*)

Arguments: Use the first form of the function to call a DLL or code resource previously registered using the REGISTER.ID function. Use the second form to simultaneously register and call a DLL or code resource.

In the first form, *register_id* is a value returned from a call of the REGISTER.ID function. *Argument1* and subsequent arguments are the arguments to be passed to the function called.

In the second form, *module_text* is a text string enclosed in quotes identifying the name of the DLL or other code resource. *Procedure* is a text string specifying the name of the function you are calling. *Type_text* is a text string specifying the name of the Windows data type returned by the function. (See the Excel Development Kit documentation and the Windows Software Development Kit documentation for more information about Windows data types.) *Argument1* and subsequent arguments are the arguments passed to the function.

REGISTER.ID

Purpose: Collects the register ID of a function in a dynamic link library. The register ID is a unique number that identifies the function to Excel.

Syntax: REGISTER.ID(*module_text, procedure, type_text*)

Arguments: *Module_text* is a text string that gives the name of the DLL or other code resource containing the function. *Procedure* is a text string that specifies the name of the function. *Type_text* is a text string specifying the name of the Windows data type returned by the function. (See the Excel Development Kit documentation and the Windows Software Development Kit documentation for more information about Windows data types.) If the function has already been registered somewhere else on a worksheet, you can omit *type_text.*

Chapter Snapshot

In this chapter, you learn about using the Analysis ToolPak provided with Excel. This bonus package of software applications enables the user to apply statistical analysis in an easy-to-use fashion. Statistics have always been frightening for most people, but after you complete this chapter and work a few of the examples—and some of your own—you'll work numbers like a pro. This chapter leads you through the following:

- ◆ Installing the Analysis ToolPak

- ◆ Understanding the analysis tools

- ◆ Using business tools

- ◆ Using engineering tools

- ◆ Using statistical tools

The examples given in this chapter should help you get started. Feel free to use and experiment with them as you want. If you can't quite master a tool or two right away, don't worry. Find some that you want to work with, and after you have mastered those, you can go back and try one of the others. The more you use these tools, the easier it becomes, and you will soon wonder how you ever managed without them!

New Riders Publishing

INSIDE
SERIES

C H A P T E R

9

Mastering Excel
Analytical Tools

Excel, along with the Analysis ToolPak, can rival—and even rise above—other software packages that are designed solely as statistical analysis packages. Using the data analysis tools in the Analysis ToolPak, you easily can perform simple or complex statistics with any amount of data. The results of the analysis then can be used as the basis of further calculations, graphed in a variety of ways, or both. Excel's robust features add an extra dimension to statistical analysis by enabling you to merge statistics into spreadsheet calculations or database operations. You can organize your data in separate workbooks or on separate worksheets of the same workbook, and still have access to it all from the data analysis tools in the Analysis ToolPak.

Installing the Analysis ToolPak

If the Data Analysis entry already appears in your **T**ools menu, skip this section—the Analysis ToolPak has already been installed in your copy of Excel. If not, use the steps that follow to install the Analysis ToolPak.

 Note Be sure to close Excel before you run Setup. If you do not, Setup first asks you to close Excel. You might as well save time by doing it now.

Installing the Analysis ToolPak Add-In

To install the Analysis ToolPak, follow these steps:

1. In the Windows File Manager, change to your Excel directory, then double-click on SETUP.EXE to run the Microsoft Excel Setup program. You also can run SETUP.EXE from the Control menu's Run command.

2. Click on the **A**dd/Remove button. A series of check boxes for the available options appear.

 Stop The items currently installed are already checked; do not uncheck those items unless you are sure you want to remove them from your system.

3. Double-click anywhere on the word Add-ins or its check box. The Microsoft Excel–Add-ins dialog box appears, showing a list of add-ins with check boxes.

4. If not already checked, click on Analysis ToolPak to select it, then click on OK and proceed with the rest of the Excel Setup, inserting the appropriate disk(s) as prompted.

 Note If Analysis ToolPak is already checked, the Analysis ToolPak is already present in your system. You can exit Setup (click on Cancel) and go on to the next section.

Adding the Analysis ToolPak to an Excel Menu

After you install the add-in tools, you must let Excel know they now are available. Use the following steps:

1. Select the **T**ools menu, then select Add-ins. After a moment, the Add-ins dialog box appears, displaying all the available add-ins, as shown in figure 9.1.

2. Click on the Analysis ToolPak check box and select OK. Click on OK in the Adding Analysis .XLL dialog box. Data Analysis then appears in the Tools menu.

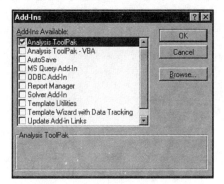

Figure 9.1

The available add-ins.

Understanding the Analysis Tools

For clarity, this discussion is split into three tool types: business tools, engineering tools, and pure statistical tools. Although all these tools are statistical in nature, they are grouped into their most commonly used fields. Their uses, however, are not restricted to any one field. Histograms, for example, are discussed in the "Business Tools" section, but also are used by engineers and statisticians.

Each section explains the use of a particular tool and provides an example of each. Many sections in this chapter contain an introductory paragraph that assumes little or no prior knowledge of statistics. These paragraphs are not intended as complete discussions of each statistical operator, but rather, are simple explanations to bridge the gap for the uninitiated into a more full explanation of each statistical tool in the ToolPak. Tools that require more prior knowledge of statistical terms than an introductory paragraph can dutifully perform do not include such a paragraph.

To use any tool in the ToolPak, select Data Analysis from the Tools menu. The Data Analysis dialog box appears, as shown in figure 9.2. Scroll through the list until you find the tool you want to use, and either double-click on it or click on it and then choose OK. You also can use the up- or down-arrow keys to scroll through the list.

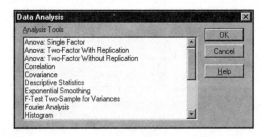

Figure 9.2

The Data Analysis dialog box.

Using Business Tools

The tools discussed in this section are statistical tools used more often in business applications than anywhere else. They include the following:

◆ Correlation

◆ Covariance

◆ Exponential Smoothing

◆ Histogram

◆ Moving Average

◆ Random Number

◆ Rank and Percentile

These tools are not only used in business applications. Generally, the tools explained in this section are the most basic and easiest to use of the statistical tools in the Analysis ToolPak. It pays to know what each one of them does, regardless of how you might plan to use them.

Most of the dialog boxes for the tools in this section have some common features, including the following:

◆ **Input Range.** In the Input Range field, enter the range of cells in a spreadsheet where the source data resides. You can enter the range in A1 or R1C1 format—depending on Excel's setting—and you can include external references.

◆ **Grouped By.** If the source data is oriented in columns, select the Grouped By Column option button. For data that is oriented in row(s), select the Grouped by Rows option button.

◆ **Labels in First Row.** If the Input Range includes labels for each column in the first row of the range, check Labels in First Row to indicate that the row does not contain data. If you have labels in the first row of data, but did not select this box, Excel assumes that the first row contains data that it can use, and Excel tries to compute the first row with the rest of the data. This mistake can either throw off your result, or generate an error message.

◆ **Output Range.** The result of the tool appears in the cell location that you indicate in the Output Range. Single-cell reference can be used for an output range, to indicate the upper left corner of the resultant data; Excel automatically expands the range to include as many cells as necessary.

◆ **New Worksheet Ply.** Selecting this option enables you to send the tool's results to a new worksheet in the same workbook. To do this, you need to check the box and supply Excel with a name for the new sheet.

◆ **New Workbook.** If you want to send the tool's results to an entirely new workbook, check this box.

Correlations

A *correlation* can indicate whether a particular set of data might be related by cause-and-effect to another set of data. The Correlation tool checks each data point against its corresponding data point in the other data set (see fig. 9.3). It returns a positive number if both sets of numbers move in the same direction (positive or negative) throughout the data. Likewise, it returns a negative number if the sets of numbers move in opposite directions (positive or negative). The more closely the sets of values move together, the higher the correlation value. A correlation value of 1 indicates that the values move exactly together, and a value of –1 indicates that they move exactly opposite.

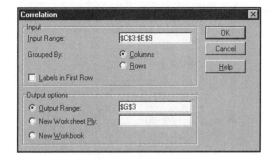

Figure 9.3

The Correlation dialog box.

If more than two sets of data are given, correlation values are returned for each set of data to every other set of data. The data to be analyzed must be located in adjacent rows or columns.

The example in figure 9.4 shows three columns from which correlations are drawn: column 1 is Average Temp, Column 2 is Sales of Ice Cream, and Column 3 is Sales of Donuts. You can see that a high correlation exists between Average Temp and Sales of Ice Cream, and very little for donut sales.

Figure 9.4

*An example of
correlation and
covariance.*

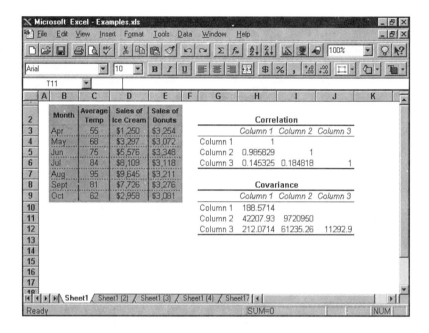

Covariances

Covariance is much like correlation, except covariances aren't restricted to numbers between –1 and +1. Thus, results from covariance can be misleading if different units or widely different data set values are compared. You might want to use covariance under special circumstances, such as when dealing with sets of closely similar data or for more in-depth statistical analysis, but correlation is useful far more often.

In the example, you can see how covariance can be misleading. The covariance of Column 1 (Average Temp) to Column 2 (Sales of Ice Cream) is 36178, but the covariance of Column 2 to Column 3 (Sales of Donuts) is 52487, or greater than that of Column 1 to 2. This fact suggests that the sales of ice cream and sales of donuts are closely related, but a look at the correlations for these columns tells you that they are not related. The correlation values are, in this case, the correct numbers—as the temperature goes up, so do ice cream sales.

Covariances can be useful in comparing, for example, two years of sales data for ice cream. The data in this case would be about the same, but would more closely show relationships because of the larger resulting numbers. For in-depth statistical analysis, the covariance results can be more useful when using them in succeeding calculations because they have not been "normalized" to 1.

You use the Covariance dialog box, shown in figure 9.5, in much the same way you use the Correlation dialog box. The results of both the correlation and covariance examples are shown in figure 9.5 to better show the relationship between the two tools.

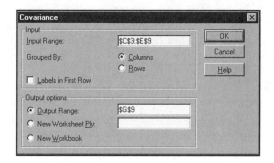

Figure 9.5

The Covariance dialog box.

Exponential Smoothing

Exponential smoothing is most commonly used to forecast trends—a forecast is generated that shows the current trend of existing data. You then can tailor a forecast using a "Damping Factor" to smooth out random variations in the data or to detect trends in the data that are delayed from their stimulus (see fig. 9.6).

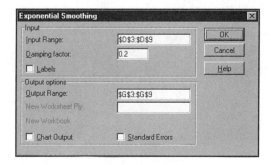

Figure 9.6

The Exponential Smoothing dialog box.

A good example is plotting mortgage applications to determine housing sales. The actual housing sales are delayed from their loan applications because of the time it takes for the lender to process the loan. This results in about a one month or so delay between mortgage applications and the desired housing sales trend. If the mortgage applications suddenly stop, housing sales will still continue for about a month; if applications suddenly abound, however, sales will not start booming for about a month.

The **D**amping factor field enables you to tune the sensitivity of the smoothed output to any variability of the input data. A larger damping factor provides smoother data. A good damping factor to use is between 0.2 and 0.3—these numbers are a good balance between highly smoothed output data (greater than 0.5) and an output that is sensitive to changes in the input data (less than 0.1).

In the example in figure 9.7, if you had data for many years of ice cream sales—and you wanted to know in general whether your business was improving or receding— you would want to choose a large damping factor (0.8, for example) to mask the seasonal variation in sales and show you the "big picture." If, however, you wanted to see how your business varied from week to week, you would probably want a small damping factor (0.1, for example) to show those weekly fluctuations in sales. These damping factors are not given as fixed numbers, but as general starting points for analysis. You will probably need to use different damping factors a few times until you get just the results you want.

Figure 9.7

Examples of exponential smoothing.

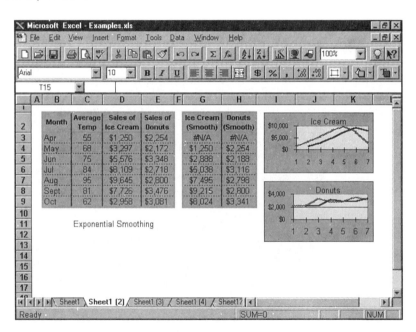

If you select the **C**hart Output option, Excel automatically generates a chart for the output data. The charts presented in this chapter, however, were generated manually for better appearance in this book. Automatic charts are quick, and usually work well for interactively displaying "pictures" of the numerical results.

If you select the **S**tandard Errors check box, Excel includes standard errors for each data point in the output data. *Errors* are how much the smoothed output data is different from the raw input data.

Notice the charted result for the Donut Sales data in figure 9.7. The smoothed data makes the sales trend more obvious than does the raw data. The raw data tends to fluctuate up and down, and it is difficult to see just from that line whether sales are growing, declining, or holding steady. The smoothed line clearly shows that sales are on the rise.

Histograms

A *histogram* counts the number of occurrences of a unique piece of information within a set of data. Each unique piece of information is called a *bin*, and the number of times each bin is repeated in a set of data is called the *frequency*.

Excel generates bins by default if you do not enter anything in the **B**in Range field. If, however, you want to show only certain bins, or explicitly declare bins, enter the bin you want to show in a specific row or column, then indicate that range in the **B**in Range field (see fig. 9.8).

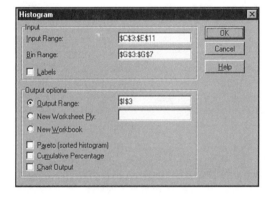

Figure 9.8

The Histogram dialog box.

You can get a Pareto histogram (not shown) by selecting the **Pa**reto check box under Output options. A *Pareto histogram* uses the same data as a standard histogram, but the bins are presented in descending order of frequency, rather than simply in order of bin numbers. The first (leftmost) bar in a Pareto chart would always be the tallest bar, and the chart would proceed in order from left to right, concluding with the rightmost bar as the shortest.

If the Cu**m**ulative Percentage check box is selected, cumulative percentages are included in the output data. *Cumulative percentage* is the percentage of data covered from the first bin to the current bin. Cumulative percentage is most useful with Pareto histograms, because it indicates the percentage of the total that the largest bins occupy. In the example, a cumulative percentage of the 10 minute bin would equal the number of times the employee was 10 minutes late for work, or 14+6+6=26 times.

Check the **C**hart Output check box if you want Excel to automatically generate charts for the output data. The chart presented in the example in figure 9.9 was, however, generated manually.

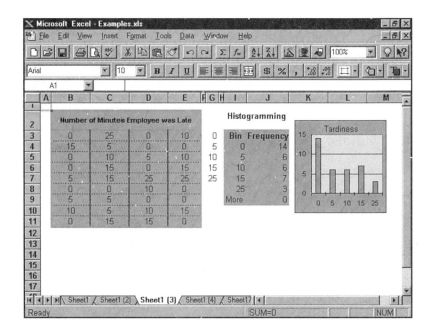

Moving Averages

A *moving average* is the average of a range of data taken from within a set of data. Moving averages are typically used in forecasting in this example, as we want to see the trend in donut sales and make some guesses from it about future sales. The input data points, which are used to generate the output data points, overlap. If, for example, three input data points are used to generate one output data point (an *interval* of 3), output data point #2 is generated from input data points #2, #3, and #4. Output data point #3 is generated from input data points #3, #4, #5, and so on.

In our donut sales example, you can see how variations in sales are averaged into one generally increasing line. Notice how the average flattens out around the fifth and sixth months. This is the result of averaging the previous three months' sales—two of which were somewhat sluggish.

Another explanation of moving averages can be made by taking a year-long set of data, using only three months worth of data for each data point in a forecast. The total set of data fell significantly, but then returned to its original value. A total average in such a case indicates a zero trend, because the beginning and the end are

at the same point—a flat trend. A moving average, however, shows a true upward trend, because only the most recent data points are used for the last few output data points.

The Moving Average dialog box is shown in figure 9.10; some examples are illustrated in figure 9.11.

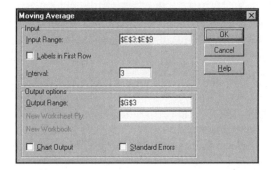

Figure 9.10

The Moving Average dialog box.

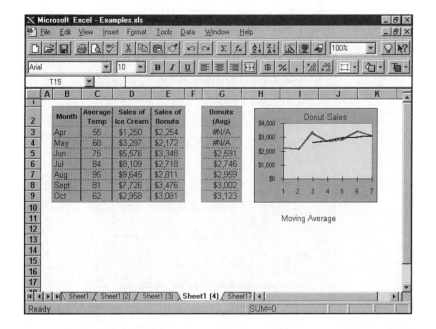

Figure 9.11

Moving average examples.

The Interval field indicates the number of data points from the input data Excel should use to create each data point in the output data.

Note The total number of output data points is determined by the following formula:

Number of input points — Interval + 1

Check the **C**hart Output check box if you want Excel to automatically generate a chart for the output data.

Use the **S**tandard Errors check box to include standard errors for each data point in the output data. These errors are the result of the differences between the raw input data and the averaged output data.

Random Numbers

Excel can generate a set of random numbers that fit certain criteria you specify in the Random Number Generation dialog box (see fig. 9.12). The most important of these criteria is *distribution*, or the chance that any random number will fall within certain limits. If you are not familiar with distributions, you might want to use the Uniform Distribution option at first, then experiment later with others. A *uniform distribution* simply generates random numbers between given upper and lower limits. There is not as much tailoring of the data available inside of those limits as there is in other distributions.

Figure 9.12

The Random Number Generation dialog box.

Random Number Generation

Number of **V**ariables:	[ ]
Number of **R**andom Numbers:	[10]
Distribution:	[Uniform ▼]

OK
Cancel
Help

Parameters

Be**t**ween [0] **a**nd [1]

Random Seed: [ ]

Output options
- ⊙ **O**utput Range: [$B$3:$B$12]
- ○ New Worksheet **P**ly: [ ]
- ○ New **W**orkbook

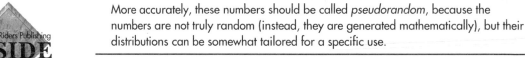

AUTHOR'S NOTE

More accurately, these numbers should be called *pseudorandom*, because the numbers are not truly random (instead, they are generated mathematically), but their distributions can be somewhat tailored for a specific use.

New Riders Publishing
INSIDE SERIES

The Number of **V**ariables field enables you to tailor the distribution of the random data by using more than one random variable to generate the random numbers. If you leave this box blank, Excel assumes one variable.

The Number of Random Num**b**ers field is where you indicate how many random numbers to generate.

In the Parameters box, your entry varies depending on the selected **D**istribution. If you use Uniform distribution, however, numbers can be given for the upper and lower limits (see B**e**tween and **a**nd) of the output data; all random numbers generated fall between the limits you specify.

Use **R**andom Seed for any set of random numbers. **R**andom Seed is the number Excel uses to initiate the mathematical process of generating pseudorandom numbers. Normally, Excel uses its own seed number, but you can enter a different number. Because the numbers are generated mathematically and are not truly random, the numbers can follow a pattern on rare occasions. The pattern, if any does exist, might not be obvious, and certainly defeats the purpose of using "random" numbers. Entering your own seed number can sometimes ward off unwanted repetition of certain numbers or sequences of numbers.

Two separate columns of random numbers are presented in the example to illustrate the use of the parameters in the Uniform distribution (see fig. 9.13). The first list is a Uniform distribution set between 0 and 1; the second is a Uniform distribution set between 0 and 10.

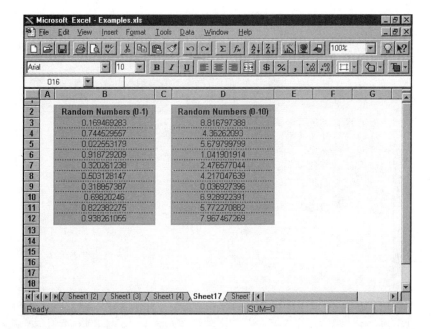

Figure 9.13

Two sets of random numbers with different parameters.

Ranks and Percentiles

Rank and Percentile generates a list of all values within a set of data, assigns each a rank from greatest to least, and generates the percentile of each data point to the top data point in the data set. This tool is most commonly used in schools and universities to calculate each student's class rank (like, 8th out of 92 in the class) and the student's percentile in the class (84 percent, or in the top 16 percent of the class). The Rank and Percentile dialog box is displayed in figure 9.14.

Figure 9.14

The Rank and Percentile dialog box.

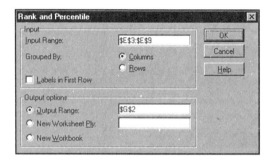

In the example in figure 9.15, a Rank and Percentile is performed on the donut sales column. The sales figures are ranked from highest to lowest sales volume so you can see at a quick glance how high and how low sales became during the plotted period of time. Each point is also ranked in order and assigned a percent value from the current highest value.

Figure 9.15

A Rank and Percentile example.

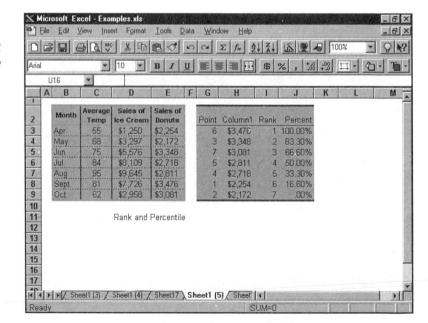

Using Engineering Tools

The tools discussed in this section are statistical tools used most often in engineering applications. These tools include the following:

◆ Fourier Analysis

◆ Sampling

As in the previous section, these tools are not dedicated to engineering use only. Although Fourier Analysis is rarely used outside of engineering circles, Sampling is a useful tool in many areas, especially where a great deal of data is analyzed.

The dialog boxes for these tools have some common features, including the following:

◆ **Input Range.** In the Input Range field, enter the range of cells in a spreadsheet where the source data resides. You can enter the range in either A1 or R1C1 format—depending on Excel's setting—and you can include external references.

◆ **Grouped By.** If the source data is oriented in columns, select the Grouped By Column option button. For data that is oriented in row(s), select the Grouped by Rows option button.

◆ **Labels in First Row.** If the Input Range entered previously includes labels for each column in the first row of the range, check Labels in First Row to indicate that the row does not contain data. If you have labels in the first row of data, but did not select this box, Excel assumes that the first row contains data that it can use, and Excel tries to compute the first row with the rest of the data. This can either throw off your result, or generate an error message.

◆ **Output Range.** The result of the tool appears in the cell location that you indicate in the Output Range. Single-cell reference can be used for an output range, to indicate the upper left corner of the resultant data; Excel automatically expands the range to include as many cells as necessary.

◆ **New Worksheet Ply.** Selecting this option enables you to send the tool's results to a new worksheet in the same workbook. To do this, you need to check the box and supply Excel with a name for the new sheet.

◆ **New Workbook.** If you want to send the tool's results to an entirely new workbook, check this box.

Fourier Analysis

Fourier analysis is most often used by engineers to translate a set of time-dependent (*time-domain*) data into a set of complex constants (*frequency-domain*) that more clearly show the frequencies of certain data. The Fourier Analysis dialog box is shown in figure 9.16.

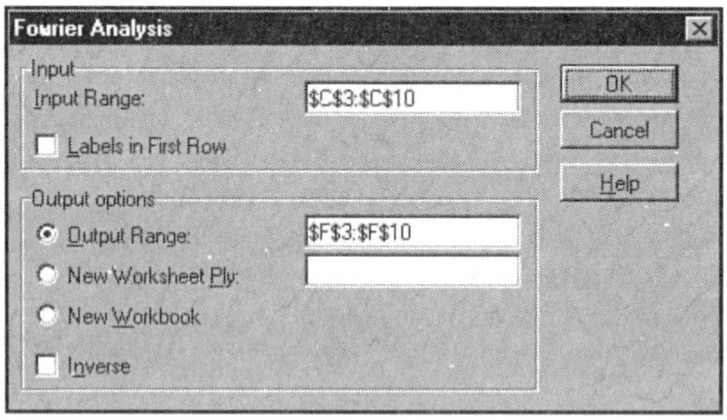

Figure 9.16

The Fourier Analysis dialog box.

Fourier Analysis	☒

Input
Input Range: `$C$3:$C$10`
☐ Labels in First Row

Output options
◉ Output Range: `$F$3:$F$10`
○ New Worksheet Ply:
○ New Workbook
☐ Inverse

OK
Cancel
Help

Excel requires that the number of input data points be a factor of 2 (2, 4, 8, 16, and so on).

An *inverse fourier* transform is available by selecting the **In**verse check box. This procedure converts frequency-domain data into time-domain data.

Two different sets of time-domain data are presented in the example to illustrate different frequency-domain outputs produced by Excel's fourier transform (see fig. 9.17).

Two standard wave forms are shown in the preceding figure. The first is a triangle wave of amplitude Vpk=2v and period t=8 milliseconds.

The "Number" column is the harmonic number of the frequency output. Harmonic 0 is DC, harmonic 1 is the fundamental frequency (in this case, 125hz), harmonic 2 is the second harmonic (250hz), and so on. The Fourier Constants column is the amplitude of the given harmonic, presented as a complex number.

Sampling

Sampling extracts a selected number of values from a set of data. Sampling helps to reduce the size of a large set of data, while changing its overall qualities as little as possible.

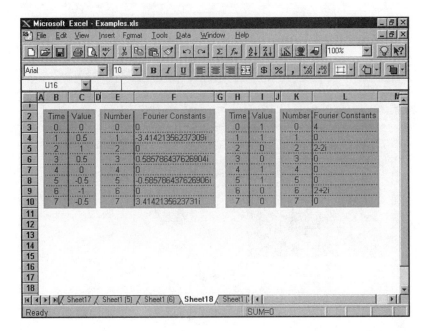

Figure 9.17

Two separate examples of fourier analysis.

Two sampling methods are available in Excel. The first method, **P**eriodic, moves down the data in order and returns every *interval* number of input data points as an output data point. You specify the interval in the Period edit box. An interval of 3, for instance, samples every third data point. The second method is termed **R**andom. Use it to generate a specified number of output data points randomly chosen from the input data. These methods can be chosen from the Sampling dialog box, displayed in figure 9.18.

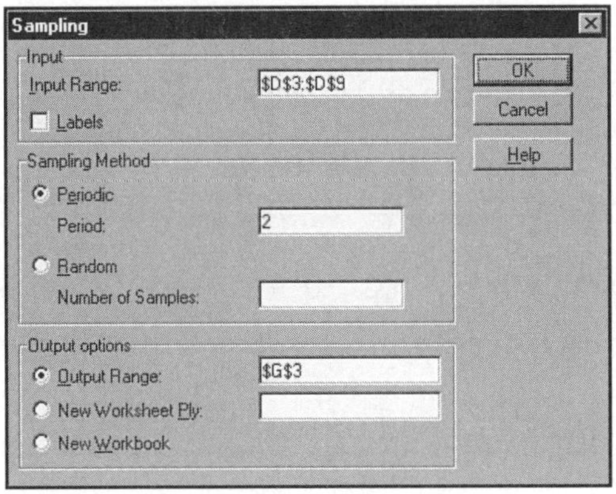

Figure 9.18

The Sampling dialog box.

Both sampling methods are shown in this figure 9.19. The ice cream sales data was periodically sampled, and the donut sales data was randomly sampled.

Figure 9.19

The results of the different types of sampling.

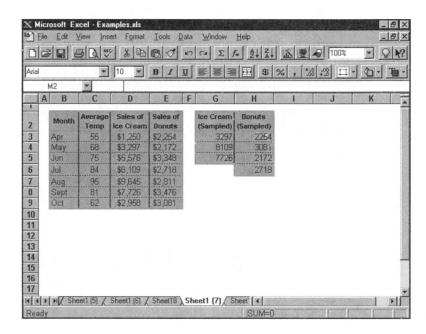

Notice that periodic samples ("Ice Cream Sales") might not include the true peak and low sales, even with a large volume of data. This fact can be especially true if the sample interval is high and only a few data points are taken for a lot of data. The data order is retained, however, and you can draw a general trend from the sampled data.

Random samples ("Donut Sales") can include the peak sales and low sales values, even if only a few samples are taken. Data order is lost, however—you have no way to track back and find out at what time each of the data points occurred. Thus, you cannot draw general trends from this sampled data. Random sampling, however, is more effective than periodic when used with distribution and average statistics.

Using Statistical Tools

The tools discussed in this final section are purely statistical tools. The tools in this group include the following:

◆ Anova

◆ Descriptive Statistics

◆ Regression Analysis

◆ Sampling Tests

These tools are not necessarily useful just to statisticians. Some (like the sampling tests) *are* better suited for those who are somewhat experienced in statistics. Descriptive statistics, however, can be very useful in many areas as they can give you easy access to such basic calculations as means (averages) and standard deviations.

The dialog boxes for these tools have some common features, including the following:

◆ **Input Range.** In the **I**nput Range field, enter the range of cells in a spreadsheet where the source data resides. You can enter the range in either A1 or R1C1 format—depending on Excel's setting—and you can include external references.

◆ **Grouped By.** If the source data is oriented in columns, select the Grouped By **C**olumn option button. For data that is oriented in row(s), select the Grouped by **R**ows option button.

◆ **Labels in First Row.** If the **I**nput Range entered previously includes labels for each column in the first row of the range, check **L**abels in First Row to indicate that the row does not contain data. If you have labels in the first row of data, but did not select this box, Excel assumes that the first row contains data that it can use, and Excel tries to compute the first row with the rest of the data. This can either throw off your result, or generate an error message.

◆ **Output Range.** The result of the tool appears in the cell location that you indicate in the **O**utput Range. Single-cell reference can be used for an output range, to indicate the upper left corner of the resultant data; Excel automatically expands the range to include as many cells as necessary.

◆ **New Worksheet Ply.** Selecting this options enables you to send the tool's results to a new worksheet in the same workbook. To do this, you need to check the box and supply Excel with a name for the new sheet.

◆ **New Workbook.** If you want to send the tool's results to an entirely new workbook, check this box.

Anova Analysis of Variance

In general, an analysis of variance, or *anova*, examines the mean values of multiple sets of data (assuming all means are equal) to determine if the mean values of samples taken from these sets also are equal. Three types of anova tools are available in Excel, as follows:

◆ **Anova: Single-Factor.** Performs a single-factor analysis of variance (see fig. 9.20). Data sets of different sizes can be used with this tool. A single-factor analysis of variance tests the effect of a single factor (one column on the sample), as shown in figure 9.21.

Figure 9.20

The Anova: Single Factor dialog box.

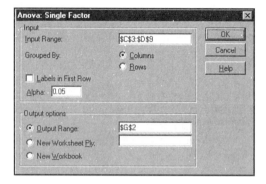

Figure 9.21

Single-Factor Anova results.

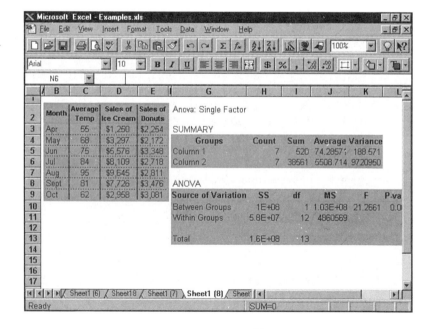

◆ **Anova: Two-Factor With Replication.** Performs a two-factor anova, including more than one sample for each group of data. Data sets must be the same size.

A two-factor anova classifies input data by two different factors. The total variation is partitioned into the part that can be attributed to each factor (each row), and the interaction of each factor.

◆ **Anova: Two-Factor Without Replication.** Performs a two-factor anova, but does not include more than one sampling per group.

Enter the anova alpha factor in the **A**lpha box. The *alpha factor* is the significance of the fit as a whole. It is the significance level of the ratio of the regression mean square value to the residual (error) mean square value.

The Anova: Two-Factor With Replication dialog box is shown in figure 9.22. It is very similar to the Anova: Single Factor dialog box. You can use data from multiple rows as a single data point by indicating the number of rows to use in the Rows Per Sample box.

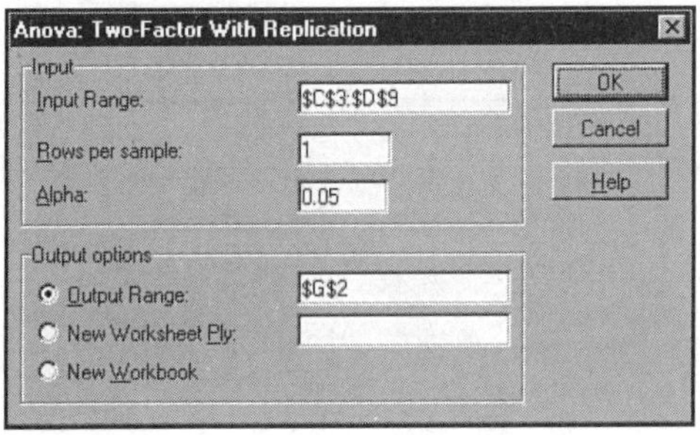

Figure 9.22

The Anova: Two-Factor With Replication dialog box.

Figure 9.23 illustrates the results of the sample data.

Figure 9.24 shows the Anova: Two-Factor Without Replication dialog box, which works in much the same way as the other two anova dialog boxes. The results of figure 9.24 are illustrated in figure 9.25.

Figure 9.23

Two-Factor With Replication results.

| File | Edit | View | Insert | Format | Tools | Data | Window | Help | | | | _|8|x| |

A	B	C	D	E	F	G	H	I	J	K	
2	Month	Average Temp	Sales of Ice Cream, Year 1	Sales of Ice Cream, Year 2		Anova: Two-Factor With Replication					
3	Apr	55	$1,250	$1,325		SUMMARY	1250	1325	Total		
4	May	68	$3,297	$3,152			68				
5	Jun	75	$5,576	$5,712		Count	1	1	2		
6	Jul	84	$8,109	$8,094		Sum	3297	3152	6449		
7	Aug	95	$9,645	$9,922		Average	3297	3152	6449		
8	Sept	81	$7,726	$7,518		Variance	#DIV/0!	#DIV/0!	#DIV/0!		
9	Oct	62	$2,958	$3,008							
10											
11							75				
12						Count	1	1	2		
13						Sum	5576	5712	11288		
14						Average	5576	5712	11288		
15						Variance	#DIV/0!	#DIV/0!	#DIV/0!		
16							84				
17						Count	1	1	2		
18						Sum	8109	8094	16203		
19						Average	8109	8094	16203		
20						Variance	#DIV/0!	#DIV/0!	#DIV/0!		
21											
22							95				
23						Count	1	1	2		

Sheet18 / Sheet1 (7) / Sheet1 (8) / **Sheet1 (9)** / Sheet

| File | Edit | View | Insert | Format | Tools | Data | Window | Help | | | | _|8|x| |

D	E	F	G	H	I	J	K	L	M	
31			Average	7726	7518	15244				
32			Variance	#DIV/0!	#DIV/0!	#DIV/0!				
33										
34				62						
35			Count	1	1	2				
36			Sum	2958	3008	5966				
37			Average	2958	3008	5966				
38			Variance	#DIV/0!	#DIV/0!	#DIV/0!				
39										
40				Total						
41			Count	6	6					
42			Sum	37311	37406					
43			Average	37311	37406					
44			Variance	3E-164	3E-164					
45										
46										
47			ANOVA							
48			Source of Variation	SS	df	MS	F	P-value	F crit	
49			Sample	8E+07	5	2E+07	65535	#NUM!	#NUM!	
50			Columns	752.08	1	752.08	65535	#NUM!	#NUM!	
51			Interaction	80367	5	16073	65535	#NUM!	#NUM!	
52			Within	0	0	65535				
53										
54			Total	8E+07	11					

Sheet18 / Sheet1 (7) / Sheet1 (8) / **Sheet1 (9)** / Sheet

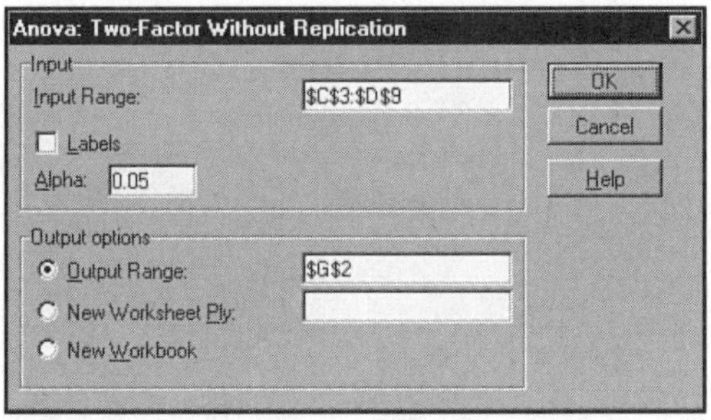

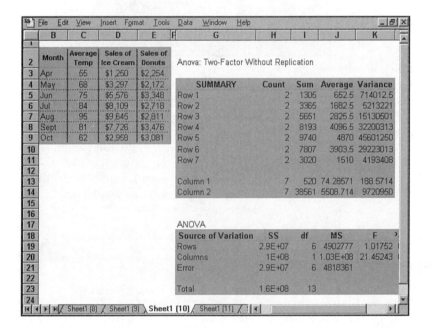

Figure 9.24

The Anova: Two-Factor Without Replication dialog box.

Figure 9.25

Two-Factor Without Replication results.

Descriptive Statistics

Descriptive statistics generate various numbers that describe properties of a data set, such as mean, standard deviation, and so on. The Descriptive Statistics dialog box is shown in figure 9.26.

Enter the desired confidence level in the Confidence Level for Mean box. The confidence level, 95 percent in this example, means that 95 percent of the time a given data point will be contained within a certain range (interval) about the mean value.

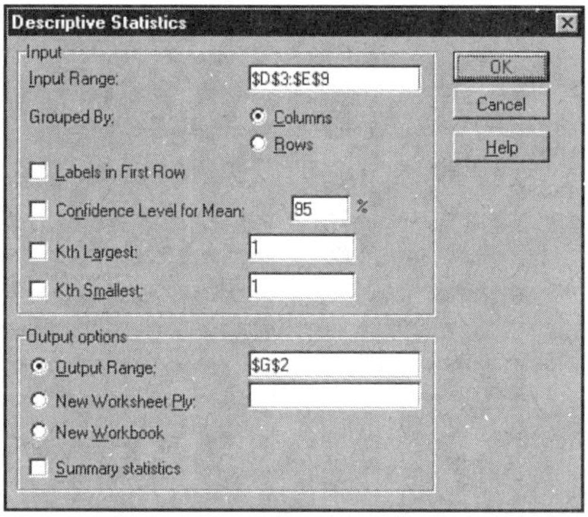

Figure 9.26

The Descriptive Statistics dialog box.

Descriptive Statistics

Input
Input Range: `$D$3:$E$9`
Grouped By: ⦿ Columns ○ Rows
☐ Labels in First Row
☐ Confidence Level for Mean: `95` %
☐ Kth Largest: `1`
☐ Kth Smallest: `1`

Output options
⦿ Output Range: `$G$2`
○ New Worksheet Ply:
○ New Workbook
☐ Summary statistics

OK   Cancel   Help

The Kth L**a**rgest and the Kth S**m**allest boxes enable you to exclude a number of data points from either the largest of the data points, or the smallest—or both. Often, in large amounts of data, a few data points can be wildly different from the rest, and this difference can introduce error into your descriptive statistics. If you want to exclude, for example, the largest two values from your analysis, enter **3** in the Kth L**a**rgest box; the analysis will then start with the third-largest data point and proceed to the S**m**allest. If then, you wanted to exclude the smallest value as well, enter **2** in the Kth smallest box. The analysis then ranges from the third-largest to the second smallest data values.

You also can ask Excel to provide **S**ummary statistics, which are shown in figure 9.27.

The descriptive statistics produced are as follows:

1. **Mean.** The average between the Kth largest and the Kth smallest values.

2. **Standard Error.** The standard error of the data.

3. **Median.** The middle value.

4. **Mode.** The mode of the data.

5. **Standard Deviation.** A measure of the data spread.

6. **Sample Variance.** Another measure of the data spread.

7. **Kurtosis.** A measure of the "tails" of a distribution, or how much of the data is far away from the mean.

8. **Skewness.** A measure of how the distribution of the data is "balanced" around the mean.

9. **Range.** The largest value used minus the smallest value used.

10. **Minimum.** The smallest value used.

11. **Maximum.** The largest value used.

12. **Sum.** The total of all data points.

13. **Count.** The number of data points used.

14. **Confidence Level.** The interval (range) within which 95 percent of the time a given data point can be found.

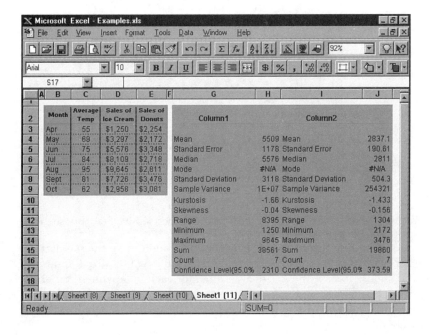

Figure 9.27

Examples of descriptive statistics for both columns.

Regression Analysis

Regression fits a smooth line (not necessarily a straight line) to a set of otherwise jagged data. This statistical tool is most often used graphically, where a straight line is superimposed on rough data. Regression enables you to more easily see a trend where the trend may not be obvious from the raw data. Statistical data is also given for each data point. Regression is also useful in reducing raw data into a mathematically simple function.

The Regression dialog box is shown in figure 9.28. Use the Input **X** and **Y** Range fields to indicate where the X and Y data resides within the spreadsheet.

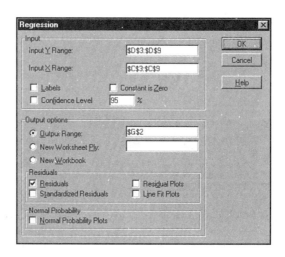

Regression uses a series of x-y values—coordinates of each data point—to calculate its results, then both the Input **Y** Range and the Input **X** Range must be entered.

The confidence level is the same as that described in the Descriptive Statistics section.

You have a variety of options for results to be displayed, in addition to the standard expression results. You can display the **R**esiduals (errors), the St**a**ndardized Residuals, or both. You can choose to have the Residuals Plotted for each independent variable. A plot of the central data with the regression line also drawn on the same graph is available by selecting L**i**ne Fit Plots. You also can specify a **N**ormal Probability Plot to be displayed as well.

The statistic result is placed in the range indicated (the single reference points to the upper left corner of the result table). You also can select **S**ummary statistics.

The results of the example are partially shown in figure 9.29.

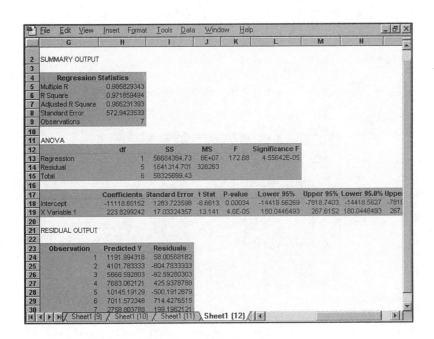

Figure 9.29

Portions of the Regression summary results.

Sampling Tests

The *sampling tests* compare certain properties of two sets of data. Five varieties of this tool are available:

◆ **Two-Sample for Variances F-Test.** Compares the variances between two sets of data.

◆ **Paired Two-Sample for Means t-Test.** Compares the means between two paired sets of data. The data should show a natural pairing of data points, such as running the same experiment twice, and must contain the same number of data points. The variances between the two sets of data are not assumed to be equal.

◆ **Two-Sample Assuming Equal Variances t-Test.** Determines whether the means of two samples are equal, based upon the assumption that the variances of the two samples are equal.

◆ **Two-Sample Assuming Unequal Variances t-Test.** Determines whether the means of two samples are equal, based upon the assumption that the variances of the two samples are not equal.

◆ **Two-Sample for Means z-Test.** Tests the probability that a sample was drawn from a certain population.

The F-Test: Two-Sample for Variances dialog box appears in figure 9.30. Enter the data range in the Input Variable **1** and **2** Range fields. Enter the alpha factor in the **Al**pha edit box. The Output options section is identical to those discussed earlier in this chapter.

Figure 9.30

The F-Test Two-Sample for Variances dialog box.

F-Test Two-Sample for Variances		

Input
Variable 1 Range: $D$3:$D$9   OK
Variable 2 Range: $E$3:$E$9   Cancel

☐ Labels   Help
Alpha: 0.05

Output options
◉ Output Range: $G$2
○ New Worksheet Ply:
○ New Workbook

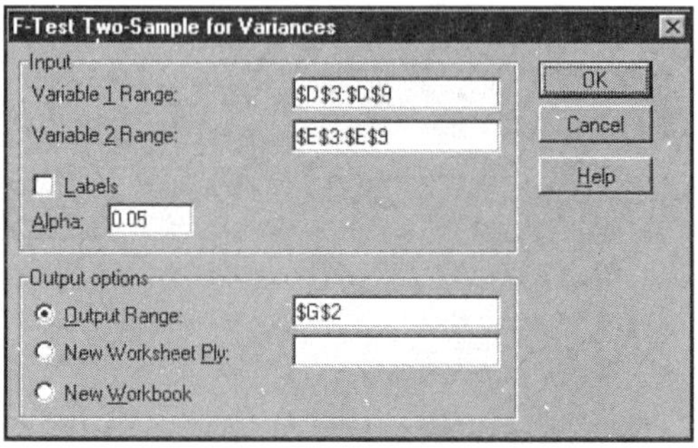

The dialog boxes for the remaining sampling test tools are all very similar and are used in much the same way. By studying figures 9.31 through 9.35, you can see the different results returned by each of these tests.

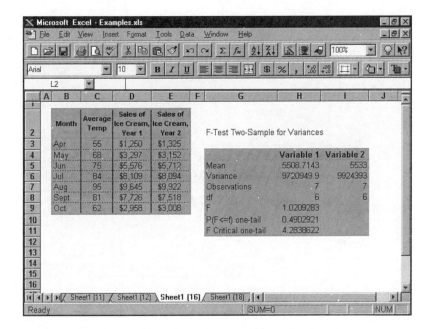

Figure 9.31

Two-sample for variances F-test results.

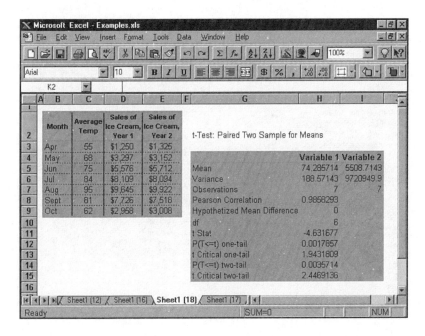

Figure 9.32

Paired two-sample for means t-test results.

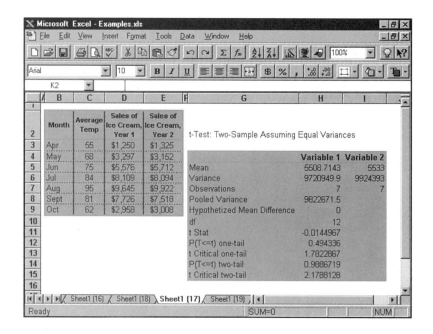

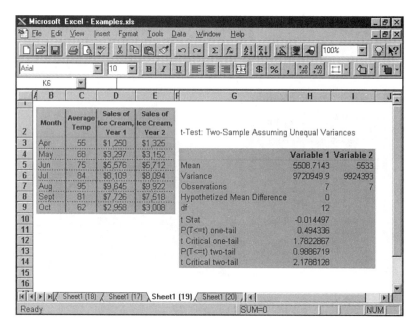

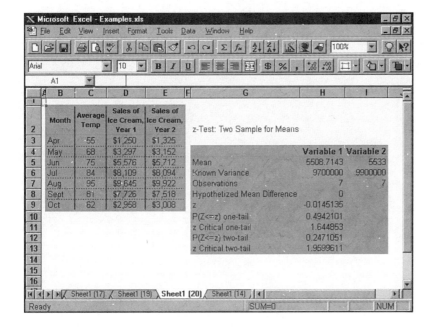

Figure 9.35

Two-sample for means z-test results.

Part II

Databases

Chapter Snapshot

Among Excel's more powerful capabilities are its excellent data-management features. Although Excel worksheets are most often used to manipulate numeric data, with a little work, your worksheets can be used as a database to store and retrieve text and other nonnumeric information. This chapter presents the following information:

- ◆ Introducing database terminology

- ◆ Using spreadsheets as database tables

- ◆ Designing a database list in Excel

- ◆ Using Excel's data filters

- ◆ Sorting data in a list

- ◆ Knowing when to use a "real" database system

As you will see, Excel for Windows 95 provides interactive, visual methods for sorting, filtering, and searching the data stored in Excel worksheets. This chapter shows you the basic technology you must master to use Excel spreadsheets as databases.

New Riders Publishing
INSIDE
SERIES

CHAPTER

10

Excel Database Basics

Businesses run on data. Customer lists, inventory control, employee records, and sales histories all are examples of common business data-management needs.

In many ways, Microsoft Excel is the ideal data-management tool for small to medium businesses and many personal data-management needs. You can use Excel spreadsheets to store and retrieve data, just like more sophisticated, specialized database management systems. Excel also is more forgiving and easier to learn than most database systems, such as Microsoft FoxPro or Borland's dBASE.

Excel has many functions specifically designed to help you sort and filter data stored in worksheets. This chapter covers sorting and filtering, as well as general database design considerations for the novice database user.

Database Terminology

The first step to learning databases is to become familiar with the specialized database terminology database experts use. The following list is by no means complete and might be Excel-specific, but is intended to provide a basic understanding of common Excel database terms.

◆ **Database.** The term "database" is used in several different ways, depending on what database system is being used. In Microsoft FoxPro and Borland dBASE, for instance, a *database* is a single table that is part of a database application. A Microsoft Access database, on the other hand, includes all of the tables, forms, and other objects that make up the application.

◆ **Table.** A database *table* is just like an Excel worksheet. An Excel database table contains rows and columns of data contained in the worksheet cells (which might be empty). A table is usually referred to as a *list* in Excel.

◆ **List.** In Excel terms, *list* is another name for a database table. Based on certain design elements (discussed later in this chapter) and the way in which it is used, Excel automatically recognizes a list on a worksheet.

◆ **Field.** A *field* is a column of data in a database table. A field contains a specific type of data, which might be alphanumeric or numeric. The fields in a table might include "Name," "Address," and "Phone Number." All fields in a database table are of the same type.

◆ **Record.** A *record* is a set of related data that corresponds to a single row in the database table. A record in a database table might be a person's name, address, and phone number.

◆ **Query.** A *query* is a request to a database to retrieve data. Normally, a query only retrieves specific information from the database table, based on parameters that you define.

In Excel terms, a *query definition* is all the information needed by Microsoft Query (an Excel add-in discussed in Chapter 11) to extract data from a source of data (like an external database). This information includes the table name(s), field name(s), and specific search criteria needed to complete the database search.

◆ **Query criteria or search criteria.** Because a *query* returns specific information from a database table or Excel list, some way must exist for specifying which

data to extract from the table. The expressions *query criteria* and *search criteria* both apply to the set of information that specifies the data to be retrieved from the Excel list.

◆ **Query design.** When using Microsoft Query, *query design* refers to the tables, relationships between tables, and other elements included in the query criteria used to extract data from an external database.

Using Spreadsheets as Database Tables

Whatever the underlying database system, a table (or list, in Excel) consists of rows and columns of data. A Microsoft Excel worksheet is perfectly analogous to a database table in FoxPro, Access, or dBASE.

Because Excel is designed primarily to handle financial or other numeric data, however, certain principles apply differently to Excel than to most other database systems.

Guidelines

Because many Excel features can be applied to only one list on a worksheet at a time, it is generally a good idea to put only one list on a worksheet. It also is a good idea to dedicate a single worksheet to maintaining a single list of data.

Surround the list with blank rows above and below and blank columns to the left and right. This arrangement makes it easy for Excel to distinguish your list from other things on the worksheet.

As you soon learn, *filtering* a list hides rows that are excluded from the list, leaving only those fields meeting the selection criteria. If you have important information on the left or right of your list, it might be hidden when you filter the list.

Using the Data List

An Excel data list can be used interactively or through macros and other automation techniques. Excel provides a number of menu options that enable you to quickly and easily filter the data contained in lists. A number of macro functions greatly enhance your ability to utilize data in Excel lists and external databases. These techniques are discussed later in this chapter.

Basic Design Elements

As already mentioned, when you build Excel data lists, worksheet columns become fields and worksheet rows serve as database records. Several other important concepts should be kept in mind, however, as you design and build Excel data lists.

Designing a Database Worksheet

As an example of a common database, consider the address and phone directory you carry in your briefcase. This phone directory is correctly thought of as a *database* of contact information. Most often, these directories are pre-printed with areas for a person's name, an address, and phone numbers.

Columns Become Fields

Each of these areas is a *field* in the directory database. If you are designing an Excel worksheet to use as a phone directory, you should add *columns* for the name, address, and phone number information.

Rows Become Records

Each row in the worksheet will serve as a database *record* and will contain all of the contact information for a person.

Allow Enough Columns

Very often, people design databases without enough fields. You'll want columns for each different type of information you might want to access. As you will soon see, it would be much easier to search for a person's last name if it appears in a column of its own, rather than being included with the first name in the "Name" column. Most databases function more efficiently if only one type of data (like the first or last name) is stored in a field.

Figure 10.1 shows an Excel worksheet containing a data list that serves as a simple address book.

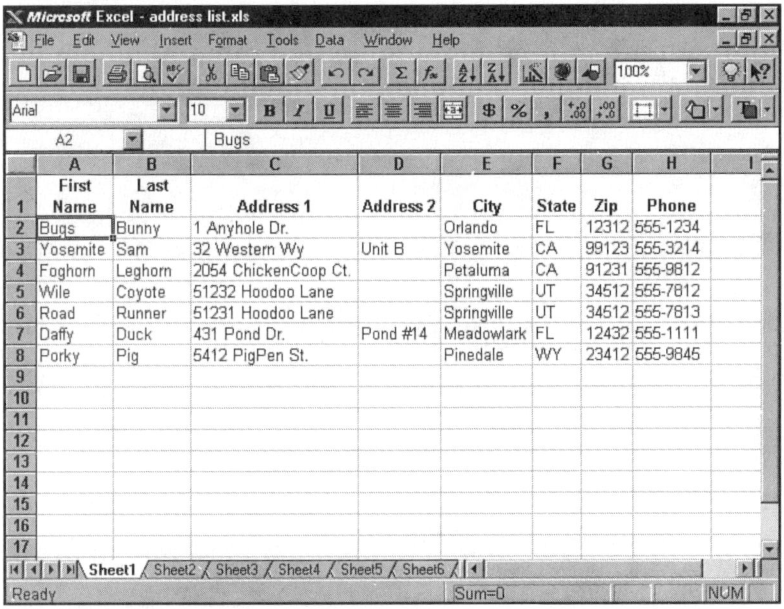

Figure 10.1

A data list on an Excel worksheet.

Use Column Labels

It is generally a good idea to use column labels on the list. Excel uses column labels when finding data in the list and for creating reports from the data.

Column labels should appear in a different font or typeface than the data stored in the column. Most often, column labels will appear in a bold typeface. It's enough to use a pattern or cell border to distinguish the column labels from the data in the columns.

If you want to separate the column labels from the data in the column, use a border along the bottom of the labels, rather than empty cells. If the column labels aren't contiguous with the data in the columns, Excel won't know that the column labels belong to the list.

Entering Data into Cells

When entering data into the cells of an Excel data list, don't put blanks at the beginning of a cell. The extra blanks will be used by Excel when sorting the list and might cause unexpected results.

Some Windows fonts (for instance, Arial) are *proportionally spaced*, which means that blanks take up less room than wide characters like "m" or "w." The extra blanks at the front of cells displayed in a proportionally spaced font can be difficult to see.

Formatting Cells

Use the same font characteristics (bold, size, and so on) for all of the cells in a column. Arbitrarily mixing typefaces can lead to some unnecessary confusion.

Name the List and Its Major Elements

After you have the basic list in place, assign a name to the entire list. If you plan to use the worksheet only to hold the data list, assign the list name by highlighting all of the columns in the list, and selecting the **N**ame option from the **I**nsert menu. The cascading menu shown in figure 10.2 will appear.

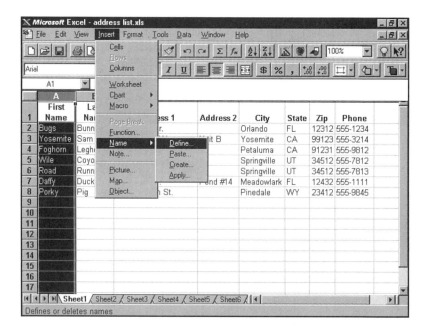

Figure 10.2

The Name cascading menu.

When you select **D**efine from the cascading menu, the Define Name dialog box appears (see fig. 10.3). Enter the name you want to assign to your data list in the Names in **W**orkbook text field.

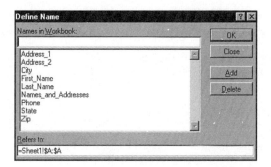

Figure 10.3

The Define Name dialog box.

Each of the columns is named by highlighting the column, and entering appropriate names in the Define Name dialog box. Later, these columns and the list can be referenced by the names assigned to them.

It's easy to find the names assigned to the list or parts of the list. Click on the down arrow next to the names box on the Formatting toolbar to reveal the list of named items in the list (see fig. 10.4).

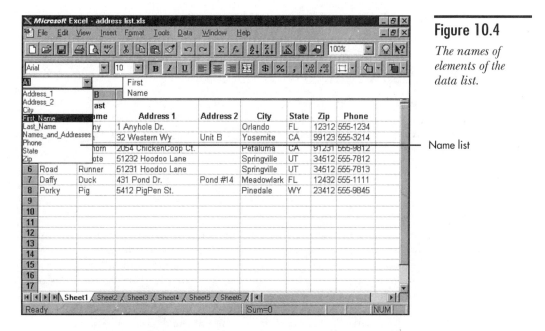

Figure 10.4

The names of elements of the data list.

Although it isn't necessary to name the items in the list, you can use the appropriate element name any time Excel requires a reference to data in the list. For instance, when sorting the list by the values in the "Last Name" column, you can use the name assigned to that column ("Last_Name") rather than a range or other reference.

Designing a Database: A Case Study

Designing a database table is a rather straightforward exercise. A little advance planning can make it much easier when it comes time to lay out the list in an Excel worksheet.

Determining the Structure

The first step is to decide what data you want the database list to manage. Expanding somewhat on the address book analogy, consider the case of Sarah Wood, the manager of a busy shoe store, who is building an Excel database to manage the commissions paid to her salespeople.

Sarah's data management needs are similar to those of most businesses. Dissimilar information (employee names, sales figures, and commission rates) will all be contained within the Excel data list. Calculations will be applied to the data in the worksheet to determine sales commissions and bonuses (Sarah's shoe store pays a monthly bonus to the top-grossing salesperson). Finally, summary reports can be used to determine which salespeople are showing the most improvement in their sales figures.

Sarah Wood's Data List

Sarah's first iteration of her worksheet is shown in figure 10.5. The names of the 10 salespeople are listed in the column labeled "Employee Name," and the gross sales by each employee for the first six months of 1995 are in the six columns to the right of the Employee Name column.

The wide disparity in gross sales is because most of the Top Shoes employees are employed only part time. The full-time employees have much higher gross sales figures than the part-time employees.

Sarah is interested in the monthly sales totals for each month, so she added a simple formula (=SUM(B2:B11)) in column B, a couple of rows below the last row of data. It is easy to copy this formula into row 13, below each column of monthly data. She also adds a column to the right of the list containing the total sales of each employee over the six-month period.

Being new to Excel, Sarah isn't sure what to do next. The data in the worksheet in figure 10.5 is somewhat difficult to work with. The rows and columns are in no particular order, so not much information can be derived.

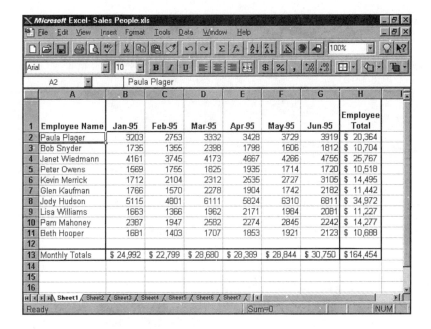

Figure 10.5

Sarah Wood's worksheet.

Sarah does understand, however, that her worksheet qualifies as an Excel database list. In any column, all the cells contain the same type of data. Each row is the sales record for one employee, so each cell in a row is related to the other cells in the same row. Sarah assigns the name "Sales95" to the range of cells from A1 to H11. Excel recognizes the column labels at the top of each column because Sarah has set their typefaces to Bold and put a thick single-line border at the bottom of each cell in the top row.

Sorting the List Alphabetically

First, Sarah wants to sort the list alphabetically. This arrangement would make it easier when entering data in the store's ledger or calculating withholding taxes.

Sorting the list by the Employee Name column is easy. All she needs to do is to click on any cell within the "Sales95" area (she chose the Employee Name column label) to inform Excel that she intends to work with the "Sales95" data list.

Next, she selects the **S**ort option from the **D**ata menu. The Sort dialog box appears (see fig. 10.6). Notice that the Sales95 list is highlighted while the Sort dialog box is open to let you know that Excel understands what area is about to be sorted.

Figure 10.6

The Sort dialog box.

Sarah opens the combo box in the **S**ort By area of the Sort dialog box by clicking on the down arrow and selects "Employee Name" from the list of names. Because Excel recognizes "Sales95" as a data list, each column label is automatically added to this list.

What Ascending and Descending Mean

Notice that there are selections for **A**scending and **D**escending for each sort option. An *ascending* sort (the default) reorders the list from the smallest number (including negative numbers) to the largest number on numeric columns. If the column is alphabetic, an ascending sort follows alphabetic order (A to Z). Columns containing date or time data are sorted from earliest date or time to latest. Remember, because all of the data within a column is of the same type (numeric, alphabetic, or date/time), Excel won't become confused by changing data types during a sort. A *descending* sort reorders the list from largest to smallest, highest to lowest, and latest to earliest.

Using Column Headings During Sorting

At the bottom of the Sort dialog box in figure 10.6 is an area (labeled My List Has) in which you can tell Excel if it has found the correct column labels. If, for some reason, your list has column labels, but Excel didn't find them (most likely because you did not use a different typeface for the column labels), the "No Header Ro**w**" option button will be selected. If you click on the "Header **R**ow" option button, Excel will use the top row of the list as column labels.

Note If Excel thinks your list does *not* have column headings, the top row of your list will be included in the sort. This can lead to unexpected changes to the list order. Always check the results of a sort. If the column headings (also called the *column labels*) have been included in the sort, undo the sort by selecting the **U**ndo option in the **E**dit menu, then check to make sure the column headings have a different appearance than the items in the list.

When Sarah clicks on the OK button, the Sales95 list is instantly sorted alphabetically, as shown in figure 10.7. If Sarah wanted the list to be sorted by the employees' last names, she probably should have put the names into the list as "Last Name, First Name." As it is, the list is nicely sorted by the employees' first names.

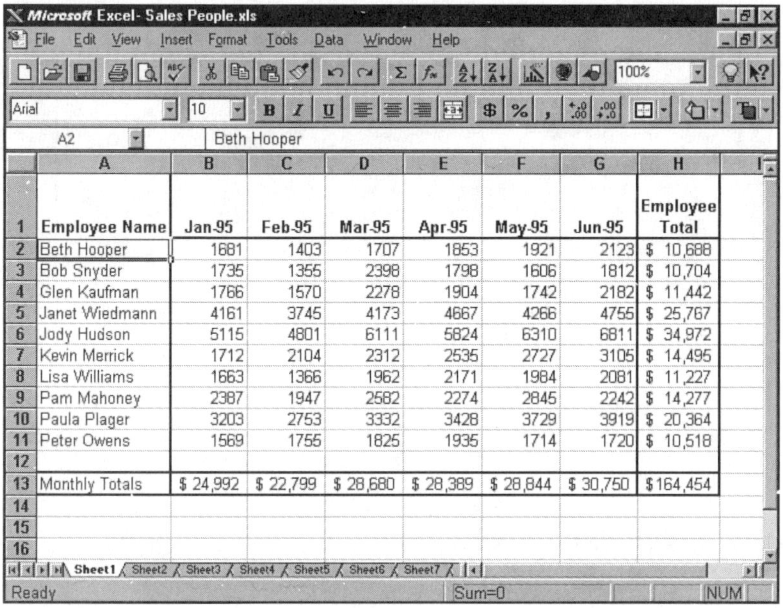

Figure 10.7

The list sorted by the Employee Name column.

	A	B	C	D	E	F	G	H
1	Employee Name	Jan-95	Feb-95	Mar-95	Apr-95	May-95	Jun-95	Employee Total
2	Beth Hooper	1681	1403	1707	1853	1921	2123	$ 10,688
3	Bob Snyder	1735	1355	2398	1798	1606	1812	$ 10,704
4	Glen Kaufman	1766	1570	2278	1904	1742	2182	$ 11,442
5	Janet Wiedmann	4161	3745	4173	4667	4266	4755	$ 25,767
6	Jody Hudson	5115	4801	6111	5824	6310	6811	$ 34,972
7	Kevin Merrick	1712	2104	2312	2535	2727	3105	$ 14,495
8	Lisa Williams	1663	1366	1962	2171	1984	2081	$ 11,227
9	Pam Mahoney	2387	1947	2582	2274	2845	2242	$ 14,277
10	Paula Plager	3203	2753	3332	3428	3729	3919	$ 20,364
11	Peter Owens	1569	1755	1825	1935	1714	1720	$ 10,518
12								
13	Monthly Totals	$ 24,992	$ 22,799	$ 28,680	$ 28,389	$ 28,844	$ 30,750	$164,454

Sorting the List Numerically

Working with a sorted list is easier than dealing with rough, unorganized data. Although the alphabetically sorted list is easier to use, it still doesn't give Sarah any direct indication of which employees are her top performers. Sarah sorts the list once more, this time choosing "Employee Total" as the **S**ort By column. She also clicks on the **D**escending button. The results of this sort are shown in figure 10.8.

From this list, it is easy to see that Jody Hudson was, by far, the highest-grossing employee for the first half of 1995 (although a case could be presented that, in such a small list, it is easy to pick out the highest number from the Employee Total column). Consider for a moment how different the situation would be if there were several hundred rows and dozens of columns in the data list. It is very difficult to pick out the highest (or lowest) number if the list spans across many screens.

More advanced sorting options are discussed later in this chapter.

Figure 10.8

*The list sorted by
Employee Total.*

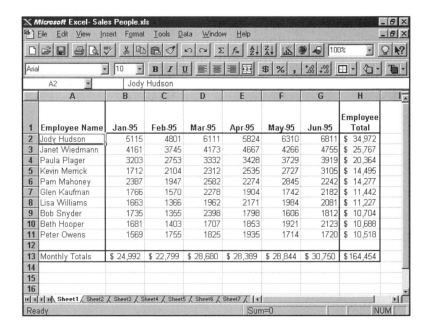

	A	B	C	D	E	F	G	H	
1	Employee Name	Jan-95	Feb-95	Mar-95	Apr-95	May-95	Jun-95	Employee Total	
2	Jody Hudson	5115	4801	6111	5824	6310	6811	$ 34,972	
3	Janet Wiedmann	4161	3745	4173	4667	4266	4755	$ 25,767	
4	Paula Plager	3203	2753	3332	3428	3729	3919	$ 20,364	
5	Kevin Merrick	1712	2104	2312	2535	2727	3105	$ 14,495	
6	Pam Mahoney	2387	1947	2582	2274	2845	2242	$ 14,277	
7	Glen Kaufman	1766	1570	2278	1904	1742	2182	$ 11,442	
8	Lisa Williams	1663	1366	1962	2171	1984	2081	$ 11,227	
9	Bob Snyder	1735	1355	2398	1798	1606	1812	$ 10,704	
10	Beth Hooper	1681	1403	1707	1853	1921	2123	$ 10,688	
11	Peter Owens	1569	1755	1825	1935	1714	1720	$ 10,518	
12									
13	Monthly Totals	$ 24,992	$ 22,799	$ 28,680	$ 28,389	$ 28,844	$ 30,750	$164,454	

Filtering Data in a List

So far, Sarah Wood has sorted her list by both alphabetic and numeric data. Excel's built-in sorting routines made these tasks quick and easy.

Her next step is to experiment with *filtering* the data in the list. Bonuses in the Top Shoes store were only paid to employees exceeding certain monthly quotas. Any full-time employee bringing in more than an average of $3,000 in sales was eligible for a tidy bonus every six months. Sarah wants to *filter out* employees who didn't make their quota.

Using AutoFilter

Obviously, Sarah wants to exclude any employees with gross sales of less than $18,000 for the six-month period covered in her list. Excel makes simple filters like this easy to do. Again, Sarah's first step is to click on a cell in the Sales95 data list. She then selects the **F**ilter option in the **D**ata menu to reveal the **F**ilter cascading menu (see fig. 10.9).

Initially, Sarah just wants a quick and easy filter, so she selects the Auto**F**ilter option. AutoFilter places drop-down arrows on each column in the data list (see fig. 10.10).

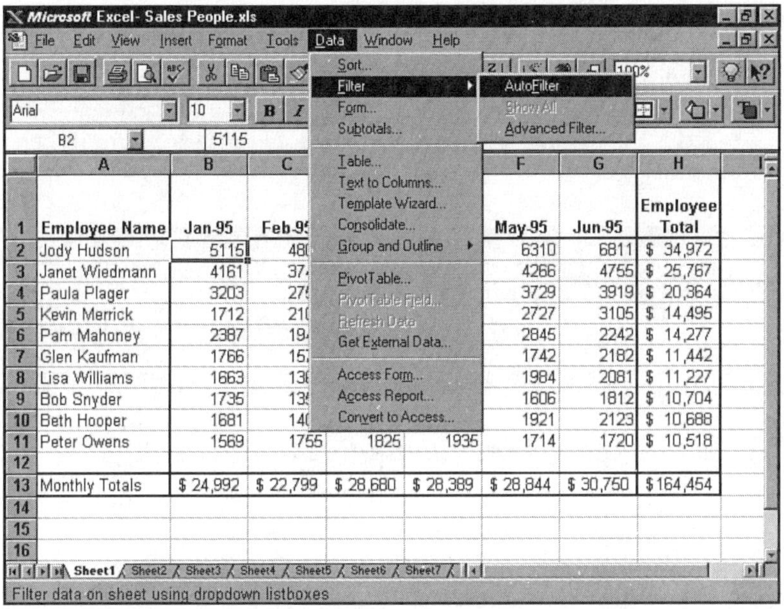

Figure 10.9

*The Filter
cascading menu.*

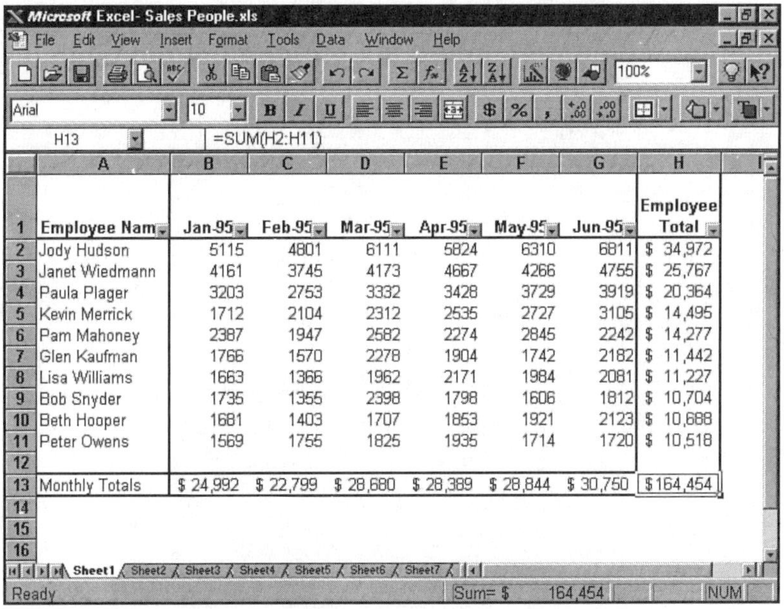

Figure 10.10

*The AutoFilter
drop-down arrows
on the data list.*

Specifying AutoFilter Criteria

When you click on the down arrows, a list of filter criteria is revealed, as shown in figure 10.11. This drop-down list contains all of the unique value in the column. By clicking on a value in this list, Sarah could quickly exclude all rows except for those that contain the value she selected.

Figure 10.11

The filter criteria list.

Filter criteria list ——

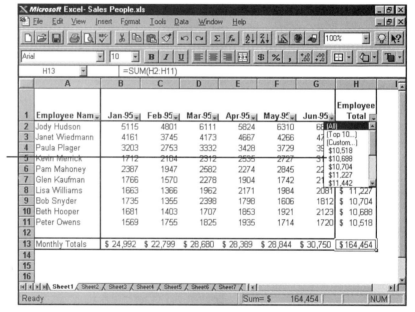

This approach, however, does not help her determine which employees have met their quota. Instead, she selects the Custom option from the list, which opens the Custom AutoFilter dialog box (see fig. 10.12). This dialog box contains fields for specifying which data should be included in the filtered data.

Figure 10.12

The Custom AutoFilter dialog box.

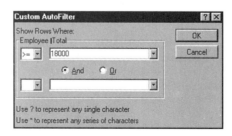

Because she wants all employees who brought in more than $18,000 in gross sales, Sarah enters 18000 in the text box in the Custom AutoFilter dialog box and clicks on the OK button. The list instantly changes to what is shown in figure 10.13.

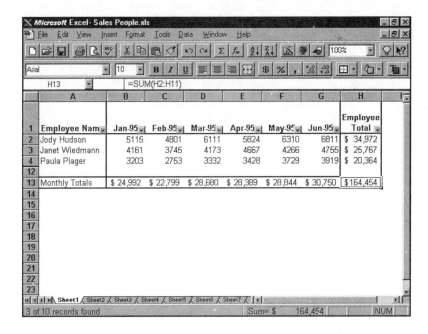

Figure 10.13

The result of the custom AutoFilter.

Although at first glance it appears that a lot of rows have been deleted from the list, look at the row numbers at the far left of figure 10.13. The row numbers indicate that all of the rows from 5 through 11 have been hidden rather than deleted. When you filter data in an Excel database list, the rows excluded by the filter are simply hidden from view.

How Filters Affect List Operations

Many list operations like printing, copying, and charting work only on displayed data. The fields hidden by a filter will not be printed or copied along with the displayed fields.

Note To leave AutoFormat, select **F**ilter in the **D**ata menu and click on Auto**F**ilter. When you return to the worksheet, all the drop-down arrows disappear.

Summing Across Hidden Rows

A couple of things are worth noting here. For instance, notice that the grand total in the lower right corner of figure 10.13 is the same as when all data was displayed (see fig. 10.10). The formula for the grand total is =SUM(H2:H11), which includes rows that are hidden from view.

Even when rows are hidden from view, Excel continues to correctly display summary data based on the hidden values.

Advanced Filters

January and February were particularly difficult months for Top Shoes. Bad weather kept away many customers and a few employees called in sick several days during this period. Sarah is interested in knowing which employees had been able to make their quotas during the bad weather, indicating a willingness to tough it out when things got bad.

Although AutoFilter is easy to use, Sarah cannot get AutoFilter to show all rows with values above $3,000 in either January or February. This more complex filter criteria requires Excel's Advanced Filter capabilities.

The advanced filter feature requires a certain amount of setup before selecting the Advanced Filter menu option. First, Sarah must specify the criteria she wishes to use for the filter. The criteria was quite simple: for the months of January and February, she needs all rows with values greater than 3000.

The advanced filter option requires Sarah to build an area on the worksheet with this information (see fig. 10.14). Just below the data list, Sarah puts exact duplicates of the column labels for the January and February data, and, below each label, the value for which she wants to search. The column labels and criteria make up the *criteria range* for the advanced filter.

 Note The labels for the criteria range must be exactly like the labels on the columns you want to filter. The best way to get exact duplicates of the column labels is to copy and paste them into the criteria range.

Next, Sarah selects the **A**dvanced Filter option from the **F**ilter cascading menu (see fig. 10.15). It is important to note that you must have the criteria range established before invoking the **A**dvanced Filter option.

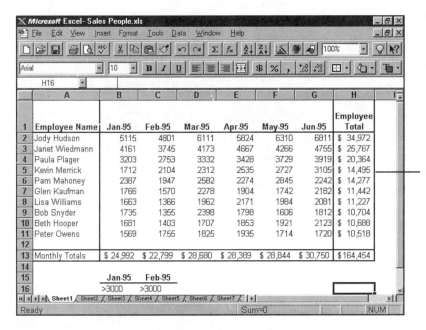

Figure 10.14

The criteria range for the advanced filter.

Criteria range

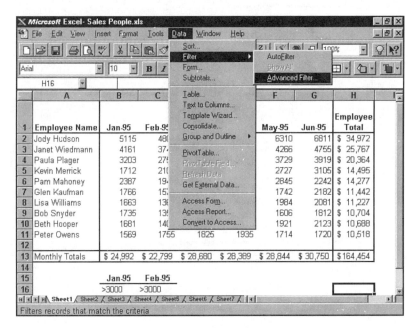

Figure 10.15

The Advanced Filter option in the Filter cascading menu.

The Advanced Filter dialog box then opens (see fig. 10.16). The **L**ist Range box is automatically filled in by Excel with the range for the Sales95 data list. Sarah has to fill in the **C**riteria Range box herself, however.

Figure 10.16

The Advanced Filter dialog box.

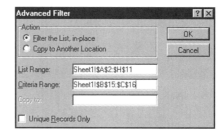

When Sarah clicks on the OK button, the data in her list is instantly filtered according to the information specified in the criteria range (see fig. 10.17). Only those rows with values above 3000 in January or February appear.

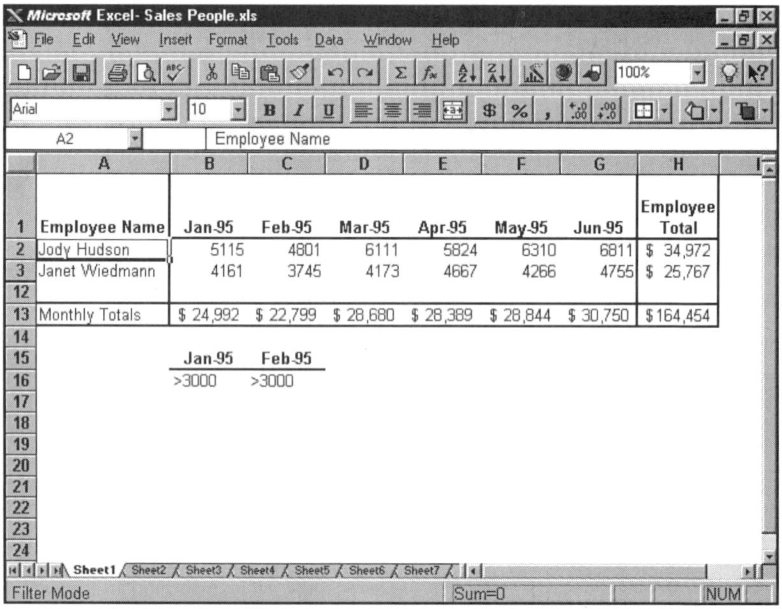

Figure 10.17

The result of the advanced filter.

	A	B	C	D	E	F	G	H
1	Employee Name	Jan-95	Feb-95	Mar-95	Apr-95	May-95	Jun-95	Employee Total
2	Jody Hudson	5115	4801	6111	5824	6310	6811	$ 34,972
3	Janet Wiedmann	4161	3745	4173	4667	4266	4755	$ 25,767
12								
13	Monthly Totals	$ 24,992	$ 22,799	$ 28,680	$ 28,389	$ 28,844	$ 30,750	$164,454
14								
15		Jan-95	Feb-95					
16		>3000	>3000					

Note To remove the advanced filter, select the **S**how All option in the **F**ilter cascade menu under the **D**ata main menu. The **S**how All option is available only when a filter has been applied to a data list.

Advanced Sorting and Filtering Features

In addition to the basic sorting and filtering operations described earlier in this chapter, Excel for Windows 95 provides a number of advanced features that extend your ability to manage lists used as databases.

Custom Sort Order

The default sort orders are simply "ascending" and "descending." When Sarah Wood wanted to see who was the highest-selling employee, she simply sorted the list by the "Employee Total" column. As you read this chapter, it might have occurred to you that it was not entirely fair to her part-time employees to include them along with the full-time employees during this sort.

Since part-time salespeople have less opportunity to sell shoes, their sales figures are naturally lower than those of full-time workers. With the current Sales95 list design, it is not possible to easily include information indicating employment status in a sort or filter.

Even a column added to the list indicating FT (for full-time) and PT (for part-time) does not provide a full solution. "PT" will always fall after "FT," because it comes after "FT" when sorted in alphabetical order. Sarah Wood wants to be able to sort by more than just FT and PT, however. She'd like to be able to use FT (full-time), TQ (three-quarter time, or 30 hours a week), and HT (half-time, 20 hours or less a week). Sorting this column alphabetically puts the half-time people at the top of the sorted list.

What Sarah needs is a "custom sort order" that appropriately sorts or filters FT, TQ, and HT columns. She first adds a new column to the list to contain the employment status, as shown in figure 10.18.

Next, Sarah needs to add the custom sort order to her Excel for Windows 95 installation. She simply opens the Options notebook by selecting **O**ptions in the **T**ools menu, and then clicks on the Custom Lists tab (see fig. 10.19).

The left half of the Custom Lists page displays the current set of custom lists. Excel is pre-installed with lists for sorting by months of the year and days of the week.

To add a list, simply enter it in the List **E**ntries box to the right of the Custom **L**ists area and then click on **A**dd. Figure 10.19 shows the Custom Lists page after Sarah enters the employment status items. When Sarah clicks on the OK button, she is returned to the Sales95 list.

Sorting the list by the Employee Total and ES columns is easy. When she selects the **S**ort option in the **D**ata menu, the Sort dialog box appears, as shown in figure 10.20.

Figure 10.18

*The Sales95 list
with the new
column added.*

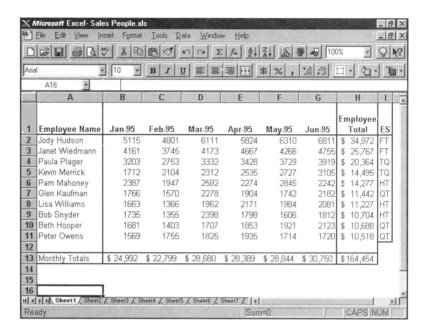

Figure 10.19

*The Custom Lists
page in the
Options notebook.*

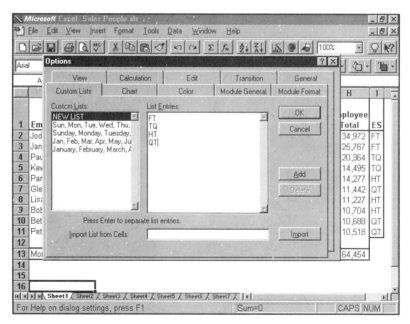

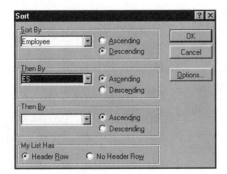

Figure 10.20

The Sort dialog box.

Sarah enters the new ES column in the **S**ort By box and the Employee Total in the **T**hen By box. This sequence means that employees will be grouped together by their employment status, then, within the employment status group, by the Employee Total column.

To make sure the new custom list is used to sort the ES column, with the **S**ort By box highlighted, Sarah clicks on the **O**ptions button in the Sort dialog box to open the Sort Options dialog box (see fig. 10.21).

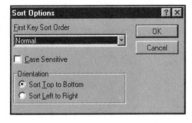

Figure 10.21

The Sort Options dialog box.

When open, the **F**irst Key Sort Order combo box shows the list of custom lists known to Excel (see fig. 10.22). Sarah selected her custom list (FT, TQ, HT, QT) from this list and clicked on the OK button.

After she sorts her list, the results are shown in figure 10.23.

A quick look at the Employee Total column shows Sarah that she has one quarter-time employee (Glen Kaufman) who has out-performed two half-time people (Bob Snyder and Lisa Williams). Either Glen Kaufman is an exceptional salesperson or Bob Snyder and Lisa Williams need a little training!

Figure 10.22

*The custom orders
that can be used
for sorting.*

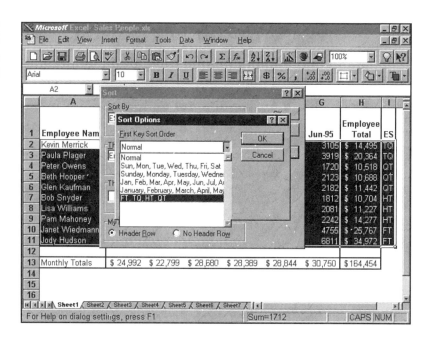

Figure 10.23

The sorted list.

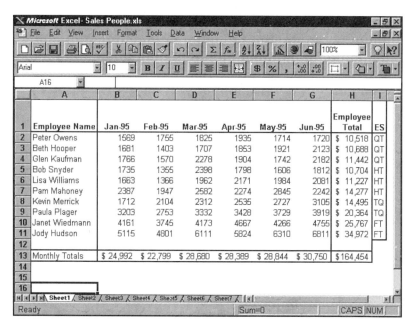

Sorting More Than Three Columns

Only three columns can be sorted at a time. If you need to sort by four or more columns, perform the sort in stages. Sorting rearranges the rows in the list; unlike filtering, this rearrangement is permanent (unless you immediately undo the sort, of course). Therefore, you should sort by the least important columns in the first pass and by the more important columns in the last pass. Sorting by the most important columns last allows those columns to wield the most influence on the arrangement on the rows in the list.

Sorting multiple columns makes sense when one of the columns is likely to contain multiple entries with the same value. The Top Shoes example is not a good candidate for a multiple-column sort, because each column contains unique values.

Sorting Selected Rows or Columns

It is possible to sort only certain rows or columns in the list. Simply highlight the rows or columns you want to sort, then proceed as if you were sorting the entire list.

Figure 10.24 shows the Sales95 list with the middle six rows marked for sorting. Rows from 4 through 9 were highlighted by clicking the mouse on the row heading for row 4 and dragging the mouse down to row 9.

Figure 10.25 shows the Sales95 list after alphabetically sorting the list by the Employee Name column. As you can see, Bob Snyder has been moved to row 4, the top of the area marked in figure 10.24.

Figure 10.26 shows the Sales95 list with the Jan-95 and Feb-95 columns sorted numerically in the ascending order of the Jan-95 column (the other columns in the list are sorted in descending order). The data in both the Jan-95 and Feb-95 columns were highlighted, but only the Jan-95 column was selected in the Sort dialog box.

Obviously, a word of caution is in order here. Notice that the data in the Sales95 list is hopelessly scrambled after sorting the Jan-95 and Feb-95 columns. The data in each row is completely different than it was before sorting. Arbitrary sorting of rows and columns can invalidate an Excel list as a reliable database.

Sorting Columns Rather Than Rows

You also can sort columns of data rather than rows. Clicking on the **O**ptions button in the Sort dialog box (which was opened by selecting the **S**ort option in the **D**ata menu) opens the Sort Options dialog box (see fig. 10.27).

Figure 10.24

The Sales95 list prepared for a partial sort.

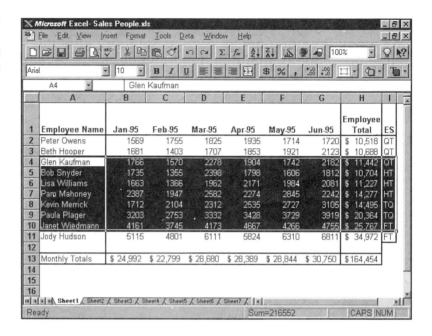

Figure 10.24

The Sales95 list prepared for a partial sort.

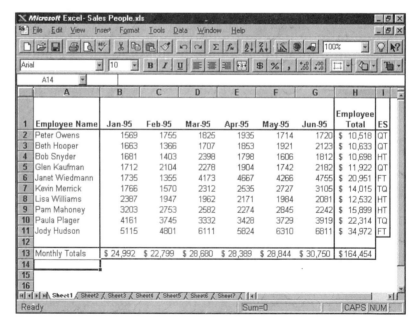

Figure 10.25

The Sales95 list after sorting rows 4 through 10.

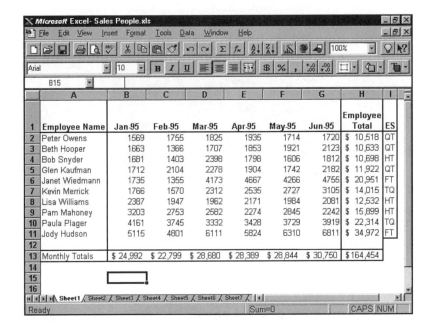

Figure 10.26

The Sales95 list with columns Jan-95 and Feb-95 resorted.

Figure 10.27

The Sort Options dialog box.

In the lower left corner of the Sort Options dialog box is an area labeled Orientation. By default, the Sort **T**op to Bottom option button is selected, meaning that sorts will rearrange the order of the rows in the list. When the Sort **L**eft to Right is pressed, the *columns* of data are sorted instead.

Copying Filtered Data to Another Location

Occasionally, you want to copy filtered data to another worksheet location. By default, an advanced filter occurs "in place." The rows that are filtered out of the data by the information in the criteria range are hidden from view, leaving only the selected rows displayed.

If you want to leave the original data list intact and want to make a copy of the filtered data somewhere else, click the Copy to Another Location option button in the Advanced Filter dialog box (see fig. 10.28).

Figure 10.28

The Copy to Another Location option button.

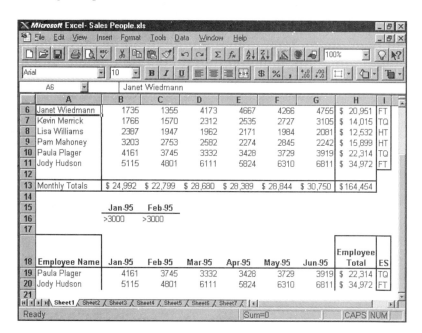

When this button is selected, the Copy **to** text box becomes active (it normally is grayed). All Excel needs is the worksheet cell in which you want the upper left corner of the filter results to appear. In figure 10.28, this location is cell A18. When you click on the OK button, Excel immediately copies the filter results to the location specified in the Copy **to** box.

Figure 10.29 shows the results of the advanced filter set up in figure 10.28. The Excel toolbars have been turned off in figure 10.29 to permit more vertical viewing space, and the overall dimensions have been scaled to 90 percent. The filtered data has been copied to the area beginning with cell A18.

Figure 10.29

Copying the result set to a different location.

New Riders Publishing

INSIDE
SERIES

Stop Be careful when using the advanced filter Copy to option. Any data already in the area specified in the Copy to will be overwritten without warning!

It is even possible to copy the results set to another worksheet. Simply include a reference to the worksheet in the Copy to box on the Advanced Filter dialog box. For instance, to copy the filter results set to the upper left corner of a worksheet named Q1-95, the entry in the Copy to box should read Q1-95!A1.

Note The destination worksheet specified in the Copy to box must already exist in the current workbook. Excel does not create a new worksheet to serve as the destination for the copy to action.

Copying Filtered Data to Another Application

If you want to copy filtered data to another Windows application, be sure to leave the filter criteria in place before the copy operation. Because the records excluded by the filter criteria are hidden, they are not copied.

Note When you copy a list from Excel to Word for Windows, the list becomes a table in Word.

Using the Excel Data Form

Excel provides an incredibly easy-to-use tool for entering new data into lists. The Excel data form displays the data from one record in a list and enables you to add, delete, or otherwise modify the field information in the list.

To open the data form for a list, put the cursor anywhere inside the list and select the Form option in the Data menu. The data form opens with the first record of the data list already displayed (see fig. 10.30).

The data form contains all the fields in the record, arranged vertically. In figure 10.30, the column labels containing dates are expressed as the numbers that Excel uses internally to store dates.

The data form also contains all the items needed to add, delete, or modify records in the data list. The data form can also be used to search for a particular record based on specific criteria entered in the form.

Figure 10.30

The Excel data form.

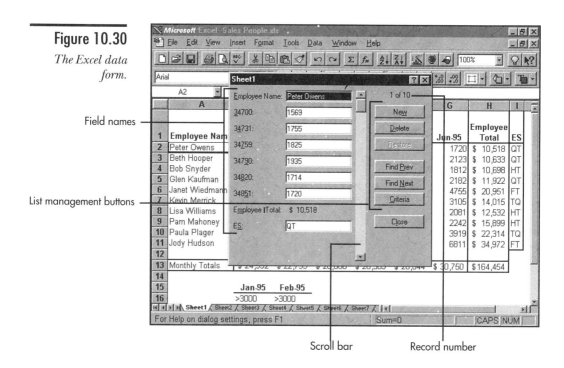

Field names

List management buttons

Scroll bar   Record number

Notice that the Employee Total field cannot be changed in the data form. The information in this field is calculated—it is the sum of all of the "month" fields in the record. Therefore, its value is dependent on other fields in the record, and it cannot be changed directly by the user.

Adding New Records Using the Data Form

A new record can be added to the list by clicking on the New button. All the fields in the form are blanked, as shown in figure 10.31, and "New Record" appears in the upper right corner of the data form. Any data filled in the fields on the data form are added to the data list when the Close button is selected.

Deleting a Record Using the Data Form

The record that appears on the form will be deleted when the Delete button is pressed. The record deletion is permanent and cannot be undone.

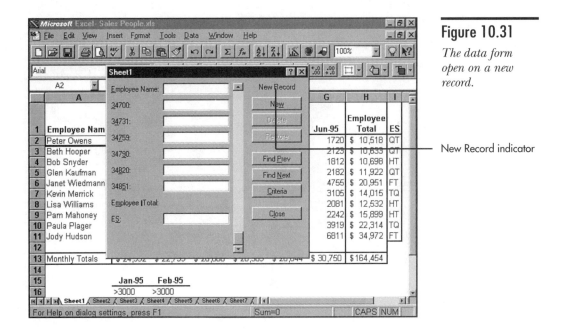

Figure 10.31

The data form open on a new record.

New Record indicator

If any data in an existing record displayed in the form is changed, the **R**estore button becomes active (by default, the **R**estore button is grayed as it appears in fig. 10.31). When pressed, the **R**estore button reverts all changes to the original condition of the record. After you move on to another record, however, the changes become permanent, and you cannot restore the record or undo changes to it.

Navigating Records Using the Data Form

The Find **P**rev and Find **N**ext buttons simply move up and down the data list, displaying records one at a time. As you move through the records, you can make changes to the displayed record or delete it using the list management buttons.

Searching for Records Using the Data Form

The **C**riteria button enables you to search for a particular record based on information you enter in the fields on the data form. After the **C**riteria button is pressed, the form clears and the scroll bar becomes inactive (see fig. 10.32). The word "Criteria" appears in the upper right corner of the form to indicate the form is ready to accept search criteria.

Figure 10.32

The Excel data form prepared to accept criteria.

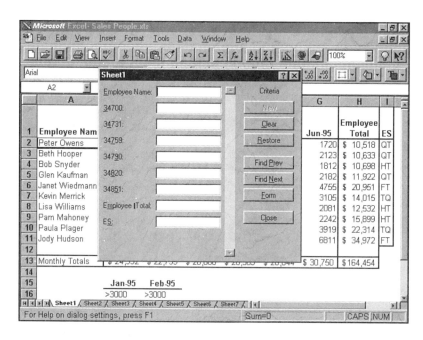

To perform a search, enter search criteria in the appropriate field and click on the Find **N**ext or Find **P**rev buttons to find the next or previous record (respectively) meeting the criteria entered in the field.

Figure 10.33 illustrates a search using the **C**riteria button.

In figure 10.33, <15000 has been entered in the E**m**ployee Total field. When the Find **P**rev or Find **N**ext buttons are pressed, Excel finds the previous or next record (respectively) with a value of less than 15,000 in the Employee Total field, as shown in figure 10.34.

Criteria can be entered in more than one field, if desired. Complex criteria can be built to narrow or broaden the search. An AND condition is implied between the criteria in multiple fields (for example, < 15000 AND > 10000).

If no records meet the search criteria, no error message is generated. Instead, the form simply displays the current field. Always check the results of the searches you conduct through the data form to be sure you've retrieved the information you intended.

Note The data form can display as many as 32 fields. If the form contains more than 32 fields (Excel worksheets can contain as many as 256 columns), the leftmost 32 fields are shown.

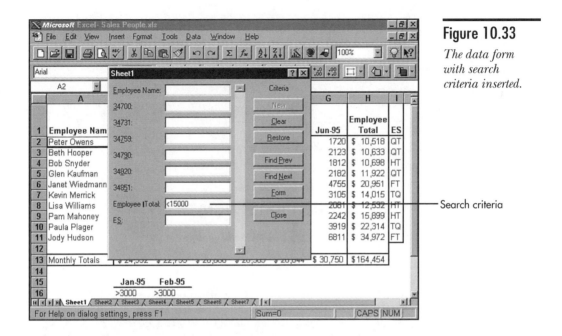

Figure 10.33

The data form with search criteria inserted.

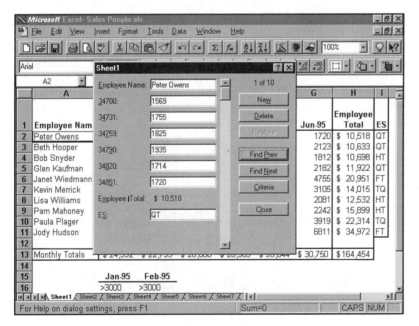

Figure 10.34

The next record with Employee Total < 15000.

Knowing When to Use a Real Database Program

Although Excel offers some very powerful list management options, it does not qualify as a full-fledged database management system. If your data management needs are complex, or if you are working with large data sets, a full-fledged database system like Microsoft Access, Microsoft FoxPro for Windows, Borland Paradox, or Borland dBASE for Windows might be more appropriate for your needs.

The Advantages of Relational Databases

First and foremost, Excel does not offer *relational* database capabilities. In a relational database system like FoxPro or Access, items in a table can be "tied" to items in another table through a *relationship* maintained and managed by the database system.

In other words, a table that contains employee names and addresses and other employment information can be related to another table that contains payroll information. Each record in the employee table has many connections to the payroll table (one connection for each paycheck that has been issued to the employee). After the employee name or other identifier has been determined, a lookup in the payroll table is very fast and efficient.

The same example in Excel would require a very large table of employee data. Each record would contain all the employment information plus payroll data for an employee. Each time a payroll check is issued, a new record would be added to the table for each employee. The new record would contain all of the employee data plus the new payroll information.

Alternatively, a new field could be added onto the end of the table to hold the new payroll information.

In either case, a simple table approach to managing complex data quickly becomes unmanageable. Relational database systems like FoxPro, Access, Paradox, and dBASE contain all the features and utilities necessary to efficiently manage the links between tables.

Databases Provide Powerful Query Capabilities

The query capabilities of relational database systems are formidable and permit rapid performance of very complex queries on large data sets. A database system built of a number of Excel tables just cannot compete with the vast capabilities of modern relational database systems.

New Riders Publishing
INSIDE
SERIES

You Can Build Powerful Forms Using a Database

Although the Excel data form (discussed earlier in this chapter) is extremely easy to use, it lacks many of the features of a true forms-oriented database system like Microsoft Access or Borland Paradox for Windows.

Forms produced by Access, Paradox for Windows, and other Windows database applications can contain routines for validating input. If, for instance, a field is expecting numeric data, and the user tries to input text in the field, the *form* notices the error and informs the user. The Excel data form cannot perform data validation.

Windows database forms can contain a wide variety of objects like text input fields, option buttons (often called *radio buttons*, because they provide selection between *mutually exclusive* options, much like the buttons on a radio), check boxes, combo boxes, selection lists, and so on.

True database forms are flexible. Because of the wealth of different objects and designs that can be used to construct forms in Access, Paradox for Windows, or FoxPro, the developer is not limited to a fixed size and shape or appearance of the form. The Excel data form is designed for a few specific tasks and cannot be modified for more complex functions.

Should You Use a Database Rather Than Excel?

There is no simple answer to the question of whether a true database is better suited to managing your data than Excel for Windows 95. The list management tools in Excel are easy to learn and use. In contrast, a product like Access or Paradox for Windows can take months (or even years) to master completely.

Generally speaking, however, Excel lists are well-suited for managing reasonably small sets (less than 1,000 records) of data or data with fewer than 20 or 30 fields. After you exceed the practical limits of Excel's list management tools (for instance, a simple sort or filter does not yield the information you need), it is time to consider a true database.

The good news is that *all* contemporary Windows database systems like Access, Paradox for Windows, and FoxPro for Windows can read and write Excel worksheets. If you discover you have outgrown Excel's list management capabilities after investing a considerable amount of time and effort building Excel worksheets to contain your data, you can always easily migrate to a Windows database system.

 Note   Microsoft Access is bundled in the Microsoft Office Professional package. If you own Microsoft Office Professional or another Windows database, you might want to import a worksheet or two in a true database table and experiment. Obviously, however, you should carefully back up your Excel worksheets before experimenting with another data management system.

Chapter Snapshot

In this chapter, you learn the power built into Microsoft Query, an add-in that's included with Excel for Windows 95. The information in this chapter enables you to directly access data stored in database tables produced by Microsoft Access and FoxPro, Borland dBASE and Paradox, and other database systems. This chapter explores the following:

♦ Understanding Microsoft Query

♦ Installing and starting Microsoft Query

♦ Mastering the Microsoft Query environment

♦ Retrieving data with Microsoft Query

♦ Building query criteria

♦ Sorting data in Microsoft Query

♦ Saving and reusing queries

♦ Transferring data from Microsoft Query to Excel

A little practice using Microsoft Query can greatly extend the data access capabilities of Excel for Windows 95.

CHAPTER
11

Using Microsoft Query

Microsoft Excel for Windows 95 provides several different ways to access data stored in external database files. As you learned in Chapter 10, because an Excel worksheet is comparable to a database table, you might find it very useful to extract data directly from database files to use within Excel.

Virtually any database can be used to supply information to Excel. Even if Excel does not contain a driver specifically designed for your database (for example, no drivers exist in Excel for Alpha Four or Lotus Approach), it is very likely your database uses a standard database format (like dBASE or Paradox) or can export its tables in one of the common formats like dBASE or Paradox or as delimited text.

Note Although not an "official" abbreviation, this chapter uses the expression MSQuery to indicate the Excel add-in application named Microsoft Query.

What is Microsoft Query?

Microsoft Query (MSQuery) is a complete, stand-alone application that enables you to retrieve data from a number of external data sources. MSQuery is added to your system when you install Excel 95 and resides in the MSAPPS\MSQUERY subdirectory under the Windows directory (which is almost always C:\WINDOWS).

MSQuery provides you with ways to perform many common database tasks: extract data from database tables, delete or modify data in databases tables, or add new data to database tables.

Understanding What Microsoft Query Does

When used within Excel, data retrieved from external database sources (like Microsoft Access and FoxPro or Borland Paradox and dBASE) can be added to Excel worksheets. Using Microsoft Query, data can be piped into Excel worksheets directly from database tables.

MSQuery is designed to build complex database queries without the aid of the entire database engine. These queries draw data from database tables and provide a mechanism for adding that data to Excel worksheets.

As this chapter shows, when you start MSQuery you find yourself inside a complete Windows application. Microsoft Query has its own menu, toolbar, and other controls. You are able to create, save, and reuse database queries from within MSQuery.

This chapter explains Microsoft Query and describes the learning that is required to put MSQuery to work for you.

Starting MSQuery

The MSQuery add-in is located in the Excel **D**ata menu. When you click on the Get E**x**ternal Data option, Microsoft Query starts up (see fig. 11.1).

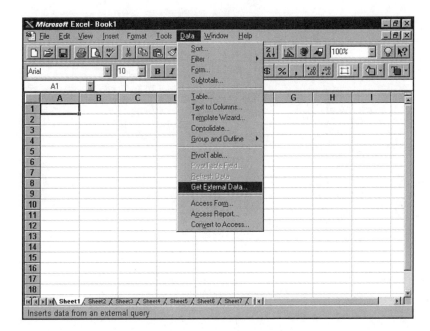

Figure 11.1

*Use Get External
Data to start
MSQuery.*

Excel still is running after the MSQuery environment appears—just behind the
MSQuery window. When started as an Excel add-in, MSQuery is able to transfer data
directly from database files into Excel. Because MSQuery includes the tools and
options necessary to extract only the data you are interested in, MSQuery is much
more efficient to use than importing the same files directly into Excel.

Although Excel can directly open only dBASE database files, most database systems
like Access, FoxPro, and Paradox are able to convert their native table formats to
dBASE. Opening a Paradox table inside Excel, therefore, would require two steps:
using Paradox to save the table in dBASE format, and opening the dBASE format file
in Excel. MSQuery enables you to work directly with the Paradox, dBASE, FoxPro, or
other database files from within Excel.

If you cannot find a Get External Data option in the **D**ata menu, the Microsoft Query
add-in has not been installed on your computer. Run the Office Setup program to
install it.

The Microsoft Query Toolbar

All of your interaction with Microsoft Query takes place through the toolbar and
menu options in the MSQuery environment. Although a complete description of the
Microsoft Query environment is not necessary at this point, it might be useful to

become familiar with the icons on the toolbar. Figure 11.2 shows the entire MSQuery toolbar. These tools are explained in table 11.1.

Figure 11.2

The Query toolbar.

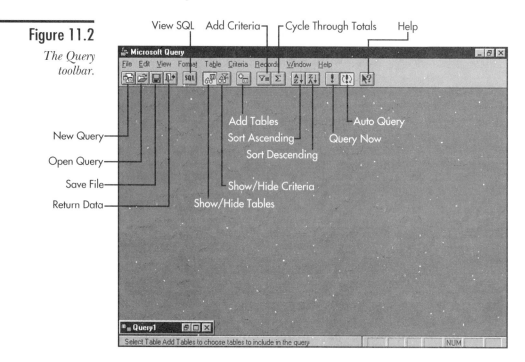

TABLE 11.1
Microsoft Query Toolbar Icons

Icon Name	Description
New Query	Begins the process of building an entirely new database query.
Open Query	Opens an existing query.
Save File	Saves the current query for future use.
Return Data	Returns you to Excel when your query activity is complete. This button is not on the toolbar when Microsoft Query is started as a stand-alone application.
View SQL	Queries generated by Microsoft Query are converted to *structured query language* (SQL) by Microsoft Query, even when the database does not require SQL. You might want to use this button to view the SQL statement during your work.

Icon Name	Description
Show/Hide Tables	Hides the "Table pane" in Microsoft Query to provide more room for the Query pane.
Show/Hide Criteria	Hides the "Query pane" in Microsoft Query to provide more room for the Table pane.
Add Tables	Opens the Add Tables dialog box so that you can add another table to the query.
Add Criteria	Automatically adds criteria to the query.
Cycle Through Totals	Provides access to a number of basic statistics for data retrieved from databases (discussed later in this chapter).
Sort Ascending	Quickly sorts columns of data in ascending order.
Sort Descending	Quickly sorts columns of data in descending order.
Query Now	Activates the query.
Auto Query	Runs the query when the query criterion is complete.
Help	Provides specific help for the objects you see in the MSQuery window.

Although most of your work with MSQuery involves little more than opening a database source, specifying which tables to examine, and building the query criteria, this chapter details each of the options available to you as you use Microsoft Query.

It is not necessary to memorize the purpose of each toolbar button. As you move the mouse cursor across the buttons, the MSQuery status bar shows you each button's function.

The rest of this chapter deals with using MSQuery to extract data from database tables. Although a Microsoft Access database is used as the example, the principles are the same for essentially any database source.

Using MSQuery to Retrieve Data

The first thing you see when you open Microsoft Query with the MSQuery add-in in Excel is the Select Data Source dialog box (see fig. 11.3). This dialog box also appears when you click on the New Query button or select New Query in the File menu of stand-alone Microsoft Query.

Figure 11.3

The empty Select Data Source dialog box.

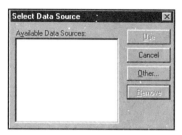

Selecting the Data Source

Microsoft Query needs to know the data source from which you want to get data. The first time MSQuery is opened, the Select Data Source dialog box is empty.

Microsoft Query needs to know what kind of data source you want to use. Clicking on the **O**ther button opens the ODBC Data Sources dialog box (see fig. 11.4).

Figure 11.4

The installed ODBC drivers.

Your system might have more or fewer ODBC drivers than shown in figure 11.4.

Note What is ODBC? Microsoft has established the *Open Database Connectivity* for Windows applications in an attempt to provide a standard application interface to the bewildering variety of database file formats that exist in the world today. Any application (like Microsoft Query) that understands ODBC can use ODBC drivers to connect to a wide variety of database files.

An ODBC driver usually is written by the database vendor and is distributed as a particular type of *dynamically linked library* (DLL). DLLs usually are stored in the Windows system directory.

When Microsoft Query is started, it checks for ODBC drivers that have been installed on the computer system. When you ask MSQuery to open a particular type of database (like Access, FoxPro, or Paradox), MSQuery uses the ODBC driver DLL to find out how to interpret the data stored in the database tables.

Figure 11.4 shows "MS Access 7.0 Database," which will be used for this example.

Adding ODBC Drivers

New ODBC drivers can be added to your system by clicking on the New button in the ODBC Data Sources dialog box. The Add Data Source dialog box, shown in figure 11.5, enables you to notify Microsoft Query of any new ODBC drivers located on your system.

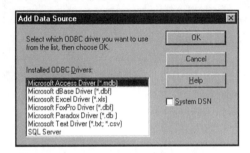

Figure 11.5

All ODBC drivers installed on the system.

Simply click on the ODBC driver you want to install in MSQuery and press the OK button. This action informs MSQuery that the ODBC driver is available and should be added to the list of drivers in the ODBC Data Source dialog box.

Note   Entirely new ODBC drivers (those not yet located on your system) are installed through the ODBC icon in Windows Control Panel.

Deleting ODBC Drivers

If you do not need to use Microsoft Query with one of the data sources shown in the list in the ODBC Data Sources dialog box, highlight it by clicking on its name one time and press the **R**emove button. This action does not remove the ODBC DLL from the Windows system directory, so the ODBC driver still is available to other Windows applications.

Opening the Data Source

After the data source has been selected in the ODBC Data Source dialog box and the OK button is pressed, Microsoft Query immediately searches for candidate database files in the active directory.

The Select Database dialog box shows all candidate databases in the active directory (see fig. 11.6). Because you selected "MS Access 7.0 Database" in the ODBC Data Sources dialog box, only Microsoft Access databases appear in the Database N**a**me list.

Figure 11.6

*All databases in
the current
directory.*

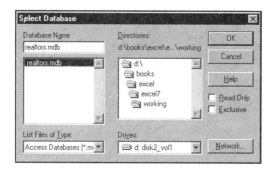

 Note   The REALTORS.MDB database is found on the *Inside Excel for Windows 95* disk.

For this example, you use the REALTORS.MDB database.

 Note   Do not be misled by the List Files of **T**ype combo box in the lower left corner of the
Select Database dialog box. Although it might appear that this list enables you to
select a different type of database file, it is there only in case your database file has
a different extension than the default for the type of database selected in the ODBC
Data Sources dialog box.

For instance, the default extension for Microsoft Access database is MDB. If, for
some reason, the Access database had a different extension, its name would not
appear in the Database N**a**me list. The List Files of **T**ype combo box enables you to
see either the Access Databases with the MDB extension or All Files in the current
directory. It does not permit you to select a different type of database file.

Adding More Database Types to the Query

Oddly enough, when the Microsoft Access database is selected, instead of being
returned to the MSQuery environment to proceed with the query, you are returned
to the Select Data Source dialog box. The only difference this time is that MSQuery
already knows that you intend to use the MS Access 7.0 Database type in your query
(see fig. 11.7).

This design permits you to add another type of database to your query. Because our
example involves only the Microsoft Access database, the **U**se button returns to the
MSQuery environment.

New Riders Publishing
INSIDE
SERIES

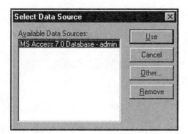

Figure 11.7

The Select Data Source dialog box.

Opening a Database Source

After the **U**se button is clicked in the Select Data Source dialog box, MSQuery opens the Microsoft Access database previously selected in the Select Database dialog box and examines the tables found within it.

In the case of REALTORS.MDB, six different tables (named "Agents," "Agencies," and so on) are in the database. The Add Tables dialog box, which opened automatically upon return to the MSQuery environment, shows the tables in the REALTORS.MDB database (see fig. 11.8).

Figure 11.8

The REALTORS.MDB database contains six tables.

The data contained in the REALTORS database includes the names and contact information for a number of different realtors and the real estate agencies for which they work, plus the selling information for several different homes.

Note   The Agents table is part of the REALTORS.MDB database on the *Inside Excel for Windows 95* disk.

When you select the Agents table and click on the **A**dd button, the Agents table is added to the current query, as shown in figure 11.9.

Figure 11.9

The Agents table has been added to the query.

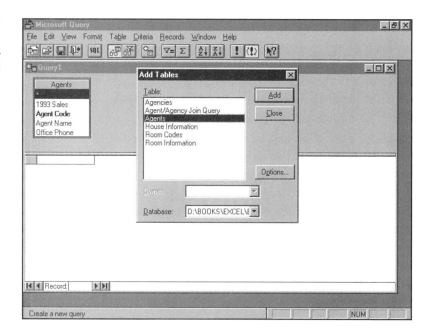

The large window on the MSQuery screen is called the *Query window*. MSQuery features a multiple document interface, which means that more than one Query window can be placed within the MSQuery environment at one time. Normally, however, you work with only one query at a time.

Displaying Data

The fields in the Agents table appear in the upper pane of the Query window. To display the data stored in the database fields, click on the field names (one at a time) in the table window in the upper portion of the Query window and drag them to the data display area in the bottom half of the Query window. Figure 11.10 shows the Query window after the "Agent Name" and "1993 Sales" fields from the Agents table have been added to the data area.

Notice that no query criteria have been applied to extract the data in figure 11.10. All the data in the Agent Name and 1993 Sales fields are displayed. None of the records in the Agents table have been excluded. This query is similar to the situation in which a database table is imported directly into Excel.

Note Instead of dragging fields to the Data pane, you can move them by double-clicking on them in the table field list.

Fields are dragged to the Data pane

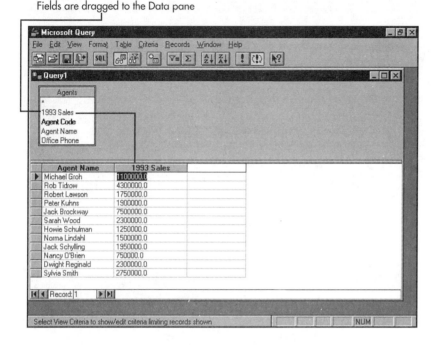

Figure 11.10
The Query window.

Understanding the Query Window

The Query window is rather complicated. It contains all of the information necessary to build complicated database queries, and although it is quite straightforward to use, it can be confusing to understand. Before we proceed with building complicated queries, a quick overview of the Query window's components is necessary.

Initially, the Query window is divided into upper and lower portions. The upper portion contains all the tables involved in the query, while the lower area contains the data retrieved by the query.

Figure 11.11 explains the default components of the Query window.

These default components are as follows:

◆ **Table pane.** The Table pane contains all of the tables included in the query. Each table window shows the database fields within the table. In the case of the Agents table, the fields are named "1993 Sales," "Agent Code," "Agent Name," and so on.

◆ **Data pane.** The Data pane displays the data extracted from the Agents table by MSQuery. The data extracted from the database source is called the *results set*.

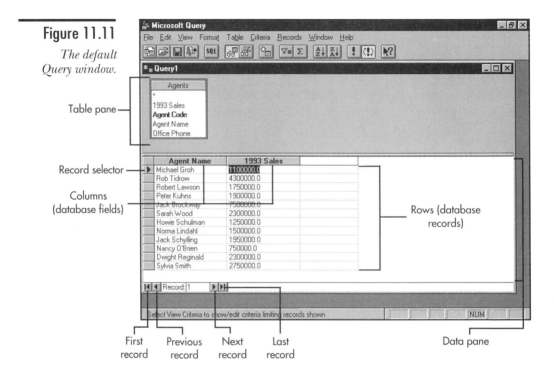

Figure 11.11

The default Query window.

◆ **Record selector.** The small triangle at the extreme left of each record in the Data pane can be used to highlight (or "select") the entire record.

◆ **Navigation ("VCR") buttons.** In the lower left corner of the Data pane are a number of highly specialized buttons that provide navigational functions to move through the records in the Data pane. Large data sets might have hundreds or even thousands of records. The VCR buttons (so named for their similarity to the control buttons on most VCRs) provide a way to quickly move through the records in the Data pane.

◆ **Columns (database fields).** Each column in the Data pane holds data from a field in the database table.

◆ **Rows (database records).** Each row in the Data pane contains the data for the selected fields for one record in the database table.

As you work your way through this chapter, you should become familiar with the various components of the Query window.

Note   Be aware of the difference between the words field and column. A *field* is the name of a specific part of a database table. Database fields normally are displayed as columns of data. In this chapter, the words field and column are used almost (but not quite) interchangeably.

Similarly, a *record* is a component of a database table. Database records normally are displayed as rows of data. All of the data items in a record are related to each other—for instance, your name, address, and phone number might make up a record in a database, and can be displayed on the screen in a row of a table.

This chapter uses the word "field" when referring to the structure of the database table, and "column" for the way in which database fields are displayed. Similarly, a "record" is a specific unit of data stored in a database that appears on the screen as a row of a table.

Selecting Individual Fields

A field is selected for display in the Data pane by clicking on its name in the table window on the Table pane and dragging it to the Data pane. If you release the field anywhere in the unoccupied area of the Data pane, the column displaying the new field's data is added to the right of the far right column currently displayed in the Data pane.

If you release the new field on top of an existing column in the Data pane, the new column is inserted in the existing column's location and the existing column is pushed to the right.

Selecting All Fields

Notice in figure 11.11 that an asterisk (*) appears at the very top of the list of fields in the Agents table. If you drag the asterisk to the Data pane, all fields in the Agents table are added to the Data pane in the order in which they were created in the Agents database table.

If you want to add all the fields to the Data pane in alphabetical order, double-click on the field list's title bar (in figure 11.11, the field list title bar says "Agents") to highlight all the fields in the list, and drag any of the fields to the Data pane. All fields are automatically added to the Data pane in alphabetical order.

Specifying Query Criteria

So far, the examples have involved working with the complete set of records from the Agents database table. In most cases, however, you do not really want to work with the complete set. Most often, you want to select only certain records from the database for display or manipulation.

A thorough understanding of constructing and using query criteria is essential to success using Microsoft Query.

What are Query Criteria?

Before you can extract specific records for a database table, you must specify the *query criteria* that MSQuery should use during its search of the database table.

Perhaps the simplest form of query criteria is something similar to "Show me the names of all real estate agents who sold more than $2,000,000 of property in 1993." Intuitively, you know that somewhere along the way, the mathematical expression "> 2000000" must figure into the query criteria.

Furthermore, you must be able to tell MSQuery that you want the criteria to be applied to the "1993 Sales" field, and that you want to see only those records whose "1993 Sales" fields contain values greater than 2,000,000.

Query criteria are not restricted to a single field, as in this simple example. You might, for instance, want to see the real estate listings of all four-bedroom (or larger) houses in the database with offering prices between $100,000 and $150,000 that have attached two-car garages and have at least two full bathrooms. This query involves no fewer than four different fields: "Number of Bedrooms," "List Price," "Garage," and "Number of Bathrooms."

It should come as no surprise that MSQuery is carefully designed to help you construct query criteria exactly like these examples.

The Add Criteria Button

So far in this chapter, you have not used the Show/Hide Criteria button on the MSQuery toolbar. By default, the Show/Hide Criteria button is not pressed, meaning that the Criteria pane of the Query window is hidden from view.

When you click on the Show/Hide Criteria button, the Query window changes, as shown in figure 11.12, to reveal the Criteria pane. The Criteria pane normally is kept hidden between the Table and Data panes.

Query grid

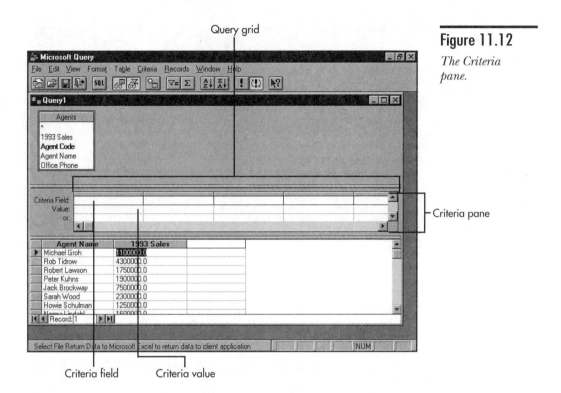

Figure 11.12

The Criteria pane.

Criteria pane

Criteria field   Criteria value

Notice that when the Criteria pane is revealed, the Data pane shrinks to accommodate the space required by the Criteria pane.

Using the Criteria Pane

The query criteria area in the Criteria pane appears as a grid, usually called the *query grid*. Each column in the query grid represents one field that is involved in the criteria. The row labeled "Value" is where you enter the *expression* you want MSQuery to apply to the data in the field when searching for records to display in the Data pane.

To add a field to the Criteria Field row of the Criteria grid, click on the name of a field in the Table pane and drag it down to the Criteria Field row, as shown in figure 11.13.

Next, enter the mathematical expression that completes the query criteria. In this case, ">2000000" yields the records of all real estate agents who sold more than $2,000,000 of real estate in 1993. The expression ">2000000" is entered into the Value row under the name of the field in the Criteria pane. The completed query criteria is shown in figure 11.14.

Figure 11.13

*Drag fields from
the table list to the
query grid.*

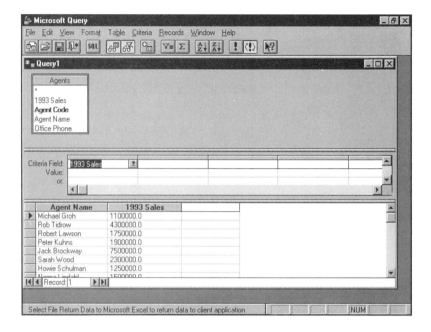

Figure 11.14

*The completed
query criteria in
the query grid.*

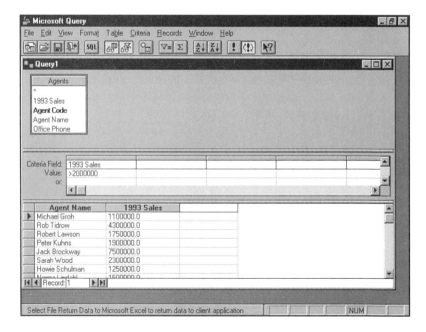

By default, the query is triggered as soon as you complete the query criteria and move the insertion point someplace else on the Query window. To test the autoquery capability of MSQuery after the ">2000000" is filled in, click the mouse on the table field list in the Table pane or use the Tab key to move to the next column in the query grid. You see the screen change, as shown in figure 11.15.

Query Now
button

Auto Query
button

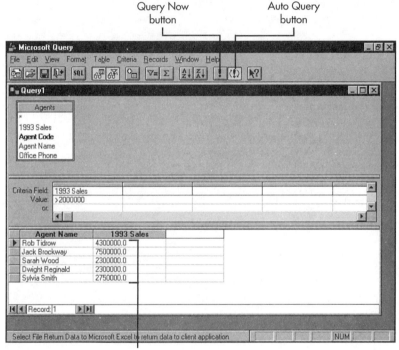

Figure 11.15

By default, the query runs automatically after the criteria is complete.

Results set

If you do not like the autoquery behavior, which can cause significant delays when the data set is very large and can hinder building complex queries (discussed later in this chapter), you can turn off the function by clicking on the Auto Query button.

Note The Auto Query button remains depressed after it has been clicked. The Query Now button, however, is a "momentary contact" button—it works only when you click it.

After the Auto Query button is released, you must explicitly trigger the query by clicking on the Query Now button on the toolbar (the Query Now button looks like an exclamation mark).

Note Notice that MSQuery does not accept commas in the expression, although you can have a space between the ">" and "2000000."

Adding Criteria to the Query Grid

Usually, a successful query requires more than simple criteria built from a single field. Most real-world exercises involve multiple fields and even multiple tables.

Adding a field to the query criteria is simple. Notice that the criteria grid has space for more than one field. Figure 11.16 shows the effect of adding fields to the criteria grid. In this case, both the List Price and Number of Bedrooms fields are examined, apparently because the user wants to see the MLS numbers and addresses of all houses with three or more bedrooms at list prices less than $150,000.

Figure 11.16

A query with two fields in the criteria grid.

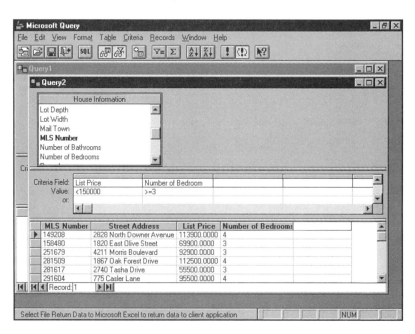

Note When adding fields to the query grid, you might find that the Auto Query feature of MSQuery gets in the way. Because Auto Query runs the query every time a criteria set (field and query criteria) is completed (for instance, List Price < 150,000), you might find that Auto Query interrupts your work. After you enter the information for the query on one field and move to another field, Auto Query runs before you can enter the information for the next field.

In all of the cases illustrated in this chapter, the data sets involved are so small that queries run pretty quickly. On larger data sets, particularly if the data source is

located on a server or another node on a network, you might find that the pause while queries run is intolerable.

Be sure to disable Auto Query if the delay becomes too intrusive.

Saving the Query

After you build a query and are satisfied that you are retrieving the data you want from the database table, you might want to save the query for reuse at a later time.

When you click on the Save Query button, the Save As dialog box opens (see fig. 11.17). Notice that the default extension for MSQuery files is QRY.

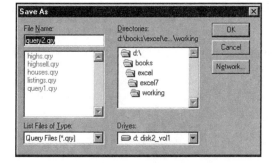

Figure 11.17

Saving the query for future use.

All the information necessary for MSQuery to rebuild the query conditions is saved in the query file: the database type and name, the table name, and the SQL statement.

You can open the query later and run or modify it as needed.

Understanding Expressions

Microsoft Query recognizes a wide variety of different expressions. Simple expressions like ">" (greater than) are easy to understand, but MSQuery can work with much more complicated expressions.

Using Comparison Operators in Query Criteria

The "greater than" sign (">") is an example of a comparison operator. When you use ">" in the query criteria, you are telling MSQuery that you want to *compare* the data in a field with the value to the right of the ">". For instance, ">2000000" means, "show me all of the records with values higher than 2000000."

MSQuery understands a number of other comparison operators as well:

< **Value less than.** Returns all records with field data less than *value*. "< 2000000" returns records with numbers like 1,500,000 and 1,900,000.

<= **Value less than or equal to.** Returns all records with field data smaller than or equal to *value*. "<= 2000000" returns 1,500,000 and 1,900,000, as well as 2,000,000.

> **Value greater than.** You saw this comparison operator in action. Returns all records with field values greater than *value*.

>= **Value greater than or equal to.** Returns all records with field data larger than or equal to *value*. ">= 2000000" returns 2,350,000 and 4,300,000, as well as 2,000,000.

= **Value equal to.** Returns only those records with field data equal to *value*. Be careful with this one, because often you might not find any records meeting this criteria. This operator often is used with text that you want to find in the database. For instance, ='Sarah Wood' in the Agent Name field returns all the records in which the agent's name is Sarah Wood.

Notice that single quotes are used around the text in expressions. Spaces within the quotes are permissible. Also, MSQuery is not case-sensitive. ='Sarah Wood' and ='sarah wood' return the same records.

<> **Value not equal to.** Returns all records with field data that are not equal to *value*.

Most of the mathematical comparison operators look like the algebraic symbols you learned in high school. A little practice is all that is necessary to master the use of these symbols in MSQuery expressions.

Note   Always remember that mathematical expressions cannot contain commas. ">2,000,000" is an illegal MSQuery expression.

Using Logical Operators in Expressions

Another category of operator uses multiple conditions when performing the search. These expressions combine the expressions or use them separately when building the query criteria:

◆ *Value1* **AND** *value2.* *Value1* and *value2* are combined for the search to narrow the results set to only those records which match both conditions. Only those records meeting both criteria are returned. Figure 11.18 illustrates an example using the And operator.

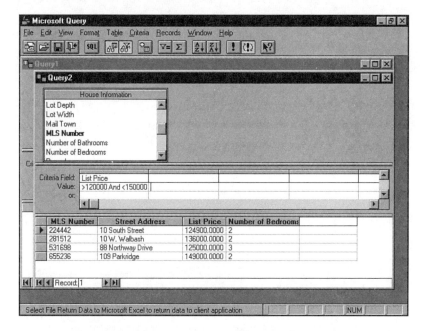

Figure 11.18

This query criteria returns only those houses with list prices between $120,000 and $150,000.

◆ *Value1* **OR** *value2.* The Or operator expands the search somewhat by returning records that match either *value1* or *value2.* In figure 11.19, The query criteria has returned all houses with list prices less than $75,000 or more than $200,000. (The results set also was sorted in ascending order on the List Price column.)

◆ **NOT** *value.* Returns all records that *do not* have value in the field. Figure 11.20 illustrates a query that returns all houses with list prices not less than $150,000 (which is almost silly, because it is the same as saying "Show me all houses with list prices *more than* $150,000).

Esoteric Operators

A few operators are not often used in expressions. For the most part, these operators are equivalent to other, more commonly used operators in expressions:

◆ **Between** *value1* **and** *value2.* Returns all records with data in the field between *value1* and *value2.* You might want to see all houses with list prices between $120,000 and $150,000, for instance. This operator is easily replaced with the And operator, as described earlier in this chapter.

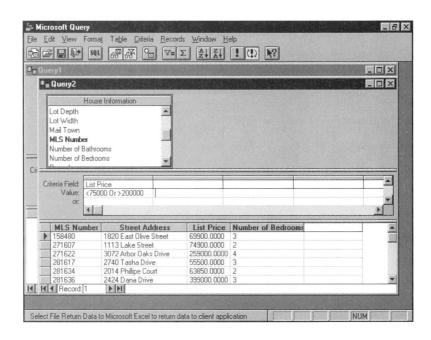

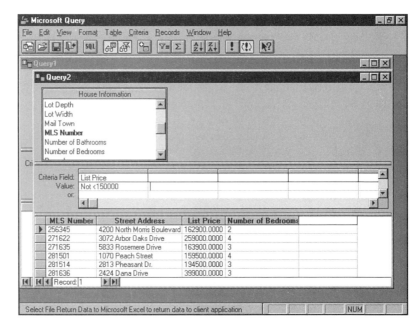

◆ **In (value1, value2, ...).** Returns records with values found in a list of values. The list of values must be enclosed in parentheses. An example might be finding the records with Agent Names In ('Sarah Wood', 'Rob Lawson', 'Rob Tidrow').

◆ **Is Null, Is Not Null.** Determines whether the value in the field is null (has no value) or not null (has a value). When used with Null, this operator returns all records with empty values in the field.

◆ **Like 'value'.** Returns values matching value, where *value* contains the wildcard character ("%"). In fact, *value* must contain the wildcard character. Figure 11.21 shows how the Like operator works. All records with Agent Name fields that begin with "Rob" have been returned in the results set.

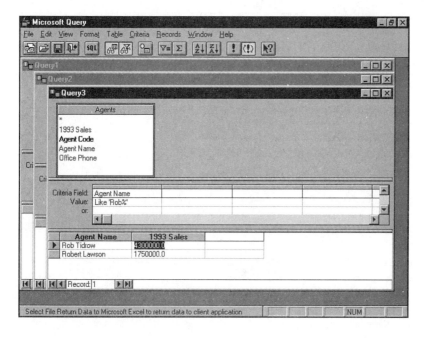

Figure 11.21

Using the Link operator to get fields with agent names beginning with "Rob."

The Like operator is very powerful and can be used to return records from fairly ambiguous query criteria.

Sorting the Results Set

The data displayed in the Data pane is difficult to use in its current condition. The records in the results set are in no order; the records appear in the order in which they were entered into the Agents database table.

Sorting the Results Set in Ascending Order

You can understand the results of a query more easily if the data is sorted in alphabetical or numeric order. Perhaps the objective of this query is to determine the best-selling real estate agent in the database. It is, therefore, useful to sort the 1993 Sales data in ascending order so that the top agent appears at the bottom of the list.

It is not necessary to highlight the entire column before sorting. Simply position the insertion point somewhere within the 1993 Sales column and click on the Sort ascending button. Figure 11.22 shows the result of an ascending sort on the 1993 Sales column.

Figure 11.22

The 1993 Sales column sorted in ascending order.

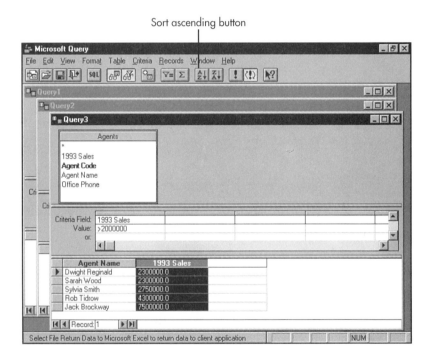

Sort ascending button

Note Sorting the data in the results set does not modify the data in the underlying database tables.

Sorting the Results Set in Descending Order

It looks a bit odd, however, to have the top sales agent at the bottom of the list. To reverse the sort order, click on the Sort descending button (see fig. 11.23).

New Riders Publishing
INSIDE
SERIES

Sort descending button

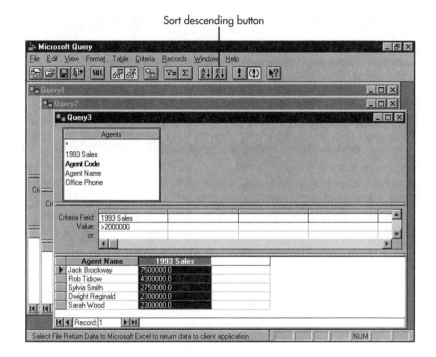

Figure 11.23

*The 1993 Sales
column sorted in
descending order.*

Sorting on Multiple Columns

Although it does not make sense in this example, you can sort on multiple columns.
Maybe the results set is so large that, even when sorted on one column in the Data
pane, it still is difficult to pick out the individual data item that is important.

Two basic methods are available for sorting multiple columns. The first method
involves sorting columns sequentially. Start with the data that is most important and
sort it first. Then, while holding down the Ctrl key, sort each column in the order of
decreasing importance, so that the least important column is sorted last.

For instance, maybe the results set includes the names of agents and all the houses
each agent has listed for sale. You might sort the houses by their Agent Code first,
then sort the column of MLS numbers next. The results set is sorted with all houses
being sold by each agent grouped together.

Note   The House Information table is part of the REALTORS.MDB database on the *Inside
Excel for Windows 95* disk.

Figure 11.24 illustrates this principle. Rather than the Agents table, the House
Information table was used for this query. The Agent Code column was sorted first;
then, while holding down the Ctrl key, the MLS number column was sorted.

Figure 11.24

*The House
Information
table.*

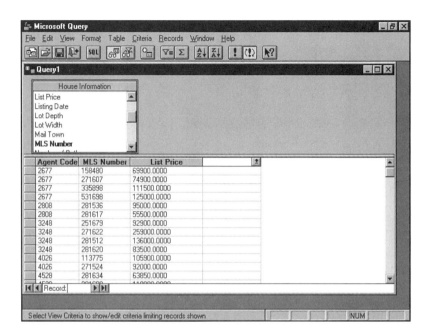

Notice that for each agent code, the MLS numbers assigned to that agent are sorted in ascending order.

Note Be sure to hold down the Ctrl key when sorting subsequent columns. Otherwise, the entire results set is sorted according to the last column sorted.

Queries on More than One Database Table

Very often, you need to use more than one table in a query. So far in this chapter, the examples have used only one table in the Table pane, and all queries have been directed to that one table. More complex queries require two, three, or more tables to provide data. In fact, multiple table queries often are used to consolidate and filter data before adding it to Excel worksheets.

Adding Tables to the Query

For the moment, return to the simple query that extracted all records from the Agents table for agents who had sold more than $2,000,000 of property in 1993 (discussed earlier in the chapter).

Suppose you want to see listing information on the houses these agents currently have listed. The only fields in the Agents table are Agent Code, Agent Name, Office Phone, and 1993 Sales. Nothing in the Agents table tells you about the houses in the database. How can you determine which houses each of these agents has listed?

The House Information table in the REALTOR.MDB database contains all the information relating to house listings, including the MLS number, list price, address, and other data. Obviously, the House Information table contains the information you want to see.

Ideally, there ought to be some way to *join* the Agents table to the House Information table so that you can see just which houses each agent has listed.

Relational databases like Microsoft Access, FoxPro, and Paradox, are the answer. Each table contains one or more *key fields,* which serves as a "connector" to tie the table to the other tables in the database.

 Note The REALTORS.MDB database described in this section can be found on the disk accompanying *Inside Excel for Windows 95.*

Joining Tables

To begin the process of joining the Agents and House Information tables, a new query is created by clicking on the New Query button. Microsoft Query "remembers" the database sources that have been used in the past and presents them in the Select Data Source dialog box (see fig. 11.25).

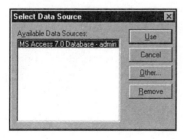

Figure 11.25

The Select Data Source dialog box.

Because the Agents and House Information tables are part of REALTORS.MDB, a Microsoft Access database, select the MS Access 7.0 Database option and click on the <u>U</u>se button.

Next, the Select Database dialog box opens, enabling you to select REALTORS.MDB from the list of Access databases in the current directory.

Next, the Add Tables dialog box opens. This time, instead of selecting only the Agents table, the House Information table is added to the Table pane, as well.

When the Select Tables dialog box is closed, the Agents and House Information tables appear in the Tables pane (see fig. 11.26). Notice that Microsoft Query has drawn a line connecting these tables.

Figure 11.26

The Agents and House Information tables in the Tables pane.

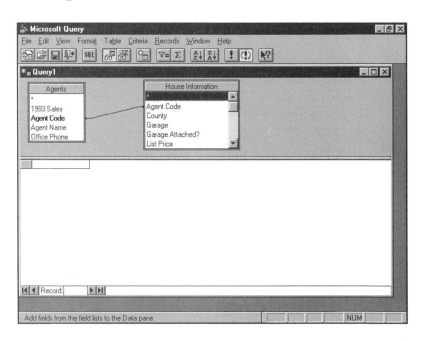

To be more specific, the line joining the Agents and House Information tables is drawn from the Agent Code field in the Agents table to the Agent Code field in the House Information table. In the Agents table, Agent Code appears in bold-face type to indicate that it is a key field for the Agents table. The Agent Code in the House Information is just another bit of data contained in this table.

The line drawn between these tables, however, represents a *relational join* between the Agents and House Information tables. Microsoft Query draws lines between fields in the field lists that the tables share. This relational join means that the Agent Code in

the Agents table can be used to find all of the corresponding Agent Code fields in the House Information table. You can, therefore, determine which houses an agent has listed by looking for the agent's code in the House Information table.

Using Joined Tables in Queries

Microsoft Query makes it easy to use joined tables in queries. Start by dragging the Agent Name field from the Agents table to the Data pane. Next, drag the MLS Number, Street Address, and List Price fields from the House Information table to the Data pane. The result looks like figure 11.27.

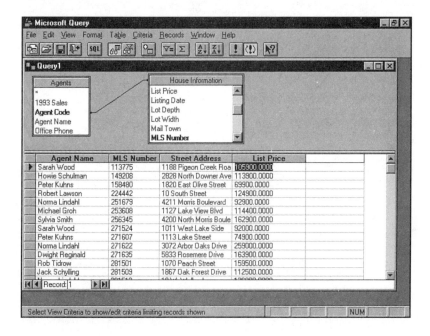

Figure 11.27

Adding fields from multiple tables to the Data pane.

Each row of data in the Data pane represents a real-estate agent's name and some information on one house that the agent has listed.

Notice that you do not need to add the Agent Code to the Data pane. MSQuery understands the relationship between these tables and brings the related data to the Data pane.

The data displayed in the Data pane is a little difficult to understand. You have a hunch that each agent has more than one house listing in the database, but at first glance, it looks as though only one house is listed for each agent. If you look more closely at the Agent Name column, you notice that Sarah Wood and Norma Lindahl appear twice, indicating that each agent has more than one house listed.

It is easy to clarify the data displayed in the Data pane. An ascending sort is applied to the Agent Name column, resulting in figure 11.28.

Figure 11.28

After sorting on the Agent Name column.

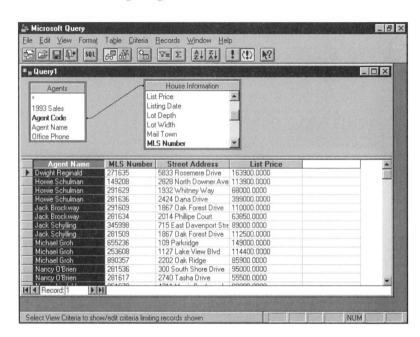

Mission accomplished! Now you easily can see that Dwight Reginald has only one house listed, while Howie Schulman has a total of three different houses in the database.

Although much more complicated multiple-table queries are possible, the principles involved are the same as presented in this example: open the database source, add the tables to the Table pane, and drag the desired fields to the Data pane. Often, sorting or other manipulation is required to make sense of the data as it is drawn from the database tables.

Automatic Joins

Microsoft Query calls the lines drawn between related tables *automatic joins* to indicate that it automatically recognizes the relationship between the tables. Sometimes MSQuery needs you to perform a *manual join* to give it a little help understanding relationships between tables.

Manual Joins

From time to time, no automatic relationship exists between tables in the Table pane. In the example described earlier in the section, the Agent Code field in the Agents and House Information tables defined a relationship between these tables. The relationship was formed in Microsoft Access at the time the tables were created.

Consider the situation in which one table comes from an Access database and another from a dBASE application. Although the data in the tables might be related (for instance, the Access application contains customer names and addresses and the dBASE table contains invoice information), no direct link exists between the tables, because they came from different applications.

Microsoft Query enables you to specify relationships between tables manually. You can create manual joins only if the tables share common fields, even if the tables were created in different applications.

Add the tables to the Table pane using the techniques discussed earlier in this chapter. Then, use the mouse to drag a common field from one of the tables to the field list of the other table. Microsoft Query understands the relationship between the tables and builds the relational join between them.

Part III

Charts

Chapter Snapshot

One of the most valuable parts of Excel is its charting function. By using this feature, you can prepare a wide variety of charts that help you communicate or analyze the information contained in your worksheets. Whether your need is based on analyzing data or presenting information, Excel's charting function will most likely suit your needs. In this chapter, you learn the following:

◆ Charting terminology

◆ Creating charts using the ChartWizard

◆ Editing and changing charts

◆ Embellishing your charts using legends, text, arrows, and graphics

◆ Determining which types of charts are better for presenting or analyzing your data

Despite the wide variety of choices available in generating your charts, Excel makes creating and formatting charts easy. Use this chapter to understand all the fundamentals involved in using charts.

CHAPTER

12

Complete Guide to Charts

E xcel for Windows 95 has one of the most complete charting functions of any spreadsheet application. In fact, it's so good that there is little need for dedicated charting programs—even for difficult technical charts. It can produce not only standard charts like bar charts and line charts, but also attractive charts with a three-dimensional appearance.

Excel also contains many tools for embellishing your charts, including the capability to add legends, text, arrows, and graphics images to your charts. You also have full control over the symbols and colors that Excel uses on your charts, and you can even use a graphics image rather than colors in certain types of charts. (For example, a chart showing auto sales might have stacked cars, as you see in many newspapers and magazines.)

Microsoft also has made creating attractive, effective charts in Excel fairly easy. A function called the ChartWizard walks you through all the steps required to quickly create a chart, previewing the eventual results at each step.

Understanding Charts

Before you begin, you need to understand the terminology used to describe the different parts of each chart. Please examine figure 12.1.

Figure 12.1

A sample line chart.

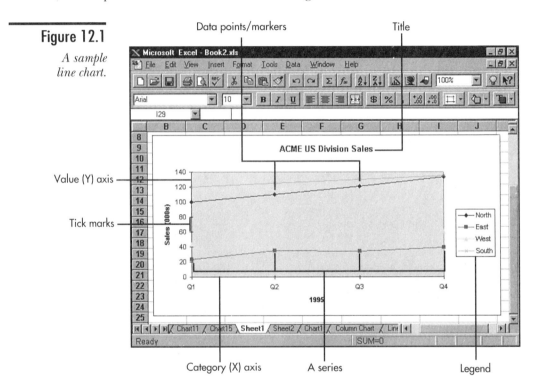

Data Points

The *data points* are the individual points on the chart. You can control the way the data points are represented by using different symbols (squares, circles, triangles, and so on) to make your chart more readable. This idea is particularly important when you are presenting black-and-white charts, as opposed to color ones.

As you learn in this chapter, certain types of charts enable you to move data points manually. When you are finished, Excel actually changes the worksheet data to match your changes to the chart—a marketing person's dream!

Series

A *series* is a group of data that forms one part of the data shown on a chart. In the sample chart in figure 12.1, each line represents a series of data. Each series of data is made up of a formula that you can see when you click on the series. If, for example, you click on the North line, you see the series formula appear in the formula bar. The series formula in this case is as follows:

```
=SERIES(Sheet1!$C$2,Sheet1!$D$1:$G$1,Sheet1!$D$2:$G$2,1).
```

Understanding and editing series formulas is covered in Chapter 14, "Advanced Charts for Business and Science."

Axes

The *axes* are the vertical and horizontal lines that show what is being charted. Excel offers many features to control these axes, including formatting, manual control of the scale shown, and double y-axes (the vertical axis).

Most charts have two axes: the *x axis*, also known as the *Category* axis, and the *y axis*, typically called the *Value* axis. Some charts also can contain a second Value (Y) axis. Certain 3D charts can be formatted to contain a *z axis* (a 3D chart can show categories along two dimensions, with the z axis normally showing the categories or values from the front of the 3D chart to back).

 Note   See Chapter 14 for more information on creating dual Value (Y) axis charts.

Legend

The *legend* defines what each series represents. In figure 12.1, the boxed legend explains that North is represented by diamonds, East by squares, West by triangles, and South by Xs. Legends can be formatted in many different ways, and you can place them anywhere in your chart.

Markers

The *markers* are the symbols (squares, diamonds, and so on) used at each intersection of the plotted data on a line chart. The markers show what the actual data is; the lines between each marker are generated by Excel simply to "connect the dots." You can control the color, type, and style of markers in Excel.

Tick Marks

Tick marks are the incremental marks that appear along each axis to measure or designate the data. The chart shown in figure 12.1 shows four tick marks along the x axis that mark where each quarter's sales are plotted, and eight tick marks along the value axis to show exactly where each value falls. Excel enables you to control the degree of detail the tick marks show, or if they are shown at all. You could, for example, show a tick mark for each month of the year. Because the chart only deals with quarterly data, however, these extra tick marks serve no purpose.

Grid

Figure 12.2 shows the same sample chart as figure 12.1, but a grid has been added. *Grids* help the reader see more easily where the chart markers line up with the axis references.

AUTHOR'S NOTE

Be careful when using gridlines. Sometimes they don't really add anything to the chart, and they can actually make it more difficult to read. The sample chart with gridlines shown in figure 12.2 is a good example. The gridlines make the chart too busy and don't really help the reader of the chart. It is easy to see where the data markers line up with the sales figures and categories without the gridlines.

Figure 12.2

A sample chart with grid lines.

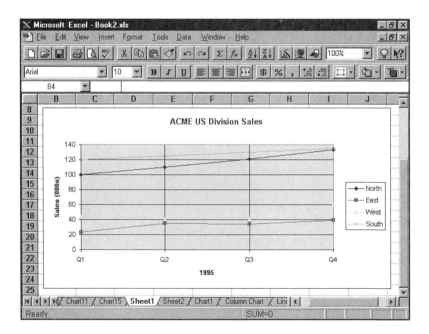

Titles

Titles are lines of text you use to label or identify elements of a chart (or the chart itself). The sample chart has a main title at the top ("ACME US Division Sales"), as well as titles attached to each axis ("1995" and "Sales (000s)").

Introducing the ChartWizard

Excel includes a powerful utility that walks you through each step of the chart creation process. This utility is called the *ChartWizard*, and it makes creating charts in Excel a snap. Not only can you use the ChartWizard to create new charts, but you also can use it to change existing charts.

Selecting Chart Data

To use the ChartWizard, you begin by selecting the data you want to plot:

1. Click and drag, or click and Shift+click, on the range of cells you want to include. Select noncontiguous ranges by holding down the Ctrl key as you select each range.

2. Click on the ChartWizard button in the toolbar. Your pointer changes to a small cross.

3. Use the cross to select the area in the workbook in which you want Excel to create the chart. Move the pointer to the upper left corner of that area, then drag down and to the right. When the chart area is where you want it to be, release the mouse button.

 Tip   Hold down the Alt key as you drag to force Excel to align the chart box with cell borders. Hold down the Shift key as you drag to force Excel to create a perfectly square chart area.

After you have selected the area in which to place the chart, the first ChartWizard dialog box appears, shown in figure 12.3.

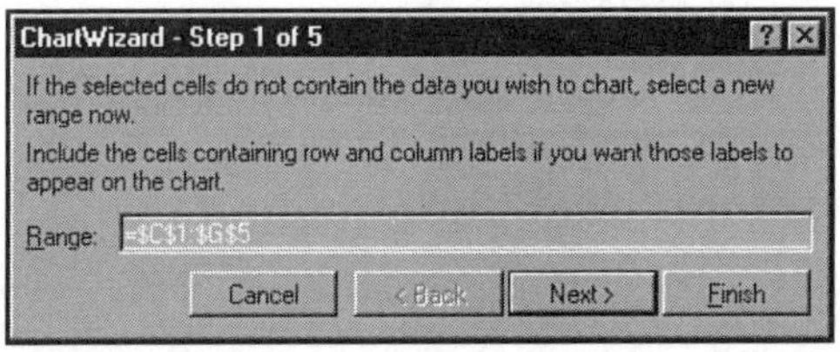

ChartWizard - Step 1 of 5

If the selected cells do not contain the data you wish to chart, select a new range now.

Include the cells containing row and column labels if you want those labels to appear on the chart.

Range: =$C$1:$G$5

Cancel | < Back | Next > | Finish

Figure 12.3

Step 1 of the ChartWizard.

Using ChartWizard Dialog Boxes

Each ChartWizard dialog box uses the buttons described in table 12.1.

TABLE 12.1
ChartWizard Dialog Box Buttons

Button	Function
Help	Get help on the current step in the ChartWizard.
Cancel	Cancel the chart.
Back	Go back to the previous steps to change your choices.
Next	Move to the next step in the ChartWizard.
Finish	Complete the chart creation process using Excel's standard chart and default chart settings.

Confirming Plot Data

The first step of the ChartWizard shows you the range of cells you have selected to create the chart. You can edit the cell ranges shown in the first dialog box, although it's typically easier just to cancel the chart and reselect the data you want to plot, reactivating the ChartWizard after you have chosen the correct ranges. You can also select the cell range with the Step 1 dialog box active, but the dialog box will remain in the foreground and hide the worksheet.

Selecting the Chart Type

The second dialog box in the ChartWizard shows you the various Excel chart types, with the default column chart already selected for you (see fig. 12.4). Choose the chart you want by clicking on it, and then clicking on the Next button or by double-clicking on the desired type.

Selecting the Chart Format

After you select the Next button, you see the third dialog box, which shows you the different ways in which the selected chart type can be formatted. Figure 12.5 shows this dialog box for three-dimensional line charts.

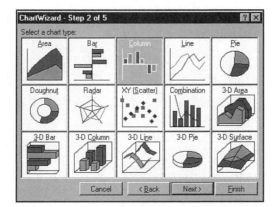

Figure 12.4

Step 2 of the ChartWizard.

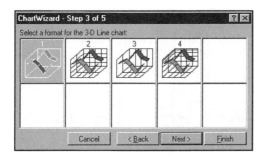

Figure 12.5

Step 3 of the ChartWizard.

Choosing Chart Options

Depending on the type of chart you selected in step 2, Excel asks you for various settings that control the way it presents the chart.

The step 4 dialog box, shown in figure 12.6, offers the following options:

◆ **Data Series in Rows or Columns.** These two option buttons control whether Excel assumes that each chart series should originate from columns in your data or from rows. If you choose **R**ows, for example, each series of the chart is created from a row in your worksheet data. When you select one of these buttons, Excel shows you a sample of that option.

Note Excel uses the "shape" of your data range to assume whether you want the data series plotted in rows or columns. If the data is wider than it is tall, for example, Excel assumes that you want the series to be plotted in the rows. If Excel guesses incorrectly, you easily can change the option button setting.

Figure 12.6

*Step 4 of the
ChartWizard*

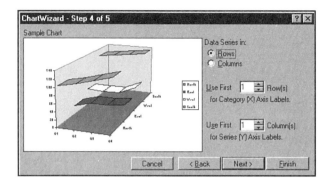

◆ **U̲se First x Row(s) for Category (X) Axis Labels.** Change the value of *x* in this setting to control the number of data rows to use to label the Category axis of the chart. If your data has no labels in the first row, set this number to 0.

◆ **Us̲e First x Column(s) for Value (Y) Axis Labels.** Change the value of *x* in this setting to control the number of data columns to use to label the Value axis of your chart. If the first column has no labels, set this number to 0.

Note   The cell range that was selected for the example included column C and row 1 (refer back to fig. 12.3). These cells do not contain the raw data, but the information they represent (column and row labels) can easily be used for axis labels. In step 4, the feature to use the first row(s) and column(s) for axis labels identified these cells for this purpose.

Adding Legends and Titles

The fifth step in the ChartWizard enables you to add titles and a legend to your chart. Enter each label in the field provided. Figure 12.7 shows this dialog box.

Figure 12.7

*Step 5 of the
ChartWizard.*

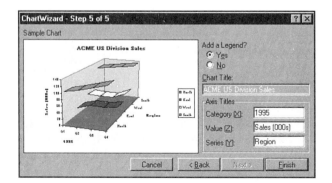

Tip You can force Excel to update or refresh the Sample Chart view immediately by pressing the Tab key.

After you click on the **F**inish button in the final ChartWizard dialog box, your chart is created, as shown in figure 12.8.

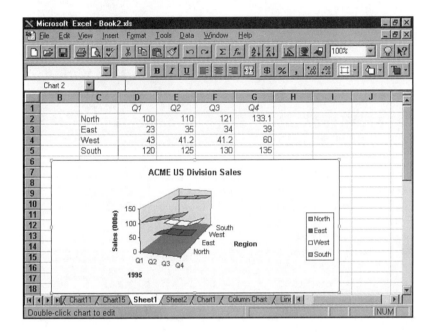

Figure 12.8

The finished chart.

Using the ChartWizard to Create a Chart Sheet

You also can use the ChartWizard to create an entire sheet in your workbook devoted to your chart. This method creates a full-page chart, as opposed to an embedded chart that coexists on the same page as the rest of your worksheet.

To create a chart page with the ChartWizard, follow these steps:

1. Select the data to be charted.

2. Click your right mouse button on the sheet tab for the current sheet. From the pop-up menu, choose Insert. This selection brings up the Insert dialog box, shown in figure 12.9.

3. Choose the General tab, then Chart icon in the dialog box and click on the OK button.

Figure 12.9

The Insert dialog box.

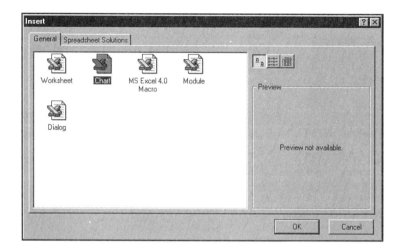

As an alternative to steps 2 and 3, pull down the **I**nsert menu and choose **C**hart. This step activates a cascading menu from which you select **A**s New Sheet to begin the ChartWizard with your selected data. Figure 12.10 shows a chart created as a separate page in your workbook.

Figure 12.10

A full-page chart in a workbook.

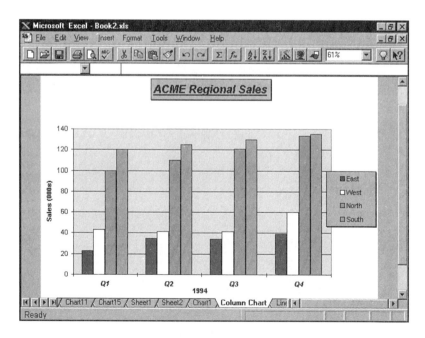

New Riders Publishing
INSIDE SERIES

Tip If you simply want a chart of your data using the Excel chart defaults, select the data you want to chart and press the F11 key to instantly create the chart.

Changing Charts

Creating charts is only half the battle. Even with the ChartWizard, you often have to format and reformat charts until you achieve the exact results you want. This section teaches you to format all of the elements of your charts.

Selecting Areas of the Chart

You can select each element of a chart simply by clicking on it. Alternatively, you can press the right arrow key repeatedly to cycle through all the selectable chart elements. You might want to try this on a couple of charts to see which parts of the chart you can select individually.

Tip To select an individual data point, click once on the point to select the entire series. Click a second time on the point to select just that data point. Alternatively, click on the series to select it, and then press the right arrow key to cycle through each data point.

Adding a New Series to a Chart

Figure 12.11 shows a chart that was created before the Europe data line was added to the table.

To add the new line of data to the chart, follow these steps:

1. Select the new data to be added.

2. Grab the border of the new data selection and drag it to the chart. When you move the mouse to the chart, the chart is enclosed in a gray line.

3. Release the mouse button. If the new series is consistent with the chart data, Excel adds the series to the chart automatically. Otherwise, the Paste Special dialog box appears, as shown in figure 12.12.

The Paste Special dialog box for charts has the following choices:

Figure 12.11

A column chart before adding a series.

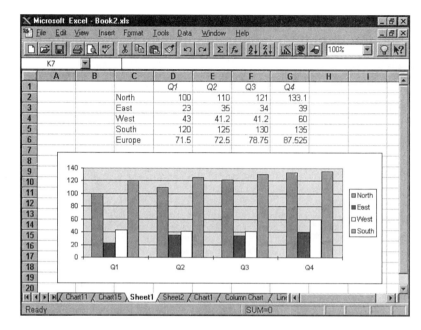

Figure 12.12

The Paste Special dialog box for charts.

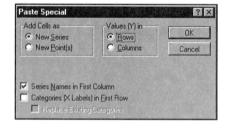

◆ **Add Cells as.** Choose between New **S**eries or New **P**oint(s). Select New **S**eries to insert the data as a separate data series. New **P**oints creates a new category with the inserted data. In this example, New **S**eries is the appropriate choice.

◆ **Values (Y) in.** Here you can choose between your pasted data being contained in **R**ows or **C**olumns. Although the data in this example obviously is in a row, you also can paste larger selections of data where this choice is not so obvious.

◆ **Series Names in First Column.** If selected, Excel uses the first column of the pasted data for the series labels.

◆ **Categories (X Labels) in First Row.** If the data you are pasting has its labels in the top row, select this check box.

◆ **Replace Existing Categories.** This option is available only if the previous selection also is checked. It specifies that the new labels should replace the existing labels in the chart.

Note Remember to include the cell(s) containing the label information, when available, so that you can take advantage of the automatic labeling features in the ChartWizard.

After you click on OK, Excel shows you the updated version of your chart (see fig. 12.13).

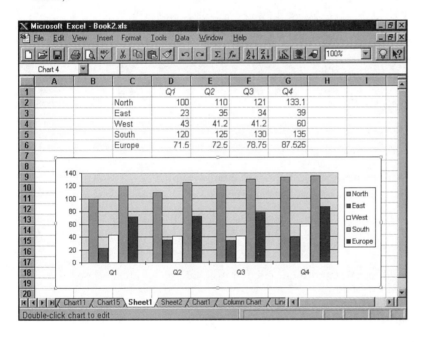

Figure 12.13

The chart with added data.

Removing a Series from a Chart

To remove a data series from a chart, follow these steps:

1. If you are working with an embedded chart, open the chart you want to edit by double-clicking on it. If the chart is on its own chart sheet, this step is not necessary, although you might need to click on the tab for the page which contains the chart.

2. Click on the series you want to remove. You should see all the parts of the series selected with small boxes visible, as in figure 12.14.

Figure 12.14

Selected series.

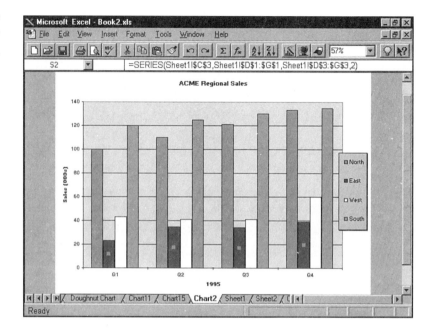

3. To remove the series, perform one of these operations:

◆ Press the Del key.

◆ Click the right mouse button on the series you want to remove, then choose Clear from the pop-up menu.

◆ Select the series and then pull down the **E**dit menu and choose Cle**a**r. This displays a cascading menu from which you can choose **A**ll (clear all series), **S**eries (clear only the selected series), or **F**ormats (removes any formatting you have applied). Select **S**eries.

Moving and Sizing Chart Elements

Many elements of the chart can be moved, including text and legends. To move a chart element, just select it and drag it to its new location. In the case of text objects in the chart, select the text object, then grab the border of the text box and drag it to a new location.

You also can resize many parts of a chart, such as the plot area or text boxes. To do so, select the object. Grab one of the small boxes in the corner, which are called *handles*. You then can drag the handle to a new position. When resizing an element by dragging one of the handles, hold down the Shift key to force the element to retain its original proportions.

Changing the Appearance of Chart Elements

Excel provides you with virtually unlimited capabilities to format your chart so that it is as pleasing and effective as possible. To format any chart element, select that chart element and click the right mouse button on the selected element. From the pop-up menu, choose Format *x*, where *x* is the name of the element you want to format. Also, rather than using the pop-up menu, you can pull down the F**o**rmat menu and choose S**e**lected Object. The actual name of the menu item changes depending on which object you have selected when you access the F**o**rmat menu.

 Tip

To instantly pull up the formatting dialog box, press Ctrl+1 after selecting the object you want to format.

Each type of object presents a different formatting dialog box, depending on what can be formatted for the selected object. For example, if you pull up the formatting dialog box with an axis selected, you see a page to change the axis scale.

The following sections show you each dialog box page and explain which types of objects apply to the dialog box page.

Patterns

Depending on what type of element you are formatting, the Patterns page has different choices available. Sometimes the different choices are subtle, like adding a check box called S**m**oothed line if you are formatting a series in a line chart. Other times the differences might be obvious, such as a section on the page for choosing tick mark styles when you are formatting an axis.

The Patterns page of the formatting dialog box is used to control the following formatting tasks:

◆ **Borders.** You can control the style, color, and weight of the line used to border the object. With some objects, you also can choose a *drop shadow*, which gives the box the appearance of depth.

◆ **Area fill.** Some objects enable you to control their fill colors and patterns. You can, for example, control the color and pattern of each bar in a bar chart or each slice of a pie chart. Also, with some charts, you can select a check box called In**v**ert if Negative, which tells Excel to reverse the color for any parts of the series that represent negative numbers.

◆ **Lines.** Some objects—notably gridlines and axes—enable you to control the style of the line with which they are drawn. You can control the color, style, and weight of these lines. Also, if you are formatting a series in a line chart, the Patterns page has a check box that enables you to select smoothed lines. On a line chart, you can use the Patterns dialog box page to select the style of the markers used for each plot point.

One example of the Patterns dialog box page is shown in figure 12.15.

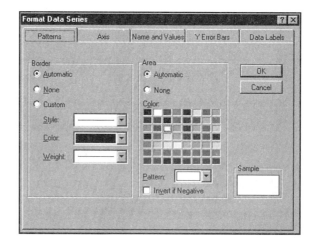

Font

If the object you are formatting is a text box or has text associated with it (such as an axis), you can use the Font page in the formatting dialog box to change the characteristics of the font used. Figure 12.16 shows the Font page.

Using AutoFormat

After you have found a chart format that you like and that you might want to use again, Excel enables you to store your formatting choices as an AutoFormat template. You then can apply these templates to a new chart and escape the drudgery of constantly reformatting your charts. AutoFormat also helps reduce error in cases where you constantly produce charts you want to format the same way.

To add to the AutoFormat table, follow these steps:

1. Start with a chart selected that contains all the formatting you want to store.

2. Pull down the Format menu and choose **A**utoFormat. The AutoFormat dialog box appears (see fig. 12.17).

    The AutoFormat dialog box initially shows you the different types of charts in the list on the left called **G**alleries. After you click on each different chart type in the **G**alleries list, you can select from the subtypes shown in the windows to the right.

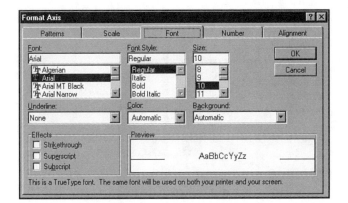

Figure 12.16

The Format Axis dialog box showing the Font page.

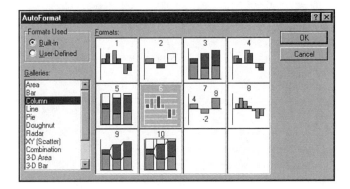

Figure 12.17

The AutoFormat dialog box.

3. To access the user-defined charts, click on the option button marked **U**ser-Defined. You now see the dialog box changed, as in figure 12.18.

   The AutoFormat dialog box already has a user-defined chart format called MS Excel 4.0. This format was the default chart in Excel 4. If you want to use it, click on the OK button.

4. Click on the Custo**m**ize button. The AutoFormat dialog box changes again, as shown in figure 12.19.

5. Click on the **A**dd button to add the current chart format to the AutoFormat system. The AutoFormat system prompts you for the name of your chart format with the dialog box shown in figure 12.20.

Note You also can select an existing format in the **F**ormats list and delete it using the **D**elete button.

Figure 12.18

*The AutoFormat
dialog box with
user-defined styles.*

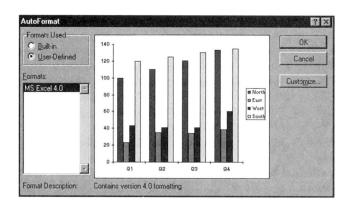

Figure 12.19

*The AutoFormat
dialog box in
Customize mode.*

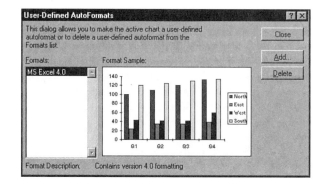

6. Type a name and a description for the chart in the fields provided and click on the OK button. The User-Defined AutoFormats dialog box reappears. To close it, click on the Close button.

After you have defined a chart in AutoFormat, it is available for all your Excel workbooks. You can apply your automatically formatted charts by accessing Format, AutoFormat. In the AutoFormat dialog box, click on the User-Defined button, then click on the name of your format in the Formats list. Finally, click on the OK button to apply the AutoFormat to the currently selected chart.

Adding Text

Excel charts have several types of text available: axis labels, attached labels, attached text, and unattached text. *Axis labels* indicate what each point on the axis labels represents; this type of text cannot be moved. *Attached labels* are titles, axis titles, and data labels. *Attached text*, although it is created in certain predefined locations, can be moved freely around the chart. Finally, you can create *unattached text* that you also can place anywhere you want in the chart.

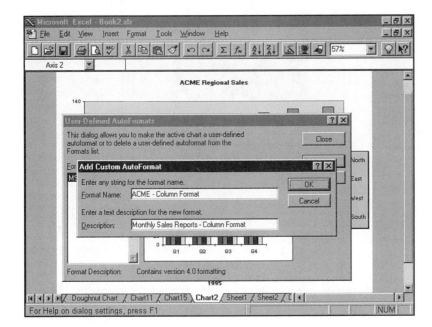

Figure 12.20

The Add Custom AutoFormat dialog box.

Creating Unattached Text

To create unattached text in an Excel chart, deselect any selected chart elements and simply start typing. Your text appears in the formula bar. After you press Enter, the text is placed in the center of the chart area. You can click on the text to select it, format it, and move it.

Creating Data Labels

Data labels are attached to each data point of the chart. For example, numbers next to each bar in a bar chart are data labels. Depending on the type of chart you are working with, several different types of labels are available.

Note A *label* is text attached to a chart element, but a *title* is text attached to the title position at the top of the chart or to the axes.

To control data labels, pull down the **I**nsert menu and choose **D**ata Labels. You see the dialog box shown in figure 12.21.

Figure 12.21

The Data Labels dialog box.

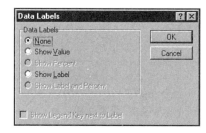

The Format Data Labels dialog box has the following choices:

◆ **None.** Suppresses all data labels

◆ **Show Value.** Places the appropriate number next to each data point

◆ **Show Percent.** Places the percentage of the total next to each data point for pie charts

◆ **Show Label.** Shows the category label next to each data point

◆ **Show Label and Percent.** Shows the category label and the percent of the total next to each data point on pie charts

Figure 12.22 shows a column chart with value data labels attached to each bar.

Figure 12.22

A column chart with value data labels.

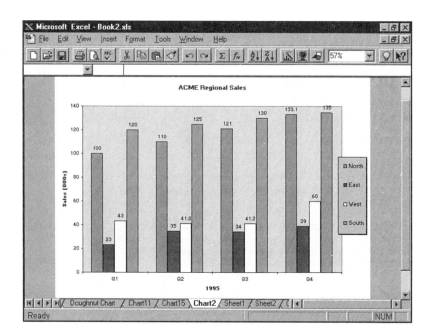

Creating Titles

To create a title, select <u>I</u>nsert, <u>T</u>itles. You see the dialog box shown in figure 12.23.

The Titles dialog box has a selectable check box for each type of title your chart can accept. In the example in figure 12.23, you see that the chart has no Value (Y) Axis title. To create one, select the check box and click on the OK button. A new text area is created next to the Value axis, ready to accept your input. Type in the text for the title and press Enter.

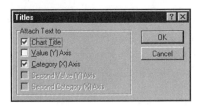

Figure 12.23

The Titles dialog box.

Changing Text Alignment

Most of the text on the Excel chart, with the exception of legend text, can be re-aligned or rotated so that you can fit more data on the page at very little cost in readability. To try these options, select the text you want to align and press Ctrl+1 to bring up the formatting dialog box for that text. Click on the Alignment page, which is shown in figure 12.24. These options are self-explanatory.

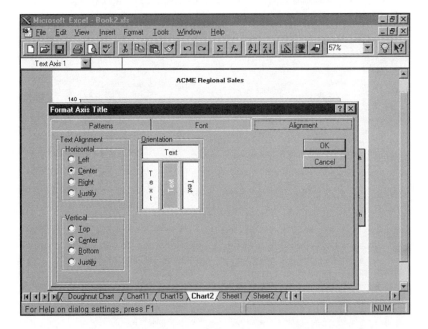

Figure 12.24

The Alignment formatting page.

Controlling Legends

You can decide whether to include a legend on your Excel charts. To delete an existing legend, select the legend and press Del or click on the Legend button in the Chart Toolbar. To create a new legend, pull down the Insert menu and choose Legend. A default legend is created, which you can then format as you want using the formatting techniques covered earlier in this chapter.

You also can change the way a legend is arranged by dragging any of its handles. As you drag the handle, an outline previews the way your legend will be arranged, from a straight vertical arrangement of legend items, to multicolumn legends, to a straight horizontal arrangement.

Controlling Axes

Controlling the axes of your charts can play a powerful role in the impact of the information you convey. For example, consider figure 12.25, which shows a line chart of an imaginary index (sort of like the Consumer Price Index). Notice that it is virtually impossible to tell what the chart is saying with all the lines grouped together so closely at the top of the chart. While the ChartWizard attempts to compensate for the range of displayed values, Excel will sometimes show zero as the bottom value axis entry.

Figure 12.25

An imaginary index chart.

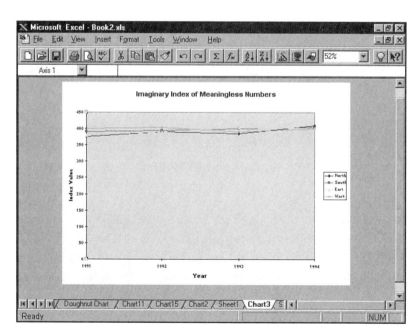

You can solve this problem by changing the Value axis scale:

1. Click on the Value (Y) axis to select it.

2. Pull down the Format menu and choose Selected Axis. The Format Axis dialog box appears.

Tip   After you have selected the object you want to format, either press Ctrl+1 to instantly pull up the formatting dialog box for that object, or click on the right mouse button and choose Format object.

3. Click on the dialog box tab labeled Scale. The Scale dialog box page is shown in figure 12.26.

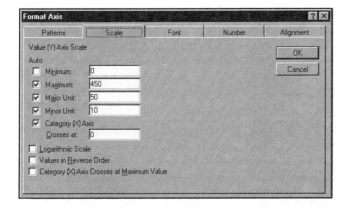

Figure 12.26

The Format Axis dialog box showing the Scale page.

Table 12.2 shows the different settings available on the Scale dialog box page.

TABLE 12.2
Scale Dialog Box Page

Setting	Purpose
Minimum	Defines the minimum point on the scale. If the check box in this field is selected, Excel uses the default value (0 or the lowest data point on the chart, whichever is lowest). Entering in a minimum value automatically deselects the check box.
Maximum	Defines the maximum point on the scale. If the check box is selected, Excel automatically uses the highest data point on the chart, rounded up to the next highest major axis number.

continues

TABLE 12.2, CONTINUED
Scale Dialog Box Page

Setting	Purpose
Major Unit	Defines the major unit used for gridline control. You can choose to have gridlines display at each major unit on the axis. You also can control the tick marks used to denote the major unit. See the following section on controlling tick marks for information about the way this page and the tick marks relate.
Minor Unit	Defines the minor unit used for gridline control. You can choose to have gridlines displayed at each minor unit on the axis. You also can control the tick marks used to indicate each minor unit on the axis.
Category (X) Axis Crosses at	Enables you to tell Excel where on the Value at axis you want the Axis Category axis to intersect. You could, for example, enter the number used in the Maximum field, which would cause Excel to place the Category axis along the top of the chart.
Logarithmic Scale	Causes Excel to use a logarithmic scale for the axis.
Values in Reverse Order	Forces Excel to reverse the default order for the Value axis, so that the lower numbers are at the top of the axis, and the higher numbers are at the bottom of the axis.
Category (X) Axis Crosses at Maximum Value	If you select this check box, Excel places the Category axis wherever the maximum value of the Value axis is. In the example chart, this would cause the Category axis to be displayed at the top of the chart.

Figure 12.27 shows the sample line chart with the Minimum value set to 370. As you can see, the chart is now much more readable, and you now can see how each region is doing with respect to the other regions. You also can discern an overall upward trend in the numbers. Although the trend is somewhat difficult to see, you can see it far easier than before when all the lines were grouped very tightly together.

AUTHOR'S NOTE

Although being able to adjust the axis measurements on your charts is a valuable tool for analysis and presentation, I have to admit that I really dislike it when newspapers make economic data more alarming than it really is by making it unclear that they

are playing with the Value axis in the charts they show. Some charts that purport to show steep economic increases or declines actually say very little (or show only very small changes) after the values used in the Value axis are considered.

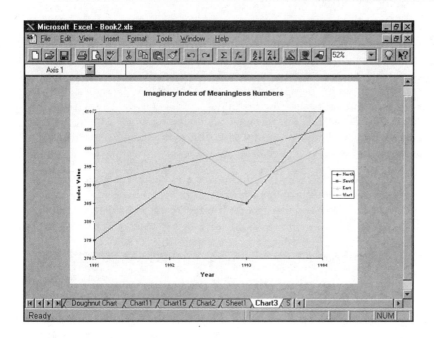

Figure 12.27

The Value axis with an adjusted scale.

Changing Axis Tick Marks

You can control the tick marks used for your charts with the Patterns page of the Format Axis dialog box for the selected axis. Select the axis and press Ctrl+1 to pull up the formatting dialog box, then click on the Patterns tab. The Patterns page is shown in figure 12.28.

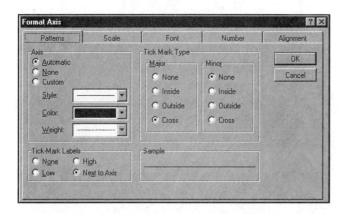

Figure 12.28

The Format Axis dialog box showing the Patterns page.

The Patterns page enables you to control whether tick marks appear for your minor and major axis numbers, what type of tick marks to use (None, Inside, Outside, or Cross), and the way the labels next to the tick marks appear. Select the options you want for the axis and click on the OK button.

Changing 3D Perspective

Excel contains six different types of 3D charts. Using a 3D chart, however, presupposes that you can change your viewing perspective. Fortunately, Microsoft did not forget to include this capability. Being able to rotate 3D charts can be critical in showing information that might otherwise be hidden, and it can also be used to change the impact that a chart has. For instance, all else being equal, viewing a chart as if you are looking up at it can have a profoundly different impact than viewing it from above looking down.

Figure 12.29 shows a 3D bar chart with the hindmost series being somewhat obscured by the other bars. You can fix this problem simply by rotating your viewpoint of the chart to the left about 1/8 turn. You can accomplish this feat using a dialog box or the nifty wireframe feature.

Figure 12.29

A 3D chart with an obscured series.

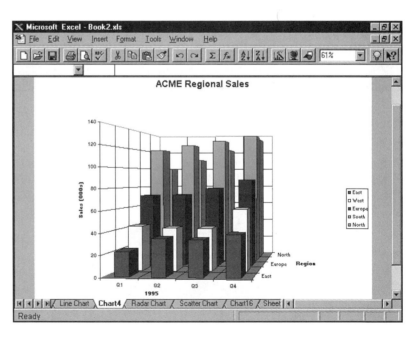

To change the perspective of the chart using the dialog box, follow these steps:

1. Pull down the Format menu and choose 3D **V**iew. You see the dialog box shown in figure 12.30.

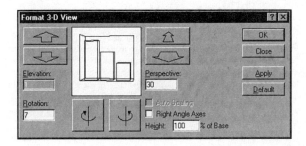

Figure 12.30

The Format 3-D View dialog box.

2. Adjust the **E**levation, **R**otation, and **P**erspective to the new viewpoint.

   The viewpoint fields are accompanied by convenient buttons that help indicate their functions. See table 12.3 for a breakdown of all the choices on the Format 3-D View dialog box.

TABLE 12.3
Format 3-D View Dialog Box Settings

Field	Function
Elevation	This field controls the height of your viewpoint and is expressed in degrees (from –90 degrees, looking up at the chart, to 90 degrees, which is looking down onto the chart). Pie charts and bar charts have different limits. The elevation for pie charts is limited to 10–80 degrees; bar charts are limited to 0–40 degrees.
Rotation	Rotation also is given in degrees, from 0–360 degrees. Bar charts are restricted from 0–44 degrees.
Perspective	Perspective controls the perceived depth of the chart. This value controls the ratio of the size of the front of the chart to the size of the rear of the chart. Perspective can range from 0–100.
Right Angle A**x**es	When this check box is selected, the axes always are displayed at right angles (90 degrees, 180 degrees, 270 degrees, and 0 degrees). Otherwise, the axes are free to be displayed at varying angles called for by the chart perspective.
Auto **S**caling	This choice is available only if Right Angle A**x**es is selected. When Auto **S**caling is selected, the chart is scaled proportionally to take up as much of the chart area as possible.

continues

TABLE 12.3, CONTINUED
Format 3-D View Dialog Box Settings

Field	Function
He**i**ght % of base	This field controls the percentage of the height of the chart in relationship to the Category axis. If you set this number to 300, for example, the chart will be three times taller than the Category axis is wide.
Apply	This button applies your changes without exiting the dialog box, so that you can see your changes before you commit to them. You might need to move the dialog box off to the side to see the chart, however. Note that when you apply your changes, they are not canceled by exiting the dialog box. Instead, the **A**pply button enables you to adjust and view your changes, enabling you to quickly readjust and view until the chart view is to your liking.
Default	When clicked on, this button returns the chart to the Excel default settings for 3D view.

3. Click on the **A**pply button to look at your changes. If you are not happy with the result, continue to adjust the values in the dialog box and click on the **A**pply button until you see what you want.

4. Click on the OK button to finalize your changes and exit the dialog box.

Excel also enables you to change the 3D view more directly by dragging handles on the chart itself, as follows:

1. Select the chart by clicking on it. Handles appear at each corner of the chart. Click on one of these handles and hold down the mouse button to begin dragging. As you drag, you see a *wireframe* (three-dimensional outline) image of your chart, shown in figure 12.31.

2. When the wireframe indicates the view you want, release the mouse button to have Excel redraw the chart based on the new perspective.

Changing Data from the Chart

In most Excel charts, you can change the value of a particular data marker directly by simply dragging it. When you do this, Excel automatically adjusts the values in the original worksheet data so that they correspond to the new data marker position.

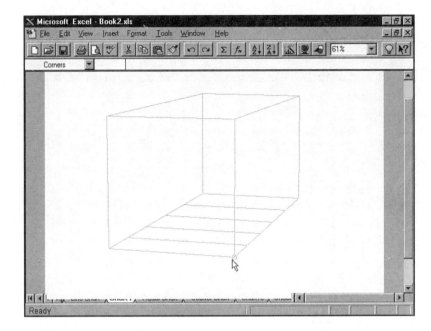

Figure 12.31

A wireframe of a 3D chart, displayed while dragging a corner.

Note If you are going to be adjusting a chart in this way, you should consider making a copy of the worksheet data on which the chart is based before manipulating the chart and changing the data.

Consider the chart and worksheet example in figure 12.32. You see a simple line chart graphing two data series. The second data series is based on the first, with 40 percent added to it.

To directly change the middle data point in the first series, follow these steps:

1. Double-click on the chart to place it in edit mode, designated by a broad border with diagonal lines, as shown in figure 12.33.

2. Click on the center data marker of the lower series once to select the series, then again to select the individual data point. After the individual data point is selected, your pointer changes to a small double-headed arrow that points up and down.

3. Drag the data point to a new position and release the mouse button to complete the change. You see as you are dragging the data marker that a small cross appears in the Value axis to help you select the new value more accurately. The formula bar displays the exact value that will be placed in the worksheet data as you drag the data marker.

Figure 12.32

A sample line chart.

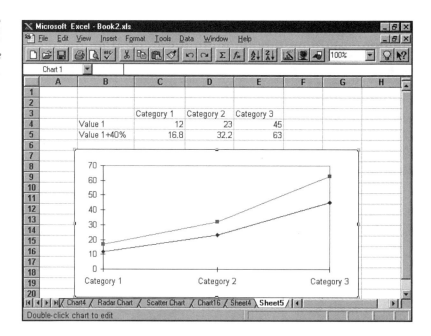

When the change is finished, the sample chart looks something like figure 12.33. As you can see, the data in the worksheet was changed automatically to be consistent with the chart data.

Figure 12.33

Moved data marker.

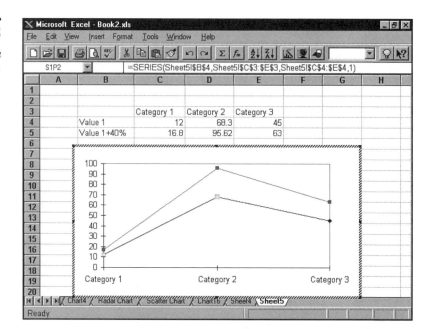

Note You see in figure 12.33 that the scale for the chart has changed from figure 12.32. Excel compensated for the broader range of values automatically.

If you move a data marker that represents the result of a calculation, Excel automatically updates the data. In this example, moving one of the markers in the top data series would also have to change the number in the lower data series, because the top data series is dependent on the lower data series.

When you move a dependent data marker, Excel automatically invokes its Goal Seek feature so that it can reverse the change to the cells that make up the formula. Figure 12.34 shows the Goal Seek dialog box after you move one of the dependent data markers.

The Goal Seek dialog box has three fields. The **S**et cell field shows the cell on the worksheet that you have changed with the data marker. The To **v**alue field shows the new value for the cell associated with the moved data marker. The final field, By **c**hanging cell, prompts you for the cell that should be changed in order for all the calculations on the worksheet to remain consistent. This field must be set to a cell that provides a constant value (in this case, cell D4 is the cell that must be changed in order for cell D5 to remain consistent). If the cell being changed is based on many constant values, the Goal Seek Status dialog box enables you to choose which one to manipulate to reverse the calculations. Select the appropriate cell by making the By **c**hanging cell field active and clicking on the cell to change. Click on the OK button to initiate the Goal Seek process.

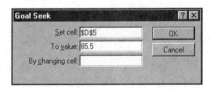

Figure 12.34

The Goal Seek dialog box.

If Goal Seek is not able to find a solution that fits all the formulas involved, it displays an error message and the Goal Seek fails. If it finds a solution, it shows you the message in figure 12.35.

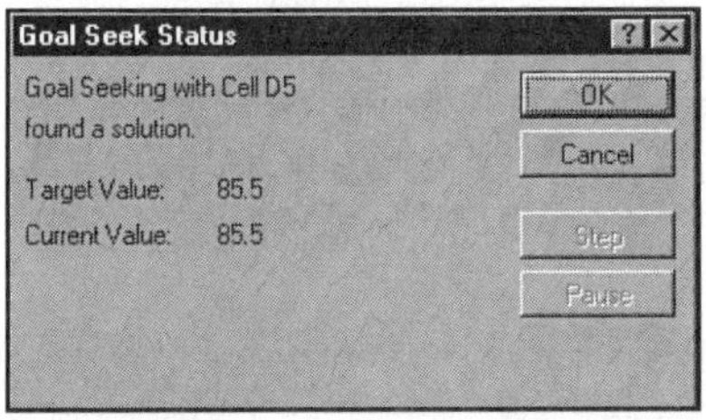

Figure 12.35

The Goal Seek Status dialog box.

Note The Goal Seek function works by trying many different values in the target cell, zeroing in on a solution until it finds one that works perfectly. Note that you might not be able to solve some formulas with the Goal Seek function. Also, if more than one possible solution exists, Excel might not choose the solution you want. Examine the results carefully before you accept the change.

Changing Chart Type

You easily can change the type of chart used to plot your data. To do this, select the chart, pull down the F**o**rmat menu, and choose Chart **T**ype. You can also click on the right mouse button after selecting the chart and choose Chart Type from the shortcut menu. Figure 12.36 shows the Chart Type dialog box.

The Chart Type dialog box is divided into two main sections—Apply to and the display of chart types. To display available two-dimensional chart types, click on the **2**-D button. The **3**-D button shows you available three-dimensional charts.

Figure 12.36

The Chart Type dialog box.

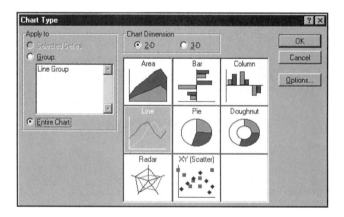

To select a new chart type, click on the chart you want in the display, then click on the OK button, or simply double-click on the chart type you want.

You also can choose to change the chart type for only selected series in the chart. Select the series you want to change before invoking the Chart Type dialog box. Then click on the **S**elected Series button before choosing a chart type. This capability enables you to form combination charts. For example, you could have some of the series plotted with lines and others plotted with bars. You can even take a single series of a line chart and plot it as a pie chart, superimposed on top of the line chart (if you want to get really wild, that is).

Guided Tour of Excel Charts

The remainder of this chapter shows you examples of each major type of chart in Excel, along with suggestions about how best to use each chart and notes about special features particular to that chart.

The different charts in Excel are not built in for aesthetic reasons. Rather, each chart specializes in showing different types of information.

AUTHOR'S NOTE

The chart you choose to present your data can have a subtle but profound impact on your audience. Different charts prompt different questions about the information and can influence your audience to come to different conclusions. Take some care in choosing the right chart for the job and in anticipating the questions that your chart might prompt.

Area Charts

Area charts work best when you want to show the relationship of different series of numbers and the way each series contributes to the total of all series. If figure 12.37 were done with a line chart, you would have to add a line to represent total sales in order to easily see the sum of all series in a given category, and even then it would be difficult to see how each one contributed to the whole.

Area charts emphasize change across the categories, particularly relative change between different series.

Area charts can show error bars and standard deviations. Access these features by selecting a particular series, pulling up its formatting dialog box (double-clicking on the series), and using the Y Error Bars page in the dialog box.

Bar Charts

Bar charts emphasize comparison of the different categories rather than emphasizing comparison across time, as column charts do. Several different subgroups of bar charts exist, including the stacked bar and 100-percent stacked bar. The *stacked bar* shows the relationships between the different series more accurately, whereas the *100-percent stacked bar* shows the percentage of the whole for each series. Figure 12.38 shows a sample bar chart.

Figure 12.37

A sample area chart.

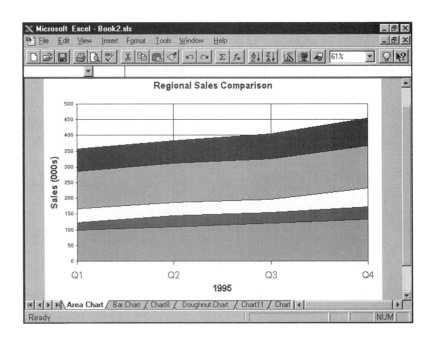

Figure 12.38

A sample bar chart.

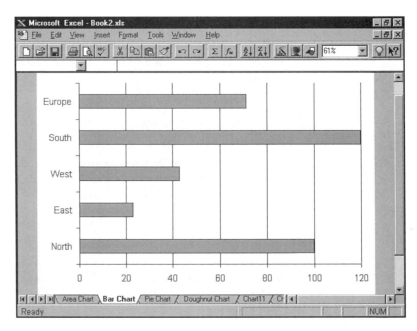

Note Bar charts, along with column charts, are an excellent place to use error bars. Typically, *error bars* are used to show the standard deviation on technical charts. To add error bars to a bar chart, select the series to which you want to add the error bars, pull down the **I**nsert menu, and choose **E**rror bars. On the dialog box page that appears, choose the style of error bars you want and define the amount of error to be shown in the Error section of the page. See Chapter 14, "Advanced Charts for Business and Science," for more information.

Column Charts

Column charts are best at illustrating the way values change over time, and they also help the reader compare different values side by side. Because time is on the horizontal access, column charts emphasize change over time. Column charts, like bar charts, can use error bars and can also be produced in a stacked column format and a 100-percent stacked format. Figure 12.39 shows a sample column chart.

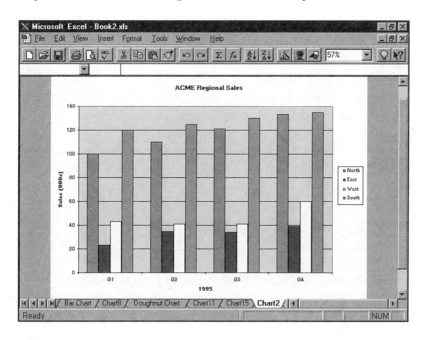

Figure 12.39

A sample column chart.

Note One key difference between a column chart and a line or area chart is that the column chart shows only discrete values across time. Line and area charts, on the other hand, presuppose activity between each data point because of the line drawn between each point.

Line Charts

Line charts emphasize trends in your data. Although line and area charts have some similarities, they also have some big differences. Area charts, for example, easily express the total of all series, but line charts do not (unless you add that as a separate series). Line charts are designed to show a trend over time, and the Category axis is almost always time-based (months, quarters, years, and so on).

If you need to show a trend using a measurement other than time on the Category axis, use a scatter chart with the data points connected by lines (one of the scatter subtypes; see the section later in this chapter on scatter charts). Because line charts are designed to use time on their Category axis, you cannot have a logarithmic scale on the Category axis, as you can with scatter charts.

Figure 12.40

A sample line chart.

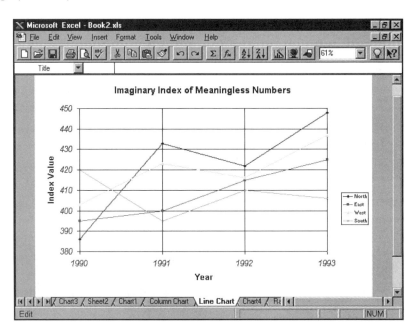

You also can add trend lines to your charts. See Chapter 14 to learn more.

Pie Charts

Pie charts always show percentages of a whole and emphasize a particular part of your data, as the emphasized Europe slice shows in figure 12.41.

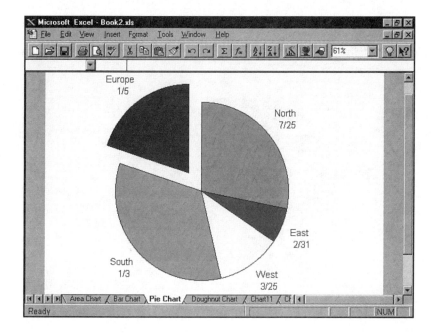

Figure 12.41

A sample pie chart.

You can rotate the pie chart by selecting the chart, pulling down the F**o**rmat menu, and selecting Pie Group from the menu. On the dialog box that appears, click on the Options tab. On this page, you can change the **A**ngle of First Slice field, which specifies the degrees at which the first pie slice appears.

Doughnut Charts

Doughnut charts are very similar to pie charts, because they show proportions of a whole. The main advantage of a doughnut chart, however, is that it enables you to compare multiple series of data, as shown in figure 12.42.

Radar Charts

Radar charts show changes between categories (see fig. 12.43). Each radiating axis from the center represents a category, and each line is a series. As you can see in category 1 (the vertical category at the top of the chart), radar charts also can be formatted to use a logarithmic scale to represent their data. Radar charts are most commonly used in Asia and Europe.

Figure 12.42

A sample doughnut chart.

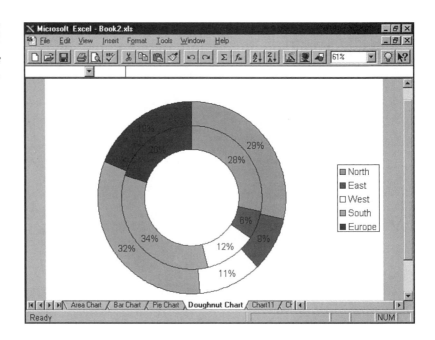

Figure 12.43

A sample radar chart.

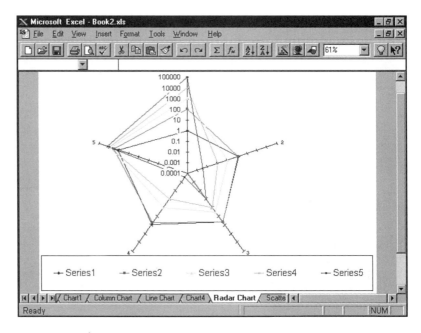

Scatter (XY) Charts

Scatter (XY) charts show the relationship between two (or more) scales. Generally, both scales are numeric measurements. In fact, the scatter chart is not really designed to show a time series, although it can if needed. A scatter chart often is used for scientific plots, and they are often seen with logarithmic scales, as shown in figure 12.44.

If you need to show the relationship between two number-based axes, but want connecting lines between the data points, you can use the scatter chart, but choose the subtype of scatter chart that connects the data markers.

Note   For more information about scatter (XY) charts, see Chapter 14.

3D Charts

The pie, bar, column, and line charts also are available in a 3D format. The 3D variants are provided for aesthetic reasons; the preceding notes for bar, column, and line charts also apply to the 3D versions of these charts. See figures 12.45–12.48 for examples of these charts.

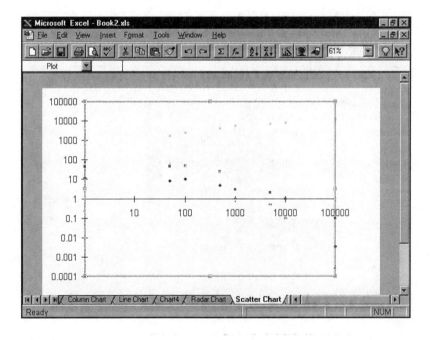

Figure 12.44

A sample scatter (XY) chart.

Figure 12.45

A 3D bar chart.

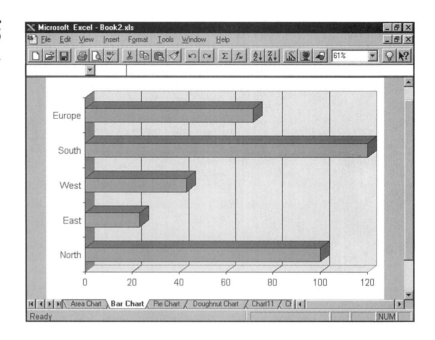

Figure 12.46

A 3D column chart.

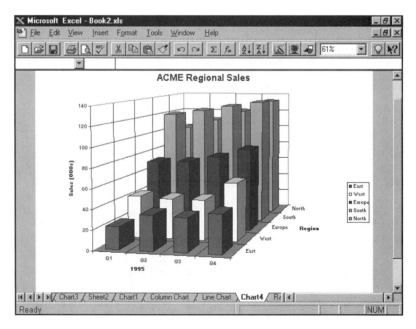

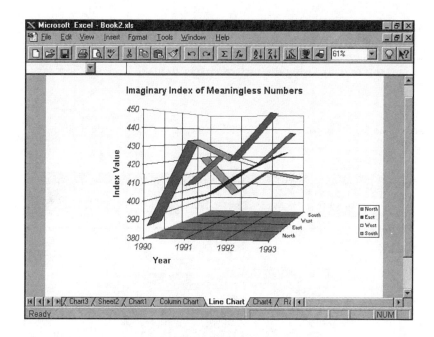

Figure 12.47

A 3D line chart.

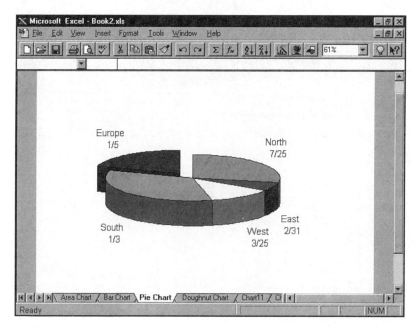

Figure 12.48

A 3D pie chart.

3D Surface Charts

The *3D surface chart*, as shown in figure 12.49, is used to help you find the best combination of two sets of data. Using the surface chart can make large sets of data easier to interpret.

 Note The colors on the 3D surface chart show different axis ranges rather than different series.

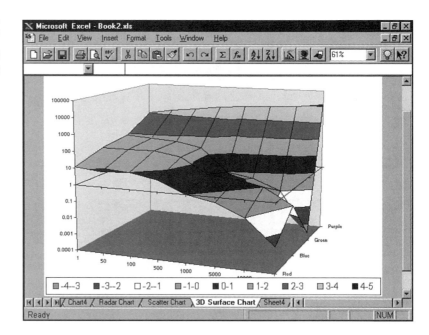

Chapter Snapshot

Not only can you use the graphics capabilities of Excel to annotate your worksheets and charts, you also can use the graphics
tools to create more complex drawings, such as organizational
charts, freehand drawings, and flow charts. In this chapter, you
learn the following tasks:

◆ Drawing and controlling graphics on your Excel documents

◆ Linking an Excel macro to a graphics object

◆ Incorporating pictures from other programs into your
  worksheets and charts

◆ Using a graphics image as your charting symbol

Even aside from the ability to annotate your charts and
worksheets with graphics, the drawing tools in Excel are almost
as good as many dedicated drawing packages. Unless you have
complex needs, you will find that most drawing tasks can be
accomplished easily and quickly in Excel.

C H A P T E R

13

Drawing and Adding Graphics to Documents

Now more than ever before, spreadsheet programs are being used not only as analysis and automation tools for numbers, but also as presentation tools. Some people might feel that graphics capabilities are more toys than serious business tools, but you can make a strong case for their use.

In addition to preparing complete presentations with spreadsheet programs such as Excel, you can use graphics capabilities to make a spreadsheet clearer for the people who need to read it. Pointing out a particular number with an arrow, placing borders around parts of the spreadsheet, or even illustrating a point graphically are all functions that have a very serious purpose—not only to show results, but to help communicate them. This capability to communicate more effectively is, in one sense, the very purpose of spreadsheets.

Spreadsheet programs such as Excel can be thought of as *decision support tools* rather than tools to crunch numbers together. Because Excel plays a role in helping people make decisions, you also must consider the ability to communicate the information as an integral part of the tool.

As you discover in this chapter, Excel for Windows 95 has a wealth of capabilities that you can put to work immediately to help convey your information more concisely, accurately, and most important, compellingly.

Enhancing Your Documents Using the Drawing Tools

This chapter makes extensive use of the Drawing toolbar. To see the Drawing toolbar on-screen, pull down the **V**iew menu and choose **T**oolbars. In the dialog box that appears, select the check box next to Drawing and then click on OK. Alternatively, click on the Drawing tool icon on the Standard toolbar to display or hide the Drawing toolbar. Yet another way to access the Drawing toolbar is to right-click anywhere on the visible toolbars, then select Drawing from the pop-up menu.

The Drawing toolbar automatically opens in floating mode. To make it part of the toolbar area, drag it left, right, up, or down until it is positioned along one of the screen borders (such as below the Standard toolbar or above the status bar at the bottom of the screen), and then release the mouse button. If you prefer to keep the Drawing toolbar in floating mode, you can reshape it by dragging its borders to a new size and shape. As you drag the borders, a frame outline shows you the new shape that you are creating.

The following sections show you ways to use the tools built into Excel to add drawings to your charts and worksheets.

 Note The drawing tools work the same way on both charts and worksheets. Although this chapter shows most of the drawing tools on a worksheet, they work equally well on a chart and function identically.

Although each drawing tool has some differences, they have many common characteristics. To use any of the drawing tools, simply click on the tool you want to use and drag it to the document to begin drawing with it.

 Tip Normally, when you click on a drawing tool and then draw something with it, the tool immediately becomes deselected as soon as you have finished drawing the object. To make a tool "stick" so that you can draw several items of the same object type, double-click on the tool. It remains selected until you click on it again to deselect it, or click on another drawing tool.

Drawing Tools Summary

Table 13.1 shows you each of the drawing tools and discusses features specific to each tool.

TABLE 13.1
Drawing Toolbar Icons

Icon	Name	Description
◥	Line	The Line tool draws straight lines. You can take a line drawn with the Line tool and make it into an arrow by bringing up the formatting dialog box and changing the **S**tyle on the Patterns page.
▢	Rectangle	Use the Rectangle tool to draw rectangles and boxes. The Patterns page of the rectangle's formatting dialog box has two check boxes: Sha**d**ow, which gives the rectangle a drop shadow, and **R**ound Corners, which rounds the corners of the rectangle. When you give a rectangle a drop shadow, Excel automatically assigns the rectangle a white color fill. Figure 13.1 shows a normal rectangle alongside one with rounded corners and a drop shadow.

 Tip After selecting the object, click on the Shadow button in the Drawing toolbar to turn the shadow on and off.

Icon	Name	Description
⬭	Ellipse	The Ellipse tool draws ovals and circles. The Patterns page of an ellipse's formatting dialog box has a check box called **S**hadow, which gives the ellipse a drop shadow.
◠	Arc	The Arc tool draws arcs that begin and end at 90 degree angles, although the arc does not have to have perfect proportions in height and width. Hold down the Shift key as you draw an arc to force it to have equal height and width measurements (in other words, 90 degrees of a circle). Figure 13.2 shows three different arcs.

continues

TABLE 13.1, CONTINUED
Drawing Toolbar Icons

Icon	Name	Description
	Freeform	The Freeform tool is very powerful. You can use it in two modes: connect mode and freehand mode. To use connect mode, select the tool and click where you want the first line to start. Move to the ending location for the line and click again. Keep repeating this point-and-click operation until you have drawn your shape. In connect mode, you can hold down the Shift key to constrain the lines to 45 degree angles. Hold down the mouse button and drag to draw in freehand mode. You can use both modes in a single object drawing. Double-click the mouse to finish drawing the object. After your object is drawn, you can use the Patterns page of the formatting dialog box to give the entire object a drop shadow by selecting the **S**hadow check box.
	Text Box	The Text Box tool enables you to draw rectangles that contain text. After the rectangle is drawn, a cursor automatically appears within the rectangle, ready for you to begin typing the text. The Text Box tool has two extra pages in its formatting dialog box: Alignment, which controls the alignment of the text in the box, and Font, which controls the font used. You also can mix fonts and styles within the box by selecting only the text you want to format before you open the dialog box. Also, the Protection page has a Lock **T**ext check box that controls the locking property of text in the box when the workbook is protected.
	Arrow	The Arrow tool enables you to draw lines with arrowheads at either end. By default, the arrowhead is automatically placed at the end of the line. Control the format of the arrowheads using the Patterns page of the Format Object

Icon	Name	Description
		dialog box, which is shown in figure 13.3. In the Arrow Patterns page, you can control the Style of the arrow (no arrowhead, open arrowhead, filled arrowhead, and double-ended arrowheads), the Width of the arrowhead (the amount of space between the end of the tines), and the Length of the arrowhead (the distance from the tip to the back of the arrowhead).
	Freehand	Using the Freehand tool, you can draw in a pure freehand mode, as opposed to the Freeform tool, which also lets you draw straight lines. Stop drawing the freehand line by releasing the mouse button after the object is drawn.
	Button	The button tool draws objects on your worksheet or chart that look just like dialog box buttons. After you have drawn the button object, a dialog box appears that enables you to specify a macro that you want to run when the button is clicked on. See the section in this chapter called "Linking Actions to Objects" for more information.
	Drop Shadow	Use this tool to add a drop shadow to an object without opening the formatting dialog box.
	Pattern	Use this tool to change the fill or line style of an object without opening the formatting dialog box.

Each of the area drawing tools (Rectangle, Ellipse, Arc, and Freeform) also have filled counterparts, which automatically fill the area of the drawing with a fill color. When you use a filled drawing tool, Excel fills the shape with a white color fill. To change the color, use the object's Patterns formatting page and select a color from the Area section of the page. You also can choose a pattern to draw the color by using the **P**attern drop-down tool. Figure 13.4 shows a drawing created using various filled objects with different colors and patterns. The filled object drawing tools are shown in table 13.2.

Figure 13.1

Two rectangles.

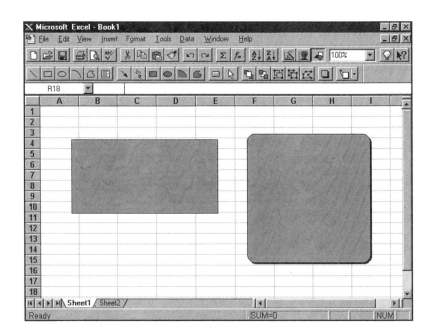

Figure 13.2

Three arcs.

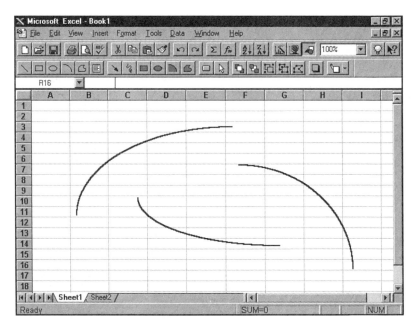

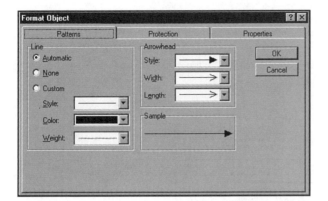

Figure 13.3

The Format Object dialog box showing the Patterns page.

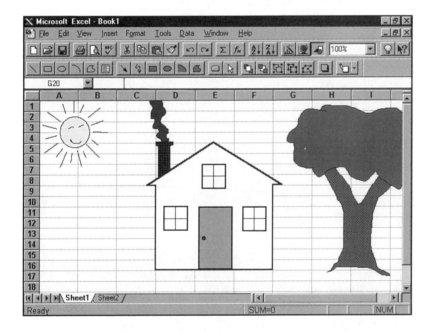

Figure 13.4

The house that Excel built.

AUTHOR'S NOTE

I prefer to be called "artistically challenged."

Note The only difference between the filled objects and their corresponding standard (outline) drawing objects are the formatting options set in the Fill section of the Patterns page. Regardless of whether you selected a filled object drawing tool or not, you can easily change one from the other and back again without having to redraw the object.

TABLE 13.2
Filled Object Drawing Tools

Icon	Tool Name
▣	Filled Rectangle
⬯	Filled Ellipse
◣	Filled Arc
◿	Filled Freeform

Understanding Constrained Drawing

Most of the drawing tools support a feature called *constrained drawing*. This feature is activated when you hold down the Shift key as you draw the object. Constrained drawing is used to ensure that a line is at a perfect 45 degree angle, that a rectangle is perfectly square, or that an ellipse is perfectly round.

Tip When you resize a drawing with the Shift key held down, Excel ensures that the drawing retains its original proportions. Also, you can select multiple objects by holding down the Shift key when you click on each object. Then, after they all are selected, hold down the Shift key while you resize one object. All objects are resized proportionately.

Formatting Graphics Objects

To format an object that you have drawn, select the object, pull down the Format menu, and choose Object. You also can select the object and press Ctrl+1 to bring up the Format Object dialog box. Alternately, use that handy right mouse button while resting the pointer on the selected object, and click on Format Object. The dialog box for a simple line object is shown in figure 13.5.

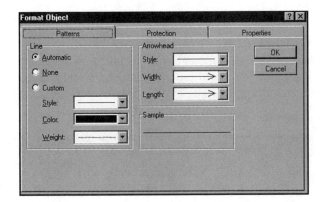

Figure 13.5

The Format Object dialog box for a line object.

The Patterns page of the dialog box controls the fill pattern and line style for the object. In addition, some objects have some special effects or attributes; these, too, are found on the Patterns page. You can, for example, choose to give a rectangle rounded corners.

Tip

You can change the fill pattern of an object by selecting the object and clicking on the Pattern button in the Drawing toolbar. You also can double-click on the object to bring up the formatting dialog box for that object.

The Protection page has a single check box called Locked. If the Locked check box is selected, the graphics object is frozen in place when the sheet is protected. The Locked check box has no effect for an unprotected worksheet.

As shown in figure 13.6, the Properties page has some very important settings that control the way an object interacts with a worksheet as the worksheet is reformatted:

◆ **Move and Size with Cells.** This selection automatically adjusts the object when the cells it is on top of are resized. Suppose, for example, you have drawn a circle that spans several columns. If you later delete a column in the area of the circle, Excel makes the circle into an ellipse to compensate for the deleted area. Similarly, when cells are resized within the area of the graphics object, the object changes shape and size so that its borders are still in the same cells.

◆ **Move but Don't Size with Cells.** Choose this option to cause the graphics object to move along with the cell in its upper left corner, but not to be resized if cells are added, resized, or deleted within the boundaries of the object.

◆ **<u>D</u>on't Move or Size with Cells.** Objects that have this option button selected are not affected by any cell insertions or deletions.

◆ **<u>P</u>rint Object.** You can control whether graphics objects print. All objects are set to print by default, with the exception of button objects. This feature can be useful to shorten the printing time when you do not need final output (printing graphic images takes longer on most printers).

Figure 13.6

The Properties page.

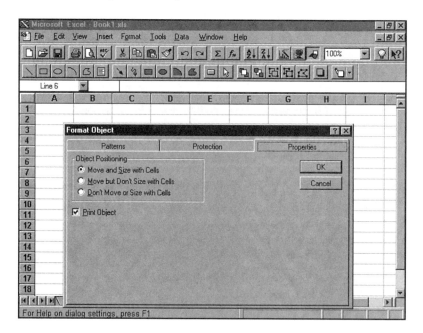

Linking Actions to Objects

Any objects you draw can be linked to macros so that they can perform actions when clicked on. To edit an object with an attached macro, you must right-click or Ctrl+click on the object to select it, because a left-click executes the macro.

 Note   Macros normally are linked to button objects you create using the Button tool, although macros can be attached to any graphic object on your worksheet or chart.

To attach an existing macro to a graphics object, follow these steps:

1. Draw the object to which you want to attach the macro.

2. Click the right mouse button on the object to bring up the pop-up menu. From the pop-up menu, choose Assign Macro to access the Assign Macro dialog box, shown in figure 13.7.

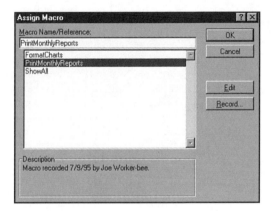

Figure 13.7

The Assign Macro dialog box.

Note Step 2 is unnecessary when you draw a button object. The Assign Macro dialog box appears automatically as soon as you finish drawing the button, although you have the option to decline assigning a macro by clicking the Cancel button or pressing Esc.

3. Choose the macro you want to assign by clicking on it in the list box. Click on the OK button to store your choice.

Tip You also can edit or record a macro from the Assign Macro dialog box. Click on the **E**dit or **R**ecord button.

To detach a macro from a graphics object, bring up the Assign Macro dialog box, clear the field titled **M**acro Name/Reference, and click on the OK button.

Controlling Graphics Objects

Excel provides six buttons to assist in the management and arrangement of your graphics objects, as detailed in table 13.3.

TABLE 13.3
Graphics Management Tools

Icon	Name	Description
	Drawing Selection	The Drawing Selection tool is used to select multiple graphics objects. You can accomplish this task in two ways. Select the tool, then drag it over the objects you want to select. As you drag, a marquee appears around the area you are selecting. After all the objects are contained within the marquee, release the mouse button to select them all. Alternatively, you can select multiple objects by holding down the Shift key as you select each object.
	Bring to Front	Click on the Bring to Front button after you have selected an object to make the object appear on top of any overlapping objects.
	Send to Back	Click on the Send to Back button after you have selected an object to push the object behind any overlapping objects.
	Group	After you select multiple objects with the Drawing Selection tool, click on the Group button to combine all the objects into a single group. When you group a collection of objects, you create a complex object made up of many other objects. You can move, resize, and reformat the complex object as a single entity. Grouping objects makes editing complex drawings easier; as you get an area of the object finished, group the objects together to keep from disturbing the object relationships.
	Ungroup	Click on the Ungroup tool after selecting a complex object to break the complex object up into its component objects.

Icon	Name	Description
![Reshape icon]	Reshape	For freehand or polygon drawings, select the drawing and click on the Reshape button to create editing handles at each curve or angle (called *vertexes*). Drag on the handles to reshape the drawing in more complex ways than are available using the normal handles. Figure 13.8 shows a freehand squiggle with the numerous Reshape handles displayed.

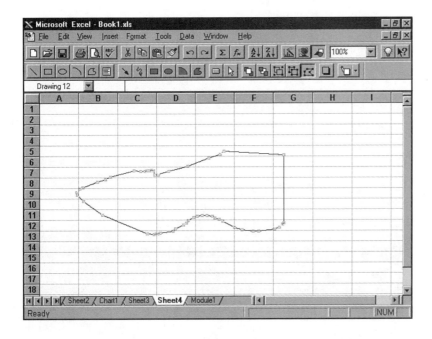

Figure 13.8

A freehand object with reshape handles.

Importing Graphics Images

Excel can import and display many different types of graphics images, including images in the following formats:

◆ Windows Bitmaps (BMP)

◆ Tagged Image Format (TIF)

◆ Encapsulated PostScript (EPS)

◆ Targa (TGA)

◆ Windows Metafile (WMF)

◆ AutoCAD format 2D (DXF)

◆ Computer Graphics Metafile (CGM)

◆ PC Paintbrush (PCX)

◆ CorelDRAW!(CDR)

◆ WordPerfect Graphics (WPG)

◆ HP Graphics Language (HGL)

◆ Macintosh PICT (PCT)

◆ Micrographx_Designer/Draw (DRW)

◆ CompuServe GIF (GIF)

◆ Kodak PhotoCD (PCD)

◆ JPEG Filter (JPG)

You can import graphics directly as long as they are stored in one of these formats. Pull down the **I**nsert menu and choose **P**icture. You see the dialog box shown in figure 13.9.

Figure 13.9

The Picture dialog box.

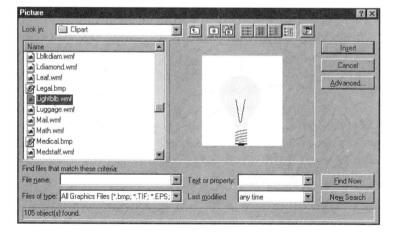

Use the Look in, File Name, Files of type, Text or property, or Last modified boxes to narrow your search to the file you want to open. Click on the Advanced button to further specify the search criteria. A useful option on the advanced page is the check box to search in subdirectories, using the location of the Look in box as the root. Select a file from the Name list box to display a preview representation of the graphic. After you have found and selected the file you want to open, click on the OK button to insert the picture into your worksheet or chart.

Inserting Graphics Using the Paste Special Command

You can insert graphics objects from virtually any Windows-based drawing program by using the program's Cut or Copy option. After the object is in the Windows Clipboard, use Paste Special in Excel to insert the object. When you do this, the Paste Special dialog box appears, as shown in figure 13.10.

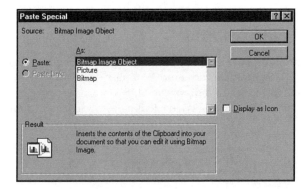

Figure 13.10

The Paste Special dialog box.

You can choose between the two option buttons on the left of the dialog box: Paste and Paste Link. Paste simply pastes the image in the format you select, but Paste Link creates a DDE link back to the application that created the drawing (in this case, Windows Paint). When you Paste Link a drawing, changing the drawing in the source application automatically updates the drawing in Excel. Also, you can double-click on a drawing that has been pasted using Paste Link to automatically load the source application with the drawing ready for editing. Similarly, you may also double-click on a Windows bitmap picture to activate the Paint program for editing, even though it was inserted using the Paste option only.

Note DDE stands for *Dynamic Data Exchange*, one of the methods that Excel can use to communicate with other Windows programs. Excel also uses OLE, which stands for *Object Linking and Embedding*. For a complete discussion of DDE and OLE, see *Inside Windows 95*, also from New Riders Publishing.

In the **A**s list box, the various options for pasting the data are listed. Click on each choice to see the comments about that type of graphics discussed in the Result box at the bottom of the dialog box.

If you select the **D**isplay as Icon check box, the graphic does not appear on the worksheet. Instead, an icon appears that represents the image's source application. Use this feature to conserve space and reduce memory requirements in complex documents. The image does not appear, but the worksheet user can click on this icon to easily open the image in its source application.

Changing Imported Images

You can resize and move imported pictures just like any other graphics objects in Excel. Because imported images likely are more complex than the other objects you work with, however, remember to hold down the Shift key as you resize the pictures to constrain the object to its original proportions. Failing to do so can ruin the quality of the image.

Using an Image for Chart Patterns

One of the more interesting features of Excel is that it enables you to use an imported image as charts patterns.

Consider the chart shown in figure 13.11. This chart could be improved and made more interesting to the audience by replacing the bars in the bar chart with an appropriate symbol. One possibility is shown in figure 13.12.

You can replace chart markers (for Line, Radar, and Scatter charts) or area fills (for Bar and Column charts) with graphics images using either of two methods. One option is to copy the image to the Clipboard in the source application, switch to your chart, select the data series you want to change, and choose **P**aste from the **E**dit menu.

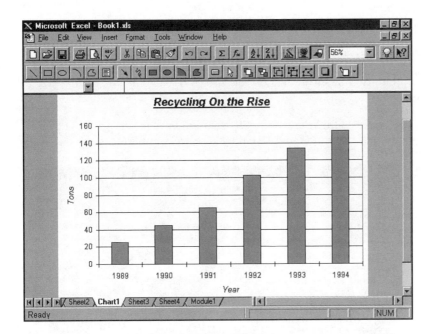

Figure 13.11

A recycling chart.

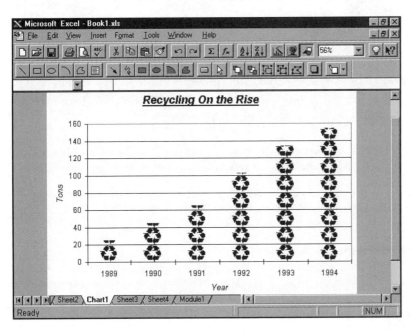

Figure 13.12

The recycling chart using symbols.

You also can import the images directly. To do this, follow these steps:

1. Select the series you want to modify.

2. Pull down the **I**nsert menu and choose **P**icture. You see the Picture dialog box shown in figure 13.13.

3. Use this dialog box to find the picture file you want to use. After you have found it, click on the In**s**ert button to replace the chart symbol with the graphics image.

Figure 13.13

*The Picture
dialog box.*

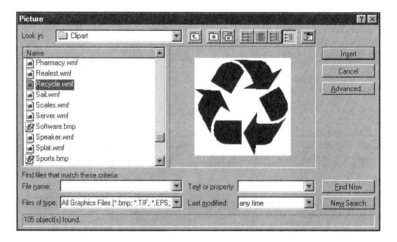

A series that has had its symbol replaced with a graphics image has some additional settings available on the Patterns page of its formatting dialog box (see fig. 13.14).

The Patterns page has these new settings available:

◆ **Stretch.** Stretches the image to cover the entire area in the bar or column rectangle. Figure 13.15 shows the graph with this choice selected.

◆ **Stack.** Keeps the image size the same, but stacks as many images as are necessary to fill up the bar or column rectangle. The preceding figure 13.12 uses the Stack option.

◆ **Stack and Scale.** Enables you to control the number of units of the Value axis that are represented by each chart image. When you select this option button, you can type a number in the **U**nits/Picture field to control the number of axis units represented per picture. By default, Excel chooses the number that shows the picture as large as possible. Figure 13.16 shows the Stack and S**c**ale option with each picture set to represent 10 units on the chart.

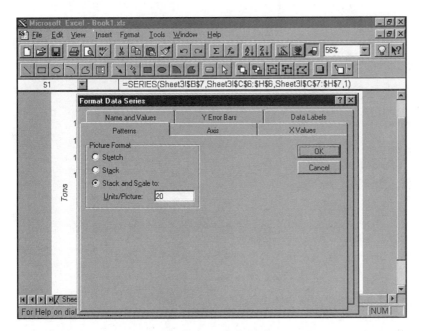

Figure 13.14

The Patterns page for chart symbols.

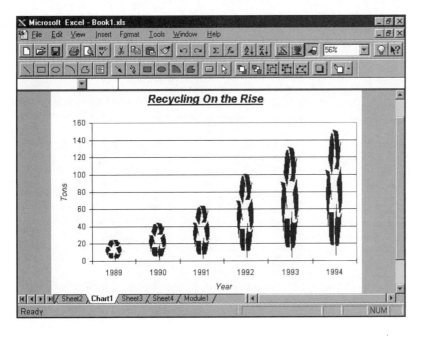

Figure 13.15

The Stretch option.

Figure 13.16

*The Stack option
with modified
scale.*

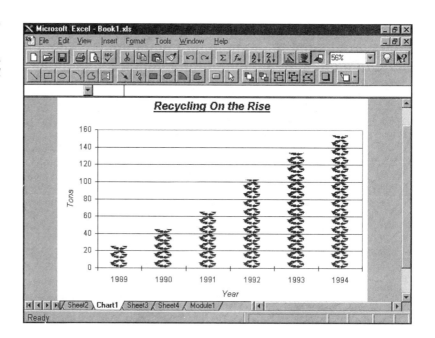

Chapter Snapshot

Excel has many advanced charting capabilities applicable to the more advanced business or technical user. In this chapter, you learn to accomplish the following:

- ◆ Editing the series formula for a chart

- ◆ Creating stock High-Low-Close stock charts

- ◆ Plotting trend lines

- ◆ Creating charts that use logarithmic scales

- ◆ Plotting missing data

- ◆ Creating multi-axis charts with dual x or y axes

- ◆ Creating error bars for many Excel chart types

As you will see, Excel has the capability to generate just about any type of chart you could want. After you have mastered the basics of Excel charts, use the information in this chapter as a reference for these more advanced chart types and for the more advanced editing tasks.

Advanced Charts for Business and Science

At times, you probably need to generate charts that require something a little more complex than simply grabbing a chunk of your worksheet and hitting the ChartWizard button. Perhaps you want to control which parts of a series of numbers are plotted, or you want to use different category references for different data series. The next sections show you ways to accomplish these tasks.

Understanding Series Formulas

When you plot data from a worksheet to a chart, Excel uses a *series formula* in the chart to indicate each series. Although you usually don't have to work directly with this series formula, understanding how to read it and how to change it can be an important step in advancing your charting skills.

The series formula indicates the workbook name, the name of the sheet in the workbook, and the cells that contain the data being charted. To display a series formula for a particular chart series, click on the series. The formula is shown in the formula bar. Figure 14.1 shows a series formula for the bottom chart series. From the formula bar, you can see that the data series is referencing Sheet1. Figure 14.2 shows the data on Sheet1 from which the example chart was plotted.

The series formula is divided into four major parameters, each separated by commas. The series formula parameters are arranged in this order:

1. **Series Name.** This parameter references the name of the series, which you also can see in the legend of your chart. In this case, the reference points to cell B1, giving the series the name "Red."

2. **Category Reference.** The second reference in the formula is to the range of cells that define the categories for the plotted data. For this series formula, the reference is to cells A2 through A9—the categories against which the data was plotted.

3. **Values Reference.** The Values Reference is the actual data that is plotted—in this case, cells B2 to B9.

4. **Order Number.** The Order Number in the series formula defines where in the order of the plotted data the series belongs. The sample series formula is for the first data series on the chart.

You can edit the series formula directly to change the data that the chart is plotting, but far easier methods are available.

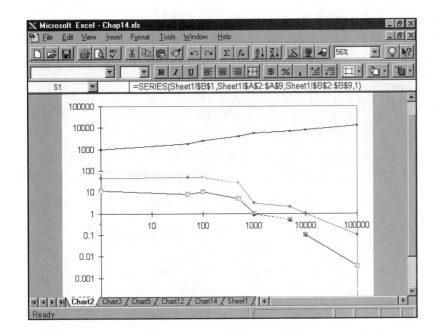

Figure 14.1

A series formula example.

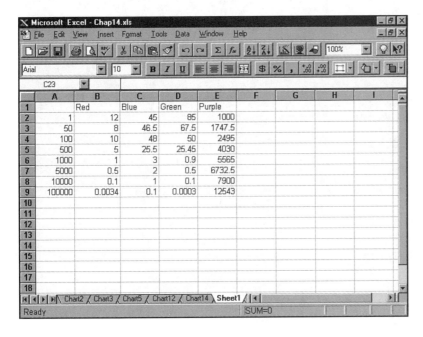

Figure 14.2

Data for the example chart.

Changing the Series Using the Format Data Series Dialog Box

You can change the series formula easily by using the Format Data Series dialog box.

1. Select the series you want to control.

2. Pull up the Format Data Series dialog box for that series. Press Ctrl+1 to do this quickly, or press the right mouse button and select Format Data Series.

3. Click on the X Values tab. You see the page shown in figure 14.3.

Figure 14.3

The X Values page.

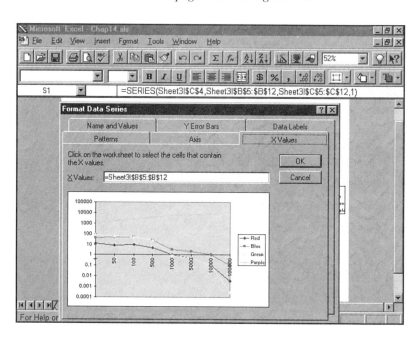

When you click on the X Values tab and then click in the series formula shown, you return to the source of the series data behind the dialog box. To change the range used for X Values, move the formatting page so that you can see the source data, then use your mouse to reselect the range.

You also can change the cells used for the series name and for the Y Values by using the Name and Values page in the dialog box, shown in figure 14.4.

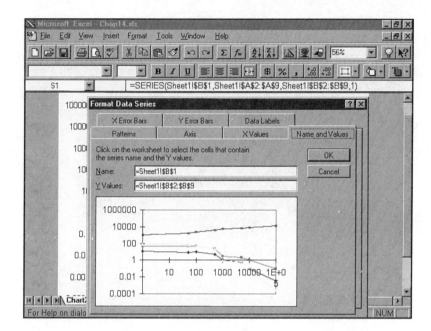

Figure 14.4

The Name and Values page.

Plotting or Adding Noncontiguous Ranges

You do not necessarily need to arrange your data so that it is contiguous before you create a chart. Excel enables you to plot noncontiguous ranges of data (such as the selection shown in fig. 14.5) or add data to an existing chart using a range that is not next to the original data. To try this procedure, follow these steps:

1. Select the first set of data to plot. If the data is not organized so that you can select the set, hold down the Ctrl key as you select each part of the set.

2. Plot the data from the first set.

3. Return to the worksheet and select the second set of data.

4. Use the **C**opy command on the **E**dit menu.

5. Switch to the chart and select the chart.

6. Use the Paste **S**pecial command in the **E**dit menu. You see the dialog box shown in figure 14.6.

Figure 14.5

Noncontiguous ranges.

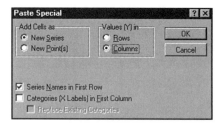

	A	B	C	D	E	F	G	H	I
1									
2									
3									
4		Category 1	Red	Blue	Green		Category	Purple	
5		1	12	45	85		100	1000	
6		50	8	46.5	67.5		5000	1747.5	
7		100	10	48	50		10000	2495	
8		500	5	25.5	25.45		50000	4030	
9		1000	1	3	0.9		100000	5565	
10		5000	0.5	2	0.5		500000	6732.5	
11		10000	0.1	1	0.1		1000000	7900	
12		100000	0.0034	0.1	0.0003		10000000	12543	
13									
14									
15									
16									
17									
18									

Figure 14.6

The Paste Special dialog box.

In the Paste Special dialog box, you can choose to add the new data as a New **S**eries or as New **P**oint(s) in existing series. You also can specify whether the values are organized in **R**ows or **C**olumns. Finally, use the three check boxes at the bottom of the dialog box to define what part of the pasted data contains the labels for the data.

When you click on OK in the Paste Special dialog box, your second set of data is added to the chart. At this point, you might want to designate that the second set of data use a different Value (Y) axis. See the section later in this chapter titled "Creating a Dual Y-Axis Chart."

Changing a Chart Using the ChartWizard

With a chart selected, click on the ChartWizard button in the Standard toolbar to redefine the chart choices. Clicking on the ChartWizard button starts a two-step process to redefine the chart. The first dialog box is shown in figure 14.7.

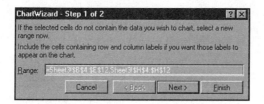

Figure 14.7

ChartWizard redefinition: step 1.

The ChartWizard takes you to the data source worksheet, if it is different from the chart's worksheet, and selects the current cell range(s). Use the first dialog box to reselect the range of cells to plot. When satisfied with your choice, click on the Next button to proceed to the second step, shown in figure 14.8.

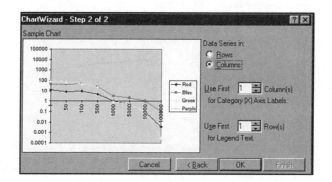

Figure 14.8

ChartWizard redefinition: step 2.

On the second dialog box of the redefinition process using the ChartWizard, you can keep or change the choices you made when the chart was originally created. See Chapter 12, "Complete Guide to Charts," for more information about these choices.

Using Advanced Charts

The remainder of this chapter shows you some of the more esoteric charts Excel can produce, as well as some charting features that are not commonly used, but that can be of great benefit when you need them.

Creating High-Low-Close Stock Charts

Excel includes a special type of line chart specifically for plotting stock market data over time in a High-Low-Close fashion. Start with your data in a format similar to the format shown in figure 14.9.

Figure 14.9

Stock market data.

	A	B	C	D	E	F	G	H	I
1	Date	Volume	High	Low	Close				
2	1/1/96	13240	91.75	88.50	89.00				
3	1/2/96	17630	90.25	87.25	88.00				
4	1/3/96	18100	88.50	86.50	87.13				
5	1/4/96	7940	87.50	86.50	87.25				
6	1/5/96	14910	87.75	85.25	86.00				
7	1/6/96	56000	84.25	81.25	83.38				
8	1/7/96	21910	85.50	84.00	84.88				
9	1/8/96	15630	85.00	83.50	84.63				
10	1/9/96	8290	84.75	83.50	83.75				
11	1/10/96	11400	84.00	82.50	82.75				
12	1/11/96	13590	85.50	82.50	84.25				
13	1/12/96	10760	84.25	82.75	83.50				
14	1/13/96	26950	83.25	80.75	81.13				
15	1/14/96	38260	80.25	78.00	78.75				
16	1/15/96	23380	80.50	78.00	80.50				
17	1/16/96	55930	79.00	76.75	79.00				
18	1/17/96	46100	81.75	76.75	77.63				

AUTHOR'S NOTE

This data was downloaded from the CompuServe MicroQuotell system, which is capable of creating comma-separated files of stock history and downloading them to your computer.

Create the chart normally, but select the Line chart type and choose the High-Low-Close subformat shown in figure 14.10, which results in the chart shown in figure 14.11.

New Riders Publishing
INSIDE
SERIES

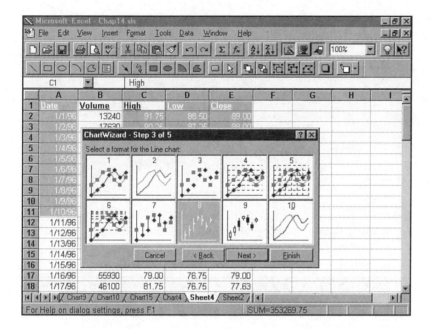

Figure 14.10

The High-Low-Close chart type.

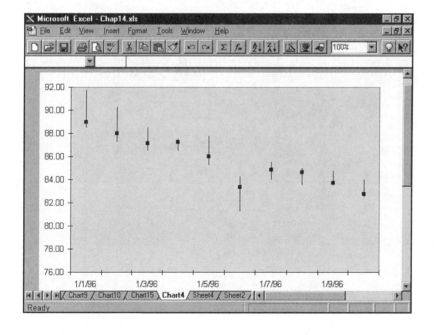

Figure 14.11

The High-Low-Close chart.

You also can create a combination chart showing the High-Low-Close chart superimposed on a column chart that shows the trading volume. To begin, make sure your data is organized in this order:

1. Date

2. Volume

3. High

4. Low

5. Close

Select the data and create the chart normally. Choose the Combination Chart type and the High-Low-Close/Volume subtype, shown in figure 14.12. The finished chart (with some minor formatting added) is shown in figure 14.13.

Figure 14.12

The High-Low-Close/Volume subtype.

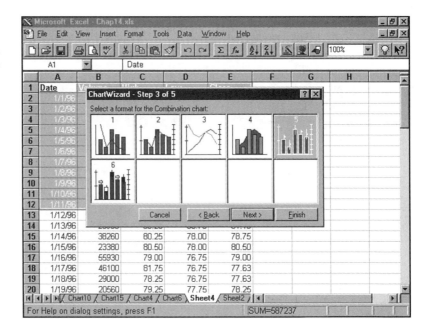

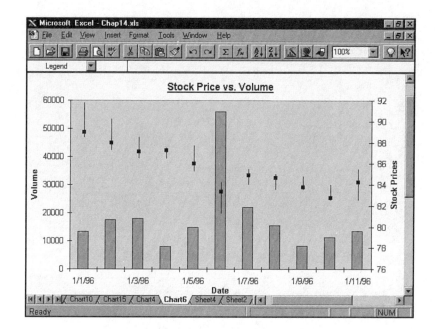

Figure 14.13

The High-Low-Close/Volume combination chart.

Creating a Dual Y-Axis Chart

When you need to compare two sets of data that are based on different scales, you do this with a dual y-axis chart. Generally, these types of charts are used to look for correspondence between two sets of data. A dual y-axis chart shows one set of data against values on the left axis of the chart, whereas the second set of data is shown against the right axis of the chart.

Examine the chart shown in figure 14.14. The top line of the chart contains numbers that are dramatically higher than the rest of the series (if the Value axis wasn't set to Logarithmic scale, you wouldn't even be able to see all the series). When this sort of spread happens, you lose the ability to discern some of the detail for both sets of data, because the chart must cover a much larger range.

Figure 14.14

A line chart with a broad range of values.

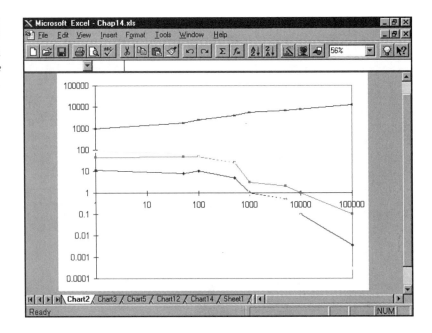

In cases like these, you might want to consider plotting the series that are different against another value category. To plot a second y axis, follow these steps:

1. Select the series that you want to plot against the second y axis.

2. Pull up the formatting dialog box for that series. (Press Ctrl+1 or double-click on the series.)

3. Click on the Axis tab. The Axis page is shown in figure 14.15.

4. Click on the option marked **S**econdary Axis. The change is previewed on the Axis page.

5. Click on OK to save your changes and return to the chart. The results are shown in figure 14.16.

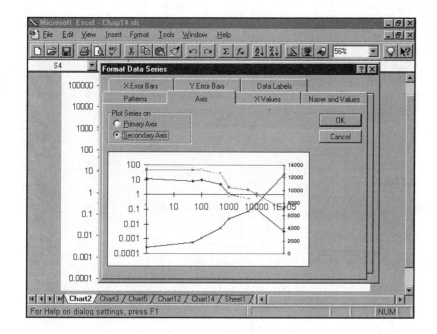

Figure 14.15

The Axis page.

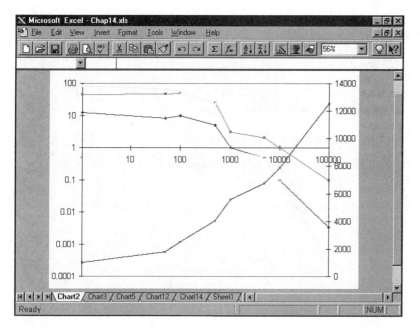

Figure 14.16

The dual y-axis chart.

Working with Error Bars

Excel has a robust error bar feature that gives you the capability to plot error bars easily.

Error bars are used to show visually the amount of uncertainty—or error—in plotted data. Excel enables you to calculate the amount of error in a number of ways, as follows:

◆ Fixed value that you enter

◆ Percentage that you enter

◆ Calculated Standard Deviation based on the mean of the plotted values

◆ Calculated Standard Error

◆ Calculated cell-by-cell error values from a worksheet

You can add error bars to area, bar, column, line, and scatter charts only. In addition, scatter charts can contain both y-axis error bars and x-axis error bars.

 Stop   If you change the chart type on a chart containing error bars from one of the allowed chart types to a different chart type, the error bars are deleted from the chart.

To add error bars to a chart, follow these steps:

1. Create the chart using one of the allowed chart types.

2. Select the series you want to show the error bars.

3. Pull down the **I**nsert menu and choose Error **B**ars. You see the formatting page shown in figure 14.17.

4. Set the parameters for the desired error bars and click on OK to add the error bars.

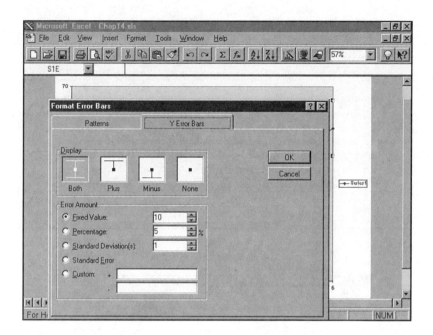

Figure 14.17

The Error Bars formatting page.

Table 14.1 details the options on the Error Bars formatting page.

TABLE 14.1
Error Bar Settings

Setting	Description
Display	In the **D**isplay section, you can choose whether you want error bars shown in both the positive and negative directions, either direction alone, or none at all.
Fixed Value	Enter an amount here to force all the error bars to be shown based on the entered number. Fixed error amounts are often given with various testing equipment, for example.
Percentage	Enter a number in the **P**ercentage field to show what percentage of each value to use as the error amount.
Standard Deviation	This choice calculates the standard deviation based on the plotted series, which then is multiplied by the value you enter in the field next to the **S**tandard Deviation option.

continues

TABLE 14.1, CONTINUED
Error Bar Settings

Setting	Description
Standard **E**rror	Select Standard **E**rror to calculate the standard error for the plotted values using a least squares method.
Custom	Use the **C**ustom setting to define the error amount based on values stored in the worksheet. Click on either the + or – field, then select the range in the worksheet that contains the appropriate error values. You must select the same number of error values as the plot contains. You also can use an array formula in these fields, such as {12,15,3,4.5,12.1}.

Figure 14.18 shows a chart with error bars calculated to plus or minus 15 percent.

Figure 14.18

Percentage-based error bars.

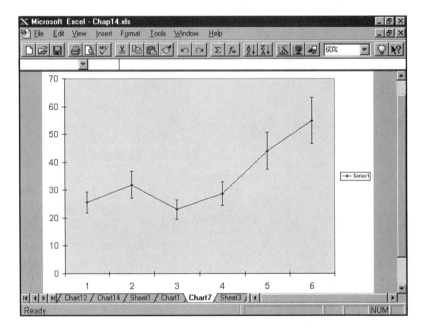

Plotting with Missing Data

If you are using Excel as a technical graphing tool, you often have to work with charts that have some of the data missing. Excel provides three different methods for accounting for missing data:

◆ Don't plot them at all.

◆ Assume that the missing data are zero.

◆ Interpolate the missing data.

You control the way Excel handles missing data through the Options dialog box. Access the Options dialog box by selecting the **O**ptions command in the **T**ools menu, then click on the Chart page of the dialog box. The Chart page is shown in figure 14.19.

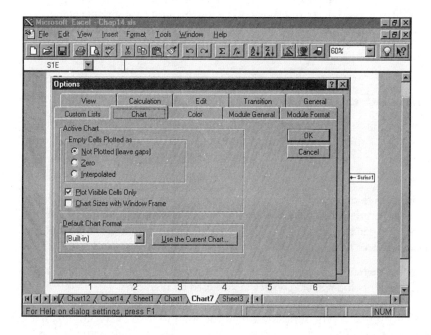

Figure 14.19

The chart page of the Options dialog box.

Table 14.2 discusses the three methods of plotting empty data points.

TABLE 14.2
Missing Data Settings

Setting	Description
Not Plotted	Often the most appropriate for bar charts or column charts, this choice simply leaves the data out of the chart. If this option is selected on line charts, two segments of the line are missing in the chart—the line before the missing data point and the line from the missing data point to the next data point. For that reason, avoid this setting on line charts.
Zero	This choice assumes the missing data are set to zero. This choice is rarely appropriate, but it might come in handy for some situations.
Interpolated	For line charts or scatter charts that use lines to connect the data points, **I**nterpolated is often the most appropriate choice. Excel continues the line through any missing data points. The point itself is not plotted for missing data.

Creating Trend Lines

Trend lines can be used to smooth fluctuations in the plotted data or to predict values forward or backward. You can base the trend lines on a number of different statistical models.

Note Trend lines are calculated using *regression analysis*. Regression analysis uses the values provided to predict the relationship between the values. After the relationship is known, it can be used to display the data in a "smoothed" fashion or to predict values that aren't given.

Note that the Moving Average trend line is not a regression-based trend line; it is used only for data smoothing and cannot be used for prediction.

To create a trend line, select the series on which you want to base the trend line. Then pull down the **I**nsert menu and choose T**r**end line. The Trendline dialog box is displayed in figure 14.20.

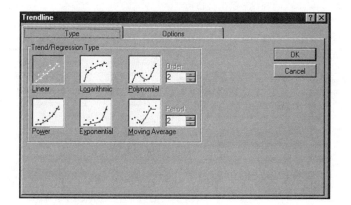

Figure 14.20

The Trendline dialog box.

In the Type dialog box page, choose the regression method that best suits your data. You might need to try different methods depending on the data you are using. To find out how well the regression method fits your data, look at the R-Squared value, which is set on the Options page of the dialog box. The closer the R-Squared value is to 1, the more accurate the trend line.

The Options page also includes a variety of other settings for controlling the trend line. Figure 14.21 shows the Options page. Table 14.3 details these settings.

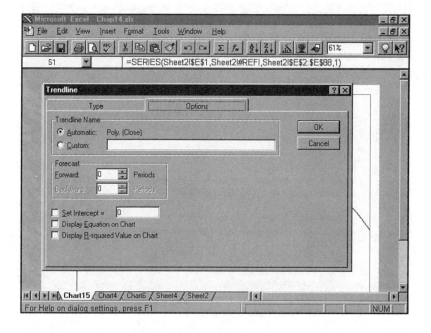

Figure 14.21

The Options page for Trendlines.

TABLE 14.3
Trend Line Options Settings

Setting	Description
Trend line Name	Use this area to define the name of the trend line, which is used for the legend on the chart.
Forecast	The Forecast section can contain the number of periods to forecast the data either **F**orward or **B**ackward.
Set Intercept	Enter a value here to force the first location of the trend line against the y axis.
Display **E**quation on Chart	Select this check box to place the formula used for the regression calculation on the chart, as shown in figure 14.22.
Display **R**-Square Value on Chart	Select this check box to display the R-Squared value on the chart. An R-Squared value closer to zero indicates that the regression is not matching the curve closely; an R-Squared value close to 1 indicates increasing accuracy in the trend line. The R-Squared value is displayed in the chart in figure 14.22.

Figure 14.22

A chart with the trend line, showing the Equation and R-Squared values.

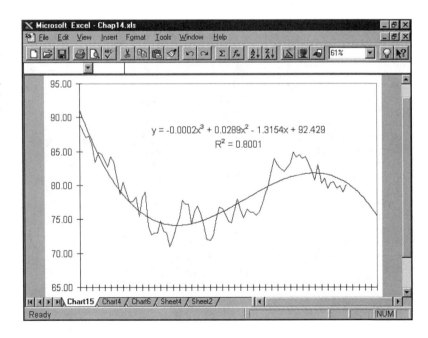

Part IV

Macros

Chapter Snapshot

Macros can save you a great deal of time and effort. After you complete the examples in this chapter, you will be able to record and execute macros to automate repetitive tasks. In this chapter, you learn the following:

◆ Recording a macro to repeat keystrokes, menu, and dialog box operations

◆ Assigning a macro to a shortcut key

◆ Creating macros for use with every workbook

◆ Saving macros

◆ Printing macros

◆ Editing existing macros

◆ Deleting macros

◆ Understanding Excel's macro languages

◆ Assigning macros to toolbar buttons

◆ Assigning macros to graphics objects

Macros make your work with Excel faster, more efficient, and even fun! In fact, the more you create and use macros, the more uses you find for them. One day you'll wonder how you ever got along without them.

CHAPTER 15

Understanding Macros

Despite Excel's impressive power and capabilities, you still might find yourself performing some operations over and over. You might begin several worksheets with the same column and row headings, or apply the same series of formats to cells time and again. Macros automate these repetitive tasks for you. A *macro* contains a series of keystrokes, menu selections, or formulas. After you create a macro, you can repeat all the operations by pressing a shortcut key combination or by selecting the macro from a list. You can even customize a toolbar to run a macro by clicking on a toolbar button.

AUTHOR'S NOTE

You might not realize it, but you've been taking advantage of the power and flexibility of macros all along. You use a macro every time you press a key combination, such as Ctrl+B to turn on boldface, and each time you click on a toolbar button. Key combinations and toolbar buttons run macros that Microsoft has already written for you. These macros perform the most frequently used Excel and Windows functions. By recording or writing your own macros, you are actually customizing Excel for the way you work.

Macros also help you design consistently formatted worksheets. You probably want each part of a multipage worksheet to have the same overall appearance, for example. If you apply the formats manually, you might format one page of the worksheet differently from another. By recording the formats in a macro, you can apply the same formats to common elements on different pages or in different worksheets.

The primary tools you learn about in this chapter are described in table 15.1. The macro tool buttons use the standard recorder symbols like the ones on your VCR or tape player.

TABLE 15.1
The Macro Tools

Tool	Name	Purpose
▶	Run	Displays the Macro dialog box to run a macro.
■	Stop	Stops recording macro instructions.
●	Record	Displays the Record New Macro dialog box for recording a macro.

Recording a Simple Macro

The easiest way to create a macro is to record it. When you record a macro, Excel saves each of the keystrokes or mouse actions that you perform so that you can quickly repeat the steps another time. Macros are recorded live, meaning Excel performs the instructions you are recording. If you are recording a macro that prints

a selected portion of a worksheet, for example, Excel actually prints that portion of the worksheet as you record the macro.

Note   If you want to create a macro without performing the actions, you have to write the macro, as explained in Chapter 16, "Using the Excel 4 Macro Language."

Before you record a macro, make sure that Excel, Windows, and your worksheet are set up exactly as you want them. Otherwise, you might have to stop recording the macro, change your settings, then record the macro again. If you want to print a worksheet, for example, make sure your printer is set up properly in the Windows environment before you start recording the macro.

To record a macro, select **R**ecord Macro from the **T**ools menu, then choose **R**ecord New Macro. The dialog box shown in figure 15.1 appears.

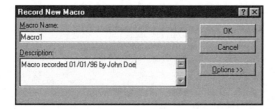

Figure 15.1

The Record New Macro dialog box.

Macro Names

In the **M**acro Name text box, you enter the macro's name. Excel suggests the name Macro1 for the first macro you record, Macro2 for the second, and so on. You can accept the suggested name or create one of your own. Enter a name that clearly illustrates the macro's function. Several months from now, you might forget the function that Macro1 performs, but you will know exactly what task is performed by the macro named Print_Worksheet.

Tip   Excel reserves some special macro names for automatic executing macros. A macro named Auto_Open, for example, will run as soon as you open the Workbook. If you usually start Excel and change to full-screen display, name the macro Auto_Open, then record the selection View Full Screen. Other reserved macro names are Auto_Close, Auto_Activate, and Auto_Deactivate.

Macro names must start with a letter and cannot contain any spaces or punctuation marks other than the underline character. Use uppercase letters or the underline character to designate separate words, such as Print_Worksheet or OpenBudget.

Stop Excel displays a warning message if you try to use a macro name that already exists. You can select Yes to replace the existing macro with a new macro or select No to enter another macro name.

Macro Description

In the **D**escription box, type a brief description of the macro. By default, the description includes the date you recorded the macro and the user name inserted when Excel was installed. If you don't care about that information, you can press the Del or Backspace keys to delete the default entry. Otherwise, place the cursor at the end of the default description and add your own comments there. Later, if you can't remember the function of the macro by its name, you can use the description to help you determine which macro you want to run.

After you have completed the macro name and description in the dialog box, click on OK to begin recording the macro. Follow these steps to record a macro that prints a worksheet:

1. Turn on your printer.

2. Select **T**ools, **R**ecord Macro, **R**ecord New Macro to display the Record New Macro dialog box. The Macro Name text box is automatically selected.

3. Type **QuickPrint** as the macro name, replacing Excel's suggested name, Macro1.

4. Select the Description text box and type **Prints an entire worksheet**.

5. Select OK.

6. Select **F**ile, **P**rint, then select OK.

7. Because your worksheet is empty, a warning box reports that there is nothing to print. Select OK to close the warning box without affecting the macro.

8. To stop recording, click on the Stop button or select **T**ools, **R**ecord Macro, **S**top Recording.

You cannot stop recording a macro while you are entering text in the formula bar—the options in the Macro submenu are dimmed. Click on the Enter box to accept your entry or press Esc to cancel it, then select **S**top Recording.

Tip   If you press an arrow key or press the Enter key to move to another cell, then stop recording, the selection of that cell is recorded in the macro. When you later run the macro, Excel will make the same selection. If you want to stop recording without moving to another cell, click on the formula bar Enter box to accept the text you just entered, then stop recording.

Do not forget to click on the Stop button or select **T**ools, **R**ecord Macro, **S**top Recording to stop recording your actions. If you forget, Excel continues to record all your operations.

Playing a Macro

To play a macro, select **T**ools, **M**acro to display the dialog box shown in figure 15.2. Double-click on the name of the macro in the list, or choose the macro and click on Run.

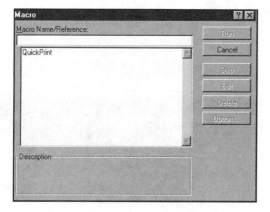

Figure 15.2

The Macro dialog box.

When you select a macro in the list, its description appears in the **D**escription box. Make sure you select the proper macro before you run it.

Excel beeps and displays a message box if it encounters an error in the macro. This beep should not occur if you recorded the macro properly. (Do not confuse an error beep with the normal system beep that sometimes occurs when computing is complete.)

Most of your macros run so quickly that they will appear to perform their tasks almost instantaneously. To stop a longer macro while it is running, however, press Esc. A dialog box appears with options to end the macro, continue running it, debug the macro to locate errors, or to go to the cell where the macro stopped. Select **E**nd to stop the macro, or select **C**ontinue to continue from where it stopped. Debugging macros is discussed in later chapters.

 Note Like figure 15.2, the option buttons in the Macro dialog box remain dimmed until you select a macro in the list box. These options are discussed later in this chapter.

When you run a macro, Excel repeats the keystrokes, menu, and dialog box actions you recorded. The pull-down menus and dialog boxes you used to record the macro do not appear, however—only the results of selecting them are repeated. Suppose, for example, that you use the Font dialog box to record a macro that formats a number of cells. When you run the macro, the fonts are applied to the cells, but the Font dialog box does not appear on-screen.

Using the Visual Basic Toolbar

You can streamline your work with macros by displaying the Visual Basic toolbar, shown in figure 15.3. Select **V**iew, **T**oolbars, click on Visual Basic, and select OK.

Figure 15.3

The Visual Basic toolbar.

For fundamental work, you need only the Run, Stop, and Record buttons. The other buttons are used for more advanced programming tasks.

 Note The toolbar is called Visual Basic because macro instructions are recorded in the *Visual Basic for Applications* (VBA) language.

Macro Record Options

You can make your macros more efficient by selecting macro options. In the Record New Macro dialog box, click on **O**ptions to expand the box, as shown in figure 15.4.

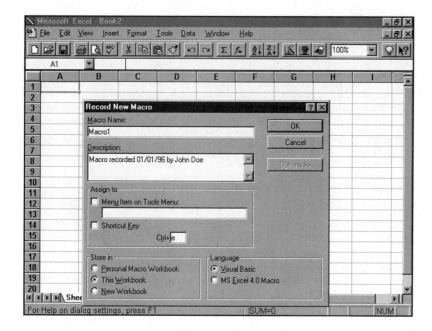

Figure 15.4

*Options on the
Record New
Macro dialog box.*

Assigning Macros for Easy Play

In the Assign to section of the dialog box, you can choose to attach the macro to the **T**ools menu, to a shortcut key combination, or both.

Assigning to the Tools Menu

To add the macro to the **T**ools menu, click on the check box next to the Me**n**u Item in Tools Menu option. Tab to the text box under the prompt, then type the text you want to appear on the menu.

Use a brief name, but one that clearly explains the task the macro performs. For example, if you were creating the QuickPrint macro and wanted to add it to the menu, use the name QuickPrint or the words "Print Worksheet."

The entry you make appears at the bottom of the Tools menu. To run the macro, select **T**ools, then click on the item, or select it and press Enter.

Note   The macro appears in the Tools menu only when the workbook is open.

Assigning Shortcut Keys

The quickest way to run a macro is to assign it to a *shortcut key*—a key you can press along with the Ctrl key to execute the macro.

To assign a shortcut key, select the Shortcut **K**ey check box. Excel suggests a default letter starting with the lowercase "e." For each macro that you assign a shortcut key, it increments the letter, skipping over those already assigned to the built-in shortcut keys, such as "a" for Select All (Ctrl+A) and "b" for Boldface (Ctrl+B). Excel displays the letters in this order:

e j k l m q t w y

These letters are followed by all 26 uppercase letters from A to Z. If you want to assign a key different from the suggested letter, click in the box next to C**t**rl+ and enter the letter you want to use.

Shortcut keys are case-sensitive. An uppercase shortcut letter actually assigns the combination Ctrl+Shift plus the letter to the macro. If you press Shift+E to enter the uppercase "e" as the shortcut key, you have to press Ctrl+Shift+E to run the macro. If you enter the lowercase "e" as the shortcut key, you only have to press Ctrl and the "e" key to run the macro.

AUTHOR'S NOTE

In the Excel help system, shortcut keys are shown with uppercase letters. For example, if you look up help on how to use the keyboard with Excel, you'll see that Ctrl+A is the shortcut key for the "select all" function and that Ctrl+B is the shortcut key for boldface. (To agree with the Excel convention, the built-in shortcut keys shown in this book also include uppercase letters.) These letters refer to the letter printed on the face of the keyboard key.

In actuality, Microsoft has assigned its built-in shortcut keys to lowercase letters. To bold, you press Ctrl and the B key by itself, not Ctrl+Shift+B. If you press Ctrl+Shift+B, Excel sounds a little warning beep reporting that the key combination is not assigned—unless, of course, you assigned it one of your own macros.

Keep this in mind when you are creating your own macros. You can assign the key combination Ctrl+Shift+B to one of your own macros, even though Ctrl+B is already used by Excel.

When you select OK in the Record New Macro dialog box, Excel displays a warning box asking if you used a shortcut key letter already assigned to another macro. The warning box asks if you want to assign the key anyway. Select No to return to the

New Riders Publishing
INSIDE
SERIES

Record New Macro dialog box so that you can enter a different letter; select Yes if you want to assign the same letter to another macro. You can record several macros assigned to the same shortcut key. When you press the shortcut key combination, however, Excel runs the macro whose name is first alphabetically. To execute another macro assigned to the same shortcut key, you must select its name from a list.

You can attach a macro to any letter key, even if the letter is assigned to a built-in Excel function. The new macro overrides the built-in function; the original assignment does not run. If you create a macro assigned to Ctrl+P, for instance, your macro runs—you can no longer use the default Ctrl+P combination to display the Print dialog box. To return the shortcut key to its original purpose, you must delete the macro, as explained later in this chapter.

Tip Don't worry if you have already recorded a macro without assigning it to the menu or to a shortcut key. Later in this chapter, you learn to set the options for a previously recorded macro.

Macro Locations

You can store a macro in any of three locations. By default, your macros are stored with the current workbook. You can use the macros whenever you open the workbook.

Since Excel version 5, global macros have no longer been stored in the global macro sheet. If you have macros from version 4, however, you can still use them.

If you want to use the macro with every workbook, store the macro in the Personal Macro Workbook, a file called PERSONAL.XLS in the EXCEL\XLSTART directory. Each time you start Excel, the workbook is automatically opened and its macros are made available for use.

Note If you just installed Excel, don't bother looking for the PERSONAL.XLS file. The file does not exist until you create a macro and save it in the personal workbook.

You also can record the macro in a new workbook. If you select this option, Excel opens another workbook just to record the macro. If you store your macro in a workbook other than the Personal Macro Workbook, you must open the workbook to access the macro; Excel does not open it automatically.

You might want to create individual workbooks for categories of macros. If you have several macros you use just to create budget worksheets, for example, you can store them together in one workbook. When you need to create a budget, open the workbook to access the macros.

AUTHOR'S NOTE

It might seem more convenient to store all of your macros in the Personal Macro Workbook so that you can use them without opening a workbook first. The use of other workbooks to divide your macros into logical groups makes sense for several reasons, however. A workbook crammed with rarely used macros takes up needed system memory and other resources. In addition, you quickly run out of unique key assignments and have to spend time scrolling through a list of macro names to locate the one you want to run.

Use the Personal Macro Workbook for macros you use on a regular basis. Use other workbooks for macros you use only periodically.

Running Macros from Workbooks

You can run a macro in any worksheet of the workbook. You might, for example, use the Title macro created later in this chapter to add headings to any worksheet in the same workbook. Keep in mind, however, that any text, numbers, or formulas entered by the macro replace contents already in the cells.

To use a macro in another workbook, you must open the workbook first. Macros in any open workbook are available for use. You can run macros in the Personal Macro Workbook in any workbook.

 Stop Before you run a macro, make sure the correct worksheet is active. Do not run a macro that sets up standard headings, for example, when the active worksheet already has headings.

If the macro you want to run is not listed in the dialog box or does not run when you press the shortcut key, the workbook in which it is located is not open. Use the **F**ile, **O**pen option to open the workbook.

Macro Language

Excel gives you two options for the language used to record your macros. By default, macros are saved in the Visual Basic language (known as VBA). Microsoft uses this powerful programming language in many of its application programs and as a stand-alone development tool.

You also can select to record your macros in the Excel 4 macro language. This programming language was used exclusively with Excel 4. If you are an experienced macro programmer in Excel 4, you might want to select this option.

Note   For more information on using the Excel 4 macro language, see Chapter 16.

AUTHOR'S NOTE

Even if you are an experienced Excel 4 macro programmer, take the time to learn VBA. VBA is becoming the common macro language for all Microsoft applications. By learning VBA now, you can transfer your new skills to other programs and build complete custom applications.

To compare the two approaches quickly, record the same macro using both languages. Then use the **A**rrange option on the **W**indows menu to display both on the screen at the same time.

Changing Macro Properties

Excel makes it easy to change the name, shortcut key, or menu assignment of an existing macro:

1. Select **T**ools, **M**acro.

2. Click on the name of the macro you want to modify, then select **O**ptions to display the dialog box shown in figure 15.5.

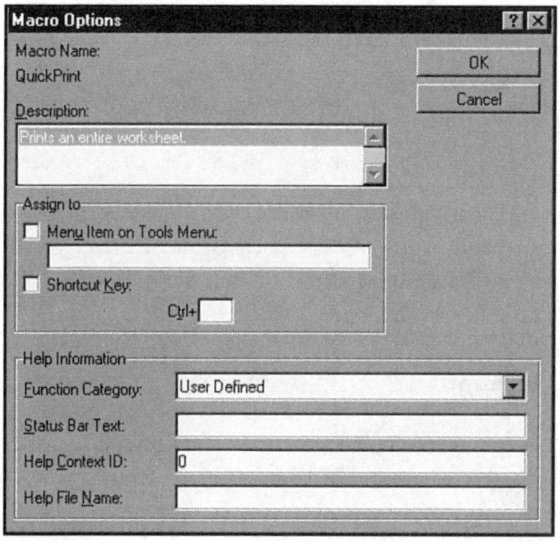

Figure 15.5

The Macro Options dialog box.

3. Set or change the desired options in the dialog box, then select OK.

Note The options in the Help Information section are used for creating custom applications.

Relative and Absolute Selection

When you record a macro that includes cell selection, you can record the operation in two ways. By default, Excel records cell selections on an *absolute* basis. If you select a cell when recording the macro, the same cell is selected when you later execute the macro. Suppose you begin recording a macro when you are in cell A1, for example. You click on cell B2 to select it, then continue recording your macro instructions. When you later run the macro, cell B2 is selected no matter where in the worksheet you are when you run the macro. If you are in cell C5, cell B2 is still selected when you run the macro.

Alternatively, you can choose to select cells using a relative reference. When you select a cell *relatively*, the macro selects a cell in relation to the currently active cell. If you start in cell A1 and select cell B2 using a relative reference, Excel selects the cell one column over and one row down from whichever cell is currently active when you later run the macro. If you run the macro when cell C5 is active, for example, cell D6 is selected. You select the method in the Record Macro submenu.

You select cells by relative reference by choosing **T**ools, **R**ecord Macro and selecting the option **U**se Relative Reference. The option is turned on when a check mark appears next to it. To change to absolute selection, deselect the option so that no check mark appears there.

Use Relative Reference is a *toggle*—a setting you turn off or on. It does not affect the way you select the cells when you record the macro, just the way they are selected when you run it later.

As another example, suppose you duplicate a series of column and row headings in several locations within an individual worksheet or on a number of separate worksheets. Rather than type the headings yourself, you record a macro to do it for you. If you used the default absolute reference, however, the headings would always appear in the same rows and columns. You would not be able to use the macro to place the headings in other locations.

In the following steps, you record a macro that enters standard row and column headings using a relative reference. You should be in Excel with a blank worksheet. Record the macro in the Personal Macro Workbook.

1. Select **T**ools, **R**ecord Macro, then select **U**se Relative Reference if it is not already selected.

2. Select cell A1.

3. Select **T**ools, **R**ecord Macro, **R**ecord New Macro to display the Record New Macro dialog box.

4. Type **Standard_Headings** as the macro name.

5. Select **O**ptions.

6. Click on the Menu Item on Tools Menu check box.

7. Select the text box under the prompt and type **Headings**.

8. Select the Ctrl+ text box and type **h**. Editing the Ctrl+ box automatically places a check mark in the Shortcut **K**ey check box.

9. Click on **P**ersonal Macro Workbook.

10. Click on OK.

11. Select cell B1.

12. Type **1st Qtr**.

13. Drag the fill handle in the lower right corner of cell B1 to cell E1.

14. Select cell A2 and type **Sales**.

15. Select cell A3 and type **Rentals**.

16. Select cell A4, type **Total**, and press Enter.

17. Click on the Stop button, or select **T**ools, **R**ecord Macro, **S**top Recording to stop recording your actions.

The cell selections were recorded using a relative reference. When you later run this macro, Excel inserts the text 1st Qtr in the cell to the right of the active cell and uses AutoFill to complete the series in the next three cells. The row headings appear in the three rows below the starting cell position.

Note   To change back to absolute cell selection for further macro recording, deselect the **U**se Relative Reference option.

Adding to a Macro

While you are recording a macro, you can stop the recorder to perform actions you don't want to record. For example, suppose that while recording a macro you want to open another worksheet to check a reference. If you open the worksheet while recording, the open instructions are recorded as part of the macro. When you later run the macro, the worksheet is opened, even though you only needed to open it as a reference that one time. To pause the recording, click on the Stop button or select **T**ools, **R**ecord Macro, **S**top Recording to stop recording your actions. When you want to continue adding instructions to the same macro, select **T**ools, **R**ecord Macro, R**e**cord at Mark.

You can use this feature if you realize that you stopped recording a macro before you performed all the operations you wanted to record. When you select R**e**cord at Mark, Excel begins recording your actions again, adding them to the end of the last macro you created.

 Note   To add instructions to a previously recorded macro, see "Setting the Recording Location" later in this chapter.

Follow these steps to insert additional instructions into the macro named Standard_Headings that you recorded in the last exercise:

1. Select cell A4.

2. Select **T**ools, **R**ecord Macro, then select **U**se Relative Reference, if it is not already selected.

3. Select **T**ools, **R**ecord Macro, R**e**cord at Mark.

4. Select cell A6 and type **Salaries**.

5. Select cell A7 and type **Supplies**.

6. Select cell A8 and type **Total**.

7. Select cell A10, type **Profit**, and click on the Enter box.

8. Click on the Stop button, or select **T**ools, **R**ecord Macro, **S**top Recording to stop recording your actions.

Exploring the Recorded Macro

When Excel records a macro, it inserts special instructions into the workbook. If you recorded your macro correctly and you are not interested in learning more about the advanced macro features discussed in Chapter 16, "Using the Excel 4 Macro Language," you don't need to view these commands.

If you want to confirm that the macro was recorded properly, or if you want to edit or delete a macro, you must display the text of the macro.

When you use the VBA language (the default setting), macros are recorded in a module. A *module* is a special type of object attached to the workbook. To display a module, click on the Last Tab button to see a tab called Module1 (see fig. 15.6). Then click on the Module1 tab to display the module.

Figure 15.6

The macro module.

Last Tab button

Tip   You can also select **T**ools, **M**acro, select the macro you want to see, and then click on **E**dit to see the workbook's module.

Your macros are listed in the order that you created them. The commands are written in VBA.

By tiling the macro sheet and your worksheet, you can get a feel for the way Excel records macros. Follow these steps to display the module and the worksheet to record an additional macro:

1. Make the worksheet the active window, then select **W**indow, **N**ew Window.

2. Click on the Last Tab button, then click on the Module1 tab to display the text of your macro.

3. Select **W**indow, **A**rrange, **T**iled and click on OK.

4. Click in the worksheet window, or press Ctrl+F6.

5. Select cell A25.

Now record a macro and watch the instructions appear in the Module window.

6. Select **T**ools, **R**ecord Macro, **R**ecord New Macro to display the Record New Macro dialog box.

7. Type **Title** as the macro name.

8. Select **O**ptions.

9. Click on the This **W**orkbook button.

10. Select OK. The macro name is added to the end of the list of existing macros. Excel scrolls the list automatically to display the macro name in the window.

11. Type **Wilson Automotive, Inc.** and press the down arrow. The recorded instruction appears in the macro sheet.

12. Type **Annual Budget**, then click on the Enter box.

13. Select cells A25 and A26.

14. Select Forma**t**, **C**ells, **A**lignment, **C**enter, then click on OK.

15. Click on the Stop button.

16. Click anywhere on the worksheet to deselect the cells. Your screen should look something like figure 15.7.

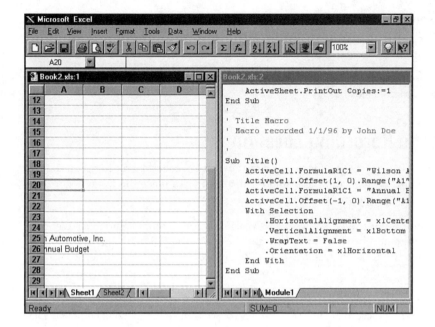

Figure 15.7

The module and worksheet tiled.

Displaying the Personal Macro Workbook

Unlike workbooks, modules, and other windows, Excel does not normally display the Personal Macro Workbook on the screen—it is hidden. To open the Personal Macro Workbook, select **W**indow, **U**nhide to display a dialog box listing the names of hidden windows. Click on PERSONAL.XLS, then select OK. Excel displays the personal workbook that contains your macros.

You can use the **A**rrange command to display the personal workbook and your other workbook on the screen at the same time.

Printing Macros

Although the macro instructions might not mean much to you, they can serve as an excellent source of reference, particularly when you record a large number of operations.

As your macros become longer and more sophisticated, you should print a hard copy of the macro list as a reference. You can study the hard copy, writing notes where you'd like to make changes.

To print a copy of your macros, display the macro sheet, or make it active if its windows are tiled, then select **F**ile, **P**rint and click on OK.

Tip Make sure the Selecte**d** Sheets option is chosen in the Print dialog box when you want to print macros.

Setting the Recording Location

You can add instructions to a macro you have already recorded by setting the recording location. When you set the recording location, you can place the newly recorded instructions at any point within a macro.

Display the Module or the Personal Macro Workbook that contains the macro to which you want to add instructions. Move the cursor to the point at which you want to insert the instructions, then select **T**ools, **R**ecord Macro, **M**ark Position for Recording.

Tip To add instructions to the end of the macro, place the insertion point before the End Sub command (see fig. 15.8).

Figure 15.8

Placement of the insertion point to add to the macro.

Click here to add to the end of the macro

```
Selection.ClearContents
ActiveCell.Offset(0, -1).Range("A1").Select
Selection.AutoFill Destination:=ActiveCell.Range("A1:D1"), Type:= _
    xlFillDefault
ActiveCell.Range("A1:D1").Select
ActiveCell.Offset(1, -1).Range("A1").Select
ActiveCell.FormulaR1C1 = "Sales"
ActiveCell.Offset(1, 0).Range("A1").Select
ActiveCell.FormulaR1C1 = "Rentals"
ActiveCell.Offset(1, 0).Range("A1").Select
ActiveCell.FormulaR1C1 = "Total"
ActiveCell.Offset(1, 0).Range("A1").Select
ActiveCell.Offset(2, 0).Range("A1").Select
ActiveCell.FormulaR1C1 = "Salaries"
ActiveCell.Offset(1, 0).Range("A1").Select
ActiveCell.FormulaR1C1 = "Supplies"
ActiveCell.Offset(1, 0).Range("A1").Select
ActiveCell.FormulaR1C1 = "Total"
ActiveCell.Offset(2, 0).Range("A1").Select
ActiveCell.FormulaR1C1 = "Profit"
End Sub
```

Display the sheet where you want to record the macro, then select **T**ools, **R**ecord Macro, R**e**cord at Mark and begin recording your macro. The new instructions are recorded at the position you set.

 Stop Make sure you set the position correctly. If you record instructions in the wrong location, your macro will not operate correctly. Suppose, for example, your macro selects a cell and enters some information into the cell. If you record new commands between these instructions, the contents will not appear where you originally intended.

Follow these steps to add instructions at the end of the Standard_Headings macro in the Personal Macro Workbook:

1. Maximize one of the workbook windows.

2. Select **W**indow, **U**nhide, OK to unhide the Personal Macro Workbook.

3. Scroll until you see the End Sub command of the Standard_Headings macro.

4. Place the cursor before End Sub, as you saw in figure 15.8.

5. Select **T**ools, **R**ecord Macro, **M**ark Position for Recording.

6. Press Ctrl+F6 to return to the worksheet window.

7. Select cell A10.

Because you are recording the macro using relative reference, you must position the insertion point in the correct cell. When you run this part of the macro, you want it to select the proper cell in relation to the previously recorded section.

8. Select **T**ools, **R**ecord Macro, then select **U**se Relative Reference, if it is not already selected.

9. Select **T**ools, **R**ecord Macro, R**e**cord at Mark.

10. Select cell A15.

11. Type **All budget figures are subject to audit** and click on the Enter box.

12. Click on the Stop button.

The new instructions appear at the end of the macro, as in figure 15.9.

Figure 15.9

The added instructions.

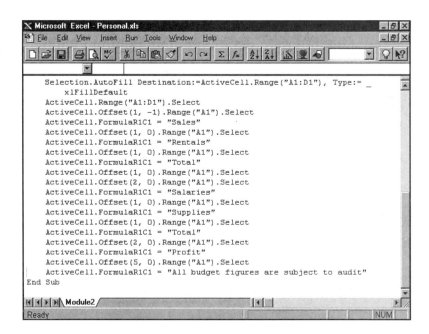

```
Selection.AutoFill Destination:=ActiveCell.Range("A1:D1"), Type:= _
    xlFillDefault
ActiveCell.Range("A1:D1").Select
ActiveCell.Offset(1, -1).Range("A1").Select
ActiveCell.FormulaR1C1 = "Sales"
ActiveCell.Offset(1, 0).Range("A1").Select
ActiveCell.FormulaR1C1 = "Rentals"
ActiveCell.Offset(1, 0).Range("A1").Select
ActiveCell.FormulaR1C1 = "Total"
ActiveCell.Offset(1, 0).Range("A1").Select
ActiveCell.Offset(2, 0).Range("A1").Select
ActiveCell.FormulaR1C1 = "Salaries"
ActiveCell.Offset(1, 0).Range("A1").Select
ActiveCell.FormulaR1C1 = "Supplies"
ActiveCell.Offset(1, 0).Range("A1").Select
ActiveCell.FormulaR1C1 = "Total"
ActiveCell.Offset(2, 0).Range("A1").Select
ActiveCell.FormulaR1C1 = "Profit"
ActiveCell.Offset(5, 0).Range("A1").Select
ActiveCell.FormulaR1C1 = "All budget figures are subject to audit"
End Sub
```

Saving Macros

A macro module is part of the workbook. When you save the workbook, the module is saved along with it. If you want to save the macros without saving the sheets, you have several alternatives. You can delete the contents of the sheets, then save the workbook. You also can copy the module to a new workbook. To copy the module, click on the module tab, then select **E**dit, **M**ove or Copy Sheet. Pull down the **T**o Book list and select (new book). Excel creates a new book that contains the module.

Tip   You also can display two workbooks on the screen, then drag the Module tab to the other workbook.

Hiding and Saving the Personal Macro Workbook

The Personal Macro Workbook is not saved when you save other workbooks. You must save the Personal Macro Workbook before you exit Excel. Display the workbook, then select **F**ile, **S**ave.

If you close the Personal Macro Worksheet when it is unhidden, its macro is not available, and you must open it again. Rather than closing it, hide it again. This removes the workbook from the display, but makes its macros accessible. To hide the worksheet, make it active and select <u>W</u>indow, <u>H</u>ide. If you don't hide the Personal Macro Worksheet, it appears on-screen the next time you start Excel.

Remember to display and select the Personal Macro Workbook before you select <u>W</u>indow, <u>H</u>ide. If you don't, the active worksheet window is hidden.

Deleting a Macro

You can delete a macro if you change your mind after recording it, or if you just want to clean out unused macros from a workbook.

To delete a macro, select <u>T</u>ools, <u>M</u>acro, click on the macro name in the list box, then select <u>D</u>elete. You also can display the module or Personal Macro Workbook, then delete the macro code by selecting it and pressing Del. Remember, you must unhide the Personal Macro Workbook if it is not listed in the Window menu.

If you delete a macro that has been added to the <u>T</u>ools menu, the list still appears in the menu. Before you delete the macro, select <u>T</u>ools, <u>M</u>acro, then select the macro in the list box. Finally, select <u>O</u>ptions. Deselect the Me<u>n</u>u Item on Tools Menu box, then select OK. This action removes the item from the menu. You can now delete the macro itself. If you delete the item before removing it from the menu, you must use the <u>T</u>ools, Men<u>u</u> Editor option to edit the menu.

To delete all your personal macros, delete the file PERSONAL.XLS from the disk. Excel creates a new one the next time you save a macro using that option.

Classifications of Macros

Excel's macro language is a powerful tool for automating worksheets. Recorded macros, however, only touch on their power and versatility. When you record a macro, you are creating a command macro, which is one of two types of macros you can create. The other type of macro is a function macro.

Command Macros

A *command macro* performs some action on the worksheet. It repeats keystrokes or selections from menus or dialog boxes. Command macros save you from repeating the same series of operations.

Macros that you record are always command macros. You can also write a command macro if you want to create it without actually performing the instructions. By writing macros, you can repeat a series of steps, make decisions based on the contents of cells, and even create interactive macros that accept input from the keyboard.

Function Macros

A *function macro* creates a user-defined function. The macro operates the same way as Excel's built-in functions to perform a calculation and return a value. It does not perform any action on the worksheet except to insert a value into a cell.

Some complex calculations that you perform might require formulas in several cells. Each formula is actually another step in the overall calculation. If you add the formulas directly in the worksheet, they could occupy a considerable amount of space. By adding all of the formulas into a function macro, you can perform the calculation using a single worksheet cell.

 Note   You cannot record an entire user-defined function macro. You have to write the macro, or perform extensive editing on a record macro.

Understanding Macro Code

Unless you decide to record macros in the Excel 4 format, your macros are constructed using the *Visual Basic for Applications* (VBA) language.

A *keyword* is a word that represents a macro language command or instruction. Every macro begins with the keyword Sub followed by the macro name and ends with the keyword End Sub. The macro instructions are called *statements*. Each statement tells Excel to perform a specific action. VBA instructions are combinations of objects, methods, properties, and variables.

 Note   Technically, the Sub and End Sub commands indicate a subroutine. Some of VBA's basic concepts are discussed here.

The VBA statement to select cell D9, for example, appears like this:

```
Range("D9").Select
```

Range is a VBA object that represents a cell or a range of cells. The range object, however, requires an argument that further identifies the object being referred to, giving the specific cell or range of cells. In this case, the object is cell D9.

The VBA statement also must specify the *method* of dealing with or using the object. The keyword Select is the method. It tells Excel what action to perform on the object—in this case, to select the cell. In the statement Range("D9:G9").Select, the object to be selected is the range of cells D9 through G9.

The statement for entering contents into a cell appears like this:

```
ActiveCell.FormulaR1C1 = "Profit"
```

The object is the currently active cell. In this case, however, you are not performing a method on the cell but defining its properties. A *property* explains the conditions or state of the object. In this statement, the property is FormulaR1C1, and it indicates that the following text will be contained in the object.

In some cases, the object has a number of properties. For example, the command to format a cell in a font is as follows:

```
Selection.Font.Name = "Arial"
```

Selection is an object that refers to the currently selected object in the worksheet. Font also is an object to be applied to the selections. But the Font object needs a property (Name) to explain the way in which it is applied. In this case, the selected cells are assigned the font named Arial.

Note Macros are not simply a record of keystrokes. The command to change a font has no reference to the Format Cell selection, which is needed to display the Font dialog box. Macro instructions are the results of your recorded actions.

A definite pattern exists for performing Excel tasks. Usually, a cell (or range of cells) is selected, then one or more properties are assigned to the selection. Suppose, for example, you record the instructions that use AutoFill to complete a series of entries. Here is a typical process:

```
Range("D9").Select
ActiveCell.FormulaR1C1 = "1st Qtr"
Selection.AutoFillDestination:=Range("D9:G9"),Type:=xlFillDefault
```

These VBA statements select a cell, enter the starting value (1st Qtr), then assign properties to the cell that complete the series.

When you select items from a dialog box, any number of properties can be included in the VBA statement. For instance, when you use the Font dialog box, you can select a font name, size, and various other character attributes. Rather than repeating the object names for every property, Excel places them in a With structure, as follows:

```
With Selection.Font
    .Name = "Arial"
    .FontStyle = "Regular"
    .Size = 10
    .Strikethrough = False
    .Superscript = False
    .Subscript = False
    .OutlineFont = False
    .Shadow = False
    .Underline = xlNone
    .ColorIndex = xlAutomatic
End With
```

The statement `With Selection.Font` indicates that all of the following properties
refer to the same object. `Name`, `FontStyle`, `Size`, and so on are properties of the
`Selection.Font` object.

You can use a similar technique to format the position of text within a cell. In the
following example, the five properties are applied to the `Selection` object:

```
With Selection
    .HorizontalAlignment = xlCenter
    .VerticalAlignment = xlBottom
    .WrapText = False
    .Orientation = xlHorizontal
    .AddIndent = False
End With
```

Streamlining Macro Selection

If you use a macro often, you can add it to a toolbar or to a graphics object. This
procedure makes the macro visible on-screen so that you don't have to remember
its shortcut key or select it from a list.

Adding a Macro to a Toolbar

Pressing the shortcut key combination is a quick way to run a macro. Still, it is easy
to forget which key you assigned to every macro you created. As you build a library
of macros, you also might run out of keys to assign.

Rather than try to remember the shortcut keys or scroll through the Run Macro
dialog box to locate the macro, you can assign the macro to a toolbar. You can then
run the macro by clicking on the toolbar button.

AUTHOR'S NOTE

Assigning a macro to a toolbar has one great advantage. When you click on the tool assigned to the macro, Excel opens the workbook in which the macro is located if it is not already open. You don't have to remember to open the workbook yourself.

You assign a macro to the toolbar using the dialog box shown in figure 15.10. Select the desired tool, then drag it onto the toolbar. You then can select the macro you want to assign to the toolbar or record a macro to assign to it. The macro sheet that contains the macro you want to assign must be open.

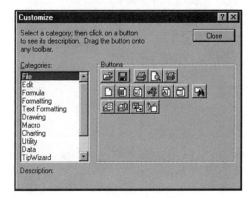

Figure 15.10

The Customize dialog box.

Follow these steps to add the Standard_Headings macro to the toolbar:

1. Point to the toolbar and click on the right mouse button to display the toolbar shortcut menu. Alternatively, use the keyboard to select **V**iew, T**o**olbars.

2. Select Customize to display the Customize dialog box.

3. Click on Custom in the **C**ategories list. (You have to scroll the list to display the option.) The tools shown in the dialog box are unassigned. They are not connected with any Excel function.

4. Drag one of the tools to the toolbar. When you release the mouse button, the Assign Macro dialog box appears.

5. Select PERSONAL.XLS!Standard_Headings or any other macro you want to assign to the tool, then click on OK. Click on **R**ecord to record and assign the macro to the tool at the same time.

6. Select Close to close the Customize dialog box.

If you select Cancel in the Assign Macro dialog box, the tool is not associated with a macro. When you first click on the macro, however, the Assign Macro dialog box appears so that you can make the assignment or record a macro.

 Tip Alternatively, you can use the keyboard to assign a macro using the **V**iew, **T**oolbars, **T**ools, Assi**g**n Macro.

Reassigning Tools

You also can assign a macro to a tool already displayed on the toolbar. Like preset key combinations, making the assignment cancels the built-in function—when you click on the tool, your macro runs instead. To assign a macro to an existing tool, follow these steps:

1. Display the toolbar that contains the button.

2. Point to the toolbar and click on the right mouse button to display the toolbar shortcut menu.

3. Select Customize.

4. Point to the button you want to change, then click on the right mouse button to display the shortcut menu shown in figure 15.11.

Figure 15.11

The Customize toolbar shortcut menu.

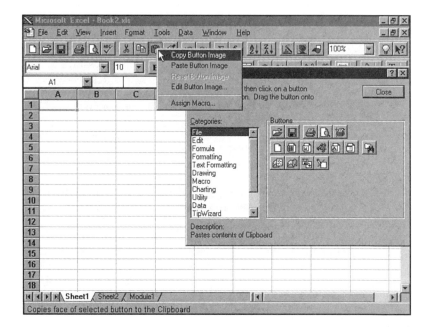

5. Select Assign Macro.

6. Select the macro you want to assign to the tool, then click on OK.

7. Close the Customize dialog box.

Only the tool on that toolbar is affected. If the same tool appears on another toolbar, it retains its original value. To reassign the tool to its original function, follow these steps:

1. Display the toolbar that contains the button.

2. Point to the toolbar and click the right mouse button to display the toolbar shortcut menu.

3. Select Customize.

4. Drag the tool off the toolbar to delete it.

5. In the **C**ategories box, select the category of the function originally performed by the tool. The tools in that category appear in the Tools panel.

6. Drag the tool to its original position on the toolbar.

Adding a Macro to a Graphics Object

In Chapter 13, "Drawing and Adding Graphics to Documents," you learned to create graphics objects. You can assign a macro to a graphics object and then run the macro by selecting the object. To assign a macro to a graphics object, follow these steps:

1. Select the graphics object.

2. Select **T**ools, Assi**g**n Macro.

3. Select the macro from the list, or select **R**ecord and then record the macro.

Chapter Snapshot

When you need to create macros, Excel gives you a choice. You can create macros in *Visual Basic for Applications* (VBA) or the Microsoft Excel 4 macro language. Even if you want to program in VBA, you should know how to use the alternative. In this chapter, you learn the following tasks and concepts:

◆ Recording a macro using the Excel 4 macro language

◆ Using existing Excel 4 macros and macro sheets

◆ Adding instructions to existing macros

◆ Deleting macros

◆ Understanding macro arguments

◆ Writing command macros

◆ Writing user-defined functions

◆ Understanding macro flow control

◆ Writing macros that make decisions

◆ Writing macros that repeat instructions

◆ Writing macros that input values

If you are new to the world of macros and programming, you should find this chapter to be a perfect introduction to programming logic and techniques. The programming skills you learn here can be applied to VBA or any other programming language.

CHAPTER

16

Using the Excel 4 Macro Language

Although *Visual Basic for Applications* (VBA) is a powerful automation and development tool, you should be familiar with another Microsoft language: the Excel 4 macro language. If you already are an experienced Excel macro programmer, you'll discover the convenience of developing important macros in the familiar environment while you learn VBA. You then can switch to VBA when your programming skills increase.

But even if you are not a programmer, you might have Excel macros that were written by others, copied from magazines, or downloaded from a bulletin board. You can use these macros in Excel, and record and write macros in the Excel 4 macro language. (From this point on, this chapter refers to the Excel 4 macro language as *the macro language.*)

If you skipped Chapter 15 because you are an experienced macro language programmer, or because you did not want to learn VBA, go back! Excel for Windows 95 incorporates some new features that can streamline recording and writing macros.

Recording a Macro

As you learned in Chapter 15, you record a macro in the macro language the same way you do in VBA. When the Record New Macro dialog box appears, however, select Options, then click on the MS **E**xcel 4.0 Macro button in the Language section.

Give the macro a name, enter a description, and assign a shortcut key just as you do for any other macro. From the recording standpoint, the process is the same as the one you learned earlier.

Table 16.1 describes the toolbar icons you use in this chapter.

TABLE 16.1
Macro Toolbar Icons

Tool	Name	Purpose
▷	Step	Steps through macro instructions one at a time.
‖	Resume	Resumes a paused macro.
⌸	Step Into	Steps through a macro, including subroutines.
⌸	Step Over	Steps through a macro, skipping over subroutines.

 Note Remember, macro names must start with a letter and cannot contain any spaces or punctuation marks other than the underline character.

New Riders Publishing
INSIDE
SERIES

Macro Locations

You can select to store a macro in one of three locations. By default, macros are stored in the current workbook. These macros are available whenever the workbook is open. You can open the workbook to access its macros from other workbooks.

If you want to be able to use the macro with every worksheet, select the Personal Macro Workbook option. The macro is recorded in the file PERSONAL.XLS, along with any VBA macros that you have written or recorded. The Personal Macro Workbook operates according to the description in Chapter 15:

◆ It is opened automatically when you start Excel.

◆ It is hidden until you select Windows Unhide.

◆ It must be saved when you exit Excel.

If you select New Workbook, Excel opens a new workbook and records your macro there. You must save the workbook before you exit Excel, and you must open the workbook to access the macros.

 Note Each time you select New Workbook, Excel opens another workbook. After you open a workbook, record other macros in it by setting the macro location.

Running Macros

You can run a macro written in the macro language just as you learned to in Chapter 15:

◆ If the macro is assigned to a shortcut key, press the key combination.

◆ If the macro is assigned to the menu, pull down the menu and select the item.

◆ If the item is assigned to a toolbar button or graphic object, point and click. If necessary, Excel opens the workbook in which the macro is located.

◆ Select **T**ools, **M**acro, then double-click on the macro in the list box, or select the macro and choose Run.

 Note All the cautions and warnings that apply to running VBA macros apply equally to macro language macros. Refer to Chapter 15 for additional information.

Follow these steps to record a macro that enters your name on a worksheet:

1. Select cell A1.

2. Select **T**ools, **R**ecord Macro, **R**ecord New Macro to display the Record Macro dialog box.

3. Type **Title** as the macro name.

4. Select **O**ptions.

5. Select the Me**n**u Item on Tools Menu option.

6. Select the text box under the prompt, then type **Title**.

7. Click on the Shortcut **K**ey check box.

8. Click on MS **E**xcel 4.0 Macro.

9. Click on OK.

10. Select cell A1.

11. Select **I**nsert, **R**ows.

12. Type your name, then press Enter.

13. Click on the Stop button, or select **T**ools, **R**ecord Macro, **S**top Recording to stop recording your actions.

 Stop   Do not forget to stop recording when you have completed the operations that you want to record. If you forget, Excel continues to record all your operations.

 Note   You can record Excel 4 macros using either relative or absolute cell references, as explained in Chapter 15.

Using Existing Macros

You can use macros written in Excel 4 without any conversion or editing. Open the macro sheet just as you did in Excel 4 and run the macro using the explanation in Chapter 15.

If you have an Excel 4 global macro sheet (the file GLOBAL.XLM in the EXCEL\XLSTART subdirectory), it opens automatically when you start Excel, and its macros are available. By default, however, the global macro sheet is hidden.

 Note   GLOBAL.XLM is a worksheet created by Excel 4 that stores macros in the Excel 4 macro language. Both the GLOBAL.XLM worksheet and the PERSONAL.XLS workbook open automatically, which might cause Excel to start slowly.

Transferring Macros

If you have macros in the global macro sheet, you can transfer them to PERSONAL.XLS. This step avoids the necessity of having both open in order to access all your global macros. To transfer the macros, open and unhide both GLOBAL.XLM and PERSONAL.XLS. Display the sheet that contains your macros in GLOBAL.XLM, then select **E**dit, **M**ove or Copy Sheet to display the dialog box shown in figure 16.1. Pull down the **T**o Book list and select PERSONAL.XLS, then OK.

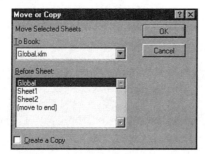

Figure 16.1

The Move or Copy dialog box.

 Tip   If you want to copy the macros so that they remain in the global macro sheet, click on the **C**reate a Copy check box.

AUTHOR'S NOTE

The Personal Macro Workbook replaced the global macro sheet functionality of Excel 4 with the release of Excel 5. Excel for Windows 95 continues to support the version 4 macro language and use of the global macro sheet. You can use both if desired, and both can store VBA and Excel 4 macros. The only reason to retain the global macro sheet, however, is for compatibility with earlier Excel versions.

continues

If you have Excel for Windows 95 on your office computer and Excel 4 on your home computer, for instance, recording macros in the global macro sheet enables you to use them with both versions.

Excel for Windows 95 has features and functions not available in earlier versions, however. Macros that contain commands for these functions do not run in Excel 4.

Exploring the Recorded Macro

As you read in Chapter 15, VBA macros are stored in modules. A module is attached to a workbook, but it does not contain the rows and columns of a worksheet.

Macro language macros are saved in macro sheets that look the same as regular worksheets. The sheets are added at the end of the workbook, following any VBA modules. Sheet tabs for worksheets that contain Excel 4 macros are labeled Macro rather than Module. Module sheets are reserved for VBA macros. To display the sheet, click on the Last Tab button on the far left of the horizontal scroll bar to find a tab called Macro1. Then click on the Macro1 tab. Your Title macro appears as illustrated in figure 16.2.

Figure 16.2

An Excel 4 macro in a macro sheet.

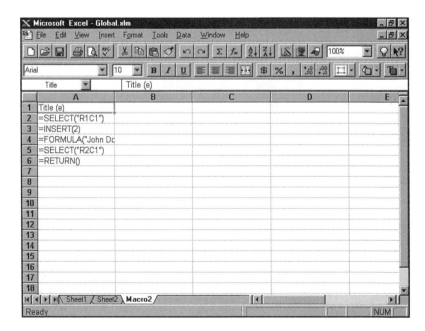

Note Macro sheets do not exist until you record an Excel 4 macro.

Each macro is listed in a column of the worksheet. The first macro you recorded is in column A, the second in column B, and so on. Row A contains the macro names and shortcut key assignments. Cell A1 in figure 16.2, for example, indicates that the column contains the macro called Title and that it is assigned to the key combination Ctrl+E.

Note The columns settings might prevent you from seeing the full text of each macro instruction. Widen the columns if necessary.

The remaining rows contain instructions in Excel's macro language. The instruction =RETURN() must end every macro. It tells Excel where to stop looking for instructions to repeat when you run the macro.

Tip By tiling the macro sheet and your worksheet, you can get a feel for the way Excel records macros.

Printing Macros

To print a copy of all the macros in the macro sheet, display the sheet and select **F**ile, **P**rint, OK. To print a copy of a specific macro, select the instructions that make up the macro and select **F**ile, **P**rint, **S**election, then OK.

Tip Widen the columns and/or change fonts to see the full text of the instructions on the printout.

Setting the Recording Location

You can use the **M**ark Position for Recording option to add commands to any macro in the macro sheet.

To add commands to the *end* of a macro, click on any cell in the macro that already contains a command, then select **T**ools, **R**ecord Macro, **M**ark Position for Recording. Return to the worksheet, then select **T**ools, **R**ecord Macro, Re**c**ord at Mark. The instructions you record will be added to the end of the macro.

To add commands within a macro, first insert enough blank rows to hold the macro commands you are adding. Select the first blank row, and then select **T**ools, **R**ecord Macro, **M**ark Position for Recording.

Stop   If you set a recording position to start in a blank cell, make sure there are enough empty cells below that position to store the entire macro. If Excel encounters a cell that already contains any contents, it will stop recording your macro and display a warning box with the message Recorder Range is Full. To continue, click on OK to remove the warning box, then insert additional blank cells in the macro.

You waste space if you record a large number of short macros and start each in a new column. This method is particularly troublesome if you want to print your macro sheet. If you record 20 short macros, for example, you must print all 20 columns for a hard copy of the macros. Instead, you can use unused rows that follow a macro's RETURN() command to record other macros.

When you set the recording position, you can start a macro in a row other than the first one. To set the position, display the macro sheet, click on the empty cell where you want to begin recording instructions, then select **T**ools, **R**ecord Macro, **M**ark Position for Recording. Change to a worksheet window, then select **T**ools, **R**ecord Macro, R**e**cord at Mark. The instructions are recorded beginning in the selected cell.

Before using the macro, you must give it a name. Change to the macro window and select the cell in which you began the macro. Select **I**nsert, **N**ame, **D**efine to display the dialog box shown in figure 16.3. Type a name for the macro, then click the **C**ommand option button in the Macro section. You can assign the macro a shortcut key by entering the keystroke in the Key:Ctrl+ box. Click on OK.

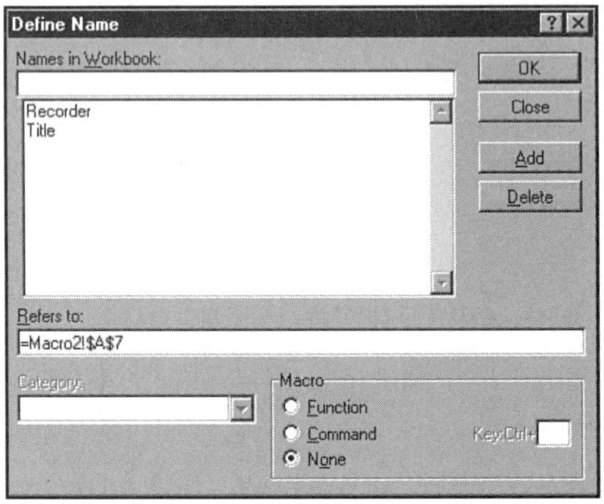

Figure 16.3

The Define Name dialog box.

The set recorder feature works only for one macro at a time. The next macro that you record is saved in the next available column.

Note   If you select a range of cells in the macro sheet (rather than clicking on just one cell), then select **T**ools, **R**ecord Macro, **M**ark Position for Recording. Excel limits the macro to that number of instructions. If you select ten cells, for example, you can only record a macro with eight steps. Remember, one cell is needed for the macro name and another cell for the RETURN() command. If you try to record more instructions than will fit in the cells, the `Recorder Range is Full` message appears, and the recorder stops.

To add macros to a previously recorded macro sheet, you must open it. Select **F**ile, **O**pen, then double-click on the name of the workbook that contains the macros.

Recording to the Global Macro Sheet

Even with the global macro sheet open and unhidden, the macro is stored in PERSONAL.XLS when you select Personal Macro Sheet as the recording location.

To store a macro in the Excel 4 global macro sheet, you must open and unhide it, then choose a cell in the sheet as the starting recording position. Record and name the macro according to the previous explanation.

Excel 4 created the global macro sheet when you selected the option from the Record Macro dialog box. Excel for Windows 95 does not create a global macro sheet for you automatically. If you want to create a global macro sheet, select **N**ew Workbook as the location. Before exiting Excel, save the workbook that contains your macros with the name GLOBAL.XLM and store it in the XLSTART subdirectory.

 Note   Remember, references in this chapter to the global macro sheet relate to the file GLOBAL.XLM, not to the personal macro workbook of Excel for Windows 95.

Hiding the Global Macro Sheet

If the global macro sheet is not hidden when you exit Excel, it appears automatically when you start Excel again. Before exiting Excel, display the sheet and select **W**indow, **H**ide. When you exit, Excel asks if you want to save the macro sheet changes, even if you saved the sheet before hiding it.

The hidden attribute is actually stored with the sheet itself. Hiding the sheet after you saved it changes the attribute. Select **Y**es to exit Excel. If you select **N**o, the sheet appears when you next start Excel, even though it was hidden.

Stop If you fail to display and select the global macro sheet before you select **W**indow, **H**ide, the active worksheet window will be hidden.

When you exit Excel, Excel asks if you want to save the changes to the global macro sheet. Select **Y**es to keep the sheet hidden when you start Excel again.

Deleting an Excel Macro

You can delete a macro if you change your mind after recording it, or if you just want to clean out macros from a macro sheet.

Note You cannot use the **D**elete option in the Macro dialog box to delete an Excel 4 macro. The Delete dialog box option only deletes Visual Basic macros.

To delete an Excel 4 macro, make the macro sheet in which the macro is stored the active window. (Remember, you must unhide GLOBAL.XLM if it is not listed in the Window menu.) Delete the contents of the cells in which the macro is stored, or delete the entire column.

Next, with the macro sheet still active, select **I**nsert, **N**ame, **D**efine, click on the macro name, then choose **D**elete.

If you simply delete the macro from the sheet, its name still appears when you list macros that can be run. If you delete just the name, the macro instructions still occupy space in the macro sheet.

Tip To delete all the macros, delete the macro sheet file from the disk. If you delete the global macro sheet file, Excel creates a new one the next time you save a macro using that option.

Understanding Excel's Macro Language

Excel's macro language is a powerful tool for automating worksheets. Like VBA, you can use it to create command macros and function macros.

Macro Command Arguments

The macro instructions recorded in the macro sheet are functions. Each macro function represents the results of a series of actions. If, for example, you select File, Open to record the actions that open a worksheet called Budget, the macro instruction might be =OPEN("C:\EXCEL\BUDGET.XLS").

The instruction contains no reference to the File menu, just the results of the operation. The function OPEN represents the selection File, Open, or clicking on the Open tool.

You should be familiar with the concept of functions. In Chapter 7, you learned to use Excel's built-in functions to perform mathematical and other operations. When you use a built-in function, you enter the equal sign, the name of the function, and an argument or arguments that explain the details of the operation. If you use the SUM function to total the values in cells A1 through A13, for instance, you enter the function like this:

```
=SUM(A1:A13)
```

The name of the function is SUM, and the argument is A1:A13, which tells Excel the way to apply the function.

Macro functions are very similar. Each macro command contains two parts, the macro function name and one or more arguments. The name indicates the type of action to be performed, such as Open to open a worksheet, Print to print a worksheet, or Select to select a cell. A macro function name is assigned to every action that you can perform using Excel.

The arguments give specific details of the action. The macro command Open, for example, needs an argument that specifies which worksheet should be opened. The arguments are contained in parentheses following the macro function name. Without the argument, Excel wouldn't know what to do with the function, just as entering =**SUM()** would be meaningless.

AUTHOR'S NOTE

If you plan only to record macros, don't worry about understanding macro arguments. Excel inserts the correct arguments for you when it records your menu and dialog box actions.

Some macro functions require only one argument; others might require quite a few. Arguments are separated by commas. Every macro function has a specific number of arguments that it can accept. The number of arguments used in the instruction depends on the task you are performing.

The macro function to select cells, for example, is named Select, and it is followed by an argument that indicates which cell should be selected. The argument lists the row, then the column of the cell. In recorded macros, columns are designated by numbers, not letters. The instruction =SELECT("R1C2"), for example, selects cell B1 using absolute reference. Think of the argument as meaning "Row 1, Column 2." The second column corresponds to column B.

Note Recorded Excel macros use R1C1 references even if you are working in A1 mode. The cell references must be enclosed in quotation marks.

Instructions for selecting cells by relative references appear like this:

```
=SELECT("R[1]C[1]")
```

The numbers in brackets indicate the distance away from the cell currently active. In this case, the notation specifies the selection of a cell one row and one column away from the current cell. The instruction =SELECT("RC[1]") means to select a cell in the same row, but one column to the right. Use positive numbers to indicate positions to the right of or below the current cell. Use negative numbers to indicate cell positions to the left of or above the cell. The instruction =SELECT("R[-1]C"), for example, indicates the cell one row above the active cell in the same column.

Both of these examples contain only one argument. If you select a range of cells, however, the command includes two arguments. The first argument is the range of cells selected, and the second is the active cell in the selected group, as in =SELECT("R1C1:R5C2","R2C1").

Arguments must be in a prescribed order. You do not need to use all the arguments, but the ones that are used must appear in their proper positions. Excel knows what each argument means by its position in the parentheses.

When Excel encounters an Open macro function, for example, it knows that the first argument lists the name of the file to open. The Open command can take up to 10 arguments, but only the first is absolutely necessary. In fact, when you record a macro that opens a workbook using the default values in the open dialog box, only one argument is listed.

Note The other arguments in the Open command specify the way in which links are updated, the text file format, and the source of the file.

When you record a macro that opens a worksheet in read-only mode, however, it appears like this:

```
=OPEN("C:\EXCEL\BUDGET.XLS",,TRUE)
```

The argument TRUE indicates read-only option is set. The extra comma between the arguments is a placeholder, indicating that TRUE is the third possible argument. The second parameter, which specifies the way links are updated, was not recorded, but a place must be left for it. This precaution ensures that Excel knows that the word TRUE refers to the third argument. When you use a placeholder, Excel applies the default arguments that would appear in that position in the command.

When the macro represents a dialog box action, the arguments specify your selections from the dialog box. But even if you select OK to accept all the default dialog box values, several arguments might be recorded. If you record the command to print a worksheet using all the default settings, for instance, it appears as follows:

```
=PRINT(1,,,1,FALSE,FALSE,1,,,300)
```

Many arguments have been omitted, but their positions are marked by placeholders. In this case, the arguments listed are the minimum that Windows needs to print the worksheet. The omitted arguments are optional.

The first argument tells Windows the range of pages you want to print. If you select the default values, the argument indicates that you want to print the entire worksheet. Because you are printing the entire worksheet, the second and third arguments, which specify a range of pages, are unnecessary. Their places are left blank.

The fourth argument in the Print command is required because it indicates the number of copies to be printed. Excel expects the value to be in the fourth argument position. The extra commas indicate the empty positions of the second and third arguments, ensuring that the fourth argument is interpreted correctly.

If you select to print specific pages in the dialog box, the value of the second argument is 2 and the next two arguments are required.

```
=PRINT(2,1,3,1,FALSE,FALSE,1,,,300)
```

 Note Some macro functions, such as Return(), can contain no arguments, although the opening and closing parentheses are still included.

Entering Data into Cells

In the macro language, the command for entering data into cells is FORMULA. The information to insert is the command's argument, enclosed in quotation marks. To insert a text string in a cell, add the text as the argument as follows:

```
=FORMULA("1st Qtr")
```

To insert a cell reference or formula, precede it with an equal sign, but also enclose it in quotation marks:

```
=FORMULA("=R1C1+R2C1")
```

The command inserts the formula to add cells A1 and A2 into the cell currently selected.

You also can designate a specific cell, other than the active cell, in which to enter the data. The syntax is =FORMULA("text", cell).

The command =FORMULA("1st Qtr", "R10C3"), for example, inserts the text in cell C10.

Writing Macros

In addition to recording a macro, you can write one directly in the macro sheet. Writing a macro enables you to take advantage of functions and commands that are not recordable.

Both VBA and the macro language contain a large number of programming commands that extend the capabilities of your macros. These commands control the flow of your macro, make decisions based on cell contents, and can repeat a series of commands.

> **AUTHOR'S NOTE**
>
> In order to write macros, you must be familiar with the macro language. Excel's Function Wizard helps you select and enter macro commands, but you still need a basic understanding of the language.

Writing a macro requires a series of steps, as follows:

1. Planning and outlining the steps or functions you want the macro to perform.

2. Displaying or opening the macro sheet.

3. Writing the macro instructions.

4. Naming the macro.

5. Testing the macro.

In the following sections, you learn the details behind each of these basic steps.

Designing a Macro

Before you write a macro, you should plan exactly what tasks the macro should perform. Most macros automate routine tasks that you perform often, such as inserting labels, formatting cells, or printing worksheets, reports, and database operations. You can also use macros to repeat a complex series of tasks that require many actions. By performing the tasks using a macro, you can ensure that the correct operations are performed each time the macro is run. You also can use macros to create complete, automated applications that include custom dialog boxes, menus, and buttons.

AUTHOR'S NOTE

You can create an application using the macro language, but VBA is better suited for sophisticated systems.

Write the steps of your macro in sentence form, each sentence explaining another step in the macro. Suppose, for instance, you have a series of workbooks that contain budget reports, and you need a macro that opens the workbooks and prints the first worksheet of each. You can outline the macro like this:

1. Open worksheet Budget1.

2. Select File, Print, Selected Sheets, OK.

3. Open worksheet Budget2.

4. Select File, Print, Selected Sheets, OK.

5. Open worksheet Budget 3.

6. Select File, Print, Selected Sheets, OK.

Note As your macros become more complex, you might need to design them in a flow chart form. A *flow chart* shows graphically the steps of the macro and the relationship between them. Flowcharting is an art in itself and requires knowledge of program flow and design.

Opening a Macro Sheet

The next step is to open the macro sheet that will contain your macro. You can use a macro sheet already attached to the workbook, or you can open a new one. To begin a new macro sheet in the current workbook, select **I**nsert, select the MS **E**xcel 4.0 Macro icon, and click on OK. The sheet appears before the worksheet already displayed. If Sheet1 is active, for example, the macro sheet appears at the start of the workbook, before Sheet1.

Excel numbers macro sheets consecutively. If you have recorded a macro already, the new sheet is labeled Macro2, the next is Macro3, and so forth.

You can write the macro by opening a macro sheet in PERSONAL.XLS, GLOBAL.XLM, or any other workbook. If you want to use the macro with every workbook, however, use the Personal Macro Workbook or the global macro sheet.

 Tip While creating and testing a macro, use a separate workbook to ensure that your work in progress does not interfere with macros that you use every day. After you complete the macro and thoroughly test it, you can copy it to any other workbook or sheet.

Writing the Macro

To write the macro, move to an empty cell. Make sure that enough empty cells are available below it to store the entire macro. Type the name you want to assign the macro in the first cell, then continue writing the macro commands, beginning each with the = sign.

 Note The macro name is optional. You assign the macro name when you use **I**nsert, **N**ame, **D**efine to name the macro.

The last line of the macro usually is =RETURN(). The line might, however, be =HALT() or even a Goto command, depending on the flow of your program logic.

Tip   Remember to start commands with the = symbol.

When you move to a cell after you complete a macro instruction, Excel checks the command to make sure it conforms to the proper syntax. It changes lowercase characters in command names to uppercase and ensures that the instruction contains the proper arguments. It displays a message box if it detects an error. Click on OK to remove the box, then correct the mistake. The checking process is not foolproof, however. It checks for syntax of commands, not for proper logic. Excel does not know if you are entering the wrong command as long as the command is properly structured.

If you are uncertain of a command's syntax, you can paste the command in the macro rather than writing it. To paste a command, select **I**nsert, **F**unction, invoking the Function Wizard. Scroll the Function Category list and select the category that contains the command you want to insert. Programming and flow control commands are in the Macro Control category. In the Function Name list, double-click on the command you want to insert, or select the command, then choose Next.

Excel displays one or more dialog boxes from which you can select the syntax desired or enter arguments.

Naming the Macro

Before using the macro, you must define its name. Select the cell that contains the macro name, then select **I**nsert, **N**ame, **D**efine. Click on the Command button in the macro section, assign a shortcut key, if desired, then select OK.

This procedure assigns the name that you use to run the macro from the Macro dialog box.

Follow these steps to write a command macro:

1. Select Sheet1.

2. Select **I**nsert, then double-click the MS **E**xcel 4.0 Macro icon to display a new macro sheet, Macro2.

3. Select cell A1, type **DateSheet**, then press Enter to select cell A2.

4. Type **=Select("R1C1")** and press Enter. Excel uppercases the command.

5. Type **=Insert(3)** and press Enter. This command inserts a row in the worksheet. The arguments correspond to the options in the Insert dialog box: 1 to shift cells to the right; 2 to shift cells down; 3 to insert a row; and 4 to insert a column.

6. Type **=FORMULA("=TODAY()")** and press Enter. The TODAY() function returns the current date. By using it as the argument of the FORMULA command, the date appears in the active cell.

7. Type **=RETURN()** and press Enter.

8. Select cell A1, the cell that contains the macro name.

9. Select **I**nsert, **N**ame, **D**efine. The label in cell A1 appears as the suggested macro name. You can enter another name if you want, but using the same label as the name makes it easier to identify your macro if you need to edit.

10. Click on the **C**ommand button in the macro section.

11. Click on OK.

12. Select **F**ile, **S**ave, type **MYMAC**, and click on OK twice.

 Tip Do not forget to select the **C**ommand button. If you fail to select it, the macro name does not appear in the Macros dialog box.

To run the macro, select **T**ools, **M**acro, then double-click on the macro name:

1. Click on the Sheet2 tab.

2. Select cell A1.

3. Type **BUDGET** and press Enter.

4. Select **T**ools, **M**acro, then double-click on the name DateSheet.

Excel runs the macro, which inserts a row and the current date.

Function Macros

A command macro performs some action on the worksheet. You also can create a function macro. A function macro operates in much the same way as Excel's built-in functions. When you want to perform some task that is not available in a built-in function, write your own.

Like a built-in function, a custom function might have arguments. An argument contains information you are "sending" to the function to process. Suppose you want to create a function that subtracts a six-percent discount. The argument needed by the function is the amount of the order. The function can then multiply the amount

by 0.94 to arrive at the discounted price. The complete function is shown in figure 16.4. Refer to it as you read the following discussion.

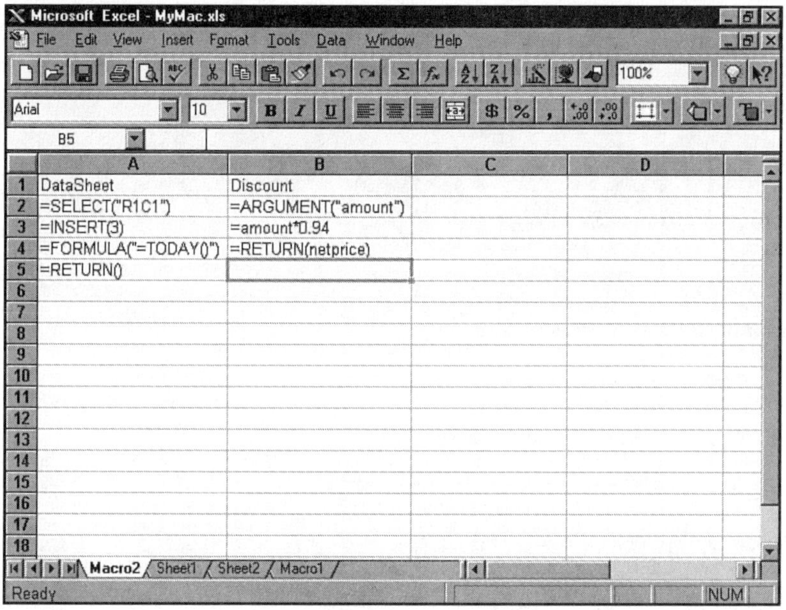

Figure 16.4

The Function macro.

You specify the argument by following the name of the macro with the ARGUMENT command. The argument of ARGUMENT is the name of the variable that contains the sales amount:

```
=ARGUMENT("amount").
```

Notice that the argument is in quotation marks. The next instruction performs the computation:

```
=amount * 0.94
```

Finally, the RETURN command sends the computed value to the worksheet. The argument of the RETURN command is the variable that contains the value, the result of the calculation:

```
=RETURN(netprice)
```

To use this function macro, you need to define two names: the macro name (discount) and the returned variable name (netprice). If you want to list the macro in the Function dialog box, you must define the macro as a function in the Define Name dialog box.

Note You do not need to define the name of the receiving argument, such as amount; the argument statement defines the name.

To create the macro, follow these steps:

1. Click on the Macro2 tab to display the macro sheet.

2. Select cell B1.

3. Type **discount** and press Enter.

4. Type **=ARGUMENT("amount")** and press Enter.

5. Type **=amount*0.94** and press Enter.

6. Type **=RETURN(netprice)** and press Enter.

Next, name the macro and the return variable.

7. Select cell B1.

8. Select **I**nsert, **N**ame, **D**efine.

9. Click on the Function button in the macro section.

10. Click on OK.

11. Select cell B3, the cell that contains the formula.

12. Select **I**nsert, **N**ame, **D**efine.

13. Type **netprice**, then select OK. The name must be the same as the returned variable in the RETURN command.

14. Click on the Sheet1 tab to return to the worksheet.

Tip When defining the name of the RETURN variable, leave the macro section set at None.

Using a Function Macro

To use custom function, you must call it from the worksheet. If the function is defined in the same workbook, you simply use its name and the proper argument:

1. Select cell C3.

2. Type **100** and press Enter.

3. Type **=discount(C3)** and press Enter.

Excel executes the function, displaying the results in the cell. Here's what Excel does:

◆ Transfers processing to the discount function

◆ Assigns the value in cell C3, the argument, to the variable amount

◆ Computes the value of amount*.94 and assigns the result to the variable netprice

◆ Returns to the worksheet, and inserts the value of netprice into the active cell

Note Like built-in functions, you can use your custom functions anywhere in the workbook, as often as you need them.

If you defined the macro as a function in the Define Name dialog box, you can paste the function using the Function Wizard. Select **I**nsert, **F**unction, scroll the Function category list, and select User-defined. Your custom functions are listed in the Function Name list. Double-click on the function to insert it into the worksheet.

Tip If your function does not appear in the Function Wizard, confirm that you clicked on the Function option in the Name dialog box. Return to the macro sheet, select the function label, then select **I**nsert, **N**ame, **D**efine. If the option is not selected, click on it, then select OK.

Using Global Functions

If you created the function in the Personal Macro Workbook, the global macro sheet, or another open workbook, you must specify the sheet name in the function call. If you added the discount function to the Personal Macro workbook, for example, call it using this syntax:

```
=PERSONAL.XLS!discount(B3)
```

If the function is in any other workbook, the workbook must be opened before it can be accessed.

Multiple Arguments

Custom functions are not limited to a single argument. If you need to send more than one cell or value to the function, you can create multiple arguments. Each argument must be included in its own ARGUMENT command, and arguments must appear in the order in which you want to call them. Suppose you want to compute the discount on the amount of the sale less any special reduction, such as a manufacturer's coupon or special promotion. You need to pass two values to the function. If the amount is in cell A3 and the reduction is in cell A4, you call the function as follows:

```
=discount(A3,A4)
```

The first argument sent to the function contains the amount of the sale; the second argument contains the reduction. The function, then, needs two arguments:

```
discount
=ARGUMENT("amount")
=ARGUMENT("reduction")
=(amount-reduction)*0.94
=RETURN(netprice)
```

If you reverse the order of the receiving or calling arguments, the function does not return the correct results. If you call the macro using the syntax =discount(A4,A3), the function assumes that cell A4 contains the amount of the sale and that cell A3 contains the reduction.

The amount of the sale then is subtracted from the reduction amount. A sale of $100, for example, and a $15 reduction is calculated as 15–100, rather than 100–15. You would be charging the customer a negative amount!

Make the change to the function macro and test it:

1. Click on the Macro2 tab to display the macro sheet.

2. Select cell B3.

3. Click the right mouse button to display the shortcut menu and select Insert.

4. Select OK to shift the cells down.

5. Type **=ARGUMENT("reduction")** and press Enter.

6. Type **=(amount-reduction)*0.94**, then press Enter.

7. Click on the Sheet1 tab.

8. Select cell C4.

9. Type **15** and press Enter.

10. Type **=discount(C3,C4)** and press Enter. Excel calculates and displays the correct results.

11. Select **F**ile, **S**ave to save the workbook.

Your macros can be as simple or as complex as they need to be.

Handling Macro Errors

When you record a macro, Excel always inserts the proper commands using the appropriate syntax. Unfortunately, mistakes can occur in our own command or function macros. Three types of errors are common, as follows:

◆ **Language.** Occurs because you used the incorrect syntax or arguments. In many cases, Excel detects the language error when you enter the command, so you can correct it before you run the macro. You can avoid these errors by inserting commands with the Function Wizard. Select the Commands option in the Function **C**ategory list to display programming commands.

◆ **Run-time.** Occurs when the macro attempts to perform a function that cannot be completed. These errors might occur, for example, when you attempt to reference a cell that contains text in a mathematical formula. When you wrote the macro, Excel had no way of knowing what the actual contents of the cell would be at run-time.

◆ **Logic.** Occurs when your commands follow the proper syntax but do not perform the intended task. These errors include calling multiple arguments in the incorrect order, using the wrong arithmetic operators in a formula, or constructing the formula incorrectly.

When Excel encounters a language or run-time error, it stops executing the macro and displays a dialog box such as the one shown in figure 16.5. The message contains the location of the macro and the cell in which the error occurs.

Figure 16.5

A Macro Error dialog box.

Tip   In most cases, Excel does not detect a logic error unless it results in a run-time error. If you enter a formula with the wrong operators (such as adding rather than subtracting numbers), for example, Excel performs the operation and displays the results without stopping. Logic errors are the most difficult to detect and correct. The best way to find logic errors is to check the results of your macros very carefully. Make certain mathematical results are correct and that the macro performs the tasks for which it was designed.

◆ **Halt.** Stops the macro. Before you select this option, note the location of the error, so you can return to the macro sheet to correct the problem.

◆ **Step.** Continues executing the macro one command at a time. It begins with the command after the one that caused the error condition.

◆ **Continue.** Continues running the macro, ignoring the error. In most cases, however, a macro does not continue to run without additional errors after one error has occurred and has been ignored.

◆ **Goto.** Stops the macro and returns to the macro sheet where the command error has occurred. This method is the best way to correct errors.

◆ **Help.** Displays help information.

Stepping Through Macros

When you select the **S**tep option, Excel displays the Single Step dialog box, shown in figure 16.6, after each command is executed. Use the options in this box to help find additional errors in the macro or to further investigate the current error.

Figure 16.6

The Single Step dialog box.

 Note   The Debug window is available only when viewing VBA modules.

The box displays four additional command buttons, as follows:

◆ **Step Into.** Performs the next command shown. If the next command calls a subroutine, the subroutine is performed step by step. You learn about subroutines later in this chapter.

◆ **Step Over.** Performs the next command that is not a subroutine call.

◆ **Evaluate.** Calculates and displays the results of each expression of a formula. Use this option if the error is in a formula.

◆ **Pause.** Removes the Single Step dialog box from the screen. To continue the macro, display the Visual Basic toolbar and click on the Resume button.

Tip You also can find errors using the VBA toolbar, even with macro language macros. To display the toolbar, select **V**iew, Toolbars, Visual Basic, OK. Display the macro sheet, then click on the Step button to single-step through the macro. The toolbar also contains Resume, Step Into, and Step Over buttons.

Understanding Flow Control

The macros you have designed so far have been linear. They perform each step of the macro in the order it appears in the macro sheet.

Recorded macros are always linear; thus, recorded macros are limited. By writing a macro, however, you can control the flow of the *program logic,* the order in which instructions are performed. You also can perform some steps based on the contents of a cell or the status of Excel at a certain point.

Designing non-linear macros requires some understanding of programming logic. If you are familiar with any computer programming language, such as BASIC, C, or PASCAL, then you should feel comfortable with the Excel 4 macro language or with VBA. The programming concepts are the same in every language; only the syntax of the commands varies.

If you are unfamiliar with programming logic, Excel's macro language serves as a good introduction. The language is easy to learn, and you can observe program results immediately by running the macro. If you understand the macro concepts already discussed in this chapter, you learn quickly the way to program in the macro language. In fact, you can transfer the skills and concepts you learn here to VBA or any other programming language.

Function Subroutines

One way to streamline your macros is to use subroutines. A *subroutine* is a section of macro instructions stored outside the macro in which they are used. A subroutine, however, is just another macro. Any macro can be used as a subroutine, even if it is not entered or designed in any special way.

Note You can even use VBA macros as subroutines in macro language macros, and macro language macros as subroutines in VBA macros. If you already have macro language macros, you can use them in VBA macros without converting or retyping them.

Suppose, for example, you want to perform the functions of the DateSheet macro within another macro. Rather than retype the instructions or copy them from macro to macro, call the macro as a subroutine. This not only saves typing, but makes your macros smaller and easier to read and understand.

To call the DateSheet macro in a macro, for example, use the command `=Datesheet()`. When Excel encounters the line in a macro, it performs the command DateSheet, then returns to the calling macro. It then continues with the commands following the call to DateSheet.

If the macro is not in the current workbook, precede the name with the workbook name, as in `=GLOBAL.XLM!Datesheet()`.

AUTHOR'S NOTE

By building a library of subroutines, you can write complex macros quickly and easily. In fact, some macros might contain little more than function calls to other macros.

Jumping to Other Instructions

One other way to perform another macro or set of instructions is to use the GOTO command. You can use GOTO to leave one macro and perform another or to begin following the commands at a named reference in the same macro. The syntax is `=GOTO(reference)`. When Excel encounters a GOTO command, it moves to the referenced location and begins to follow the macro instructions found there. After completing the instructions at that location, however, the macro does not return to the instructions after the GOTO command. This behavior is the opposite of a subroutine call, which performs the instructions in the subroutine, then returns to the instruction after the call.

Tip The GOTO statement is not recommended, because you can lose control over your macro. To perform other macros, use a subroutine call. To bypass a set of instructions, use the IF command. To repeat a series of instructions, use the FOR or the WHILE commands. You learn about these commands later in this chapter.

Making Decisions

You might not always want to perform every instruction in a macro. Some commands might be *conditional*, meaning you might want to perform them in some situations, but not in others.

The discount function macro illustrated previously subtracted a six-percent discount on a sales amount. Each time you called the function, the reduction was taken regardless of the sale amount. A purchase of $1,000 would be reduced by the same percentage as a purchase of just one dollar.

In reality, the discount might be applied only to purchases over a certain amount, or a different discount rate might be applied to various levels of purchases.

You can write separate functions for each discount amount, but you need to know which function to call when you create the worksheet. You cannot, for instance, use the same function call for every purchase.

The solution is to write a function macro that contains conditional instructions. The percentage of the discount, or whether one is subtracted or not, varies with the amount of the order. The same function can be called no matter what the purchase amount. The function decides the proper discount rate. The command that performs this decision is the IF command. The IF command has several forms, but they all are based on a condition:

```
if(condition)
```

The condition is a logical test that can be TRUE or FALSE. Usually, the test compares two values, as in `if(amount > 100)` or `if(B4 < B5)`.

In the first example, the condition is TRUE if the value of the amount is greater than 100. In the second example, the condition is TRUE if the contents in cell B4 are less than the contents of cell B5. The condition can use the following operators:

=	equal
>	greater than
<	less than

>=   greater than or equal

<=   less than or equal

<>   not equal

Making Fundamental Choices

The most basic use of the IF command decides between two alternatives. The syntax is as follows:

```
If(condition, TRUE-command, FALSE-command)
```

If the condition is TRUE, the TRUE-command is performed. If the condition is FALSE, the FALSE-command is performed:

```
if(amount>100, amount * 0.94, amount)
```

In this command, if the value of amount is greater than 100, then amount is multiplied by 0.94 to apply the discount. If amount is 100 or less, then no discount is applied. The command could be used in a function macro like this:

```
discount
=ARGUMENT("amount")
=if(amount>100, amount * 0.94, amount)
=RETURN(netprice)
```

You also can use the command to perform alternate subroutines. One subroutine would be performed if the condition were TRUE, another if the condition were FALSE, as in the following example:

```
=if(amount>1000, specialrate(), standardrate())
```

When the condition is TRUE, because the amount is over $1,000, the specialrate macro is called and performed. Otherwise, the standardrate macro is called.

Any macro or macro command can be performed as part of the conditional.

Change the discount macro to provide a decision based on the purchase amount. The macro uses two arguments, but you need to consider only the value of amount in the condition:

1. Click on the Macro2 tab to display the macro sheet.

2. Select cell B4, the cell that contains the formula in the discount macro.

3. Edit the formula so that it reads **=if(amount>100, (amount-reduction)*0.94, amount-reduction)**, then press Enter.

4. Press Enter.

5. Click on the Sheet1 tab.

6. Select cell C3.

7. Type **101,** then click on the Enter box.

8. Select cell C4, type **0**, then click on the Enter box. Notice the results of the function cell reflect the discount, 94.94.

9. Select cell C3 again, type **100**, then click on the Enter box. Now no additional discount is applied.

10. Select **F**ile, **S**ave to save the workbook.

Performing Multiple Commands

The basic syntax of the IF command allows it to perform only one command or subroutine call on a TRUE or FALSE condition. Often, the logic of your macro requires that a number of commands be executed. You can use another syntax of the IF command, called IF END.IF():

```
IF(condition)
    instructions
END.IF()
```

You can have as many instructions between the IF and END.IF commands as you need. When the condition is TRUE, all the instructions are performed, then the macro continues with the command following END.IF. When the condition is FALSE, none of the instructions between the IF and END.IF commands are performed, and the macro goes directly to the command following END.IF.

You must understand that the instructions following the END.IF command are *always* executed. They are not dependent upon the condition being TRUE or FALSE. You might, however, want to perform an alternate series of commands only when the condition is FALSE. For this, use the IF ELSE END.IF structure:

```
IF(condition)
    instructions to perform when the condition is true
ELSE()
    instructions to perform when the condition is false
END.IF()
```

This structure provides alternate sets of commands. If the condition is TRUE, the commands between the IF and the ELSE() instructions are performed. Those commands between the ELSE() and the END.IF are ignored.

When the condition is FALSE, the commands between the ELSE() and the END.IF() are performed, and those commands between the IF and ELSE() are ignored.

You can use the command in all types of macros, even command macros such as the following:

```
=IF(amount>100)
=          (amount-reduction)*0.94
=          send.mail(client,"Special discount",FALSE)
=ELSE()
=          (amount)
=          printinvoice()
=END.IF()
=SAVE()
=CLOSE()
```

If the condition is TRUE, the special discount is applied and the worksheet is transmitted via Microsoft Mail. If the condition is FALSE, no discount is applied and a custom function, called printinvoice, is called.

In either case, the worksheet is saved, then closed using Excel's built-in functions.

 Tip The instructions following the END.IF are performed regardless of the condition.

Yet another possible use of the command is to combine IF with the ELSE.IF structure, as follows:

```
IF(condition)
   instructions
ELSE.IF(condition)
   instructions
END.IF()
```

Using this syntax, one set of instructions is performed when the condition is TRUE. If the condition is FALSE, however, a second IF condition is tested.

 Tip For the second set of instructions to be performed, the first condition must be FALSE and the second condition must be TRUE. If both are FALSE, no instructions between the IF and END.IF() commands are executed.

Repeating Commands with Loops

In addition to making decisions, a macro can repeat a series of instructions. Programming commands that cause repetition are called *loops*. Why would you want to repeat commands? Perhaps you might want to insert text or values in a series of cells, or perform a step repeatedly until some condition is TRUE or a certain event occurs. Excel provides several ways to repeat instructions.

Fixed Repetitions

When you know or can determine the exact number of times you want to repeat the instructions, use the FOR-NEXT loop. The syntax for this loop is as follows:

```
FOR(counter_text, starting_num, ending_num, step_num)
```

The functions of the arguments follow:

◆ Counter_text is a name, similar to a variable, which counts the number of repetitions. Its value changes with each repetition of the loop so that Excel will know when the maximum value has been reached.

◆ Starting_num sets the first value that the counter_text will contain.

◆ Ending_num determines the last value of the counter text. The repetition stops when the counter_text is above this value.

◆ Step_num determines the way in which the counter_text value is incremented with each repetition. The number is optional. If you omit it, the counter increments by one with each loop.

When the step number is not included or is set at 1, the loop repeats from the starting to the ending number. The command FOR("counter",1,10) would repeat a series of instructions 10 times. During the first repetition, the value of counter is set at 1. During the second repetition, the value is 2. After the tenth repetition, the value of counter is 11, and the process stops.

Every FOR command must be matched with a NEXT() command. During the loop, Excel repeats all the instructions between the FOR and NEXT() commands. Consider this macro:

```
=SELECT("R1C1")
=FORMULA("1")
=FOR("counter",1,19)
=SELECT("RC[1]")
=FORMULA("=RC[-1]+1")
```

```
=NEXT()
=RETURN()
```

The macro numbers the top row of the worksheet from 1 to 20. Enter it now:

1. Click on the Macro2 tab to display the macro sheet.

2. Select cell C1.

3. Type **loop** and press Enter.

4. Type =**SELECT("R1C1")** and press Enter.

5. Type =**FORMULA("1")** and press Enter. Now use the Function Wizard to enter the FOR loop.

6. Select **I**nsert, **F**unction.

7. Scroll the Function Category list and select Macro Control.

8. Scroll the Function Name list and select For.

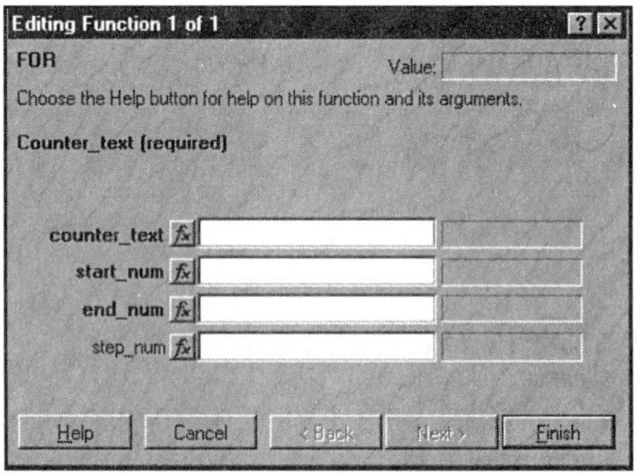

Figure 16.7

The Function Wizard dialog box showing the FOR command.

9. Select Next to display the dialog box shown in figure 16.7.

10. Type **counter** in the counter_text box, then press Tab.

11. Type **1** in the start_num box and press Tab.

12. Type **19** in the end_num box, then select Finish. The completed command is inserted in the cell.

13. Press Enter.

14. Type =**SELECT("RC[1]")** and press Enter.

15. Type **=FORMULA("=RC[-1]+1")** and press Enter.

16. Type **=NEXT()** and press Enter.

17. Type **=RETURN()** and press Enter.

18. Now name the macro. Select cell C1.

19. Select **I**nsert, **N**ame, **D**efine.

20. Click on the Command button in the macro section.

21. Click on OK.

22. Click on the Sheet4 tab to return to the worksheet.

23. Select **T**ools, **M**acro, and double-click on the loop macro. The macro numbers the first 20 columns.

Here is the way that the macro works.

1. The SELECT command selects cell A1.

2. The FORMULA command inserts the number 1 in cell A1.

3. The FOR command sets up a loop that repeats 19 times, incrementing the value of counter from 1 to 19. When counter becomes 20, the loop stops.

4. The SELECT command selects the cell in the next column. This relative reference means "one cell over in the same row."

5. The FORMULA command inserts into the cell the value of the previous cell plus 1.

6. The NEXT command repeats the loop.

7. The RETURN command ends the macro.

You can perform any number of instructions between the FOR and NEXT() commands, even call other macros as subroutines.

Tip   While you are learning to write loops, practice with a small number of repetitions. When you are certain your macro operates correctly, increase the number of repetitions to the final setting.

A variation of the FOR-NEXT loop is FOR.CELL-NEXT. This loop repeats once for each cell in a designated range of cells, using the following syntax:

```
FOR.CELL(reference, area, skip_blanks)
  instructions
NEXT()
```

With each repetition, Excel uses the next cell in the range. The loop stops after it reaches the last cell. The reference is the name Excel gives to the currently selected cell. The actual cell being referenced changes with each repetition.

Skip_blanks is set at either TRUE or FALSE. When set at TRUE, Excel skips blank cells that it encounters in the range. When set at FALSE, Excel operates on blank cells. The default setting is FALSE.

As an example, suppose you have a worksheet that contains price information in the first 20 columns of row 5. To increase all prices by 10 percent, create a macro with these commands:

```
=FOR.CELL("prices","R5C1:R5C20",TRUE)
=FORMULA(prices*1.1,prices)
=NEXT()
=RETURN()
```

The FOR.CELL loop repeats for each of the cells in the range. It does not perform any operation on blank cells—only on those that already contain values.

Using the WHILE Loop

Sometimes you do not know the exact number of times you want to repeat a series of instructions. In these instances, use the WHILE-NEXT loop. The loop uses this syntax:

```
WHILE(condition)
  instructions
NEXT()
```

The instructions within the loop are repeated as long as the condition is TRUE.

 Stop   You must ensure that the condition eventually becomes FALSE; otherwise, the loop continues until you press Esc to stop it.

The condition can reference a cell value or a named variable. Before using the loop, however, you must know the initial state of the condition. If you want to perform the

loop at least one time, you must ensure that the condition is initially TRUE. This task usually is accomplished using the SET.VALUE command. The command assigns an initial value to a named cell on the macro sheet.

Getting User Input

Suppose you want to create a macro that enables the user to select the number of columns to number. Rather than include the ending number in the FOR loop, you want to input a number and use it as a variable. The command to input a number is as follows:

```
=INPUT("Enter a number",1,"Input Macro",,,,)
```

The syntax for this command is the following:

```
=INPUT(text, type, title, default, x-position, y-position,
help-reference)
```

Note The INPUT command inputs a value into a cell in the macro sheet, not into the worksheet. You must name the INPUT command cell, then you can use the name as a variable in another macro command.

The type represents the type of value expected:

0	Formula
1	Number
2	Text
3	Logical
4	Reference
8	Error
64	Array

Tip Most of the parameters of the INPUT command are used for special purposes. Include the first three parameters, then omit or use placeholders for the rest, as shown in the example.

You must enter a number greater than zero, however, to actually number the columns. You want to design a macro that repeats the INPUT command until a number greater than zero has been entered. Follow these steps:

1. Click on the Macro2 tab to display the macro sheet.

2. Select cell C2.

3. Select **I**nsert, **C**ells, OK.

4. Type **=SET.VALUE(count,0)** and press Enter. This command ensures that the input is performed.

5. Select cell C5, then select **I**nsert, **C**ells, OK.

6. Type **=WHILE(count<1)** and press Enter.

7. Select **I**nsert, **C**ells, OK.

8. Type **=INPUT**("Enter a number:",1,"Input Macro",,,,), then press Enter.

9. Select **I**nsert, **C**ells, OK.

10. Type **=NEXT()** and press Enter.

11. Select cell C8, the cell that contains the FOR loop.

12. Edit the contents to **=FOR("COUNTER",1,COUNT-1)**, then click on the Enter box.

The completed macro is shown in figure 16.8. The FOR loop now contains a variable for the ending number. The value is the amount entered in response to the INPUT command less 1. Now name the INPUT command as the count variable.

13. Select cell C6.

14. Select **I**nsert, **N**ame, **D**efine.

15. Type **count**, then select OK.

16. Click on the Sheet5 tab to return to the worksheet.

17. Select **T**ools, **M**acro, and double-click on the loop macro. A dialog box appears, as shown in figure 16.9.

18. Type **10**, to number 10 columns, then press Enter.

Programming in the macro language can be a rewarding experience. Take your time and try to record as many of the instructions as possible. Then, display the macro sheet, insert cells, and enter additional commands that you need to perform the desired task.

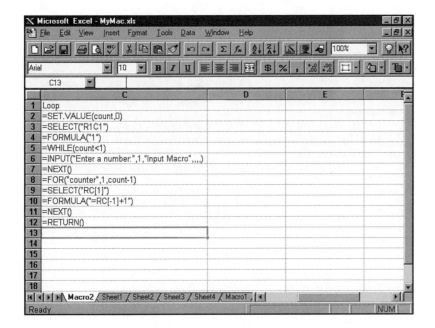

Figure 16.8

The completed macro using the WHILE and INPUT commands.

Figure 16.9

The Input Macro dialog box.

Chapter Snapshot

You can use this chapter as a quick guide to finding descriptions of Excel's macro functions. Specifically, this chapter contains the following:

- ◆ A list of the available macro functions in Excel

- ◆ Variable names associated with each function

- ◆ One-line descriptions of each function

The Complete Macro Language Function Reference

This chapter provides a list of Excel for Windows 95's macro functions and a brief description of each function's purpose. This chapter is not intended to serve as a complete startup guide to using macros, but as a ready reference for you to use after you become familiar with the functions.

Each function's variable names (shown within the parentheses) attempt to be reasonably self-explanatory. Variable names with a suffix of _*text* will require a text string enclosed in quotes or a reference to a cell containing text information. Likewise, variables ending with _*num* expect a numeric value. Variables that take a TRUE or FALSE value are often identified with _*logical*. When Excel evaluates logical expressions, a 0 indicates FALSE, and a 1 or nonzero number indicates TRUE. You don't need to use these exact variable names in your macros—you can use any name, or simply a value. Further information about macro functions can be found in the *Excel User's Guide* or Excel's Help system.

Note   The parameter list of certain functions only references the manual because those functions have multiple permissible syntaxes. See your *Excel User's Guide* or online help for greater detail.

A1.R1C1(logical)

Sets display of row and column headings to A1 or R1C1 format.

ABSREF(Offset, Reference)

Returns the absolute reference of the cells that are offset from the reference cells by a given amount.

ACTIVATE(window_text, pane_num)

Switches to a different window or pane.

ACTIVATE.NEXT(workbook_text)

Switches to the next window or the next worksheet in the workbook.

ACTIVATE.PREV(workbook_text)

Switches to the previous window or the previous worksheet in the workbook.

ACTIVE CELL

Returns the full reference of the active cell.

ACTIVE.CELL.FONT(font, font_style, size, strikethrough)

Sets the character font attributes for the currently active cell.

ADD.ARROW

Adds an arrow to the active chart.

ADD.BAR(bar_num)

Creates a new menu bar and returns the menu bar ID number.

ADD.CHART.AUTOFORMAT(name_text, desc_text)

Adds the format of the active chart to the AutoFormat list of custom formats.

ADD.COMMAND(bar_num, menu, command_ref, position1, position2)

Adds a command to a menu.

ADD.LIST.MENU(text, index_num)

Refer to Excel's online help for description of parameters.

ADD.MENU(bar_num, menu_ref, position1, position2)

Adds a menu to a menu bar.

ADD.OVERLAY()

Adds an overlay to a 2D chart.

ADD.TOOL(bar_id, position, tool_ref)

Adds buttons to a toolbar.

ADD.TOOLBAR(bar_name, tool_ref)

Creates a new toolbar with specified buttons.

ADDIN.MANAGER(operation_num, addinname_text, copy_logical)

Refer to Excel's online help for function description and parameters.

ALERT(message_text, type_num, help_ref)

Displays a dialog box and waits for user button press.

ALIGNMENT(horiz_align, wrap, vert_align, orientation, add_indent)

Aligns the text of the selected cells.

ANOVA1(InputRange, OutputTopLeftCell, RowOrColumn, FirstRowLabels, Alpha)
or
ANOVA1?(InputRange, OutputTopLeftCell, RowOrColumn, FirstRowLabels, Alpha)

Performs single-factor analysis of variance.

ANOVA2(InputRangeWithLabels, OutputTopLeftCell, NumRowsPerSample, Alpha)
or
ANOVA2?(InputRangeWithLabels, OutputTopLeftCell, NumRowsPerSample, Alpha)

Performs two-factor analysis of variance with replication.

ANOVA3(InputRange, OutputTopLeftCell, FirstRowLabels, Alpha)
or
ANOVA3?(InputRange, OutputTopLeftCell, FirstRowLabels, Alpha)

Performs two-factor analysis of variance without replication.

APP.ACTIVATE.MICROSOFT(app_ID)

Activates a different Microsoft application.

APP.ACTIVATE(ApplicationTitle, ImmediateOrWaitToSwitch)

Switches to another application.

APP.MAXIMIZE()

Maximizes the Excel window.

APP.MINIMIZE()

Minimizes the Excel window.

APP.MOVE(x_num, y_num)

Moves the Excel window.

APP.RESTORE()

Restores the Excel window to its previous size and location.

APP.SIZE(x_num, y_num)

Changes the size of the Excel window.

APP.TITLE(text)

Changes the title of the Excel workspace.

APPLY.NAMES(name_array, ignore, use_rowcol, omit_col, omit_row, order_num, append_logical)

Replaces definitions with their respective names.

APPLY.STYLE(style_text)

Applies a style to the current selection.

ARGUMENT(argument_text, data_type, dest_ref)

Describes the arguments used in a custom function.

ARRANGE.ALL(arrange_num, Active_doc, sync_horiz, sync_vert)

Rearranges or resizes open windows and icons.

ASSIGN.TO.OBJECT(macro_ref)

Assigns a macro to the currently selected object.

ASSIGN.TO.TOOL(bar_id, position, macro_ref)

Assigns a macro to a tool.

ATTACH.TEXT(attach_to_num, series_num, point_num)

Attaches text to parts of the selected chart.

AUTO.OUTLINE()

Refer to Excel's online help for function description and parameters.

AXES(XPrimary, YPrimary, XSecondary/ZPrimary, [Ysecondary])

Sets chart axes to visible or hidden.

BEEP(tone_num)

Sounds a tone.

BORDER(outline, left, right, top, bottom, shade, uutline_color, left_color, right_color, top_color, bottom_color)

Adds a border and background color to selected cells.

BREAK()

Interrupts a program loop.

BRING.TO.FRONT()

Places the selected object on top of all other objects.

CALCULATE.DOCUMENT()

Calculates the active worksheet.

CALCULATE.NOW()

Calculates all open workbooks.

CALCULATION(type_num, iter, max_num, max_change, update, precision, date_1904, recalc_before_save, save_extlink, excel_or_lotus_calc, excel_or_lotus_formulas)

Controls calculation.

CALLER

Returns information about the item that called the macro currently running.

CANCEL.COPY()

Cancels the marquee after copy or cut.

CANCEL.KEY(enable, macro_ref)

Specifies action taken when user interrupts a macro.

CELL.PROTECTION(locked, hidden)

Controls cell protection and display.

CHANGE.LINK(old_text, new_text, type_of_link)

Changes a link from one workbook to another.

CHART.ADD.DATA(ref, rowcol, titles, categories, replace, series)

Refer to Excel's online help for function description and parameters.

CHART.TREND(type, ord_per, forecast, backcast, intercept, equation, r_squared, line_text)

Adds a trendline to the active chart.

CHART.WIZARD(long, ref, gallery_num, type_num, plot_by)

Assists in formatting a chart. Refer to Excel's online help for parameter descriptions.

CHECK.COMMAND(bar_num, menu, command, check, position)

Adds or removes a check mark from a command in a menu.

CHECKBOX.PROPERTIES(value, link, accel_text, accel2_text)

Sets the associated properties of a check box.

CLEAR(type_num)

Clears series or formats from selection.

CLEAR.OUTLINE()

Refer to Excel's online help for function description and parameters.

CLEAR.PRINT.AREA()

Refer to Excel's online help for function description and parameters.

CLEAR.ROUTING.SLIP(reset_only_logical)

Clears the routing slip.

CLOSE(save_logical, route_logical)

Closes the active window.

CLOSE.ALL()

Closes all windows.

COLOR.PALETTE(file_text)

Copies a color palette from another workbook.

COLUMN.WIDTH(width_num, ref, standard, type_num, standard_width)

Changes column widths.

COMBINATION(type_num)

Changes the format of the active chart.

CONSOLIDATE(source_refs, function_num, top_row, left_col, create_links)

Consolidates data on multiple worksheets to a single worksheet.

CONSTRAIN.NUMERIC(numeric_only)

Constrains handwriting recognition to numbers and punctuation only.

COPY(from_reference, to_reference)

Copies data or objects into the Clipboard.

COPY.CHART(HowToCopy)

Copies a chart.

COPY.PICTURE(appearance_num, size_num, type_num)

Copies chart or cells to the Clipboard as graphics.

COPY.TOOL(bar_id, position)

Copies a button face to the Clipboard.

CREATE.NAMES(top, left, bottom, right)

Creates names from text labels.

CREATE.OBJECT(_)

Draws an object on a worksheet. Refer to Excel's online help for a description of parameters.

CREATE.PUBLISHER(NewFile, Appearance, Size, Format)
or
CREATE.PUBLISHER?(NewFile, Appearance, Size, Format)

Publishes selection to an edition file (Macintosh).

CUSTOM.REPEAT(macro_text, repeat_text, record_text)

Allows custom commands to be repeated using the Repeat command.

CUSTOM.UNDO(macro_text, undo_text)

Enables you to customize the Undo and/or Redo commands.

CUSTOMIZE.TOOLBAR(category)

Refer to Excel's online help for function description and parameters.

CUT(from_reference, to_reference)

Cuts data or objects into the Clipboard.

DATA.DELETE
or
DATA.DELETE?()

Deletes data that matches the current criteria in the current database.

DATA.FIND(EnterOrExitFindMode)

Selects records in the database range that match criteria in the criteria range.

DATA.FIND.NEXT
or
DATA.FIND.NEXT?()

Finds the next matching record in the database.

DATA.FIND.PREV
or
DATA.FIND.PREV?()

Finds the previous matching record in the database.

DATA.FORM

Displays the data form.

DATA.LABEL(show_option, auto_text, show_key)

Refer to Excel's online help for function description and parameters.

DATA.SERIES(row_col, type_num, date_num, step_value, stop_value, trend_check)

Enables you to enter an incremental series on a worksheet.

DEFINE.NAME(name_text, refers_to, macro_type, shortcut_text, hidden_text, function_num, local_or_global_logical)

Defines a name on the active worksheet.

DEFINE.STYLE(_)

Creates and changes styles. Refer to Excel's online help for function description and parameters.

DELETE.ARROW()

Deletes the selected arrow.

DELETE.BAR(bar_num)

Deletes a custom menu bar.

DELETE.CHART.AUTOFORMAT(name_text)

Deletes a custom format from AutoFormat.

DELETE.COMMAND(bar_num, menu, command, subcommand)

Removes a command from a menu.

DELETE.FORMAT(format_text)

Deletes a given custom number format.

DELETE.MENU(bar_num, menu, submenu)

Deletes a menu or submenu.

DELETE.NAME(name_text)

Deletes a name.

DELETE.OVERLAY()

Deletes all overlays from a chart.

DELETE.STYLE(style_text)

Deletes a style from the active workbook.

DELETE.TOOL(bar_id, position)

Deletes a button from a toolbar.

DELETE.TOOLBAR(bar_name)

Deletes a custom toolbar.

DEMOTE(row_col)

Demotes (groups) the selected rows or columns in an outline.

DEREF(CellReference)

Returns the value of the cells in a reference.

DESCR(InputRange, OutputTopLeftCell, RowOrColumn, FirstRowLabels, SummaryStatistics, ReportLargestData, ReportSmallestData, ConfidenceLevel)
or
DESCR?(InputRange, OutputTopLeftCell, RowOrColumn, FirstRowLabels, SummaryStatistics, ReportLargestData, ReportSmallestData, ConfidenceLevel)

Generates descriptive statistics.

DIALOG.BOX(dialog_ref)

Displays a predefined dialog box.

DIRECTORY(PathToChangeTo)

Sets a directory path or returns the current path.

DISABLE.INPUT(logical)

Disables all mouse and keyboard input.

DISPLAY(_)

Controls screen displays. Refer to Excel's online help for function description and parameters.

DOCUMENTS(IncludeAddInWorkbooks, [NameSelectionCriteria])

Returns the names of the open workbooks, sorted alphabetically.

DUPLICATE()

Duplicates the selected object.

ECHO(logical)

Specifies whether screen updating is on or off while a macro is running.

EDIT.COLOR(color_num, red_value, green_value, blue_value)

Defines a color.

EDIT.DELETE(shift_num)

Removes cells from the worksheet.

EDIT.OBJECT(VerbNumberForApplication, MacroPauseWhileEditing)

Starts the application to edit the selected object.

EDIT.REPEAT()

Repeats prior action.

EDIT.SERIES(series_num, name_ref, x_ref, y_ref, z_ref, plot_order)

Adds a new series formula to chart.

EDIT.TOOL(bar_id, position)

Refer to Excel's online help for function description and parameters.

EDITBOX.PROPERTIES(validation_num, multiline_logical)

Refer to Excel's online help for function description and parameters.

EDITION.OPTION(PublisherOrSubscriber, EditionName, CellReference, EditionOption, PublishScreenOrPrint, ChartSize, FileFormatNumber)

Sets options or actions to a specified publisher or subscriber.

ELSE()

Begins a group of formulas to be executed if the preceding IF function returns a FALSE value.

ELSE.IF(logical_test)

Begins a group of formulas to be executed if the preceding IF function returns a FALSE value and if logical_test is TRUE.

EMBED(ObjectCreatorClass, AreaToCopy)

Displayed in the formula bar when an embedded object is selected.

ENABLE.COMMAND(bar_num, menu, command, enable, submenu_command)

Enables or disables a custom menu command or custom menu.

ENABLE.OBJECT(object_id_text, enable_logical)

Enables or disables the referenced object.

ENABLE.TIPWIZARD(state)

Refer to Excel's online help for function description and parameters.

ENABLE.TOOL(bar_id, position, enable)

Enables or disables a button on a toolbar.

END.IF()

Ends a group of formulas associated with the preceding IF function.

ENTER.DATA(logical)

Enables data entry into unlocked cells in the current selection.

ERROR(enable_logical, macro_ref)

Specifies action to be taken when an error is encountered during execution of a macro.

ERRORBAR.X(include, type, amount, minus)

Refer to Excel's online help for function description and parameters.

ERRORBAR.Y(include, type, amount, minus)

Refer to Excel's online help for function description and parameters.

EVALUATE(ExpressionToEvaluate)

Evaluates a formula or expression and returns the result.

EXECUTE(DDEChannel, CommandText)

Executes commands over an existing DDE link.

EXEC(ProgramName, WindowMaxOrMin, [RunInBackground])

Starts another program.

EXPON(InputRange, OutputTopLeftCell, DampingFactor, StandardErrors, GenerateChart)

Performs exponential smoothing; predicts a value based on the forecast for the prior period.

EXTEND.POLYGON(array)

Adds vertices to a polygon.

EXTRACT(UniqueRecordsOnly)
or
EXTRACT?(UniqueRecordsOnly)

Finds database records that match the criteria defined in the criteria range and copies all found records into a separate extract range.

FCLOSE(FileNumber)

Closes the specified file.

FILE.CLOSE(save_logical, route_logical)

Closes the active workbook.

FILE.DELETE(file_text)

Deletes a file from disk.

FILES(SourceDirectory)

Returns the names of all files in the specified directory.

FILL.AUTO(destination_ref, copy_only)

Copies a cell into a range of cells.

FILL.DOWN()

Copies the top cell row into the rest of the selection.

FILL.GROUP(type_num)

Copies the contents of the current selection to the same area on all other worksheets in the group.

FILL.LEFT()

Copies the right cell column into the rest of the selection.

FILL.RIGHT()

Copies the left cell column into the rest of the selection.

FILL.UP()

Copies the bottom cell row into the rest of the selection.

FILTER(FieldNumber, Criteria1, Operation2With1, Criteria2)
or
FILTER?(FieldNumber, Criteria1, Operation2With1, Criteria2)

Filters lists of data by column.

FILTER.ADVANCED(CopyList, SourceRef, CriteriaRange, CopyRange, UniqueOnly)
or
FILTER.ADVANCED?(CopyList, SourceRef, CriteriaRange, CopyRange, UniqueOnly)

Sets options for filtering a list.

FILTER.SHOW.ALL

Displays all items in a filtered list.

FIND.FILE()

Enables searching for files.

FONT.PROPERTIES(font, font_style, size, strikethrough)

Sets the font for the Normal style. Refer to Excel's online help for a full description of the parameters.

FOPEN(FileName, ReadWriteAccess)

Opens a file and returns a file ID number.

FOR(counter_text, start_num, end_num, step_num)

Defines a program loop, defining the structure for the number of iterations of the group of functions.

FOR.CELL(ref_name, area_ref, skip_blanks)

Defines a program loop, repeating the group of functions for each cell in the range.

FORMAT.AUTO(format_num, number, font, alignment, border, pattern, width)

Formats the selection from a format gallery.

FORMAT.CHART(layer_num, view, overlap, angle, gap_width)

Formats a chart. Refer to Excel's online help for function description and complete list of parameters.

FORMAT.CHARTTYPE(apply_to, group_num, dimension, type_num)

Refer to Excel's online help for function description and parameters.

FORMAT.FONT(_)

Sets font formatting. Refer to Excel's online help for function description and parameters.

FORMAT.LEGEND(position_num)

Formats a legend on a chart.

FORMAT.MAIN(type_num, view, overlap, gap_width, vary, drop)

Formats a chart. Refer to Excel's online help for a complete function description and parameters.

FORMAT.MOVE(_)

Moves the selected object. Refer to Excel's online help for function description and parameters.

FORMAT.NUMBER(format_text)

Formats numbers in selected cells.

FORMAT.OFFSET(XPosition, YPosition)

Moves the selected object.

FORMAT.OVERLAY(type_num, view, overlap, gap_width, vary)

Formats an overlay chart. Refer to Excel's online help for complete function description and parameters.

FORMAT.SHAPE(vertex_num, insert, reference, x_offset, y_offset)

Reshapes a polygon.

FORMAT.SIZE(_)

Changes the size of a selected object. Refer to Excel's online help for complete function description and parameters.

FORMAT.TEXT(x_align, y_align, orient_num, auto_text, auto_size, show_key, show_value)

Formats the selection.

FORMULA(formula_text, reference)

Enters a formula into the active cell or reference.

FORMULA.ARRAY(formula_text, reference)

Enters an array formula into the active cell or range.

FORMULA.CONVERT(FormulaText, A1ToR1C1, R1C1ToA1, FormulaReferenceType, BaseForRelativeReferences)

Converts cell references between styles or types.

FORMULA.FILL(formula_text, reference)

Enters the same formula in a range of cells.

FORMULA.FIND(text, in_num, at_num, by_num, dir_num, match_case)

Selects the text to find.

FORMULA.FIND.NEXT()

Finds the next cell meeting the FORMULA.FIND criteria.

FORMULA.FIND.PREV()

Finds the previous cell meeting the FORMULA.FIND criteria.

FORMULA.GOTO(reference, corner)

Sets the cursor to a named area or reference.

FORMULA.REPLACE(find_text, replace_text, look_at, look_by, active, match_case)

Finds and replaces characters.

FOURIER(InputRange, OutputTopLeftCell, Inverse, FirstRowLabels)
or
FOURIER?(InputRange, OutputTopLeftCell, Inverse, FirstRowLabels)

Performs a Fourier transform.

FPOS(FileNumber, SetPosition)

Sets the current position within an open file.

FREADLN(FileNumber)

Reads characters from the open file, beginning at the current position within the file and continuing to the end of the line.

FREAD(FileNumber, NumberOfBytesToRead)

Reads a specified number of characters from the open file, beginning at the current position within the file.

FREEZE.PANES(logical, col_split, row_split)

Freezes or unfreezes existing panes.

FSIZE(FileNumber)

Returns the number of bytes in the open file.

FTESTV(DataSetOneInputRange, DataSetTwoInputRange, OutputTopLeftCell, FirstRowLabels)
or
FTESTV?(DataSetOneInputRange, DataSetTwoInputRange, OutputTopLeftCell, FirstRowLabels)

Performs a two-sample F-test.

FULL(logical)

Sets Full size.

FULL.SCREEN(logical)

Sets Full screen.

FWRITELN(FileNumber, TextToWrite)

Writes text to the open file, beginning at the current position in the file. Text is followed by a carriage return and linefeed.

FWRITE(FileNumber, TextToWrite)

Writes text to the open file, beginning at the current position in the file.

FUNCTION.WIZARD()

Refer to Excel's online help for function description and parameters.

GALLERY.3D.AREA(type_num)

Changes the active chart to a 3D area chart.

GALLERY.3D.BAR(type_num)

Changes the active chart to a 3D bar chart.

GALLERY.3D.COLUMN(type_num)

Changes the active chart to a 3D column chart.

GALLERY.3D.LINE(type_num)

Changes the active chart to a 3D line chart.

GALLERY.3D.PIE(type_num)

Changes the active chart to a 3D pie chart.

GALLERY.3D.SURFACE(type_num)

Changes the active chart to a 3D surface chart.

GALLERY.AREA(type_num, delete_overlay)

Changes the active chart to an area chart.

GALLERY.BAR(type_num, delete_overlay)

Changes the active chart to a bar chart.

GALLERY.COLUMN(type_num, delete_overlay)

Changes the active chart to a column chart.

GALLERY.CUSTOM(name_text)

Changes the active chart to a custom chart.

GALLERY.DOUGHNUT(type_num, delete_overlay)

Changes the active chart to a doughnut chart.

GALLERY.LINE(type_num, delete_overlay)

Changes the active chart to a line chart.

GALLERY.PIE(type_num, delete_overlay)

Changes the active chart to a pie chart.

GALLERY.RADAR(type_num, delete_overlay)

Changes the active chart to a radar chart.

GALLERY.SCATTER(type_num, delete_overlay)

Changes the active chart to an XY (scatter) chart.

GET.BAR

Returns the number of the active menu bar.

GET.CELL(InformationType, CellsToGetInfo

Returns information about a cell.

GET.CHART.ITEM(CoordinatesToReturn, PointIndexOnChart, ItemText)

Returns the position of a point on a chart item.

GET.DEF(DefinedName, SheetContainingName, TypesOfNames)

Returns the name of an area, value, or formula in a workbook.

GET.DOCUMENT(TypeOfInformation, [DocumentName])

Returns information about a worksheet in a workbook.

GET.FORMULA(CellReference)

Returns the full contents of a cell.

GET.LINK.INFO(LinkPath, TypeOfInformation, TypeOfLink, CellReference)

Returns information about the specified link.

GET.NAME(DefinedName, [TypeOfInformation])

Returns the definition of a name.

GET.NOTE(CellReferenceAttached, StartingCharNumber, NumberOfCharactersToReturn)

Returns a note.

GET.OBJECT(TypeOfInformation, ObjectID, StartingCharNumber, NumberOfCharactersToReturn)

Returns information about the specified object.

GET.PIVOT.FIELD(TypeNumber, PivotFieldName, PivotTableName)

Returns information about a field in a pivot table.

GET.PIVOT.ITEM(TypeNumber, PivotItemName, PivotFieldName, PivotTableName)

Returns information about an item in a pivot table.

GET.PIVOT.TABLE(TypeNumber, PivotTableName)

Returns information about a pivot table.

GET.TOOLBAR(TypeOfInformation, ToolbarID)

Returns information about a toolbar(s).

GET.TOOL(TypeOfInformation, ToolbarID, ButtonPosition)

Returns information about a toolbar button(s).

GET.WINDOW(TypeOfInformation, [WindowTitle])

Returns information about a window.

GET.WORKBOOK(TypeOfInformation, [WorkbookName])

Returns information about a workbook.

GET.WORKSPACE(TypeOfInformation)

Returns information about the workspace.

GOAL.SEEK(target_cell, target_value, variable_cell)

Calculates values necessary to achieve a specific goal.

GOTO(reference)

Redirects the execution of a macro to a specified label.

GRIDLINES(x_major, x_minor, y_major, y_minor, z_major, z_minor)

Enables you to turn chart gridlines on or off.

GROUP()

Creates one object from selected objects.

HALT(cancel_close)

Stops all macros.

HELP(help_ref)

Starts or switches to Help and displays the custom Help topic specified.

HIDE()

Hides the active window.

HIDE.DIALOG(cancel_logical)

Cancels the current dialog box and hides it from view.

HIDE.OBJECT(object_id_text, hide_logical)

Hides or displays the given object.

HISTOGRAM(InputRange, OutputTopLeftCell, BinRangeReference, IncludePareto, CumulativePercents, GenerateChart, FirstRowLabels)
or
HISTOGRAM?(InputRange, OutputTopLeftCell, BinRangeReference, IncludePareto, CumulativePercents, GenerateChart, FirstRowLabels)

Performs a histogram calculation.

HLINE(num_columns)

Scrolls through the active window by a given number of columns.

HPAGE(num_windows)

Scrolls horizontally through the active window by a given number of windows.

HSCROLL(position, col_logical)

Scrolls horizontally through the active window by percentage or by column number.

IF(logical_test)

Begins a group of formulas to be executed if logical_test is TRUE.

INITIATE(ApplicationName, TopicText)

Opens a DDE channel and returns the channel number.

INPUT(message_text, type_num, title_text, default, x_pos, y_pos, help_ref)

Displays a dialog box and waits for user input.

INSERT(shift_num)

Inserts blank cells in the active worksheet.

INSERT.OBJECT(ObjectClass, SourceFileName, LinkToFile, DisplayAsIcon, FileContainingIcon, IconNumber, LabelBelowIcon, AttachedTemplateName)
or
INSERT.OBJECT?(ObjectClass, SourceFileName, LinkToFile, DisplayAsIcon, FileContainingIcon, IconNumber, LabelBelowIcon, AttachedTemplateName)

Creates an embedded object whose data is supplied by another application.

INSERT.PICTURE(file_name, filter_number)

Inserts a picture into the active worksheet.

INSERT.TITLE(_)

Refer to Excel's online help for function description and parameters.

JUSTIFY()

Refer to Excel's online help for function description and parameters.

LABEL.PROPERTIES(accel_text, accel2_text, 3d_shading)

Sets the label text and appearance.

LAST.ERROR

Returns the cell reference in which the last macro worksheet error occurred.

LEGEND(logical)

Adds or removes a legend from a chart.

LINE.PRINT(_)

Refer to Excel's online help for function description and parameters.

LINK.COMBO(link_logical)

Refer to Excel's online help for function description and parameters.

LINK.FORMAT()

Refer to Excel's online help for function description and parameters.

LINKS(SourceWorkbookName, TypeOfLink)

Returns an array of the names of all workbooks referenced in the specified workbook.

LIST.NAMES()

Lists all names defined on the active worksheet.

LISTBOX.PROPERTIES(range, link, drop_size, multi_select)

Refer to Excel's online help for function description and parameters.

MACRO.OPTIONS(macro_name, description, menu_on)

Refer to Excel's online help for function description and parameters.

MAIL.LOGOFF()

Disconnects the user's mail session.

MAIL.LOGON(name_text, password_text, download_logical)

Begins a mail session for the specified user.

MAIN.CHART(type_num, stack, 100, vary, overlay, drop, hilo, overlap%, cluster, angle)

Same as FORMAT.MAIN().

MCORREL(InputRange, OutputTopLeftCell, RowOrColumn, FirstRowLabels)
or
MCORREL?(InputRange, OutputTopLeftCell, RowOrColumn, FirstRowLabels)

Performs a correlation calculation.

MCOVAR(InputRange, OutputTopLeftCell, RowOrColumn, FirstRowLabels)
or
MCOVAR?(InputRange, OutputTopLeftCell, RowOrColumn, FirstRowLabels)

Performs a covariance calculation.

MERGE.STYLES(document_text)

Merges all styles from another workbook into the active workbook.

MESSAGE(logical, text)

Displays messages in the status bar.

MOVE(NewXPosition, NewYPosition, WindowName)

Same as WINDOW.MOVE.

MOVE.TOOL(from_bar_id), from_bar_position, to_bar_id, to_bar_position, move_copy_logical, width)

Moves or copies a toolbar button to another toolbar.

MOVEAVG(InputRange, OutputTopLeftCell, Interval, StdErrors, GenerateChart, FirstRowLabels)
or
MOVEAVG?(InputRange, OutputTopLeftCell, Interval, StdErrors, GenerateChart, FirstRowLabels)

Performs a moving averages calculation.

NAMES(WorkbookName, IncludeHiddenNames, [NameSelectionCriteria])

Returns the specified names defined in the specified workbook.

NEW(type_num, xy_series, add_logical)

Creates a new workbook or opens a template.

NEW.WINDOW()

Creates a new window for the active workbook.

NEXT()

Ends a program loop.

NOTE(add_text, cell_ref, start_char, num_chars)

Creates or edits a note.

OBJECT.CONVERT(ConvertToClass)

Converts an OLE object to another class type.

OBJECT.PROPERTIES(placement_type, print_object)

Determines the way in which the selected object(s) is attached to cells beneath.

OBJECT.PROTECTION(locked, lock_text)

Changes the protection of the selected object(s).

ON.DATA(document_text, macro_text)

Runs a macro when data is received via a DDE link.

ON.DOUBLE.CLICK(sheet_text, macro_text)

Runs a macro when you double-click on any cell, object, or item.

ON.ENTRY(sheet_text, macro_text)

Runs a macro when data is entered into any cell.

ON.KEY(key_text, macro_text)

Assigns a macro to a key combination.

ON.RECALC(sheet_text, macro_text)

Runs a macro when a given worksheet is recalculated.

ON.SHEET(sheet_text, macro_text, activate_logical)

Runs a macro when a sheet is made the active sheet.

ON.TIME(time, macro_text, tolerance, insert_logical)

Runs a macro at a given time.

ON.WINDOW(window_text, macro_text)

Runs a macro when a given window has the focus.

OPEN(file_text, update_links, read_only, format, Prot_pwd)

Opens a workbook. Refer to Excel's online help for function description and complete list of parameters.

OPEN.LINKS(document_text1, document_text2, read_only, link_type)

Opens workbooks linked to a particular worksheet.

OPEN.MAIL(Subject, Comments)

Opens the mail utility.

OPEN.TEXT(file_text, file_origin, start_row, file_type)

Uses the TextWizard to open a text file in Excel. Refer to Excel's online help for a complete description of parameters.

OPTIONS.CALCULATION(type_num, iter, max_num)

Sets worksheet calculation settings. Refer to Excel's online help for a complete description of parameters.

OPTIONS.CHART(display_blanks, plot_visible, size_with_window)

Sets chart settings.

OPTIONS.EDIT(incell_edit, drag_drop, alert, enter_move, fixed, places, copy_logical, update_links)

Sets worksheet editing options.

OPTIONS.GENERAL(R1C1_mode, dde_on, sum_info, tips)

Sets general Excel for Windows 95 settings. Refer to Excel's online help for a complete description of parameters.

OPTIONS.LISTS.ADD(string_array, row_col_logical)

Adds a new custom list.

OPTIONS.LISTS.DELETE(list_num)

Deletes a custom list.

OPTIONS.LISTS.GET(import_ref, list_num)

Imports a custom list from an external reference.

OPTIONS.TRANSITION(menu_key, menu_key_action)

Sets compatibility with other spreadsheets. Refer to Excel's online help for a complete description of parameters.

OPTIONS.VIEW(formula, Status, Notes, show_info, object_num)

Sets various view settings.

OUTLINE(auto_styles, row_dir, col_dir, create_apply)

Creates an outline and defines settings.

OVERLAY(type_num, stack, 100, vary, overlap, drop, hilo)

Refer to Excel's online help for function description and parameters.

PAGE.SETUP(header, footer, left, right, top, bottom, row_col_heading, grid, center_horiz, center_vert, orient, paper_size, scale, first_page_num, Page_order, b&w_logical, Quality, header_margin, footer_margin, Print_notes, draft)

Controls the appearance of the worksheet on the page.

PARSE(parse_ext, destination_ref)

Distributes the contents of the current selection to fill multiple columns.

PASTE(to_reference)

Pastes data or objects from the Clipboard into the active cell(s).

PASTE.LINK()

Pastes data or objects from the Clipboard into the active cell(s) and establishes a link to the source of the data or objects.

PASTE.PICTURE()

Pastes a picture from the Clipboard into the active cell(s).

PASTE.PICTURE.LINK()

Pastes a picture from the Clipboard into the active cell(s) and establishes a link to the source of the data or objects.

PASTE.SPECIAL(_)

Pastes the given components from the copy area into the current selection. Refer to Excel's online help for a complete description of parameters.

PASTE.TOOL(bar_id, position)

Pastes a button face from the Clipboard to a toolbar position.

PATTERNS(_)

Changes the appearance of the selection. Refer to Excel's online help for a complete description of parameters.

PAUSE(no_tool)

Pauses a macro.

PIVOT.ADD.DATA(TableName, PivotFieldName, NewName, FieldPosition, FieldFunction, CalculationToField, BaseField, BaseFieldItem)

Adds data to a PivotTable.

PIVOT.ADD.FIELDS(TableName, RowArray, ColumnArray, PageArray, AddToTable)

Adds fields to a PivotTable.

PIVOT.FIELD(TableName, PivotFieldName, Orientation, DestinationPosition)

Pivots a field within a PivotTable.

PIVOT.FIELD.GROUP(StartDate, EndDate, SizeOfGroups, Periods)
or
PIVOT.FIELD.GROUP?(StartDate, EndDate, SizeOfGroups, Periods)

Creates groups within a PivotTable.

PIVOT.FIELD.PROPERTIES(TableName, PivotFieldName, NewName, Orientation, CalculationToApply, Formats)

Changes the properties of a field inside a PivotTable.

PIVOT.FIELD.UNGROUP

Ungroups all selected groups within a PivotTable.

PIVOT.ITEM(TableName, PivotFieldName, PivotItemName, Position)

Moves an item within a PivotTable.

PIVOT.ITEM.PROPERTIES(TableName, PivotFieldName, PivotItemName, NewName, Position, Show, ActivePage)

Changes the properties of an item within a PivotTable.

PIVOT.REFRESH(TableName)

Refreshes a PivotTable.

PIVOT.SHOW.PAGES(TableName, PageField)

Creates new worksheets in the workbook that contains the active cell.

PIVOT.TABLE.WIZARD(TypeOfData, Source, Destination, TableName, RowGrandTotal, ColGrandTotal, SaveData, ApplyAutoFormat, AutoPage)
or
PIVOT.TABLE.WIZARD?(TypeOfData, Source, Destination, TableName, RowGrandTotal, ColGrandTotal, SaveData, ApplyAutoFormat, AutoPage)

Creates an empty PivotTable.

PLACEMENT(Type)
or
PLACEMENT?(Type)

Same as OBJECT.PROPERTIES.

POKE(DDEChannel, DestinationItem, DataSourceReference)

Sends data to another application via DDE.

POST.DOCUMENT(database)

Refer to Excel's online help for function description and parameters.

PRECISION(logical)

Sets precision to be precision displayed.

PREFERRED()

Changes the format of the active chart to the default.

PRESS.TOOL(bar_id, position, down)

Formats a button to appear normal or pressed.

PRINT(range_num, from, to, copies, draft, preview, print_what, color, feed, quality, y_resolution, selection)

Prints the active workbook.

PRINT.PREVIEW()

Previews pages of the active workbook on the screen prior to printing.

PRINTER.SETUP(printer_text)

Changes the default printer.

PROMOTE(rowcol)

Promotes (ungroups) the selected rows or columns in an outline.

PROTECT.DOCUMENT(contents, windows, password, objects)

Adds or removes document, worksheet, or object protection. Refer to Excel's online help for a complete description of parameters.

PTTESTM(DataSetOneInputRange, DataSetTwoInputRange, OutputTopLeftCell, FirstRowLabels, Alpha, MeanDifference)
or
PTTESTM?(DataSetOneInputRange, DataSetTwoInputRange, OutputTopLeftCell, FirstRowLabels, Alpha, MeanDifference)

Performs a paired two-sample t-test for means.

PTTESTV(DataSetOneInputRange, DataSetTwoInputRange, OutputTopLeftCell, FirstRowLabels, Alpha)
or
PTTESTV?(DataSetOneInputRange, DataSetTwoInputRange, OutputTopLeftCell, FirstRowLabels, Alpha)

Performs a two-sample t-test assuming unequal variances.

PUSHBUTTON.PROPERTIES(default_logical,cancel_logical)

Refer to Excel's online help for function description and parameters.

QUERY.GET.DATA(ConnectionString, QueryText, KeepQueryDefn, KeepFieldNames, KeepRowNumbers, Destination)
or
QUERY.GET.DATA?(ConnectionString, QueryText, KeepQueryDefn, KeepFieldNames, KeepRowNumbers, Destination)

Builds a new SQL query using supplied information.

QUERY.REFRESH(CellReference

Refreshes data in a data range written by a query.

New Riders Publishing
INSIDE
SERIES

QUIT()
Exits Excel.

RANDOM(OutputRange, NumberOfVariables, NumberOfDataPoints, DistributionType, Seed, From/Mean/Probability/Lambda/InputRange, To/StdDev/NumberOfTrials, [Step, NumberOfRepeats,])NumberOfSeqsRepeat
or
RANDOM?(OutputRange, NumberOfVariables, NumberOfDataPoints, DistributionType, Seed, From/Mean/Probability/Lambda/InputRange, To/StdDev/NumberOfTrials, [Step, NumberOfRepeats, NumberOfSeqsRepeat])
Generates a given number of pseudo-random numbers.

RANKPERC(InputRange, OutputTopLeftCell, RowOrColumn, FirstRowLabels)
or
RANKPERC?(InputRange, OutputTopLeftCell, RowOrColumn, FirstRowLabels)
Performs a rank and percentile calculation on a set of data.

REFTEXT(ReferenceToConvert, A1OrR1C1)
Converts a cell reference to an absolute reference.

REGISTER(DLLName, DLLFunctionName, DataTypes, FunctionNameToWizard, ArgumentNames, FunctionOrCommand, FunctionCategory, ShortcutKey, ReferenceToHelp, FunctionDescription, Argument1, ..., Argument21)
Registers the given DLL and returns the ID.

REGRESS(InputYRange, InputXRange, YInterceptZero, FirstRowLabels, ConfidenceLevel, SummaryOutputTopLeftCell, IncludeResiduals, IncludeStdzdResiduals, ResidualsPlots, RegressionLinePlots, ResidualsOutputTopLeftCell, NormalProbPlots, ProbOutputTopLeftCell)
or
REGRESS?(InputYRange, InputXRange, YInterceptZero, FirstRowLabels, ConfidenceLevel, SummaryOutputTopLeftCell, IncludeResiduals, IncludeStdzdResiduals, ResidualsPlots, RegressionLinePlots, ResidualsOutputTopLeftCell, NormalProbPlots, ProbOutputTopLeftCell)
Performs linear regression analysis.

RELREF(Offset, Reference)

Returns the reference of a cell relative to a given cell.

REMOVE.LIST.ITEM(index_num, count_num)

Removes an item from a custom list.

REMOVE.PAGE.BREAK()

Removes manual page breaks.

RENAME.COMMAND(bar_num, menu, command, name_text, submenu_command)

Changes the name of a menu or menu command.

RENAME.OBJECT(new_name)

Renames the selected object or group.

REPLACE.FONT(font_num, name_text, size_num, bold, italic)

Defines a new font for the current selection. Refer to Excel's online help for a complete description of parameters.

REPORT.DEFINE(ReportName, SectionsArray, ContinuousPageNumbers)

Creates or replaces a report definition.

REPORT.DELETE(ReportName)

Removes a report definition from the active workbook.

REPORT.GET(TypeOfInformation, ReportName)

Returns information about reports defined for the active workbook.

REPORT.PRINT(ReportName, NumberCopies, ShowPrintDialog)
or
REPORT.PRINT?(ReportName, ShowPrintDialog)

Prints a report.

REQUEST(DDEChannel, TypeOfInformationRequested)

Requests an array from a DDE link.

RESET.TOOL(bar_id, position)

Resets a tool button to its default button face.

RESET.TOOLBAR(bar_id)

Resets toolbars to the defaults.

RESTART(level_num)

Removes a given number of Return statements from the return stack.

RESULT(type_num)

Sets the type of data a macro or custom function returns.

RESUME(type_num)

Resumes a paused macro.

RETURN(value)

Returns a macro to its calling routine.

ROUTE.DOCUMENT()

Routes the document using its routing slip.

ROUTING.SLIP(recipients, subject, message, route_num, return_to_sender, track_status)

Adds or edits the routing slip attached to the current workbook.

ROW.HEIGHT(height_num, reference, standard, type_num)

Changes the row height in a reference.

RUN(reference, step)

Runs a macro.

SAMPLE(InputRange, OutputTopLeftCell, SamplingMethod, SamplingRateOrNumber, FirstRowLabels)
or
SAMPLE?(InputRange, OutputTopLeftCell, SamplingMethod, SamplingRateOrNumber, FirstRowLabels)

Performs sampling of a set of data.

SAVE()

Saves the active workbook.

SAVE.AS(document_text, type_num, prot_pwd, backup, write_pwd, read_only)

Saves a file under new name or attributes.

SAVE.COPY.AS(document_text)

Saves a copy of the current file and attributes to a new file name.

SAVE.TOOLBAR(bar_id, filename)

Saves toolbar definitions to a given file.

SAVE.WORKBOOK(document_text, type_num, prot_pwd, backup, write_pwd, read_only)

Same as SAVE.AS.

SAVE.WORKSPACE(name_text)

Saves the current workbook(s) as a workspace.

SCALE(_)

Scales a chart. Refer to Excel's online help for function description and parameters.

SCENARIO.ADD(scen_name, value_array, changing_ref, scen_comment, locked, hidden)

Defines a scenario.

SCENARIO.CELLS(changing_ref)

Defines the changing cells for a scenario model.

SCENARIO.DELETE(scen_name)

Deletes a scenario.

SCENARIO.EDIT(scen_name, new_scenname, value_array, locked, hidden)

Edits a scenario.

SCENARIO.GET(TypeOfInformation, ScenarioName)

Returns information about defined scenarios.

SCENERIO.MERGE(source_file)

Refer to Excel's online help for function description and parameters.

SCENARIO.SHOW(scen_name)

Recalculates using a scenario and displays the result.

SCENARIO.SHOW.NEXT()

Recalculates using the next scenario and displays the result.

SCENARIO.SUMMARY(result_ref, report_type)

Generates a table summarizing the results of all scenarios.

SCROLLBAR.PROPERTIES(value, min, max, inc, page, link)

Refer to Excel's online help for function description and parameters.

SELECT(_)

Selects a cell(s) or changes the active cell. Refer to Excel's online help for a complete list of parameters.

SELECT.ALL()

Selects the entire worksheet.

SELECT.CHART

Selects a chart.

SELECT.END(direction_num)

Selects the cell at the edge of the range in a given direction.

SELECT.LAST.CELL()

Selects the last cell that has data.

SELECT.LIST.ITEM(index_num, selected_logical)

Selects the specified member of a custom list.

SELECT.PLOT.AREA

Selects the plot area of the active chart.

SELECT.SPECIAL(type_num, value_type, levels)

Selects groups of cells that have similar characteristics.

SELECTION

Returns the full reference of the current selection.

SEND.KEYS(KeyCombination, WaitForActions)

Sends a series of keystrokes to the active application.

SEND.MAIL(recipients, subject, return_receipt)

Sends the active workbook to recipients.

SEND.TO.BACK()

Sends selected object(s) behind all other objects.

SERIES(NameReference, CategoriesReference, ValuesReference, PlotOrder)

Represents a data series in the active chart.

SERIES.AXES(axis_num)

Refer to Excel's online help for function description and parameters.

SERIES.ORDER(chart_num, old_series_num, new_series_num)

Refer to Excel's online help for function description and parameters.

SERIES.X(x_ref)

Refer to Excel's online help for function description and parameters.

SERIES.Y(name_ref, y_ref)

Refer to Excel's online help for function description and parameters.

SET.CONTROL.VALUE(value)

Sets the currently selected control to the value supplied.

SET.CRITERIA

Defines the name Criteria for the selected range.

SET.DATABASE

Defines the name Database for the selected range.

SET.DIALOG.DEFAULT(object_id_text)

Refer to Excel's online help for function description and parameters.

SET.DIALOG.FOCUS(object_id_text)

Refer to Excel's online help for function description and parameters.

SET.EXTRACT

Defines the name Extract for the selected range.

SET.LIST.ITEM(text, index_num)

Sets the indexed item of the current list to the text value.

SET.NAME(name_text, value)

Defines a name to refer to a value.

SET.PAGE.BREAK()

Sets manual page breaks.

SET.PREFERRED(format)

Changes the default format used to create a new chart.

SET.PRINT.AREA(range)

Defines the print area for the workbook.

SET.PRINT.TITLES(titles_for_cols_ref, titles_for_rows_ref)

Defines the print titles for the active worksheet.

SET.UPDATE.STATUS(LinkedFilePath, UpdateMethod, TypeOfLink)

Sets automatic or manual updating of a link.

SET.VALUE(reference, values)

Changes the value of cells on the macro worksheet without changing any formulas within those cells.

SHEET.BACKGROUND(file_name, filter_number)

Refer to Excel's online help for function description and parameters.

SHORT.MENUS(logical)

Sets short menus.

SHOW.ACTIVE.CELL()

Scrolls the window until the active cell is visible.

SHOW.BAR(bar_num)

Displays a menu bar.

SHOW.CLIPBOARD()

Displays the Clipboard contents in a new window.

SHOW.DETAIL(rowcol, rowcol_num, expand, show_field)

Expands or collapses detail.

SHOW.DIALOG(dialog_sheet)

Refer to Excel's online help for function description and parameters.

SHOW.INFO(logical)

Controls the display of the Info window.

SHOW.LEVELS(row_level, col_level)

Displays row and column levels of an outline.

SHOW.TOOLBAR(bar_id, visible, dock, x_pos, y_pos, width)

Hides or displays a toolbar.

SIZE(Width, Height, WindowName)

Same as WINDOW.SIZE.

SLIDE.COPY.ROW

Copies the selected slides to the Clipboard.

SLIDE.CUT.ROW

Cuts the selected slides to the Clipboard.

SLIDE.DEFAULTS(EffectNumber, Speed, AdvanceRate, SoundFileName)
or
SLIDE.DEFAULTS?(EffectNumber, Speed, AdvanceRate, SoundFileName)

Specifies the default values for transitions in a slide show.

SLIDE.DELETE.ROW

Deletes the selected slides.

SLIDE.EDIT(EffectNumber, Speed, AdvanceRate, SoundFileName)
or
SLIDE.EDIT?(EffectNumber, Speed, AdvanceRate, SoundFileName)

Modifies attributes of the selected slide.

SLIDE.GET(TypeOfInformation, SlideShowDocName, [SlideNumber])

Returns information about a slide or the entire slide show.

SLIDE.PASTE(EffectNumber, Speed, AdvanceRate, SoundFileName)
or
SLIDE.PASTE?(EffectNumber, Speed, AdvanceRate, SoundFileName)

Pastes the Clipboard as the next available slide.

SLIDE.PASTE.ROW

Pastes multiple slides from the Clipboard into the current selection.

SLIDE.SHOW(InitialSlideNumber, Repeat, DialogTitle, AllowNavigationKeys, AllowDialogBoxControl)

Starts a slide show.

SOLVER.ADD(ConstraintCellReference, Relation, Formula)

Adds a constraint to the current problem.

SOLVER.CHANGE(ConstraintCellReference, Relation, Formula)

Changes the right side of an existing constraint.

SOLVER.DELETE(ConstraintCellReference, Relation, Formula)

Deletes a constraint from the current problem.

SOLVER.FINISH(KeepFinalSolution, ReportArgumentsArray)

Displays a dialog box with the arguments and results when Solver is finished.

SOLVER.GET(TypeOfInformation, ScenarioSheetName)

Returns information about the current settings for Solver.

SOLVER.LOAD(LoadSourceReference)

Loads previously saved Solver problem specifications.

SOLVER.OK(SetTargetCell, MaxMinValue, ValueOf, ByChanging)

Specifies basic Solver options.

SOLVER.OPTIONS(MaxTime, Iterations, Precision, AssumeLinear, StepThrough, Estimates, Derivatives, Search, IntTolerance, Scaling)

Specifies the available Solver options.

SOLVER.RESET

Removes all cell selections and constraints from the Solver parameters and restores all Solver option settings.

SOLVER.SAVE(DestinationReference)

Saves the Solver problem specification on the worksheet.

SOLVER.SOLVE(UserFinish, ShowMacroReference)

Begins Solver.

SORT(rows_or_cols, sort_key1, order1, sort_key2, order2, sort_key3, order3, header, custom_sorting, m_Match_case)

Sorts rows or columns within the selection.

SOUND.NOTE(cell_ref, erase_logical)

Records or erases sound in a cell note.

SOUND.PLAY(cell_ref, file_text, resource)

Plays the sound from a cell note or a file.

SPELLING(custom_dic, ignore_uppercase, always_suggest)

Checks the spelling of words in the current selection.

SPELLING.CHECK(WordOrReference, CustomDictName, IgnoreUppercaseWords)

Checks the spelling of a word.

SPLIT(col_split, row_split)

Splits the active window into panes.

SQL.BIND(ConnectionNumber, ResultColumn, CellReference)

Specifies the location at which results from a SQL query are placed.

SQL.CLOSE(ConnectionNumber)

Closes a connection to an external data source.

SQL.ERROR

Returns error information from a SQL operation.

SQL.EXEC.QUERY(ConnectionNumber, QueryText)

Queries an external data source.

SQL.GET.SCHEMA(ConnectionNumber, InfoType, QualifierText)

Returns information about the structure of a data source in a given connection.

SQL.OPEN(ConnectionString, OutputReference, DriverPrompt)

Establishes a connection with an external data source.

SQL.RETRIEVE.TO.FILE(ConnectionNumber, DestinationFile, FirstRowColumnNames, ColumnDelim)

Retrieves results from data source and places them in a file.

SQL.RETRIEVE(ConnectionNumber, DestinationCellReference, MaxColumns, MaxRows, FirstRowColumnNames, FirstColumnRowNumbers, NamedRange, FetchFirst)

Retrieves results from data source.

STANDARD.FONT(name_text, size_num, bold, italic, underline)

Sets the default font characteristics.

STANDARD.WIDTH(standard_num)

Sets the default column widths of new worksheets.

START()

Refer to Excel's online help for function description and parameters.

STEP()

Single-steps a macro—useful for debugging.

STYLE(Bold, Italic)
or
STYLE?(Bold, Italic)

Same as FORMAT.FONT.

SUBSCRIBE.TO(SourceFileName, SourceFileFormat)

Inserts contents of a given edition at the current selection point.

SUBTOTAL.CREATE(AtEachChangeIn, UseFunctionNumber, AddSubtotalTo, Replace, PageBreakBetweenGroups, SummaryBelowData)
or
SUBTOTAL.CREATE?(AtEachChangeIn, UseFunctionNumber, AddSubtotalTo, Replace, PageBreakBetweenGroups, SummaryBelowData)

Generates a subtotal in a list or a database.

SUBTOTAL.REMOVE

Removes all subtotals.

SUMMARY.INFO(title, subject, author, keywords, comments)
Generates summary info for the active workbook.

TAB.ORDER()
Refer to Excel's online help for function description and parameters.

TABLE(row_ref, column_ref)
Creates a table based upon input values and formulas.

TERMINATE(DDEChannel)
Closes a DDE channel.

TEXT.BOX(add_text, object_id_text, start_num, num_chars)
Replaces characters in a text box or button.

TEXT.TO.COLUMNS(destination_ref, data_type, text_delim, consecutive_delims, tab_delims, semicolon_delims, comma_delims, space_delims, custom_delims, other_char_delims, field_info)
Parses text into columns of data.

TEXTREF(ReferenceAsText, A1OrR1C1)
Converts text to absolute cell references.

TRACER.CLEAR()
Clears all tracer arrows on the worksheet.

TRACER.DISPLAY(direction, create)
Activates formula tracers showing relationships among cells.

TRACER.ERROR()
Activates formula tracers showing error values in cells.

TRACER.NAVIGATE(direction, arrow_num, ref_num)
Moves the selection from one end of the tracer arrow to the other.

TTESTM(DataSetOneInputRange, DataSetTwoInputRange, OutputTopLeftCell, FirstRowLabels, Alpha, MeansDifference)
or
TTESTM?(DataSetOneInputRange, DataSetTwoInputRange, OutputTopLeftCell, FirstRowLabels, Alpha, MeansDifference)

Performs a two-sample t-test for means, assuming equal variances.

UNDO()

Reverses (in most cases) the last action.

UNGROUP()

Separates a grouped object into individual objects.

UNHIDE(window_text)

Displays a hidden window.

UNLOCKED.NEXT()

Moves the next unlocked cell in a protected worksheet.

UNLOCKED.PREV()

Moves the previous unlocked cell into a protected worksheet.

UNREGISTER(RegisterID)

Unregisters the given DLL.

UPDATE.LINK(link_text, type_of_link)

Updates a link.

VBA.ADD.WATCH

Refer to Excel's online help for function description and parameters.

VBA.CLEAR.BREAKPOINTS

Refer to Excel's online help for function description and parameters.

VBA.DEBUG.WINDOW

Refer to Excel's online help for function description and parameters.

VBA.END

Refer to Excel's online help for function description and parameters.

VBA.INSERT.FILE

Refer to Excel's online help for function description and parameters.

VBA.INSTANT.WATCH

Refer to Excel's online help for function description and parameters.

VBA.MAKE.ADDIN

Refer to Excel's online help for function description and parameters.

VBA.OBJECT.BROWSER

Refer to Excel's online help for function description and parameters.

VBA.PROCEDURE.DEFINITION

Refer to Excel's online help for function description and parameters.

VBA.REFERENCES

Refer to Excel's online help for function description and parameters.

VBA.STEP.INTO

Refer to Excel's online help for function description and parameters.

VBA.STEP.OVER

Refer to Excel's online help for function description and parameters.

VBA.TOGGLE.BREAKPOINT

Refer to Excel's online help for function description and parameters.

VIEW.3D(elevation, perspective, rotation, axes, height%, autoscale)

Adjusts the view of the active 3D chart.

VIEW.DEFINE(ViewName, PrintSettingsInView, RowColumnSettingsInView)

Defines or redefines a view.

VIEW.DELETE(ViewName)

Deletes a view from the active workbook.

VIEW.GET(TypeOfInformation, NameOfView)

Returns an array of views from the active workbook.

VIEW.SHOW(ViewName)
or
VIEW.SHOW?(ViewName)

Shows a view.

VLINE(num_rows)

Scrolls through the active window by a given number of rows.

VOLATILE(logical)

Defines whether a custom function is recalculated whenever a calculation occurs on the worksheet.

VPAGE(numwindows)

Scrolls vertically through the active window by a given number of windows.

VSCROLL(position, row_logical)

Scrolls vertically through the active window by percentage or by row number.

WAIT(serial_number)

Pauses a macro until a given time.

WHILE(logical_test)

Defines a program loop, repeating the enclosed group of functions until the logical_test becomes FALSE.

WINDOW.MAXIMIZE(window_text)

Changes the active window to full size.

WINDOW.MINIMIZE(window_text)

Changes the active window to an icon.

WINDOW.MOVE(x_pos, y_pos, window_text)

Moves the active window.

WINDOW.RESTORE(window_text)

Changes the active window from maximized or minimized to its previous size.

WINDOW.SIZE(width, height, window_text)

Changes the size of the active window.

WINDOW.TITLE(text)

Changes the title of the active window.

WINDOWS(TypesOfWorkbooks, [NameSelectionCriteria])

Returns the names of the given Excel windows.

WORKBOOK.ACTIVATE(sheet_name, new_window_logical)

Activates a worksheet.

WORKBOOK.ADD(name_array, dest_book, position_num)

Moves a worksheet between workbooks.

WORKBOOK.COPY(name_array, dest_book, position_num)

Copies a worksheet between workbooks.

WORKBOOK.DELETE(sheet_text)

Deletes a worksheet(s) from the current workbook.

WORKBOOK.HIDE(sheet_text, very_hidden)

Hides worksheets in the active workbook.

WORKBOOK.INSERT(type_num)

Inserts a worksheet(s) into the current workbook.

WORKBOOK.MOVE(name_array, dest_book, osition_num)

Moves a worksheet(s) between workbooks or within a workbook.

WORKBOOK.NAME(oldname_text, newname_text)

Renames a worksheet in a workbook.

WORKBOOK.NEW
or
WORKBOOK.NEW?()

Adds a worksheet to a workbook.

WORKBOOK.NEXT()

Activates the next worksheet in the active workbook.

WORKBOOK.OPTIONS(sheet_name, bound_logical, new_name)

Renames a worksheet in a workbook.

WORKBOOK.PREV()

Activates the previous worksheet in the active workbook.

WORKBOOK.PROTECT(structure, windows, password)

Controls the protection of workbooks.

WORKBOOK.SCROLL(numsheets, firstlast_logical)

Scrolls through the worksheets in a workbook.

WORKBOOK.SELECT(name_array, active_name, replace)

Selects a worksheet(s) in the active workbook.

WORKBOOK.TAB.SPLIT(ratio_num)

Sets the ratio of the tabs to the horizontal scrollbar.

WORKBOOK.UNHIDE(sheet_text)

Unhides a worksheet(s) in the active workbook.

WORKGROUP(name_array)

Creates a group.

WORKSPACE(fixed, decimals, r1c1, scroll, status, formula, alt_menu_key, ignore_remote, move_after_enter, command_underlines, standard, note, nav_keys, menu_key_action, drag_drop, show_info, cell_editing)

Changes the workspace settings for a workbook.

ZOOM(magnification)

Zooms the display in the active window.

ZTESTM(DataSetOneInputRange, DataSetTwoInputRange, OutputTopLeftCell, FirstRowLabels, Alpha, MeansDifference, DataSetOneVariance, DataSetTwoVariance)

or

ZTESTM?(DataSetOneInputRange, DataSetTwoInputRange, OutputTopLeftCell, FirstRowLabels, Alpha, MeansDifference, DataSetOneVariance, DataSetTwoVariance)

Performs a two-sample z-test for means, assuming known variances.

Part V

Excel Tools

Chapter Snapshot

Microsoft includes additional Excel tools that are not part of the basic Excel software. The tools covered in this chapter are broken out into "add-ins," which you can choose to enable and use if you want. These tools provide a variety of added functions, including the following:

- Examining Excel's additional financial, statistical, and engineering functions

- Saving workbooks automatically

- Managing reporting on multiple views and scenarios

- Performing an electronic slide show with Excel charts and worksheets

- Exploring a tool called the Solver, which performs more advanced What-If functions than Goal Seek performs (Goal Seek is built into Excel, whereas Solver is an add-in)

- Examining View Manager, which saves multiple versions of the same workbook

Getting the most out of these tools is an important aspect of mastering Excel. The Solver, for example, is a powerful tool that can be used to solve difficult problems. Likewise, the View Manager is an invaluable tool for performing various analysis functions in Excel. And enabling the AutoSave add-in frees you from worrying about saving your workbooks every so often.

Using Excel Add-Ins

Excel for Windows 95 contains many additional features that are not part of the core Excel program. You can add these additional capabilities to Excel selectively, so that you use only the features you want. This chapter shows you the way to add, remove, and use the various add-ins that Excel provides.

Installing Excel Add-Ins

You can install the optional add-in tools at the same time you install Excel. If you did not choose to install them at that time, however, you can make them a part of Excel by using the Microsoft Excel Setup program in your Excel folder.

Using the Add-In Manager

After the add-ins are installed on your computer, you can incorporate them into Excel so that they appear on the Excel menus just like any other command. You control the status of the add-ins by using the Add-In Manager. Access the Add-In Manager by pulling down the **T**ools menu and choosing the Add-**I**ns command. The Add-Ins dialog box is shown in figure 18.1.

Figure 18.1

The Add-Ins dialog box.

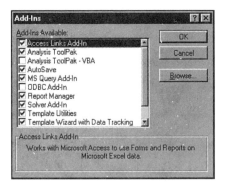

In the dialog box, select or deselect the check boxes to control which add-ins appear on the Excel menus. You also can click on the Help button to find out more about the add-ins available for Excel.

Note   Depending on the speed of your computer, accessing the Add-Ins menu might take a while. Also, selecting new add-ins might take several minutes when Excel installs them after you click on the OK button from the Add-Ins dialog box.

Analysis

Access the analysis tools by pulling down the **T**ools menu and choosing **D**ata Analysis from the menu. This operation causes the Data Analysis dialog box to appear, as shown in figure 18.2.

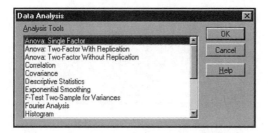

Figure 18.2

*The Data
Analysis
dialog box.*

To use any of the analysis tools, select a tool in the list and then click on the OK button. This procedure causes the dialog box for that tool to appear on your screen. For example, selecting Random Number Generation shows the dialog box in figure 18.3.

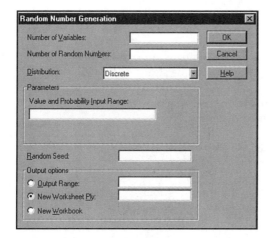

Figure 18.3

*The Random
Number
Generation
dialog box.*

The data analysis tools are very extensive. They are covered in detail in Chapter 9, "Mastering Excel Analytical Tools."

AutoSave

Nothing is more frustrating than spending lots of time on a workbook, only to have your computer crash for some reason with your work unsaved. Although you can help prevent this problem by learning to do frequent saves of your work, you also can use the AutoSave add-in to save automatically.

Access the AutoSave function by pulling down the **T**ools menu and choosing AutoSave. You can see the dialog box shown in figure 18.4.

Figure 18.4

*The AutoSave
dialog box.*

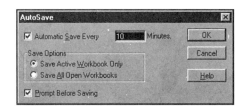

In this dialog box, you can control several functions, as follows:

◆ **Whether to perform the automatic save.** Select or deselect the check box marked Automatic **S**aveEvery.

◆ **The number of minutes between automatic saves.** Change the value in the **M**inutes field.

◆ **Whether to save the active workbook or all open workbooks.** Use the two option buttons in the Save Options box to choose. If you have many workbooks open, but are not modifying more than one of them at a time, you can speed up the AutoSave process by choosing Save Active **W**orkbookOnly. If, however, you are using a single workbook that modifies the other workbooks (by means of a macro, for instance), choose to Save **A**ll open workbooks to ensure that all of your work is saved.

◆ **Whether you are prompted before every automatic save.** Select or deselect the check box marked **P**rompt Before Saving in order to control this option.

Report Manager

Excel enables you to define separate reports in your workbooks. You can use these defined reports to generate multiple reports from your workbooks in one operation.

To set up the reports, access the Report Manager by pulling down the **V**iew menu and choosing **R**eport Manager. You can see the Report Manager dialog box, shown in figure 18.5.

To print predefined reports, select the reports from the dialog box and click on the Print button. To add new reports to the dialog box, click on the **A**dd button, which brings up the dialog box shown in figure 18.6.

You define each report by specifying its name, the sheet in the workbook on which scenario the report is located, and which view you want to show. After you have defined the first report, click on the **A**dd button to create it. When you have several reports defined, use the Move Up and Move Down buttons to reorganize the order of the reports.

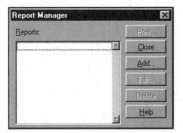

 Note   See the last section in this chapter for more information about the View Manager.

Solver

The Goal Seek function in Excel is fairly limited when you need to solve problems
that have many factors influencing the outcome or when you need to apply constraints to the solution. Excel contains an add-in called the Solver, however, which
can deal with finding optimal solutions to such problems. Examples of problems to
which the Solver might be applied include the following:

◆ Finding optimal scheduling for employees

◆ Maximizing return on investment while keeping within a defined risk in a
complex portfolio

◆ Modeling engine performance, given certain physical constraints and engineering data

◆ Maximizing profit by choosing product mix

These examples suggest only a few of the uses for the Excel Solver. It is an incredibly powerful tool that you can use to help solve extraordinarily difficult problems. Figure 18.7 shows an example problem for which the Solver is suited.

Figure 18.7

An example Solver problem.

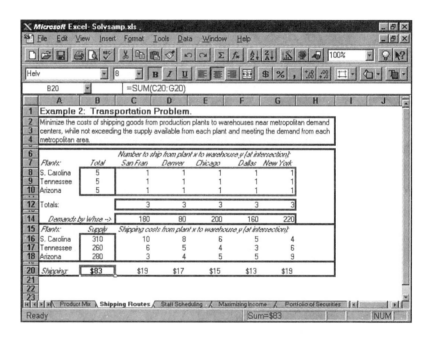

In order to understand the way Solver works, you must understand the structure of the example problem.

Row 7 shows the five warehouses: San Francisco, Denver, Chicago, Dallas, and New York. Cells A8:A10 show the three plants. The numbers at the intersection of the plants and warehouses contain the number of packages to ship to each warehouse from each plant. These numbers are *seeded* with 1s to give the Solver something from which to start. To the left and bottom of the table are the totals shipped from each plant and the totals received from each warehouse. To begin, each warehouse ships five packages, one to each plant.

Below the ship table, cells C14:G14 contain the numbers of packages demanded by each warehouse. One constraint for a successful solution is to find a method that makes certain that each warehouse gets the number of packages it requires.

The bottom table, cells C16:G18, contains the shipping costs from each warehouse to each plant. Cells B16:B18 contain the amount available to ship from each plant.

The bottom line in the worksheet contains the total shipping cost for each warehouse, with the total of all shipping costs shown in cell B20.

At first glance, the worksheet looks somewhat complex, but when you study it, you probably realize that it really is quite simple. It contains no complex math and should be understood easily.

The problem for the Solver can be stated as follows:

◆ Minimize total shipping costs

◆ Meet the demands of each warehouse

◆ Do not exceed the supply available from each plant

Note This worksheet is perfect for this discussion. In real life, however, you are likely to need to add timing constraints, along with production rate at the plants, and so forth. Models such as this one can always be made more complicated, however. The real trick in modeling a complex problem is in finding the least complicated way for you to meet your goals.

After the worksheet is set up, you can access the Solver by pulling down the **T**ools menu and choosing Sol**v**er. This operation displays the main dialog box of the Solver, as shown in figure 18.8.

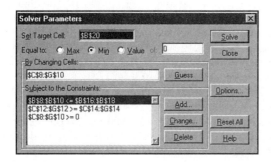

Figure 18.8

The Solver Parameters dialog box.

Table 18.1 discusses the settings in the Solver Parameters dialog box.

TABLE 18.1
Solver Parameters Dialog Box Settings

Setting	Description
S**e**t Target Cell	The key goal to be met by the Solver, it indicates a single cell on the worksheet.
Equal to	The Equal to box enables you to tell the Solver what you want it to do with the target cell. You can choose to find the maximum value possible by choosing the **M**ax button, the minimum value possible by choosing the **M**in button, or a set goal amount defined in the **V**alue field. In this example, you want to minimize shipping costs, so the **M**in button is selected.
By Changing Cells	Indicate in this field which cells on the worksheet should be changed in an attempt to find the optimal solution, or click on the **G**uess button.
Guess	Click on the **G**uess button to cause the Solver to determine which non-formula cells go into the cell indicated in S**e**t Target Cell. These cells are entered automatically into the **B**y Changing Cells field. When you choose **G**uess, Excel examines the target cell, and then moves back through all calculated cells until it finds the cells that do not contain formulas, but are part of the target cell's solution.
S**u**bject to the Constraints	This list box lists all of the constraints in the problem. As you can see, three are set already. The first constraint, B8:B10 <= B16:B18, indicates that the cells in B8:B10 (the total shipped from each plant) must be less than or equal to the values in cells B16:B18 (the amount each plant has available). The second constraint, C12:G12 >=C14:G14, indicates that the total amount shipped to each warehouse must be greater than or equal to the amount required by the warehouse. The final constraint, C8:G10 >= 0, tells the Solver that the amount shipped to each warehouse must be greater than or equal to zero for each plant. This constraint (obvious in real life) keeps the Solver from suggesting solutions that include some negative shipments to certain plants, but still meet the other constraints.

To define a constraint, click on the **A**dd button. The Add Constraint dialog box appears, as shown in figure 18.9.

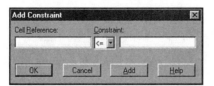

Figure 18.9

The Add Constraint dialog box.

Indicate the cell reference for the constraint in the field provided. Then select a constraint type by clicking on the down arrow in the middle of the dialog box. Possible constraints are >=, =, <=, and Int. Int requires that the values in the cell reference cells be full integers. (If you are trying to find optimal schedules, for example, you can't very well schedule part of a truck, or part of a person.) After you have chosen the constraint, you can enter the value of the constraint in the **C**onstraint field. Click on OK to return to the Solver dialog box, or click on **A**dd to store the constraint but keep the Add Constraint dialog box on-screen to define additional constraints.

You can control the behavior of the Solver with the Solver Options dialog box, accessed through the **O**ptions button. Figure 18.10 shows the Solver Options dialog box, and table 18.2 shows its settings.

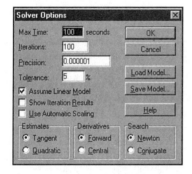

Figure 18.10

The Solver Options dialog box.

TABLE 18.2
Solver Options Dialog Box Settings

Setting	Description
Max **T**ime	Sets the maximum amount of time that the Solver can use to solve the problem. You can enter a value as high as 32,767 seconds in this field.
Iterations	Limits the maximum number of iterations that the Solver can take. You can enter up to 32,767 in this field.

continues

TABLE 18.2, CONTINUED
Solver Options Dialog Box Settings

Setting	Description
Precision	This field controls the precision that the Solver uses to find solutions. You can enter a value here between 0 and 1. A smaller number (fewer decimal places) indicates greater precision. This value controls the tolerance used for constraints.
Tol**e**rance	The Tolerance settings are used when you solve problems that have integer constraints. When you add integer constraints, you require the Solver to solve many subproblems in finding the answer to the larger problem. The value you enter in this field controls the percentage error allowed in the optimal solution. Use this field to speed up the Solver for problems with integer constraints.
Assume Linear **M**odel	If all of the relationships in a particular problem are linear, selecting this check box can make the Solver run faster.
Show Iteration **R**esults	If this check box is selected, the Solver stops on each iteration to show you the results in progress. This option can be useful in learning why the Solver is arriving at solutions, which do not seem to be correct, and can suggest additional constraints that keep the Solver on the right track for a correct solution.
Use Automatic Scaling	When you solve a problem where the inputs and outputs have an order of magnitude differences (such as percentage yield on very large dollar investments), you can get more accurate results by enabling this check box.
Estimates	The two choices in the Estimates box tell the Solver how to come up with the initial estimates used for the solving process. Choose Ta**n**gent for the Solver to use linear extrapolation from a tangent vector. Choose **Q**uadratic for the Solver to use Quadratic Extrapolation.
Derivatives	You can choose between **F**orward differencing and **C**entral differencing for estimating partial derivatives for the target and constraints. Use **C**entral differencing when the Solver gives you a message saying that it cannot improve on the results already obtained.

Setting	Description
Search	When the Solver comes up with an estimate during an iteration, it must decide in which direction to search to proceed to the optimal solution. **N**ewton searching is the default method, but it can consume large amounts of memory for complex problems. In such cases, use C**o**njugate searching, which is slower, but requires less memory.
Save Model	Click on this button to save the Solver parameters for the problem to a cell range. This operation saves the information on the main Solver dialog box, such as the target cell and constraints, but not the options set in the options dialog box. To work on a Solver problem over multiple sessions with Excel, use this option to save your parameters, and then use the **L**oad Model option to reload the parameters when you return to your workbook.
Load Model	Click on this button to load a model from a cell range.

After changing the Solver options, click on the OK button to return to the main Solver dialog box. To solve for the optimal solution, click on the **S**olve button. When the Solver has finished calculating, it shows you the results, as shown in figure 18.11.

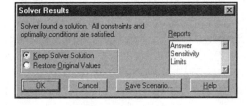

Figure 18.11

The Solver Results dialog box.

In the completion dialog box, you can choose to view reports of the actions taken by the Solver. Click on each type of report you want to see in the **R**eports box before clicking on OK to complete the Solving process. The results of the example worksheet are shown in figure 18.12.

View Manager

You can use the View Manager to store different *views* of your worksheet without being required to maintain different sheets in your workbook. You might, for example, create different views that show various levels of detail and use the View

Manager to switch quickly between the different views. The View Manager stores aspects of your current view, such as zoom level, pane and window positions, gridline appearance, and so on.

First, you should create a view of the completed worksheet so that you can quickly switch back to it at any time. To create this first view, follow these steps:

1. Pull down the **V**iew menu and choose **V**iew Manager. You see the View Manager dialog box, shown in figure 18.13.

2. Click on the **A**dd button to bring up a new dialog box, which enables you to control which aspects of the current view to save (see fig. 8.14).

3. In the Add View dialog box, enter the name to be used for the current view in the **N**ame field.

4. If you want current print settings stored in the view, select the **P**rint Settings check box. If you want hidden row and column status to be saved, select the Hidden **R**ows & Columns check box. Click on the OK button to save the view and exit the View Manager.

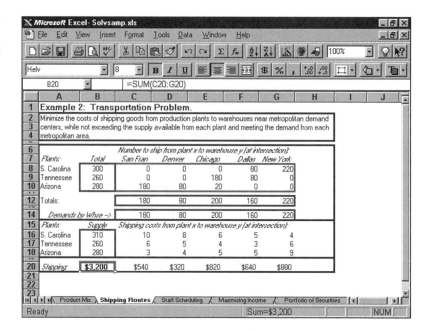

Figure 18.12

The completed Solver example.

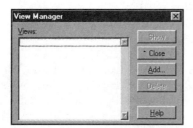

Figure 18.13

The View Manager dialog box.

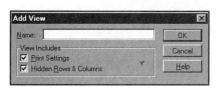

Figure 18.14

The Add View dialog box.

Now, you can create another view that you would like to store. When you have completed changing the worksheet viewing components to suit your taste, activate the View Manager again and add the new view.

After you have added the views you want to store, switch between them by activating the View Manager, choosing the view you want in the dialog box, and then clicking on the **S**how button to display the worksheet instantly in the stored fashion.

Chapter Snapshot

Many people use Microsoft Excel at work and, consequently, interact with others in the company that also use Excel. Wouldn't it be nice if Excel helped you work more collaboratively within your organization? What if it let you more effectively manage shared files, for example? Fortunately, it does all this and more.

In this chapter, you learn about the following:

◆ Sharing Excel files on a network

◆ Tracking control information for shared files

◆ Preserving the security of your files

◆ Using shared lists in Excel

◆ Creating customized templates for your workgroup

One of the biggest benefits that networks bring companies is the ability to rapidly share and process information within workgroups. Taking advantage of the features shown in this chapter will increase the efficiency of you and your Excel-using peers.

C H A P T E R

19

Excel in Workgroups

Most tightly-knit groups within a company that use a network set up and use shared areas on the common file server in which everyone in the workgroup can access and save files. This sort of structure greatly expands the ability of the workers in the department to get their jobs done, particularly in organizations that ask every worker to get more done with less. Taking advantage of the power of your network to enable your peers to work more smoothly together can pay large, if subtle, dividends.

Excel supports this model of information sharing. It has features that make working together easier and more manageable.

Sharing Files on a Network

If you often work on files that are stored in areas to which many others have access, you will often try to open a file that someone else is already working on, or they will try to open a file that you are using and changing. Dealing with this simple and common occurrence is important in making sure that confusion doesn't ensue.

Excel warns you when you try to open a file that someone else is already using. When someone first opens a file for editing, that file is locked on the file server, such that another user cannot modify it while it's locked. Excel helps you deal with this gracefully by warning you with the File Reservation dialog box, shown in figure 19.1.

Figure 19.1

When you try to open a file that someone else is using, you see this dialog box.

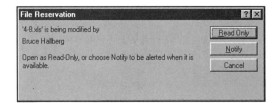

You have four ways of dealing with the dialog box shown in figure 19.1: you can select Cancel and try again later, hoping that the file is free then; you can call the other person on the phone (if you know who he is) and ask him to close the document so you can use it; you can select **N**otify and have Excel tell you when the other person is finished working with it automatically; or you can click on the OK button and make a copy of the document.

Making a copy of the document means that whatever is saved to the disk at that moment will be loaded into your computer, with the indicator (Copy) appearing after the file name in the title bar of the application. You can then freely edit the file.

Using the **N**otify feature means that the file will be opened for Read-Only viewing. When the other person finishes working with the file, you will be told with the dialog box shown in figure 19.2. Choosing Read-**W**rite will then reopen the document that they saved, with their changes intact.

If you opened a file in Read-Only mode, you cannot save it to the original file name, although you can certainly save additional changes to a new file name.

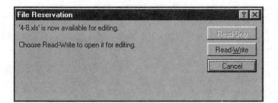

Figure 19.2

When you choose Notify and the document becomes available, you see this dialog box.

Using Excel's Shared Lists

New to Excel for Windows 95 is the ability for more than one person to edit a single file at the same time, much like a multiuser database program. In order to do this productively, however, you need to understand how the feature works.

Shared lists only let you add, change, or delete data. You cannot make formatting changes to the shared list file, or add or change formulas. This is why these workbooks are called *shared lists*—they are primarily used for list management duties within Excel. The following are two good examples of where you want to use this feature:

◆ A workgroup may keep a schedule of their shared "to-do" items in Excel (a finance department's period closing schedule would be a good example). Shared lists let all the members maintain the list simultaneously, adding and deleting items as needed.

◆ You may have some kind of departmental database that you keep in Excel workbooks. Perhaps it is a list of people that request information from different people within the department. Each person can add the relevant data simultaneously. The person who is responsible for sending out the information can also access the file to see what they have to do.

Any time you maintain lists of data in Excel where you want more than one person to access and maintain the data simultaneously is potentially a candidate for the shared list feature.

The first person who opens a workbook has the responsibility for turning on the Shared Lists feature so that others can have concurrent access to the file. You do this through the File menu's Shared Lists command. Selecting this for the first time brings up the dialog box shown in figure 19.3.

Figure 19.3

Before using a shared list workbook, enable multiuser editing with the check box shown in the Shared Lists dialog box.

 Note Once you designate a workbook as a shared list, the setting persists until you turn off the feature, even through successive saves and opens.

After turning on the Multi-User check box, Excel immediately does a Save As of the file, so that the file on the shared network drive is immediately saved with the Shared List setting enabled. This first save after enabling multiuser access is required in order for others to access the file in a multiuser fashion.

 Note You can change the formatting and formulas in a shared list workbook, but only after turning off the shared lists feature. When you finish your formula or formatting changes, you can re-enable shared lists so that others can access the revised file.

The key to understanding shared list workbooks is knowing how conflicts within a file are sorted out—some are sorted out automatically, while others require intervention when you save the file.

Let's look at both cases. First, say that two people are working on a single workbook. One person inserts a row of data and saves his or her copy of the file. The other person has not inserted that new row. What happens when the second person goes to save their version of the file? The answer is that the new row added by the first person is automatically inserted into the second person's workbook during the save. Inserting a row would not generally cause a conflict with any other work the second person did, so it's updated automatically. Excel does tell you when it does this, however, with the dialog box shown in figure 19.4.

More tricky is the case where a change that the first user makes conflicts with something the second user has done within the file. For example, the first person changes the text in a cell in one way, while the second person makes a different change to the same cell. How does Excel handle that?

When the second person goes to save their copy of the workbook and there is a conflict like the one presented in the previous paragraph, they see the Conflict Resolution dialog box, shown in figure 19.5.

New Riders Publishing
INSIDE
SERIES

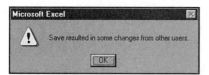

Figure 19.4

Changes that don't present a conflict are updated automatically at the time of saving the file.

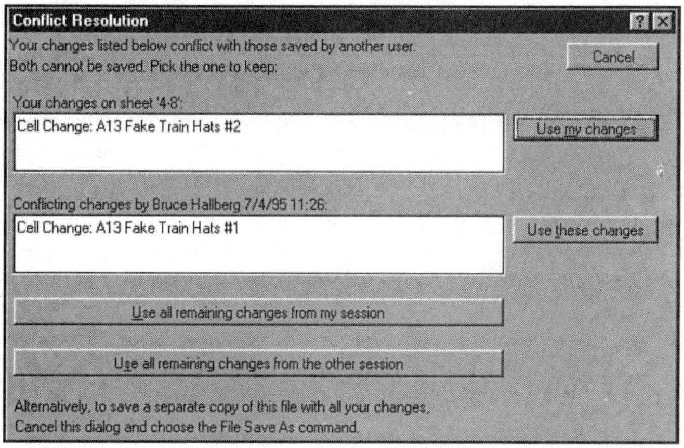

Figure 19.5

Trying to save information that conflicts with what another user has done causes this dialog box to display.

This dialog box is relatively self-explanatory. You can choose to do one of the following:

◆ Make your change succeed, in which case the first person's conflicting change is overwritten.

◆ Use the other person's change, in which your conflicting change is overwritten by theirs.

◆ Save the file with your changes to a new file name that doesn't conflict with the main file. This is a good strategy when you're not sure which change should prevail, or when you simply want to save your changes for reference at some other time, but want to accept the other person's changes for the time being.

You can also click on the two bottom buttons in the dialog box in which you elect to resolve all conflicts with the other person's changes or with your own changes.

Excel offers you two tools that let you more easily manage shared lists: the ability to view who is using the file at any given time, and the Conflict History sheet.

At any time that you're working on a shared list workbook, you can see who else is working on it by accessing the S<u>h</u>ared Lists command in the <u>F</u>ile menu. The Status tab shows you who has the file open for editing, and when they opened it (see fig. 19.6).

Figure 19.6

The Shared Lists dialog box shows you who else is using the file.

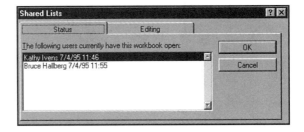

Excel also lets you keep track of any conflicts in the file, as a sort of audit-trail that can help you sort out problems. To see this, make sure the Show <u>C</u>onflict History check box (on the Editing tab of the Shared Lists dialog) is selected. When you do this, your workbook will have a Conflict History sheet, like the one shown in figure 19.7.

Figure 19.7

You can view the history of conflicts in the file in the Conflict History sheet.

	A	B	C	D	E	F
1	Action Type	Date	Time	Who	Change	Sheet Location
2						
3	Won	7/4/95	12:02:46 PM	Kathy Ivens	Cell Change	8-Ap
4	Lost	7/4/95	12:02:51 PM	Bruce Hallberg	Cell Change	8-Ap
5	Won	7/4/95	12:02:54 PM	Bruce Hallberg	Cell Change	8-Ap
6	Lost	7/4/95	12:02:46 PM	Kathy Ivens	Cell Change	8-Ap

Setting Document Properties

One of the tricks to making effective use of Excel in a shared environment involves using the file properties to track information about a particular file. With these properties, you can track items such as the following:

◆ Author

◆ Subject

◆ Keywords

◆ Comments

◆ Custom properties, such as editor, client name, and a host of other choices

To access the file's properties, pull down the File menu and choose Properties. The Summary tab contains the main tracking information, shown in figure 19.8.

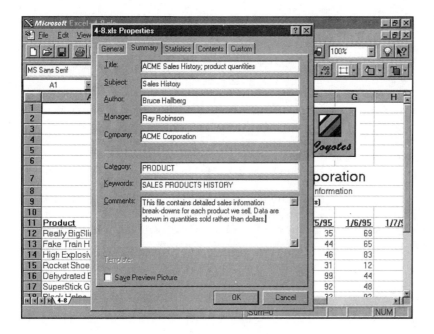

Figure 19.8

You can save summary information about the files you work on in the Summary tab.

Excel also includes a host of custom file properties that you can make good use of. These are found in the Custom tab of the Properties dialog box (see fig. 19.9).

Figure 19.9

Use custom properties to track more detailed information about your files.

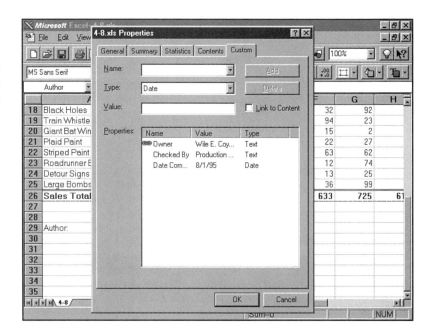

Access the custom properties using the **N**ame drop-down list—there are over 25 different properties available to you. After choosing a custom property, choose its data type in the **T**ype drop-down list (choose from Text, Number, Date, or Yes/No). Then, type the information into the **V**alue field. Finally, click on the **A**dd button to store the property. Existing properties show in the **P**roperties window.

You can develop some more complicated mechanisms using the **L**ink to Content check box. When selected, you can link a property to data contained in the file itself. For instance, you can reference named cells in Excel, or bookmarks in Word. You must have defined the named cells or bookmarks first, however.

Routing Files

If you use Microsoft Exchange, or a similar compatible e-mail system, you can route your Excel files to others on your e-mail system. You access this feature by choosing Add **R**outing Slip in the **F**ile menu. You see the Routing Slip dialog box shown in figure 19.10.

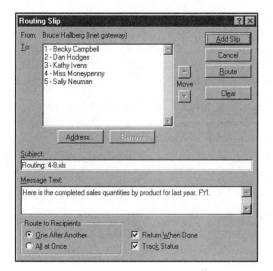

Figure 19.10

Use routing slips to easily distribute Excel files to others in the company.

Add recipients using the **A**ddress button. Type a subject and message text so that the recipients will know why they are getting the file. Then, choose your routing method. You can choose to send the file to A**l**l at once or **O**ne after another. Selecting the Trac**k** Status check box causes an e-mail message to be automatically sent to you each time a recipient forwards the file onto the next person. You can also choose to have the file automatically sent back to you once the last person is finished with it.

After filling in the Routing Slip, choose the **A**dd Slip button to store the routing slip, or the **S**end button to put the file into your e-mail outbox.

Maintaining Security

When working in a shared environment, protecting the security of your documents can be important. You can do this with your Excel files with file-specific passwords.

To add a password to an Excel file, simply choose the Save **A**s command in the **F**ile menu. Then, click on the **O**ptions button to reveal the dialog box shown in figure 19.11.

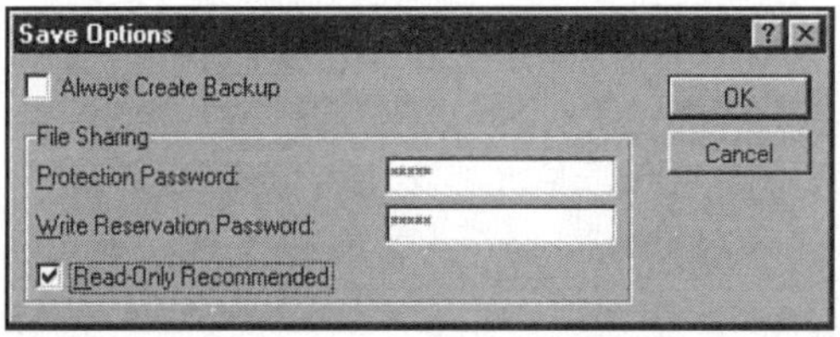

Figure 19.11

Use the Save Options dialog box to add password protection to your files.

There are two different passwords you can set: **P**rotection Password and **W**rite Reservation Password. The protection password denies access to the file entirely unless the individual knows the password. The write reservation password lets anyone open the file in read-only mode, but they can only make changes to the file if they know the write reservation password.

You can also specify that a file be **R**ead-Only Recommended. If this check box is selected, Excel will warn the person opening the file that he or she should open it in read-only mode. While users have the choice of going ahead and opening it with write access, this check box causes Excel to remind them that they should be careful in doing so.

Setting Up Workgroup Templates

In Excel, when you go to create a new file using the **N**ew command in the **F**ile menu, you see a tabbed dialog box that lists possible files and templates on which you can base your new file. Excel creates the standard tabs and files when you first install it.

A workgroup may have many additional template files that are used specifically within the group. You can create special Workgroup Templates that contain these group-specific files. When you do this, they appear in the File New dialog box as if they are part of Excel.

Files that you would like to appear in the File New dialog box must be placed in the Excel Templates directory, which is in the directory into which you installed Excel. You can create new folders within Templates; these appear automatically as new tabs in the File New dialog box.

After creating these folders and files, any time you use the File New command you automatically see the tabs and files that you placed in the Templates folder, as shown in figure 19.12.

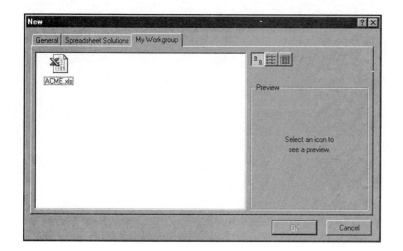

Figure 19.12

*Once you've set
up new templates,
they appear auto-
matically in the
New dialog box.*

Part VI

Appendixes

New Riders Publishing
INSIDE
SERIES

Getting Excel Help

When you are learning and using Excel for Windows 95, questions inevitably arise, and your work comes to a screeching halt until you find answers. As a general rule, you should become a little familiar with where and how to find information before you really need it. This appendix uncovers all those places you can go for help, including the following:

◆ The Excel program

◆ Reference materials

◆ Online help

◆ Microsoft support

If you know where to look, you can get fast relief and proceed with work as planned.

Experts estimate that as many as 98 percent of the people who call for software support already had the answer to their questions available in the manuals that came with their programs. You should not be surprised, then, to learn that Microsoft charges for telephone support—after all, it costs money to hire all those employees to read the manual to people who call.

Why do so many people call for software support, anyway? With a large, complex program like Excel for Windows 95, it is sometimes hard to know where to begin to look for answers.

Running the Tutorial

One of the first things to know is the correct terminology. Clearly, you might find it difficult to look up an answer when you are having a problem with a "whatcha-macallit," only to find out that the Excel program refers to it as a "thingy." Utilizing the tutorial that comes with Excel is a great way to start learning the correct terminology.

Note The first time you start Excel after installing it on your computer, Excel automatically presents you with its built-in tutorial. If you are new to Excel, spend the time to run this tutorial. It is a good way to get your feet wet with Excel.

To start the tutorial, use the following steps:

1. Pull down the **H**elp menu.

2. Choose Quick Preview.

The Quick Preview function is divided into four lessons; each one takes about seven minutes to complete. These lessons cover getting started, new features in Excel for Windows 95, getting help while you work, and a special preview for people moving to Excel from Lotus 1-2-3. After you have mastered the information in the Quick Preview, choose **E**xamples and Demos from the **H**elp menu to get more comprehensive information about a wide variety of Excel topics. Many of these topics include demonstrations on ways to accomplish different tasks, along with explanatory text and pictures.

Using Excel Help

After you have progressed through the tutorial, take some time to browse through the Help feature that comes with the Excel program. If you did not install Help (yes, it does take up some extra disk space), you should install it now. To begin the Excel Help, simply click on the word **H**elp in the upper right corner of the Excel Window.

You also can access help for specific parts of the screen, toolbar buttons, and so on, by clicking on the Help button on the Standard toolbar. Your cursor changes to a pointer with a question mark. Point to the part of Excel with which you want

additional help, then click on the left mouse button. You also can use this method to choose menu commands to get help.

Using Excel Wizards

In Excel for Windows 95, Microsoft has included Wizards for various functions. A Wizard (ChartWizard, Function Wizard, TextWizard, Answer Wizard, and so on) automatically starts up when you begin using the tool it accompanies. Each Excel Wizard is discussed in its appropriate place in this book. They help make Excel more "user-friendly" by walking you through different procedures step- by-step.

Tip
Take advantage of Excel's new Answer Wizard. This Wizard is unlike any you've used in Excel before because it takes your plain-English question, interprets what you want to know, and then presents you with a selection of topics to choose from that will help you get rolling with the function or feature you want to use.

Viewing Demonstrations of Excel Features

You do not need to go to the nearest computer store for a quick demonstration of ways to use various functions. Click on **H**elp, then select **E**xamples and Demos for a helpful sneak preview.

Reading the Manual

The manuals that come with Excel actually are quite good and are fairly complete, unlike many computer software manuals. Their only real shortcoming is that various topics are not explained terribly well; they are, however, well laid out. The manuals are a great place to look when you have a question about Excel (if you can't find it in *this* book, of course!).

Reading This Book

Inside Excel for Windows 95 is a useful resource for you, also. The book is written and organized for maximum reference value. See the Introduction for organization information, type conventions, and special icons. Whether you are a beginner or an advanced Excel user, this book will provide a wide range of helpful information and valuable advice.

Getting Excel Help on CompuServe

If none of the help resources already mentioned answer your questions, do not pick up the phone to call (and pay for) Microsoft's Excel help line just yet. Instead, pick up the phone and call *CompuServe Information Service* (CIS) to get a CompuServe account.

Nearly all large (or even moderately-sized) software or hardware companies today provide help on CIS, and Microsoft is no exception. This support is a win-win situation—companies that have their own CIS forums find that it takes far fewer people to support *a lot* more users, and it costs you considerably *less* money to get support on CIS than it does to call the help line.

Understanding CompuServe

If you are not familiar with CIS, take a few minutes to read this section.

You can think of CompuServe as the world's largest computer *bulletin board system* (BBS). A real bulletin board contains messages to specific people and general information for everyone. CIS has everything a real bulletin board has and a whole lot more. In addition to the business-related forums, it has many hobby- and interest-related categories, as well as tremendous databases of information.

The cost to access CompuServe varies with the pricing plan you select, as well as the country in which you reside. For United States residents, it costs approximately $10–18 per hour.

 Note You can greatly reduce your costs by using an automatic navigational program. An *autonav* program can go online and offline very quickly, picking up most of the information you need at full speed—because you told it what to get before it went online. Most autonav programs are available for downloading from CompuServe, although they are published independently. Good programs to evaluate include OzCIS, TapCIS, CISOP, and CsNAV, to name a few, although there are other good programs as well. If you decide to keep and use these shareware programs, you need to register and pay for the programs with the respective software companies.

The best part about CompuServe is that the nearest node (telephone access number) is usually only a local telephone call away. Every major city, and lots and lots of smaller ones, have a CompuServe node.

New Riders Publishing
INSIDE
SERIES

In addition to accessing CompuServe and all it has to offer, you can do the following:

◆ Send and receive Internet, MCI, and MHS mail

◆ Send postal letters (which later are printed at certain CompuServe locations and mailed as regular U.S. postal mail)

◆ Send faxes

◆ Access Internet World Wide Web pages, UseNet news and mail groups, and much, much more

CompuServe provides a lot of different services. Some of these services cost a little extra.

Tip   For a complete guide to CompuServe and its many uses, see New Riders Publishing's *Inside CompuServe, Third Edition*, by Richard Wagner.

Getting Started on CompuServe

You can open a CompuServe account in a number of ways, as follows:

◆ Contact a friend who already has a CompuServe account—your friend receives some usage credit for referring you, and you receive a usage credit for signing up.

◆ Call CompuServe Information Service at 1-800-848-8990 or 1-614-529-6887.

◆ Browse your local computer software store for a box that says "CompuServe" on the side. It contains all the information and software you need to go online and get started immediately.

Note   As soon as you get a CompuServe account, go to the Practice area (**GO PRACTICE**) to practice posting and reading messages. This forum is free of connect time charges so that you do not have to pay to learn. You can also find some useful information in the libraries there. (Libraries are discussed later in this appendix.)

Setting Up Your Computer

All you need to use CompuServe is a modem attached to your computer. If you do not have a CompuServe access program, you also need some communications software, which you can find in any computer retail store or catalog. That's it!

Talking to Microsoft on CompuServe

If you have other Microsoft programs, you should be happy to know that Microsoft
supports all of them on CIS without a surcharge other than the normal CIS fees. To
get to the top level menu of all the Microsoft services on CompuServe, type **GO
MICROSOFT** from any ! prompt.

Note You navigate through CompuServe using "GO" commands. CompuServe, in its
ASCII rendition, is not pretty, and it might seem a little cryptic. CompuServe uses an
exclamation mark for its prompt. At any ! prompt, you can type **HELP** to get the
help you need. The prompt also is where you type **GO** words.

Three main areas in the Microsoft forums provide the support you need for getting
help with Excel. These areas are discussed in the next three sections.

Accessing the Excel Forum

Each forum on CompuServe is divided into several sections to better categorize
questions and answers and the conversations that occur. The Excel forum sections (at
the time this book was written) are set up as shown in figure A.1.

Figure A.1

*The Microsoft
Excel Forum
Message Section
Menu.*

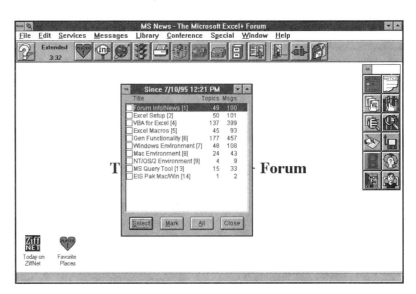

You can see that your questions should be posted in Section 6, "Gen Functionality." In
case you are wondering, the numbers to the right of the message sections indicate the
number of topics, or *message threads* (conversations) on the message board, followed
by the total number of messages in that section.

Microsoft forums change frequently, so by the time you read this, Section 6 may indeed be called "AccessLinks." Be sure to check the section you want to view or post a message to before you post it, simply to save the sysop (system operator, or overseer of the forum) some time and to help you get a speedier reply.

If you need to post a question on the message board, keep the following guidelines in mind:

◆ **Be Polite.** Even if you are frustrated, keep your temper in check. That old adage "You can catch more flies with honey than with vinegar" applies just as much on CompuServe as it does anywhere else. People are more willing to be helpful if you are courteous.

◆ **Once is enough.** Do not post the same message more than once on a forum. If your message is in the wrong place, the sysop moves it to the correct message section or lets you know where you might post the message for a better response. Remember that people do not like to pay to download or read the same message more than once.

◆ **Be concise.** Provide all the pertinent information, but do not wander from the point too much. For instance, including such items as "I stayed up for 82 hours straight trying to solve this problem" does not help in providing people with the information they need to answer your question. You should include the following information in your message:

  ◆ The version of Excel you are using.

  ◆ Your operating system (DOS, OS/2, and so on) and version number.

  ◆ Your hardware manufacturer and model.

  ◆ The keystrokes that you used just prior to having a problem (if applicable). Try to reproduce the problem before you report it.

  ◆ If you receive an error message, write down the exact wording so that you can include it in your message.

Most forums try to provide answers within 24 hours. Some questions are answered in a matter of an hour or two, and most are answered within the targeted 24-hour period. Do not despair, however, if your question is not answered immediately.

In addition to the sysops, a lot of knowledgeable people tend to "hang out" on the forums (including many of the people involved in writing and producing this book). If your question is answered by someone other than a Microsoft employee, chances are fairly high that the person is well-informed. Very rarely do you receive incorrect answers or bad advice anywhere on CompuServe. Because the messages are visible to be read by anyone with a CompuServe account, people correct information they know is wrong.

> **Note** One of the things that makes a support forum on CompuServe so viable is that advice to one person can be read by all people who choose to read the messages. If you pay attention to what other people are asking, you might not need to post your own question, because it might have already been asked and answered. You might also be able to avoid some pitfalls or mistakes by reading what others are doing.

Using the Microsoft Knowledge Base

You might not even need to post a question on Microsoft's Excel forum if you utilize Microsoft's Knowledge Base. The Knowledge Base is a special database that formerly was available only to Microsoft Technical Support personnel—the people you talk to when you call Microsoft Support. Now, you can use it in your own home or office at no cost over and above the regular CompuServe charges.

To get to the Microsoft Knowledge Base, simply type **GO MSKB**, or select it from the Microsoft main menu (**GO MICROSOFT**). However you get there, you should end up at a menu that looks like figure A.2.

Figure A.2

The Microsoft Knowledge Base main menu.

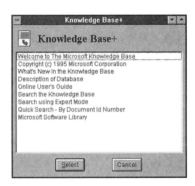

You should read item 4—Description of Database—and item 5—Online User's Guide—before you try to use the database. This area cannot be automated with an auto-navigational program, and the clock is ticking while you are online. Learning the way in which the Knowledge Base works before spending lots of time with it pays off in reduced connect-time charges.

Accessing the Microsoft Software Library

Another valuable area is the Microsoft Software Library. As you can see from the menu shown in figure A.2, you can choose selection number 9, or you can go there directly by typing **GO MSL**. This library contains all sorts of files, including device

drivers, samples, information files, sample spreadsheets, and even macro code samples. These sample files not only serve as good examples, but might also be a good starting point for a project.

You can utilize this area much better by finding out what information you want to download beforehand in the Knowledge Base. (You cannot automate access to this area, either.) This area is particularly cryptic, as shown in figure A.3.

Figure A.3

The Microsoft Software Library main menu.

Finding Other Files

CompuServe is rich with all types of resources, including many shareware programs, add-ons, and files. (*Shareware* is try-it-before-you-buy-it software—Excel is *not* shareware, although many of the tools available for download from CIS are.)

CompuServe File Finder is the central place to go to find out where all the Excel shareware files might be found. Type **GO FILEFINDER** to get there, and start with a keyword search of "EXCEL." You need to have additional selection criteria in mind because so many files containing keywords of Excel exist. As of the date of this book, a keyword search for EXCEL in Filefinder found 407 files that had the word "Excel" in their descriptions.

Again, this area of CompuServe cannot be auto-navigated—have some idea of what you are looking for before you go there.

Talking to Macmillan Publishing

Macmillan Publishing also maintains a forum on CompuServe where many of the authors, editors, and other readers hang out (**GO MACMILLAN**). New Riders Publishing is a division of Macmillan Publishing, and you can post a message there if you have a question or comment about the book. This area is not intended for technical support for Excel, but rather for comments about Macmillan Publishing books.

If you do not want everyone with a CompuServe account (more than one million people) to see your comments about this book, you can send messages directly to persons involved with this book. New Riders can be reached at CompuServe ID 70031,2231, and author Bruce Hallberg's private CompuServe ID is 76376,515.

Calling Microsoft

If you still have not found the answer to your question in the Microsoft Excel help system, demos, tutorial, wizard, manual, or this book, and you cannot find what you are looking for on CompuServe (which is very unlikely), you should call Microsoft for support.

 Note   Before you call Microsoft, take a look at the Common Questions in the help files, as well as the README file that was installed with Excel. You might be able to save yourself some time and money by finding the answers you need there.

Like your CompuServe messages, make sure you have the following information handy before you call:

◆ The version of Excel you are using, along with the serial number, which you can find in the Excel box or by accessing **A**bout from the **H**elp menu.

◆ Your operating system and version number.

◆ Your hardware manufacturer and model.

◆ The keystrokes you used just prior to having a problem (if applicable). Try to reproduce the problem before you report it.

◆ If you receive an error message, write down the exact wording so that you can include it in your message.

Microsoft has two calling plans; each one costs a lot more money and takes more time than any of the options listed previously.

Accessing Free Support

Between the hours of 6:00 a.m. and 6:00 p.m. Pacific time, Microsoft has a free support line available (although you do have to pay for the long-distance phone charges). This number is 206-635-7070. Because this number is for free support, you should expect a fair amount of time on hold. You hear status messages regarding the average time spent waiting, so you can judge whether to stay on the line or try again later.

Accessing Paid Support

Microsoft offers "priority access" support 24 hours a day, 7 days a week, excluding holidays. The numbers vary depending on the payment plan you choose. Here are the numbers:

◆ 1-900-555-2100. The cost is $2 per minute ($25 maximum), and the charges appear on your telephone bill.

◆ 1-800-936-5700. The charge is $25 per "incident" and can be billed to your VISA, MasterCard, or American Express.

An "incident" means that if the question or problem cannot be taken care of with one telephone call, no additional fee is charged for calls until the problem is resolved.

 Note If you want to tell Microsoft what you would like to see in the next version of Excel, then you need to call 1-206-936-WISH.

Using Other Telephone Support

Microsoft offers telephone support to people with special needs. If you have hearing difficulties, you can call Microsoft's text telephone (TT/TDD) at 1-206-635-4948 between 6:00 a.m. and 6:00 p.m. Pacific time, Monday through Friday (excluding holidays).

For faxes, and to receive recorded answers to questions commonly asked, you can dial Microsoft's FastTips telephone number at 1-800-936-4100, 24 hours a day, 7 days a week. You also can receive articles concerning technical subjects (solving installation problems, resolving compatibility problems, and so on) via the FastTips line.

Finding Excel Training

If you are really stumped about all this Excel business, you might want to consider some formal training courses. In addition to local PC stores that offer many training courses, Microsoft has officially sanctioned training courses and centers around the United States. Call 1-800-227-4679 between 6:30 a.m. and 5:30 p.m. Pacific time to find out the location nearest you.

Closing Advice

As you can see by browsing this appendix, lots of help options are open to you when working with Excel. To overcome likely problems, keep the following advice in mind when you are working with any software program:

◆ **Be patient.** Expect to take some time to look through this book, the help files in the Excel program, and the manuals. Excel is a large, complex program, and it might take some time and experimentation to find the right answers.

◆ **Take frequent breaks.** It does not matter if you walk your kids or pet your dog, but do take frequent breaks. You are better off in the long run.

◆ **Take small steps.** Try one thing at a time—do not make lots of changes all at the same time. Lots of changes can cause confusion and can make a mess even worse. It also makes it harder to retrace your steps if you have a crash or get an error message.

◆ **Look out for bugs.** Programmers are human, and humans do make mistakes. Although Excel is exceptionally clean compared to many software programs, you might run into an occasional problem that is rooted in the program itself. Again, patience is the key here. If you think you have found a software bug, it is very important that you write down all the information concerning the bug and report it to Microsoft. Often, they have fixes for bugs already reported and can send those fixes to you for a nominal fee.

◆ **Have fun!** Remember, the future of Western civilization is not at stake here. Maintain your perspective.

APPENDIX

B

Keyboard Shortcuts

This appendix contains a number of useful keyboard shortcuts. Learning the following keys can make you more productive with Excel. Use the following tables as a handy reference guide.

Tables B.1–B.3 lists the keys you use to enter and edit data. Use these keys to navigate your documents, access the Clipboard functions, and control calculations in your documents. You'll use some shortcuts more often than others.

TABLE B.1
Entering Data

Key or Key Combination	Action
F2	Edits the current cell.
Enter	Completes an action.
Esc	Cancels an act.
F4	Repeats the last act (Redo).
Ctrl+Z	Undoes the last act (Undo).
Ctrl+Shift++ (plus sign)	Inserts new blank cells.
Ctrl+– (hyphen)	Deletes the selected object or cells.
Del	Clears the selected area of formulas and data; when editing a cell, deletes the character to the right of the current cursor position.
Ctrl+X	Cuts the selection.
Ctrl+C	Copies the selection.
Ctrl+V	Pastes to the selection.
Backspace	Edits the formula after clearing the cell entry, or backspaces over a character; when editing a cell, erases the previous character.
Shift+F2	Edits a cell note.
F3	Pastes a name into a formula.
Shift+F3	Activates the Function Wizard.
Ctrl+F3	Defines a name.
Ctrl+Shift+F3	Creates names from cell text.
F9 or Ctrl+= (equals sign)	Calculates all documents in all open workbooks; if you highlight a section, calculates only that section.

Key or Key Combination	Action
Shift+F9	Calculates the active document.
Alt+=	Inserts the AutoSum formula.
Ctrl+; (semicolon)	Enters the date.
Ctrl+Shift+: (colon)	Enters the time.
Ctrl+D	Fills down.
Ctrl+R	Fills right.
Enter	Moves down through a selection.
Shift+Enter	Moves up through a selection.
Tab	Moves right through a selection.
Shift+Tab	Moves left through a selection.
Ctrl+Shift+A	Completes the punctuation for you when you first type in a valid function name in a formula.
Alt+Down arrow	Activates the AutoComplete list.

TABLE B.2
Editing Data

Key or Key Combination	Action
Ctrl+X	Cuts the selection to the Clipboard.
Ctrl+C	Copies the selection to the Clipboard.
Ctrl+V	Pastes the selection from the Clipboard.
Del	Clears the selection of formulas and data.
Ctrl+Shift++	Inserts blank cells.
Ctrl+−	Deletes the selected calls.
Ctrl+Z	Undoes the last act.

TABLE **B.3**
Working in Cell Entries

Key or Key Combination	Action
=	Starts a formula.
Alt+Enter	Inserts a carriage return.
Arrow keys	Moves one character up, down, left, or right.
Backspace	Deletes the character to the left of the insertion point, or deletes the selection.
Ctrl+´ (apostrophe)	Copies the formula from the cell above the active cell into the current cell.
Ctrl+' (single quote)	Alternates between displaying results or formulas in cells.
Ctrl+A	Displays the Function Wizard if a valid function name is typed in a cell.
Ctrl+Alt+Tab	Inserts a tab.
Ctrl+Delete	Cuts text to the end of the line.
Ctrl+Enter	Fills a selection of cells with the current entry. Select the cells, type the information, then press Ctrl+Enter.
Ctrl+Shift+"	Copies the value from the cell above the active cell into the current cell.
Ctrl+Shift+:	Inserts the time.
Ctrl+Shift+Enter	Enters the formula as an array formula.
Del	Deletes the character to the right of the cursor, or deletes the entire selection.
Enter	Completes a cell entry.
Esc	Cancels an entry.
F2	Edits cell entry.
F4	Toggles current reference between absolute and relative references.

Key or Key Combination	Action
Home	Moves to the start of a line.
Shift+Tab	Stores the cell entry and moves to the previous cell in the row or range.
Tab	Stores the cell entry and moves to the next cell in the row or range.

The workbook metaphor in Excel creates the need for key shortcuts useful for moving between your workbook documents. Table B.4 shows the keys that accomplish these moves, as well as the keys for navigating among and within open Excel windows.

TABLE B.4
Moving In and Between Documents

Key or Key Combination	Action
Alt+PgDn	Moves right one screen.
Alt+PgUp	Moves left one screen.
Arrow key	Moves one cell in the direction of the arrow key pressed.
Ctrl+6	Toggles between hiding objects, displaying objects, and displaying placeholders for graphic objects.
Ctrl+7	Toggles the Standard toolbar.
Ctrl+A	Selects the entire worksheet.
Ctrl+Down arrow	Moves down to the edge of any filled cells or to the end of the document.
Ctrl+End	Moves to the lower right corner of the worksheet.
Ctrl+Home	Moves to cell A1.
Ctrl+Left arrow	Moves left to the edge of any filled cells.
Ctrl+PgDn	Moves to the next sheet in the workbook.

continues

TABLE B.4, CONTINUED
Moving In and Between Documents

Key or Key Combination	Action
Ctrl+PgUp	Moves to the previous sheet in the workbook.
Ctrl+Right arrow	Moves right to the edge of any filled cells or by one screen width.
Ctrl+Shift+* (asterisk)	Selects the current region (contiguous filled cells).
Ctrl+Shift+Arrow key	Extends the selection to the edge of any contiguous filled cells in the direction of the arrow key pressed.
Ctrl+Shift+End	Extends the selection to the lower right corner of the worksheet.
Ctrl+Shift+Home	Extends the selection to the beginning of the worksheet.
Ctrl+Shift+Spacebar	With an object selected, selects all objects on a sheet.
Ctrl+Spacebar	Selects the entire column or all columns for the current selection.
Ctrl+Up arrow	Moves up to the edge of the current data region.
Home	Moves to the beginning of the row (Column A).
PgDn	Moves down one screen.
PgUp	Moves up one screen.
Scroll Lock	Turns scroll lock on or off.
Shift+Arrow key	Extends the selection by one cell in the direction of the arrow key pressed.
Shift+Backspace	Collapses the selection to the active cell.
Shift+Home	Extends selection to the beginning of the row.
Shift+End	Extends selection to the end of the row.

Key or Key Combination	Action
Shift+PgDn	Extends the selection down one screen.
Shift+PgUp	Extends the selection up one screen.
Shift+Spacebar	Selects the entire row.
Tab	Moves among the unlocked cells in a protected worksheet.

Excel contains a special shortcut key mode called End mode, which you enter by pressing the End key. When End mode is active, the END indicator appears on the right side of the status bar. Use the keys listed in table B.5 to jump around your document in ways that you cannot accomplish with other shortcut keys.

TABLE B.5
End Mode Keys

Key or Key Combination	Action
End	Turns End mode on or off.
End,Arrow key	Moves by one block of data within a row or column.
End,Enter	Moves to the last filled cell in the current row.
End,Home	Moves to the lower right corner of the worksheet.
End,Shift+Arrow key	Extends the selection to the end of the data block in the direction of the arrow.
End,Shift+Enter	Extends the selection to the last cell in the current row.
End,Shift+Home	Extends the selection to the lower right corner of the worksheet.

Excel also allows a different keyboard mode, similar to End mode, when you activate the Scroll Lock key. To use any of the keys in table B.6, make sure Scroll Lock is on.

TABLE B.6
Scroll Lock Keys

Key or Key Combination	Action
End	Moves to the lower right cell in the window.
Home	Moves to the upper left cell in the window.
Left or right arrow	Scrolls the screen left or right one column.
Shift+End	Extends the selection to the lower right cell in the window.
Shift+Home	Extends the selection to the upper left cell in the window.
Up or down arrow	Scrolls the screen up or down one row.

Primarily used for data entry, the keys listed in table B.7 show you how to move around a data-entry area—any series of cells you have selected before entering data.

TABLE B.7
Moving Within Selected Cells

Key or Key Combination	Action
Enter	Moves from top to bottom within the selection.
Shift+Enter	Moves from bottom to top within the selection .
Tab	Moves from left to right within the selection; if at far right in selection, wraps to left side of next row.
Shift+Tab	Moves from right to left within the selection or to far right of previous row.
Ctrl+. (period)	Moves clockwise to the next corner of the selection.

The shortcut keys listed in table B.8 do not really fall into any single category, but instead are miscellaneous Excel key shortcuts that you will rarely use. When you do need them, however, they can really come in handy. Of particular interest are the shortcuts that use the left and right brackets ([or]). These keys select cells that contribute to the active cell or that rely on the data in the active cell.

Table B.8
Special Cells

Key or Key Combination	Action
Ctrl+Shift+? (question mark)	Selects all cells that contain notes.
Ctrl+Shift+*	Selects a range of filled cells around the active cell.
Ctrl+/ (forward slash)	Selects the entire array, if any, to which the active cell belongs.
Ctrl+[(left bracket)	Selects all cells that are referred to by the formula in the selected cell.
Ctrl+Shift+{ (left brace)	Selects all cells directly or indirectly referred to by cells in the selection.
Ctrl+] (right bracket)	Selects all cells whose formulas refer to the active cell.
Ctrl+Shift+} (right brace)	Selects all cells that directly or indirectly refer to the active cell.
Ctrl+\ (backward slash)	Selects cells with contents that are different from the selected cell in current column.
Ctrl+Shift+| (vertical bar)	Selects cells with contents that are different from the selected cell in each column.
Alt+;	Selects all visible cells in the current selection.

The shortcuts listed in table B.9 are not Excel shortcut keys, but are Windows shortcuts that you might find helpful.

Table B.9
Switching Windows

Key or Key Combination	Action
Alt+Esc	Moves to next application.
Alt+Shift+Esc	Moves to previous application.
Alt+Tab	Shows the next Windows application.
Alt+Shift+Tab	Shows the previous Windows application.

continues

TABLE B.9, CONTINUED
Switching Windows

Key or Key Combination	Action
Ctrl+Esc	Activates the Windows Task List.
Ctrl+F4	Closes document.
Ctrl+F5	Restores window size.
Ctrl+F6	Moves to next window.
Ctrl+Shift+F6	Moves to previous window.
Ctrl+F7	Move window command.
Ctrl+F8	Size window command.
Ctrl+F9	Minimizes window.
Ctrl+F10	Maximizes window.

Excel power users quickly learn that using the mouse actually slows them down. Having to move your hands away from the keyboard is an impediment to the fastest possible use of Excel. If you are trying to use your mouse as little as possible, use the keys in table B.10 to navigate Excel (or Windows) dialog boxes.

TABLE B.10
Dialog Boxes

Key or Key Combination	Action
Tab	Moves to the next section in the dialog box.
Shift+Tab	Moves to the previous section in the dialog box.
Arrow key	Moves within the section of the dialog box (radio buttons, list boxes).
Spacebar	Selects the active button.
Any letter key	Moves to the item beginning with that letter in an active list box.

Key or Key Combination	Action
Alt+any letter key	Selects the item with that underlined letter (hot keys).
Enter	Chooses the default command button (it is surrounded with a thick black line).
Esc	Cancels the dialog box.

Most people spend quite a bit of time formatting their worksheets. The keys in table B.11 are useful for performing a variety of quick formatting tasks.

TABLE B.11
Formatting Data

Key or Key Combination	Action
Alt+´ (apostrophe)	Activates the style dialog box.
Ctrl+Shift+~ (tilde)	Applies the General number format.
Ctrl+Shift+$ (dollar sign)	Applies the currency format with two decimal places.
Ctrl+Shift+% (percent sign)	Applies the percentage format.
Ctrl+Shift+^ (carat)	Applies the exponential number format.
Ctrl+Shift+# (pound sign)	Applies the standard date format.
Ctrl+Shift+@ (at sign)	Applies the standard time format.
Ctrl+Shift+&	Applies the outline border.
Ctrl+Shift+_ (underscore)	Removes all borders.
Ctrl+B	Toggles bold.
Ctrl+I	Toggles italic.
Ctrl+U	Toggles underline.
Ctrl+5	Toggles strikethrough.
Ctrl+9	Hides rows.

continues

TABLE B.11, CONTINUED
Formatting Data

Key or Key Combination	Action
Ctrl+Shift+((open parenthesis)	Unhides rows.
Ctrl+0 (zero)	Hides columns.
Ctrl+Shift+) (close parenthesis)	Unhides columns.

If you are using the Excel outlining features, use the shortcuts in table B.12 to quickly promote and unhide selected outline groups.

TABLE B.12
Outlining

Key or Key Combination	Action
Alt+Shift+Left Arrow	Ungroups a row or a column.
Alt+Shift+Right Arrow	Groups a row or a column.
Ctrl+8	Displays or hides the outline symbols.
Ctrl+9	Hides selected rows.
Ctrl+Shift+(	Unhides selected rows.
Ctrl+0 (zero)	Hides selected columns.
Ctrl+Shift+)	Unhides selected columns.

Table B.13 lists keys you use to work with AutoFilter in your database files.

TABLE B.13
Shortcut Keys for AutoFilter

Key or Key Combination	Action
Alt+Down arrow	Displays list for selected column label.
Alt+Up arrow	Closes list for current column.

Key or Key Combination	Action
Up arrow	Chooses previous item in list.
Down arrow	Chooses next item in list.
Home	Selects first item in list.
End	Selects last item in list.
Enter	Filters the list using selected item.

Table B.14 lists the keys you use to work with the PivotTable Wizard.

TABLE B.14
Shortcut Keys for PivotTable Wizard

Key or Key Combination	Action
Alt+P	Moves selected field to page area.
Alt+R	Moves selected field to row area.
Alt+C	Moves selected field to column area.
Alt+D	Moves selected field to data area.
Alt+L	Shows PivotTable field dialog box.
Alt+Down arrow	Displays page field list.
Alt+Up arrow	Closes page field list.
Alt+Shift+Right arrow	Groups selected PivotTable items.
Alt+Shift+Left arrow	Ungroups selected PivotTable items.

Table B.15 lists keys you can use to control printing your selection and navigate the Print Preview function.

TABLE B.15
Printing and Print Previewing

Key or Key Combination	Action
Ctrl+P	Activates the Print dialog box.
Arrow keys	Moves around page when zoomed in.
Up or down arrow	Moves by one page when zoomed out.
PgUp, PgDn	Moves by one page when zoomed out.

Sometimes you might have trouble selecting certain chart items. The item you want might be very small or too close to another chart item. When this problem arises, switch to the keys in table B.16 for assistance.

TABLE B.16
Selecting Chart Items

Key or Key Combination	Action
Down arrow	Selects the previous group of items.
Up arrow	Selects the next group of items.
Right arrow	Selects the next item within the group.
Left arrow	Selects the previous item within the group.

Most Windows users should already be familiar with the keystrokes used to speed up working with menus. Take a quick look at table B.17, however, to make sure that you are making full use of the shortcut keys available for navigating menus.

TABLE B.17
Keys for Working in Menus

Key or Key Combination	Action
Alt or F10	Activates the menu bar.
Shift+F10	Activates the shortcut menu.

New Riders Publishing
INSIDE
SERIES

Key or Key Combination	Action
Alt+Backspace or Ctrl+Z	Undoes the last command.
F4	Repeats the last command.
Esc or Ctrl+. (period)	Cancels the menu.
Spacebar	Displays Control menu.
Letter key	Selects the menu or option that contains the underlined letter.
Left or right arrow	Selects the menu to the left or right.
Down or up arrow	Selects the next or previous command on the menu.
Enter	Chooses the selected command.
Down or up arrow	Selects the next or previous command on the menu.
Left or right arrow	Toggles selection between main menu and submenu.

Use the shortcut keys in table B.18 to access the most frequently used items in the Excel **F**ile menu.

TABLE B.18
File Commands

Key or Key Combination	Action
Ctrl+N	New workbook.
Ctrl+O	Open.
Ctrl+S	Save.
F12	Save As.
Ctrl+P	Print.
Alt+F4	Closes Excel.

Use the shortcut keys in table B.19 to access the most frequently used items in the Excel Edit menu.

TABLE B.19
Edit Menu Command Keys

Key or Key Combination	Action
Ctrl+Z	Undo.
F4	Repeat.
Ctrl+X	Cut.
Ctrl+C	Copy.
Ctrl+V	Paste.
Ctrl+D	Fill Down.
Ctrl+R	Fill Right.
Delete	Clear Contents.
Ctrl+_	Deletes the selected cells.
Ctrl+F	Displays the Find dialog box.
Ctrl+H	Displays the Replace dialog box.
Ctrl+Shift+F	Find Next.
Ctrl+Shift+E	Find Previous.
F5	Go To.

TABLE B.20
Insert Commands

Key or Key Combination	Action
Ctrl+Shift++	Activates Insert dialog box.
Shift+F11	Inserts new worksheet.

Key or Key Combination	Action
F11	Inserts new chart sheet.
Ctrl+F11	Inserts new Excel 4.0 macro sheet.
Ctrl+F3	Activates the Define Name dialog box.
F3	Activates the Paste Name dialog box.
Shift+Ctrl+F3	Activates the Create Names dialog box.

Use the shortcuts in table B.21 to access the most common items in the Excel Format menu.

TABLE B.21
Format Menu Commands

Key or Key Combination	Action
Ctrl+1	Format Cells tabbed dialog box.
Ctrl+9	Hide rows.
Ctrl+Shift+(	Unhide rows.
Ctrl+0 (zero)	Hide columns.
Ctrl+Shift+)	Unhide columns.
Alt+´ (apostrophe)	Activates the Style dialog box.

Although many of the keys listed in table B.22 are listed in other sections of this appendix, this table contains all the function key shortcuts for easy reference.

TABLE B.22
Function Keys

Key or Key Combination	Action
F1	Help.
Shift+F1	Help for current function.

continues

TABLE B.22, CONTINUED
Function Keys

Key or Key Combination	Action
F2	Activates the formula bar.
Shift+F2	Edit Note.
Ctrl+F2	Info window.
F3	Paste Name dialog box.
Shift+F3	Function Wizard.
Ctrl+F3	Define Name command.
Ctrl+Shift+F3	Create command.
F4	Toggles between relative and absolute references.
Ctrl+F4	Closes the window.
Alt+F4	Closes Excel.
F5	Go To command.
Ctrl+F5	Restores window size.
F6	Next pane.
Shift+F6	Previous pane.
Ctrl+F6	Next window.
Ctrl+Shift+F6	Previous window.
F7	Checks spelling.
Ctrl+F7	Move command.
F8	Toggles Extend Mode.
Shift+F8	Toggles Add mode.
Ctrl+F8	Size command.

Key or Key Combination	Action
F9	Calculates all.
Shift+F9	Calculates active sheet.
Ctrl+F9	Minimizes the workbook.
F10 *	Activates the menu bar.
Shift+F10	Activates the shortcut menu.
Ctrl+F10	Maximizes the workbook.
F11	Inserts new chart sheet.
Shift+F11	Inserts new worksheet.
Ctrl+F11	Inserts new Excel 4.0 macro sheet.
F12	Save As command.
Shift+F12	Save command.
Ctrl+F12	Open command.
Ctrl+Shift+F12	Print command.

Index

N

PLUG YOURSELF INTO...

THE MACMILLAN INFORMATION SUPERLIBRARY™

Free information and vast computer resources from the world's leading computer book publisher—online!

FIND THE BOOKS THAT ARE RIGHT FOR YOU!

A complete online catalog, plus sample chapters and tables of contents give you an in-depth look at *all* of our books, including hard-to-find titles. It's the best way to find the books you need!

● STAY INFORMED with the latest computer industry news through our online newsletter, press releases, and customized Information SuperLibrary Reports.

● GET FAST ANSWERS to your questions about MCP books and software.

● VISIT our online bookstore for the latest information and editions!

● COMMUNICATE with our expert authors through e-mail and conferences.

● DOWNLOAD SOFTWARE from the immense MCP library:
   - Source code and files from MCP books
   - The best shareware, freeware, and demos

● DISCOVER HOT SPOTS on other parts of the Internet.

● WIN BOOKS in ongoing contests and giveaways!

TO PLUG INTO MCP: ➜ WORLD WIDE WEB: **http://www.mcp.com**

GOPHER: gopher.mcp.com

FTP: ftp.mcp.com

WANT MORE INFORMATION?

CHECK OUT THESE RELATED TOPICS OR SEE YOUR LOCAL BOOKSTORE

CAD and 3D Studio

As the number one CAD publisher in the world, and as a Registered Publisher of Autodesk, New Riders Publishing provides unequaled content on this complex topic. Industry-leading products include AutoCAD and 3D Studio.

Networking

As the leading Novell NetWare publisher, New Riders Publishing delivers cutting-edge products for network professionals. We publish books for all levels of users, from those wanting to gain NetWare Certification, to those administering or installing a network. Leading books in this category include *Inside NetWare 3.12*, *CNE Training Guide: Managing NetWare Systems*, *Inside TCP/IP*, and *NetWare: The Professional Reference*.

Graphics

New Riders provides readers with the most comprehensive product tutorials and references available for the graphics market. Best-sellers include *Inside CorelDRAW! 5*, *Inside Photoshop 3*, and *Adobe Photoshop NOW!*

Internet and Communications

As one of the fastest growing publishers in the communications market, New Riders provides unparalleled information and detail on this ever-changing topic area. We publish international best-sellers such as *New Riders' Official Internet Yellow Pages, 2nd Edition*, a directory of over 10,000 listings of Internet sites and resources from around the world, and *Riding the Internet Highway, Deluxe Edition*.

Operating Systems

Expanding off our expertise in technical markets, and driven by the needs of the computing and business professional, New Riders offers comprehensive references for experienced and advanced users of today's most popular operating systems, including *Understanding Windows 95*, *Inside Unix*, *Inside Windows 3.11 Platinum Edition*, *Inside OS/2 Warp Version 3*, and *Inside MS-DOS 6.22*.

Other Markets

Professionals looking to increase productivity and maximize the potential of their software and hardware should spend time discovering our line of products for Word, Excel, and Lotus 1-2-3. These titles include *Inside Word 6 for Windows*, *Inside Excel 5 for Windows*, *Inside 1-2-3 Release 5*, and *Inside WordPerfect for Windows*.

Orders/Customer Service **1-800-653-6156**   Source Code **NRP95**

New Riders Publishing   201 West 103rd Street ◆ Indianapolis, Indiana 46290 USA

REGISTRATION CARD

Inside Excel for Windows 95

Name _____ Title _____

Company_____ Type of
business _____

Address _____

City/State/ZIP _____

Have you used these types of books before? ☐ yes ☐ no

If yes, which ones? _____

_____

How many computer books do you purchase each year? ☐ 1–5 ☐ 6 or more

How did you learn about this book? _____

Where did you purchase this book? _____

Which applications do you currently use? _____

_____

Which computer magazines do you subscribe to? _____

_____

What trade shows do you attend? _____

_____

Comments: _____

_____

_____

Would you like to be placed on our preferred mailing list? ☐ yes ☐ no

☐ **I would like to see my name in print!** You may use my name and quote me in future New Riders
products and promotions. My daytime phone number is: _____

New Riders Publishing   201 West 103rd Street ◆ Indianapolis, Indiana 46290 USA

Fax to **317-581-4670**   Orders/Customer Service **1-800-653-6156**   Source Code **NRP95**